Soviet Military Policy

International Security Readers

Strategy and Nuclear Deterrence (1984)

Military Strategy and the Origins of the First World War (1985)

Conventional Forces and American Defense Policy (1986)

The Star Wars Controversy (1986)

Naval Strategy and National Security (1988)

—published by Princeton University Press

Soviet Military Policy (1989)

Conventional Forces and American Defense Policy, revised edition (1989)

—published by The MIT Press

Soviet Military Policy

AN *International Security* READER

EDITED BY
Sean M. Lynn-Jones
Steven E. Miller
and Stephen Van Evera

THE MIT PRESS
CAMBRIDGE, MASSACHUSETTS

The contents of this book were first published in *International Security* (ISSN 0162-2889), a publication of The MIT Press under the sponsorship of the Center for Science and International Affairs at Harvard University. Except as otherwise noted, copyright in each article is owned jointly by the President and Fellows of Harvard College and the Massachusetts Institute of Technology.

Jack Snyder, "Richness, Rigor, and Relevance in the Study of Soviet Foreign Policy," *IS* 9, no. 3 (Winter 1984/85); Franklyn Griffiths, "The Sources of American Conduct: Soviet Perspectives and Their Policy Implications," *IS* 9, no. 2 (Fall 1984); Jack Snyder, "The Gorbachev Revolution: A Waning of Soviet Expansionism?" *IS* 12, no. 3 (Winter 1987/88); Stephen M. Meyer, "The Sources and Prospects of Gorbachev's New Political Thinking on Security," *IS* 13, no. 2 (Fall 1988); Fritz W. Ermarth, "Contrasts in American and Soviet Strategic Thought," *IS* 3, no. 2 (Fall 1978). Copyright © 1978 by the President and Fellows of Harvard College. Raymond L. Garthoff, "Mutual Deterrence and Strategic Arms Limitation in Soviet Policy," *IS* 3, no. 1 (Summer 1978). Copyright © 1978 by the President and Fellows of Harvard College. Dimitri K. Simes, "Deterrence and Coercion in Soviet Policy," *IS* 5, no. 3 (Winter 1980/81); Donald MacKenzie, "The Soviet Union and Strategic Missile Guidance," *IS* 13, no. 2 (Fall 1988); Matthew A. Evangelista, "Stalin's Postwar Army Reappraised," *IS* 7, no. 3 (Winter 1982/83); Richard Ned Lebow, "The Soviet Offensive in Europe: The Schlieffen Plan Revisited?" *IS* 9, no. 4 (Spring 1985); Benjamin S. Lambeth, "Uncertainties for the Soviet War Planner," *IS* 7, no. 3 (Winter 1982/83). Copyright © 1982 by the RAND Corporation. Reprinted with permission of the RAND Corporation, Santa Monica, CA.

Selection and preface, copyright © 1989 by the President and Fellows of Harvard College and the Massachusetts Institute of Technology.

ISBN 0-262-12142-5 (hard)
    0-262-62066-9 (paper)

Contents

The Contributors

SEAN M. LYNN-JONES is Managing Editor of *International Security* and a Research Fellow at the Center for Science and International Affairs, Harvard University.

STEVEN E. MILLER is Co-editor of *International Security* and a Senior Research Fellow at the Stockholm International Peace Research Institute (SIPRI).

STEPHEN VAN EVERA is an Adjunct Fellow at the Center for Science and International Affairs, Harvard University.

JACK SNYDER is Associate Professor in the Political Science Department and the Harriman Institute for the Advanced Study of the Soviet Union at Columbia University.

FRANKLYN GRIFFITHS is Professor of Political Science and Acting Director of the Centre for Russian and East European Studies at the University of Toronto.

STEPHEN M. MEYER is Associate Professor of Political Science at MIT.

FRITZ W. ERMARTH is Chairman of the National Intelligence Council of the Central Intelligence Agency.

RAYMOND L. GARTHOFF is a Senior Fellow at the Brookings Institution.

DIMITRI K. SIMES is a Senior Associate at the Carnegie Endowment for International Peace.

DONALD MACKENZIE is a Lecturer in Sociology at the University of Edinburgh.

MATTHEW A. EVANGELISTA is Assistant Professor in the Department of Political Science at the University of Michigan.

RICHARD NED LEBOW is Professor of Government and Director of the Peace Studies Program at Cornell University.

BENJAMIN S. LAMBETH is a Senior Staff Member of the RAND Corporation.

Acknowledgments

The editors gratefully acknowledge the assistance that has made this book possible. A deep debt is owed to all those at the Center for Science and International Affairs, Harvard University, who have played an editorial role at *International Security*, including Paul Doty, Joseph S. Nye, Jr., Albert Carnesale, Michael Nacht, Ashton Carter, Derek Leebaert, Barbara Degen, Melissa Healy, Lisbeth Tarlow Bernstein, Lynn Page Whittaker, Teresa Pelton Johnson, Mary Ann Wells, and Maude Fish. Special thanks go to Ann Callahan and Lisa Grumbach for their skill and diligence in preparing the volume for publication.

Preface | Sean M. Lynn-Jones

For over 45 years, the Soviet Union has maintained one of the world's two largest concentrations of military power. U.S. defense planners have had no choice but to pay close attention to Soviet capabilities and intentions. And no country can afford to ignore Soviet military power, whether it regards the USSR as a likely threat or a potential ally. The sheer size of the Soviet arsenal makes Soviet military policy an inescapably significant issue in world politics.

If the USSR's military posture is among the most important issues in international security studies, it is also one of the most analytically perplexing. The Soviet Union makes its defense policy in a different cultural and political context that creates the potential for misunderstanding by Western analysts. Information is scarce and conclusions must be drawn from scattered pieces of evidence. Analysts confront the problem of determining when official pronouncements are meant as propaganda and when they reflect actual Soviet policy.

Mikhail Gorbachev's rise to power in 1985 and his sometimes startling series of reforms have changed the setting of Soviet military policy and, quite frequently, confounded students of Soviet politics. Gorbachev's ambitious agenda for *glasnost* (openness) and *perestroika* (restructuring) may lead to far-reaching changes in traditional patterns of Soviet defense policy. More information on Soviet defense programs has become available, but the rapid pace of change in Soviet foreign policy complicates the analytical task of understanding, let alone predicting, Soviet international behavior.

Regardless of the future of Gorbachev's "new thinking," the study of Soviet military policy will remain as essential as it is challenging. Western analysts will continue to assess Soviet nuclear and conventional military capabilities, to uncover and explicate the military doctrine that governs the use of Soviet forces, and to attempt to understand the course of Soviet foreign policy. The essays in this volume present important perspectives on these questions.

The study of Soviet foreign policy offers a context for understanding Soviet military doctrine and strategy. Lenin and subsequent Soviet leaders have professed adherence to Clausewitz's dictum that "war is the continuation of politics by other means." The first section of this volume thus explores the broader political factors that shape defense policy in the Soviet Union.

In "Richness, Rigor, and Relevance in the Study of Soviet Foreign Policy," Jack Snyder offers a framework for analyzing Soviet behavior. Lamenting the slow progress toward understanding Soviet actions, he argues that a systematic approach is essential when data are scarce and urges Sovietologists to adopt a more scientific approach based on the comparative case study method. Even when Western analysts lack information on the processes that produce Soviet decisions, it is still possible to compare behavior across cases to develop generalizations. Snyder points out that such an approach still requires detailed historical work on individual cases. The traditional empirical richness of Soviet studies would provide the basis for more systematic development of theories that examine problems of policy choice.

How the Soviets understand the sources of U.S. foreign policy may offer important clues to Soviet foreign policy. Franklyn Griffiths examines "The Sources of American Conduct: Soviet Perspectives and Their Policy Implications" and finds that Soviet specialists on the United States have developed four images of U.S. government and policy-making: (1) domination of the state by a unitary monopoly bourgeoisie; (2) domination of the state by a divided monopoly bourgeoisie; (3) domination of a relatively self-sufficient state by the whole bourgeoisie and a divided monopoly stratum; and (4) a more self-sufficient and autonomous state. Each of these images is associated with a different tendency in Soviet foreign policy, ranging from a coercive isolationism that displays no concern for U.S. public opinion to, at the other extreme, a democratic isolationism that would seek internal reform and democratization in a stabilized international setting. Griffiths argues that the second and third images were favored in the Brezhnev era. He concludes that the four tendencies he outlines describe the main dispositions of the Soviet regime and will continue to shape its conduct toward the United States.

In the two succeeding essays, Jack Snyder and Stephen Meyer offer perspectives on the implications of Mikhail Gorbachev's new thinking for Soviet defense policy. Snyder argues in "The Gorbachev Revolution: A Waning of Soviet Expansionism?" that Soviet expansionist behavior and strategic concepts have been rooted in Stalinist domestic institutions, particularly the militant Communist Party and the command economy. Gorbachev's restructuring has been prompted by Soviet economic needs and the interests of new constituencies, including urban professionals and the intelligentsia. Gorbachev's changes in the Soviet domestic order could produce a radically different foreign policy that reduces military spending, promotes a durable détente, and accelerates Soviet involvement in the world economy.

Stephen Meyer presents a different perspective on the causes of Gorbachev's policies in "The Sources and Prospects of Gorbachev's New Political

Thinking on Security." He suggests that Gorbachev's new thinking is not the result of deterministic forces; instead, it is an attempt by Gorbachev to regain control of the Soviet defense agenda so that he can devote more resources to his industrial and economic program. Underlying forces in Soviet society may have had some influence on the changes in Soviet ideas on security, but the key factor is the persona of the general secretary. Gorbachev's new thinking may bring about revolutionary changes in Soviet military policy, but some new concepts may be rejected unless they are institutionalized. Meyer explicates Gorbachev's doctrinal innovations on issues such as avoiding nuclear war, reasonable sufficiency, and defensive defense and then assesses the likely counterarguments and prospects for each aspect of the new thinking.

The role of nuclear weapons in Soviet strategy has been an important issue in analyses of Soviet military policy. In the late 1970s, a debate emerged between Western analysts who claimed that the Soviet Union believed that it could emerge victorious in a nuclear war and those who suggested that Western concepts of deterrence had been embraced in the Kremlin. Although this debate flared up over ten years ago, it has had substantial influence on U.S. thinking about arms control policy and offers a context for present discussions of Soviet strategy and intentions. Part II accordingly presents several important viewpoints on how the Soviet Union regards nuclear weapons.

Fritz Ermarth and Raymond Garthoff put forth contending perspectives on Soviet nuclear doctrine. In his essay, "Contrasts in American and Soviet Strategic Thought," Ermarth declares that there are fundamental differences in U.S. and Soviet strategic ideas. Unlike American concepts of assured destruction, Soviet strategic doctrine is based on the assumption that the Soviet Union could achieve a meaningful victory should deterrence fail, and it holds that strategic forces and plans for war-fighting are an effective means of preventing nuclear war and serving Soviet foreign policy goals. He also warns that the Soviet Union has not accepted stability as a principle and that failure to understand Soviet doctrine may lead to excessive confidence in arms control.

In "Mutual Deterrence and Strategic Arms Limitation in Soviet Policy," Garthoff draws upon confidential Soviet military literature to support his conclusion that in the 1960s the Soviet Union recognized that there is a stable strategic balance that provides mutual deterrence based on mutual retaliatory capability. He also reviews the SALT negotiating history and finds additional evidence suggesting Soviet acceptance of the role of arms limitations in maintaining deterrence at reduced levels of armaments.

Dimitri Simes offers another perspective on the debate over Soviet strategic doctrine in his essay, "Deterrence and Coercion in Soviet Policy." He argues that false dichotomies, such as that between Mutual Assured Destruction and "war-fighting," have clouded Western analyses of Soviet nuclear strategy. Simes suggests that the Soviet Union has come to see nuclear war as unwinnable, but Soviet military planners also believe that only a credible war-fighting capability can maintain nuclear deterrence. Civilian members of the Soviet Politburo accord the military considerable autonomy in determining Soviet concepts of military operations. Attempts to change the war-fighting aspects of Soviet doctrine would provoke significant resistance and could only take place in the context of a fundamental restructuring of the Soviet political process.

The accuracy of Soviet ballistic missiles has been a significant element in debates over Soviet nuclear strategy. Donald MacKenzie's essay, "The Soviet Union and Strategic Missile Guidance," gives an overview of the development of Soviet missile guidance technology. He suggests that Soviet missile accuracies are the result of strategic goals, not technological determinism. The Soviet pursuit of missile accuracy indicates an interest in counterforce targeting, but not a simple reliance on a first strike against U.S. strategic forces. On several occasions, the Soviet Union has sacrificed increased accuracy for greater survivability. Moreover, MacKenzie points out that some Soviet missiles appear to have been fitted with lower accuracy guidance systems and configured for second-strike missions, but he concedes that it is difficult to come to definitive conclusions about Soviet nuclear strategy solely by drawing inferences from the pattern of deployed forces.

In addition to Soviet nuclear strategy, the Soviet conventional threat to Western Europe has occupied much of the attention of Western analysts and policymakers. Since the end of World War II, the Soviet Union has maintained significant ground forces in its western regions and in Eastern Europe. Most analysts have argued that Moscow has adopted an offensive doctrine for these forces. The capability and intentions of the Soviet Union to implement this apparently offensive strategy have thus become central issues in the debate over Soviet military policy. Part III of this volume consists of several examinations of Soviet conventional forces and of the offensive threat they pose.

Matthew Evangelista reassesses the Soviet conventional threat to Western Europe in the late 1940s and early 1950s. In "Stalin's Postwar Army Reappraised," he takes issue with the prevailing image of an overwhelming Soviet force confronting token U.S. and West European opposition. Using declassified intelligence assessments of the period, Evangelista faults contemporary commentators for not taking into account the considerably smaller size of Soviet divisions compared to their Western counterparts, the weaknesses in the Soviet transportation system and logistics, and the widespread use of Soviet troops for reconstruction and occupation duties. He suggests that the Soviet threat was exaggerated to build public support for NATO and for U.S. spending on its atomic arsenal.

In "The Soviet Offensive in Europe: The Schlieffen Plan Revisited?" Richard Ned Lebow questions not only the ability of the Soviet Union to execute a blitzkrieg against Western Europe but also whether such a strategy makes sense from a Soviet standpoint. He suggests that breakdowns in command and control, logistical failures, sheer physical exhaustion, and the general "friction" of war would probably prevent a rapid Soviet victory. A Soviet offensive might bog down and a lengthy war of attrition could ensue, much as it did in 1914. Even if the Soviet forces did achieve an early breakthrough, they would face the likely use of nuclear weapons by NATO. Lebow concludes that a defensive conventional strategy would not only be stabilizing, but would better serve Soviet political goals.

Benjamin Lambeth, in "Uncertainties for the Soviet War Planner," examines how the Soviet leadership might assess the likelihood of success in a major war. He finds much evidence of uncertainties and anxieties in Soviet military writings and points out that the Soviet Union has generally been risk-averse. In contemplating an invasion of Western Europe, Soviet leaders would have to worry about their rigid command structure, the reliability of Warsaw Pact allies, and the risk of a two-front war against NATO and the Chinese. These factors, as well as other uncertainties and a general lack of Soviet combat experience, may inspire caution in the Kremlin.

This collection of essays by no means exhausts the range of issues in Soviet military policy. The upheaval set in motion by Gorbachev's *perestroika* will give students of Soviet foreign policy many topics to analyze in the coming years. These essays provide a framework for thinking about Soviet military policy and a starting point for further analysis.

Part I:
The Foreign Policy Context

Richness, Rigor, and Relevance in the Study of Soviet Foreign Policy

Jack Snyder

$\mathbf{A}$ short time ago, a group of senior specialists in the study of Soviet foreign policy gathered to assess the state of their field. Though none disputed the view that "we know more now than we did a decade ago," they also felt that the field was making disturbingly slow progress in identifying the empirical disagreements about Soviet behavior that underlie Western policy disputes and in investigating them systematically. The explanation for these shortcomings was laid at least in part on the field's traditional tendency to sacrifice "rigor" in the interests of "richness" and short-run policy relevance.

Many saw the richness/rigor dilemma simply as one of too few hours in the day. People cannot be expected to achieve a well-rounded knowledge of the language, history, society, and politics of the Soviet Union, while also mastering the arcane theories and methods of a social science discipline. In this view, the solution is more years spent in graduate school training. Another view is that rigor and richness are inherently incompatible and that the dubious benefits of greater rigor would not outweigh the corresponding sacrifice of detail, nuance, intuition, and plain common sense. Pointing to the failure of past attempts to make a "behavioral revolution" in the study of Soviet foreign policy, some experts argue that it is wiser to recognize the unavoidable limitations of the field.

Compounding the richness/rigor dilemma is the trade-off between rigorous basic research and policy applications. In a field in which the leading experts inevitably become involved in current policy analysis and even policymaking itself, there is a tendency to neglect the replenishment of the intellectual capital on which policy analysts draw. As one participant put it, policy analysis itself suffers when its roots in basic research are not nourished.

I would like to thank Robert Cutler, Alexander Dallin, Matthew Evangelista, Robert Jervis, Friedrich Kratochwil, Deborah Larson, Herbert Lin, and Deborah Palmieri for their helpful comments.

Jack Snyder is an Assistant Professor in the Political Science Department at Columbia University.

International Security, Winter 1984/85 (Vol. 9, No. 3) 0162-2889/84/030089-20 $02.50/0

What is needed is a way to minimize the trade-off between rigor, on one hand, and richness and relevance, on the other. This task may not be as insurmountable as it seems. Between the extremes of quantitative methodology and journalistic narrative lies the promising middle ground of the comparative case study method. When properly carried out, the case study approach is no less scientific than more daunting methodologies. Indeed, in the early stages of theory-building, the richness of the case study is an advantage, not a shortcoming, and does not greatly conflict with the requirements of rigor. Systematic methods of this kind can be easily incorporated into the normal training of area studies specialists and adapted to the established habits of those who are already practicing their trade. The best analysts in the field have always used a rough-and-ready version of the scientific method, which after all is nothing more than a self-conscious, systematic application of common sense rules of inference.

The notorious scarcity of reliable data in the Soviet field does nothing to reduce the importance of explicit attention to theory and method. As Kremlinologists have long understood, the worse the data the greater the need for sophisticated techniques to make the most of it. Likewise, the unavoidable policy focus of research in this field does not mean that there is no role for theory. Rather, it means that researchers should pay special attention to theories that examine problems of policy choice and the effects of variables that policymakers can manipulate. Arguably, this kind of theory-based analysis could be more policy-relevant than much of the narrative work traditionally produced by Soviet specialists. Implementing this kind of research strategy will require, first, a clear understanding of what the scientific method is and, second, a practical sense of how to apply it under the special conditions of the study of Soviet foreign policy.

Misconceptions of Science

One reason that people resist the use of the scientific method in Soviet studies and other social fields is that they idealize science, mistaking the trappings of the physical sciences for the essence of science itself. Science is not only quantifiable experimentation in a laboratory, but rather a method of inquiry that can be profitably carried out by a variety of techniques and with varying degrees of precision, as much or as little as the subject matter allows. For practical purposes, the scientific method can be characterized in terms of five fundamental elements.[1]

1) CAUSAL GENERALIZATION. Scientific hypotheses posit an "if, then" relationship between two variables, expressed in general form. For example, a popular hypothesis in the recent literature on international political economy holds that, if power is concentrated in the hands of a single hegemonic state, free trade will result, and conversely, if power is dispersed among a number of states, protectionism will result.[2]

2) OPERATIONAL DEFINITIONS OF VARIABLES. Explicit rules are established for the measurement of variables in order to avoid arbitrary, ad hoc assessments of each particular case. Thus, it is necessary to specify whether the openness of the trading system should be measured by tariff levels or trade flows. Operational definitions should be precise enough so that any two researchers using the same definitions would be able to reach the same conclusion about the "degree of concentration of power" or "the degree of openness of the trading system" in the case under investigation.

3) COVARIATION. Tests are carried out not only to determine whether the hypothesized cause is present when the hypothesized consequence is, but also to see whether the outcome is different when the cause is absent. Thus, to establish covariation, it would be necessary to show both that hegemony is related to free trade and that the dispersal of power is related to protectionism.

4) CONTROLLED COMPARISON TO ELIMINATE ALTERNATIVE EXPLANATIONS. Tests are designed to try to rule out alternative explanations for the observed

---

1. For caveats and elaboration, see Ernest Nagel, *The Structure of Science* (New York: Harcourt, Brace & World, 1961). For a somewhat different approach that also emphasizes case studies, see Alexander George, "Case Studies and Theory Development," Paper presented to the Second Annual Symposium on Information Processing in Organizations, Carnegie-Mellon University, October 15–16, 1982. See also his "The Causal Nexus Between 'Operational Code' Beliefs and Decision-Making Behavior," in Lawrence S. Falkowski, *Psychological Models in International Politics* (Boulder, Colo.: Westview Press, 1979), pp. 95–124. George offers criticisms of the use of controlled comparisons to eliminate alternative explanations and argues instead for a process-tracing method. For a more fundamental attack on the philosophical assumptions of positivistic methods in the social sciences, see Karl-Otto Apel, "The A Priori of Communication and the Foundation of the Humanities," in Fred R. Dallmayr and Thomas A. McCarthy, eds., *Understanding and Social Inquiry* (Notre Dame, Ind.: University of Notre Dame Press, 1977), pp. 292–315.
2. Stephen Krasner, "State Power and the Structure of International Trade," *World Politics*, Vol. 28, No. 3 (April 1976), pp. 317–347.

outcomes. For example, an alternative to the hegemonic thesis might hold that free trade occurs during peaks of the international business cycle, while protectionism occurs during international depressions. Testing should focus on periods in which the alternative hypotheses would predict opposite outcomes, i.e., periods of hegemony and depression or periods of dispersed power and prosperity.

5) DEDUCTIVE THEORY. In a mature science, hypotheses are part of a logical, deductive framework, shaped like a pyramid. At the apex are theoretical assumptions and abstract theorems derived from them; at the base are empirically testable hypotheses stating the implications of these theorems in a variety of contexts. For example, the hegemonic explanation for free trade is said to be an empirical application of the more abstract "collective goods" theorem, a mathematical demonstration of the relationship between the relative size and number of actors and the likelihood that goods benefiting the whole group will be provided.[3]

Even the physical sciences do not entirely live up to this idealized version of the scientific method. There are gaps in the logic of most theoretical frameworks, and as Thomas Kuhn has shown, arbitrary judgment can play a considerable role in the evaluation of experimental results.[4] These imperfections do not prevent scientific progress, however, even in fields like meteorology, which cannot rely on artificially controlled experiments and consequently must isolate the effects of variables by the systematic observation of natural occurrences.

---

3. George's process-tracing method, which "attempts to identify the intervening steps or cause-and-effect links between an independent variable and the outcome of the dependent variable," might be added as a sixth component of the scientific method. Process-tracing is "not purely descriptive," he stresses, since it uses "generalizations of one kind or another to support each step in the postulated causal sequence." ("Case Studies and Theory Development," p. 19.) One of George's students has criticized Krasner's article on process-tracing grounds. He shows that even when Krasner's independent and dependent variables covary, the intervening steps that the theory would predict are absent, implying that the covariation is coincidental. (Timothy McKeown, "Hegemonic Stability Theory and 19th Century Tariff Levels in Europe," *International Organization*, Vol. 37, No. 1 [Winter 1983], pp. 73–91.) Process-tracing, conceived of as a testing strategy based on the idea that a theory may make a whole series of predictions within a single case, offers a partial solution to the problem of "too many variables, too few cases." Still, this is nothing more than a multi-step variant of the test of covariation. Moreover, it does not obviate the need for controlled comparison to eliminate alternative explanations that might also be able to trace a plausible process producing the observed outcome.
4. Thomas S. Kuhn, *The Structure of Scientific Revolutions*, 2nd ed. enl. (Chicago: University of Chicago Press, 1970). But in the long run, standards of proof are not arbitrary, according to Imre Lakatos, "Falsification and the Methodology of Scientific Research Programmes," in Imre Lakatos and Alan Musgrave, eds., *Criticism and the Growth of Knowledge* (London: Cambridge University Press, 1970), pp. 91–196.

If the physical sciences stand near one end of the continuum of scientific rigor, approximating but not quite achieving the scientific ideal, the common sense inference processes used in everyday life stand near the less rigorous end. Nowadays, cognitive psychologists portray the man-in-the-street as a "naïve scientist," who tries to use the scientific method in solving his daily problems but tends to use it badly.[5] He makes causal generalizations, observes covariation, may even look for evidence that would rule out alternative explanations, and so on. But his thinking is flawed by its lack of system and use of shortcuts. For example, people focus inordinately on vivid cases or first-hand information, ignoring underlying probabilities. They fail to consider non-events (dogs that should have barked, but didn't). They rarely stop to ask whether evidence that fits their own view might also fit others. And surprisingly, the thinking of non-scientists may be even more rigidly determined by theories than that of scientists, who qualify their generalizations and are more sensitive to disconfirming evidence. Even scientists, however, are susceptible in some measure to the same biases as the man-in-the-street.[6]

In short, it is an error to overestimate the pristine perfection of the natural sciences and the difference between the scientific method and everyday reasoning processes. Defenders of traditionalist approaches to the study of social relations often make this mistake, arguing that their explanations are— and must be—"wholistic" and "particularistic" and thus have nothing in common with the method of the natural sciences, which is "analytic" and "generalizing."[7] However, philosophers of science who examine these wholistic explanations claim that the use of tacit causal generalizations is rampant in them.[8] Like the man-in-the-street, traditionalists are using the scientific method, but in an unself-conscious, unsystematic way. It is debatable

5. Alexander L. George, *Presidential Decisionmaking in Foreign Policy* (Boulder, Colo.: Westview Press, 1980), pp. 58–61; Richard Nisbett and Lee Ross, *Human Inference* (Englewood Cliffs, N.J.: Prentice-Hall, 1980); David Kahneman, Paul Slovic, and Amos Tversky, eds., *Judgment under Uncertainty: Heuristics and Biases* (New York: Cambridge University Press, 1982).
6. On scientists' biases, see Kahneman and Tversky, "Belief in the Law of Small Numbers," in Kahneman, Slovic, and Tversky, eds., *Judgment under Uncertainty*, pp. 23–31. For some examples from international politics, see Robert Jervis, *Perception and Misperception in International Politics* (Princeton: Princeton University Press, 1976); and Ernest R. May, *"Lessons" of the Past* (New York: Oxford University Press, 1973).
7. For this argument, see Philip Tetlock et al., "Political Psychobiography," *Micropolitics*, Vol. 1, No. 2 (1981), pp. 191–213.
8. Nagel, *Structure of Science*, chapter 15, "Problems in the Logic of Historical Inquiry," pp. 547–592. Apel offers a rebuttal to this claim.

whether this lack of system enhances the analyst's ability to take nuances and complex interrelationships into account. Social psychologists have found that people tend to overestimate the amount of data and the complexity of the thought processes that they use in making judgments. For example, members of university admissions committees think that they are making evaluations on the basis of subtle cues and diverse considerations; in fact, they tend to be heavily swayed by one or two crude indicators.[9] Flexible, wholistic approaches may be useful for generating insights worthy of scientific examination, but more rigorous procedures must be used in validating those insights.

Another error is to confuse the trappings of science for its substance. There are many studies in the Soviet and international fields that are laden with jargon, diagrams, and numerical manipulation, but nonetheless manage to omit several of the five elements of the scientific method listed above. Just as the trappings of science may be present without its substance, so too the scientific method does not require the use of arcane techniques. Following the lead of Alexander George and Richard Smoke, a number of recent studies in the national security field have adopted the comparative case study method.[10] Most of these studies begin with an explicit theory or theories (balance of power, deterrence, bureaucratic, or cognitive), derive hypotheses from them that are relevant to a particular application, and test the hypotheses on a few case studies. All of the case studies are presented in chronological narrative style without jargon or quantification. Although each of these works has shortcomings, especially in using the technique of controlled comparison to eliminate alternative explanations, collectively they are successful enough to demonstrate that the research strategy is workable. They also show that the advantages of a straightforward, narrative style do not have to be sacrificed in the pursuit of generalization and rigor. Finally,

---

9. Robert Jervis, "Deterrence and Perception," *International Security*, Vol. 7, No. 3 (Winter 1982/83), p. 20; Robert Abelson, "Script Processing in Attitude Formation and Decision Making," in John Carroll and John Payne, eds., *Cognition and Social Behavior* (Hillsdale, N.J.: Lawrence Erlbaum, 1976), pp. 33–45.

10. Alexander L. George and Richard Smoke, *Deterrence in American Foreign Policy* (New York: Columbia University Press, 1974); Richard Smoke, *War: Controlling Escalation* (Cambridge: Harvard University Press, 1977); Barry R. Posen, *The Sources of Military Doctrine* (Ithaca: Cornell University Press, 1984); John J. Mearsheimer, *Conventional Deterrence* (Ithaca: Cornell University Press, 1983); Richard Ned Lebow, *Between Peace and War* (Baltimore: Johns Hopkins University Press, 1981); Jack Snyder, *The Ideology of the Offensive* (Ithaca: Cornell University Press, 1984). Note also Robert Jervis, *Perception and Misperception*, chapter 6.

they are all concerned with questions of direct policy significance (e.g., the conditions for deterrence, the barriers to military innovation, the sources of strategic instability), and their authors have drawn on their theoretical findings in doing policy analysis of a more conventional type.[11] In sum, this body of literature suggests that the trade-offs among richness, rigor, and relevance may not be as acute as many specialists in Soviet foreign policy assume.

Data Limitations of the Soviet Field

It is frequently argued that the limited data available to students of Soviet foreign policy precludes the use of scientific theories and methods. For better or for worse, Soviet studies is inherently an art, not a science, in this view. Thus, the kind of skill that needs to be developed is not so much analytic rigor as a "finger-tip feel," achieved through immersion in primary sources, that cannot be reduced to set rules of inference. Without minimizing the value of immersion and intuition for Soviet studies or indeed any other science, it might be argued that theoretical and comparative approaches are even more indispensable when direct evidence is scarce and unreliable than when it is plentiful. An example from the study of Soviet military doctrine shows why this is the case.[12]

American nuclear strategists, seeking a rational use for nuclear weapons in the event that NATO's conventional defenses are routed, have for a long time pondered the feasibility of a limited nuclear war in which the U.S. and the Soviet Union would refrain from attacking each other's cities. One stumbling block has been the Soviets' persistent denial that nuclear war could be kept limited. According to Soviet doctrine, once nuclear exchanges have begun, the only way to limit damage to the Soviet Union is through unrestrained, disarming, decapitating attacks on U.S. war-making capabilities. "Intrawar deterrence" is said to be (a) impossible and (b) a ploy designed to salvage the coercive value of nuclear weapons despite the loss of U.S. strategic superiority. Precisely because the latter accusation is largely true, Soviet statements about limited nuclear war cannot be taken at face value. The

11. John J. Mearsheimer, "Why the Soviets Can't Win Quickly in Central Europe," *International Security*, Vol. 7, No. 1 (Summer 1982), pp. 3–39; Barry R. Posen, "Inadvertent Nuclear War? Escalation and NATO's Northern Flank," *International Security*, Vol. 7, No. 2 (Fall 1982), pp. 28–54.
12. The following discussion is based on Jack Snyder, *The Soviet Strategic Culture: Implications for Limited Nuclear Operations*, Rand Report R-2154-AF (Santa Monica, Calif.: Rand, September 1977).

Soviets have a clear interest in feigning the belief that nuclear escalation is inevitable, since this would degrade the credibility of the U.S. threat to initiate the use of nuclear weapons in areas where the Soviets enjoy conventional superiority. Consequently, doctrinal pronouncements by themselves do not constitute satisfactory evidence of the Soviets' real views.

An alternative to relying on Soviet statements is to infer doctrine from force posture. Indeed, at one point, some American analysts were arguing that the Soviets' growing capability to fight a limited counterforce war belied their doctrinal statements.[13] However, those capabilities were the same as would be needed to carry out an unrestrained but well-coordinated series of disarming, decapitating strikes, and therefore could not be used to choose between the alternative hypotheses.

Since direct evidence from statements and force posture is inconclusive, a third approach would be to infer Soviet thinking indirectly by developing a theory of the determinants of military doctrine and asking what doctrine the theory would "predict" in the Soviet case. A military doctrine, like any belief system, is rooted in the sociological characteristics, historical experiences, and parochial outlook of the people who develop it. Pursuing this line of reasoning, we should try to identify the circumstances that led to the development of limited nuclear war doctrines in the U.S. and then compare them to the formative experiences shaping Soviet strategic thinking. In the U.S. case, two factors stand out. First, doctrinal debates were dominated by civilian defense intellectuals, whose analytical bent and training led them to think of the use of force as a political tool for coercive bargaining in a mixed-motive game. Second, the problems of extended deterrence and rational first use in the European theater focused American thinking on the suicide-or-surrender dilemma and possible limited war solutions. This way of thinking became so ingrained in the American strategic culture that even central strategic exchanges came to be viewed through this prism.

The forces shaping the Soviet strategic culture were quite different. Detailed exposition of doctrine was carried out exclusively by military officers, whose operational bent and training led them to think in terms of a zero-sum struggle to disarm the enemy. Political limitations on the use of force tend to conflict with the military's desire for operational autonomy and with its belief that both sides will be unable to resist seizing the advantages of

13. For example, Fritz W. Ermarth, "Contrasts in American and Soviet Strategic Thought," *International Security*, Vol. 3, No. 2 (Fall 1978), pp. 148–149.

surprise and "the initiative" in trying to disarm the other. Likewise, thinking about the European theater led the Soviets away from limited war concepts, just as it led Americans towards such notions. For the Soviets, Europe was not an extended deterrence problem, giving rise to schemes for limited first use. Instead, it was an overlap problem, giving rise to the fear that a limited "theater" war would damage Russia almost as much as a strategic exchange.

In short, a strategic culture approach would predict the development of limited war thinking in the United States and its absence in the Soviet Union. In this way, it reinforces the view that Soviet denunciations of such notions are not merely propaganda but also reflect the thinking that would probably guide Soviet wartime actions. Crucial to reaching this conclusion were the use of the comparative method and general social science theories, especially the application of organization theory and cognitive theory to the question of the doctrinal preferences of the military. It should be noted that a research agenda for checking these findings would entail further work both on the theoretical dimension and on its application to the Soviet case. Is it true that military professionals are usually hostile to limited war doctrines? What accounts for exceptions to this rule? Does the Soviet case fit the pattern of these exceptions? To answer these questions, students of Soviet military doctrine must not only be good Sovietologists, but they must also be conversant with the relevant theoretical literature and other cases that can be used as points of comparison.[14]

To return to the main point, it was precisely the lack of reliable, direct evidence of Soviet views on limited nuclear war that necessitated the use of theoretical, comparative techniques. This is not a quirk of the present example. Indeed, theoretical assumptions, usually implicit, underlie all interpretations of Soviet published statements. For example, Dina Spechler's study of Soviet media treatment of the October War assumed that variations in press commentary reflect actual differences of opinion.[15] However, when her analysis is reread in light of new research on the workings of the Soviet media, many of her findings seem at least superficially consistent with a

---

14. Two excellent discussions of theory and method in the study of Soviet military policy are: Stephen Meyer, "Soviet Defense Decision-making," UCLA Occasional Paper No. 33; and Matthew Evangelista, "Why the Soviets Buy the Weapons They Do," *World Politics*, Vol. 36, No. 4 (July 1984).

15. Dina Spechler, "Internal Influences on Soviet Foreign Policy: Elite Opinion and the Middle East," Hebrew University of Jerusalem, Soviet and East European Research Centre, Paper No. 18, December 1976.

number of alternative explanations: articulation of group interests, leadership politics, functional differences in focus of attention, tailoring propaganda to different audiences, and so on.[16] To try to rule out some of these alternatives, it would be necessary to find circumstances in which they would predict different patterns of press commentary. Thus, the policymaking and editorial processes would be treated as a "black box," the contents of which would be inferred from its inputs and outputs.[17]

Sovietologists have long understood the idea of using inference to peer into the black box of Soviet decision-making. What they have not understood is the importance of alternative theories in guiding these inferences. For example, an influential Rand study argues that the inability to see into the foreign policymaking black box virtually requires the Sovietologist to adopt some kind of rational actor model.[18] Dubious about the value of applying organizational process and politics models when direct evidence is scarce, the Rand team contends that "with a weak data base the range of behaviors compatible with the characteristics imputed to the organizations in question (from a 'general understanding' of the way organizations function) may be very extensive."[19] But the rational actor model suffers from precisely the same problem. Unless a rational actor's preference structure is known in detail, his actions will be even harder to predict than those of most routine-loving organizations. What is most important, however, is that different models of the decision-making process *do* make different predictions about behavior, at least in some circumstances. Consequently, a choice among models should be made on the basis of observed patterns of inputs and outputs, not a priori on the grounds of insufficient evidence.

This line of argument raises an even more fundamental question about the implications of limited data for the way Soviet foreign policy should be studied. If it is true that most of what is known about the contents of the black box (i.e., Soviet aims, motivations, and decision-making processes) is inferred from observable inputs and outputs, why dwell on the black box?

16. Lilita Dzirkals, Thane Gustafson, and A. Ross Johnson, *The Media and Intra-Elite Communication in the USSR*, Rand Report R-2869 (Santa Monica, Calif.: Rand, September 1982).
17. See the method used by Robert Cutler, "Soviet Debates over the Conduct of Foreign Policy toward Western Europe: Four Case Studies, 1971–1975" (Ph.D. dissertation, University of Michigan, 1982).
18. Arnold L. Horelick, A. Ross Johnson, and John D. Steinbruner, *The Study of Soviet Foreign Policy: A Review of Decision-Theory-Related Approaches*, Rand Report R-1334 (Santa Monica, Calif.: Rand, December 1973), p. 42.
19. Ibid., p. 37.

Why not be satisfied to study patterns of inputs and outputs without becoming unduly preoccupied with unobservable intervening variables? To drive a car successfully, it is important to know that the accelerator makes it go and the brake makes it stop; a detailed understanding of what goes on under the hood to achieve these results is usually not essential. Likewise, the most useful kind of knowledge about Soviet foreign policy may be how it behaves in certain kinds of situations and how it responds to the policies of other states. To develop and test generalizations of this kind, we may not always need to agonize over "what Khrushchev must have been thinking." Rather, we should devote more effort to comparing and contrasting patterns of behavior across cases.

There are many theories of international politics and foreign policy that can be tested by observing either behavior alone or behavior plus a modest amount of internal evidence. Propositions from deterrence or spiral theories can be tested by examining patterns of response to threats and concessions. Hypotheses about the effects of the balance of power can be tested without access to Politburo transcripts. Even "operational code" theories can be tested by observing how the Soviets probe commitments and manage risks. Access to Soviet writings was important in the initial formulation of hypotheses about the Bolshevik operational code, but not in verifying their application to crisis decision-making. This does not mean that direct evidence about internal processes should be ignored, but simply that we should adopt a research strategy that makes the most systematic use of the best available information. At least for some areas of inquiry, that strategy should be to use the comparative case method as a way of drawing inferences largely from observable behavior.

Implementing the Scientific Method in the Soviet Context

Exhortations to be more rigorous are of little value without a specific program for carrying this out. How can students of Soviet foreign policy overcome the hurdle posed by each of the five elements of the scientific method? Drawing examples from some of the best studies in the field, suggestions for a more satisfactory implementation of the scientific method will be discussed.

1) CAUSAL GENERALIZATION
Many writers on Soviet foreign policy, especially those who produce detailed historical accounts, are accustomed to explaining events without explicit

generalizations. They believe that generalization means overgeneralization, forcing a unique confluence of circumstances to fit a prefabricated, simplistic model that ignores decisive nuances, contextual differences, or complex interrelationships. However, theory does not have to be a Procrustean bed. Even complex, unique events can be described as the outcome of a number of variables interacting in a particular way. As long as each link in the chain of cause and effect can be "covered" by a plausible generalization, the scientific method is satisfied.[20] Science prefers simplicity on utilitarian grounds, but does not demand it.

It can even be argued that oversimplification is less likely when causal generalizations are stated explicitly and all the steps in the argument are meticulously presented. For example, all the rich detail in Vojtech Mastny's *Russia's Road to the Cold War* has very little to do with its ultrasimple bottom line: "Russia's striving for power and influence far in excess of its reasonable security requirements was the primary source of conflict, and the Western failure to resist it early enough an important secondary one."[21] Nowhere does Mastny show how his evidence supports this conclusion and refutes others; the conclusion just grows out of the narrative in a way that seems persuasive because of a few strategically deployed quotations from Litvinov. It is of course this concluding assertion that everyone remembers, while the particularistic nuances of the narrative are soon forgotten.[22] The origins of the Cold War are reduced to a generic deterrence failure, with necessary and sufficient causal conditions lost in the mass of detail. Unlike Mastny, deterrence *theory* offers several hypotheses about the conditions in which "resisting early" is beneficial as well as conditions in which it is likely to be counterproductive or irrelevant.[23] Mastny's study would have been much more useful and persuasive if he had systematically marshaled his evidence

20. Sidney Verba, "Some Dilemmas in Comparative Research," *World Politics*, Vol. 20, No. 1 (October 1967), pp. 111–127.
21. Vojtech Mastny, *Russia's Road to the Cold War* (New York: Columbia University Press, 1979), p. 283.
22. See, for example, John Lewis Gaddis, "The Emerging Post-Revisionist Synthesis on the Origins of the Cold War," *Diplomatic History*, Vol. 7, No. 3 (Summer 1983), pp. 175–176. Mastny's well-supported argument that Stalin had no fixed aims for territorial conquest could be seen as providing a fairly direct, logical link between Mastny's evidence and his conclusions about the need to resist early. Perhaps this is so, but George and Smoke's analysis of the problem of deterring an opponent who uses flexible tactics to pursue a strategy of minimum and maximum aims suggests to me that early resistance is likely to provoke a challenge to deterrent commitments in such cases. See *Deterrence in American Foreign Policy*, pp. 540–547.
23. Jervis, *Perception and Misperception*, chapter 3.

to show which *type* of conditions existed in his case. In other words, even in explaining a single case, theory and generalization play a crucial role. Implementing this strategy does not require oversimplification, which is a vice that historians and political scientists must both strive to avoid.

2) CONSTRUCTING HYPOTHESES AND MEASURING VARIABLES
It is quite possible to engage in abstraction and generalization without constructing testable "if, then" hypotheses. Indeed, the hallmark of the Soviet studies field is the insightful, synthesizing book or article that pronounces broad generalizations on the basis of examples, quotations, and a general feel for what makes the Soviet Union tick. The master of this method is Adam Ulam, whose latest work, *Dangerous Relations*, demonstrates the creative possibilities of this approach as well as its analytical limitations.[24] Ulam is not reluctant to generalize, arguing for example that future Soviet "decisions on foreign policy in all likelihood will depend on the Kremlin's perception of the condition of the West. We say condition rather than policies, for, as we have seen during the past twelve years, it has been Moscow's reading of the strengths and weaknesses . . . of the entire community of democratic nations that has been mainly instrumental in shaping the USSR's foreign policy."[25] This is a generalization but not yet a testable, causal hypothesis. For that, it would be necessary to state what kinds of Soviet policies are predicted when the West is weak and divided and, conversely, what policies are predicted when the Soviet Union is the weaker side. Ulam's discussion of the 1970s and his policy prescription ("the West recouping its strength and vitality") suggest that Western weakness produces Soviet assertiveness.[26] But his treatment of the 1940s suggests the reverse: "The USSR did not see itself as yet strong enough to be friendly with the democracies."[27] As Ulam and others have shown, the problem in this period was that each side was vulnerable to the policies of the other and that self-defense was seen as requiring the exploitation of the other's weakness.[28] Where, then, does Ulam stand? Is he a correlation of forces theorist, arguing for deterrence through unity and strength, or is he a security dilemma theorist, focusing on the role

24. Adam Ulam, *Dangerous Relations* (New York: Oxford University Press, 1983).
25. Ibid., p. 314.
26. Ibid., p. 315.
27. Ibid., p. 15.
28. See especially William Taubman, *Stalin's American Policy* (New York: Norton, 1982), chapter 7, on the Marshall Plan and the response of the French communists.

of *mutual* vulnerability in producing conflict spirals? Both hypotheses emphasize "conditions" rather than "policies" as the underlying cause of conflict, but their prescriptions for creating stabilizing conditions are quite different. When does each model apply? How do we know that the lessons of the 1940s are not relevant for the 1980s? In short, Ulam generalizes, but he does not offer "if, then" hypotheses that can be tested by the evidence he offers and used to support his policy conclusions.

Even studies that show a concern for theory and method often fail to develop clear "if, then" hypotheses. Hannes Adomeit, for example, begins *Soviet Risk-taking and Crisis Behavior* with a lengthy discussion of theories of deterrence, bargaining, and crisis decision-making.[29] He even lists some testable hypotheses developed in that literature. But when the case studies arrive, the theories and hypotheses are replaced as explanatory tools by "factors of risk-taking," such as "ideology," "domestic factors," and "interests." These obviously are not causal variables but loose umbrella categories used to organize the case study material. Most of the analysis conducted under the rubric of each category is ad hoc. For example, there is no clear prediction of types of domestic circumstances that should promote or discourage risk-taking. The most satisfactory category is "ideology," which includes some fairly specific hypotheses about the Bolshevik operational code. Adomeit treats the operational code as a constant, prescribing a set formula of limited probes and controlled pressure that the Politburo uses to manage the risks of expansionism. Although Adomeit does not tell us how a Bolshevik "knows when to stop," his operational code notion is not entirely nonfalsifiable, since he does admit that the Soviet fait accompli strategy for emplacing missiles in Cuba does not fit the limited-probe formula.[30] This is an improvement on Alexander George's virtually non-falsifiable treatment of Soviet risk calculation (they must have thought the risks were low), but it would be better still if Adomeit could identify the conditions that led the Soviets to abandon their operational code in this case.[31]

---

29. Hannes Adomeit, *Soviet Risk-Taking and Crisis Behavior* (Boston: Allen & Unwin, 1982).
30. Ibid., p. 319.
31. George and Smoke hypothesized that deterrence will succeed if the would-be initiator concludes that the risks are incalculable and uncontrollable. Thus, they conclude that Khrushchev must have believed that he could control the risks in the Cuban missile crisis, and they show how he could plausibly have held such a belief. This may constitute an interesting thought experiment, but in no way can it be considered a test of their hypothesis, since they present no evidence to refute the opposite view that Khrushchev believed he might lose control over events

A more fundamental source of difficulty is Adomeit's use of "risk-taking" as his dependent variable, i.e., that which he seeks to explain. Actions are not inherently risky or cautious; the riskiness of an action can only be judged in comparison with other options. In the Prisoner's Dilemma game, for example, cooperative behavior is the "risky" course of action. Cautious players who want to minimize their maximum loss will behave aggressively. Consequently, "riskiness" is not an elemental variable that can be measured by direct observation. Rather, it is a second-order characterization that only distracts us from the key first-order questions: Under what conditions does deterrence succeed or fail? What conditions produce what types of deterrence failure (fait accompli, controlled pressure, limited probe, etc.)? Under what conditions does a Bolshevik decide to retreat from the brink to his fallback position?

For the elegant handling of the definition and measurement of a dependent variable in the Soviet field, one could do no better than a study by William Zimmerman and Robert Axelrod of the lessons of Vietnam as portrayed by various Soviet press organs.[32] At least one senior Soviet specialist points to this article as *the* model for methodologically sophisticated work in the field. Indeed, Zimmerman and Axelrod's measurement of the commentary of nine newspapers on a left-right scale (i.e., militancy versus peaceful coexistence) leaves little to be desired. The problem is that all of their effort goes into measuring this one variable. Virtually no systematic effort is devoted to identifying the causes of these left-right variations. The authors assert that this finding in itself shows that Soviet foreign policymaking is "polyarchic," but many Soviet specialists have argued that variations in media treatment of an issue can be explained in other ways: for example, division of labor in a unified propaganda strategy or emphasis of different aspects of an issue due to different functional concerns.[33] To convince skeptics, Zimmerman and Axelrod should have paid as much attention to the problem of eliminating alternative explanations as they did to measuring their dependent variable. For that matter, even if one takes for granted that policy differences underlie variations in press commentary, it would be interesting to know whether

---

but figured he had no choice. George and Smoke, *Deterrence in American Foreign Policy*, pp. 463–466, 527–529.
32. William Zimmerman and Robert Axelrod, "The 'Lessons' of Vietnam and Soviet Foreign Policy," *World Politics*, Vol. 34, No. 1 (October 1981), pp. 1–24.
33. See Dzirkals, Gustafson, and Johnson, *The Media and Intra-Elite Communication*.

these disputes are rooted in leadership politics, institutional interests, generational cleavages, or some other cause. In short, Zimmerman and Axelrod do provide a model for the sophisticated measurement of a dependent variable, but they do not use scientific techniques in explaining the outcomes that they so meticulously observe.

3 AND 4) ESTABLISHING COVARIATION AND ELIMINATING ALTERNATIVES
Once an "if, then" relationship between two variables has been hypothesized and rules for measuring them have been established, the next step is to examine some cases to see if the expected relationship holds. A mistake that is often made at this stage is neglecting to examine cases with contrasting outcomes. If the scholar is interested in studying the causes of military intervention, for example, his natural inclination will be to look at several instances of intervention to identify similarities among them. A more revealing method would be to look at instances of both intervention and non-intervention to identify differences as well as similarities. An excellent example of the use of this method in the Soviet field is Christopher Jones's study of Soviet military intervention in Eastern Europe.[34]

Jones examines one case of Soviet military intervention (Czechoslovakia) and four cases of non-intervention (Yugoslavia, Poland in 1956, Rumania, and Albania). In all five cases, Jones contends that the Soviets sought to unseat an independent Communist regime and replace it with a "Muscovite" faction, but four times they acquiesced rather than use force. (Hungary is placed in a separate category on the grounds that Nagy was heading an anti-communist movement, not a local communist regime.) The standard explanation for these outcomes, Jones says, is that "the Soviets resorted to military intervention only when certain ideological or strategic issues were at stake. . . . East European Communists who avoided challenging the Soviets in these particular areas were able to break free of Soviet control."[35] In contrast, Jones holds that a single factor is sufficient to explain all five cases: whether or not the local Communists showed that they were "willing to go to war in defense of their national sovereignty."[36]

---

34. Christopher Jones, "Soviet Hegemony in Eastern Europe: The Dynamics of Political Autonomy and Military Intervention," *World Politics*, Vol. 29, No. 2 (January 1977), pp. 216–241.
35. Ibid., p. 216.
36. Ibid., p. 240.

Although Jones does establish that "willingness to fight" covaries with the outcome in each case, he neglects to show that alternative explanations fail to correlate with these outcomes. Despite his aim of refuting the conventional explanations that stress strategic importance and/or ideological deviation, he does not even attempt to measure these variables to see whether they might also fit the outcomes. One parsimonious alternative explanation seems at least superficially persuasive for all five cases and Hungary as well: namely, the erosion of the "leading role" of the Party. Hungary was the extreme case of the Communists' loss of control; Czechoslovakia was just at an earlier stage on the slippery slope, both in Moscow's view and perhaps in reality. In contrast, the other four Parties had disagreements with Moscow, but their power to control non-Communist forces was not in jeopardy. This alternative explanation is particularly troublesome for Jones because it can use many of his own arguments about the role of the legitimacy factor in deterring Soviet interventions. As Hungary shows, the prospect of armed resistance is not what makes intervention illegitimate; rather, legitimacy hinges on the credibility of the argument that intervention is the only way to prevent anti-communists from reversing the gains of socialism. The point here is not that Jones is necessarily wrong, but that merely establishing covariation is insufficient to prove that he is right. It is also necessary to show that the most likely alternative explanations do not covary with the outcome.

There are several ways to use case studies to try to eliminate alternative explanations. One technique is the "most similar case" comparison, which compares cases that are similar in all major respects except the outcome and the hypothesized cause. Jones might try to argue, for example, that Poland in 1956 was similar to Czechoslovakia in 1968 in most respects (e.g., strategic importance, degree of ideological deviation, degree of party control over society) except for the willingness to fight and the outcome. Often, however, the "most similar case" will be the same country in an earlier time period. Thus, Jones might try to argue that the Soviets did not invade Czechoslovakia in July 1968 because they were uncertain about the likelihood of Czechoslovak resistance. Some analysts have argued, in fact, that the purpose of the Cierna negotiations in early August was to gather intelligence on this point and/or to lull the Czechs, making military surprise easier to achieve. Another technique for eliminating alternative explanations is the "least similar case" comparison, which seeks cases that are different in all major respects except for the outcome and the hypothesized cause. Thus, Jones might argue that

Poland and Rumania were different in all respects (strategic value, ideological deviation, firmness of party control) except their willingness to fight and the outcome (no intervention).

A final possibility is variously termed the "crucial case," "hard case," or "least likely case" method. The goal here is to find a case in which (1) the hypothesized cause and the strongest challenger make opposite predictions, and (2) the challenger has the home-court advantage. The classic example is Robert Michels's test for the Iron Law of Oligarchy. Reasoning that if any organization is run democratically it should be the German Social Democratic Party, he showed that it was an oligarchy and hence that no organization can be democratic.[37] Similarly, Graham Allison implies that the Cuban missile crisis is something like a crucial case for choosing between the rational actor model and his organizational model, since crisis decision-making should be harder to explain in organizational terms than more routine policy processes.[38]

If all of these methods fail to rule out an important explanation, it may indicate that the "competing" explanatory variables are not truly independent of each other. For example, it might be that strong local Communist Parties—precisely because they are strong, well organized, legitimate, and nationalist—are also those that can most credibly threaten effective military resistance. If so, strong local party control might be the underlying cause of Soviet non-intervention and threatened resistance might be an intervening variable. Or the link between threatened resistance and Soviet acquiescence might be spurious: the legitimacy per se of the local party is what deters Moscow, and not the threat to fight.[39]

It should be noted that all of these comparative techniques are not replacements for detailed historical analyses of the kind traditionally carried out by students of Soviet foreign policy. Detailed case studies must be done in order to have something to compare. And "measuring variables" in this context can hardly be reduced to a mechanical procedure; the judgment of an experienced area specialist is indispensable in deciding which cases fit into which categories. The theoretical side of the enterprise mainly comes into play at two points: (1) suggesting variables that should be taken into account

---

37. See the discussion by Harry Eckstein, "Case Study and Theory in Political Science," in Fred I. Greenstein and Nelson W. Polsby, eds., *Strategy of Inquiry*, Vol. 7 of *Handbook of Political Science* (Reading, Mass.: Addison-Wesley, 1975), pp. 79–137.
38. Graham T. Allison, *Essence of Decision* (Boston: Little, Brown & Co., 1971).
39. On spuriousness, see Jervis, *Perception and Misperception*, chapter 6.

and (2) drawing inferences from the completed cases. Even in these areas, feedback between richness and rigor is vital. Do the variables highlighted by theory seem to be a proper focus for studying the case? If not, should the theory be adjusted? One reason that exclusively statistical methods are dangerous in a young science is that they do not provide sufficient richness to support this feedback between theory and history. In sum, theoretical, methodological, and area studies skills are complementary in this kind of research process.

5) DEDUCTIVE THEORY

Theories are an efficient way to store and retrieve knowledge; they allow us to aggregate our past experiences and learn from them in a systematic way. They also help us to feel our way through unfamiliar terrain and estimate the probable consequences of our actions. Exceptionally efficient are general theories, which allow us to organize a great variety of data, and tightly deductive theories, which allow us to anticipate what we will find around the next corner if the trail of evidence leaves major gaps.

These are familiar utilitarian reasons for wanting to group isolated hypotheses into a deductive theory, composed of many related hypotheses and increasing levels of abstraction. A less familiar notion is that, by placing a hypothesis in a coherent theoretical structure, we can feel more certain that it is true. For example, the hegemonic stability explanation for free trade would be less persuasive if it could not be deduced from collective goods theory.[40] Likewise, Jones's hypothesis would be more compelling if he had placed it in the context of deterrence theory generally and, more specifically, linked it to the findings of Glenn Snyder and Paul Diesing regarding the importance of perceptions of legitimacy for deterrent outcomes.[41] Standing alone, Jones's argument seems a bit arbitrary, notwithstanding the fact that it seems to fit the cases. Put in the context of Snyder and Diesing's arguments about the key role of legitimacy in determining the "balance of interests" (as well as their varied cases supporting that proposition), Jones's hypothesis begins to appear more imposing.

In short, linking hypotheses in deductive theories makes them more useful. When direct evidence is indecisive, deduction also helps us to assess the

40. McKeown, "Hegemonic Stability Theory," makes precisely this charge.
41. Glenn H. Snyder and Paul Diesing, *Conflict among Nations* (Princeton: Princeton University Press, 1977), pp. 184, 498–499.

validity of those hypotheses. Finally, when a number of factors covary, deduction also helps us to determine which variables are causes, which are effects, and which are merely spurious.

Conclusions

The scientific method, if properly understood, complements rather than conflicts with the traditional approach of students of Soviet foreign policy. Surprisingly, the data limitations of the Soviet field actually enhance the importance of explicit attention to theory and scientific methodology. Relatively small changes in the way analysis is conducted could improve the rigor and value of many studies. These changes would not entail great costs in terms of richness or policy-relevance. Recent literature in the international politics field, which employs a method of controlled comparison of narrative case studies, shows that richness, rigor, and relevance can go hand-in-hand. Soviet specialists should benefit greatly from the theories and the methods employed in this literature. In turn, international theory would be greatly enriched if students of Soviet foreign policy would contribute their own special skills and insights to those theoretical debates.

The Sources of American Conduct

Franklyn Griffiths

Soviet Perspectives and Their Policy Implications

$\mathbf{A}$ new way of thinking and talking about Soviet foreign policy is needed, one that allows ready recognition of diversity in the outward behavior of a society whose leaders are bent on the containment of diversity within. The experience of the liberal democracies demonstrates that a dual policy of concurrent resistance and cooperation in dealing with the U.S.S.R. suffers in the absence of public recognition of dualism in Soviet conduct. But how to contest the widespread assumption that the Soviet leaders are single-minded expansionists without falling into the other error of implying that the regime is divided into coalitions of moderates and diehards whose presence cannot be demonstrated with assurance? The answer is to be had in the identification of contrasting tendencies in the behavior of the Soviet Union that persist irrespective of momentary internal configurations of the regime.

Western analysts have debated the sources of Soviet foreign conduct for many years now. The effort to define and explain the opponent's behavior, sometimes referred to simply as "the threat," has seen the emergence of three main schools of thought which continue to vie for acceptance.[1] This article seeks to promote a new synthesis suited to the needs of Western policy in the latter half of the 1980s and beyond.

Some would explain Soviet conduct primarily by reference to what the U.S.S.R. is or is supposed to be—a totalitarian political order that is irrevocably committed to world domination, that stays its hand only when confronted with superior force, and that invariably exploits Western good will in the furtherance of its aggressive aims. President Reagan's vision of the Soviet Union as an empire of evil is not far removed from this eccentric evaluation. It is however far removed from the data of Soviet behavior, as will be seen.

A more empirical assessment is associated with mainstream Western thinking about the containment of Soviet power. For this school of thought, the explanation of Soviet actions centers more on what the Kremlin does and less on what the Soviet system "is." A wider range of Soviet responses to Western moves is in principle allowed, mainly because the Soviet leaders are viewed not only as ideological thinkers but as realists who accommodate when forced to do so. Indeed, the elements of a tendency analysis lie buried in the foundations of Western thinking about containment: as

Franklyn Griffiths is Professor of Political Science and Acting Director of the Centre for Russian and East European Studies at the University of Toronto.

1. See the penetrating accounts in William Welch, *American Images of Soviet Foreign Policy* (New Haven: Yale University Press, 1970) and William Zimmerman, "Rethinking Soviet Foreign Policy: Changing American Perspectives," *International Journal*, Vol. 35, No. 3 (Summer 1980), pp. 548–562. Zimmerman especially is relied upon here.

International Security, Fall 1984 (Vol. 9, No. 2) 0162-2889/84/020003-48 $02.50/1

George F. Kennan put it in 1947, the "expansive tendencies" in Soviet policy were accompanied by "tendencies which must eventually find their outlet in either the break-up or the gradual mellowing of Soviet power."[2] An overriding preoccupation with Soviet expansionism and with the mechanics of countervailing force has, however, served to inhibit the emergence of a comprehensive understanding of Soviet tendencies and how they might figure in a more balanced Western approach to the U.S.S.R.

Both schools of thought—they have been called "essentialist" and "mechanist" respectively—have relied heavily on strategic conceptions in accounting for Soviet behavior. In common with more conservative Soviet assessments of the politics of American policymaking, to be considered below, it is felt that the opponent is best understood in terms of its ability to implement a strategy, or even "plan," devised by a small group of individuals at the pinnacle of the political system. This readiness to attribute a high level of centralization, intentionality, and self-control in the making of Soviet policies has been challenged by a growing body of research since the early 1960s.

A third, process-oriented school succeeded in drawing attention to what may be regarded as the quasi-pluralist character of Soviet politics and policymaking, to the presence of foreign policy debates and the use of ideology in advancing contrasting evaluations of the external setting, and to the complex linkages between Soviet domestic and foreign policy.[3] Not only was participation in the Soviet policy process shown to be more extensive, but the degree of Soviet responsiveness to Western actions seemed to be greater than previously recognized. At the same time, the dark side of Soviet domestic and foreign operations received less emphasis as hope rose for cooperation with the U.S.S.R. and ultimately for internal reform of the Soviet regime.

Hope for change in relations with the Soviet Union seemed to be vindicated in the early 1970s as American policymakers led the way in derogating the significance of ideology in Soviet policy, in seeking the creation within the Soviet Union of vested interests in good behavior, and in acting broadly as though the Soviets were capable of offering an alternative to relentless expansionism in their dealings with the West. Just what this alternative was never received a proper explanation. Nor was there a public understanding of what might be required of the West to sustain it. The result was an excessive swing towards optimism about the future of East–West relations, and then the inevitable disillusion. With disillusion came a return to prominence of

---

2. "The Sources of Soviet Conduct," *Foreign Affairs*, Vol. 25, No. 4 (July 1947), pp. 575, 582.
3. See, for example, Marshall D. Shulman, *Stalin's Foreign Policy Reappraised* (Cambridge, Mass.: Harvard University Press, 1963); H. Gordon Skilling and Franklyn Griffiths, eds., *Interest Groups in Soviet Politics* (Princeton: Princeton University Press, 1971); Jerry F. Hough, *How the Soviet Union Is Governed* (Cambridge, Mass.: Harvard University Press, 1979); Alexander Dallin, "The Domestic Sources of Soviet Foreign Policy," in Seweryn Bialer, ed., *The Domestic Context of Soviet Foreign Policy* (Boulder, Colo.: Westview Press, 1981), pp. 335–408; and Jerry F. Hough, *Soviet Policy Debates about the Third World* (Washington, D.C.: Brookings, forthcoming).

one-sided strategic explanations of Soviet conduct, and then an immoderate commitment to containment and confrontation with the U.S.S.R.

Experience shows that each of the available schools of thought on the sources of Soviet policy is inadequate when relied upon exclusively. Each captures and overstates selected aspects of a complex reality that must somehow be understood in its totality. The task of providing a new synthesis should be accomplished in a way that reduces the risk of oversimplification and excess in Western conduct. It should also produce a central concept that is simple enough to be readily understood and used by individuals who do not have professional knowledge of Soviet affairs. The analysis that follows seeks to meet this need mainly by establishing the proposition that there is an array of conflicting tendencies in the behavior of the Soviet system towards the United States. It does so primarily by examining stated Soviet perceptions of American foreign and military policymaking as reported in the published work of Soviet specialists during the Brezhnev era.

Perceptions of the American policy process as presented in the open by specialists may well diverge substantially from the operational evaluations of Soviet decision-makers. Where Soviet decision-making itself is concerned, the assessment of what is going on within the United States is likely to be only one of a great many considerations that shape Soviet conduct towards the principal adversary. Persistent variations in the writing of specialists as they consider the workings of the American system do nevertheless reveal a good deal about the predispositions of the regime in its approach to relations with the United States. This is because the things specialists say in public about the U.S. policy process reflect the proclivities of the leadership, and are advanced in part to justify pre-existing preferences for Soviet policy towards America. By backtracking from stated specialist conceptions of American politics as put forward over an extended period of time, we stand to gain an initial understanding of Soviet tendencies, of what they tend to do in dealing with the United States.

Representing predispositions to act in given ways, tendencies are by definition future-oriented. To the degree that the tendencies in Soviet policy towards the United States can reliably be specified, it should be possible to reduce uncertainty both in anticipating what next in the Soviet Union's American policy, and in understanding it when it happens. As well, knowledge of contrasting tendencies in Soviet conduct that is derived from Soviet perceptions, as distinct from an external view of things, should add to the efficiency of policy towards the U.S.S.R. Knowing more about the structure of Soviet thinking about their relations with the United States, governments and attentive publics in the liberal democracies might be more discriminating in the use of resources to underwrite tendencies that deserve encouragement, while simultaneously acting to resist unwanted variants of Soviet conduct.

Greater economy in the commitment of resources and greater steadfastness in public support for a dual policy are essential prerequisites for a reduction in the severity of East–West conflict. To the degree that a tendency analysis of Soviet policy meets not only the foreign policy but the domestic political needs of dualism in Western and especially United States conduct, it should further the cause of East–West cooperation while encouraging measured responses to the continuing requirements of competition.

Perception and Policy

To begin with, it may be noted that leadership change in the Soviet Union provides an occasion for change in the overall approach of the regime to the United States. Stalin, Khrushchev, and Brezhnev each presided over the evolution of a distinctive orientation to the principal adversary. Under each, there was a departure from the governing perceptions and policies of the previous era. As of the spring of 1984, it is too early to speak with confidence about the policy predispositions of Konstantin Chernenko and his associates. It may however be assumed that short of an experience with nuclear confrontation, the Soviet need to be inventive in its relations with the United States will remain limited.[4] We may therefore expect the current leadership (or its successor if Chernenko's tenure in office proves brief) to reassemble bits and pieces of recombinant policy and analysis to meet the needs of the U.S.S.R., and to do so without deviating abruptly from the line laid down in Brezhnev's last years. Nevertheless, the potential for change in Soviet relations with America is there, as it was under Andropov. Given the varied assessments and practices that have at one time or another found favor in Moscow in its dealings with the United States, the repertoire of behavior on which the present Soviet leadership might eventually draw is quite broad.

Since the first months of the Soviet era, decision-makers in Moscow have tended to look within the capitalist countries, the United States included, for non-working class social forces (later called "reserves") that can be turned to advantage.[5] The quintessential instance of this practice is to be found in secret Soviet preparations for the Genoa Economic Conference of 1922. In the face of intra-party opposition, Lenin secured support for a tension-reducing policy aimed at utilizing the electoral process in the West to strengthen the influence of liberals and pacifists, to weaken the "war party," and thereby to face Moscow with governments more inclined to accept Soviet terms for political-military stabilization and trade expansion.[6] This line of policy was

---

4. A cogent discussion of the regime's ability to cope with a variety of domestic problems in the remainder of the 1980s is to be found in Timothy J. Colton, *The Dilemma of Reform in the Soviet Union* (New York: Council on Foreign Relations, 1984).
5. See, for example, the references of the Commissar for Foreign Affairs to conflicting tendencies in Berlin on the Russian question in 1918, to "farsighted" members of the German ruling class, and to the Soviet "tactic . . . of opposing the interests of German industry and trade to the military government." G.V. Chicherin, *Stati i rechi po voprosam mezhdunarodnoi politiki* [Articles and Speeches on Questions of International Politics] (Moscow: Sotsekgiz, 1961), p. 228. Similar perceptions and tactics are evident in Chicherin's discussion of Soviet policies towards Japan in 1918, Estonia in 1919–1920 (the "first experiment in peaceful cohabitation with bourgeois states"), and the United States in 1921. Ibid., pp. 60, 135–143, 171–179. Where the United States was concerned, Chicherin differentiated between regional groupings of finance capital, some of which were more favorably disposed to Soviet Russia than others.
6. To undercut the position of those who relied on the "Soviet threat," and to underwrite the electoral appeal of pacifist and liberal candidates, Soviet Russia was to propagate a "proletarian pacifism" centered on proposals for arms regulation, trade expansion, and other forms of collaboration that stopped just short of what existing Western governments could accept. For details, see Franklyn Griffiths, *Genoa plus 51: Changing Soviet Objectives in Europe*, Wellesley Paper

based on an ideologically vulnerable evaluation of the politics of policymaking in the West, one that emphasized the presence of conflicting tendencies in the ruling class and the relative autonomy of the imperialist state.

Intra-party argumentation in favor of the attempt to penetrate and manipulate the opponent's policymaking processes was however suppressed as Stalin put his own mark on the foreign policy of the Soviet Union. Although Leninist unorthodoxy experienced a brief resurgence after World War II, the predominant requirement of the regime in Stalin's last years was to mobilize and control its own population in an international setting of confrontation with the West. Specialists were ordered to produce a propaganda image of the United States according to which only the worst could be expected. The vision here was one of a very tightly controlled American society in which the "monopolies"—the leading industrial corporations, banks, and investment houses plus the tiny financial oligarchy that controlled these operations— did pretty well as they wanted in pursuing a policy of unrelieved hostility towards the U.S.S.R. Needless to say, this view of the American system effectively negated the possibility of conducting a policy of tension-reduction and negotiation modelled on the Genoa precedent. Though Soviet foreign policy was in practice conducted with a more subtle assessment in mind,[7] the official need to know about the inner political workings of American capitalism was presumably rather limited, there being little immediate prospect of an end to confrontation and a policy of fixed position.

At the outset of the Khrushchev era, the Soviet leadership embarked on a campaign to make their country into a global power without, however, raising the risks of nuclear war and the costs of being prepared for it. Lacking the capabilities required to force American acceptance of a rapid change in the world correlation of forces (the global balance of strength and advantage between competing social systems), and preferring not to go all out in acquiring them, Moscow needed American restraint and a degree of cooperation as well. As Khrushchev and some of his colleagues looked to the United States, they evidently saw a Presidency that might, with Soviet assistance, be taken over or substantially influenced by the liberal wing of the bourgeoisie acting through the Democratic Party. Internal evidence of an interest in utilizing the Presidential electoral process is to be found in a greater Soviet readiness after the mid-1950s to differentiate between conflicting tendencies in American policy and policymaking,[8] and in the appearance of esoteric references to the Genoa policy of

No. 4 (Toronto: Canadian Institute of International Affairs, 1973), pp. 23–32. The precedent of Soviet policy at Genoa became a point of reference for those in the Soviet Union who subsequently favored the use of a détente posture—propaganda restraint, concessions, and agreements—to strengthen moderation in the making of Western foreign and military policies. For one of a good many examples that relate to the contemporary United States, see V.V. Zhurkin, SShA i mezhdunarodno-politicheskie krizisy [The U.S. and International Political Crises] (Moscow: "Nauka," 1975), pp. 302–303.

7. William Taubman is quite convincing on this point. See his Stalin's American Policy (New York: Norton, 1982), esp. pp. 135–138.

8. Among Soviet leaders, Khrushchev and O.V. Kuusinen led the way in distinguishing between conflicting tendencies in U.S. politics and policies. See, for example, their speeches in Pravda,

1922 as having contemporary significance.[9] The operative image of the United States
in the Khrushchev era would seem to have been one of an American pluralism in
which no single stratum had a monopoly of influence over the office of the Presidency,
in which a broad-based reformist coalition could use the electoral process to wrest
away or diminish the control over the executive branch exercised by the more reactionary elements of the ruling class.

Soviet policymakers in the Khrushchev era accordingly acted to lower tensions with
the United States in Presidential election and pre-election years. Simultaneously, they
endeavored to create the impression of nuclear-missile strength and pressed for
unilateral advantage, primarily in Europe and primarily in the off years. Hence the
Soviet interest in the three détentes of the Eisenhower and Kennedy Presidencies.
Hence the use of a détente posture and its association with a policy of pressure in a
two-track effort to achieve three goals: to subvert the influence of American advocates
of strength, to deny American politicians the opportunity to exploit the Soviet threat,
and to give Americans greater strength in the conviction that "sobriety" and "moderation" were appropriate in U.S. foreign and military policy. Khrushchev accordingly
took credit for the election of President Kennedy.[10] By 1963–1964, as the Soviet global
offensive foundered, Moscow found itself making headway in the elaboration of an
improved bilateral relationship with the United States.

April 23, 1960 (Kuusinen), January 25, 1961 (Khrushchev), and December 15, 1963 (Khrushchev).
For specialist commentary differentiating between opposed tendencies in American conduct,
see I.M. Lemin, "Monopolii i vneshnyaya politika" [The Monopolies and Foreign Policy], in M.
Rubinshtein et al., eds., *Monopolisticheskii kapital SShA posle vtoroi mirovoi voiny* [U.S. Monopoly
Capital after World War II] (Moscow: Izd-vo AN SSSR, 1958), pp. 647–670; N. Inozemtsev,
"'Atomnaya politika' SShA: proekty i deistvitelnost" [The "Atomic policy" of America: Plans
and Reality], *Mirovaya ekonomika i mezhdunarodnye otnosheniya* (hereafter *MEMO*), No. 3 (1958),
p. 41; G. Trofimenko, "Borba v SShA po voprosam vneshnei politiki" [Struggle in the U.S. over
Foreign Policy], ibid., No. 9 (1958), pp. 106–116, and "SShA: politicheskii kurs i vnutrennaya
borba" [The U.S.: Internal Struggle over the Political Course], ibid., No. 4 (1959), pp. 56–57; F.
Burlatskii, *Pravda*, July 25, 1963; Yu. Arbatov, ibid., August 13, 1963; and I.M. Lemin et al.,
eds., *Dvizhushchie sily vneshnei politiki SShA* [The Motive Forces of U.S. Foreign Policy] (Moscow:
"Nauka," 1965), esp. pp. 48–54, 510.
9. On July 22, 1959, the first of a series of hitherto secret documents pertaining to Soviet policy
at the time of the Genoa Conference was sent to press. V.I. Lenin, *Leninskii sbornik* [Lenin
Miscellany], Vol. 36 (Moscow: Institut Marksizma–Leninizma, 1959), pp. 451–455. See also
Kuusinen, *Pravda*, April 23, 1960, for the first high-level reference to Genoa; Khrushchev, ibid.,
January 25, 1961; and B.N. Ponomarev, ibid., April 23, 1963. Still more revealing Genoa documents were published in *Pravda* on April 12 and 22, 1964.
10. Television interview with N.S. Khrushchev, National Broadcasting Company, July 12, 1967.
Cited in James N. Rosenau, "Introduction," in Rosenau, ed., *Linkage Politics* (New York: Free
Press, 1969), p. 1. For a contemporary account that suggests Khrushchev had influenced the
outcome of the 1960 election, see V.G. Korionov and N.N. Yakovlev, *SSSR i SShA dolzhny zhit
v mire* [The U.S.S.R. and U.S.A. Must Live in Peace] (Moscow: Gospolitizdat, 1961), pp. 108,
115. See also the reference to Genoa and to the need for "growing pressure of the peoples on
the governments, so that the advocates of war and the arms race and their allies are pushed
out of the management of affairs of state and their place occupied by sober-minded figures
. . . ," in A.A. Arzumanyan, "Vernyi put obespecheniya prochnogo mira mezhdu narodami"
[The True Way of Insuring Lasting Peace Among Peoples], *Kommunist*, No. 4 (1962), pp. 27, 35.

Following Khrushchev's removal and the onset of full-scale military intervention in Vietnam by a liberal Democratic President who had just routed a conservative Republican, those in Moscow who were not already convinced doubtless came to see the limitations of the Presidential electoral process as a point of entry in attempting to moderate American policy.[11] More important, the new Soviet leadership appears to have given up the Khrushchevian and indeed Leninist attempt to further the creation of a reformist political coalition in the United States.[12] As well, they put an end to Khrushchevian reformism in the Soviet Union. Yielding in larger measure to the established Soviet interests, they reduced the urgency of the need for moderation in American conduct. Instead, they placed greater emphasis on the creation of Soviet strength and external constraints on the United States to display "realism," to adopt a more accurate assessment of American capabilities in a less enabling world. The United States was in effect to be dealt with as it stood.[13] Correspondingly, the Soviets' operational conception of the American system would seem to have altered from the pluralism envisaged in the Khrushchev years to one that stressed the interconnections of the state with monopoly capital, the limited ability of American monopoly capitalism to adapt policy to new requirements, and the workings of the political mech-

---

11. That Brezhnev may have had some learning to do is indicated by his comment on the 1964 Presidential election: "The defeat of the American 'ultras' is a good lesson for all adherents to the policy of adventure and reaction." Quoted in E.A. Ivanyan, *Belyi dom: prezidenty i politika* [The White House: Presidents and Politics] (Moscow: Politizdat, 1975), p. 383.

12. With one exception, the Soviet Union did not move to establish a détente with the United States in a Presidential election or pre-election year after 1964. The exception, in 1972, saw Moscow indirectly but clearly indicate a preference for the Republican incumbent over a left-liberal challenger who, even if he had been an effective contender, would not likely have been preferred by a Soviet regime bent on "businesslike" dealings with America. Internal Soviet commentary after 1964 also shows a decline in leadership references to the Genoa policy and to Lenin's key phrase of 1922, "It is not a matter of indifference to us whether we have to deal with representatives of the bourgeois camp who are attracted to a military solution of the problem or . . . to pacifism. . . ." Similarly, Brezhnev-era specialist discussions of Soviet policy in 1922 became less frequent, less revealing, and more wooden. For an example of the latter, see S. Tikhvinskii, "Lenin, Genuya, Sovremennost" [Lenin, Genoa, Present-day Conditions], *MEMO*, No. 4 (1982), pp. 3–17. An exceptionally informative piece is, however, to be found in A.O. Chubaryan, "V.I. Lenin i Genuya" [V.I. Lenin and Genoa], *Istoriya SSSR*, No. 2 (1970), pp. 36–50.

13. Accepting an American system whose behavior was not susceptible to reliable moderation from within, the efforts of the Brezhnev–Kosygin and later the Brezhnev regime to intervene directly in the politics of American policymaking would seem to have been confined to tactical operations exemplified by the Washington lobbying of the Soviet embassy, the extension of support to the Nixon Administration in turning back the Mansfield amendment on U.S. force reductions in Europe, and momentary increases in Jewish emigration as a means of undercutting Congressional opponents of expanded trade relations. Also significant is the commitment in 1982 not to use nuclear weapons first, which would seem to have been made in part to undercut American arguments that Moscow planned a disarming first strike; and the series of official comments on the suicidal nature of nuclear war, which evidently sought to mute the "Soviet threat" by qualifying Soviet interests in nuclear "war-fighting" and victory. To some in Moscow, these latter statements on the character of nuclear war doubtless had the additional advantage of being true.

anism centered in Washington—bureaucratic politics, congressional–executive relations, and the like.

As of mid-1972, the Brezhnev regime's American policy appeared to be yielding results as a militarily much more capable Soviet Union joined a Republican administration in a celebration of "realism" that promised to expedite the process of favorable change in the correlation of forces while also meeting immediate Soviet security and economic needs. A decade later, the Soviet effort to induce greater "realism" in American behavior had been reduced to a shambles. Having endeavored to create external constraints on American forwardness and abilities to resist the rise of the Soviet Union to a position of equality, they had left it to successive American administrations to maintain domestic support for a continuation of détente. But they were presented with Presidents increasingly incapable of delivering on matters of importance. And then, in 1980, a mounting sense in the United States of Soviet expansionism and American loss of position contributed to the election of a President determined to recreate situations of strength. Though the capacity of the Reagan Administration to succeed in this was readily questioned in Moscow, the Soviets at the end of the Brezhnev era were faced with a protracted, expensive, and dangerous capability race with an aroused opponent unless the 1984 Presidential election yielded a change of emphasis in American policy.

The continued deterioration of American–Soviet relations since Brezhnev provides good reason for the new leadership to follow its predecessors in altering the thrust of the overall Soviet effort to deal with the United States. But in moving to meet the American challenge, Chernenko and his colleagues will not have a free hand. Aside from foreign and domestic constraints, they will in effect have to manage the acquired response patterns of the Soviet system. In principle, the repertoire they will be drawing upon ranges from a Stalinist acceptance of confrontation, to a return to the Khrushchevian effort to promote reformism in the politics of American policymaking. In practice, the preferred course represents an amalgam of long-standing operational procedures. In greater or lesser measure, leadership decisions will serve to rearrange these patterns of behavior to produce a composite line of action that is adapted to perceived Soviet needs. In short, Soviet policy will consist of a set of tendencies.

Though little is known about the foreign policy preferences of the present leadership, the perennial specialist discussion of the American political process provides the Western observer with a narrow window through which Soviet tendencies may be studied in detail. A set of integrating conceptions or images of the United States is maintained and updated by a corps of analysts whose job year in and year out is to report on U.S. affairs and to contribute to the Communist Party's evaluation of developments in the capitalist world, America included. The producers of this knowledge presumably structure it in part with the interests of the consumer in mind. Certainly the studies published by specialists are actively structured by the consumer: the simple fact that one of the specialist images was personally sponsored by Stalin has meant that its status, and consequently the standing of alternative images, is a function of the regime's attitude toward Stalin and Stalinism. Contrasting specialist images of the American system may therefore be taken to reflect broad variations in the corporate political interests and policy preferences of the regime. Once we have these specialist images in focus, we should be in a position to infer something about the tendencies of the post-Brezhnev Soviet Union in its dealings with the United States.

Images of the American Policy Process

Soviet thinking on the politics of American foreign and military policies may strike the Western reader as strange and forbidding, if not irrelevant. The Soviet reader would doubtless find an elaborate American discussion of nuclear deterrence equally difficult to assimilate. The comparison is intentional. Soviet national security thinking would seem ultimately to be expressed in the language of political economy, and not in military-strategic terms. The observations that follow provide an opportunity to begin to look at the requirements of national security from a Soviet point of view. As well, it should be emphasized that the literature we are about to consider is written by Soviets for Soviets. It is impenetrable to all but the most determined external observer. As such, it minimizes the risk of disinformation that sometimes comes with Western reliance on published Soviet sources. It allows us to listen to Soviets talking amongst themselves about the political economy of national security.

The specialist literature since 1945 yields four images of the U.S. political process. Each of these images has evolved in the course of protracted and sometimes polemical discussion of the opposing social system. Each has also responded to change in the political economy of American capitalism. Each however retains certain core attributes that remain unchanged. To simplify what might otherwise become an excessively complicated discussion, the account that follows is confined to the literature of the Brezhnev era as it concerns the American policy process and the role of the Presidency as represented in each of these images, designated I–IV.[14] In each case our concern is not so much with details as with the overall Soviet conception of how the United States makes policy and where the Presidency fits into the scheme of American political life.

Moving from conservative to innovating conceptions, we begin with a brief look at the Stalinist assessment of how America is ruled. Originally authorized by the dictator himself in his *Economic Problems of Socialism in the U.S.S.R.* (1952), Image I centers on the capacity of the monopolies to subordinate the apparatus of the American state to

---

14. An earlier study by the author examined the literature from 1945 to 1970: Franklyn Griffiths, "Images, Politics and Learning in Soviet Behaviour toward the United States," Ph.D. dissertation, Columbia University, 1972. This paper updates the analysis to 1982. For several reasons there is no Soviet theory of American capitalism as such, nor is there a theory of the American political process. The Western observer is instead presented with semi-theoretical discussions of capitalism "in general," and with descriptive accounts of American internal politics that tend to avoid theoretical generalization. Soviet images of the American political process must therefore be derived from the literature on contemporary capitalism as well as those publications that deal explicitly with the United States. For detail on the derivation of images which centers on Soviet debate over the nature of state-monopoly capitalism, see Griffiths, "Images, Politics and Learning," pp. 117–123.

their own interests.[15] Dominating the economic life of the country, the media of mass communication, and the electoral process, the financial oligarchy which stands at the peak of the monopoly bourgeoisie is seen invariably to have its man in the White House, its men in key positions throughout the executive branch and Congress, and therefore a monopoly of control over domestic and foreign policy. Striving for profit above all, the monopolists use the state to maintain their exploitation of the working class, to oppose socialism in every way, and to wage predatory wars. Internally the subordinated state penetrates all aspects of social life, appearing as a kind of Leviathan that puts America under the heel of the financiers.[16] On the other hand, economic development and the business cycle in particular cannot effectively be regulated, owing to the "anarchy" of production engendered primarily by competition among monopolists. Despite the capacity of the American oligarchy to deny all progressive political change or reform, the anarchy of production is expected sooner or later to bring the whole system down in the midst of socialist revolution.

The image here is one of a totalitarian order in which politics virtually disappears except between the mass of the oppressed and the exceedingly privileged few. The Democratic and Republican parties are seen to be decisively similar, so much so that the United States becomes essentially a one-party state governed for the monopolists by the Democratic–Republican Party.[17] There is no real separation of powers and no significant congressional-executive interaction.[18] Even the existence of a separate military-industrial complex may be questioned.[19] If there is any significant within-system politics, it is the result of monopoly competition for profit, which leads to differences within the ruling stratum over policy for the subordinated state. These differences

---

15. I.V. Stalin, "Ekonomicheskie problemy sotsializma v SSSR" [Economic Problems of Socialism in the U.S.S.R.], *Bolshevik*, No. 18 (1952), esp. p. 23. For Brezhnev-era evaluations that conform to the subordination thesis, see I.I. Kuzminov, "K voprosu o nauchnoi polemike" [On the Question of Scientific Polemics], in Kuzminov et al., eds., *Metodologicheskie problemy politicheskoi ekonomii* [Methodological Problems of Political Economy] (Moscow: "Mysl," 1965), pp. 255–299; M.F. Kovaleva, *K voprosu metodologii politicheskoi ekonomiki kapitalizma* [On the Question of the Methodology of the Political Economy of Capitalism] (Moscow: "Mysl," 1969), esp. pp. 118–119; A. Nutsubidze, *Imperializm ili 'transformirovannyi kaptializm'* [Imperialism or "Transformed Capitalism"] (Tbilisi: Metsnireba, 1970), pp. 54–56; G.G. Boichenko, *Politicheskaya organizatsiya SShA* [Political Organization of the U.S.A.] (Minsk: Izd-vo BGU, 1970), pp. 464–465; and I.I. Beglov, *SShA: sobstvennost i vlast* [The U.S.A.: Property and Power] (Moscow: "Nauka," 1971), pp. 505, 525–526.
16. The voice of the Bolshevik theoretician N.I. Bukharin is heard here. In fact, one analyst ventured to run two pages of Bukharin's writing on the capitalist system as though it were from Lenin. A.G. Kulikov, *Generalnye shtaby monopolii* [The General Staffs of the Monopolies] (Moscow: "Mysl," 1969), pp. 6–7.
17. Beglov, footnote 15 above, p. 381. See also Kovaleva, fn. 15, p. 160 and R.S. Ovinnikov, *Uoll Strit i vneshnyaya politika* [Wall Street and Foreign Policy] (Moscow: "Mezhdunarodnye otnosheniya," 1980), p. 30.
18. Boichenko's lengthy study of American "political organization," fn. 15, mentions the Congress hardly at all in discussing the relationship of political actors to what is in effect a unitary apparatus of state.
19. Beglov, fn. 15, pp. 39–43.

are resolved in peak business associations such as the National Association of Manufacturers or the Chamber of Commerce, which may proceed to issue instructions to
the apparatus of state.[20] The President is accordingly viewed as the puppet of the
financial oligarchy. Though he may be very vigorous in the exercise of his powers,
he has no significant policymaking role or influence on matters of importance except
as the executor of the monopolists' wishes. Quite simply, he takes dictation.
    What we have here is essentially the transposition of Soviet and Russian political
thinking in the interpretation of an alien reality. Nothing happens by chance. Everything is controlled and directed from a single point, the elaborate façade of democracy
notwithstanding. If there is disarray, it has a hidden purpose. The oligarchs murmur
and the state acts. Otherwise, leading personnel in the apparatus of state are fully
primed to anticipate the wishes of the super-rich. Though there may be differences
among the oligarchs, they do not add up to anything of significance. And while the
state is a powerful instrument, it is in no way an actor in its own right. The imperialist
state does not have any real self-sufficiency in relation to the monopolists.[21] Hierarchy
and subordination, not conflict and bargaining among actors endowed with a measure
of autonomy, are the order of the day in the United States. That these are characteristically Russian as well as Soviet views of political life is suggested by Lenin's pre-
revolutionary comments to the effect that Russians were inclined to underrate the
self-sufficiency of the state in their own country.[22]
    Image II stresses conflict among the monopolists and accords the apparatus of state,
most notably the Presidency, greater leeway in implementing policy for the ruling
stratum. An attempt is made here to reconcile the proposition of monopoly rule with
some of the evidence of the daily riot of American political life and perceived "zigzags" in U.S. foreign and military policy. The existence of a number of family and
regional groupings of finance capital is emphasized—Rockefellers, Morgans, du
Ponts, etc.—each of which is seen to have a particular set of domestic and foreign
policy interests depending on the character of its foreign investments and the extent
of its involvement in defense as opposed to civilian production.[23] The state apparatus,

20. Kulikov, fn. 16, pp. 42–44, 72, 79; Boichenko, fn. 15, pp. 464–465; and Beglov, fn. 15, pp.
508–509, who demurs in noting that direct instructions are not required for leading officials and
politicians whose outlook is in any event that of monopoly capital. Ovinnikov, fn. 17, p. 29,
also asserts that the basic direction of U.S. foreign policy is "dictated by the co-ordinated course
of the monopolies" and is not the product of "spontaneous competitive struggle" among different groups of monopolists.
21. Kovaleva, fn. 15, pp. 165, 221–222. Ovinnikov, fn. 17, insists that the leading groups of
U.S. monopoly capital have coalesced into a "central financial complex." Based on Wall Street
and dominated by the Rockefellers, this complex is said to work out the basic course of American
foreign policy which is implemented by top officials who "well appreciate the real limits into
which their self-sufficiency must be entered" (p. 32).
22. See, for example, V.I. Lenin, "Pismo 'Severnomu soyuza RSDRP'" [Letter to the "Northern
Union of the RSDRP"] (April 1902), Polnoe sobranie sochinenii [Complete Collected Works], Vol.
6 (Moscow: Gospolitizdat, 1959), p. 363.
23. The principal analyst on this question has been V.S. Zorin: Dollary i politika Vashingtona
[Dollars and Washington Politics] (Moscow: "Mezhdunarodnye otnosheniya," 1964); Nekorovan-

while fused with and subordinate to monopoly capital as in Image I, now becomes an arena of monopoly competition and also a very active economic as well as political instrument of the ruling stratum.

Although peak business associations remain a major channel for monopoly access to the state, policy is made by interaction among monopoly representatives who are positioned throughout the executive branch, in both houses of Congress, and in the apparatus of the two major political parties which are not viewed as being identical.[24] Despite the monopolies' control over the electoral process as a consequence of the great amounts of money that are required to win, elections are not wholly illusory: in voting, the mass of the population decides which particular coalition of monopolists will dominate the Presidency and the Congress.[25] The state apparatus accordingly possesses some slight autonomy or "self-sufficiency" *vis-à-vis* the internally divided ruling stratum.[26] In particular, the President acts not so much on the direct instructions as on behalf of the general interests of big business.

Responding to the long-term requirements of monopoly capital as a whole and in the face of opposition from certain monopoly groupings, the Kennedy Administration and its successors in the 1960s and early 1970s are seen to have greatly increased the already significant role of the state in economic and social life.[27] They endeavored to regulate the business cycle for purposes of economic growth, to accelerate scientific and technological development, and to generate increased productivity—all as a

nye koroli Ameriki [The Uncrowned Kings of America], 2nd ed. (Moscow: Politizdat, 1967); "Monopolii i Vashington" [The Monopolies and Washington], *SShA: ekonomika, politika, ideologiya* (hereafter *SShA*), No. 7 (1978), pp. 27–37; and "'Novoe' i staroe v politike Vashingtona" ["New" and Old in the Policy of Washington], *Kommunist*, No. 3 (1982), pp. 105–115. Zorin is a purveyor of socialist pornography which takes the form of portraits of American plutocrats that are to be examined by the Soviet reader in the privacy of his own room, if he has one.

24. On the matter of differentiation between the parties, see N.N. Yakovlev, ed., *SShA: Politicheskaya mysl i istoriya* [American Political Thought and History] (Moscow: "Nauka," 1976), pp. 301–302; and A.N. Yakovlev, *Ideologiya amerikanskoi 'imperii'* [The Ideology of the American "Empire"] (Moscow: "Mysl," 1967), p. 69, where it is asserted that America's rulers reserve the dirtiest foreign policy tasks for the Democratic Party in view of the fact that it has a broader social base. For other aspects of the state-monopoly relationship, see the comments of A. Kokoshin, "Monopolii i vlast" [The Monopolies and State Power], *Kommunist*, No. 5 (1982), pp. 108–112.

25. This is the thrust of Ivanyan's *Belyi dom*, fn. 11. See also O.A. Feofanov, *SShA: reklama i obshchestvo* [American Advertising] (Moscow: "Mysl," 1974), who notes the need of politicians as well as corporations to develop attractive public images, pp. 142, 195–207.

26. N.N. Inozemtsev et al., eds., *Leninskaya teoriya imperializma i sovremennost* [The Leninist Theory of Imperialism and the Contemporary World] (Moscow: "Mysl," 1977), pp. 221–222; M.S. Dragilev and V.I. Mokhov, *Leninskii analiz monopolisticheskogo kapitalizma i sovremennost* [The Leninist Analysis of Monopoly Capitalism and the Contemporary World] (Moscow: "Vysshaya shkola," 1970), p. 167; and A.N. Yakovlev, ed., *SShA: ot 'velikogo' k bolnomu* [The United States from "Great" to Sick] (Moscow: Politizdat, 1969), pp. 133–134.

27. V.M. Shamberg, *SShA: problemy i protivorechiya gosudarstvenno-monopolisticheskogo regulirovaniya ekonomicheskogo rosta* [The U.S.: Problems and Contradictions in State-Monopoly Regulation of Economic Growth] (Moscow: "Nauka," 1974), pp. 5–7, 49; and Yu.I. Bobrakov and V.A. Fedorovich, eds., *SShA: gosudarstvo i ekonomika* [The U.S.: The State and the Economy] (Moscow: "Nauka," 1976), pp. 547–577.

means of creating the resources necessary not only for defense production, but for class peace through increased personal consumption ("state-monopoly maneuvering").[28] All of this was seen for a while to have led not only to a reduction in the anarchy of capitalist production, but to the strengthening of state-monopoly tendencies in the development of American monopoly capitalism, if not the actual replacement of monopoly capitalism by state-monopoly capitalism. As well, compared to Image I, the military-industrial complex looms large as a major manifestation of state-monopoly processes.[29] It also becomes something of a "law" of capitalist development that the executive branch, charged with vast new functions as compared with the era prior to the New Deal, increases in power relative to the Congress despite the setbacks suffered by the Presidency after Watergate.[30] Although the economic crisis of 1974–1975 and the ensuing conditions of inflation and stagnation revealed, beyond question for Image II analysis, the inability of the capitalist system to stabilize itself by means of state-monopoly measures, state intervention is said to remain a significant "reserve" of the system. As such, it makes unlikely the sudden collapse which is anticipated in Image I assessments.[31] Thus, while imperialism does not change in its essentials, it is in principle capable of limited adaptation.

The Image II view of adaptive processes in the political economy of the United States has them originating not so much in endogenous factors as in the changing correlation of forces between capitalism and socialism—in the preference of the monopolists and the state for an economic and political strategy of maneuver that involves greater reliance on the inner resources of the capitalist system as a way of avoiding the need for basic change in American–Soviet relations.[32] At the same time, the changing global correlation and the deepening general crisis of capitalism are said to oblige the consideration of policy adaptations that may run counter to the innate aggressiveness of imperialism.[33] A "far-sighted" segment of the ruling class takes

28. See, for example, N.N. Inozemtsev, Sovremennyi kapitalizm: novye yavleniya i protivorechiya [Contemporary Capitalism: New Phenomena and Contradictions] (Moscow: "Mysl," 1972), pp. 24–26, 37, 49, 116–117; and Yakovlev, fn. 26, pp. 14–15, 35–36.
29. Yakovlev, fn. 26, Chapter 3; V.S. Zorin, ed., SShA: problemy vnutrennei politiki [The U.S.: Problems of Internal Politics] (Moscow: "Nauka," 1971), pp. 357–368; and A. Gromyko, Vneshnyaya politika SShA: uroki i deistvitelnost [U.S. Foreign Policy: Lessons and Reality] (Moscow: "Mezhdunarodnye otnosheniya," 1978), passim.
30. V.A. Tumanov, in F.M. Burlatskii and V.E. Chirkin, eds., Politicheskie sistemy sovremennosti [Contemporary Political Systems] (Moscow: "Nauka," 1978), pp. 165–166, 174; and A.A. Mishin, "Amerikanskaya doktrina 'sderzhek i protivoves' i sovremennost" [The American Doctrine of "Checks and Balances" in Contemporary Conditions], Sovetskoe gosudarstvo i pravo (hereafter SGP), No. 7 (1981), pp. 93–94.
31. N.N. Inozemtsev et al., eds., Uglublenie obshchego krizisa kapitalizma [The Deepening of the General Crisis of Capitalism] (Moscow: "Mysl," 1976), pp. 9, 21–22; and Inozemtsev, fn. 28, p. 36.
32. Shamberg, fn. 27, pp. 47–48; Bobrakov and Fedorovich, fn. 27, pp. 547–548; and A.V. Anikin, ed., Sovremennyi monopolisticheskii kapitalizm: Soedinennye Shtaty Ameriki (Contemporary Monopoly Capitalism: The United States] (Moscow: "Mysl," 1982), pp. 7, 23.
33. Shamberg, fn. 27, p. 47; Inozemtsev, fn. 26, p. 25; Inozemtsev, fn. 28, p. 22; and, more skeptically, Yakovlev, fn. 24, pp. 308–310.

note of the consequences of nuclear war and the increasing unreality of a policy of world domination.[34] Competing "realistic" and "aggressive" tendencies are thus to be noted in American policy—"realism" in the moderation of American goals and in a readiness to improve U.S.–Soviet relations, and "aggressiveness" *inter alia* in the use of a temporary stabilization of foreign relations to pave the way for a return to policies of global predominance as had occurred by the early 1980s.[35]

What then of the policymaking role and influence of the Presidency? The mechanism of the dictatorship of monopoly capital makes it certain that the President is the instrument of the winning coalition of monopolists. His behavior conforms broadly to the correlation of forces within the ruling stratum.[36] His constitutional powers are however formidable and he dominates the foreign policy process within the limits allowed by the monopolists. In the making of individual decisions he can accomplish a great deal. But his capacity is more limited where the overall strategy of the United States is concerned. Among other things, he must contend with the military-industrial complex and the bureaucracy if he is of a mind to alter American policy in the direction of greater "realism." Add to this the congressional opponents of "realism" and the activity of right-wing organizations in attacking the advocacy of moderation in external affairs, and the picture is one of an American ship of state that steers to the right.

Despite the evident inadequacy of this approach to the interpretation of American political behavior, Image II does alert the Soviet observer to significant interactions occurring within the United States. Where Image I envisages an imperfect monism, the Image II emphasis on competition in the ruling stratum makes it possible to discern some of the diversity on the American political scene. Very few Soviet analysts have however been bold or patient enough to attempt to demonstrate the interconnections between the economic interests of groupings of monopoly capital and the conduct of the Presidency. When they do, they encounter difficulties similar to those met by Western analysts who apply the "conflict model" of factional strife in the Soviet leadership to the interpretation of Soviet policy: how to identify the factions and to demonstrate their effects on policy outcomes. Instead, the Image II analyst typically assumes the existence of groupings of U.S. monopoly capital and goes on to write as though he knows what he is talking about. Sprinkling his work with references to the domination of the monopolies, he may proceed to run an account that is comparatively factual, in its coverage of electoral affairs, public opinion,

---

34. Gromyko, fn. 29, pp. 32, 101–102, 259–263; Inozemtsev, fn. 28, pp. 106–110; and Inozemtsev, fn. 31, p. 10.
35. Anikin, fn. 32, p. 23. See also Inozemtsev, fn. 31, pp. 10, 82–83; Gromyko, fn. 29, pp. 101–102, 260; Zorin, fn. 29, p. 396; and N.N. Yakovlev, fn. 24, pp. 191–192. Zorin (1982), fn. 23, provides an explanation of the return to "aggressiveness" in the late 1970s and early 1980s that stresses the ability of conservatives and militarists to exploit a shift to the right in American political life.
36. Ivanyan, fn. 11, pp. 14–15, 383; and Gromyko, fn. 29, pp. 31–32, 280, on which the remainder of this paragraph is based.

bureaucratic politics, and so on. Why then the reluctance to move clearly to an analysis of political process as such?

The answer in part is that Soviet images of the American system and the role of the Presidency are constructed only partly with the United States in mind. Image II is a limited but significant response to the limitations of Image I. Its meaning may be reduced to the caution, "Don't oversimplify the thesis of subordination." According to Leninist orthodoxy, imperialism is not a policy but an inevitability under conditions of monopoly capitalism. To venture into a forthright political analysis of the sources of American conduct would be to risk viewing imperialism as a matter of choice within the existing social framework. It would become possible to consider reforming American policy. Soviet reformism might as a result become more viable. On moving to Image III we enter reformist terrain.

Where Image II views the American political process in terms of a truncated or sawed-off pluralism, Image III is less reservedly pluralist. The political power of monopoly capital is reduced, the self-sufficiency and power of the state increase correspondingly, and non-monopoly actors enter the field of view more directly. Simultaneously, political factors come to the fore and economic determinants of behavior diminish in importance. The outcome is a construct in which no single stratum has decisive power on all the issues, in which coalition behavior cuts across class lines, and in which the apparatus of state plays a mediating role in implementing policy for the whole American bourgeoisie and the monopolists in the first instance.

Although monopoly capital remains clearly the single most potent social force and is coalesced with the state by means similar to those described in Image II analyses, economic concentration is far from complete. In addition to monopoly capital, which has yielded some ground to "collective" capitalists such as pension and mutual funds, there are the populous non-monopoly formations of the ruling class to be considered.[37] Moreover, within the corporation itself, managers tend to be the predominant figures. They seek to make profit for all shareholders.[38] As occurs with the state, where political executives take over from the monopolists as the dominant operational force, the large corporation is the corporation of the whole bourgeoisie as well as the instrument of monopoly capital.[39] In addition, the middle strata come into focus—employees, small businessmen, intellectuals, students, farmers, and so on—as social and political actors. As to the American working class, it too appears in altered form, the industrial proletariat having become a minority as a consequence of the scientific and technological revolution and the growth of service industry.[40] Conflicting attitudes on domestic and foreign affairs—attitudes that are not derived directly from the individual's relationship to the means of production[41]—come into being and cut

37. S.A. Dalin, SShA: poslevoennyi gosudarstvenno-monopolisticheskii kapitalizm [Postwar American State-monopoly Capitalism] (Moscow: "Nauka," 1972), pp. 34, 494–496.
38. Ibid., pp. 63–66.
39. Ibid., pp. 65–66, 70, 78.
40. Ibid., pp. 359–369.
41. A. Galkin, "Neocapitalism and the Facts," International Affairs (Moscow), No. 11 (1968), p. 31.

across class lines to yield conflicting tendencies in American political behavior.[42] Not only is monopoly capital in need of social support, but the operative alignments in American politics link a heterogeneous monopoly bourgeoisie with other strata and classes into coalitions, as seen for example in the trade union movement and a section of the business community working primarily through the Democratic Party for policies of state economic intervention.[43]

If American society is less rigidly stratified and monopoly capital is less potent a force than is made out in Images I and II, the state is a more imposing presence. In particular it has a substantial and growing self-sufficiency in relation to monopoly capital, the ruling class as a whole, and in relation to society as a whole.[44] Its relative autonomy arises *inter alia* from competition among monopolists and from growth in its own size and complexity as it performs a widening array of functions.[45] Decentralization in the mechanism of state itself, as in the congressional-executive relationship, also reflects "the pluralism of interests of different groupings of the ruling class."[46] In no way therefore is the state to be viewed as wholly subordinate to monopoly capital.[47] Rather, in intervening in economic and social life and in conducting a foreign and defense policy whose substance is much the same as in Image II, the state acts in the interests of the whole bourgeoisie, albeit with clear bias towards

42. G.A. Arbatov provides an extensive discussion of conflicting tendencies in American foreign policy in *The War of Ideas in Contemporary International Relations* (Moscow: Progress Publishers, 1973), esp. pp. 223–247. This volume is an accurate and slightly updated translation of G.A. Arbatov, *Ideologicheskaya borba v sovremennykh mezhdunarodnykh otnosheniyakh* (Moscow: Politizdat, 1970). For ease of reference, the English-language text is used here. Any points cited that are not made in the original Russian version are indicated as such. For other comment on tendency conflict, see also N.N. Inozemtsev, ed., *Politicheskaya ekonomiya sovremennogo monopolisticheskogo kapitalizma* [The Political Economy of Contemporary Monopoly Capitalism], Vol. 2 (Moscow: "Mysl," 1970), p. 190; A.A. Gromyko and V.V. Zhurkin, eds., *SShA: nauchno-tekhnologicheskaya revolyutsiya i tendentsii vneshnei politiki* [The Scientific and Technological Revolution and Tendencies in American Foreign Policy] (Moscow: "Mezhdunarodnye otnosheniya," 1974); and G.A. Trofimenko, "Amerikanskii podkhod k mirnomu sosushchestvovaniyu s Sovetskim Soyuzom" [The American Approach to Peaceful Coexistence with the Soviet Union], *SShA*, No. 6 (1978), pp. 18–31, and No. 7 (1978), pp. 38–53.
43. See, for example, V.O. Pechatov, *Demokraticheskaya partiya SShA* [The Democratic Party of the United States] (Moscow: "Nauka," 1980), pp. 189–194; and V.P. Androsov, *Profsoyuzy SShA v usloviyakh gosudarstvenno-monopolisticheskogo kapitalizma* [American Trade Unions under Conditions of State-monopoly Capitalism] (Moscow: "Nauka," 1971), pp. 337–338.
44. Inozemtsev, fn. 42, Vol. 1, p. 378, and Vol. 2, p. 178; V.E. Guliev, *Sovremennoe imperialist-icheskoe gosudarstvo* [The Modern Imperialist State] (Moscow: "Mezhdunarodyne otnosheniya," 1973), pp. 66–67, 70–100; I.D. Levin and V.A. Tumanov, eds., *Politicheskii mekhanizm diktatura monopolii* [The Political Mechanism of the Dictatorship of the Monopolies] (Moscow: "Nauka," 1974), pp. 8–15; and E.L. Kuzmin, *Ideinoi bankrotstvo burzhuaznoi demokratii* [The Intellectual Bankruptcy of Bourgeois Democracy] (Moscow: "Mezhdunarodnye otnosheniya," 1977), pp. 26–30.
45. Guliev, fn. 44, p. 97; and Kuzmin, fn. 44, pp. 29–30.
46. V.A. Savelyev, *SShA: Senat i politika* [The Senate and American Politics] (Moscow: "Mysl," 1976), p. 172. See also A.M. Belonogov, *Belyi Dom i Kapitolii: partnery i soperniki* [The White House and Congress: Partners and Rivals] (Moscow: "Mezhdunarodnye otnosheniya," 1974), pp. 3–4.
47. Guliev, fn. 44, p. 67; Levin and Tumanov, fn. 44, p. 15; and Kuzmin, fn. 44, pp. 26–27, 29.

the monopolies.[48] It acts as "coordinator" for the ruling class, and in so doing may be responsive to the interests of the working class as well.[49] In brief, the Image III evaluation sees the state as being sufficiently autonomous *vis-à-vis* monopoly capital to raise the possibility of its use by a broad-based coalition to weaken the position of the most conservative elements of the ruling class.[50]

Taken as a whole, the Image III assessment envisages the American system as a self-regulating entity that works to the benefit of the ruling class and first of all the monopoly bourgeoisie without there being a single point of control from which directives are issued to the state.[51] Though monopoly capital "rules" in the sense of being the single most powerful non-state actor, the established social order is maintained by means of a decentralized political process that centers on the state. The system tends therefore to be regarded not as a more or less modernized or adapted form of monopoly capitalism, as in Image II.[52] Rather it is viewed as a manifestation of state-monopoly capitalism whose principal feature is the unification of two relatively autonomous forces, the state and monopoly capital, to produce a new economic mechanism that represents substantial forward movement in the preparation of organizational and material preconditions for socialism. We see here the beginnings of an open recognition that imperialism has not only adapted but changed since Lenin's day, and this as a result of internal or "immanent" processes as well as the need to respond to adverse change in the world correlation of forces.[53]

Viewed through a third image optic, the President stands at the center of a maelstrom of influences. While he is granted a greater degree of autonomy in relation to

48. Arbatov, fn. 42, pp. 49, 56; Dalin, fn. 37, pp. 70, 78; Guliev, fn. 44, p. 67; Levin and Tumanov, fn. 44, pp. 13–14; Inozemtsev, fn. 42, Vol. 2 (2nd ed., 1975), p. 184; and Kuzmin, fn. 44, pp. 29–30.
49. Inozemtsev, fn. 42, Vol. 1, p. 399; N.S. Yulina, *Burzhuaznye ideologicheskie techeniya v SShA* [Bourgeois Ideological Currents in the U.S.] (Moscow: "Nauka," 1971), pp. 12–13; A.A. Popov, *SShA: gosudarstvo i profsoyuzy* [Trade Unions and the American State] (Moscow: "Nauka," 1974), p. 211; Inozemtsev, fn. 42, Vol. 1 (2nd ed., 1975), p. 362; Savelyev, fn. 46, p. 3; and O.A. Zhidkov, *SShA: antitrestovskoe zakonodatelstvo na sluzhbe monopolii* [U.S. Anti-trust Legislation in the Service of the Monopolies] (Moscow: "Nauka," 1976), pp. 6, 29, 48.
50. Androsov, fn. 43, pp. 31–32; Zhidkov, fn. 49, pp. 172–175; Guliev, fn. 44, p. 97; Popov, fn. 49, pp. 215–218; Inozemtsev, fn. 42, Vol. 1 (2nd ed., 1975), p. 12; and Kuzmin, fn. 44, pp. 29, 52. Arbatov, fn. 42, p. 270, refers to the possibility of depriving "hawks" of all political influence.
51. Arbatov, in an implicit criticism of Image I interpretations and the work of A.G. Kulikov in particular (fn. 16), argues that American policies are the product of political struggle and conflicting evaluations of the situation, as opposed to being the outcome of the work of a General Staff. Arbatov, fn. 42, pp. 232–233.
52. Compare, for example, the more conservative Image II presentation of Dragilev and Mokhov, fn. 26, with the relatively venturesome treatment in Inozemtsev, fn. 42, where an attempt is made to reconcile Lenin's thesis of the virtual omnipotence of monopoly capital with evidence of change in the nature of the capitalist system since Lenin wrote in 1916.
53. Arbatov, for example, indirectly commented in 1974 on the relevance of the Leninist theory of imperialism in noting that as a consequence of the scientific and technological revolution within the capitalist countries, U.S. foreign investment was going primarily to Western Europe and Canada, not to the developing countries. Gromyko and Zhurkin, fn. 42, p. 21. Lenin's theory, it will be recalled, stressed the need of the imperialist countries for spheres of foreign investment in the colonial areas.

monopoly capital than is the case with Image II, he is exposed to a broader array of forces. Aside from carrying on with what amounts to "a practically unending electoral campaign,"[54] he must deal with big business and its privileged access to the executive branch, and with an immense bureaucracy that is rife with departmental rivalry, that puts up tendentious and self-serving recommendations to him, and that organizes political support for policy in addition to playing an active role in its formulation and implementation.[55] As well, he is faced with a military establishment whose foreign policy role has increased as a result of its involvement in negotiations for strategic arms limitation,[56] with a Congress that has cut into the power of the executive since Watergate,[57] with public opinion that is shaped by the media and pollsters as well as the Administration,[58] with mass organizations and "interest groups" of the left and the right,[59] with the military-industrial complex and the diverse interests of the ruling class as a whole, with demands issuing from the international environment, and so on. All of this and more may be considered in some detail in Image III presentations, which tend to be considerably more empirical and to rely more heavily on American sources than is the case with Image II analyses.

For example, the President is on occasion presented with a National Security Adviser who is attempting to advance his own foreign policy strategy against the preferences of the Secretary of State.[60] In the Senate, the President is confronted with cleavages that run not so much on party lines as between "Congressional" and "Presidential" parties.[61] Public opinion may have a substantial effect on his actions and success: fearing public reaction to a forthright admission that altered international realities had forced a modification of America's long-standing globalist strategy, the Nixon Administration presented U.S.–Soviet détente to the American people as a breakthrough for the United States, with the result that when the inevitable difficulties arose the way was clear for charges that the public had been deceived.[62] And where the preferences of the ruling class as a whole are concerned, Presidents are obliged to deal with complex and changing attitudes such as those which conditioned the move away from détente after the early mid-1970s.[63]

54. S.B. Chetverikov, *Kto i kak delaet politika SShA* [Who Makes Policy in the United States and How] (Moscow: "Mezhdunarodnye otnosheniya," 1974), p. 27.
55. Ibid., pp. 29–32.
56. R.G. Bogdanov and A.A. Kokoshin, *SShA: informatsiya i vneshnyaya politika* [Information and American Foreign Policy] (Moscow: "Nauka," 1979), p. 43.
57. See, esp., S.B. Chetverikov, "Vneshnepoliticheskaya rol kongressa SShA" [The Foreign Policy Role of the U.S. Congress], *SGP*, No. 12 (1981), pp. 113, 117–118; also Savelyev, fn. 46, pp. 4, 172; and E.I. Popova, *Amerikanskii Senat i vneshnyaya politika* [The American Senate and Foreign Policy] (Moscow: "Nauka," 1978), pp. 5–6, 116.
58. Chetverikov, fn. 54, p. 176; and Yu. A. Zamoshkin, ed., *Amerikanskoe obshchestvennoe mnenie i politika* [Public Opinion and Politics in America] (Moscow: "Nauka," 1978), pp. 113–115, 121. See also Arbatov, fn. 42, pp. 49, 246–247, on the need to mold and hold public opinion.
59. Chetverikov, fn. 54, pp. 12, 39, 167; and Bogdanov and Kokoshin, fn. 56, pp. 15–17.
60. Bogdanov and Kokoshin, fn. 56, pp. 34–35.
61. Savelyev, fn. 46, pp. 44–45.
62. Trofimenko, fn. 42 (*SShA*, No. 7, 1978), pp. 38–39.
63. A.A. Kokoshin, "Gruppirovki amerikanskoi burzhuazii i vneshnepoliticheskii kurs SShA" [Groupings of the American Bourgeoisie and U.S. Foreign Policy], *SShA*, No. 10 (1981), pp. 3–

In the midst of all of this the President endeavors to shape domestic and foreign policy to meet the needs of the ruling class. His personal views count here, as does his decision-making style.[64] His decisions inevitably amount to a compromise in which domestic considerations, including bureaucratic politics, affect his capacity to solve problems abroad. In fact, he does not solve problems. Rather he picks from among options that are developed by his personal staff and the bureaucracy and that rely heavily on the "reservoir of decisions" of previous administrations.[65] While there is no discussion of the sources of Presidential success in policymaking in the literature under review here, in large part the President would seem to succeed or fail to the degree that his decisions serve to maintain and add to the coalition that brought him into the White House.

Finally, brief mention should be made of a fourth image that represents the outlook of what broadly may be called Soviet Eurocommunism. We are dealing here with a set of conceptions that to some extent remained academic during the Brezhnev era. Politically, they seem to have been ahead of their time. And in terms of research, they appeared to be concerned more with theory than with a developed empirical view of the American political process and the role of the Presidency.

As early as 1967, Soviet readers were informed that certain West European Communist parties, later to be called Eurocommunist, no longer accepted Lenin's theory of imperialism as originally stated in 1917. The foreign comrades argued *inter alia* that Lenin's identification of imperialism with monopoly capitalism was not applicable when monopoly capitalism had been replaced by state-monopoly capitalism. They accordingly asserted the need for a "two-phase theory of the imperialist stage," according to which monopoly capitalism gives way to a reformist state-monopoly capitalism that allows the working class new opportunities to use the state to eliminate the monopolies.[66] The Institute of the World Economy and International Relations (IMEMO) of the U.S.S.R. Academy of Sciences, which was (and is) the leading institution in Soviet studies of contemporary capitalism, refused to accept such a view. Instead it favored the notion of the "adaptation" of monopoly capitalism, which soon found its way into Brezhnev's speeches and party documents. In 1969–1973,

14. Distinguishing between three groupings of the American ruling class (large and smaller corporations engaged mainly in defense contracting, old and new multinationals, and millions of medium-sized and small businesses producing for the domestic market), Kokoshin argued that all three came to favor increasingly nationalist and chauvinist policies as a consequence of the "undialectical" approach of the multinationals towards détente, the deterioration of U.S. global positions, the panic-producing effects of two energy crises and increased foreign economic competition, and other developments such as the events in Iran and Afghanistan. For an assessment oriented more to foreign policy considerations as such, see G.A. Trofimenko, "Osnovnye postulaty vneshnei politiki SShA i sudby razryadki" [The Basic Postulates of U.S. Foreign Policy and the Fate of Detente], *SShA*, No. 7 (1981), pp. 3–14.
64. Chetverikov, fn. 54, p. 174.
65. Ibid., pp. 171–172.
66. N.N. Inozemtsev et al., eds., *Uchenie V.I. Lenina ob imperializme i sovremennost* [Lenin's Teaching on Imperialism and the Contemporary World] (Moscow: "Nauka," 1967), pp. 155–159, 225.

however, the political economist S.I. Tyulpanov of Leningrad State University undertook to secure acceptance of the "two-phase theory of the imperialist stage."[67] In so doing, he took up the theme, long espoused by the controversial economist E.S. Varga and reasserted in a posthumous volume published late in 1964, of the predominant role of the state in advanced capitalist society.[68]

Writing in what could soon be seen as the twilight of the Keynesian era in Western economic development, Tyulpanov argued that since the 1950s a series of qualitative changes had occurred in the aims, scope, and character of the activities of the state, in the productive forces, relations of production, social structure, and political institutions of bourgeois society.[69] These changes arose primarily from internal processes,[70] and not from external variables as suggested in Image II. Taken together, they allowed it to be said that monopoly capitalism had grown into state-monopoly capitalism, thereby marking the achievement of a new phase in the imperialist stage.

For Tyulpanov, the predominance of state-monopoly processes signified a weakening of the positions of monopoly capital and an "important regrouping" within the ruling class as a consequence of the assertion of the "state principle."[71] The autonomous regulatory role of the market had been subverted, as had the equivalent political role of legislative bodies, the press, and political parties.[72] In both domains, market relations had been replaced by state-monopoly institutions as the main determinant of social processes, in effect by a limited form of corporatism. The state nevertheless had a growing self-sufficiency in relation to an ever more highly concentrated mo-

---

67. S.I. Tyulpanov, ed., *V.I. Lenin i problemy sovremennogo kapitalizma* [V.I. Lenin and Problems of Contemporary Capitalism] (Leningrad: Izd-vo LGU, 1969), esp. pp. 25, 30; S.I. Tyulpanov and S.I. Yakovleva, "Krupnoe nauchnoe sobytie" [A Big Scientific Event], *Vestnik Leningradskogo universiteta* (Seriya ekonomika), No. 11 (1971), pp. 131–136; S.I. Tyulpanov and V.L. Sheinis, *Aktualnye problemy politicheskoi ekonomii sovremennogo kapitalizma* [Current Problems in the Political Economy of Contemporary Capitalism] (Leningrad: Izd-vo LGU, 1973); and S. Tyulpanov, "Istoricheskoe mesto gosudarstvenno-monopolisticheskogo kapitalizma" [The Historical Place of State-monopoly Capitalism], *MEMO*, No. 10 (1973), pp. 103–109. Tyulpanov and Sheinis, *Aktualnye Problemy* (1973), summarize the case for the two-phase theory on pp. 6–14. Tyulpanov is an interesting figure. A retired general, he is said to have been a close personal friend of General A.A. Epishev, head of the Main Political Administration of the Soviet armed forces, who sometimes stayed in Tyulpanov's apartment when visiting Leningrad. Tyulpanov, who evidently was convinced that imperialism had changed markedly since Lenin's day, was thus host to the man who was responsible for a stream of military-indoctrinational articles that stressed the inability of imperialism to change.
68. See E.S. Varga, *Ocherki problemam politekonomii kapitalizma* [Notes on the Political Economy of Capitalism] (Moscow: Politizdat, 1965), pp. 45–46; and E.S. Varga, "Reshayushchaya rol gosudarstva v voennom khozyaistve kapitalisticheskikh stranakh" [The Decisive Role of the State in the Wartime Economy of the Capitalist Countries], *Mirovaya ekonomika i mirovaya politika*, No. 1 (1945), pp. 11–21.
69. Tyulpanov, *V.I. Lenin* (1969), fn. 67, pp. 21–23; and Tyulpanov and Sheinis, fn. 67, pp. 6–7.
70. Tyulpanov and Sheinis, fn. 67, p. 64.
71. Tyulpanov, *V.I. Lenin* (1969), fn. 67, p. 6; Tyulpanov and Yakovleva, fn. 67, p. 136; and Tyulpanov and Sheinis, fn. 67, pp. 12, 90–92.
72. Tyulpanov and Sheinis, fn. 67, pp. 12–13.

nopoly capital, and was to be regarded as a force with its own specific interests.[73] It generalized the interests of the "subsystem of private enterprise," and was subject to control by a state-monopoly elite.[74] All of this signified a remarkable forward movement in the preparation of preconditions for socialism in the capitalist world.

In referring to the role of the state-monopoly elite, Tyulpanov cited the work of A.A. Galkin, who had been the first to propose the use of elite analysis in the study of capitalist society. Differentiating between political, economic, bureaucratic, military, and prestige elites, Galkin viewed the American political elite as consisting of the President and Cabinet, the staff of White House personal advisers, all members of the Senate, state governors, and others.[75] Although coalescence or circulation between the monopolies and the apparatus of state had rendered the boundary between the economic and political elites increasingly diffuse, the different situations of the different elites led to diverging views of the interests of the ruling class and "society as a whole."[76] Where the economic elite saw things from the viewpoint of big business, the political elite could approach problems from a position that represented the larger interest.[77] Viewed from this standpoint, big business became only a "decisive pressure group" on a political elite that had far more to consider than the preferences of the ruling class alone.[78] Here and in the work of other Soviet political sociologists and political scientists, we see signs of an interest not only in Western analytical concepts, but in breaking through the constraints of a class-centered analysis and into an empirical consideration of the working political processes of capitalist society.

F.M. Burlatskii, for example, sought support for the concept of the political system in making a comparative analysis of capitalist and socialist political life.[79] As was the case with the work of Tyulpanov and Galkin, Burlatskii's assessment of the capitalist system was centered on the apparatus of state. Coalesced with monopoly capital and able to operate with considerable autonomy, the state was in a position to act as

---

73. Ibid., pp. 78–94, 92.
74. Ibid., pp. 88, 94.
75. A. A. Galkin, "Pravyashchaya elita sovremennogo kapitalizma" [The Ruling Elite of Contemporary Capitalism], *MEMO*, No. 3 (1969), p. 79.
76. Ibid., p. 83.
77. Ibid. See also Galkin's comment on the capacity of the state to act against the interests of the ruling class as a whole: "Krizis politicheskoi sistemy kapitalizma: istoria i sovremennost" [Crisis of the Political System of Capitalism: Past and Present], *Rabochii klass i sovremennyi mir* (hereafter *RKSM*), No. 1 (1978), p. 65.
78. Galkin, fn. 75, pp. 77, 85. Galkin accordingly rejected the "extreme" view that monopoly capital in and of itself was the ruling elite, that the function of the political elite was essentially to mask the real relations of power. Ibid., p. 75.
79. F.M. Burlatskii, *Lenin. Gosudarstvo. Politika* [Lenin. The State. Politics] (Moscow: "Nauka," 1970), p. 118. See also F.M. Burlatskii, "Politicheskaya sistema obshchestva: ponyatie i elementy" [The Political System of Society: Concepts and Elements], in Burlatskii and Chirkin, fn. 30, p. 8. The political system is here defined as "a relatively closed system that ensures the integration of all elements of society and its very existence as a single organism that is centrally managed by a political power, the heart of which is the state, which expresses the interests of the economically dominant classes."

regulator and arbiter in the resolution of differences within the ruling class and between capital and labor.[80] It had a "free hand" in seeking to preserve the existing political and social order, and could function with substantial autonomy in relation to the ruling class itself.[81] In short, whereas Images I–III envisaged the government and politics of advanced capitalist society in terms of official responses to a broadening array of political and social forces, Burlatskii and Galkin[82] joined Tyulpanov in emphasizing the role of the state as an autonomous actor in its own right.

Image IV analyses of the American policy process and the policymaking role of the President are lacking in the literature under consideration here. All three authors considered would nevertheless seem to have envisaged a substantially modified U.S. imperialism in which monopoly capital had lost a good deal of political ground in the course of the transition to the state-monopoly phase. The rapacity and aggressiveness that were once regarded as inevitable features of American policy had to some extent become matters of political choice.[83] As well, the heightened role of the state was not primarily the result of the deepening general crisis of capitalism, as Image II had it. Rather it originated in inherent processes in the development of the capitalist system, and in "the consciousness of the ruling class or more accurately its most far-sighted and influential representatives."[84] Where Image I sees the state as an iron-heeled Leviathan that serves the interests of the monopolies in domestic and foreign affairs, Image IV envisages it as the well-heeled creature of the state-monopoly phase that stands above society and is capable of being responsive as well as repressive in its relatively autonomous operations to maintain the existing social order.

By way of overall comment on the four images discussed here, we may note that each was organized around certain persistent conceptions or stated beliefs, whereas the specifics and the authority of each were subject to significant change in the course of the Brezhnev era. The core attributes may be summarized as follows: subordination of the state and political life to an essentially unitary monopoly bourgeoisie (Image I); domination of the state and political life by an internally divided monopoly bourgeoisie (Image II); domination of a relatively self-sufficient state by the whole bourgeoisie and a divided monopoly stratum in the first instance (Image III); and the increasing self-sufficiency of the state and the state-monopoly or political elite as

---

80. Burlatskii (1970), fn. 79, pp. 256–257.
81. Ibid., p. 260. The apparatus of the American state is seen to have gained considerably in size, autonomy, and significance in the political process, its self-sufficiency being attributable in part to the extreme complexity of the decision-making process as such. Ibid., pp. 256, 259.
82. The views of both are rehearsed in F. Burlatskii and A. Galkin, Sotsiologiya. Politika. Mezhdunarodnye otnosheniya [Sociology. Politics. International Relations] (Moscow: "Mezhdunarodnye otnosheniya," 1974).
83. Tyulpanov regarded the U.S. military-industrial complex as a "secondary phenomenon" offset by forces in the ruling class interested in a limitation if not a reduction of armaments. Tyulpanov and Sheinis, fn. 67, pp. 74–75. Similarly, Burlatskii, echoing Varga, asserted that the postwar activization of U.S. foreign policy was based primarily on political and ideological considerations. Burlatskii (1970), fn. 79, p. 256. Cf. E.S. Varga, Kapitalizm dvadtsatogo veka [Twentieth Century Capitalism] (Moscow: Gospolitizdat, 1961), p. 117.
84. Tyulpanov and Sheinis, fn. 67, p. 88.

actors in their own right (Image IV). Despite the persistence of these core attributes, the work of specialists was subject to a process of modification that left the discussion in November 1982 quite different from that of October 1964. These modifications occurred in two phases which first saw support drain away from Image I, and then from Image IV as well.

During the period to 1973, the elaboration of innovating assessments that had begun under Khrushchev continued but with diminishing momentum. By 1970, Image I and its leading exponents in the Communist Party of the Soviet Union (C.P.S.U.) Central Committee's Academy of Social Sciences had effectively been discredited. As a result, Image II also became a repository for tempered Image I assessments, M.S. Dragilev of Moscow State University being a principal spokesman for what may be called the conservative coalition until his death in 1975. On the other hand, IMEMO, which had spearheaded the process of analytical innovation in the Khrushchev years, withdrew to a position that favored Images II and III at the expense of IV. The volumes edited and written by its director, N.N. Inozemtsev, tended to straddle the midpoint in the debate, now veering to Image II, now to Image III. Deprived of its previous institutional support, Image IV was pressed forward principally by S.I. Tyulpanov of Leningrad State University after 1969. Tyulpanov endeavored to move the discussion into areas not previously addressed by E.S. Varga, the leading Image IV analyst of the Khrushchev and indeed the Stalin eras. In so doing, he indicated that his principal opponent was M.S. Dragilev.[85] Meanwhile, the Institute of U.S. Studies, founded in 1967 and later renamed U.S. and Canadian Studies, joined IMEMO in putting out Image II and III presentations. Its director, G.A. Arbatov, indicated a preference for Image III presentations.

As of the onset of détente with the United States in 1972–1973, the specialist discussion had experienced a consolidation that benefitted innovating perceptions. Though continuing criticism of the subordination thesis in the 1970s suggested that it retained influence behind the scenes or outside the confines of specialist discourse, Image I had been taken out of play.[86] Image II consequently gained in support. As well, Image III presentations indicated a readiness to absorb concepts and detail from Image IV assessments that would have been contentious some years earlier. And Image IV analysis was promising to break new ground.

In the remainder of the Brezhnev era, the discussion swung back towards positions of greater orthodoxy. Image IV was put on ice by 1974. This would seem to have been a consequence of the Western economic crisis, which reinforced Image II skepticism as to the economic and political capabilities of the capitalist system for self-regulation and effective competition with "socialism." In addition, the crystallization of Eurocommunism, and the unwillingness of the C.P.S.U. to concede in dealing

---

85. Ibid., p. 10.
86. In November 1970, the Academy of Social Sciences had been the recipient of a Central Committee resolution calling for measures to improve the quality of its work. See A.L., "Leninskie traditsii v podgotovke teoreticheskikh kadrov" [Leninist Traditions in the Preparation of Theoretical Cadres], *Voprosy ekonomiki*, No. 1 (1972), p. 156.

with it, may well have obliged Soviet Eurocommunist specialists to fall silent. Tyul-panov nevertheless retained a position on the editorial board of the IMEMO journal through the end of the Brezhnev period. More importantly, IMEMO itself tilted increasingly towards an Image II view of things after 1975, this at the expense of Image III analyses. This left the Institute of U.S. and Canadian Studies somewhat exposed as a producer of Image II and III studies by mid-decade. As U.S.–Soviet relations deteriorated in years that followed, innovation in the specialist analysis of the American political process, and of the political economy of capitalism more generally, was arrested. Though there were exceptions, increasingly conservative assessments of American conduct and prospects came to prevail. As of November 1982, Images I and IV had both been reduced to the status of off-stage presences in a specialist discussion that increasingly favored Image II at the expense of Image III commentary.

Four Tendencies

The perennial discourse of specialists on the sources of American conduct has, to borrow the Marxist phrase, a relative self-sufficiency. It is in part an analytical and scholarly exercise in which scientific knowledge is a principal aim, in which analysts have some degree of individual and collective autonomy. But it is also a political exercise in which the work of analysts is shaped by the varied interests of the regime, and in which competing assessments of the principal adversary express competing policy preferences for Soviet domestic as well as foreign affairs. The Image III writer S.A. Dalin, for example, took part in the discussion as a scholar with no administrative position or recognizable political influence. And yet we find Dalin disagreeing with Dragilev's assertion that state-owned industry was merely a form of collective own-ership for the financial oligarchy. Dalin argued that if this were so, foreign communist parties, and by extension the C.P.S.U., would not be supporting the nationalization of industry.[87] The appeal in this instance was not to the empirical data, but to the need for analysis to coincide with declared policy. This kind of argumentation, though not met frequently, is evident in writing from positions across the board. It suggests that rank-and-file specialist assessments contain a subtext in which policy preferences are expressed for those able to read between the lines.

Where leading participants are concerned, for instance Inozemtsev and Arbatov, who both became Central Committee members in the 1970s, the policy corollaries are often easier to read. In fact, they may be out in the open. Inozemtsev was to be found condemning Image I expectations of capitalist stagnation and collapse as lead-ing to an incorrect assessment of the correlation of forces, hindering the selection of criteria for economic competition, weakening the strategy and tactics of the interna-tional communist movement, and as justifying "passivity" and the awaiting of "ex-traordinary cataclysms."[88] Similarly, Arbatov, in arguing for a differentiated analysis

---

87. Dalin, fn. 37, p. 113.
88. Inozemtsev, fn. 42, Vol. 2, p. 375.

of conflicting tendencies on questions of foreign and military policy in the capitalist ruling class, warned against "artificially increasing the number of our enemies" by employing a sectarian or Image I evaluation.[89] Lesser participants could themselves be quite explicit on occasion, pointing for instance to the need for a correct understanding of developments within the United States and other capitalist countries so as to assure proper Soviet use of foreign economic experience in economic competition with capitalism, and in according a greater role to the state in *Soviet* economic life.[90] Furthermore, characterizations of the American political process offered by senior and lesser specialists alike were frequently accompanied by statements purporting to describe existing Soviet policy towards the United States. Defining American behavior and Soviet policy in diverse ways, they in effect advanced contrasting preferences for Soviet conduct.

To the extent we are able to surface the policy subtexts that accompanied the various images propagated by analysts working outside the decision-making arena, we should be in a position to begin to specify a set of conflicting predispositions or tendencies that figured in the regime's approach to the United States during the Brezhnev era,[91] and that may be expected to persist under the present leadership. In view of the relative scarcity of Image I and IV evaluations in the literature under review here, the corresponding tendencies are necessarily obtained more by inference than by reference to specific texts, which are more plentiful for Images II and III.

COERCIVE ISOLATIONISM

In the absence of powerful countervailing considerations, Image I would orient the Soviet viewer towards a policy of confrontation with the United States. It would do so actively by depicting the American system in terms that left the U.S.S.R. no other choice, and passively by screening out information that might be employed to justify an alternative course for Soviet policy. Active and passive effects are obtained by the use of a simple concept: the subordination of the state to the monopolies.

Frontal opposition to the United States is the appropriate response for the Image I observer who could expect little but the worst from the American government. Owing to the omnipotence of the most reactionary stratum of the ruling class and its unity of purpose on issues of importance, the policies implemented by the President would

---

89. Arbatov, fn. 42, p. 122.
90. For references to "common laws of development" for capitalist and socialist systems, and to the increased role of the state in the U.S.S.R., see V.E. Guliev and E.L. Kuzmin, *Gosudarstvo i demokratiya: kritika antimarksistskikh teorii* [The State and Democracy: A Critique of Anti-Marxist Theories] (Moscow: "Yuridicheskaya literatura," 1975), pp. 28–29. Inozemtsev also cited "objective laws" apparently applicable to socialist as well as capitalist economic development in discussing the need to learn from Western economic practice. Inozemtsev, fn. 28, p. 54. Much of the Soviet literature on the American system can be read as an indirect commentary on Soviet political life, for example on the State-Party ("State-Monopoly") relationship.
91. A discussion of tendencies in Soviet politics is available in Franklyn Griffiths, "A Tendency Analysis of Soviet Policy-making," in Skilling and Griffiths, eds., *Interest Groups in Soviet Politics*, pp. 335–377.

be inevitably and exclusively hostile to the Soviet Union. High levels of defense preparedness and political vigilance would be mandatory for the U.S.S.R., as would the readiness to repress counterrevolutionary activity promoted within the socialist camp by the United States. Furthermore, since not only the American but all capitalist governments are subordinated by the monopolies, the Image I observer would be inclined to favor not merely a posture of confrontation in relation to the United States, but a two-camp foreign policy.[92] Selective détente with America's allies could accordingly be seen as inappropriate or of dubious value in view of the reactionary nature of capitalist states. As well, the fact of subordination would make illusory many of the ideological and political compromises accepted by the communist parties of the capitalist countries, and by the C.P.S.U., in an effort to utilize the electoral or parliamentary path to power.[93] Since the dictatorship of the proletariat is thought to be virtually impossible to achieve prior to the anticipated economic and political collapse of modern monopoly capitalism, opportunities would be taken to exploit the greater revolutionary potential of the developing areas, and to deprive imperialism of the markets and raw materials on which it depends.[94]

At the same time, an Image I assessment would arm the Soviet viewer with a sense of certainty in resisting intra-party attempts to conciliate the United States. He would be predisposed to reject information suggesting that the President was susceptible to any constraints other than those originating from monopoly capital or social forces diametrically opposed to the American government within the United States and in the world arena. Public opinion, electoral considerations, congressional-executive conflict, bureaucratic politics—all this and more would be discounted in view of the President's subordination. Gestures of restraint or conciliation from the United States would accordingly be regarded as attempts to deceive and disorient. If members of

92. Arbatov hinted at the existence of a positive view of confrontation in the C.P.S.U., in referring to the presence in the communist movement of "sectarian groups and individuals who contend that imperialism's old, traditional policy . . . is more preferable from the standpoint of the revolution." Arbatov, fn. 42, p. 238.
93. See, for example, the criticism of the "parliamentary path" in K.I. Zarodov, *Leninizm i sovremennye problemy perekhoda ot kapitalizma k sotsializmu* [Leninism and Contemporary Problems of the Transition from Capitalism to Socialism], 2nd ed., rev. (Moscow: "Mysl," 1981), pp. 53, 252–253. Zarodov argued that Stalin favored the "peaceful" path; he also noted, evidently with approval, that the Communist Party of the United States left open the question of whether socialist revolution would be "non-peaceful" or peaceful. Ibid., pp. 249, 56.
94. Zarodov cited Lenin on the difficulty of revolution in the advanced capitalist countries. Ibid., pp. 37–38. It is necessary however to reach back to the Khrushchev years for a clear Image I statement of the comparative revolutionary advantage in the developing areas: V.F. Khlepikov et al., eds., *O gosudarstvenno-monopolisticheskom kapitalizme* [On State-monopoly Capitalism] (Moscow: Izd-vo AON i VPSh pri TsK KPSS, 1963), p. 58. For evidence of the extraordinary continuity of Image I thinking, compare Kovaleva (1969), fn. 15, with I.I. Kuzminov, *O gosudarstvenno-monopolisticheskom kapitalizme* [On State-monopoly Capitalism] (Moscow: Gospolitizdat, 1949). A criticism of the view that "the most important if not the sole path" to the destruction of capitalism was to deny it the markets and raw materials of the developing countries is to be found in I.A. Sokolov, "Leninskaya teoriya i sovremennyi imperializm" [Leninist Theory and Modern Imperialism], *SShA*, No. 1 (1970), p. 38.

the ruling class appeared to be opposing U.S. policies, it would probably be regarded as the result of their having been put up to it: "hawks" and "doves" would be acting in preassigned roles with intent to mislead.[95] Clearly there would be no conflicting tendencies in American conduct. Nor would any credence be given to the view that the electoral process or public opinion might be used by the Soviet Union to moderate American conduct from within. Party members proposing to negotiate and otherwise to come to terms with the United States would accordingly be resisted. And if negotiations there had to be, they would best be used as an occasion for anti-imperialist propaganda designed to expose the real character of American policy to the peoples of the world.[96]

By the same token, neither the C.P.S.U. nor foreign communism would have grounds for concern with Western perceptions of the "Soviet threat" or the "communist menace." Monopoly capitalism being immutably hostile and incapable of progressive change short of socialist revolution, any Soviet argumentation suggesting that Moscow and the communist movement should exercise restraint so as not to make matters worse would be rejected. Threats and opportunities along the Soviet periphery would be dealt with forcibly and with little concern for Western public reaction, as would select opportunities in the Third World. Counter-propaganda and strength, not unilateral restraint and negotiation, would be viewed as the best answer to the monopolies' attempt to play on the Soviet threat. Fulminating passivity and the awaiting of "extraordinary cataclysms" would in effect be the order of the day. Though a fortress Russia would seek to weaken the United States and its allies by making use of reliable forces in distant areas, it would not compete actively for global influence among the "non-aligned."

The symbols, slogans, and policy preferences accompanying Image I texts tend to stress coercion and unilateral action, whether it be in the domestic and international conduct of the American government, or in Soviet and international communist behavior. They also point to a perceived need for high levels of mass mobilization and enforced unity within the U.S.S.R. Were Soviet policies to be constructed exclusively on the basis of an Image I assessment of the United States, the Soviet Union would quickly isolate itself from all but those it was able to subordinate, thereby

---

95. I.M. Lemin, writing in the heyday of Image I assessments, argued that Churchill's opposition to Munich had been "a distinct game, with previously assigned roles, which was used by the British Government to make itself sought after in negotiations with Hitler, to tilt the latter to agreement." I. Lemin, *Obrazovanie dvukh ochagov voiny i borba SSSR za kollektivnuyu bezopastnost* [The Formation of Two Foci of War and the Soviet Struggle for Collective Security] (Moscow: "Pravda," 1951), p. 32. By 1958 Lemin had reversed course in arguing that it would be "entirely incorrect" to regard differences among U.S. policymakers as a display of "previously assigned roles." Lemin (1958), fn. 8, p. 647. Subsequently he argued more strongly still for recognition of the importance of conflict among American decision-makers. Lemin (1965), fn. 8, chapter 1.
96. Chubaryan, fn. 12, p. 36, observed that the intra-party debate over Lenin's proposals for Genoa in 1922 bore a powerful resemblance to the discussion going on in 1969–1970. If so, a sectarian preference was expressed in Moscow for the utilization of East–West negotiation as a propaganda opportunity prior to and during the early months of the Strategic Arms Limitation Talks.

reproducing an acute Cold War setting conducive to the reimposition of Stalinist totalitarianism within the U.S.S.R. and Eastern Europe. We may therefore infer from Image I presentations a tendency to what may be called "coercive isolationism" in specialist thinking about policy towards the United States.

EXPANSIONIST INTERNATIONALISM

Image II is more complex and allows for greater flexibility in Soviet conduct. If its policy corollaries alone were to guide Soviet behavior towards the United States, the U.S.S.R. would strive for global expansion in conditions of East–West détente and limited cooperation with Washington. This line of policy flows from an assessment of the American system that (a) gives the Soviet Union a choice other than confrontation, and (b) directs attention to the importance of external factors, principally the growth of Soviet power, in weakening an adversary that can alter its methods but not its essence as a hostile force. The proposition that authorizes Image II preferences for simultaneous expansion and tension-reduction is that of the domination of the American state by an internally divided monopoly bourgeoisie.

Owing to the presence of competition within the dominant stratum and the capacity of the monopolists to employ the state, not ineffectively at times, in a "goal-directed strategy of adaptation" aimed at meeting the needs of struggle with "socialism,"[97] the United States is neither likely to collapse internally nor to pursue a policy of unmitigated hostility towards the U.S.S.R. Conflicting tendencies in the orientation of the American monopoly bourgeoisie towards the Soviet Union are, moreover, seen to present opportunities to advance Soviet interests in ways that are denied when the adversary is viewed as monolithic in its rapacity and belligerence.[98] Rather than waiting for the millennial transformation of American capitalism, Image II analysis suggests an active interest in encouraging the erosion of American aggressiveness and global power. Since monopoly capital remains in firm control of the American political process, there would be clear limits on the capacity of the United States to deviate from a policy of strength as a consequence of internal political developments. A premium would therefore be placed on the furtherance of an external setting or correlation of forces that gradually disabled or "paralyzed" American imperialism.

Perceived Soviet successes in altering the global correlation and in demonstrating the unreality of American efforts to create situations of strength accordingly yield the assertion that it is not imperialism but the "conditions of its existence" that have changed.[99] Or, "The aggressive nature of imperialism has not changed and cannot change, it refrains from the use of arms only under pressure of the objective international situation. . . ."[100] As well, support for national liberation movements not

97. M.S. Dragilev et al., eds., Gosudarstvenno-monopolisticheskii kapitalizm: Obshchie cherty i osobennosti [State-monopoly Capitalism: General and Specific Features] (Moscow: Politizdat, 1975), p. 23.
98. Inozemtsev, fn. 66, p. 33.
99. Inozemtsev, fn. 26, pp. 24–25, 194; Inozemtsev, fn. 28, pp. 23, 106–110; and Inozemtsev, fn. 31, pp. 76–77.
100. N.N. Inozemtsev et al., eds., Mirovoi revolyutsionnyi protsess i sovremennost [The World Revolutionary Process Today] (Moscow: "Nauka," 1980), p. 114.

wholly subordinated to the Soviet interest would be viewed with approval. The Angolan events of 1975, for example, are depicted as part of a larger process that serves to deliver "the strongest blow at the positions of capitalism as a whole, as a world social system."[101] Image II assessments may thus be taken to favor a Soviet policy of military might and global power projection that aims to outdo the United States and its allies in creating situations of strength.

As American positions weaken and the general crisis of capitalism deepens, the United States is obliged to call upon its "reserves." Reserve capabilities such as the use of the military-industrial complex to impose a defense-spending burden on the Soviet Union,[102] or state economic intervention to promote economic growth and scientific and technological innovation, do allow the American monopolists some room for maneuver. But ultimately they fail to prevent the decline of American abilities to resist the worldwide advance of "socialism." Global competition with an increasingly debilitated United States is nevertheless taxing and dangerous for the U.S.S.R., which also calls upon its "reserves." As specified in Image II texts, the reserves of the Soviet Union include "inter-imperialist contradictions" and the presence of "far-sighted representatives of the capitalist system."[103] Lowered tension, as well as strength, is essential in the exploitation of both types of reserve.

Image II is associated with the view that the Atlantic Alliance is prone to greater disarray in conditions of diminished international tension.[104] By seeking to reduce tension through propaganda restraint, support for broad-front tactics of the communist movement, and a commitment to East–West negotiations, the Soviet Union could be expected not only to weaken allied support for U.S. policy positions, but to add to its own economic and political strength. On the last point, Image II analyses indicate an interest in utilizing Western economic capabilities and experience, American included, to bolster the capacity of the Soviet system to finance simultaneous increases in defense production and personal consumption.[105] Soviet efforts to pro-

---

101. Inozemtsev, fn. 31, pp. 74–75. See also Inozemtsev, fn. 100, p. 114, for an endorsement of Soviet support for the Afghan "revolution." N.N. Yakovlev, fn. 24, pp. 173–174, 194, looked forward to the day when "socialism is the absolutely decisive force" and opposed any attempt to "compromise" the policy of peaceful coexistence by subordinating Soviet dealings with third states to considerations of American–Soviet coexistence.

102. On the military-industrial complex as a "reserve" bearing on the Soviet economy, see Zorin, fn. 29, pp. 368, 69. For mention of other "reserves," see Bobrakov and Fedorovich, fn. 27, p. 565; and Inozemtsev, fn. 26, p. 197.

103. See Inozemtsev, fn. 28, p. 134, and "Leninskaya teoriya imperializma i sovremennost" [The Leninist Theory of Imperialism Today], *MEMO*, No. 12 (1977), p. 91, for references to differences between Western countries as a "reserve." For comments on the "far-sighted" as "reserves," see Inozemtsev, fn. 28, p. 109, and Zorin, fn. 29, p. 368.

104. N.N. Yakovlev, fn. 24, p. 196. This assessment may have been changing as the Brezhnev years drew to a close. As one observer noted, "In the past, it used to be assumed that inter-imperialist contradictions tend to exacerbate in periods of relative international calm and to abate during periods of crisis as a result of the self-preservation instinct of the Western ruling circles." L. Vidyasova, "Inter-imperialist Contradictions and Imperialist Foreign Policy," *International Affairs* (Moscow), No. 3 (1982), p. 82.

105. Inozemtsev's observations that modern capitalist practice allowed both objectives to be met simultaneously (fn. 28, pp. 49, 116), and that the Soviet Union could learn from capitalist

mote détente and economic cooperation would however be centered on Western Europe insofar as the use of inter-imperialist contradictions were a primary aim. Image II evaluations thus point not only to a policy of strength and forwardness aimed at containing and ultimately isolating the United States, but to an interest in tension-reduction as a means of depriving America of reliable allies and increasing the capacity of the U.S.S.R. to compete militarily and economically.

As to the "far-sighted" or "realistic" elements in the West, they would be exploited in a two-track effort to weaken and isolate the most reactionary wing of the monopoly bourgeoisie. Whereas Image I commentaries make no mention of nuclear weapons, Image II presentations explain the emergence of "realism" among American and West European elites as a consequence of the unprecedented destructiveness of modern warfare, and of the effects of the changing world correlation of forces on the viability of policy from situations of strength.[106] Favorable changes in the correlation of forces are seen to sharpen the conflict of tendencies in Western policymaking.[107] Efforts to increase Soviet capabilities and otherwise to alter the global balance of advantage would therefore serve to reduce the predominance of the "aggressive" elements in the foreign and military decision-making of capitalist countries.

On the other hand, reduced international tension serves to increase the political influence of "far-sighted" elements.[108] So also does Soviet diplomacy.[109] Their presence in and about the governments of America's allies would presumably be regarded as an asset in the exploitation of NATO differences, and in the realization of direct economic and security benefits for the Soviet Union in Europe. Their presence in the American ruling stratum would enhance nuclear deterrence, which is understood in terms of a favorable correlation of competing forces in the opponent's policymaking arena, and not primarily in terms of the disposition of military capabilities as such.[110] The activities of U.S. "realists" could also be expected to reduce overreaction to the growth of Soviet power, and to strengthen American readiness to cooperate on terms acceptable to the U.S.S.R. As occurs with Image II views on the use of inter-imperialist differences, global expansion goes hand in hand with a détente posture in the utilization of elite-level differences within capitalist countries.

---

experience (ibid., p. 54), are suggestive. So also is his recognition that while U.S. defense expenditures rose significantly between 1954 and 1970, they declined as a proportion of G.N.P. (pp. 116–117).
106. Ibid., p. 106; and Inozemtsev, fn. 31, pp. 82–89.
107. Inozemtsev, fn. 31, pp. 82, 10.
108. Inozemtsev, fn. 100, p. 108.
109. Inozemtsev, fn. 28, p. 110. See also the comments that the Soviet Union "carefully" analyzed and took "into account" conflicting tendencies in American politics and policies, in A.N. Yakovlev, fn. 24, pp. 190–191, and Gromyko, fn. 29, pp. 102, 260.
110. A comment from an observer standing outside the discussion on the characteristics of the American system is relevant here: "The prospect of unavoidable defeat in war has a deterrent [sderzhivayushchii] effect on the organizers of military campaigns, causes differentiation in their ranks, prompting the more far-sighted . . . to manifest more sobriety and moderation in policy." K. Bochkarev, "Borba za mir i razvitie mirovogo revolyutsionnogo protsessa" [The Fight for Peace and the Development of the World Revolutionary Process], *Kommunist vooruzhennykh sil*, No. 22 (November 1964), pp. 18–19.

This much granted, Western "realists" are not to be regarded as "friends" of the U.S.S.R.[111] Though they may be opposed to the military-industrial complex,[112] and may favor the use of nonmilitary "reserves" in competing with the Soviet Union,[113] their interest is limited to tactical modifications of the common policy line of monopoly capital.[114] They also link détente to a freeze on social development the world over.[115] Nor are "realists" likely to be very influential in the United States, American policies towards the Soviet Union being affected *inter alia* by "the passion of the 'liberals' for moralizing, their reeling and inconsistency in foreign affairs."[116] Add to this the Image II view of the American political process as being effectively closed to non-monopoly actors in the absence of mass movements of protest, and the prospect is at best one of limited and tactical agreements with the United States. Though America's allies may read the "objective situation" as necessitating relatively broad if still essentially tactical cooperation with Moscow, the lack of a similar assessment in Washington would leave the Soviet Union with little option but to persist with a détente-oriented effort to promote favorable change in the correlation of forces between different social systems. In effect, cooperation and the encouragement of American "realism," as for example in negotiations for strategic arms limitation, would be sought more in the expectation of constraining U.S. belligerence than in the hope of achieving much in the way of substantive agreement.

The tendency in Soviet thinking about policy towards the United States that is connoted by Image II presentations may be referred to as "expansionist internationalism." In common with the coercive isolationism of Image I, expansionist internationalism points to a heavy requirement for military capabilities, and to an interest in the acceleration of revolutionary change in the Third World. But in contrast to the self-isolation and passivity that flow from Image I assessments of the opposing social system, the expansionist tendency in specialist comment entails a vigorous global effort to contain and isolate the United States. Two-camp confrontation gives way to a détente posture and the exploitation of divisions between and within Western countries. Though a radical transformation of U.S. foreign and military policies is the ultimate goal of Soviet expansionist thinking, the opponent is perceived in a manner that inhibits the thought of acting to modify its conduct through direct bilateral action aimed at a *modus vivendi*. The expansionist orientation thus suggests a preoccupation not with the development of U.S.–Soviet bilateral relations as such, but with the furtherance of an international context in which America has less and less choice but to come to Soviet terms. Limited agreements with the United States may be feasible and desirable, but not at the cost of compromising the capacity of the U.S.S.R. to

---

111. Inozemtsev, fn. 31, p. 83. N.N. Yakovlev, fn. 24, is emphatic on this point.
112. Zorin, fn. 29, p. 368.
113. Inozemtsev, fn. 28, pp. 109–116; and Inozemtsev, fn. 26, p. 197.
114. Gromyko, fn. 29, pp. 4–5, 32, 263. See also A.N. Yakovlev, fn. 24, pp. 16, 432. On the other hand, an Image II presentation edited by Inozemtsev includes the assertion that capitalism was obliged to make concessions that went far beyond the tactical in their significance. Inozemtsev, fn. 31, p. 77.
115. Inozemtsev, fn. 100, pp. 145–146.
116. Gromyko, fn. 29, p. 32.

promote continued change in the correlation of forces. Hence a preference for improved relations with America's allies and the maintenance of a less tense but still remote relationship with America itself.

REFORMATIVE INTERNATIONALISM

In contrast to the clear sense of policy direction that accompanies Image II assessments of the American system, the foreign policy and military corollaries of Image III appear to be somewhat indeterminate. Where Image II draws attention to inherent limits on the capacity of the United States to cooperate with the U.S.S.R., Image III filters the information in a way that allows for greater variety in American conduct as the result of interaction among non-monopoly as well as monopoly actors who make diverse demands on a relatively autonomous apparatus of state. Internal political conflict, conditioned *inter alia* by changes in the correlation of forces and in the consequences of modern warfare,[117] is seen to incline American behavior in either a militaristic and "aggressive" or a relatively moderate and "realistic" direction. Should American policies take on an "aggressive" cast, the Image III viewer might well lend support to an expansionist Soviet effort to contest and otherwise demonstrate the unworkability of U.S. globalism.

But to the extent that American politics and policies are seen to entail a readiness to cooperate with Moscow, Image III analyses suggest an interest not only in encouraging American moderation, but in working out a long-term stabilization of political and military relations with the main opponent. Indeed, as distinct from the fixed expectation of political-military rivalry connoted by Image II presentations, Image III signals a preference for a reformation of East–West and Soviet–American relations in which military-strategic forms of conflict are replaced, as circumstance allows, by forms that stress economic and ideological competition. The construct that both allows for a greater measure of cooperation in Soviet policy and accounts for the relatively wide range of behavior that may in principle be expected from the United States is that of the domination of a relatively self-sufficient apparatus of state by the whole bourgeoisie and the heterogeneous stratum of monopolists in the first instance. The tendency in specialist thinking about Soviet policy that is associated with this image of the American system will be called "reformative internationalism."

Evidence for the presence of a reformative tendency in Soviet thinking about policy towards the United States could be extracted from Image III analyses taken together with Image III references to the contemporary significance of the Genoa policy of 1922. Fortunately, there is an easier way: Arbatov chose to provide Soviet readers with an exposition of the reformative case in the early 1970s. If it is assumed that he acted as spokesman for a more widespread policy preference in the specialist discussion at that time, we should be able to get a fix on the reformative tendency by concentrating on what he had to say.

---

117. For comments on changes in the correlation of forces and the nature of war as causative factors, see Arbatov, fn. 42, pp. 230–232, 246, 264–265; Dalin, fn. 37, pp. 499–500; and Inozemtsev, fn. 42, Vol. I (2nd ed., 1975), p. 11.

Stressing the existence of conflicting tendencies in the orientation of the American ruling class and its dominant stratum towards foreign and military affairs, Arbatov indirectly agreed with the Image II assessment that such differences were inherently tactical in nature.[118] But in the evaluation of "realistic" (also called "moderate," "liberal," or "reformist") tactics and their significance, he diverged substantially from Image II argumentation. For a variety of reasons, the American ruling class had been obliged to evolve a "'dialectical'" or dual policy that envisaged concessions and compromises, as well as pressure and divisive cooperation in relations with the Soviet Union and its allies.[119] In this more "subtle and differentiated anti-communism," military power was employed increasingly as a "shield" for other foreign policy tactics that included economic, scientific, technological, and cultural relations, and "even certain forms of cooperation" with the Soviet bloc.[120] In developing these ties, the United States aimed not only at the erosion of socialism, but at the avoidance of nuclear war.[121] Moreover, where previously it had been thought that imperialist aggressiveness would increase as the correlation of forces shifted to its disadvantage, now it could be said that, "Among the more sober-minded and far-sighted representatives of the bourgeoisie the trend toward [acceptance of peaceful coexistence] will become more and more pronounced as socialism grows stronger and the hollowness of any other political line is laid bare."[122] Evidently the United States was moving into an era in which frontal opposition to the U.S.S.R. would gradually be replaced by more subtle forms of struggle.

Presented with a choice between different forms of struggle between different social systems, Arbatov noted, communist parties, and therefore presumably the C.P.S.U., sought to direct the conflict into "channels that would bring no calamities."[123] A proper distinction between opposed tendencies in American behavior was therefore of "very great significance."[124] Indeed, it spelled "the difference between a thermonuclear war and a policy envisaging methods of struggle [consistent with] peaceful coexistence. . . ."[125] To the extent that "realism" succeeded in influencing American policy, it was possible for U.S.–Soviet relations to enter a channel in which the danger of nuclear war diminished and the prospects for cooperation increased.[126] Demands made within the United States for the avoidance of confrontation and for a normalization of relations with the Soviet Union could therefore "dovetail" with Soviet policy.[127] Arbatov accordingly found it appropriate to speak of "a sphere of coinciding interests" between the Soviet Union and the United States—a possibility not admitted

---

118. Arbatov, fn. 42, pp. 225, 229.
119. Ibid., pp. 227, 225, 235–236, 238.
120. Ibid., pp. 236, 241, 59.
121. Ibid., pp. 236, 241, 246, 232, 264–265.
122. Ibid., pp. 226, 245–246.
123. Ibid., p. 275.
124. Ibid., p. 226.
125. Ibid., pp. 225–226.
126. Ibid., p. 245.
127. Ibid., p. 237 (a point not made in the Russian-language version of 1970).

in Image II commentary and all but explicitly denied by Image I.[128] Not only was the Soviet Union advised to distinguish between conflicting tendencies in American conduct, but as well it stood to gain from an effort to strengthen American "realism" by negotiation and other means aimed at translating the inevitable struggle of different social systems from political-military into "non-military" forms.[129] To the extent that Moscow was successful in this, ideological and economic competition would come to coexist with efforts to strengthen peace, to cooperate, and to promote a stabilizing "mutual dependence."[130]

Aside from reducing the likelihood of nuclear war, the goals of a reformative emphasis in Soviet policy, as presented by Arbatov, included a reduction in the burden of defense spending on the Soviet economy, the creation of external conditions favoring more rapid Soviet economic and political development including higher living standards and the development of "socialist democracy," and also a continued worldwide evolution towards "socialism."[131] On the latter point, Arbatov argued that the decisive contribution of the U.S.S.R. to the revolutionary movement lay in the success of Soviet economic policy and in the "force of socialist example."[132] In so doing, he indicated a preference for reciprocal ("complete parity" was the phrase[133]) American–Soviet non-intervention in the developing areas, as distinct from an expansionist effort to intervene competitively on behalf of revolutionary movements. More was evidently to be gained from an endeavor to reinforce the Vietnam-induced reluctance of the United States to intervene, thereby allowing Moscow to gain the benefits of inevitable social change in the Third World at reduced cost and risk. Viewed from this standpoint, what later transpired in Angola, the Horn of Africa, South Yemen, Indochina, and Afghanistan would not have been met with unqualified approval. Whatever its advantages as viewed from an expansionist perspective, Soviet forwardness would have been seen as risking an increase in international tension, inviting a rebirth of American interventionism, justifying a more vigorous American prosecution of the arms race, and impeding strategic arms negotiations. All of this follows from the recognition that American advocates of strength made a practice of "using" international developments to further their case in policy debate within the United States.[134] Ultimately the result would be to undercut the capacity of the

---

128. G.A. Arbatov, "Nauchno-tekhnicheskaya revolyutsiya i vneshnyaya politika SShA" [The Scientific and Technological Revolution and U.S. Foreign Policy], in Gromyko and Zhurkin, fn. 42, p. 35.
129. Arbatov, fn. 42, pp. 275, 265, 225–226, including a footnote reference to Genoa. See also G.A. Arbatov, "Sobytie vazhnogo mezhdunarodnogo znacheniya" [An Event of Great International Significance], SShA, No. 8 (1972), p. 7.
130. Arbatov, fn. 42, pp. 274–275. The reference to "mutual dependence" is in Arbatov, fn. 128, p. 37.
131. Arbatov, fn. 42, pp. 306–308. That Arbatov had the continued spread of socialism in mind is generally evident in his work, and is clear in his insistence that the U.S.S.R. could provide no "guarantees" against revolution and the spread of communist ideas. Ibid., p. 269.
132. Ibid., pp. 259, 304, 313.
133. Ibid., p. 269. See also S.M. Menshikov, Sovremennyi kapitalizm [Contemporary Capitalism] (Moscow: "Mysl," 1981), pp. 14–15, where a "code of behavior" is spelled out.
134. G.A. Arbatov, "Administratsiya Niksona u srediny distantsii" [The Nixon Administration at Mid-course], SShA, No. 8 (1970), p. 13.

U.S.S.R. to prevail on the front of economic construction, which ultimately determined "everything."[135]

Arbatov's presentation of the aims and means of reformative internationalism was thus centered on bilateral negotiation and mutual restraint in distant areas—a reversal of the expansionist recipe. In responding to the threat of nuclear war and the opportunity costs of being prepared for it ("waste"[136] and retarded rates of Soviet economic and political development), a sufficiency of military power was clearly required. It was needed to deter the United States by promoting realism and weakening traditional thinking, to bring America to the negotiating table, and to prevent adverse change in the correlation of forces. But otherwise, nonmilitary forms of struggle were to be favored, as opposed to the accumulation of military might and power-projection capabilities, in supporting processes of global change in which an increasingly "realistic" United States could acquiesce. A dual policy that combined "firmness . . . with flexibility" was appropriate in dealing with America.[137] Though Image II texts also communicated a preference for a two-track policy towards the United States, the "firmness" track was clearly to be emphasized. From an Image III standpoint, however, a greater measure of "flexibility" was appropriate in taking advantage of opportunities to direct American–Soviet relations towards increased cooperation and nonmilitary competition.

This much granted, Arbatov stressed the contingent nature of the "realist" line in American policies and politics. It was the product of internal political conflict which saw an unrelenting effort by reactionaries to reassert the strategy of strength.[138] The occurrence of "disagreements" in American–Soviet relations was inevitable.[139] Economic and political crises might also affect American conduct adversely.[140] If a "realist" were elected to the White House, he would be under pressure to conciliate the conservative opposition and to incorporate its preferences into official policy.[141] Furthermore, even if American conservatives were entirely isolated and eliminated as a political force, the threat of nuclear war would remain: there would likely be tensions, local conflicts, and the continuing possibility of "'accidental'" war caused by simple error.[142] The reformation of American–Soviet relations was thus to be viewed as a lengthy and difficult process.

How then was the Soviet Union to moderate American foreign and military policies? Aside from following a dual policy of pressure and cooperation aimed at ordering American choices from without, the U.S.S.R. stood to gain from an effort to intervene directly in the politics of American policymaking on behalf of the "realist" coalition. This latter point was the meaning of Image III references to the Genoa policy of

---

135. Arbatov, fn. 42, p. 304.
136. Mention is made of "aimless waste" in Arbatov, fn. 129, p. 7. See also the reference to war as "becoming pointless." Arbatov, fn. 42, p. 273.
137. Arbatov, fn. 129, p. 9.
138. Arbatov, fn. 42, pp. 232–234.
139. Arbatov, fn. 129, p. 7.
140. Arbatov, fn. 42, p. 228.
141. Ibid., p. 227.
142. Ibid., pp. 270–271.

1922.[143] Specifically, the Soviet Union was being advised to take up a détente posture in which it would (1) actively mute the "Soviet threat" by avoiding "frightening words" and presumably deeds, (2) learn to speak the political language of American moderates so as to engage them in dialogue, (3) advance a "pacifist programme" designed to reinforce the arguments of "realists" and expose "traditionalists" as the unreasoning advocates of belligerence, and (4) do "everything possible and even the impossible" to increase the electoral strength of "realists"—all to bring forth administrations capable of reaching agreements with the U.S.S.R. and shaping a favorable American public opinion in return.[144]

In sum, Soviet diplomacy was to implement a set of procedures aimed not only at structuring the external context in which decisions on U.S. foreign and military policy were made, but also at modifying American public opinion.[145] As well, Moscow was to utilize the relative self-sufficiency of the Presidency to alter the balance of forces within the American ruling class.[146] To the extent that these efforts were successful, the Soviet Union and the United States would both find themselves pursuing dual policies that allowed for a growing measure of bilateral cooperation in the midst of continuing conflict.

Contrary to the thrust of reformative thinking about policy towards the United States, the years that followed Arbatov's presentation of the argument for a dual policy oriented towards greater collaboration saw the Presidency become less and less useful for the promotion of an American "realism" whose social base steadily narrowed. Faced with weaker Presidents, fundamental American questioning of the role of the state in economic and social life, the growth of congressional-executive rivalry, the rightward shift of American public opinion, the increasing disability of the Democratic Party, and finally the capacity of the Reagan Administration to mobilize public support for a return to policies of strength, those favoring a reformative emphasis in Soviet policy could only have been dismayed. Add to these considerations a growing awareness of impediments to cooperation arising from the need to

143. See, for example, ibid., p. 226; G.A. Arbatov, *Pravda*, May 4, 1971; Popova, fn. 57, p. 6; and Zhurkin, fn. 6, pp. 302–304.
144. Implications of the Genoa policy for the Soviet Union in the early 1970s are discussed in Griffiths, fn. 6, pp. 23–32. "Doing the impossible" may well have included proceeding with the May 1972 summit following the American bombardment of Hanoi and the mining of North Vietnamese harbors, so as to assist in the reelection of a "realist" to the White House. That there was opposition to going ahead with the 1972 summit was stated to the author by a Central Committee member in an interview in Moscow in April 1979.
145. Cf. Arbatov, fn. 42, p. 41: "In the ideological struggle the basic aim of any class is to bring the largest number of people under the influence of its ideas and to tear them away from the spiritual influence of the class adversary." And: ". . . ideological propaganda is used by a class as a means of undermining the spiritual unity of the class adversary and ensuring to itself the broadest possible influence in his ranks." Ibid.
146. A direct interest in employing the state to influence the ruling class is suggested by Arbatov's observations that the strategic arms agreements of 1972 undermined the "aggressive" elements, and that détente and a normalization of relations would strengthen the hand of the moderates. Ibid., pp. 235, 253 (both observations added in 1973 version).

deal simultaneously with the Senate and the President,[147] and from the greater responsiveness of the Congress itself to local interests and political action committees,[148] and the American scene as viewed from Moscow by the end of the Brezhnev era became one that all but denied the immediate utility of a reformative perspective. For those who nevertheless clung to a preference for reformative internationalism as of November 1982, the choice would seem to have been one of keeping the option of cooperation open and otherwise limiting damage in American–Soviet relations, or of lending support to an expansionist effort to constrain American choices by making clear the futility of a renewed globalism.

DEMOCRATIC ISOLATIONISM

Finally, some brief remarks may be ventured on the policy corollaries of the very few Image IV texts that have been considered here. When compared with reformative internationalist preferences for a gradual liberalization of American foreign and military policies, Image IV evaluations suggest an interest in more rapid and far-reaching transformations in American–Soviet relations, in the nature of American capitalism, and ultimately in the nature of the Soviet system as well. Indeed, the principal goal implied by Image IV writings appears to be the internal reform and democratization of Soviet "socialism" in a stabilized international setting. The tendency connoted by Image IV texts will therefore be referred to provisionally as "democratic isolationism."

Having discussed in unusual detail the consequences of a war fought with nuclear weapons, Burlatskii and Galkin stated that self-regulating global mechanisms based on the spontaneous interaction of competing forces were no longer an acceptable means of assuring international stability.[149] Instead, they suggested, the prevention of nuclear war required the adoption of a strategy of "planned general peace" that consisted of "conscious, goal-directed and effective actions" in which the Soviet Union and the United States were in effect to lead the way.[150] Just how general peace was to be planned and brought about was not made clear. Evidently an evolving American capitalism whose differences with the U.S.S.R. were essentially political, and in which the state played an increasingly autonomous role, was capable of taking part in such an exercise. Evidently the Soviet Union was in a position to reduce the severity of the political conflict that stood in the way of broadening cooperation to avert nuclear war. Tyulpanov's presentation of the case for the two-phase theory of the imperialist stage suggested several ways in which the Soviet Union could improve the prospects for American–Soviet cooperation and for the evolution of American capitalism itself.

---

147. Bogdanov and Kokoshin, fn. 56, pp. 47–48, report as justified West European opinions to the effect that negotiation with American administrations is impossible without considering the position of the Congress from the very outset. Another Image III observer, Chetverikov, fn. 57, pp. 117–118, while commenting that the President remained the predominant force despite the growth of congressional power, makes note of a Presidential practice of referring to congressional constraints in an attempt to extract "additional concessions" from the Soviet Union.
148. Chetverikov, fn. 57, pp. 113–114.
149. Burlatskii and Galkin, fn. 82, p. 282.
150. Ibid., pp. 282, 291–302.

Given that the sources of qualitative change in the capitalist system were primarily endogenous, a vigorous Soviet effort to advance the cause of socialism by acting to alter the world correlation of forces would have been seen as inherently misguided in the view of Tyulpanov and those for whom he spoke. Rather, Soviet policy should have been seeking to create conditions conducive to the realization of inner "democratic transformations" of the American system that had become possible with the advent of the state-monopoly phase of imperialism. Indirect Soviet military interventions in the developing countries would accordingly have met with disapproval, as would other military moves that served to brace the forces of order and constrain the forces of movement in America. Furthermore, to the degree that the C.P.S.U. began to speak the language not merely of Eurocommunism but of the Italian Communist Party,[151] the overt Soviet political threat to American capitalism could also be reduced. While this line of policy could have been expected initially to produce an American–Soviet accommodation similar to that implied by Image III assessments, the underlying aim would have been to further the socialist transformation of American society, as distinct from encouraging a moderation of American foreign policy.

Tyulpanov's readiness to accede explicitly to Eurocommunist positions would also seem to contain an implied criticism of the Communist Party of the United States. The C.P.U.S.A., as Soviets well knew, had failed to make itself into a mass organization or an influential force in the American political process. The willingness of Burlatskii and Galkin to supplement an unamended class-against-class analysis with methodologies derived from American experience also suggested a belief that a class-based strategy such as that pursued by the C.P.U.S.A. could profitably be altered to fit the requirements of effective action in a context that differed markedly from European social settings. Image IV presentations may accordingly be read as indicating a preference for change in the policies of the C.P.U.S.A.—perhaps even its dissolution as occurred under the leadership of Earl Browder in the mid-1940s. What Browder sought to accomplish—to diffuse the "communist threat" and to deploy the resources of the Party in support of a New Deal coalition that included "men of vision and understanding" from the business community[152]—was, after all, not that far removed even from reformative internationalist thinking in the C.P.S.U. in the 1960s

---

151. Circumstantial evidence suggests that Tyulpanov favored a view of the capitalist system more in keeping with that of the Italian (P.C.I.) than the French Communist Party (P.C.F.). Though it had espoused a two-phase theory of the imperialist stage, the P.C.F. analysis of contemporary capitalism retained a strong admixture of orthodoxy, which made it little different in practice from an Image II Soviet assessment. See *Le capitalisme monopoliste d'état*, 2 vols. (Paris: Editions sociales, 1971).
152. See Earl Browder, *Teheran: Our Path in War and Peace* (New York: International Publishers, 1944), pp. 73–74. A related line of argument is to be found in James S. Allen, *World Monopoly and Peace* (New York: International Publishers, 1946), esp. pp. 254–258. Allen was closely associated with Browder. When the Soviet debate on developments in the capitalist system resumed after 1945, the leading Image I analyst, I.I. Kuzminov, made a point of attacking not only the Image IV views of E.S. Varga, but also the work of Allen. See, for example, Kuzminov, fn. 94, pp. 47–75. The postwar origins of Image IV Soviet thinking would seem to have been directly and positively related to Browderism in the C.P.U.S.A.

and 1970s. But again, from a democratic isolationist perspective, any underlying preference for change in the strategy of the C.P.U.S.A. would likely have been aimed more at a rapid and far-reaching "democratization" of the American system than at its liberalization.

To the degree that Image IV evaluations of the United States were accepted by the C.P.S.U. and acted upon in its external relations, the Soviet political order would also be opened to reform. Aside from the fact that the building of bridges to European communist parties critical of Soviet internal practices would place questions of democratization higher on the Soviet policy agenda, the propagation of a new and less intimidating official assessment of the United States within the U.S.S.R. could only serve to undercut practices and institutions that relied upon the presence of a formidable external menace. It would do so by legitimizing alternative preferences for domestic policy held in check by officially sanctioned assertions of the presence of a more or less implacable principal adversary.

Although a direct linkage between Image IV evaluations of the United States and a preference for internal reform cannot be demonstrated on the basis of the evidence under review here, indirect links are to be found in Burlatskii's long-standing commitment to democratization,[153] and in the severe criticism of the Soviet regime contained in Varga's "Testament," which began to circulate in the Soviet Union in the late 1960s.[154] It is also the case that over the years Image IV analyses have offered the most forthright Soviet criticisms of Stalinist evaluations of the capitalist system, and implicitly of Stalinism itself. If to this we add signs of an Image IV propensity to derogate the value of global political-military rivalry with the United States in favor of high levels of cooperation, the tentative conclusion that an inward-looking preoccupation with internal reform and democratization lies at the basis of the Image IV orientation to foreign affairs may be allowed to stand.

The shortage of direct evidence for the isolationist tendencies at either end of the spectrum of specialist policy preferences suggests that both lacked regime support in the course of the Brezhnev years. This is in contrast to the status of the two internationalist tendencies that coexisted at the center: both are relatively easily documented; both would seem to have been endowed with legitimacy. Yet it remains true that expansionist preferences were articulated more frequently and with greater assurance than was the case for the reformative orientation towards the United States. Indeed, had Arbatov not been explicit in making the case for a line of policy that emphasized collaboration with the principal adversary in the early 1970s, the Western analyst would be obliged to rely heavily on subtext or inference in specifying reformative internationalist preferences. Accordingly, if we are to select one tendency that predominated in the specialist literature of the Brezhnev era on the political economy of contemporary capitalism and the American policy process in particular, it must be expansionist internationalism.

153. F.M. Burlatskii, *Gosudarstvo i kommunizm* [The State and Communism] (Moscow: Sotsekgiz, 1963).
154. Eugen Varga, "Political Testament," *New Left Review*, No. 62 (July–August 1970), pp. 31–43.

Structure in Soviet Policy

Taken together, the four tendencies identified here constitute a repertoire of specialist predispositions for Soviet policy towards the United States as they existed in the period 1964–1982, and as they may be expected to persist in the years ahead. These tendencies were articulated by individuals and, it would appear, in the interaction of informal groups and coalitions. They do not allow us to speak with assurance about the subjective perceptions and policy preferences of individuals or groupings of specialists. But they do tell us something about the orientations of the specialist community as a whole. The distinction is an important one.

Depending on the issue, the application of intra-party controls, the state of American–Soviet relations, and a host of other variables, a set of specialists or an individual such as Arbatov who might personally have favored an Image IV assessment and a reformative emphasis in Soviet policy towards the United States could have found themselves publicly presenting an Image III evaluation and privately endorsing an expansionist policy prescription on a given issue. We are not in a position to establish reliable correlations between the public pronouncements and the behind-the-scenes activities of specialists, or between their stated perceptions and their personal policy preferences as individuals. What we have before us is evidence not so much of subjective as of what may be called transactional perceptions and preferences—stated beliefs and predispositions that may or may not correspond accurately to subjective thinking, and that are the product more of influence and power relationships than of an unfettered search for the true and proper.

Though the Soviet data allow only very little to be said about the subjective orientations of individuals and informal groups, they do permit us to speak with confidence about enduring patterns in the overall body of communication among specialists during the Brezhnev era. Persistent regularities can readily be discerned in the published arguments of the community of professionals engaged in perennial discussion and debate about American capitalism and Soviet policy towards the United States. In short, we have before us a set of tendencies that tells us a good deal about the long-standing policy predispositions of the corps of Soviet specialists taken as a whole. Might these also be the tendencies of the Soviet political system, or more precisely of the regime insofar as it is not commensurate with the system as a whole?

To demonstrate conclusively that we have isolated the repertoire of established response patterns of the Soviet regime as it deals with its principal adversary, we would have to widen the analysis very considerably. We should consider variations in official action towards the United States during the Brezhnev years, in official statements including the speeches of leaders, in the print and electronic media as they concerned American affairs and American–Soviet relations, and in the *samizdat* literature as well. An inquiry of this kind would yield not only a more finely textured and less ideological presentation of uniformities in the Soviet approach to the United States, but an indication of the effects of persistent preferences originating from outside the regime on the relative influence of tendencies within the regime itself. Additional patterns of policy preference could, for example, be identified on the middle ground between expansionist and reformative internationalism. More copious evidence of support for the two isolationist tendencies might also be uncovered, thereby offsetting a possible bias towards expansionist internationalism in the literature under review here.[155] Anti-war and indeed pacifist attitudes among the Soviet intelligentsia and in the population at large could as well be found to provide a social base outside the regime for the democratic isolationist orientation towards the United States, as might Great Russian nationalist and chauvinist sentiment in the case of coercive isolationist responses. In addition, contrasting orientations towards China, which do not figure in the literature under consideration here, could be factored into the analysis. Most important for practical purposes, an enlarged inquiry stands to provide indicators for assessing the relative strength of the various tendencies, and for marking changes in the correlation among them. This much granted, there are reasons to believe that the four tendencies outlined here do begin to describe the main predispositions of the regime in its dealings with the United States.

For one thing, it is a task of senior specialists and lesser commentators to lend meaning to incoming information on American affairs and American–Soviet relations, to assist in defining centrally important features of the context in which foreign and domestic policies are made, and to do so in a manner consistent with the requirements of the Party. Though an examination of a more extensive body of data would undoubtedly produce a better understanding of Soviet tendencies, it would not likely offer a major improvement on the capacity of the specialist literature to inform us as to how Soviets themselves put the pieces together for purposes of policy discussion. Secondly, to the extent that the comments of specialist producers of integrated assessments are structured year in and year out to conform to the varied needs of consumers in senior positions in the Party, tendencies that are observable in specialist discourse should reflect, however indirectly, the propensities of the leadership in its dealings with America. Though the corps of specialists is by no means wholly conformist or wholly politicized in its assessments, the outer perimeters of debate and the character of discussion within these confines are clearly regulated by a leadership that remains willing to admit some diversity of expert analysis and policy prescription.

---

155. Bias may arise, for example, from the responsibilities of IMEMO in articulating the formal ideology of the regime on developments in the capitalist world at large. The effect of IMEMO presentations could thus be to skew the distribution of opinion on the United States in particular. As well, we should be aware of possible bias in our own minds as we assess the significance of Soviet tendencies. Experience of political life in the liberal democracies suggests that power flows from the center of the policy spectrum, that positions to the right and left of center are deprived of influence the further they go. Russian and Soviet experience suggests however that the center is inherently weak. Hence the extraordinary variety of Soviet political controls to ensure that the center not only holds but dominates. Hence also the Soviet propensity to overrate the strength of the far right and far left in American politics—this evidently in an uncritical transposition from domestic Soviet experience to the evaluation of policy processes abroad. The appropriate framework in considering the correlation of forces in Soviet policymaking on relations with America may therefore be one that has the flanks exerting significant effects on the center. If this is so, the two "isolationist" tendencies could prove to be more potent than the Western observer might initially think.

As well, the Central Committee status of key spokesmen such as Inozemtsev and Arbatov supports the view that senior participants were voicing preferences distributed more widely within the Party. But aside from these considerations, which relate to the inner workings of the regime, a correspondence is to be observed between the set of tendencies under discussion here and variations in the outward behavior of the Soviet Union between 1964 and 1982.

As of the Twenty-third C.P.S.U. Congress early in 1966, for example, the correlation of tendencies in the Soviet Union's American policy had altered substantially in comparison with the situation at the time of Khrushchev's removal late in 1964. The tactics, slogans, and symbols of reformative internationalism—negotiation, arms agreements, détente, and positive internal Soviet references to "concessions"—had been withdrawn as the Vietnam War intensified and the new leadership revealed an aversion to reformism in foreign and domestic affairs. Democratic isolationist commentary—on themes such as "what disarmament will bring," or democratization of the Soviet system as conveyed by the notion of the "state of the whole people"—had been suppressed and offset by a resurgence of coercive isolationist preferences evinced in an attempted rehabilitation of Stalin and the reappearance of a two-camp propaganda on American–Soviet relations. Expansionist internationalism was clearly the order of the day as Moscow vigorously supported the intention of the North Vietnamese to defeat the United States in Indochina, maintained an arm's length bilateral relationship with Washington while greatly increasing Soviet armed strength, and endeavored to cultivate America's European allies in a renewed emphasis on the effort to extrude the United States from Western Europe.

Six years later, the correlation of tendencies in Soviet policy had assumed different proportions. Notwithstanding a second unsuccessful effort to rehabilitate Stalin at about the time strategic arms limitation talks began with the United States late in 1969, the force of coercive isolationist preferences had diminished by the time of the Moscow summit of 1972. The fortunes of democratic isolationism had correspondingly improved, as seen in the authorization of arguments favoring a basic revision of Soviet thinking and practice in regard to the United States and other advanced capitalist countries. This change in the relative influence of the two flanking tendencies would seem to have occurred in two phases. First, in 1969–1970, there appears to have been a polarization of preferences within the regime, as reflected in the strengthening of coercive and democratic isolationist impulses simultaneously. And then, in 1970–1971, as Brezhnev assumed the role of preeminent spokesman on foreign affairs and the way was cleared both for the Twenty-fourth Congress and for détente in Europe, coercive isolationist preferences evidently lost ground and the reformative inclination to negotiate directly with the main opponent began to gain at the expense of expansionism. This shift at the center was presumably a response to the attainment of approximate equivalence in strategic nuclear weapons, to the ensuing improvement in the Soviet arms bargaining position, and to evidence that a debilitated America was prepared to do business. As well, the opening for reformative internationalism would seem to have been widened by the onset of Sino–American cooperation, by a marked deterioration in Soviet economic performance, and by a perceived opportunity to apply American as well as Western European economic capabilities in stimulating Soviet economic growth and military strength in a manner that diminished the need for reform of the Soviet system.

As of the summit of 1972, reformative internationalism would seem to have approached a position of parity with expansionism in Soviet policy towards the United States. Cooperation with American allies was being pursued very actively and in an expansionist mode, as was the growth of strategic and conventional military capabilities in a setting of limited agreements on strategic arms control and leadership assertions of Soviet support for revolutionary transformations in the developing areas. Simultaneously, an attempt was being made, in SALT and in the development of American–Soviet economic relations, to alter the terms of competition with a seemingly more accommodating principal adversary. Any further accession of strength to reformative internationalism in Soviet policy would depend not only on the results of bilateral cooperation, but on the capacity of both sides to accept the risks of political and military demobilization in the midst of continuing rivalry.

A decade later, in November 1982, the relative strength of the tendencies in Soviet conduct had altered substantially once again. On the flanks, democratic isolationist argumentation had effectively been closed off since the mid-1970s, whereas coercive isolationist responses had acquired greater prominence in the effective repression of dissent, in the military intervention in Afghanistan, in the effort to intimidate the population of Poland, and in the reassertion of two-camp rhetoric in Soviet comment on American policy and American–Soviet relations. At the center of the policy spectrum, reformative internationalism had been reduced to overt reaffirmations of readiness to negotiate unaccompanied by any great flexibility in practice, but possibly accompanied by covert efforts to avoid Soviet action liable to underwrite the Reagan Administration's campaign to remobilize America. As to expansionist internationalism, after having recovered much of the ground lost in the experiment with reformative internationalism in the early 1970s, it too was increasingly muted as a consequence of the Reagan Administration's ability to deny Moscow the reduced tension that was essential to the pursuit of unilateral gain at acceptable levels of risk and cost. Soviet operations in the developing areas were consequently marked by notable restraint. On the other hand, cleavages in the Atlantic alliance and the appearance of mass antinuclear movements in the major NATO countries, the United States included, promised to hamper President Reagan's remobilization effort, if not to force the United States into a posture of restraint and cooperation with Moscow. Evidently preferring to face the NATO countries with the consequences of their decision to deploy new American intermediate-range nuclear weapons in Europe, the Brezhnev leadership sought to influence the impending West German election by pressing the cause of détente in Europe and continuing with its deployment of intermediate-range missiles. The net result, as compared with the situation in 1966 or 1972, was remarkable passivity in the American policy of a regime whose preferences added up to residual expansionism shaded by a very largely immobilized reformative internationalism and a propensity to strike out in coercive isolationist fashion.

Three brief cuts into Soviet policy over a period of eighteen years do not provide a test of the fit between the tendencies articulated in specialist discussion and the behavior of the regime towards the United States. Nor do they offer a detailed explanation of shifts in the correlation of these tendencies. But they do indicate that variations in the regime's American policy can readily be described in terms of change in the relative influence of tendencies derived from the specialist literature. If to this we add the circumstantial evidence that specialists echo foreign policy preferences distributed more widely within the regime, we may conclude that the conflicting tendencies exhibited in specialist discourse did broadly reflect the repertoire of established response patterns in Soviet behavior towards the principal adversary between 1964 and 1982.

Soviet actions are not likely to be well understood when they are viewed in terms of a unilinear, internally consistent policy whose direction is deliberately changed by the leadership as circumstance requires. The evidence assembled here suggests that Soviet conduct is better regarded as internally contradictory, consisting of a series of persistent tendencies whose relative strength alters in response to international and domestic situational variables. As is the case with the specialist community, these tendencies are best read as uniformities in the behavior of the regime taken as a whole. Democratic isolationism aside, they represent tried and tested ways of dealing with situations that face the U.S.S.R. As is shown by the meager results of the effort since 1945 to promote democratic isolationism as a legitimate orientation to domestic and foreign affairs, the basic predispositions of the regime cannot readily be altered by lesser participants in the policy process. Nor is the leadership itself in a position to change these predispositions in short order. On the contrary, the established tendencies of the regime serve to structure the performance of leaders and lesser actors alike. Barring the appearance of a leader with dictatorial powers, or a crisis that forced the consideration of radically new responses, those engaged in the making of policy towards the United States must conform to the acquired response patterns of the regime, or fail.

But if structure in the form of dominant tendencies constrains and channels the conduct of actors within, these actors nevertheless remain free to alter the inflection of policy on specific issues, and thereby to modify the correlation of tendencies in the overall approach of the regime towards America. Though individual decision-makers and those on the perimeter of the decision-making arena could well hew to particular orientations for policy towards the United States, we have no real way of knowing whether this is so. Under the circumstances, Soviet policymakers are best seen as "uncommitted thinkers" who produce a mobile consensus as together they vary the correlation of regime tendencies in processing a continuous sequence of issues that relate to America.[156] The result is a policy that at once displays remarkable continuity and a propensity to oscillate as tendencies are combined and recombined to produce an array of responses to the United States.

---

156. Cf. John D. Steinbruner, *The Cybernetic Theory of Decision* (Princeton: Princeton University Press, 1974), esp. pp. 129–131.

Soviet Tendencies, Western Choices

As of May Day 1984, the new Soviet leadership under Konstantin Chernenko was confronted with one foreign policy issue of overriding importance: the capacity of the Reagan Administration to persist in its chosen course. For their part, the Soviet leaders appeared fully determined to hold to the line laid down in Brezhnev's last years. No substantial foreign policy departures having occurred during Andropov's fifteen months, Chernenko insisted that "Continuity is not an abstract notion, but a live, real cause. And its essence comes down to moving forward, without stopping."[157] But sooner or later something had to give. Continuity in American and Soviet policy alike spelled an inexorable deterioration of political relations, higher levels of defense spending, and an increased likelihood of armed conflict between global rivals incapable of avoiding one another indefinitely.

Viewed from Moscow, the situation could have been expected to break in the aftermath of the Presidential election of November 1984—which is to say in the course of preparations for the Twenty-seventh C.P.S.U. Congress in 1986 Chernenko and his colleagues may accordingly have seen themselves as approaching an intersection in their relationship with the United States. As they endeavored to "move forward without stopping," they would act on the logic of the situation as they saw it. They would also draw on the established predispositions of the regime in deciding whether or not to turn, and, if so, which way to go.

Refusing to break with a dominant preference for expansionist internationalism, the Soviet leadership could continue straight through at the intersection. It would do so in the expectation of traversing some rough road and then regaining smooth surface after 1984. Slighting U.S. electoral considerations, it would match the American military buildup as necessary, strive to maintain East–West cooperation in Europe, and promote Western disarray by eventually presenting the United States with carefully chosen distant-area challenges on which NATO could be expected to divide. The outcome would be an expansionism that inclined towards coercive isolationism, towards selective détente in Europe, and still further away from a reformative orientation in relations with the United States. If a wholly unremitting Republican administration was returned, established Soviet tendencies could however be recombined to yield a new pattern: coercive internationalism that relied still more heavily on new Soviet strategic and force projection capabilities, and less on East–West détente, as a means of reducing the risks of renewed forwardness. In either event, Moscow would stick to the view that an Image II America whose reach exceeded its grasp was ultimately incapable of preventing progressive change in the world correlation of forces. By staying the course and making prudent defense and foreign policy decisions that maintained the Soviet capacity to compete economically, Moscow would eventually secure from Republican and Democratic administrations alike the advantages of political as well as military-strategic equality.

---

157. *Pravda*, February 14, 1984.

Secondly, the regime could in principle veer to the right and, under a cloud of leftist slogans, retreat into a fortress Russia policy that stressed coercive isolationism at the expense of reduced tension with Western Europe as well as the United States. A vigorous commitment to this line of action, while authorizing continued forays into the developing world, would represent a repudiation of virtually everything attempted by the Soviet Union in its foreign relations since the death of Stalin. As such, it must be considered less than likely. The destruction of a Korean airliner over Soviet territory and the subsequent readiness of the regime to accept the self-isolating consequences of an unwillingness to take responsibility does however indicate that coercive isolationism remains a live option in the repertoire of Soviet response patterns. So also does Moscow's readiness to break off strategic arms negotiations with the United States, and to target Western Europe as well as the United States with increased numbers of nuclear weapons since November 1983.

Finally, the American policy of the Soviet Union could be modified to give greater emphasis to reformative internationalism. Here the critical factor would be a Soviet judgment as to the likelihood of a renewal of American "realism" following the 1984 election. Faced with a Republican administration that seemed able to cope with budgetary deficits, alliance dissention, public resistance, and other variables, Moscow would certainly reject a tilt towards reformative internationalism as tantamount to appeasement. But given a Democratic President determined to ·negotiate a reversal in the trend of American–Soviet relations, or a Republican administration that was obliged to backtrack, Soviet expansionism could be offset by an attempt to strengthen the coalition of "realism" and to lend it a mass base. In pursuing this option, the regime could draw on past practice in generating a dual policy that combined a Khrushchevian peace offensive with the active political use of military capabilities that were lacking in the Khrushchev era. Endeavoring to intervene in the politics of American foreign and military policy, Moscow could associate incremental atmospheric and substantive concessions with new nuclear weapons deployments and other moves designed to bring home to the American people the potential for mutual annihilation and the need for mutually advantageous cooperation. Specifically, negotiations and displays of Soviet strength would be used to exploit the relative self-sufficiency of the American Presidency on behalf of a gradual demilitarization of U.S.–Soviet bilateral and Third World operations.

Again, a leadership whose actions thus far display marked continuity with those of Brezhnev's last years may be expected to persist in a dominant if not an exclusive preference for an expansionist course. Persistence could just suffice. And yet there is potential for change in the correlation of Soviet tendencies in the period that leads up to the Twenty-seventh Congress and the revised party Programme that will be unveiled there. Disability and death within an aged leadership will surely affect the regime's programmatic thinking and operational outlook, as will the effects of foreign policy continuity on the Soviet economy. More important for our purposes, developments in Western and particularly American politics and policies will serve to shape Soviet behavior. The results may be with us for some time to come.

Although the extent to which Soviet actions depend upon Western conduct cannot be determined with assurance, Western choices are clear. We can act as though coercive isolationism is the tendency we prefer to see as uppermost in Soviet policy. This—a debilitated and inward-looking Russia—would appear to be the prime purpose of the Reagan Administration and its supporters in Britain and Western Europe. Alternatively, we are in a position over a period of time to help bring reformative internationalism, to say nothing of democratic isolationism, towards primacy of place. North Americans and West Europeans whose main concern is with arms control and peace action, and who have little or no understanding of Soviet foreign policy, would seem implicitly to favor a reformation of Soviet conduct. Third, we can act in a manner that serves to maintain expansionism as the leading tendency in Soviet policy. This has been the net consequence of the Reagan Administration's efforts, which have not thus far been viewed as credible in Moscow, and of disunity and disorientation in the Western alliance as a whole. To my way of thinking, there is no doubt whatsoever that the principal aim of the liberal democracies should be to encourage reformative internationalism in Soviet behavior.

This is not the place to discuss the specifics of a Western effort to subvert coercive isolationism, to frustrate expansionism, and to promote reformative responses from the Soviet Union. Clearly it is a two-track policy that is required, one that offers firm resistance to Soviet forwardness, and that simultaneously holds forth the prospect of cooperation in a manner which negates expansionist assumptions and substantiates reformative argumentation within the regime. The real problem is not what to do. It is how to create preconditions in the West for the conduct of a dual policy in the first place.

In the absence of a commonly accepted framework for the evaluation of Soviet behavior in its entirety, such as existed in the period between the late 1940s and early 1960s, we in the liberal democracies suffer from a growing inability to impart shared meaning to events and issues in our relationships with the Soviet Union. The lack of a common perspective also diminishes the capacity for consensus, not only among Western governments but between governments and peoples, on what we ultimately want from the Soviets and how to go about getting it. The rise of fear and skepticism in public attitudes towards national and international security policy adds new urgency to the need for a vision of what—aside from interminable nuclear rivalry, Cold War, and nuclear winter—might be accomplished in our dealings with the Soviet Union.

So strongly are we inclined to consider policy towards the Soviet Union on an issue-by-issue basis, and to occupy ourselves with the specifics of East–West affairs, that the thought of considering and attempting to act on Soviet foreign policy in its entirety must seem to be of little practical use in dealing with the agenda of the day. This way we flounder. We have been poorly served by a fragmented, excessively complex, and largely unintelligible mode of discourse about policy towards the Soviet Union that attributes excessive significance to military-strategic detail and overstates the evident Soviet commitment to expansionism. What we need is a simple and intelligible conception of Soviet conduct towards the West and towards the United States in particular—one that draws attention to diversity in Soviet foreign policy as a whole, and that alerts Western publics and policymakers to the potential for cooperation as well as the requirements of conflict with the U.S.S.R. Some of us need it more than others.

In the American movie "North Dallas Forty," a football coach is seen exhorting his players as they prepare to view film of an opposing team's play. What does he say? He urges them to study the other team's tendencies. American–Soviet relations are certainly not a football game. But if football coaches and players can evaluate and act upon an opponent's tendencies, the task should not exceed the ability of policymakers and publics concerned with the future of East–West relations.

The Gorbachev Revolution: A Waning of Soviet Expansionism?

Jack Snyder

$\mathbf{M}$any Americans have long believed that Soviet expansionism stems from pathological Soviet domestic institutions, and that the expansionist impulse will diminish only when those institutions undergo a fundamental change.[1] The Gorbachev revolution in Soviet domestic and foreign policy has raised the question of whether that time is close at hand. At home, Mikhail Gorbachev, General Secretary of the Communist Party of the Soviet Union, has attacked many of the old Stalinist institutions as obsolete and self-serving, while promoting greater freedom of expression, contested elections at local levels, and an increased role for market mechanisms in the Soviet economy.[2] Abroad, Gorbachev has made some substantial concessions from former Soviet positions, especially in accepting the Reagan Administration's "zero option" as the basis for an agreement on Intermediate-Range Nuclear Forces (INF). In a more fundamental departure, he has also proposed to restructure NATO and Warsaw Pact conventional force postures and operational doctrines along strictly defensive lines.[3]

In assessing these developments, I will address the following questions. First, how fundamental and permanent are Gorbachev's domestic changes, and why are they occurring? Second, how new and how permanent is the

I would like to acknowledge helpful suggestions and criticisms from Seweryn Bialer, Douglas Blum, Hope Harrison, Ted Hopf, Robert Legvold, Michael MccGwire, Mark Pekala, James Richter, Cynthia Roberts, Elizabeth Valkenier and several participants at a Rand Corporation seminar, and financial support from the National Council for Soviet and East European Research.

Jack Snyder is Associate Professor in the Political Science Department and the Harriman Institute for the Advanced Study of the Soviet Union at Columbia University.

1. Such views are cited and briefly summarized in Alexander Dallin and Gail Lapidus, "Reagan and the Russians: United States Policy Toward the Soviet Union and Eastern Europe," in Kenneth Oye, ed., *Eagle Defiant* (Boston: Little, Brown, 1983), pp. 191–236, esp. 232–33.
2. For an overview and evaluation of these changes, see Seweryn Bialer, "The Education in Progress of Mikhail Gorbachev," *Foreign Affairs*, Vol. 66, No. 2 (Winter 1988), and Bialer, "Gorbachev's Move," *Foreign Policy*, No. 68 (September 1987) pp. 59–87.
3. A useful, analytical overview is Robert Legvold, "The New Political Thinking and Gorbachev's Foreign Policy," forthcoming.

International Security, Winter 1987/88 (Vol. 12, No. 3)
© 1987 by the President and Fellows of Harvard College and of the Massachusetts Institute of Technology.

"new thinking" in Soviet foreign policy? Is it just a dressed-up version of former General Secretary Leonid Brezhnev's approach to détente, which America found so unsatisfactory? Is it simply a tactic to buy time until Russia can regain its competitive strength? Or is it a qualitatively new development, organically and permanently rooted in the new domestic order that Gorbachev is creating? Third, how should the United States react to Gorbachev's policies? What influence might American policy have on the depth and direction of the domestic reforms? What opportunities has the new Soviet thinking created for enhancing Western security, and how can the West take advantage of them?

A definitive analysis of the Gorbachev revolution is hardly possible at this stage, since the process is still only beginning to unfold. Nonetheless, it is important to have working hypotheses about the causes and consequences of the reforms, since timely American policy choices may hinge in part on that analysis. In that spirit, I advance four main arguments.

First, historical Soviet expansionism and zero-sum thinking about international politics have largely been caused by the nature of Soviet Stalinist domestic institutions, especially the militant Communist Party and the centralized command economy geared toward autarkic military production. These institutions, their authoritarian methods, and their militant ideology were necessary for the tasks of "extensive economic development"—namely, mobilizing underutilized labor and material resources and overcoming bottlenecks—in conditions of imminent foreign threat.[4] After these tasks were accomplished, the Stalinist institutions hung on as atavisms, using the militant ideology and the exaggeration of the foreign threat to justify their self-serving policies.[5] The offensive form of détente practiced by First Secretary Nikita Khrushchev and by Brezhnev was an attempt to satisfy simultaneously these atavistic interests and also newly emerging, post-Stalinist groups, especially the cultural and technical intelligentsia. As recently as the period

---

4. The theory underpinning this analysis is based on Alexander Gerschenkron, *Economic Backwardness in Historical Perspective* (Cambridge, Mass.: Belknap, 1962). Current Soviet analyses are similar. Note Gorbachev's Unita interview, *Pravda*, May 20, 1987 (*Foreign Broadcast Information Service, Soviet Union* [FBIS], May 20, 1987) on the imprint socialism bears from the "grim" conditions in which it was built—intervention, civil war, economic blockade, "the military provocations and constant pressure from imperialism."
5. Following the usage of Joseph Schumpeter, *Imperialism and Social Classes* (London University Press, 1951; original edition, 1919), and also that of Gerschenkron, I use the term "atavism" to mean a group or institution that continues to carry out a task that, due to changing conditions, has become dysfunctional for society.

when Yuri Andropov was General Secretary, in Harry Gelman's view, "the entrenched influence of the military and the ideologues" suppressed the lessons that the reformist intelligentsia was learning about Soviet geopolitical overextension of the late 1970s.[6]

Second, Gorbachev is aiming for nothing less than smashing the power of the entrenched Stalinist interest groups. He realizes that the extensive model of development has run into a dead end, because fallow labor and material resources have run out. There are no more reserves to mobilize. Consequently, new institutions are needed to address the tasks of "intensive development" in a modern economy—namely, efficient allocation of already-mobilized resources and sensitivity to user needs. In the Soviet reformers' view, the old institutions and the ideas associated with them have become fetters on production, serving only their own vested interests. As Gorbachev told the January 1987 Central Committee plenum:

theoretical notions about socialism in many ways remained on the level of the 1930s and 1940s, when society was tackling entirely different problems. . . . What took place was a kind of translation into absolutes of the forms of the organization of society that had developed in practice. Moreover, such notions, in point of fact, were equated with the essential characteristics of socialism, regarded as immutable and presented as dogmas leaving no room for objective scientific analysis.[7]   ⊙

According to his diagnosis, atavistic institutions and ideas must yield to new methods that allow greater initiative and autonomy from below.[8]

Third, the requirements of intensive development and the interests of Gorbachev's principal constituency, the intelligentsia, propel new thinking in foreign policy and arms control. These include a more organic Soviet involvement in the capitalist world economy, a reduced defense burden, and the durable détente that this requires. This is more fundamental and far-reaching than a short-lived desire to buy time or digest geopolitical gains. The new conception of détente, moreover, explicitly eschews the Brezhnevian idea of one-way benefits flowing from an improved "correlation of forces," the loose index of political and military trends that the Soviets invoke when

6. Harry Gelman, *The Brezhnev Politburo and the Decline of Détente* (Ithaca: Cornell, 1984), p. 215.
7. *Pravda*, January 28, 1987; *Current Digest of the Soviet Press* (CDSP), Vol. 39, No. 4, p. 1. These themes were reiterated in Gorbachev's speech on the anniversary of the Bolshevik revolution, New York *Times*, November 3, 1987, pp. A11–13.
8. See especially the economic reform program ratified by the June 1987 Central Committee plenum, *Pravda*, June 27, 1987; FBIS, June 30, 1987.

discussing the balance of power. As Gorbachev told a Soviet national television audience, "today one's own security cannot be ensured without taking into account the security of other states and peoples. There can be no genuine security unless it is equal for all and comprehensive. To think otherwise is to live in a world of illusions, in a world of self-deception."[9]

Fourth, to promote the favorable aspects of the new foreign policy, the United States should (1) avoid extremely aggressive competitive behavior that might push the reforms in a militarized direction, (2) reciprocate genuine Soviet concessions to avoid discrediting the conciliatory line, and (3) bargain hard for structural changes in Soviet foreign trade institutions and in offensive conventional military postures in Europe. These latter changes, toward which Gorbachev appears favorably inclined anyhow, would be good in themselves and would work to institutionalize the new foreign policy in Soviet domestic politics.

In presenting these arguments, I will first explain how Stalinist domestic institutions fostered Soviet expansionism, and second, trace the effects of Gorbachev's domestic innovations on Soviet foreign policy. In concluding, I will discuss policy implications for the West.

The Old Institutions and Old Ideas

The need for forced-draft industrialization in the face of intense threats from more advanced societies shaped the militant institutions and ideas of Stalin's revolution from above.[10] These institutions and ideas lived on for decades, dominating domestic political coalitions and driving foreign and security policies in a militant, expansionist direction. It is against these atavistic institutions and ideas that Gorbachev and the reformers must contend.

THE INSTITUTIONS AND IDEAS OF STALIN'S REVOLUTION FROM ABOVE
Stalinist institutions were marked by their origins in the attempts of an autocrat to whip his backward society to modernize in the face of foreign competition. In this process, international pressure provided both the motive and the opportunity to smash obsolete institutions and replace them with

---

9. *Izvestiia*, August 19, 1986, as cited by Legvold in "The New Political Thinking".
10. When I use the term institution, I mean not only bureaucratic organizations, but also established ways of organizing social relationships, such as the institution of central planning or of the market.

more efficient, centrally controlled ones.[11] "Old Russia . . . was ceaselessly beaten for her backwardness," Stalin warned at the height of the First Five-Year Plan. "We are fifty or a hundred years behind the advanced countries. We must make good this lag in ten years. Either we do it or they crush us."[12]

The tsars, too, had tried to spur revolutions from above for much the same reason but, as Stalin explained, "none of the old classes . . . could solve the problem of overcoming the backwardness of the country."[13] Instead, they were barriers to the needed transformation. Then, between 1917 and 1921, all of these old urban and elite classes, including the old working class, were swept away by war, revolution, foreign intervention, and civil war. The Bolsheviks were not immediately strong enough to break the peasantry and mobilize the material and labor surpluses needed for rapid industrialization. During the 1920s, however, they were able to form a vanguard of social transformation from the ranks of the new working class, which was younger and less tainted with reformist trade-unionism than the old working class had been.[14]

This revolution had institutional and intellectual consequences. Institutionally, its implementation required a more militant mobilizing party, the strengthening of repressive police institutions, and a more centralized authoritarian economic structure to overcome bottlenecks and to assert the priority of military-related heavy industrial production. By the late 1930s, the revolution also drew upward from the new working class a politically dependent, hothouse technical elite—what Stalin called "a new Soviet intelligentsia, firmly linked with the people and ready en masse to give it true and faithful service."[15] This was the Brezhnev generation, for which the Great Purges cleared the way.

Intellectually, these institutions and personnel were motivated and tempered by an ideology of political combat and the exaggeration of internal and external threats. This mobilized energies when pecuniary rewards were lacking, justified repression, and legitimated the priority of resource allocations

---

11. For a state-building perspective on the Bolshevik revolution, see Gerschenkron, *Economic Backwardness*, and Theda Skocpol, *States and Social Revolutions* (Cambridge: Cambridge University, 1979).
12. Quoted in Isaac Deutscher, *Stalin* (New York: Oxford, 1949), p. 328.
13. Ibid., p. 321.
14. Sheila Fitzpatrick, "The Russian Revolution and Social Mobility," *Politics and Society*, Vol. 13, No. 2 (1984), pp. 124–126.
15. Speech to the March 1939 Party Congress, quoted in Sheila Fitzpatrick, "Stalin and the Making of a New Elite, 1928–1939," *Slavic Review*, Vol. 38, No. 3 (1979), pp. 377–402.

for the military-industrial complex. According to the definitive study of the enlistment of workers in the campaign to collectivize agriculture:

The recruitment drive took place within the context of the First Five-Year Plan mobilization atmosphere. The Stalin leadership manipulated and played upon popular fear of military intervention and memories of civil war famine, rekindled by the 1927 war scare and the grain crisis of the late 1920s. The dominant motifs of the First Five-Year Plan revolution were military and the imagery was that of the Russian civil war. The working class was called upon to sacrifice for the good of the cause and the preservation of the nation. The state sought to deflect working class grievances away from systemic problems and toward the 'external' and the 'internal' enemies—that is, the 'kulak,' the 'bougeois' specialist, the Nepmen, and the political opposition [inside the Party] all said to be in league with the agents of international imperialism.[16]

Though this paranoid, pressure-cooker atmosphere was largely generated from above by Stalin and his allies, recent studies have stressed that it was readily internalized and exploited by the upwardly mobile militants that were Stalin's shock troops. During the collectivization campaign and the later purges, these young radicals exaggerated the threat of foreign subversion to push campaigns to extremes and to sweep away the older bureaucratic elite that was blocking their path to social advancement.[17]

STALINIST ATAVISMS AND THE POLITICS OF EXPANSION

These institutions and ideas lived on as atavisms after the period of rapid social mobilization that had created them. As early as the late 1940s, the institutional instruments of mobilization were turning into tools for justifying the interests of these Stalinist institutions. The role of orthodox ideology in

---

16. Lynne Viola, "The Campaign of the 25,000ers: A Study of the Collectivization of Soviet Agriculture, 1929–1931" (Princeton University dissertation in history, October 1984), p. 59, also available as *Best Sons of the Fatherland: Workers in the Vanguard of Collectivization* (New York: Oxford, 1986). For Stalin speeches clearly showing the manipulation of the 1927 war scare for factional and mobilizational purposes, see Jane Degras, *Soviet Documents of Foreign Policy, II, 1925–1932* (London: Oxford, 1952), pp. 233–37, 301–02. While Stalin was trumpeting the threat in public, a briefing to the Politburo from Foreign Minister Chicherin argued flatly that the idea of an imminent danger of war was utter nonsense. See Michal Reiman, *Die Geburt des Stalinismus* (Frankfurt: Europaische, 1979), p. 37.
17. Viola dissertation, p. 29; J. Arch Getty, *Origins of the Great Purges* (Cambridge: Cambridge University, 1985). For a debate on the new social history of the Stalin period, see the essays by Fitzpatrick, Stephen Cohen, and other commentators in *Russia Review*, Vol. 45, No. 4 (October 1986). Wolfgang Leonhard recounts that the new intelligentsia was so steeped in the militant ideology of the revolution from above that, when given access to the foreign press, "we could hardly summon up any interest" in viewpoints couched in "expressions which were so entirely meaningless to us." Only Trotskyite publications were dangerous, he explains, because they "wrote in our own language." *Child of the Revolution* (Chicago: Regnery, 1958), p. 235.

shaping society, the priority of allocation of resources to the military-industrial complex, and petty interference by party bureaucrats in day-to-day economic administration now functioned more to justify their own continuation than to serve the needs of development.

Foreign policy ideas played an important role in rationalizing and reconciling group interests. By the 1950s, four schools of thought in Soviet grand strategy had emerged: one supported by the military-industrial complex, a second by party militants, a third by the intelligentsia. The fourth, offensive détente, resulted from the efforts of political entrepreneurs like Khrushchev and Brezhnev to form coalitions among the other three. For the sake of analytical convenience, these outlooks can be divided along two dimensions: first, whether imperialism's hostility toward socialism is conditional or unconditional upon Soviet actions, and second, whether offense is the best defense in international politics. See Figure 1.

MOLOTOV: WESTERN HOSTILITY IS UNCONDITIONAL; THE DEFENSE HAS THE ADVANTAGE. Vyacheslav Molotov, one of Stalin's henchmen, argued that Soviet efforts to relax tensions with the West would not reduce the imperialists' hostility, but would only reduce vigilance within the socialist camp. However, he saw very few opportunities to exploit imperialist vulnerabilities through offensive action, for example arguing against Khrushchev that the Third World and Yugoslavia were inextricably tied to the opposing camp. Attempts to woo them by reforming Russia's Stalinist image would only lead to unrest in Eastern Europe, he accurately predicted. Consequently, the Soviet Union should adopt a hedgehog strategy of autarky, internal repression, and the forced-draft development of Russia's military-industrial base.[18]

Figure 1.

	Defense has the advantage.	Offense has the advantage.
Western hostility is unconditional.	Molotov	Zhdanov
Western hostility is conditional.	Malenkov Gorbachev	Khrushchev Brezhnev

18. David J. Dallin, *Soviet Foreign Policy after Stalin* (Philadelphia: Lippincott, 1961), esp. pp. 229, 332–33; Mohamed Heikal, *Sphinx and Commissar* (London: Collins, 1978), pp. 90–92; Uri Ra'anan, *The USSR Arms the Third World* (Cambridge, Mass.: M.I.T. Press, 1969), chapter 4.

The constituencies for this outlook were, first, the old Stalinist henchmen like Molotov himself, and second, the military-industrial complex. Stalinists like Molotov and Lazar Kaganovich, weaned on Stalin's strategy of "socialism in one country," saw a militant defense as the best way to secure the revolution. As Stalin put it in 1923, "of course, the Fascists are not asleep. But it is to our advantage to let them attack first; that will rally the working class around the communists."[19] Since Molotov's prestige and legitimacy hinged on being Stalin's chief lieutenant, especially in foreign affairs, his interests as well as his habits were served by being the guardian of orthodoxy.

A more enduring constituency for this hedgehog strategy lay among the military-industrial interests. When Khrushchev moved to limit military spending and simultaneously to provoke foreign conflicts, for example, a powerful leader of the opposition was Frol Kozlov, whose political base was rooted in Leningrad's military-oriented economy.[20] In Kozlov's view, which became so prominent in the Brezhnev era, the methodical development of Soviet military strength was the prerequisite for successful dealings with the West.

ZHDANOV: WESTERN HOSTILITY IS UNCONDITIONAL; OFFENSE HAS THE ADVANTAGE. Party Secretary Andrei Zhdanov represented a different brand of militancy. Like Molotov, he believed that Soviet concessions would not diminish the aggressiveness of the West, but he was distinctive in arguing that a political offensive was the best defense against imperialism's hostile onslaught. As part of his militant Cominform strategy, for example, Zhdanov promoted the use of violent strikes by Western Communist parties as a means to prevent the implementation of the Marshall Plan, which Zhdanov saw as the groundwork for an American policy of rollback of Communism in Eastern Europe.[21]

19. E.H. Carr, *Twilight of the Comintern, 1930–1935* (New York: Pantheon, 1982), p. 27.
20. On the political economy of Kozlov's Leningrad, see Blair Ruble, *Leningrad: Shaping the Face of a Soviet City* (forthcoming in the Franklin K. Lane Studies in Regional Governance, 1988), p. 33 and passim. On the budgetary and foreign policy stance of Kozlov and other military-industrial figures in the late Khrushchev period, see Carl Linden, *Khrushchev and the Soviet Leadership* (Baltimore: Johns Hopkins, 1966), pp. 50–54 and passim; Sidney Ploss, *Conflict and Decision-Making in Soviet Russia* (Princeton: Princeton University, 1965), pp. 216–34; Christer Jonsson, *Soviet Bargaining Behavior: The Nuclear Test Ban Case* (New York: Columbia, 1979), pp. 133–208; Michel Tatu, *Power in the Kremlin* (New York: Viking, 1970). Hannes Adomeit, *Soviet Risk-Taking and Crisis Behavior* (London: Allen and Unwin, 1982), p. 262, points out that Kozlov was apparently not a risk-taker.
21. Gavriel Ra'anan, *International Policy Formation in the USSR: Factional "Debates" during the Zhdanovshchina* (Hamden, CT: Archon, 1983). Werner Hahn, *Postwar Soviet Politics* (Ithaca: Cor-

The constituency for the Zhdanovite strategy was the party bureaucracy and its orthodox ideologues, who needed a strategic ideology to use as a weapon in struggles against a competing faction led by Malenkov. As early as 1941, Malenkov was attempting to promote the professional interests of the new technical elite against meddling party bureaucrats. He decried the "know-nothings" and "windbags" in the party bureaucracy who exercise "petty tutelage" over industrial experts, reject sound technical advice, and spout empty quotations about "putting the pressure on."[22] The war greatly increased the autonomy of technical experts, so by 1945 Stalin needed to redress the institutional balance of power and turned to Zhdanov to promote a "party revival."

Zhdanov used foreign policy ideas as a weapon in this domestic political struggle. He inflated the threat of ideological subversion from abroad in order to justify the priority of ideological orthodoxy at home. He argued for the thorough communization of Eastern Europe, including East Germany, relying heavily on the mobilizing skills of the party to carry it out.[23] And he emphasized the strategic value of Communist fifth columns in the West.

Upon Zhdanov's death in 1948, the heir to his strategy and position in the Central Committee Secretariat was Mikhail Suslov, who defended the Zhdanov line against Malenkov's criticism that it had served only to unify and militarize the West.[24] Until Suslov's own death in 1982, he served as the

---

nell, 1982), sees Zhdanov as relatively moderate, especially in comparison with the party militants that succeeded him, like Suslov. In fact, Zhdanov's constituencies did lead him to be "moderate" on some foreign and security issues at least some of the time—e.g., limits on defense spending (to undercut Malenkov's heavy-industrial base), opportunities for foreign trade (a Leningrad interest), communization of Eastern Europe by political (not police) methods. But the suggestion that Zhdanov was actually opposed to the Cominform policy that he implemented so vigorously is certainly at odds with the memoirs of the European Communists who lived through it. See Ruble, *Leningrad*, pp. 30–32; Jerry Hough, "Debates about the Postwar World," in Susan J. Linz, *The Impact of World War II on the Soviet Union* (Totowa, NJ: Rowman and Allenhead, 1985), p. 275; Eugenio Reale, *Avec Jacques Duclos au Banc des Accusés* (Paris: Plon, n.d.), pp. 10–11 and passim. Zhdanov's Cominform speech is reprinted in Myron Rush, *The International Situation and Soviet Foreign Policy* (Columbus: Merrill, 1969).
22. William McCagg, *Stalin Embattled* (Detroit: Wayne State, 1978), p. 117 for this quotation; passim for the interpretation on which this paragraph is based.
23. On this point see also Timothy Dunmore, *Soviet Politics, 1945–1953* (New York: St. Martin's, 1984), pp. 116–117, and Radomir Luza, "Czechoslovakia between Democracy and Communism, 1945–1948," in Charles S. Maier, *The Origins of the Cold War and Contemporary Europe* (New York: New Viewpoints, 1978), pp. 73–106.
24. Ronald Letteney, "Foreign Policy Factionalism under Stalin, 1949–1950" (Ph.D. dissertation, Johns Hopkins University, School of Advanced International Studies (SAIS), 1971), passim but especially p. 197, quoting a Suslov speech in *Pravda*, November 29, 1949. See also Marshall Shulman, *Stalin's Foreign Policy Reappraised* (New York: Atheneum, 1969), pp. 118–120.

proponent of militant and ideologically orthodox means for promoting progressive change abroad and as the enforcer of the party's corporate interests in the domestic coalition-making process.[25]

MALENKOV: WESTERN HOSTILITY IS CONDITIONAL; THE DEFENSE HAS THE ADVANTAGE. Georgi Malenkov, chairman of the Council of Ministers, in contrast, believed that Western aggressiveness could be diminished by Soviet self-restraint, and that defensive advantages dominated the international system. Malenkov's view dovetailed with the arguments of Eugene Varga, who contended that institutional changes in the American state during World War II had made it a stronger but less aggressive international competitor, more able to control the heedlessly aggressive impulses of the monopoly capitalists.[26] Malenkov argued that the imperialists had become realistic and sane enough to be deterred by a minimum atomic force, so that defense budgets could be safely cut and the heavy-industry priority reversed.[27] Moreover, he argued, Soviet political concessions in Europe would split the West, defuse its aggressiveness, and revive the close Soviet-German relations that had existed in the 1920s. There is evidence that Malenkov warned on similar grounds against invading South Korea.[28]

Malenkov sought a constituency for these views among the urban middle class and the cultural and technical intelligentsia. The charges leveled by Zhdanovite inquisitors against Varga's book read like a sociological profile of Malenkov's would-be constituency: "technical" and "apolitical," suffering

25. On Suslov and the International Department ideologues, see Roy Medvedev, *All Stalin's Men* (Garden City, N.Y.: Anchor, 1984), chapter 3; Arkady Shevchenko, *Breaking with Moscow* (New York: Knopf, 1985), pp. 180, 190–1, 220, 262; Bruce Parrott, *Politics and Technology in the Soviet Union* (Cambridge: M.I.T. Press, 1985), pp. 193–8; also, the works cited above by Gelman, Tatu, Linden, and Ploss.

26. G. Ra'anan, *International Policy Formation*, pp. 64, 68–70; Hough in Linz, *Impact of World War II*, pp. 268–74; Shulman, *Stalin's Foreign Policy*, pp. 32–34, 111–17; Parrott, *Politics and Technology*, pp. 82–91; Letteney, "Foreign Policy Factionalism," pp. 61–2, 65.

27. Herbert Dinerstein, *War and the Soviet Union* (New York: Praeger, 1959), chapter 4.

28. Letteney, "Foreign Policy Factionalism," p. 330. Letteney also provides indirect but voluminous evidence that Malenkov and his allies criticized the 1948 Berlin policy as having justified the formation of NATO and the deployment of American nuclear forces within striking distance of the Soviet Union; pp. 56, 77, 82–3, quoting *Izvestiia*, February 12, 1949; March 19, 1949; July 22, 1949. Note also that Zhdanov appointees ran Soviet policy in Germany until the lifting of the blockade in 1949, when they were replaced by Malenkov–Beria men. See Ann Phillips, *Soviet Policy toward East Germany Reconsidered: The Postwar Decade* (Westport, CT: Greenwood, 1986), p. 34. Authors like Dunmore who portray Malenkov as a belligerent cold warrior during this period present virtually no evidence to support their view. It is likely, however, that Malenkov supported the military buildup at this time, because it led to the return to power of his wartime heavy industry cronies. See Jeremy Azrael, *Managerial Power and Soviet Politics* (Cambridge: Harvard, 1966), chapter 5. I am indebted to Dr. Azrael for a helpful discussion of these issues.

from "empiricism," "bourgeois objectivism," and a "non-party" outlook.[29] Malenkov's conception that the foreign threat is manageable through concessions served the interests of the intelligentsia by removing the major justification for oppressive petty tutelage over them by party ideologues and bureaucrats, for the economic priorities that enriched the military at the expense of their living standard, and for a renewal of the purges.[30]

Malenkov's strategy failed, however, because the class that Malenkov hoped to recruit was subject to counter-pressures: many worked in the military-industrial complex, and many had benefited from Stalin's "Big Deal", receiving some of the minimal trappings of petty bourgeois status and lifestyle in exchange for absolute political loyalty to the orthodox regime.[31] Even a decade later, Kosygin still found that this stratum constituted an inadequate social base for a similar strategic ideology.[32]

KHRUSHCHEV AND BREZHNEV: WESTERN HOSTILITY IS CONDITIONAL; OFFENSE HAS THE ADVANTAGE (OFFENSIVE DÉTENTE). Khrushchev and Brezhnev shared the Malenkov-Varga thesis that "realists" in the West made possible a relaxation of international tension, but they coupled this with a belief in offensive advantage in international politics. Imperialism could behave in a heedlessly aggressive manner, they believed, but prudent forces within the capitalist camp, especially the bourgeois state and public opinion, could restrain the most reckless of the monopoly capitalists. The influence of such realists could be strengthened by Soviet policy in two ways: first, Soviet efforts to shift the world correlation of forces, including the military balance, to the advantage of socialism, would cause Western realists increasingly to shun the dangers of direct confrontation; second, Soviet projection of an image of restraint in the methods by which it pursues its expansionist goals would lull the West. These two elements would reinforce each other, according to Khrushchev and Brezhnev. The increased strength of the socialist camp would leave imperialism little choice but to accept détente on terms favorable to socialism. Détente in turn would weaken imperialism by hindering its counterrevolu-

29. Franklyn Griffiths, "Images, Politics, and Learning in Soviet Behavior toward the United States" (Columbia University dissertation, 1972), pp. 40–41.
30. Ploss, *Conflict and Decision-Making*, p. 68; Boris Nicolaevsky, *Power and the Soviet Elite* (N.Y.: Praeger, 1965), chapter 3, esp. p. 153; Roger Pethybridge, *A Key to Soviet Politics* (London: Allen and Unwin, 1962), pp. 30–36.
31. Vera Dunham, *In Stalin's Time: Middleclass Values in Soviet Fiction* (Cambridge: Cambridge University Press, 1976).
32. Parrott, *Politics and Technology*, pp. 182–86, 190, 197; Gelman, *The Brezhnev Politburo*, p. 85 and passim; Heikal, *Sphinx and Commissar*, p. 194.

tionary interventions in the Third World. The success of the strategy depends, in their view, on active measures to improve the Soviet position at the expense of the West, not simply the passive acceptance of a stalemate or balance.[33] As Khrushchev put it: "Peace cannot be begged for. It can be safeguarded only by an active purposeful struggle."[34]

In promoting this conception, Khrushchev and Brezhnev were acting as political entrepreneurs, cementing a broad political coalition with a strategic ideology that promised something for everyone: progressive change for Suslov and the ideologues; military modernization and enhanced national security for the military-industrial constituencies; détente and increased foreign trade for the cultural and technical intelligentsia. The problem was that this political formula worked at home but not abroad. In practice, it led to overcommitted, contradictory policies that provoked the hostility of the West, revealing (as Gorbachev put it) that its strategic vision was "a world of illusions."[35]

This process played itself out somewhat differently under the two leaders, reflecting the different political uses to which Krushchev and Brezhnev put the strategy of offensive détente. To both Brezhnev and, in his early period, Khrushchev, offensive détente was a strategic ideology that served to legitimate the outcome of political logrolling. But in the period between 1958 and 1962, Khrushchev tried to use offensive détente as a tool to escape the contraints of his logrolled coalition, provoking the worst of the cold war crises as a consequence.

Khrushchev's version of the strategy of offensive détente relied on nuclear technology and especially on the inter-continental ballistic missile (ICBM), which was to serve as a cheap cure-all. Khrushchev believed it would change the correlation of forces and lead to détente with the West, a favorable

33. Franklyn Griffiths, "The Sources of American Conduct: Soviet Perspectives and Their Policy Implications," *International Security*, Vol. 9, No. 2 (Fall 1984), pp. 3–50; and Raymond Garthoff, *Détente and Confrontation* (Washington: Brookings, 1985), pp. 36–68, elaborate on and qualify these basic themes.
34. Quoted by Adomeit, *Soviet Risk-Taking*, p. 224.
35. My interpretation closely parallels that of James Richter, "Action and Reaction in Khrushchev's Foreign Policy: Leadership Politics and Soviet Responses to the International Environment" (Ph.D. dissertation, University of California at Berkeley, 1988). Richter's very important dissertation, based on exhaustive research in primary source material, is in some respects an application to foreign policy of George Breslauer's authority-building argument, which *inter alia* showed how the Soviet coalition-making process leads to overcommitted, "taut" policy platforms. George Breslauer, *Khrushchev and Brezhnev as Leaders* (London: Allen and Unwin, 1982), esp. p. 288.

political settlement in Europe, low cost security, and the freeing of resources for a rise in Soviet living standards.[36] Such arguments were an attractive element in Khrushchev's political platform during the succession struggle.[37] They had the further advantage that they could not fully be tested until the ICBM was actually produced. By 1958, Khrushchev had his ICBM and was eager to move on to the next phase of his domestic game plan, in which he would cap military expenditures and increase investment in chemicals and other sectors that would benefit agricultural and consumer production.[38] However, the West refused to play its part. Instead of becoming more "realistic," the Americans rejected pleas for a summit, refused to move toward recognition of the German Democratic Republic, and seemed headed toward the nuclearization of the Bundeswehr.[39]

Khrushchev sought to push on with his budgetary reversal of priorities despite this, but several Politburo members balked. "Until the aggressive circles of the imperialist powers reject the policy of the arms race and preparations for a new war, we must still further strengthen the defenses of our country," said Suslov. This had been "the general line of our party . . . in the period 1954–1957," and implicitly it had been Khrushchev's own personal pledge during the succession struggle. Thus, Suslov called on Khrushchev to "honestly fulfill [the Party's] duties and promises before the Soviet people."[40] The Berlin crisis offered Khrushchev a way out of this impasse. Using it as a lever to gain a summit, the recognition of the German Democratic Republic, and progress on the test ban, Khrushchev hoped to demonstrate that the correlation of forces had already changed enough to achieve détente

36. Richter, adding nuances, develops a similar argument from an analysis of leadership speeches, which can be corroborated by a variety of other kinds of sources. See Arnold Horelick and Myron Rush, *Strategic Power and Soviet Foreign Policy* (Chicago: University of Chicago, 1966) on nuclear diplomacy; Parrott, *Politics and Technology*, pp. 131, 158–163, and 171–72 on the political role of nuclear and other high technology policies; ibid, p. 137, for Khrushchev's ideas about "the social significance of the ICBM"; Heikal, *Sphinx and Commissar*, pp. 97–98, 128–129, for an exposition to Nasser of Khrushchev's strategic theory.
37. As early as 1954, Khrushchev had used nuclear strategy as a successful political weapon against Malenkov and, in a passage from a speech that his colleagues excised from the *Pravda* version, Khrushchev bragged that "we were even quicker than the capitalist camp and invented the hydrogen bomb before they had it; we, the Party and the working class, we know the importance of this bomb." Wolfgang Leonhard, *The Kremlin without Stalin* (Westport, CT: Greenwood, 1975), p. 88. Richter, however, shows that the mature form of Khrushchev's strategic ideology, featuring optimistic reliance on the ICBM and popular forces promoting progressive political change, was not fully worked out until later.
38. For some minor qualifications, see Breslauer, pp. 67–71.
39. Jack Schick, *The Berlin Crisis, 1958–1962* (Philadelphia: University of Pennsylvania, 1971).
40. *Pravda*, March 12, 1958. Richter alerted me to this speech.

on favorable terms, allowing radical cuts in conventional forces and a leveling off of nuclear expenditures.[41]

This attempt to use offensive détente to escape from the constraints of political promises helped put Khrushchev on the slippery slope that led to his replacement in 1964 by the team of Brezhnev and Kosygin. Brezhnev learned from this that offensive détente could not be used to escape the strictures of coalition politics, but he did not learn that offensive détente was an inherently self-defeating policy. Indeed, the story of his own coalition-building strategy suggests that he thought that the distribution of political power in the 1960s still made offensive détente an indispensable tool in domestic politics.[42]

At first, Brezhnev maneuvered to create a coalition on the moderate left. He attracted ideologues and the moderate military with a foreign policy stressing support for "progressive" Third World states, notably the Arabs, and a military policy that emphasized a huge conventional buildup, while opening the door to nuclear arms control. This isolated Kosygin and Podgorny on the right, who were vulnerable because of their insistence on reduced defense spending, and Shelepin on the extreme left, who apparently hoped to use a platform of even more reckless Third World adventures and flat-out nuclear arms racing to attract a heterogeneous coalition of the military, radical ideologues, and Great Russian chauvinists.[43] But soon a flaw appeared in Brezhnev's policy of moderate appeasement of the cartels of the left. The strategy was extremely expensive, making him vulnerable to Kosygin's charge that it was wrecking the economy and scuttling indispensable reforms.

To counter this charge, Brezhnev developed a revised version of the "correlation of forces" theory and the strategy of offensive détente. The improved military balance and the liberation of progressive forces in the Third World would encourage realism in the West, leading to détente, arms control, and technology transfers that would solve the Soviet Union's economic problems without Kosygin's structural reforms. The memoirs of defector Arkady Shev-

41. Linden advanced the hypothesis that, in some general way, a victory in Berlin would give Khrushchev the prestige he needed to check his domestic opponents and push on with his economic program. Richter, however, is the first to clarify this argument conceptually and to show in convincing detail how it worked.
42. The following reconstruction draws on Gelman, Parrott, and Richter.
43. For Shelepin's probable stance, in addition to sources cited by Gelman and Parrott, see Joan Barth Urban, "Contemporary Soviet Perspectives on Revolution in the West," *Orbis* Vol. 19, No. 4 (1976), pp. 1359–1402, especially p. 1379.

chenko show graphically how these pie-in-the-sky arguments were crafted to appeal to the delegates to the 1971 Party Congress, which ratified the strategy and for the first time gave Brezhnev a commanding political advantage over his rivals.[44] Despite this political victory, Brezhnev was nonetheless stuck with a strategy that was overcommitted and expensive. Through the mid-1970s, he fought a running battle with Marshal Grechko and the military over the budgetary implications of détente in general and SALT in particular. Only after 1976, with Grechko's death and the installation of a civilian defense minister, did strategic force procurement flatten out and nuclear warfighting doctrines wane.[45] The battle revived, however, as a result of the Reagan defense buildup, with Chief of the General Staff Nikolai Ogarkov insisting that it would be a "serious error" not to increase military outlays. In the wake of the Polish crisis, however, the civilians were more worried about the danger of cutting social programs, and Ogarkov was fired.[46]

Signs of growing skepticism about backing radical Third World regimes also began to surface in 1976,[47] but could not proceed very far until Suslov's death in 1982. A year later, Andropov himself was stressing the need to limit the cost of Soviet counterinsurgency wars in support of pseudo-Marxist regimes, noting that "it is one thing to proclaim socialism, but another to build it."[48]

Thus, through the failure of Brezhnev's strategy of offensive détente, some of the intellectual and political precursors to Gorbachev's new thinking were already in place.

---

44. Shevchenko, *Breaking with Moscow*, pp. 211–212.
45. Bruce Parrott, *The Soviet Union and Ballistic Missile Defense* (Boulder: Westview, 1987), pp. 27–39, on resource allocation debates in the mid-1970s; Michael MccGwire, *Military Objectives in Soviet Foreign Policy* (Washington: Brookings, 1987), pp. 61–2, 108–112, and Richard F. Kaufman, "Causes of the Slowdown in Soviet Defense," *Soviet Economy*, Vol. 1, No. 1 (January–March 1985), pp. 9–32, on military policy changes in 1976–7. See also Jeremy Azrael, *The Soviet Civilian Leadership and the Military High Command, 1976–1986* (Santa Monica: Rand R-3521-AF, June 1987).
46. Parrott, *BMD*, pp. 46–7; see also Garthoff, *Détente and Confrontation*, p. 1018, fn. 21. Mark Pekala has discovered an Aesopian piece in *Kommunist vooruzhennykh sil* No. 24 (December 1984), which portrays an alleged attempt by Trotsky in 1923 to exploit a period of foreign threat and leadership transition and illness to militarize the party and the country at the expense of the party's program of economic reform and restoration, which required decreased military expenditures. Translated in JPRS-UMA-85-027, April 19, 1985. Cynthia Roberts notes that this piece is full of historical inaccuracies, further suggesting that it had a current policy motivation.
47. Elizabeth Valkenier, "Revolutionary Change in the Third World: Recent Soviet Assessments," *World Politics*, Vol. 38, No. 3 (April 1986), pp. 415–434, esp. 426.
48. *Pravda*, June 16, 1983; CDSP, 35:25, p. 8.

BACKDROP TO GORBACHEV'S REVOLUTION

In sum, Soviet expansionist behavior and strategic concepts have had their roots in the institutional and intellectual legacy of Stalin's revolution from above. Atavistic interests with a stake in military-industrial budget priorities and militant promotion of "progressive change" abroad have exploited the ideological baggage of Stalinism to legitimate the continuation of their dominant social role. When Malenkov tried to change this, pushing forward new ideas and a new social constituency, Stalin was quoted to justify his removal from office: "In face of capitalist encirclement . . . 'to slacken the pace means to lag behind. And those who lag behind are beaten.'"[49] To gain power, an innovator like Khrushchev had to distort his policies to try to attract or outflank the atavistic interests and ideas, leading to contradictions and overcommitment at home and abroad.

Though foreign policy ideas tended to line up with the interests of groups and coalitions, this was not entirely the result of conscious manipulation. Sometimes conscious manipulation did occur, as in Stalin's trumped-up war scare of 1927. More often, it was probably semi-conscious, as in Brezhnev's packaging of the "correlation of forces" theory for the 1971 Congress. Sometimes it may have been the result of unconscious motivated bias.[50] Khrushchev reports spending several sleepless nights grappling with the implications of atomic weaponry, until it came to him that these fearful instruments would never be used, but could nonetheless be of great political significance.[51] The connection between ideas and interests was also sustained by the political selection process. Thus, Khrushchev and Brezhnev prevailed in the succession struggle in part because of their strategies of offensive détente, whether or not they adopted those strategies for consciously political reasons.

Though I have stressed the role of the domestic environment, I do not mean to argue that Soviet policy-making has been utterly oblivious to its international environment. Most episodes of Soviet belligerence or expansionism have had international triggers—like the Marshall Plan, the rearming of West Germany, the U-2 affair, the Jackson-Vanik Amendment and the

49. *Pravda*, January 24, 1955; CDSP, 6:52, p. 6.
50. For applications of this branch of psychological theory to foreign policymaking, see Richard Ned Lebow, *Between Peace and War* (Baltimore: Johns Hopkins, 1981), chapter 5.
51. Heikal, *Sphinx and Commissar*, pp. 96–7.

post-Vietnam syndrome—that made the strategic arguments of some Soviet factions more plausible, some less plausible.[52]

Moreover, the Soviet Union has typically been able to learn from negative feedback from its counterproductive aggressive policies, leading to at least tactical retreats. For example, the failure of the Berlin blockade and the West's reaction to the invasion of South Korea strengthened the hand of Malenkov and other leaders who wanted to reverse the confrontational Soviet policy. This differentiates the Soviet Union from Imperial Germany and Japan, which were so enmeshed in institutionally rooted strategic ideologies that policy failures produced not learning, but ever more reckless attempts to break out of their own self-encirclement.[53] Though the Soviet Union pays more attention to the realities of its environment than they did, objective conditions are nonetheless an insufficient explanation for even the milder Soviet case of self-encirclement. As Churchill asked in 1949, "why have they deliberately acted for three long years so as to unite the free world against them?"[54] Insofar as the answer lies in the peculiar domestic institutional and intellectual inheritance from Stalin's revolution from above, a sharp break with that domestic order under Gorbachev should produce a radically different foreign policy.

Emergent Institutions and Thinking Under Gorbachev

Just as the requirements of extensive development gave rise to the old institutions and ideas of the revolution from above, so too the requirements of intensive development are forcing their replacement by new institutions and ideas. Restructuring for intensive development in both the domestic and foreign areas is creating some new institutions and changing the relative power and interests of many old ones. The military-industrial complex, old-style ideologues, and autarkic industrial interests are in eclipse. Civilian defense intellectuals, reformist ideologues, and supporters of liberalized trade policies among the intelligentsia are gaining influence and trying to

---

52. The clearest cases are perhaps the U-2 (Tatu, *Power in the Kremlin*, part one) and Jackson-Vanik (Gelman, *The Brezhnev Politburo*, p. 161; Urban, "Contemporary Soviet Perspectives," p. 1379).
53. For example, Woodruff Smith, *The Ideological Origins of Nazi Imperialism* (New York: Oxford, 1986). This is another case where Gerschenkron's perspective is helpful.
54. Shulman, *Stalin's Foreign Policy Reappraised*, p. 13.

force changes that would institutionalize the policies they prefer. The emphasis on two-way security and the deepening of economic interdependence in Gorbachev's new foreign policy thinking grows directly from the new domestic institutions he is promoting and the political constituencies that he is relying on.

FORCES FOR CHANGE

Four factors are impelling the Gorbachev reforms: the objective requirements of the stage of intensive development, the discrediting of old institutions, the gradual strengthening of the constituency for change as a result of natural processes of modernization, and ironically, the Stalinist legacy of centralized institutions suited to the task of social transformation from above.

First, there is the objective need for restructuring for the tasks of intensive development. As Western experts have argued for a long time, the success of a mature post-industrial economy depends on efficient resource allocation and sensitivity to user demand. These require decentralized price formation, competition among suppliers, and profit-oriented success criteria.[55] Gorbachev's economic reforms, some of them already enacted into law, seem to be heading precisely in this direction, though how far they will go remains in doubt.[56]

Second, these objective needs have become increasingly and widely recognized, as the policy failures of the late Brezhnev period have discredited most of the key Stalinist institutions—the administrators of the centralized economy, the militant "combat party," and the military-industrial complex. Economic stagnation, in particular, has led to the widespread conviction that the old institutions and the ideas that legitimated them have become fetters on production, atavistic organs surviving only to their own benefit. *Pravda* commentators explain that "individual and group egoism" on the part of "bureaucratic and technocratic elements who were guided solely by their immediate interests" lead to "stagnation" in the period after the "October 1964 plenum."[57] Likewise, Suslov-style ideologues are now called "Old Believers"—the term for proponents of an especially archaic version of Russian

---

55. For a summary of and citations to this literature, see Bartlomiej Kaminski, "Pathologies of Central Planning," *Problems of Communism*, Vol. 36, No. 2 (March–April 1987), pp. 81–95.
56. For a variety of perspectives, some quite skeptical, see *Soviet Economy*, Vol. 2, No. 4 (October–December 1986).
57. G. Smirnov, the new head of the Institute of Marxism-Leninism, "The Revolutionary Essence of Renewal," *Pravda*, March 13, 1987; CDSP 39:1, pp. 15–16.

Orthodox Christianity—who promote a dogma that "smacks of romanticism. They carry on about dangers, they issue warnings, and they admonish against overdoing things [i.e., overdoing the reforms]. Essentially what they are defending is not even centralism, but centralism's vehicle—the bureaucratic administrative apparatus," but they "could be easily swept aside by a mass movement of the working people based on the will of the Party leadership."[58]

This kind of criticism has also been extended into the realm of foreign and security policy. Many Soviet political leaders and scholars have implicitly criticized the Brezhnev era's overoptimism about new Marxist-Leninist regimes in Third World.[59] Recently, a Soviet commentator has explicitly criticized the logical contradictions and willful optimism among the orthodox ideologues, like many of those coordinating Third World policy in Brezhnev's Central Committee International Department.[60] Similarly, in the foreign trade area, the president of the Soviet Academy of Sciences was fired after warning that an "import plague" was stifling the development of homegrown technology and thus jeopardizing national security, and his research institutes were charged with nepotism and failure to promote productive young scientists.[61]

In the wake of the German Cessna landing in Red Square, the military has come in for even more fundamental rebukes. Boris Yeltsin, candidate Politburo member and then Moscow party secretary, told officers of the Moscow Military District that they manifest a "bourgeois mentality," acting "as though they are apart from society." "Rudeness, boorishness, and intimidation," widespread within the officer corps, "give rise to toadies, boot-lickers, sycophants, and window-dressers . . . . An atmosphere of smugness, boasting, and complacency emerged everywhere. This atmosphere deprives active people of initiative and the ability to assert a correct viewpoint" and encourages a "style that blunts the cutting edge of the idea of the motherland's

---

58. Gavriil Popov, "Restructuring the Economy," *Pravda*, January 20 and 21, 1987; CDSP, 39:3, p. 4. Popov was one of the main speakers at a meeting on economic reform attended by most of the Politburo just before the June 1987 plenum. Philip Hanson and Elizabeth Teague, "Party Conference Prepares for Plenum," Radio Liberty Report #228/87, June 15, 1985.
59. Francis Fukuyama, *Moscow's Post–Brezhnev Reassessment of the Third World* (Santa Monica: Rand R-3337-AF, February 1986).
60. G. Mirskii, "K voprosy o vybore puti i orientatsii razvivaiushchikhsia stran," *Mirovaia ekonomika i mezhdunarodnye otnosheniia* [MEiMO] No. 5 (May 1987), pp. 70–81.
61. A.P. Aleksandrov, *Pravda*, February 27, 1986; CDSP, 38:9, p. 9; Yegor Ligachev's criticism of research institutes in *Pravda*, October 2, 1986; CDSP, 40:8, p. 9.

security."[62] In short, the prevailing diagnosis blames all of the encrusted Stalinist institutions, with the partial exception of the KGB:[63] the orthodox combat party, the "administrative-voluntarist methods" of the command economy,[64] the military-industrial complex, autarkic industry.

A third factor promoting the emergence of the reforms is the strengthening of the constituency that naturally favors it, the cultural and technical intelligentsia. These urban, middle-class professionals have two strong motives to support a campaign for domestic restructuring: first, it will increase their professional autonomy from arbitrary bureaucratic interference, and second, it will increase their relative income. Inside the cocoon of the old system, the intelligentsia has been steadily growing in size and independence as a natural result of the gradual modernization of the economy and social structure. Between 1959 and 1979, the number of people with full higher education tripled, as did the number with secondary educations.[65] Thus, there is now in place a precondition of restructuring for intensive development, much as the wartime destruction of the old urban classes and the rise of a new working class in the 1920s were preconditions of restructuring for extensive development.

To some extent, the intelligentsia may still be divided between those who want to keep the system that provides their sinecures and those who have professional and economic interests in changing the system so they can earn more and have more to buy. As a whole, however, the professional middle class is not only larger but also more politically alert than the Brezhnev generation, the cohort of Stalin's "Big Deal." For example, though some journalists have not succeeded in making the transition to *glasnost*, the many who have are sufficient for Gorbachev's purposes.

A fourth factor favoring the reforms is, ironically, a Stalinist legacy: the strong administrative powers available to the top leadership. This includes power over both personnel and the potent propaganda instruments of the Soviet system. Gorbachev can also call upon the traditional argument of the modernizing Russian autocrat—either we reform or we will be unable "to

---

62. As reported in *Krasnaia zvezda*, June 17, 1987; FBIS, June 17, 1987, pp. V2–V4. See also unsigned essay, "Armiia i usloviiakh demokratizatsii," *Kommunist* 14 (Sept. 1987), pp. 117–19.
63. Alexander Rahr, "Restructuring in the KGB," Radio Liberty Report No. 226–87, June 15, 1987.
64. Anatolii Butenko, Moscow State University Professor and analyst at Oleg Bogomolov's institute on the bloc economy, *Moskovskaia Pravda*, May 7, 1987; FBIS, May 26, p. R5.
65. Ruble, *Leningrad*, p. 16, citing *Narodnoe khoziaistvo SSSR v 1980g: Statisticheskii ezhegodnik* (Moscow: Finansy i statistiki, 1981), p. 27, and previous volumes.

bring the motherland into the twenty-first century as a mighty, prospering power."[66] This "Russia-was-beaten" argument is one that Gorbachev has used very sparingly, however, perhaps to avoid some of the implications of its prior invocations. He does not want to play into the hands of those who might prefer a more traditional, authoritarian, militarized revolution from above, legitimated by trumpeting the foreign threat. He wants a reform that creates "workers who are computer literate, with a high degree of culture," free to show initiative.[67]

In summary, the forces favoring radical change in domestic institutions and ideas are objective economic needs plus the clout of a strengthened professional class and an already strong reforming leadership. One prominent reformer puts it this way:

Who does want changes? It's the far-sighted political leaders and management personnel and the outstanding people in science and the cultural sphere. They understand that in the twenty-first century the present variant of development will be dangerous for the country. Further, it's the leading contingent of the working class and of collective farmers, engineers and technicians who are striving to improve their lives and who want to earn more, but to earn it by their own labor, without any finagling. And it is the segment of the intelligentsia that is interested in scientific and technical progress.[68]

DOMESTIC RESTRUCTURING

Intensive development requires central authorities and the grass roots to gain in power, while mid-level bureaucrats must lose it. The power relationships in Soviet society must thus be re-shaped from an inverted pyramid into an hour-glass configuration. These requirements in practice call for some marketization of the economy, democratization of decisionmaking at the local level, a less inhibited press, and a curtailment of the role of local party organs in economic administration. These changes are needed both to break resistance to reform and to improve economic efficiency once the reforms are underway.

In terms of the institutional structure of power, Gorbachev's problem is to devise a system that will make an end run around the recalcitrant mid-level "transmission belts" of the Stalinist system—the government ministries and

---

66. Gorbachev to the Twentieth Komsomol Congress, April 16, 1987; FBIS, April 17, 1987, R3.
67. Ibid., R10.
68. Popov, "Restructuring the Economy," p. 4.

the regional party prefects, so-called because their whole raison d'être is to pass along information and orders in a command economy. Transforming Stalin's pyramid of power into an hourglass configuration means that, at the bottom of the hourglass, increased responsibility devolves onto the local level, through partial marketization and democratization. At the top, the power of the central authorities to set overall policy is being strengthened.[69] Reformist economists like Abel Aganbegyan are taking over direction of the "commanding heights" of the economy from the old-style central planners. They rely increasingly on the manipulation of "economic levers" rather than on administrative directives.[70] Similarly, reforming ideologues like Aleksandr Yakovlev are using centralized agitation and propaganda institutions to mobilize and guide the newly empowered locals.[71]

Gorbachev is not trying to build his constituency by collecting a winning coalition from pieces that are already on the board, as Brezhnev did. This would be a losing game for Gorbachev, as most existing organized interests stand to lose from the changes. Instead, like Stalin, Gorbachev is trying to empower new constituencies, working through new institutions and transforming old ones. Thus, in the economic sphere, Gorbachev promotes private or cooperative entrepreneurial ventures, increases in the service sector of the economy at the expense of blue collar jobs, the closing of unprofitable factories, and increased wage differentials.[72] Within the party itself, Gorbachev and Yeltsin call for a prime party task to be the training of new cadres with a liberal education and big-picture outlook, instead of petty tutelage over the economy.[73] More broadly, by increasing press and artistic freedom, Gor-

---

69. This is directly reflected in the June plenum resolution on economic reform, *Pravda*, June 27, 1987; FBIS, June 30. See also Tat'iana Zaslavskaia, "The Novosibirsk Report," *Survey*, Vol. 27, No. 1 (Spring 1984), pp. 83–109, and other works cited in George Weickhardt, "The Soviet Military-Industrial Complex and Economic Reform," *Soviet Economy*, Vol. 2, No. 3 (July–September 1986), pp. 193–220, esp. 211, 220.
70. Philip Taubman, "Architect of Soviet Change," New York *Times*, July 10, 1987, p. D3.
71. Says Central Committee Secretary Vadim Medvedev: "We have succeeded in literally stirring up the masses, even those who previously used to be far from politics, and have succeeded in making them active participants in the restructuring in the outlying areas. The truth expands and reinforces its social base." *Pravda*, May 17, 1987; FBIS, May 27.
72. New York *Times*, July 4, 1987, pp. 1–2; Washington *Post*, June 27, 1987, p. A24.
73. For Gorbachev, see *Pravda*, Janury 28, 1987, CDSP, 39:6, pp. 8, 13. Yeltsin told the Party Congress that the Party is so "enmeshed in economic affairs that they have sometimes begun to lose their position as agencies of political leadership. It's no accident that the structure of the Central Committee's departments has gradually become all but a copy of the ministries. Many people have simply forgotten what true party work is." *Pravda*, February 27, 1986; CDSP, 38:9, p. 5.

bachev hands power to the intelligentsia, who can for the most part be counted on to use it against his opponents. Gorbachev's campaign for economic reform was getting nowhere until he unleashed the journalists to denounce the self-interested conservatism of his opponents and to expose their corruption. Thus, *glasnost* is desired as an end in itself by the creative intelligentsia, but for Gorbachev it is a sledgehammer to smash the opposition "by force of public pressure."[74]

RESTRUCTURING FOREIGN POLICY

In foreign and security policy, the old institutions and ideas of extensive development favored military-industrial spending, autarky, tension with the West, and militant support for progressive change abroad. Intensive development, in contrast, favors a deeper participation in the international division of labor, less costly military and Third World policies, and consequently a policy line that avoids upsetting stable relations with the West. Oleg Bogomolov, the prominent director of the institute that studies the socialist bloc's economy, puts it this way:

Previously we reasoned: the worse for the adversary, the better for us, and vice versa. But today this is no longer true; this cannot be a rule anymore. Now countries are so interdependent on each other for their development that we have quite a different image of the solution to international questions. The worsening of the situation in Europe will not at all help the development of the socialist part of Europe; on the contrary, the better things are going in the European world economy, the higher the stability and the better the prospects for our development.[75]

The changes in foreign policy are being caused both by the needs of a reformed economy and by the interests of Gorbachev's main political constituency, the intelligentsia.

In the international economic sphere, the reformers argue that the Soviet Union must make the transition from primary-product exports to a new pattern of "intensive foreign trade," featuring machine exports and schemes for joint production with foreign firms.[76] The reformers recognize that this

---

74. Gorbachev in Krasnodar, *Pravda*, September 20, 1986; CDSP, 38:38, p. 5.
75. Czech TV interview, FBIS, April 16, 1987, p. F2. Bogomolov, who exemplifies the importance of the connection between the domestic and international aspects of the economic reform, was also one of the speakers at the June pre-plenum conference. Hanson and Teague, "Party Conference." For one of many similar statements on global economic and security interdependence from Gorbachev, see his speech of February 16, 1987; FBIS, February 17, p. AA22.
76. V. Shastitko, *Pravda*, May 22, 1987; FBIS, June 23, p. S2.

will require greater independence for individual firms to conclude profitable deals on their own initiative. Preliminary reforms along these lines have already been implemented.[77]

Such reforms create the danger, however, that "the 'monopoly' of the Ministry of Foreign Trade could give way . . . to a 'monopoly' of many ministries which have gained the right to foreign economic activity."[78] Unless domestic prices are pegged to world levels, traders will have an incentive to extract rents by exploiting arbitrary price discrepancies, instead of making profits by creating real value. An even more radical solution to this problem, advocated by some prominent Soviet economists and intellectuals, would be convertibility of the ruble into hard currency at market rates. This would allow "more flexible involvement in trade on the world market" and would create "a yardstick with which to measure the effects of restructuring" of the domestic economy.[79] Thus, the push for more intensive international trade, which the West could encourage, may give added impetus to domestic structural changes that Gorbachev says he wants anyway.

In the military sphere, radical changes in Soviet nuclear and conventional postures are taking a place on Gorbachev's agenda, largely because the military is no longer the powerful political participant in the Soviet ruling coalition that it was under Brezhnev. Gorbachev has promoted minions, not independently powerful allies, to oversee the military, and has created a civilian defense think-tank to provide him with alternative strategic analysis.[80] This has allowed him to seek structural changes in Soviet military posture that would stabilize the military competition and reduce its economic burden in a permanent way. The most notable, which I will discuss in more detail later, is a change of Warsaw Pact conventional forces from an offensive

77. Charles Mathias, Jr., "Red Square, Just Off Wall St.," New York *Times*, July 20, 1987, p. 19.
78. V. Shastitko, *Pravda*, May 22, 1987; FB1S, June 23, p. S3.
79. Gennadi Lisichkin, of the Institute for the Study of the Socialist World Economy, quoted by Agence France Presse, June 29, 1987; FBIS, July 1, 1987. See also Bill Keller, "New Struggle in the Kremlin: How to Change the Economy," New York *Times*, June 4, 1986, pp. 1, 6, citing Nikolai Shmelyov, *Novyi Mir*, "Avansi i dolgi," (June 1987), pp. 142–158, esp. 153.
80. New York *Times*, May 31, 1987. The civilian think-tank is a section, headed by Alexei Arbatov, within the Institute for World Economy and International Relations (IMEMO). The central committee staff is also playing a more prominent role in arms control policy under Anatoly Dobrinin. Stressing the importance of military advice from civilian scientists like Roald Sagdeev, director of the Institute of Space Research, and Evgenii Velikhov, vice-president of the Soviet Academy of Sciences, is Matthew Evangelista, "The Domestic Politics of the Soviet Star-Wars Debate," in Harold Jacobson, William Zimmerman and Deborah Yarsike, eds., *Adapting to SDI* (forthcoming). Robert Hutchinson, "Gorbachev Tightens Grip on Soviet High Command," *Jane's Defense Weekly* 23 (June 13, 1987), pp. 1192–94.

to a defensive configuration. If institutionalized, this would of course be less easily reversible than a mere policy change.

The taming of the military creates the possibility for the change from conventional offense to defense, and Western responses could forward implementation of this change, but there is nothing in Gorbachev's reformed system that absolutely demands it. In the long run, the large-scale production of high-technology, offensive military forces would not necessarily be incompatible with the logic of intensive development.

The logic of the reform and its constituency is also affecting Third World policy, though here its effects may be weaker and mixed. On one hand, some of Gorbachev's key supporters are reform-minded ideologues, like Alexander Yakovlev, who are basically internationalist in outlook. They would be loath to relinquish the idea of a global role for the Bolshevik party. The desire to participate more deeply in the world economy also favors a continued Soviet drive for international influence. On the other hand, the reformers are clearly sensitive to the economic and political costs of futile military involvements in extremely backward societies. Given this particular mix of constraints, it is natural that ideologues like Yakovlev and Karen Brutents have hit upon the promotion of Soviet political and economic relationships with large, prospering Third World countries—the Mexicos and the Argentinas—as the new, relatively benign incarnation of Soviet progressive internationalism.[81]

EMERGING SECURITY CONCEPTS AND IMPLICATIONS FOR THE FUTURE

Gorbachev and his allies have propounded strategic concepts that facilitate their own domestic program, just as leaders of the old Stalinist institutions rationalized their interests in terms of images of the adversary and assumptions about the relative advantages of offense and defense. Because the military-industrial complex, the orthodox ideologues, and autarkic interests are in eclipse, images of unappeaseable opponents and offensive advantage are also in eclipse. Because the power of the intelligentsia is increasing, its ideas are on the rise. Like Malenkov, the Gorbachev reformers see a world in which the defense has the advantage and aggressive opponents can be demobilized by Soviet concessions and self-restraint. This similarity in stra-

---

81. On this development, see Valkenier, "Revolutionary Change in the Third World," and the other works reviewed in George Breslauer, "Ideology and Learning in Soviet Third World Policy," *World Politics* 39:3 (April 1987), pp. 429–448.

tegic ideology is rooted in the rough similarity of their domestic goals and their domestic political constituencies.

However, because some of the domestic incentives for Gorbachev's new thinking may be ephemeral, some aspects of the new thinking might not survive unless they are institutionalized, for example, in arms control agreements. Offense-oriented, as well as defense-oriented, lower-budget, higher-technology strategies would be consistent with economic reform. At present, attacking the old, offensive military policies may give Gorbachev added arguments to use against holdovers from Brezhnev's top brass, but this is a transitory incentive. In such conditions, where the domestic base for desirable new defense-oriented strategies ideas is tenuous, American diplomacy might play a role in institutionalizing such strategies and promoting their domestic base.

IMAGE OF THE ADVERSARY. Gorbachev and his circle see America as innately hostile, but they believe that America's aggressiveness can be defused through Soviet self-restraint and concessions. Initially, some western Sovietologists feared that Gorbachev's foreign policy would come to be dominated by the ideas of Alexander Yakovlev, whom they saw as an inveterate America-hater. The author of several monographs excoriating America's messianic imperialism, Yakovlev has portrayed America as aggressive, but declining, eventually to be abandoned by other capitalist powers more amenable to détente:

The distancing of Western Europe, Japan, and other capitalist countries from U.S. strategic military plans in the near future is neither an excessively rash fantasy nor a nebulous prospect. It is dictated by objective factors having to do with the rational guaranteeing of all their political and economic interests, including security . . . . As time goes by, we will witness the establishment of new centers of strength [and potential Soviet trading partners] such as Brazil, Canada, and Australia, not to mention China.[82]

Yakovlev admits, however, that America is far from collapsing and that splitting NATO through a separate détente with Europe is not a feasible prospect in the short run.[83]

Others in Gorbachev's circle, like journalist Alexander Bovin, go much further in portraying a more united, but tamer imperialism. Bovin argues

---

82. Interview in *La Repubblica*, May 21, 1985; FBIS, May 24, 1985, pp. CC1.
83. See Yakovlev's "Mezhimperialisticheskie protivorechiia—sovremennyi kontekst," *Kommunist* No. 17 (November 1986), pp. 3–17.

that in response to the economic crisis of the mid-1970s, the capitalist powers have agreed to regulate their economic competition internationally in much the same way that the bourgeois state regulates capitalism domestically. "A new transnational model of imperialism is being created before our eyes," says Bovin.[84] Thus, he extends Varga's analysis one step further, implying that a major engine of imperialist aggressiveness, the inability of the monopolies and capitalist states to act in their own long-run enlightened self-interest, is coming under rational control. This is the old Kautskyite heresy of cooperative "ultraimperialism," which Lenin railed against because he realized that it cut to the core of his theory of the sources of aggressive imperialist behavior.[85]

More important than the degree of imperialism's aggressiveness, however, is the question of how that aggressiveness can be reduced. Yakovlev believes that a crucial link in American aggressiveness is the ability of "the colossal, all-penetrating and all powerful propaganda machine" to whip up a "jingoistic fever" among the masses.[86] The way to counteract this, he argues, is through effective, substantive Soviet peace proposals, which constrain even the worst cold warriors to reciprocate in order to save face with their own public.[87] This way of looking at the problem not only gives pride of place to Yakovlev's personal skills as a propagandist, but it also reflects Yakovlev's previous experiences, battling jingoistic *Russian* nationalists for control of the press in the early 1970s.[88] In this way, Yakovlev has developed a view of imperialism that reconciles the interests and outlook of reformist ideologue-activists, like himself, with those of Gorbachev's broader constituency in the intelligentsia, exemplified by Bovin.

Gorbachev has adopted this strategy as his own, explaining it this way to *Time* magazine:

If all that we are doing is indeed viewed as mere propaganda, why not respond to it according to the principle of "an eye for an eye, a tooth for a tooth"? We have stopped nuclear explosions. Then you Americans could take

84. *Izvestiia*, June 13, 1987; FBIS, June 19.
85. See Lenin's *Imperialism: The Highest Stage of Capitalism*, in James E. Connor, ed., *Lenin on Politics and Revolution* (New York: Pegasus, 1968), pp. 130–131.
86. Alexander Yakovlev, *On the Edge of the Abyss: From Truman to Reagan* (Moscow: Progress, 1985; Russian ed., Molodaia gvardiia, 1984), p. 13.
87. Yakovlev, "Istoki ugrozy i obshestvennoe mnenie," *Mirovaia ekonomika i mezhdunarodnye otnosheniia* [MEiMO] 3 (1985), pp. 3–17, esp. 8–12.
88. Alexander Yanov, *The Russian New Right* (Berkeley: Institute of International Studies, Research Series #35, 1978).

revenge by doing likewise. You could deal us yet another propaganda blow, say, by suspending the development of one of your new strategic missiles. And we would respond with the same kind of "propaganda." And so on and so forth. Would anyone be harmed by competition in such "propaganda"? Of course, it could not be a substitute for a comprehensive arms-limitation agreement, but it would be a significant step leading to such an agreement.[89]

Complementing this notion that convincing arms control proposals demobilize Western aggressiveness is its converse: that Soviet geopolitical misbehavior provokes the West and plays into the hands of cold war propagandists. Thus, "some comrades," including some of Gorbachev's closest foreign policy advisers, have been brave enough to argue that "rash" Soviet actions in Afghanistan "provoked" the anti-Soviet turn in American foreign policy.[90]

Of course, even Khrushchev understood that superficial concessions could demobilize the West, buying time and preparing the ground for a strategy of offensive détente. But the articulation of the correlation of forces theory by Khrushchev and Brezhnev clearly signaled their intentions from the outset of their détente diplomacy. There is nothing analogous to the correlation of forces theory in Gorbachev's strategic arguments. On the contrary, he insists that this kind of one-way approach to security constitutes a "world of illusions."

OFFENSE AND DEFENSE IN MILITARY STRATEGY. The most significant aspect of Gorbachev's new thinking is his explicit understanding of the security dilemma: that security must be mutual to be stable, and that offensive means to security undermine this goal.[91] Consistent with this, Gorbachev and his circle have spoken out against nuclear counterforce and conventional offense. Measures must be taken, he says, to "rule out the possibility of surprise

---

89. *Time,* August 28, 1985.
90. Vadim Zagladin, "Sovremennyi mezhdunarodnyi krizis v svete leninskogo ucheniia," MEiMO, No. 4 (April 1984), p. 4, criticizing such views. For this and other examples, see Douglas Blum, "Soviet Perceptions of American Foreign Policy after Afghanistan" (Columbia University), paper delivered at the annual meeting of the International Studies Association, April 1987, forthcoming in Robert Jervis and Jack Snyder, eds., *Strategic Beliefs and Superpower Competition in the Asian Rimland.* Thomas Bjorkman and Thomas Zamostny, "Soviet Politics and Strategy toward the West," *World Politics,* Vol. 34, No. 2 (January 1984), pp. 189–214, show that Bovin argued publicly that the invasion of Afghanistan had provoked such a reaction and that others who are now close to Gorbachev have expressed similar views.
91. For a theoretical discussion, see Robert Jervis, "Cooperation under the Security Dilemma," *World Politics* Vol. 32, No. 2 (January 1978), pp. 167–214.

attack. The most dangerous types of offensive arms must be removed from the zone of contact."[92] The elimination of the military from the Soviet ruling coalition was a prerequisite to this intellectual revolution.

At the nuclear level, Yakovlev and others have argued that America cannot succeed in overturning the deterrent stalemate, which is objectively quite stable.[93] Bovin agrees "theoretically" with an *Izvestiia* reader who writes that "the USSR can deter the United States with a considerably lower quantity of strategic weapons. Parity is not mandatory" for deterrence, so the Soviets should move for propaganda coup by making unilateral cuts.[94] Likewise, Bovin notes that "the building and deployment of hundreds of new [SS-20] missiles must have cost a huge amount of money. And if we agree to destroy these missiles: Why then were they built?"[95]

Increasingly, Soviet civilian defense intellectuals are writing about the "de-stabilizing" nature of "counterforce concepts," which might "make easier, especially in a situation of sharp crisis, the taking of a suicidal decision to begin an aggression."[96] Perhaps one reason for their concern is that the Soviet military continues to think in terms that, at best, blur the distinctions between nuclear preemption, launch on warning, and retaliation. Invoking the kind of formula that has traditionally been a euphemism for preemption, Marshal Akhromeev says that "combat readiness of the Soviet Armed Forces is being constantly enhanced which allows [them] to prevent a possible enemy aggression at any time and in any conditions, and also to deliver a crushing retaliatory blow should war be unleashed by the enemy anyway."[97]

Some Western critics have pointed out, however, that Soviet "new thinking" in the nuclear area may not be to the advantage of the West. The

---

92. *Pravda*, February 14, 1987; CDSP, 39:7, p. 23.
93. Yakovlev, MEiMO, No. 3 (1985), pp. 10–11. See also Vitalii Zhurkin, "O strategicheskoi stabil'nosti," *S.Sh.A.* No. 1 (1986), p. 16. For similar thinking by Gorbachev and Dobrynin underpinning their resistance to matching SDI, Parrott, *BMD*, p. 75.
94. *Izvestiia*, April 16, 1987; FBIS, April 22, pp. CC8; see also R. Sagdayev, A. Kokoshin, "Strategic Stability Under the Conditions of Radical Nuclear-Arms Reductions," (Moscow, April, 1987).
95. E. Teague, "Polemics over 'Euromissiles' in the Soviet Press," Radio Liberty 113/87 (March 20, 1987), citing *Moscow News*, March 8, 1987. This query provoked a neuralgic and unconvincing rebuttal in the subsequent issue of the *Moscow News* by the general who had been in charge of INF policy in the General Staff.
96. Zhurkin, "O strategicheskoi stabil'nosti," p. 15.
97. Akhromeev, "Soviet Military Science and the Art of Warfare," *International Affairs*, No. 5 (May 1985), p. 85. Akhromeev, appointed Chief of the General Staff upon Ogarkov's removal in September 1984, had been Ogarkov's Deputy Chief, and thus is a holdover from the hierarchy of the late Brezhnev period.

agreement to scrap the INF (Intermediate Nuclear Force) capabilities of both sides, for example, still leaves Western Europe under the shadow of the Red Army's formidable conventional offensive force posture. But Gorbachev has made important overtures in that area as well. The official Warsaw Pact position is that both sides should "reduce their forces to equal and minimum levels that will exclude waging any offensive operations against each other, so that the reductions will bring about such forces on both sides that will be sufficient only for defense."[98] Civilian journals in the Soviet Union have endorsed West European proposals to eliminate "highly mobile tank units" and "strike aircraft" in order to achieve the "goal of reorganizing the armed forces of the sides, such that defensive actions would be guaranteed greater success than offensive operations.[99]

The new defense-oriented thinking on conventional strategy seems to be taking on an operational cast. For some time, articles discussing the advantages of large-scale defensive conventional operations have been appearing in military journals, though articles on conventional offense still predominate.[100] Colonel-General M.A. Gareev, deputy chief of the General Staff, has said that one of the "main tenets of the *military-technical* aspect of military doctrine" is its "profoundly defensive direction." This represents a distinct break from the traditional position, which held that, while the "socio-political" character of Soviet military doctrine was defensive, its military-technical aspect stressed the operational benefits of the offensive. Military officers warn, however that defensive operations must not be passive. Rather, they should lead to a vigorous counteroffensive. The Warsaw Pact Chief of Staff insists, consequently, that a defensive strategic stance requires no restructuring of Soviet forces. This, of course, is in direct contradiction to Gorbachev's call for changes in force posture.[101]

98. Viktor Karpov, BBC TV, May 18, 1987; FBIS, May 21, p. AA1.
99. V. Avakov and V. Baranovskii, "V interesakh sokhraneniia tsivilizatsii," MEiMO, No. 4 (1987), p. 30. Even more explicit are A. Kokoshin and V. Larionov, "Kurskaia bitva v svete sovremennoi oboronitel'noi doktriny," MEiMO, No. 8 (August 1987), pp. 32–40, and Lt. Gen. Mikhail Mil'shtein et al., roundtable discussion, "Of Reasonable Sufficiency, Precarious Parity, and International Security," *New Times*, No. 27 (July 13, 1987), pp. 18–21; FBIS, July 16, 1987, pp. AA1.
100. For example, Colonel P.A. Savushkin, "Evoliutsiia vzgliadov na oboronu v mezhvoennye gody," *Voenno–istoricheskii zhurnal*, No. 1 (1987), pp. 37–42. See also Michael MccGwire, "Military Logic Changes Foreign Policy," *Newsday*, June 14, 1987, p. 4.
101. Moscow TV news conference with Gareev, June 22, 1987; FBIS, June 23, 1987, emphasis added. Interview with Army General A. I. Gribkov, chief of the staff of the Warsaw Pact Joint

Such heel-dragging suggests that Gorbachev could not have proceeded as far as he has with the articulation of a non-offensive military doctrine without the curtailment of the military as a significant factor in the Soviet ruling coalition. Circumstantial evidence suggests that a major cause of the increased role of the conventional offensive in Soviet strategy in the 1960s and 1970s was the increased political clout of the military under Brezhnev. Now that political conditions have changed, the strategy can change also.

It has been suggested that the rise of the Soviet "conventional option" stemmed from a rational desire to prevent nuclear escalation should war occur, and that this made sense as a reaction to NATO's shift from massive retaliation to a strategy of flexible response.[102] In fact, the conventional option makes no sense as a strategy for preventing escalation or as reaction to flexible response, since the decisive conventional offensive that it envisions would create precisely the conditions that would trigger nuclear escalation by NATO. Oddly enough, Soviet doctrinal discussions of the mid–1960s, when the conventional option emerged, seem to recognize this. They portray flexible response largely as a cover for a nuclear warfighting strategy and anticipate that the collapse of NATO's front would almost surely trigger nuclear use.[103] The most that can be said is that the Soviets' offensive conventional option is, on a superficial level, less obviously mismatched with flexible response than with NATO's massive retaliation strategy, which had preceded it.

The rise of the offensive conventional option appears to have had more to do with military organizational interests and civil-military relations than with rational strategy. In the middle and late 1950s, the Soviet military justified large conventional forces as necessary to press home the victory after an initial nuclear exchange. Many troops would die, so many were needed if enough were to survive. Khrushchev, however, argued that nuclear weapons

---

Armed Forces, *Krasnaia zvezda*, Sept. 25, pp. 2–3, as translated in FBIS, September 30, 1987, pp. 5–8. Thanks to Stephen Meyer for this citation.

102. MccGwire, *Military Objectives*, pp. 29–35.

103. Marshal V.D. Sokolovskii and General Major M.I. Cherednichenko, "On Contemporary Military Strategy," *Kommunist Vooruzhennykh Sil'* (April 1966), reprinted in William R. Kintner and Harriet Fast Scott, *The Nuclear Revolution in Soviet Military Affairs* (Norman: University of Oklahoma, 1968), p. 264. Colonel D.M. Samorukov, "Combat Operations Involving Conventional Means of Destruction," *Military Thought (Voennaia mysl',* a restricted circulation journal), No. 8 (August 1967), reprinted in *Selected Readings from Soviet Military Thought*, Part I, p. 175. I am grateful to Mark Pekala for sharing his analysis on this and on the following point.

alone would be decisive, and that lean conventional forces were best suited for exploiting the effects of nuclear strikes. When Khrushchev renewed his pressure for ever deeper troop cuts in 1963–64, the military needed a new, more attractive argument for sizeable conventional forces.[104]

Thus, although the conventional offense was weak on strategic logic, it was strong on political logic. It suited the military's needs, because carrying out the conventional offensive would be such a demanding task that huge expenditures would be required.[105] It was attractive to the political leadership, because it gave them the illusion of retaining civilian control over the escalation process. Finally, it provided common ground for Brezhnev's tacit deal with Marshal Grechko: Brezhnev would name Grechko, not the civilian Ustinov, to the vacant post of Defense Minister; Grechko would also get his conventional buildup and nuclear counterforce programs. In return, Grechko would endorse Brezhnev's claim to be the "supreme commander in chief" and cooperate with Brezhnev in heading off an expensive ABM (anti-ballistic missile) race. According to Sovietological reconstructions, an arrangement roughly along these lines jelled around the time of the December 1966 plenum and an extraordinary Defense Council meeting in April 1967.[106]

In short, now that domestic political conditions have changed, the civilians have no reason to remain bound to a costly and destabilizing conventional military strategy, which Ned Lebow has aptly labeled "the Schlieffen Plan revisited."[107] However, Colonel General N.F. Chervov, of the General Staff's arms control directorate, has warned that "one should not expect unilateral steps on the part of the Warsaw Pact. The NATO countries must take practical steps to meet the Warsaw Pact halfway."[108] Indeed, it is not entirely clear

---

104. Linden, *Khrushchev*, pp. 191–2, and Thomas Wolfe, *Soviet Strategy at the Crossroads* (Cambridge: Harvard, 1965), pp. 149–152, offer analyses sensitive to domestic political and budgetary aspects of arguments about conventional strategy in this period. For evidence relating early conventional-option thinking to this budgetary setting, see Wolfe, pp. 121–23, 131.

105. For a theoretical statement explaining this and other reasons for professional militaries' preference for offensive strategies, see Barry Posen, *The Sources of Military Doctrine* (Ithaca: Cornell, 1984), esp. p. 49.

106. Edward L. Warner, *The Military in Contemporary Soviet Politics* (New York: Praeger, 1977), pp. 94, 100, 165, on ABM changes and Grechko; MccGwire, *Military Objectives*, App. A, on conventional option and December plenum; Benjamin Lambeth, *The Soviet Strategic Challenge* (Princeton: Princeton University, forthcoming), ch. 4 on the Defense Ministership and the April meeting.

107. Richard Ned Lebow, "The Soviet Offensive in Europe: The Schlieffen Plan Revisited?" *International Security*, Vol. 9, No. 4 (Spring 1985), pp. 44–78.

108. TASS, June 22, 1987; FBIS, June 23, AA3. Arguing for unilateral Soviet reductions, however, are three scholars from the United States and Canada Institute, Vitaly Zhurkin, Sergei Karaganov, and Andrei Kortunov, "Reasonable Sufficiency—Or How to Break the Vicious Circle," *New Times* 40 (Oct. 12, 1987), pp. 13–15; FBIS, Oct. 14, pp. 4–7.

that the civilians care as much about actually implementing a new defensive conventional doctrine as they do about announcing it. Vladimir Petrovskii, the deputy minister of Foreign Affairs, may have revealed more than he intended in saying that "already the very fact of the proclamation of the doctrine is having a salutary effect on the climate and situation in the world."[109] Thus, the West should respond to the Soviets' call for an experts' conference on the restructuring of conventional doctrines as a way of institutionalizing a trend that otherwise might slip away.

OFFENSE AND DEFENSE IN GEOPOLITICAL STRATEGY. To some extent, the new thinking about offense and defense also appears in a geopolitical context. Gone are Suslov, Boris Ponomarev, and the other old-style ideologues who were associated over the years with the Comintern, the Cominform, and more recently the International Department of the Central Committee.[110] Gone, too, is the bandwagon imagery of their "correlation of forces" theory.[111] Progressive change in the Third World is now universally portrayed as slow, reversible, and problematic. Gorbachev is prone to admonish visiting dignitaries from backward client states that "no country is secure against the desire of its vanguard to skip over unavoidable stages."[112]

Military conquest, even of backward states, is seen as difficult. This new view seems to be held even by military officers, suggesting that it may simply reflect learning rather than institutional change. In Grechko's time, the military had been a major enthusiast for Third World involvement and later reportedly favored the intervention in Afghanistan.[113] But this recent Yugoslav interview with Marshal Kulikov, the Warsaw Pact commander, demonstrates a new ambivalence about the use of force:[114]

Q: If a country lacks an operative army as big as, for instance, the Warsaw Pact or NATO, but possesses an armed people willing to fight and a wide concept of defense, can such a country be defeated?

---

109. Ibid. p. AA4.
110. On the intertwining of these personal and institutional histories, see Elizabeth Teague, "The Foreign Departments of the Central Committee of the CPSU," Radio Liberty Reports, October 27, 1980; Leonard Schapiro, "The CPSU International Department," *International Journal*, Vol. 32, No. 1 (Winter 1976–77), pp. 41–55.
111. Ted Hopf, "Soviet Inferences from Their Victories in the Periphery," (Columbia University) paper presented at the annual meeting of the International Studies Association, April 1987, forthcoming in Jervis and Snyder, *Strategic Beliefs*.
112. *Pravda*, February 11, 1987; CDSP, 39:6, 19.
113. Francis Fukuyama, *Soviet Civil–Military Relations and the Power Projection Mission* (Santa Monica: Rand R-3504-AF, April 1987).
114. Zagreb *Danas*, April 14, 1987; FBIS, April 21, 1987, AA11.

Kulikov: Which country?
Q: Any country.
Kulikov: A victory may be attained. Indeed only for a time, for it is something else to rule such a country. World public opinion, other factors, all that is present. It is very difficult to defeat a people determined to defend itself.

Asked specifically about Afghanistan, Kulikov remarks that it is difficult to generalize lessons from it: "I tell you that war in Afghanistan is very strange."

Other Soviet officials, however, have been more willing to generalize. Noting that the Soviet Union has backed whichever side was on the defensive in the Iran–Iraq war in order to prevent the conquest of either, a Soviet U.N. delegate went on to claim that on principle the Soviet Union "does not support materially or in any other form the party that is on the offensive, and I think this is of some importance."[115]

Some caveats should be mentioned about the geopolitical aspects of the new thinking. First, even under Brezhnev, the line was that Soviet military power was used to "defend the gains of socialism," as in Ethiopia and Afghanistan, not to export revolution through military offensives. For example, the Soviets refused to allow the Ethiopians to roll Soviet-supplied tanks across the border into Somalia. Second, a number of instances of increased aggressiveness of Soviet Third World behavior might be noted under Gorbachev.[116] Perhaps the most important is the stepped-up cross-border bombardment of Pakistan. Though Gorbachev may want very badly to extricate himself from the mistakes of his predecessors, considerations of prestige and domestic politics may make it hard to take the direct route out. Like Nixon in Vietnam, Gorbachev may feel compelled to adopt a "Christmas bombing" strategy of extrication through massive escalation of the war into Pakistan. Though this seems unlikely at present, it underscores the need to use diplomacy, and not just military pressure, to help Gorbachev find a way out of Afghanistan.[117]

ALTERNATIVE TRAJECTORIES OF CHANGE

In the preceding sections I have been discussing logical developments of institutions, policies, and ideas, given the assumption that Gorbachev will

115. New York Times, January 12, 1987. For other evidence, Blum, "Soviet Perceptions", p. 36.
116. Harry Gelman, "The Soviet Union, East Asia and the West: The Kremlin's Calculation of Opportunities and Risks," in East Asia, the West and International Security, Adelphi Paper No. 217 (London: International Institute for Strategic Studies, Spring 1987), pp. 3–26.
117. For background on Soviet positions, see Bohdan Nahaylo, "Towards a Settlement of the Afghanistan Conflict: A Chronological Overview," Radio Liberty 16/87, January 11, 1987.

enjoy a significant degree of success in implementing his domestic reforms. Structural changes have made this a possibility, and the decisions of the June 1987 plenum, which ratified an ambitious economic reform plan and promoted three Gorbachev allies to the Politburo, make it even more likely.[118] Nonetheless, other scenarios deserve mention, especially insofar as the international environment might have some effect on their likelihood.

One cause of concern stems from the character of some of Gorbachev's closest allies. Yakovlev is essentially an ideologue and a propagandist. Though he seems to have devised a stunning formula for modernizing those roles, there is still a danger that some of their traditional content will sneak back in—and if not for Yakovlev personally, then for his underlings or successors. Likewise, Lev Zaikov, the overseer of the defense industries, has his roots in Leningrad's high technology military sector.[119] His orientation toward technological modernization makes him an appropriate backer for Gorbachev's restructuring, but it is hard to forget the role played by previous Leningrad party chiefs—Frol Kozlov and Grigorii Romanov—in backing big defense budgets. It would not be difficult to imagine Zaikov aligning with modernizing elements in the military, like Marshal Ogarkov, who favor a more militarized version of the reforms. Some research suggests that there are circles in the military who favor economic restructuring, but not of the market-oriented kind. Instead, their notion may be to advance some of the more successful practices of the hierarchical defense sector as a model for the economy as a whole.[120]

Another source of danger lies at the periphery of the reform coalition. Yegor Ligachev, the second secretary of the party, has supported the general idea of reform, but has often voiced reservations about the pace and direction of change. In the arts, he calls for "vivid and profound images of Communists" to counterbalance what he sees as the excessively critical outpouring under *glasnost*.[121] In the foreign trade area, he warns about the excesses of the "'imported purchases' craze."[122] Moreover, his arguments for détente and reform take on an offensive, Brezhnevian caste:

The restructuring is unbreakably linked with the USSR's vigorous peaceloving policy. On the one hand, its scope depends on the reliability of peace,

118. New York *Times*, June 27, 1987.
119. Ruble, *Leningrad*, chapter 2.
120. Weickhardt, "Soviet Military-Industrial Complex", pp. 214–15, 225.
121. *Teatr*, No. 8 (August 1986); CDSP, 38:44, p. 1.
122. *Pravda*, October 2, 1986; CDSP, 38:40, pp. 8–9.

on the stability of the international situation. On the other hand, the renewal imparts still greater dynamism and intensity to the foreign policy activity of the CPSU and the Soviet state, strengthens the foundations for their struggle for peace.[123]

Thus, if Gorbachev's radical program runs into obstacles, Ligachev will be there to put his stamp on a scaled-down version that retains many of the features of the Soviet domestic order and foreign policy under Brezhnev.

A final possibility is the least likely but the most worrisome. It is possible that Gorbachev may fail spectacularly, but only after he has so stirred up the social and political system that returning to a Ligachev-type solution is impossible. In that case, a variety of nefarious actors might be able to enter the political process. For example, glasnost has allowed the extreme Great Russian nationalists to emerge from the shadows and go so far as to compare the current liberal trends in Soviet culture to the German invasion of June 1941.[124] In the past, Shelepin tried to tap this source of political energy, linking it to a heterogeneous would-be coalition that was to attract the KGB, the radical military, and Khrushchevite populists.[125] He had almost no success with this project, but in a more wide-open political environment, an analogous coalition might form around a militarized, xenophobic version of the reforms.

Two factors might make these adverse trajectories more likely. One would be the discrediting of Gorbachev's version of the domestic reforms through dramatically poor economic performance. The second, interacting with the first, would be a hostile international environment, in which SDI was being deployed,[126] Eastern Europe was asserting its autonomy, and Soviet clients were losing their counterinsurgency wars in Afghanistan, Angola, and Ethiopia. This would discredit the international assumptions and requirements of the Gorbachev-style reforms, and possibly promote a more militarized version.

Alternate Views of Gorbachev's Reforms

I have argued that Gorbachev appears to be aiming for a change in the Soviet Union's fundamental institutions. In the past, these institutions, many of

123. TASS, April 17, 1987, reporting on Ligachev's interview with visiting Congressman Jim Wright; FBIS, April 20.
124. *Literaturnaia Rossiia*, March 27, 1987.
125. On the chauvinist radical right, see John B. Dunlop, *The Faces of Contemporary Russian Nationalism* (Princeton: Princeton University, 1983), esp. pp. 217–27; Felicity Barringer, "Russian Nationalists Test Gorbachev," New York *Times*, May 24, 1987, p. 10.
126. For this argument on SDI, see Parrott, *BMD*, chapter 5.

them rooted in Stalin's revolution from above, supported militant expansion-ism and offensive, zero-sum approaches to security. They also promoted the offensive approach to détente taken by Khrushchev and Brezhnev. Gorbach-ev's new domestic coalition and institutional innovations are likely to call forth and sustain a new, less militant foreign policy. This is true both because the old institutions are being checked or swept away by reforms, and also because of the new system's inherent need for more stable relations with the advanced capitalist countries.

Making this argument in a brief article, I have not been able to address fully some important rival theories. One is that Gorbachev's new thinking in foreign policy is not rooted in domestic institutions, but simply reflects lessons drawn from the failures of Brezhnev's foreign and security policies. If so, those lessons, like previous swings of the right/left pendulum in Soviet history,[127] could be as easily unlearned as they were learned. The validity of this objection hinges in part on how closely I—and the sources I have cited—have established the links between particular strategic ideas and the groups and coalitions that support them. Some Sovietologists, arguing for cognitive or international explanations of Soviet foreign policy, have questioned these domestic political connections, pointing out that the top leader himself has often been the source of expansionist policies and concepts.[128] What this argument has missed, however, is the extent to which the General Secretar-ies' policies and concepts were a response to a variety of domestic political pressures, identical to none of them individually, but caused by the need to manage all of them simultaneously.

Proponents of a second theory would hold that I have placed too much emphasis on the particularities of Stalin's revolution from above, and not enough on earlier pathologies of Leninism or of Russian autocracy.[129] Here, I would argue that Stalin's system, with its hypercentralism, authoritarian-ism, xenophobia, and military orientation, was a kind of apotheosis of those earlier patterns. If Gorbachev has broken Stalin's pattern, he has broken his predecessors' as well.

Finally, there is the theory that all great powers behave aggressively be-cause of the consequences of international anarchy or for other reasons.

---

127. Putting these developments in this light is Francis Fukuyama, "The Tenth Period of Soviet Third World Policy," paper presented at the Harvard Center for International Affairs national security conference, Cape Cod, Massachusetts, June 1987, forthcoming in *Problems of Communism*.
128. Adomeit, *Soviet Risk-Taking*, pp. 188–193.
129. For example, Richard Pipes, "Militarism and the Soviet State," *Daedalus* 109 (Fall 1980), pp. 1–12.

While this may be true, there has nonetheless been a significant range in the aggressiveness of great powers, a good deal of it due to variations in their domestic systems. The Soviet Union under Brezhnev was already less pathological than some of the great powers that have populated the twentieth century. Gorbachev's Russia as I have extrapolated it should be still less aggressive.

Policy Prescriptions for the West

In order to make the most of the opportunities presented by the new thinking, American policy should follow three guidelines. First, the U.S. should avoid mounting intense geopolitical challenges, like a Strategic Defense Initiative deployment or rollback attempts on the Soviet periphery, that would force the reforms to move in a militarized direction. Military-oriented, authoritarian revolution from above is the normal pattern of Russian response to intense pressure from its environment. Moderate international pressure helps Gorbachev, because it makes reform seem necessary, but intense pressure is likely to hurt him, since it makes an Ogarkov-type reform seem more appropriate.

Second, the U.S. should continue to reciprocate meaningful Soviet concessions, like the Soviet INF offers, to avoid discrediting the new thinking, parts of which may be quite fragile. Malenkov's fate is instructive in this regard. On one hand, it is true that the West's vigorous military response to the invasion of South Korea undoubtedly helped proponents of a less assertive Soviet foreign policy in the Kremlin, by discrediting the former hard line. On the other hand, once that point was proved, further American intransigence hurt proponents of a relaxation of tension after they came to power. Herbert Dinerstein has shown how Malenkov's political career foundered in part on America's unhelpful reactions to his strategic innovations.[130]

Gorbachev is much stronger politically, but the same rule applies. America's reaction to Afghanistan probably worked in his favor, by discrediting the expansionist, militarist aspects of the old Brezhnev line. But further Western intransigence certainly would not help him, since he has implicitly promised that his strategy of competitive peace "propaganda" will lead to a more stable superpower relationship.

---

130. Dinerstein, *War and the Soviet Union*, chapter 4.

Third, the United States should press hard for meaningful restructuring of the Soviet foreign trade system and of the Soviet Army's offensive conventional posture in Europe. The West should be firm in tying Soviet membership in the General Agreement on Tariffs and Trade (GATT) and the International Monetary Fund (IMF) to some restructuring of Soviet price-setting practices, which it can justify as insurance against Soviet dumping of goods at prices below their cost of production. The U.S. should also take up Soviet offers to discuss changes in conventional force postures from offense to defense.[131] These are measures that could have important side-effects on Soviet domestic structure, deepening the reform and strengthening its institutions. Gorbachev may want to take these steps anyway, but unless America takes an active role and offers to meet him half way, they may be hard for Gorbachev to push through.

Finally, let me reinforce the qualifications with which I opened the argument. Social science does not predict the future. At best, it generates expectations about future outcomes, assuming that certain causal conditions are present. Thus, I could be wrong either because my theory about the domestic sources of Soviet expansionism is flawed, or because Gorbachev's reforms will not make sufficient changes in the causal variables to affect the outcome.

All the evidence is not yet in on the Gorbachev revolution. Nonetheless, it is important to advance hypotheses as best we can, in part so that we can recognize the relevant evidence when it does come in, and in part because our own interim actions may affect the outcome. Some of the most positive aspects of Gorbachev's new thinking, especially his interest in defensive conventional strategies, may be short-lived if the West creates an environment that is inhospitable to their survival.

---

131. I will discuss these changes in more detail in the next issue of *International Security*.

The Sources and Prospects of Gorbachev's New Political Thinking on Security

Stephen M. Meyer

$\mathbf{I}$n his short time as General Secretary, Mikhail Gorbachev has beyond a doubt revitalized the discourse on Soviet military doctrine in both the Soviet Union and the West. Under the banner of "new political thinking" on security, Soviet academics, Party, military, and other government officials are re-examining many long-standing tenets of Soviet security policy.[1] Some of the ideas being articulated are doctrinally and ideologically revolutionary in the context of traditional Soviet security policy. Indeed, the ongoing doctrinal dialogue, if carried to its logical extreme, could imply even greater changes in Soviet military policy than those associated with Khrushchev's doctrinal initiatives of the late 1950s and early 1960s.

It is also possible that this new political thinking on security could remain just that—thinking—with little long-term impact on the basic forces, capabilities, and approaches that underlie Soviet military policy. Or, following a short-term shift in military policy, there could be a subsequent regression to more standard Soviet security formulations, as happened after Khrushchev's ouster.

The author would like to thank Judyth Twigg and Matthew Partan for their comments on earlier drafts of this article.

Stephen M. Meyer is Associate Professor of Political Science at the Massachusetts Institute of Technology.

1. Gorbachev's new political thinking on security is concerned primarily with the tenets of Soviet military doctrine. Formal definitions aside, Soviet military doctrine broadly addresses the questions: (1) What are the greatest external dangers facing the Soviet Union? (2) What are Soviet options for coping with those dangers? (3) What kinds of military capabilities are required? (4) How much is enough, and how should it be allocated? More formal discussions of the content and scope of military doctrine can be found in: S.F. Akhromeyev, "Doktrina predot-vrashcheniya voyny, zashchity mira i sotsializma," *Problemy mira i sotsializma*, No. 12 (December 1987), pp. 26–27; G. Kostev, "Nasha voyennaya doktrina v svete novogo politicheskogo mysh-leniya," *Kommunist vooruzhennykh sil*, No. 17 (September 1987), pp. 10–13; L. Semeyko, "Vmesto gor oruzhiya. . . O printsipe razumnoy dostatochnosti," *Izvestia*, August 13, 1987, p. 5. Kostev is a vice admiral in the Soviet Navy, and a professor. Semeyko is a senior researcher at the Institute of USA and Canada. (Translations and transliterations from the Russian are by the author, except where otherwise noted.)

International Security, Fall 1988 (Vol. 13, No. 2)
© 1988 by the President and Fellows of Harvard College and of the Massachusetts Institute of Technology.

Therefore, in considering the potential impact of this new security thinking on Soviet defense policy in the years ahead, it is essential to assess both the likelihood of realization and the durability of the new thinking over time. Can these ideas serve as the foundation for a long-term framework for Soviet military policy in the decades to come? Are they credible principles to which future Soviet political and military leaders could easily subscribe, or are they merely a temporary doctrinal structure with little staying power?[2]

I will argue that conceptual elements of Gorbachev's new thinking on security are first and foremost tools for gaining control of the Soviet defense agenda. The new thinking is highly specific to Gorbachev's approach to rebuilding the Soviet economic-industrial base, and is decidedly not the result of deterministic forces driving Soviet defense or foreign policy. While some of his notions are easily incorporated into more traditional Soviet security frameworks, and thus readily adopted by future Soviet general secretaries, other aspects are quite antithetical to conventional Soviet thinking, and threaten important institutional interests. As is true for all of Gorbachev's programs, there are powerful political and institutional forces that must be coerced or co-opted into implementing policy. Thus, the durability of the entire new thinking framework—which would have far more radical implications for Soviet defense policy—depends on Gorbachev's ability to institutionalize its conceptual elements in political and military decision-making.

However, many of the more radical embellishments on the new thinking offered by Soviet academics are not presently part of Gorbachev's framework. Confusion among Western observers over what the Soviet leader has, and has not, advocated has created some unrealistic expectations about future directions in Soviet defense policy.

The discussion that follows is divided into three major sections. First, the purpose and the process behind Gorbachev's effort to stimulate doctrinal discussion are reviewed. Without this context, any effort to separate substance from noise in the new thinking would be futile. Next, the major elements of Gorbachev's new political thinking on security are examined,

---

2. I reject immediately the argument that the ongoing doctrinal dialogue in the Soviet Union is mere propaganda (disinformation), though there is no doubt it is being propagandized. The breadth and scope of the discussion and the variety of fora where it is occurring are such that one cannot dismiss the seriousness of the substance under consideration. Careers have been staked on some of these issues. The subsequent disruptions to the domestic political body have been significant; some rather obvious policy actions, consistent with the principles of the new thinking, have been taken.

along with the critiques of the "old thinkers." This article concludes with an assessment of the implications of both the substance and process of the new political thinking for future Soviet security policy.

ENGINES OF DOCTRINAL CHANGE

Mikhail Gorbachev became general secretary of the Communist Party of the Soviet Union in March 1985. The first unambiguous hint of his effort to recapture the defense agenda appeared in the preparatory work for the draft program of the 27th Party Congress. Gorbachev and his associates in the Central Committee Secretariat proposed a cryptic, though signficant, change in the standard formulation of the Party's commitment to defense resource allocation.[3] The 27th Congress became a kind of watershed, after which one doctrinal principle after another was subjected to review, discussion, and revision.[4] From that point on, Gorbachev's new political thinking on security grew by accretion.

What would compel the new general secretary to assume the arduous task of revising Soviet military doctrine while still in the throes of consolidating his leadership position? Previous general secretaries had waited until after they had firmly established themselves to take on the national security establishment. For answers, some Western analysts look to rational military-strategic analysis: In recognition of the awesome power of nuclear weapons and the futility of nuclear war, they say, the Soviet leadership since late 1966 has systematically been altering doctrine to reduce the likelihood of nuclear war. By this analysis, Gorbachev's new political thinking on security is merely the logical extension of Soviet military-strategic trends spanning the last twenty years.[5]

---

3. The old formulation was an open and absolute framework: "The party will do [provide] everything necessary to reliably defend the homeland." The new form is a closed and relative framework: "The party will do everything to ensure that the imperialist countries do not attain military superiority." There was some internal debate over this change in wording when the draft appeared, apparently initiated by those who felt this new formulation represented a weakening of the Party's commitment to defense. The new wording was retained in the final program. See *Programma kommunisticheskoy partii Sovetskogo Soyuza, Novaya redaktsiya* (Moscow: Politizdat, 1986), p. 115. Information on the internal debate is based on interviews with Soviet officials and academics in Moscow during fall 1987.
4. Gorbachev claims that the philosophical-political basis for the Washington summit—thus also, by implication, for the new political thinking on security—was the 27th Party Congress. See "Vystupleniye M. S. Gorbachev po sovetskomu televideniyu," *Krasnaya zvezda*, December 15, 1987, p. 1.
5. For some imaginative speculation on this point see Michael MccGwire, *Military Objectives in Soviet Foreign Policy* (Washington, D.C.: Brookings, 1987).

Others have suggested that deterministic forces within Soviet society produced an inevitable and irreversible shift in doctrine. In particular, a shift from extensive economic growth to intensive growth, and the expansion of the Soviet "intellectual class"—for whom defense holds a lower priority—are seen as important engines of change.[6]

Curiously, both of these explanations put little or no weight on the personae of the Soviet leadership—and in particular, on the man who is general secretary. Rather, they hold that Soviet leaders are compelled to change policy by deterministic forces beyond their control: by the military-technological revolution, or by social-economic evolution.

These putatively new "engines" for the new political thinking on security have, however, long been present. Soviet leaders have been aware of, and have even publicly warned of the destructiveness of nuclear war for over 30 years. Similarly, efforts to shift the relative contributions of extensive and intensive growth in the Soviet economy have been underway for over a decade; and despite assertions to the contrary, there is no obvious indication that the size, the composition, or the character of the policy-relevant "intellectual elite" in the Soviet Union has changed significantly in 15 years.[7] Indeed, most of the Soviets identified as "new thinkers" by Western scholars have been around since the early 1970s. While these underlying "forces" may quite plausibly influence policy trends in general, they fail to answer the most important question: Why are significant changes to Soviet military doctrine suddenly being proposed *now*? Why weren't they raised five, ten, or fifteen years ago; or five, ten, or fifteen years in the future?

If one looks carefully at the history of military doctrinal change in the Soviet Union, one inescapable conclusion is clear: individual general secretaries do matter. Individual perceptions, impressions, recollections, and biases affect significantly the articulation and elaboration of the Soviet de-

---

6. See Jack Snyder, "The Gorbachev Revolution: A Waning of Soviet Expansionism?" *International Security*, Vol. 12, No. 3 (Winter 1987/88), pp. 93–131. Extensive growth refers to the use of additional capital and labor to increase economic output. Intensive growth refers to increasing the productivity of existing capital and labor to increase output.

7. Snyder argues that the growth of the intellectual elite can be gauged by the increase in the number of individuals with higher education. Ibid., p. 112. There is no reason to assume, however, that higher education is in any way correlated with the rise and expansion of an "intelligentsia" class in the USSR. Many of the people who are naturally part of this "class"— artists, writers, poets, etc.—often do not have higher education degrees. At the same time, it is most unlikely that Party bureaucrats, engineers, scientists, literary figures, and industrial managers—all with higher education—share similar socio-philosophical and intellectual perspectives.

fense agenda.[8] It is not so much a matter of "personalities" as it is personal policy agendas, priorities, and images of what has gone before and what needs to be done now. In this respect, there is no reason to believe that Andropov or Chernenko (had they lived), or Romanov (had he been selected instead of Gorbachev) would have chosen to travel Gorbachev's path of doctrinal reform.

When Gorbachev came to power his only obvious aim was economic revitalization. There is no evidence—or reason to believe—that he was contemplating a grand scheme for defining a new defense agenda. He quickly learned, however, that there were at least two forces that constrained economic change. One was the entrenched attitude of the bureaucracy and labor force towards responsibility, accountability, and authority. Thus, *glasnost* and democratization were born out of the need to create accountability and responsibility by basing rewards and sanctions on performance, not position.[9]

The other constraining force was the defense agenda—not simply the existing defense budget. The problem was not the resources that were already going to the military, so much as the future resource commitments implied by threat assessments and requirements derived from traditional thinking. More elbow room for economic *perestroika* (restructuring) required lifting the shadow of a further Soviet military buildup in the 1990s and beyond, which in turn meant that Gorbachev had to gain control over and restructure the Soviet defense agenda.

At the same time, global political and economic trends seemed to have raised doubts among the Gorbachev coterie about the long-term foundation of Soviet superpower status. By the time Gorbachev became general secretary, Soviet superpower status was precariously balanced on a single leg:

---

8. I am not suggesting an explanation based on personality types or psychological profiles, though these may be important variables. I merely wish to argue that individuals—even individuals from a fairly homogeneous cohort—make a difference in the Soviet system. A complete examination of the evidence is presented in my *Defending the USSR: Building Soviet Military Power* (forthcoming). For studies outside the national security area see the very interesting work of Valerie Bunce, "Leadership Succession and Policy Innovation in Soviet Republics," *Comparative Politics*, Vol. 11, No. 4 (July 1979), pp. 379–402; Bunce, "The Succession Connection: Policy Cycles and Political Change in the Soviet Union and Eastern Europe," *American Political Science Review*, Vol. 74, No. 4 (1980), pp. 966–977; and Philip Roeder, "Do New Soviet Leaders Really Make a Difference? Rethinking the 'Succession Connection'," *American Political Science Review*, Vol. 79, No. 4 (1985), pp. 958–977.
9. This derivation for *glasnost* and *perestroika* was described in interviews in Moscow and Boston with two of Gorbachev's advisers. See also Gorbachev's comments in "Otvety M.S. Gorbacheva na voprosy gazety 'Vashington post' i zhurnala 'Nyusuik'," *Krasnaya zvezda*, May 24, 1988, p. 2.

military power. The building of Soviet military power had, indeed, been a noteworthy achievement of previous regimes, but it was now threatened with rapid depreciation by the Western technological challenge. Meanwhile as Soviet military power was growing, Soviet communism had declined significantly as a political-economic and social model for the world: Soviet political and economic influence was spotty at best, and Soviet technological power was falling further behind world standards. From Gorbachev's perspective, rebuilding the political, economic, and social bases underlying Soviet superpower status were intimately tied to economic reform that, in turn, had important implications for defense.[10]

Seen in this light, Gorbachev's agitation for new political thinking on security is more a product of instrumental necessity than of military-strategic enlightenment. Given the problems facing the Soviet economy as he (and his advisers) perceived them, his impressions of what had been attempted in the past and the reasons for their failure, and the goals he set, gaining control of the defense agenda was necessary. At the same time, Gorbachev and his allies do not appear to be affected by the traditional Soviet philosophical-ideological blinders that restricted the flexibility of some of his predecessors and many of his current colleagues.[11] Thus, a broader array of approaches has found its way onto the Gorbachev defense agenda.

CHANGING THE PROCESS

The skepticism that has greeted Gorbachev's doctrinal agenda in Western policy circles is easily understood. Some of the items on Gorbachev's list, such as complete denuclearization by 2000, smack more of propaganda than serious policy.

Compounding doubts is the deadening effect on Western thinkers of the eighteen-year rule of the Brezhnev regime. Comfortable with the glacial nature of its institutional-consensus style of decision-making, long-time Western students of Soviet military policy now have trouble imagining how the kinds of novel statements emanating from the Gorbachev regime could be anything but propaganda. Certainly there is little reason to expect radical shifts in thinking from the long-dominant bureaucracies of the Ministries of Defense and Foreign Affairs.

---

10. "Rech' tovarishcha Gorbacheva," *Krasnaya zvezda*, October 2, 1987, p. 2.
11. This includes a view of an inimical and hostile world that engenders an "us versus them" mentality, a basic distrust of foreign ideas, and a need for autocracy.

What this line of thinking fails to recognize, however, is that Gorbachev has been altering the Soviet process of national security policy-making. In the Soviet system, substantive change almost always requires process change and organizational restructuring. This is due in large part to the natural inclinations of institutional actors to resist changes in their organizational roles, missions, and resource allocations.[12]

Gorbachev has brought policy initiation out into the open; under his predecessors public doctrinal discussions reflected decisions already taken.[13] Most importantly, Gorbachev—adopting a policy Andropov appears to have set in motion—has moved to take back the defense agenda–setting function from the military bureaucracy and to redistribute it between the general secretary's office (as Khrushchev did at the very end of the 1950s) and the Central Committee staff.[14] Having become well acquainted with the institutional

---

12. When Khrushchev attempted to institute radical changes in doctrine and strategy, he also found it necessary to create a new armed service that would be institutionally committed to his approach. So the Strategic Rocket Forces were born. Even within the Ministry of Defense, changes in strategy and force concepts almost always coincide intriguingly with force reorganizations. The multiple reorganizations of the Air Force and Air Defense Forces over the last decade are cases in point.

13. Soviet Chief of the General Staff Marshal Sergei Akhromeyev claims that Soviet military doctrine is *in the process* of reformulation. S. F. Akhromeyev, "Slava i gordost' sovetskogo naroda," *Sovetskaya rossiya*, February 21, 1987, p. 1. Of course styles differ. Khrushchev set the agenda, along with his staff devised policy options, and then announced decisions. Often, only a handful of Politburo members knew what to expect. The professional military, for the most part, was an institutional bystander, left to implement policies with which it often disagreed. Public doctrinal discussions, therefore, were part of the implementation phase of policy-making (including post-decision drum beating)—when the political leadership attempted to inform the elite, justify the action, and cajole the skeptical. Brezhnev, in contrast, cultivated an institutional-consensus approach to defense policy making. Ideas and policy options were put forward by the responsible organizations, heavily dominated by the Ministry of Defense. This dominance was reinforced by the fact that the General Staff served as the staff for the Defense Council, and the chief of the General Staff acted its secretary. While decision selection remained the prerogative of the Politburo (and Defense Council), control of the agenda-setting and option-development functions could be potent instruments for steering political leaders to desired decisions. Public doctrinal discussions during Brezhnev's tenure were little more than post-decision elaborations of policy, as all the key individuals and institutions were already well aware of the outcome. I suspect that a noteworthy exception was Brezhnev's 1977 Tula speech, which marked the beginning of his effort to recapture the defense agenda-setting function. See "Rech' tovarishcha L.I. Brezhneva," *Krasnaya zvezda*, January 1977, pp. 1–3.

14. The establishment of the Committee of Soviet Scientists for Peace and Against Nuclear War (hereafter called the Committee of Soviet Scientists) under General Secretary Yuri Andropov appears to have begun largely as a propaganda effort. At the same time, Andropov is alleged to have been searching for an institutional alternative to the General Staff—a Soviet analogue to the U.S. National Security Council staff—as a source of defense policy advice and analysis. Andropov died before this plan could be implemented. (This information derives from interviews with Soviet officials and academicians in Moscow, Washington, New York, and Boston in late 1987 and 1988, hereafter cited as "interviews.") There are indications that Soviet academics,

inclinations and the performance of the traditional national security structure during both the Andropov and Chernenko regimes, Gorbachev has turned instead for new ideas—at least for now—to non-military professionals in the Ministry of Foreign Affairs, the Central Committee staff, and the Academy of Sciences.[15]

As a result, these new actors find themselves in a kind of competition—both among themselves and with the more traditional national security bureaucracy—to catch the general secretary's ear and to provide him with new ways of thinking about old problems. They appear to be aware that their influence and impact on Soviet security policy will in the long term be determined in large part by their near-term success in supplying the general secretary with new ideas that have visible and immediate payoffs.[16] A string of flops could see Gorbachev turn back, willingly or otherwise, to more traditional centers of national security advice.[17]

Of course, the Ministry of Defense continues to be an essential actor in defense policy by sheer virtue of its expertise and its responsibilities for implementing defense policy. With the reduction and limitation of its agenda-setting responsibilities, some of its long-standing avenues of influence have been narrowed. However, while the Ministry of Defense may now share agenda-setting functions with other institutional actors, it remains the primary source of detailed analysis and is still the primary implementer of defense policy. Thus, the Ministry of Defense may find that it still has a

---

acting through the Committee of Soviet Scientists, have subsequently begun to evolve into a new institutional source of advice on security issues in general, and nuclear weapons issues in particular. (Based on interviews.) As a result of this process, Soviet academics have also begun to have access to high level policy information. See A. Arbatov, "Glubokoye sokrashcheniye strategicheskikh vooruzheniy," (Part 1) *Mirovaya ekonomika i mezhdunarodnyye otnosheniya* (MEMO), No. 4 (1988), pp. 21–22. Aleksey Arbatov is head of the disarmament and security department at the Institute of World Economy and International Relations (IMEMO). His department is in becoming the locus for serious academic research on general purpose forces.

15. The Gorbachev regime's use of personnel from the Academy of Sciences and the Central Committee staff was confirmed by Central Committee Secretary Anatoly Dobrynin in a recent article: A. Dobrynin, "Za bez'yadernyy mir, navstrechu 21 veku," *Kommunist*, No. 9 (1986), pp. 21, 26. Foreign ministry personnel are also more heavily involved than in the past in the early stages of security-related agenda-setting and policy option formulation. Based on interviews.

16. This competition was described by several Soviet institutional "competitors" in interviews.

17. Where Snyder sees these "intellectuals" as being the engines of new political thinking, I see the current prominence of non-military national security "intellectuals" in the Soviet Union as a byproduct—a consequence—of Gorbachev's quest for new political thinking. Where Snyder sees Gorbachev worrying about this constituency, I see them worrying about his continued willingness that let them play in defense politics. See Snyder, "The Gorbachev Revolution," pp. 110–115.

potent ability to affect defense policy through its continuing roles in policy option formulation and implementation.[18]

ANALYTIC CAVEATS

Like Khrushchev, Gorbachev's effort to recast Soviet military doctrine has created a great deal of confusion and uncertainty in what was a very stable policy environment. Yet things are even more tentative today because Gorbachev and the new thinkers are still engaged in agenda-setting and option formulation.

Meanwhile, the burgeoning of *glasnost* has resulted in a significant increase in the "noise" found in Soviet discussions of military doctrine. Many of the ideas being tossed about by Soviet "new thinkers" represent little more than personal views. The competition for influence among the new thinkers further reinforces this tendency, as each attempts to get his own ideas on the national agenda.[19] Thus, it would be a mistake to assume that the entire ensemble of arguments articulated under the banner of new political thinking—even those things presented by Gorbachev—reflect accepted decisions on Soviet military doctrine.

Noteworthy counterarguments to aspects of the new political thinking on defense are already beginning to appear. For the most part, these counterarguments are being voiced by professional military officers; but such exchanges do not reflect a purely civil-military rift. First, these criticisms would not appear in such a diversity of party, government, and media fora without significant high-level political support. The civilians who control these information organs are allowing—if not encouraging—probing questions about the new political thinking on security. Second, the professional military's specialized expertise, its institutional role in the national security bureaucracy, and its defense policy implementation functions make it the logical authoritative counter-voice against significant departures from previous defense policies. However, the military lacks the political power to launch an independent campaign against the new political thinking on security. As in

---

18. To be sure, military-technical considerations remain important to policy deliberations. Gorbachev has noted that all preparations for the Washington summit were discussed in the Politburo, and that everything was considered from a military-technical viewpoint. "Vystupleniye M. S. Gorbachev po sovetskomu televideniyu."
19. Interviews. Some of the more provocative arguments by individuals such as Yevgeniy Primakov, Vitaly Zhurkin, and Deputy Chief of the General Staff General-Colonel Gareyev were emphatically characterized as their personal views, not government policy.

war, the men in uniform may be on the front lines, but elements of the political leadership are in command.

Moreover, the professional military is not a homogeneous body; service agendas and priorities differ, as do the views of individual military leaders. There are parts of Gorbachev's doctrinal agenda that segments of the Soviet military could find quite acceptable. For example, the Air Defense Forces might be quite pleased with greater emphasis on defensive operations in military planning. Other segments would have reason to be less pleased— e.g., the Strategic Rocket Forces could not find much comfort in the reduction in emphasis on nuclear forces.

The discussion that follows identifies each of the major elements of the new thinking. Each core concept is examined and placed in context, significant variants are described, and the instrumental utility of the concept is discussed. The traditionalists' or old thinkers' critiques are then presented, followed by an examination of the possible points of convergence between the new and old thinking on security.

The Gorbachev Doctrinal Framework

Given its instrumental origins, it is not surprising that Gorbachev's defense agenda has emerged piecemeal, rather than as a single master blueprint. Nevertheless, by mid-1987 the basic threads of Gorbachev's new political thinking on security had been articulated:

—War prevention is a fundamental component of Soviet military doctrine;
—No war—including nuclear war—can be considered a rational continuation of politics; and inadvertent paths to nuclear war are as likely, if not more likely, than deliberate paths;
—Political means of enhancing security are more effective than military-technical means;
—Security is mutual: Soviet security cannot be enhanced by increasing other states' insecurity;
—Reasonable sufficiency should be the basis for the future development of the combat capabilities of the Soviet armed forces;
—Soviet military strategy should be based on "defensive" (non-provocative) defense, not offensive capabilities and operations.

WAR PREVENTION IN SOVIET MILITARY DOCTRINE

War prevention has always been a keystone of Soviet national security policy. It was certainly a fundamental part of Stalin's policy vis-à-vis Nazi Germany in the late 1930s and early 1940s. Though Stalinist military doctrine assumed that a cataclysmic war between capitalism and socialism was inevitable, Stalin's goal was to postpone that eventuality as long as possible.

One of Khrushchev's first moves toward de-Stalinization was the revocation of the principle of the "inevitability of East-West war." As first secretary he demonstrated that—crisis-provoking policies notwithstanding—he was not actually eager to go to war and would do what was necessary to avoid it.

Brezhnev proved to be even more cautious, shying away from actions that posed a risk of direct confrontation. Yet, despite this strong and enduring *de facto* policy of avoiding war, war avoidance never attained a formal place in Soviet military doctrine.[20]

NEW THINKING. One of the hallmarks of Gorbachev's new political thinking on security was the formal shift in emphasis in military doctrine to prevent war. Authoritative Soviet political and military sources now unambiguously state that preventing war is the fundamental goal of Soviet military doctrine.[21] Gorbachev has also chosen to re-emphasize that the Party does not consider nuclear war between East and West to be inevitable.[22] This places a stamp of ideological correctness on the redirection of military doctrine towards avoiding war.

The formal inclusion of war prevention in Soviet military doctrine provides Gorbachev with a legitimate doctrinal basis for trading off current forces and future increments of military power (which might be useful should war occur), for increments of politico-military stability (which might reduce the probability of war). This lends greater weight generally to politico-military considerations (such as strategic stability), and particularly places politico-diplomatic efforts, such as arms control and actions that reduce regional and international tensions, on par with military technical efforts. It offers a doctrinal basis for attempting to reduce tensions and engage in truly cooperative behavior.

---

20. This curious fact is also noted by Akhromeyev, "Doktrina predotvrashcheniya voyny," p. 25.
21. D.T. Yazov, "Voyennaya doktrina Varshavskogo Dogovora—doktrina zashchity mira i sotsializma," *Krasnaya zvezda*, July 28, 1987, p. 2; Akhromeyev, "Slava i gordost'," p. 1.
22. *Programma kommunisticheskoy partii*, p. 50.

COUNTERPOINT AND CONVERGENCE. The incorporation of war prevention into Soviet military doctrine is perhaps the least controversial component of the new thinking. Indeed, it is not really a substantive change at all, but more of a political highlighting. An inability to develop the high-confidence capabilities that would provide for meaningful victory in strategic nuclear war has long tempered Soviet military doctrine and strategy, notwithstanding propaganda to the contrary.[23] There do not appear to be any overt disagreements with the thesis that war between socialism and capitalism can be avoided indefinitely.

There are differences of opinion, however, over the best strategy for preventing nuclear war. In particular, skeptics take a much more pessimistic view of intentions of the West. As would be expected, as policy moves from concept to implementation, disputes arise, as described in detail below.

INADVERTENT VS. DELIBERATE PATHS TO NUCLEAR WAR

Closely related to the theme of nuclear war prevention is the new emphasis on inadvertent paths to nuclear war. In the past, the problem of accidental nuclear war received cursory treatment in Soviet military doctrine. Deliberate paths to nuclear war were the dominant scenarios.[24] The new thinkers, however, have given the threat of inadvertent nuclear war equal, if not greater prominence.

NEW THINKING. The new thinking argues that in the contemporary era, war, especially nuclear war, cannot be considered a rational continuation of politics; and that inadvertent paths to nuclear war are as likely, if not more likely, than deliberate paths.

For the new thinkers, the deliberate path to nuclear war—the cold rational decision to initiate a nuclear strike for political gain—is an increasingly remote possibility.[25] The roots of this view were discernible in Brezhnev's 1977 Tula

---

23. See Stephen M. Meyer, "Soviet Nuclear Operations," in Ashton B. Carter, John D. Steinbruner, and Charles A. Zraket, eds., *Managing Nuclear Operations* (Washington, D.C.: Brookings, 1987), chapter 15.

24. See Stephen M. Meyer, "Soviet Perspectives on the Paths to Nuclear War," in Graham T. Allison, Joseph S. Nye, Jr., and Albert Carnesale, eds., *Hawks, Doves, and Owls* (New York: Norton, 1985), chapter 7, pp. 167–205.

25. See Vitaly Zhurkin, Sergei Karaganov, and Andrei Kortunov, "Vyzovy bezopasnosti—staryye i novyye," *Kommunist*, No. 1 (1988), pp. 43, 46. In Gorbachev's speech in Murmansk in fall 1987 he noted that if one gauged the threat facing the Soviet Union by the rhetoric and statements of Western leaders, then the threat would not appear to be declining. However, he pointedly observed, such words are always forgotten in a few days. See "Rech' tovarishcha Gorbacheva," p. 2.

speech, where he argued that the aggressor could not expect to fight and win a nuclear war.[26] But Brezhnev only went half-way, leaving unresolved the question of the defender's—presumably the Soviet Union's—prospects of winning a nuclear war.

Gorbachev and the new thinkers have gone much further. Nuclear war is not war in the traditional sense and cannot, therefore, be considered a rational means for seeking political goals—even for capitalist states.[27] The risks of nuclear escalation inherent in any East-West military engagement imply that war in general can no longer be considered a means for achieving political goals.[28]

Instead, the new thinkers perceive a growing threat of inadvertent nuclear war. They see an obvious tradeoff here: while ever greater quantities of nuclear arms make deliberate nuclear war unthinkable, they simultaneously raise the likelihood of nuclear war by accident or miscalculation. Higher levels of nuclear armaments, they argue, could even undermine the deterrent value of strategic nuclear parity.[29] Hence, they see parity *at lower levels* as enhancing Soviet security with respect to both deliberate and inadvertent causes of nuclear war.

In the new thinking, therefore, nuclear war is portrayed as a threat in its own right—irrespective of its political content. The great danger, as one Central Committee consultant put it (in most un-Marxist terms) is that "nuclear war could begin and end without political decisions."[30] In other words, technology, not politics, might be the cause of nuclear war.

---

26. "Rech' tovarishcha L.I. Brezhneva," p. 2.

27. See Yu. Zhilin, "Faktor vremeni v yardernyy vek," *Kommunist*, No. 11 (1986), p. 115. This is a serious revision of a long-standing Leninist principle of military doctrine.

28. Gorbachev is quoted to this effect by Akhromeyev, "Doktrina predotvrashcheniya voyny," p. 25. Reinforcing this image, Soviet discussions have begun to emphasize that the presence of nuclear power plants, chemical industry facilities, and hydroelectric complexes in the likely theater of war means that the destructiveness of conventional war will be unprecedented. See comments by Akhromeyev in "Dogovor po RSD-RMD: Protsess ratifikatsii," *Vestnik ministerstva inostrannykh del SSSR*, No. 5 (March 15, 1988), p. 23; also Zhurkin, Karaganov, and Kortunov, "Vyzovy bezopasnosti—staryye i novyye," p. 43. There is, of course, a strong propagandistic element at work here, but the issue is nonetheless a valid one.

29. This notion was sanctioned by Gorbachev in "Politicheskiy doklad tsentral'nogo komiteta KPSS XXVII s'yezdu KPSS," *27th S'yezd KPSS, Stenograficheskiy otchet #1* (Moscow: Politizdat, 1986), p. 88.

30. Yu. Zhilin, "Faktor vremeni," p. 120. It is important to realize how heretical this notion is from the standpoint of traditional Marxist-Leninist ideology, which holds that all international conflict is class-based. War is seen as an act of political and political-economic purpose and therefore *must* begin with political decisions. In contrast, the new thinkers seem to be particularly concerned with the way in which military technology is eroding decision-making time. Ibid.,

The new thinkers—Gorbachev included—have also expanded this discussion to the ideological front, arguing that, contrary to traditional Marxist-Leninist interpretations, capitalism need not be inherently militaristic.[31] Thus, the argument that the threat of nuclear war is technological rather than political becomes ideologically acceptable.

What is the instrumental utility of making inadvertent nuclear war a serious threat to Soviet security while simultaneously downplaying the threat of deliberate attack? This notion establishes the ideological and doctrinal context for reducing the role of military power in Soviet foreign policy in general, and for undertaking major strategic force reductions in particular. It is the basis for arguing that Soviet security can be increased by reducing strategic forces in step with corresponding Western reductions. This is not a repudiation of past Soviet policies. Rather, it is an ideological justification: the East-West security dilemma has reached a qualitatively new stage, driven by new technologies and capabilities for destruction, while at the same time capitalism is maturing to a less militaristic stage. Thus, new approaches to security become possible, if not required.

COUNTERPOINT. While it initially scoffed at the dangers of its own accidental or "unsanctioned" nuclear use in the 1960s, in subsequent years the Soviet military has implemented measures designed to limit the possibility of such events.[32] Since the early 1980s, technological and procedural changes have been underway to decrease further the likelihood of unsanctioned or unauthorized Soviet nuclear use.[33] Thus, it is clear that the military's appreciation of the dangers of inadvertent nuclear war has grown over time.

Nevertheless, military analysts have attempted to restore some "balance" to the consideration of accidental versus deliberate paths to nuclear war in doctrinal discussions. While acknowledging the dangers of accidental nuclear

---

pp. 119–120; Dobrynin, "Za bez'yadernyy mir," p. 19. Ye. Velikhov, "Prizyv k peremenam," *Kommunist*, No. 1 (1988), pp. 50–51.
31. M. S. Gorbachev, "Oktyabr' i perestroyka; Revolyutsiya prodolzhayetsya," *Kommunist*, No. 17 (1987), pp. 31–32; Ye. Primakov, "Leninskiy analiz imperializma i sovremennost'," *Kommunist*, No. 9 (1986), p. 109; G. Arbatov, "Militarizm i sovremennoye obshchestvo," *Kommunist*, No. 2 (1987), pp. 113–114.
32. See Meyer, "Soviet Nuclear Operations."
33. These include mechanical and electronic control systems, personnel reliability programs, and new handling and deployment methods. (Interviews.) The issue was first broached publicly by former Minister of Defense Dmitri Ustinov in 1982; see D. Ustinov, "Otvesti ugrozu yadernoy voyny," *Pravda*, July 12, 1982, p. 2, and remains an important consideration. See D.T. Yazov, *Na strazhe sotsializma i mira* (Moscow: Voyenizdat, 1987), p. 32. General of the Army Yazov is Minister of Defense.

war, they insist that—contrary to the new thinkers' hopes—the West continues to believe quite firmly that war is a continuation of politics, and thus the threat of deliberate attack to the Soviet Union is real. For these Soviet observers the physical evidence is obvious: the West continues to buy the forces it needs to start either a nuclear war or a conventional war.[34] Accordingly, as Minister of Defense Dmitri Yazov emphasizes, the Soviet armed forces must be prepared to fight all forms of war—nuclear or conventional.[35]

The issue here seems to be one of the perception of relative risk. How far can the Soviet Union go in implementing measures to reduce the risk of accidental nuclear war before impinging on militarily important capabilities, and thereby raising the risk of deliberate nuclear war? The suggestion by some new thinkers that unilateral Soviet moves may be desirable is seen by more traditional ideological elements in the Soviet leadership as increasing the danger of aggressive American behavior. This would in turn, they believe, increase the likelihood of a U.S.–Soviet confrontation and, ultimately, nuclear war.

CONVERGENCE. While most Western discussions treat the threat of accidental nuclear war as a technical problem, it is first and foremost a political-ideological issue in Soviet discussions. This means that in Soviet policy-making the relative emphasis placed on inadvertent war versus deliberate war scenarios is more a matter of political-ideological interpretation than military-technical analysis. Thus, it is unlikely that there will ever be convergence on this issue. Gorbachev and the new thinkers must highlight the dangers of inadvertent nuclear war; the ideological conservatives and the military establishment must emphasize the dangers of deliberate nuclear war.

The relative dominance of scenarios of inadvertent war over those of deliberate war will continue as long as it is useful to the Gorbachev program and there is no consensus against it in the political leadership. In other words, Gorbachev or a like-minded future General Secretary does not need a consensus to support this view; the absence of a consensus against it is sufficient.[36]

---

34. D. T. Yazov, *Na strazhe sotsializma i mira* (Moscow: Voyenizdat, 1987), pp. 30–32; V. Serebryannikov, "S uchetom real'nostey yadernogo veka," *Kommunist voorezhennykh sil*, No. 3 (1987), pp. 10, 13–15; D. Volkogonov, "Imperativy yadernogo veka," *Krasnaya zvezda*, May 22, 1987, pp. 2–3. Serebryannikov is a General-Lieutenant of Aviation, Doctor of Philosophy, and professor; Volkogonov is a General-Colonel, Doctor of Philosophical Sciences, and professor. He is now the head of the Ministry of Defense's Military Historical Institute.
35. Yazov, *Na strazhe sotsializma i mira*, p. 31.
36. Khrushchev was able to implement many of his most controversial programs because the

POLITICAL MEANS OF GUARANTEEING SECURITY

Given the new thinking on war avoidance and accidental war, an increased emphasis on political means of guaranteeing security begins to look attractive. Of course, political means have always figured prominently in Soviet security policy. Treaties, agreements, and political-economic relationships have long been used to create a better security environment.[37] However, few if any of the Soviet Union's international partners have been seen as reliable or benign. Therefore, the Soviet political leadership viewed military power as the fundamental basis for maintaining Soviet security. Political means were merely an adjunct to military-technical means.

NEW THINKING. Here again Gorbachev established the initial direction of the discussion. In concert with the new emphasis on war avoidance, Gorbachev argued that "new realities" meant that political means, rather than military-technical means, had become the primary tools for guaranteeing the security of the Soviet Union. He posited that political means may be the only means for ultimately solving Soviet security problems.[38]

This evolution towards political solutions is portrayed as a consequence of the military technologies of the "nuclear-space" era: modern weapons make it impossible for states to defend themselves by military-technical means alone. War means catastrophe. Negotiations and diplomacy, therefore, can buy the Soviet Union more security than could allocation of additional defense rubles.[39] Reducing the threat facing the Soviet Union accomplishes more than countering it. An example of this approach was offered by Chief of the General Staff Sergei Akhromeyev when he was asked why the Soviet Union was giving up more weapons than the United States in the INF (intermediate-range nuclear forces) Treaty. He replied that it was worth the trade since the removal of the American Pershing II and GLCMs (ground-launched cruise missiles) completely eliminated the threat of limited nuclear war to the European USSR.[40] From this perspective, similarly, halting American Strategic Defense Initiative (SDI) deployments via negotiation would be seen as far more efficient and effective than developing and deploying countermeasures.

---

opposition was unable to organize against him. He rarely had a majority of the political leadership supporting him.
37. For a Soviet history of these efforts, see A.A. Gromyko and B.N. Ponomarev, *Istoriya vneshney politiki SSSR,* Volumes 1 and 2 (Moscow: Nauka, 1986).
38. "Politicheskiy doklad," p. 86.
39. Ye. Primakov, "Novaya filosofiya vneshney politiki," *Pravda,* July 10, 1987, p. 4.
40. See A. Gorokhov, "Na puti yadernomu razoruzheniyu," *Pravda,* December 16, 1987. p. 4.

COUNTERPOINT. Not surprisingly, Gorbachev's emphasis on political means for guaranteeing Soviet security—and the consequent subordination of military-technical means—provoked a reaction from more traditional national security elements. For example, Minister of Defense Yazov and First Deputy Chief of the General Staff Varennikov felt compelled to point out that while, from the Soviet perspective, providing for security may seem to be increasingly a political task, the United States and NATO do not appear to see it that way.[41] These critics point out that the West remains committed to attaining military-technical superiority over the Soviet Union and the Warsaw Pact, adducing as evidence alleged Western failures to respond to unilateral Soviet initiatives and U.S. duplicity in arms control.[42] Politburo member Ligachev, in his statement before the Supreme Soviet Foreign Affairs Commission reviewing the INF Treaty, noted that there are many questions about the U.S. commitment to comply with arms control in general, and the INF Treaty in particular.[43]

As a consequence, more traditional thinkers argue, such thinking may be correct, but implementation of such policies is premature: Political means cannot work without the equal balance of adequate military-technical means. Military writers warn that if the adversary perceives weakness (i.e., an absence of military-technical preparedness), it will not be restrained from aggression.[44]

Until mid-1987 Marshal Akhromeyev—the military man most closely identified with Gorbachev's new political thinking on security—appeared to give unflinching support to Gorbachev's views on the dominance of political means over military-technical means of providing security. This is interesting, since Akhromeyev's primary responsibility as chief of the general staff is to guarantee the military-technical security of the Soviet state. However, by fall

---

41. Yazov, *Na strazhe sotsializma i mira*, pp. 5–20; V. Varennikov, "Na strazhe mira i bezopasnosti," *Partiynaya zhizn*, No. 5 (1987), pp. 11–12. General Varennikov is the First Deputy Chief of the General Staff. There is a curious impression that General Yazov has been a supporter of Gorbachev's new political thinking on security. This is clearly not the case. Even a cursory reading of Yazov's comments reveals that while he "mouths the words," he summarily criticizes the ideas and alters their meaning.
42. See Yazov, *Na strazhe sotsializma i mira*, p. 19; Marshal V.G. Kulikov, "Strazh mira i sotsializma," *Krasnaya zvezda*, February 21, 1988, p. 2. Marshal Kulikov is commander in chief of the Warsaw Pact and a first deputy Minister of Defense.
43. Of course, Ligachev never said that these were his questions, but the implications were obvious. See "Protsess ratifikatsii Dogovora po RSD-RMD nachalsya V Prezidiume Verkhovnogo Soveta SSSR," *Vestnik ministerstva inostrannykh del SSSR*, No. 4 (March 1, 1988), pp. 12–19.
44. Varennikov, "Na strazhe mira i bezopasnosti," p. 12.

1987 he had shifted the tone of his argument towards a more cautious view, arguing that military-technical solutions make equally important contributions to avoiding war and to restraining the aggressive impulses of probable enemies.[45]

CONVERGENCE. There is general appreciation in the Soviet Union that peacetime military activities have important political dimensions, and Soviet military procurement and deployment decisions do take into account a reading of the political environment. It follows that political efforts—whether improving the international environment, improving bilateral relations, or engaging in arms control—can affect military requirements. To the extent that defense resources are constrained in the USSR—i.e., that the defense constituency cannot do everything it would like at once—then political actions can help sort out military-technical priorities.[46] For example, if political accommodation and arms control could at least constrain, if not eliminate, the need to counter SDI, then R&D (research and development) and procurement priorities could continue to emphasize improving systems for conventional war. Obviously, this is one part of a politico-military strategy that both new and old thinkers can agree on.

In the West, Gorbachev's call for increased reliance on political means is always interpreted in the most benign fashion. There is, however, a side to this approach that should make it more worrisome to the West, while also making it more acceptable to Soviet traditionalists. That is: political means also include active measures to divide and weaken NATO politically. They also imply enhancing Soviet political authority around the world as a counterweight to American political presence. This is, of course, a direct copy of Khrushchev's strategy. To the extent that enhanced use of political means can increase Soviet political "presence" while weakening the political bonds of the Western Alliance, then the new thinkers and the traditionalists will find common ground.

---

45. Compare and contrast Akhromeyev, "Slava i gordost'," and Akhromeyev, "Doktrina predotvrashcheniya voyny." It is as though two different individuals wrote those articles. Perhaps this change in tone is due to: (1) his failure to be named Minister of Defense after Marshal Sokolov's ouster; (2) peer pressure from his more traditional colleagues; or (3) concern over the growing influence of the non-military "new thinkers" on defense policy. For whatever reason, Akhromeyev has changed his tone toward the Gorbachev defense agenda.
46. There are two forms of resource constraints that must be considered: explicit constraints imposed by decisions to limit resource flows to defense, and implicit constraints that reflect scarcity of resources in the Soviet economy (e.g., microprocessors).

SECURITY IS MUTUAL

Since the end of World War II, Soviet military doctrine seems to have viewed the Soviet security dilemma as a zero-sum game: the USSR's own security could best be guaranteed by posing an overwhelming threat to its neighbors, whether putative adversaries or friends. For a prime example of the application of this approach, one need only recall the massive Soviet buildup of nuclear and conventional forces facing China beginning in 1964. It is impossible to determine whether the underlying intent was eventual conquest, a somewhat less ambitious goal of political-economic dominance, merely deterrence by defense, or some combination of these. But the basic fact remained that Soviet leaders felt that Soviet security was enhanced by increasing the insecurity of the Soviet Union's neighbors.

NEW THINKING. Gorbachev's new political thinking turns this zero-sum view on its head. Now, say the new thinkers, Soviet security must be viewed as inevitably intertwined with American and, indeed, global security.[47] Security is a mutual problem. Once again this is presented as a direct consequence of the nature of nuclear war. Since no country can defend itself by military-technical means alone, national and international security are indivisible; the other side's security concerns must be taken into account.[48]

Obviously, this has important implications for military policy. First, it means that decisions about new weapons and deployments must be based on more than just military-technical and military-operational criteria. How other countries' perceptions of threat will be affected must be assessed; the military power of one state must not even *appear* to threaten other states.[49] Second, it means that political solutions, rather than military-technical ones, come to the forefront of policy.[50] This, in turn, presupposes a willingness to take into account the interests of adversaries and, above all, to make concessions.[51] There can be no denying that, since the beginning of 1987, traces of this principle have been reflected in Soviet political-military behavior.

47. Gorbachev, "Politicheskiy doklad," p. 87; Dobrynin, "Za bez'yadernyy mir," p. 24. Interestingly, this has been a theme in the Soviet academic-institute literature for a number of years.
48. Dobrynin, "Za bez'yadernyy mir," p. 24; Primakov, "Novaya filosofiya."
49. Semeyko, "Vmesto gor oruzhiya."
50. Vitaly Zhurkin, Sergei Karaganov, and Andrei Kortunov argue that relying exclusively on military-technical means is, by definition, setting one's own security against the security of others. "Reasonable Sufficiency—Or How to Break the Vicious Circle," *New Times*, No. 40 (October 12, 1987), pp. 13–15; and "O razumnoy dostatochnosti," *SShA: Ekonomika, politika, ideologiya*, No. 12 (1987), p. 14. Zhurkin is the Director of the Institute for West European Studies. Karaganov and Kortunov are senior researchers at the Institute for the Study of the United States and Canada.
51. Zhurkin, Karaganov, and Kortunov, "Reasonable Sufficiency," p. 13; Zhurkin, Karaganov,

COUNTERPOINT. Disagreements over the thesis of interdependent security have a distinctly philosophical and ideological flavor. Critics of the idea of the mutuality of security take refuge in Marxist-Leninist orthodoxy: It is the political-social essence of a state, not its force posture, that determines whether its doctrine is threatening (offensive) or non-threatening (defensive).[52] The Soviet Union and the Warsaw Pact states cannot be perceived as a threat by anyone, they argue, because they are classless socialist societies. Thus, Soviet military preparations for the legitimate defense of socialism cannot threaten anyone no matter what the scale of those efforts.

Skeptical Soviet commentators observe that, despite Soviet peaceful initiatives and numerous concessions, the West continues to build raw military-technical power with the aim of acquiring military superiority.[53] The failure to induce the United States to join the unilateral Soviet nuclear test moratorium is one often-cited example. At the same time, they detail what they describe as past U.S. duplicity in arms control. Indeed, they note that even as the INF agreement, with numerous Soviet concessions, was being signed, the West was already planning ways to circumvent the agreements by deploying "compensating" nuclear forces.[54] In short, there appears to be a substantial body of opinion—political and military—that rejects the premise that anything the USSR might do to enhance its security could be interpreted as threatening to truly peaceful states.

CONVERGENCE. It is not obvious where there are significant points of convergence here. The suspension of the historically dominant "us-them" dichotomy in Soviet ideology and foreign policy would seem to be heavily dependent on the context (for example, the World War II alliance against the Nazis), the political power of the general secretary, and personalities. This perspective is likely to affect Soviet military doctrine only as long as the general secretary has the political capabilities to pursue policies along this line. There is no reason to assume that this view of the mutuality of security has any independent durability over time.

---

and Kortunov, "O razumnoy dostatochnosti," p. 14; and Dobrynin, "Za bez'yadernyy mir," p. 24.

52. Yazov, *Na strazhe sotsializma i mira*, p. 29; Akhromeyev, "Doktrina predotvrashcheniya voyny;" and Kostev, "Nasha voyennaya doktrina," p. 10.

53. Varennikov, "Na strazhe mira i bezopasnosti," p. 11; Yazov, *Na strazhe sotsializma i mira*, pp. 16, 19; Kostev, "Nasha voyennaya doktrina," pp. 9–10.

54. Yazov, *Na strazhe sotsializma i mira*, p. 19; Akhromeyev, "Doktrina predotvrashcheniya voyny," pp. 23–24. American and British suggestions that NATO must build up its theater nuclear firepower to compensate for the removal of the INF systems has been a major theme in Soviet political and military discussions.

REASONABLE SUFFICIENCY

Of all the ideas falling under the umbrella of new political thinking on security, none is more enigmatic than the notion of "reasonable sufficiency." There is general agreement among Soviet new and old thinkers that the Soviet defense posture should be based on sufficiency.[55] Differences emerge when the issues of "what is sufficient?" and "how is sufficiency determined?" are addressed.

Moreover, there is a curious—some might say comedic—disagreement among new thinkers over the meaning of the term and how it differs from past Soviet policy. For some Soviet commentators, it connotes a shift away from the action-reaction policy of the past to one of internal determination of defense requirements. Soviet weapons programs and deployments in the past were largely the product of reactions to Western programs, it is explained. Now—under reasonable sufficiency—the Soviet Union will procure only those weapons that are necessary to fulfill the defense goals it sets for itself. Correspondingly, the characteristics of those weapons would be a function of Soviet-determined requirements, not emulatory or reactive behavior.

Other Soviet spokesmen describe reasonable sufficiency in precisely opposite terms. Unlike the past, they say, where Soviet weapons programs and deployments were determined by internally-set defense requirements and goals, now the Soviet Union will procure new weapons only in strict reaction to Western military deployments. Reasonable sufficiency implies the strict maintenance of parity by matching Western military efforts.

It is quite clear that these are two completely opposite notions of what Soviet defense policy was, and what reasonable sufficiency implies. This division of views does not break down along obvious institutional lines, nor does it divide among new and old thinkers. It suggests confusion, not political or institutional alignment. Ironically, Gorbachev's best interests are served by this confusion, making reasonable sufficiency a wild card that can be applied as the situation suits him. Reasonable sufficiency can be invoked to call into question any defense program that the general secretary perceives as superfluous to Soviet security.

NEW THINKING. The notion of reasonable sufficiency first appeared in Gorbachev's political report to the 27th Party Congress, where he said that

---

55. Brezhnev first raised the notion of sufficiency for defense in his Tula speech in 1977. See "Rech' tovarishcha L.I. Brezhneva," p. 2.

the Soviet Union would limit its nuclear potential to levels of reasonable sufficiency.[56] But he qualified this by stating that the character and level of reasonable sufficiency would be determined by the actions of the United States and NATO. In other words, Gorbachev's invocation of reasonable sufficiency was along the lines of the second interpretation noted above: an action-reaction formulation. Later, reasonable sufficiency was generalized to the entire military posture, and was purportedly adopted as the basis for Warsaw Pact military planning in May 1987.[57]

One of the clearest elaborations of the conceptual underpinnings of reasonable sufficiency was written by Lev Semeyko, a senior researcher at the Institute for the Study of USA and Canada, in the government newspaper *Izvestia* in August of 1987.[58] The old political thinking, he argued, assumed that "more is better" in security affairs; acquiring military superiority over an opponent was a necessary and sufficient condition for victory in war. In contrast, the new political thinking—as captured by the notion of reasonable sufficiency—recognizes that this is no longer the case.

Reasonable sufficiency, according to Semeyko, has three dimensions: political, military-technical, and economic. The political aspect captures the non-aggressive orientation of Soviet military doctrine. Priority is placed on political solutions to security issues (through arms control, for example). The military dimension of reasonable sufficiency ties together several other principles of the new political thinking on security. The military power of the Soviet Union must be sufficient to absorb any attack under the worst imaginable conditions, and to rebuff the enemy, while at the same time not be so great as to threaten the security of other states. There should be no unreasonable surplus of military potential.[59] Manifestations of reasonable sufficiency should be evident in the structure, character, composition, and deployment of Soviet forces.

Lastly, Semeyko argues that the economic aspect of reasonable sufficiency recognizes that there is a law of diminishing returns in the arms race: marginal improvements of military power come at ever greater cost. However,

---

56. "Politicheskiy doklad," p. 90.
57. "O voyennoy doktrine gosudarstv uchastnikov Varshavskogo Dogovora," *Krasnaya zvezda*, May 30, 1987, pp. 1–2.
58. Semeyko, "Vmesto gor oruzhiya," p. 5.
59. On this point others have been far more explicit, arguing that the notion of accumulating enough military power to balance all potential adversaries simultaneously is unrealistic and dangerous. See Zhurkin, Karaganov, and Kortunov, "Reasonable Sufficiency," p. 14; and, by the same authors, "O razumnoy dostatochnosti," p. 20.

those increments of military power add less and less to the net military capability of the state.

Confusion and disagreement among the new thinkers reared its head once they attempted to flesh out the policy implications of reasonable sufficiency. Consonant with Gorbachev's economic agenda, some of the discussions accented the political and economic implications of reasonable sufficiency. They posited that the underlying purpose of current U.S. military policy was to manipulate the arms race to bleed the Soviet economy, in part by compelling the Soviet Union to buy inappropriate military hardware (a thesis echoed by Gorbachev.)[60] Reasonable sufficiency could neutralize this Western strategy via resort to *asymmetric* responses: reacting to U.S. and NATO actions with offsetting rather than emulating responses. Here the goal is to maintain strict parity of potentials and capabilities, not parity of categories of weapons. Thus, for example, the Soviet Union would respond to SDI with an offensive buildup, not an "SDI-skiy" program.[61]

Others have pushed the bounds of asymmetry further, into the domain of unilateral Soviet actions. They argue for a unilateral restructuring of Soviet forces, consistent with reasonable sufficiency and with other tenets of the new thinking on security.[62] That is, the Soviet Union would not wait for the West to agree to mutual force changes. Rather, the Soviet Union could go forward in restructuring its military as it desired—keeping in mind that all such changes would represent a net increase in Soviet security.[63]

---

60. Primakov, "Novaya filosofiya"; Zhurkin, Karaganov, and Kortunov, "Vyzovy bezopasnosti," pp. 47–48; and "Rech' tovarishcha Gorbacheva," p. 3.

61. Zhurkin, Karaganov, and Kortunov, "Reasonable Sufficiency," p. 14. These authors elaborate further in, "O razumnoy dostatochnosti," pp. 16–17. It is important to understand that some Soviet writers are using the word "asymmetry" primarily to connote differences between the technical forms of the threat and the response. They mean non-emulating responses, which presumes that equivalent military potential is retained and that resource requirements would be more manageable (by Soviet standards).

62. Zhurkin, Karaganov and Kortunov, "O razumnoy dostatochnosti," pp. 17–20; Semeyko, "Vmesto gor oruzhiya." Only one military officer, General-Colonel Gareyev, a deputy chief of the General Staff, initially seemed to endorse the unilateral restructuring of Soviet forces. See "Voyennaya doktrina organizatsii Varshavskogo Dogovora i eye prelomleniye v mezhdunarod-noy politika," *Vestnik Ministerstva Inostrannykh Del SSSR*, No. 1 (June 22, 1987), pp. 52–62. However, it is reported that Gareyev was disappointed with that particular press conference, feeling that his views were not properly reported. Irrespective of Gareyev's actual views, other Soviet military officials asserted that this idea was not the position of the Ministry of Defense. (Interviews.) It should be kept in mind that the Soviet forces have been undergoing unilateral restructuring—what military analysts have traditionally referred to as force modernization—on an almost continual basis since 1946. Gareyev may have been referring to ongoing changes in Soviet forces.

63. Zhurkin, Karaganov and Kortunov, "O razumnoy dostatochnosti," pp. 18. See also Gareyev's comments in "Voyennaya doktrina organizatsii Varshavskogo Dogovora." Some involved

Negotiated deep reductions in strategic forces is a concept that has been embraced by all the new thinkers. Mutual reductions of 50% are seen as the first logical step of the process, and as such is the official Soviet negotiating position in START (Strategic Arms Reduction Talks).[64] The new thinkers argue, however, that the ultimate near-term goal should be mutual cuts of 95% in strategic forces.[65]

Even the possibility of unilateral Soviet force reductions has been suggested.[66] Past unilateral measures such as the Soviet nuclear test moratorium did not undermine the Soviet Union's security, or so they argue. Unilateral reductions (restructuring), in combination with bilateral and multilateral actions, could contribute significantly to Soviet security by reducing the overall level of the East-West military confrontation.[67]

COUNTERPOINT. In contrast to the new thinkers, those associated with the more traditional national security establishment focus attention on the military dimension of sufficiency. Acknowledging that the "old way of thinking"—that security was proportional to military forces deployed—can no longer be considered valid in the strategic nuclear arena, they center their concern on the importance of maintaining strict parity.[68] This involves careful analysis, forecasting of Western military trends, and timely procurement of forces needed to compensate for any deviations from strict parity.

The centrality of strategic nuclear parity is captured by the refusal of the skeptics to use the term "reasonable sufficiency." Instead they prefer to speak in terms of "defensive sufficiency," or just "sufficiency." While acknowledging the foolhardiness of matching every Western military development with

---

in the development of this new political thinking have argued that if the USSR waits for mutual agreements, nothing will ever happen. They fear political inertia and stressed the belief that there is a three-year window to redirect Soviet military policy. Soviet military officials disagreed with Gareyev's emphasis on unilateral restructuring. (Interviews.)

64. A. Arbatov, "Glubokoye sokrashcheniye," (Part 1) pp. 10–22; and by the same author, "Glubokoye sokrashcheniye strategicheskikh vooruzheniye," *MEMO*, No. 5 (1988), pp. 18–30.

65. *Strategic Stabilnost' v usloviyakh radikal'nykh sokrashcheniye yaedernykh vooruzheniy* (Moscow: Komitet sovetskkh uchenykh v zashchitu mira, protiv yadernoy ugrozy, 1987).

66. Zhurkin, Karaganov, and Kortunov, "O razumnoy dostatochnosti," pp. 17–20. I believe that this pushing of the policy boundaries is a direct consequence of the competition for influence among the new thinkers, and between this group and the more traditional elements in Soviet national security policy. As such, I fail to find any evidence that such notions reflect policy at the present time.

67. This is not a widely shared perspective among new thinkers, and some openly disagree with their colleagues who advocate unilateral Soviet reductions in the name of reasonable sufficiency.

68. Yazov, "Voyennaya doktrina"; Varennikov, "Na strazhe mira i bezopasnosti"; Serebryannikov, "S uchetom real'nostey yadernogo veka," p. 10.

a duplicate Soviet effort, they nonetheless emphasize the importance of possessing every type of weapon and maintaining strict strategic parity.[69]

Sufficiency in general purpose forces is allowed more latitude by the skeptics, perhaps because "strict" parity is impossible to define for highly complex conventional force structures. Here the criteria are given as: forces and means sufficient to ensure the peaceful work of socialist labor, and sufficient to defend the socialist alliance reliably.[70] Sufficiency is not necessarily pegged to parity or even equivalence; it can mean superiority as perceived by the other side.

While the more traditional thinkers agree that asymmetries in the European theater need to be corrected, they marshal considerable evidence demonstrating that all but a few of the meaningful asymmetries favor NATO.[71] In particular, they include naval forces in their assessments, arguing that to count only land forces biases the picture against the Warsaw Pact. Thus, one cannot talk about alleged Soviet advantages in land forces absent consideration of U.S. naval power when theater balances are calculated.[72] When all is considered, they assert, the Warsaw Pact military posture today is at the level of sufficiency.

In this respect, all military references to *perestroika* (restructuring) within the last year have been explicitly restricted to discipline, morale, and attitude issues.[73] They have summarily excluded any notion that *perestroika* is related to force structure questions. For the military, *perestroika* means improving the work habits of officers and soldiers, not changing the basic configuration of Soviet forces. These commentators correspondingly reject the suggestion that unilateral reductions could improve Soviet security; indeed, they argue that

69. Kostev, "Nasha voyennaya doktrina," p. 12; Yazov, *Na strazhe sotsializma i mira*, pp. 33–34.
70. See Yazov, "Voyennaya doktrina"; Yazov, *Na strazhe sotsializma i mira*, pp. 33–34, defines sufficiency as having forces sufficient to carry out the tasks of collective defense. Of course, military commentators proclaim that the Pact does not possess superiority and does not seek it, but they never dismiss its utility from a military standpoint (as they do dismiss the utility of strategic nuclear superiority). Akhromeyev, "Doktrina predotvrascheniya voyny," p. 26, defines sufficiency as having just enough forces to attain their objectives!
71. See, for example, V. Chernyshev, "O disbalansakh i asimmetrii," *Krasnaya zvezda*, January 28, 1988, p. 3.
72. Interviews. See S.F. Akhromeyev, "Chto kroyetsya za bryussel'skim zayavleniyem NATO," *Krasnaya zvezda*, March 20, 1988, p. 3. Soviet military spokesmen have added a new wrinkle to this issue by discussing NATO naval forces as "mobile groups" capable of devastating offensive actions against the rear areas of the Warsaw Pact. This is an explicit effort to develop a counter to Western concerns about Soviet tank army mobile groups (so-called operational maneuver groups).
73. See Yazov, *Na strazhe sotsializma i mira*, pp. 44–56; Kulikov, "Strazh mira i sotsializma," p. 2. Gareyev's early statement suggesting otherwise is an anomaly. See footnote 62.

such actions would magnify the threat.[74] Unilateral restructuring might be permissible, they suggest, but only as a means of improving the Soviet military posture, not of reducing force capabilities.

CONVERGENCE. There is good reason to believe that reasonable sufficiency will remain a political concept that will avoid explicit operational definitions. Otherwise, the idea would lose its political utility as a wild card for Gorbachev. However, as a consequence, some areas of convergence are likely.

The concept of strategic nuclear sufficiency has been on the professional military's agenda at least as far back as since at latest the early 1980s. Then Chief of the General Staff Nikolai Ogarkov very explicitly called into question the military utility of procuring additional nuclear weapons.[75] Given present-day military-technical and economic realities, strategic parity appears to be the endpoint of Soviet nuclear planning for the foreseeable future for both new and old thinkers alike. Strategic parity at lower levels is a corollary that is also acceptable, though divergence is likely to grow in proportion to the size of the proposed reduction in forces.[76]

The convergence points with respect to conventional forces are harder to detect. The traditionalist view—quite strongly expressed in a number of documents—is that sufficiency exists *now* on the Warsaw Pact side of central Europe.[77] Thus, sufficiency at lower levels in the theater is possible, but only with strictly matched compensating reductions on the NATO side.[78]

---

74. Akhromeyev, "Doktrina predotvrashcheniya voyny," p. 26; statements by General-Colonel Chervov in "Voyennaya doktrina organizatsii Varshavskogo Dogovora," p. 56. Chervov is the head of the General Staff directorate concerned with treaties and arms control. In contrast to the new thinkers' positive view of Khrushchev's unilateral conventional force cuts in the late 1950s and early 1960s, authoritative Soviet military spokesmen have described those episodes as "sorry experiences" that hurt Soviet security while providing only temporary economic benefits. See the interview with General Tret'yak, in Yuri Teplya, "Reliable Defense First and Foremost," *Moscow News*, No. 8 (1988), p. 12. Tret'yak, a General of the Army, was named commander in chief of the Air Defense Forces following the Matthias Rust affair. Interestingly, Tretyak was approved for that post by Gorbachev just eight months prior to this interview.

75. N.V. Ogarkov, "Zashchita sotsializma: opyt istorii i sovremennost'," *Krasnaya zvezda*, May 9, 1984, p. 2. Ogarkov suggested that some elements in the military did not subscribe to his notion that additional nuclear weapons had little marginal military utility.

76. Chervov, "Voyennaya doktrina organizatsii Varshavskogo Dogovora," p. 60; Yazov, "Voyennaya doktrina Varshavskogo Dogovora."

77. Noting that Warsaw Pact forces already are sufficient for defense, one military writer points out that in the future sufficiency can be maintained by: (1) keeping the present force levels on both sides, (2) mutual reductions to lower levels, or (3) increases to higher levels. He observes that, of course, the Soviet Union prefers the second alternative. P. Skorodenko, "Voyennyy paritet i printsip razumnoy dostatochnosti," *Kommunist vooruzhennykh sil*, No. 10 (1987), p. 17. See also Yazov, *Na strazhe sotsializma i mira*, pp. 33–41.

78. On this issue Gorbachev seems to be more in line with the old thinkers than he is with the new thinkers. See his interview in "Otvety M.S. Gorbacheva," p. 1.

Another apparent convergence point may be found on the question of reducing asymmetric advantages in the theater. Given the skeptics' portrayal of the situation in Europe as one favoring NATO, it is not hard for them to agree with the general principle of reducing advantages even through unilateral action. Of course, it is NATO asymmetric advantages that interest them, and NATO unilateral reductions. More usefully, the traditional thinkers seem prepared to consider the mutual reduction of asymmetries as part of formal agreements on the balance in Europe.[79]

DEFENSIVE DEFENSE

The Soviets have always maintained that their military doctrine was "defensive." This meant that the Soviet Union would only resort to military force when the "gains of socialism" were threatened. Its only goal in war would be defense of the socialist world. To support that defensive doctrine, however, the Soviet Union had a decidely offensive military strategy.[80] Its forces were configured and deployed to carry any conflict onto the territory of its opponent—to defeat and occupy its adversaries in theaters of war adjacent to the Soviet Union.

The new concept of "defensive defense" represents a significant departure from this formula; with it, Gorbachev's new political thinking crosses from the realm of doctrine to the realm of military strategy.

NEW THINKING. Defensive defense connotes a force posture and military strategy sufficient to repel a conventional attack, but incapable of conducting a surprise attack with massive offensive operations against the territory of the other side.[81] It is a military strategy of offensive self-denial: Soviet theater forces would be configured and deployed to stop an attack, hold against further penetration of Warsaw Pact territory, and then push enemy forces

79. V. Tatarnikov, "Do uroveney razumnoy dostatochnosti," Krasnaya zvezda, January 5, 1988, p. 3. Here again they insist strongly on including the naval balance as a major element of the asymmetric force balance. (Interviews.) See also Akhromeyev, "Chto kroyetsya za bryussel'skim zayavleniyem NATO."
80. Strategy refers to the operational principles for employing forces in war. See "Strategiya voyennaya," Voyennyy entsiklopedicheskiy slovar' (Moscow: Voyenizdat, 1986), pp. 711–712; P.A. Zhilin, "Istoriya voyennogo iskutsstva" (Moscow: Voyenizdat, 1986), p. 406. General-Lieutenant Zhilin, recently deceased, was head of the Military Historical Institute of the Ministry of Defense. See footnote 1 on doctrine.
81. A. Kokoshin, "Razvitiye voyennogo dela i sokrashcheniye vooruzhennykh sil i obychnykh vooruzheniy," MEMO, No. 1 (1988). See also the Warsaw Pact declaration: "O voyennoy doktrine gosudarstv—uchastnikov Varshavskogo Dogovora," Za novoye politicheskoye myshleniye v mezhdunarodnykh otnosheniyakh (Moscow: Politizdat, 1987), p. 564.

back to the border. This defensive force would not possess the capabilities to threaten the other side's territory.[82]

Proponents of defensive defense argue that the mutual fear of surprise attack in Europe can be eliminated by restructuring existing forces—that is, replacing offensive weapons with defensive weapons.[83] Thus, their motivation for this shift is partially military-political. They also point out that conventional weapons represent the largest part of a state's military spending. At least superficially then, the combination of reasonable sufficiency and defensive defense suggests an opportunity for significant reductions of the defense burden.[84]

COUNTERPOINT. Among all the activities of the new thinkers, none strikes more at a traditional preserve of Soviet military professionalism than this intrusion into the realm of military strategy for theater war. As the strongest proponents of defensive defense point out, moreover, nothing is as much anathema to traditional Soviet military thinking as is a defense-dominant theater strategy and force posture.[85]

The opposing voices have reacted with according vigor. First, they strongly assert that individual weapons systems cannot be isolated from a complex conventional force structure and characterized as offensive or defensive. How a weapon is employed—the strategy that dictates its use and the purposes to which it is put—determines whether it is offensive or defensive.[86]

82. A. Kokoshin and V. Larionov, "Kurskaya bitva v svete sovremennoy oboronitel'noy doktriny," *MEMO*, No. 8 (1987), pp. 32–40, at p. 37, argue that the idea of needing to carry the war to an enemy's territory from the very beginning of the conflict is unscientific and non-analytic, and that it precludes proper thinking about defense! All Soviet participants in these discussions—pro and con—are adamant that the notion of "defensive defense" applies only to theater warfare. In their view, it cannot apply to strategic or theater nuclear war. (Interviews.) In particular, while agitating for movement towards mutual defensive postures in the theater, Soviet "new thinkers" reject the idea that the U.S. and the USSR could move to mutual strategic defensive defense along the road suggested by President Reagan in his SDI speech of March 1983. This philosophical and doctrinal inconsistency is explained by the vast destructiveness of nuclear weapons, which they claim invalidates any notion of defensive postures at the strategic nuclear level. The implications of this curious—but not surprising—perspective are discussed in greater detail below.
83. Zhurkin, Karaganov, and Kortunov, "Vyzovy bezopasnosti," p. 45; Kokoshin and Larionov, "Kurskaya bitva"; Kokoshin, "Razvytye voyennogo dela."
84. In fact, they ignore the possibility that a defensive posture could be more expensive than an offensive posture. The costs of establishing defense production lines based on new weaponry, new output requirements, new product mixes, etc. would be staggering.
85. Kokoshin and Larionov, "Kurskaya bitva," p. 33.
86. For example, Marshal of the Armor Troops Losik makes the case that tanks are a vital system for defensive operations, see O. Losik, "Issledovaniye opyta tankovykh armiy," *Krasnaya zvezda*, March 8, 1988, p. 2. General-Lieutenant Zhilin offers the idea that some forms of nuclear

Second, one cannot successfully defend one's territory or allies without ultimately carrying the attack to the enemy (the still indeterminate 8-year Iran-Iraq War is a good example). Pure defense is not a viable military strategy. Regardless of whether a military force is operating at the tactical, operational, or strategic level, the opposing force must ultimately be routed and expelled—it cannot merely be slowed and exhausted.[87] From the perspective of the old thinkers, defensive operations do have an important role, in this respect, by providing time for Soviets forces to regroup and, if it has not been possible to begin offensive operations at the start of the war, to move to the counteroffensive.[88] The successful defensive operation is one that allows for a quick and powerful shift to the offensive.

Third, military history demonstrates the inferiority of purely defensive strategies. The reliable defense of the homeland cannot be based on ahistorical concepts.

Fourth, once again the ideological argument is made: that the Soviet military posture could be considered provocative, irrespective of its technical attributes, flies in the face of classical Marxist-Leninist teachings. Socialist states cannot, by definition, have military doctrines or postures that are threatening.[89] Thus, there are serious ideological issues to consider.

CONVERGENCE. Many Western students of Soviet military affairs were pleasantly surprised when, following the new thinkers' discussions of "defensive defense," they detected increased attention to defensive actions in Soviet military writings. Unfortunately, appearances in this instance are deceiving.[90]

---

weapons give defensive capabilities to the troops to stop enemy offensives; P.A. Zhilin, *Istoriya voyennogo iskusstva*, p. 416. The view that weapons could not be neatly categorized as offensive or defensive was vehemently repeated in interviews with Soviet military officials in Moscow.
87. Yazov, *Na strazhe sotsializma i mira*, p. 33, points out that a combination of offensive and defensive capabilities is necessary for security. In his view, counter-offensive capabilities do not contradict a defensive doctrine. This fundamental point actually predates the new thinking; see P.A. Zhilin, *O voyne i voyennoy istorii* (Moscow: Voyenizdat, 1984), p. 437. See General Tret'yak's comments regarding the need for attack capabilities to defeat the enemy, in Teplya, "Reliable Defense," p. 12.
88. This is confirmed in both military writings and exercises. See P.A. Zhilin, *Istoriya voyennogo iskusstva*, p. 414; by the editors of the *Voyenno-istoricheskiy zhurnal*, "Itogi diskussii o strategicheskikh operatsiyakh Velikoy Otechestvennoy voyny 1941–1945," *Voyenno-istoricheskiy zhurnal*, No. 10 (1987), pp. 8–24. For a typical contemporary tactical exercise report, see V. Efanov and V. Pryadkin, "Stoykost' oborony—Reportazh s ucheniya 'Druzhba-88'," *Krasnaya zvezda*, February 6, 1988, p. 1.
89. It is reported that in U.S. Secretary of Defense Frank Carlucci's March 1988 meeting with Soviet Minister of Defense Yazov, Yazov insisted that the Soviet military posture in Europe is already defensive. See George Wilson, "Soviet Military Chief Calls Forces Defensive," *Washington Post*, March 17, 1988, p. 38.
90. If one simply "dropped in" on the Soviet military literature during the past year it would

In fact the Soviet military already had a burgeoning interest in defensive operations prior to Gorbachev's rise to power. By the early 1980s a number of studies on defensive operations were underway, conducted under the auspices of the General Staff, and a series of high-level military conferences explored the role of defensive operations in combat.[91] There is little doubt that one of the most visible military commentators on defensive defense— General-Colonel Gareyev, believed to have headed the Military-Science Directorate of the General Staff at that time—directed much of the work.[92] What the military had in mind, however, was something quite different from the new thinkers' ideas on defensive defense.

The primary impetus for the military's interest in defensive operations was the realization that the Soviet theater posture was premised on a number of questionable assumptions: (1) that the USSR would know when war was imminent; (2) that Soviet political leaders would be able to make timely decisions to enable the armed forces to seize the initiative on the battlefield and begin the war with offensive operations; (3) that the war would be waged on NATO territory; and (4) that NATO would not have the forces or means to wage offensive war against the Pact in Eastern Europe. Evolving American concepts such as AirLand Battle and Follow-on Forces Attack, which advocated deep strikes against second-echelon forces, as well as more radical NATO proposals for counteroffensive strikes against Pact territory, evidently started ringing alarm bells in the Soviet Ministry of Defense.

---

be easy to find an article or two that appeared to support the view that the military is busy turning defensive defense into operational concepts. One would not understand, however, the context of those articles nor would one realize, for example, that *Voyenno-istoricheskiy zhurnal*, (the Military Historical Journal) had been running articles on strategic defensive operations since the end of the 1970s (see footnote 91), or that *Voyennyy vestnik* (Military Herald) had devoted a special issue to defensive operations each year since 1983 (see footnote 93).

91. Yu. Maksimov, "Razvitiye vzglyadov na oboronu," *Voyenno-istoricheskiy zhurnal*, No. 10 (1979), pp. 10–16. M.M. Kozlov, "Organizatsiya i vedeniye strategicheskoy oborony po opytu Velikoy Otechestvennoy voyny," ibid., No. 12 (1980), pp. 9–17; M. M. Kozlov, "Osobennosti strategicheskoy oborony i kontranastupleniya i ikh znacheniye dlya razvitiya sovetskogo voyennogo iskusstva," ibid., No. 10 (1981), pp. 28–35. The culminating conference is reported in M.M. Kozlov, *Akademiya generalnogo shtaba* (Moscow: Voyenizdat, 1987), p. 185. General of the Army Maksimov was appointed Commander in Chief of the Strategic Rocket Forces in 1985. General of the Army Kozlov was Head of the General Staff Academy from 1979 until 1987.

92. Many Western observers have pointed to Gareyev as an example of an influential figure who appears to be "on board" the train of defensive defense. In fact Gareyev's latest book clearly shows that this perception of his views is wrong. See M.A. Gareyev, *Sovetskaya voyennaya nauka* (Moscow: Znaniye, 1987). I suspect that some tendentious editing of the general's comments by the Soviet news agency TASS may have misled some readers. See "Doktrina predotvrashcheniya voyny," *Krasnaya zvezda*, June 23, 1987, p. 3, and compare it with a more complete transcript of the press conference in "Voyennaya doktrina organizatsii Varshavskogo Dogovora." See also footnote 62.

The need for increased emphasis on defensive operations, then, grew out of military pessimism (or realism). Changes had already occurred in military planning and training at the tactical and operational levels by the time Gorbachev came to power.[93] Some evidence suggests that there have even been corresponding procurement and force structure changes within the Soviet and Warsaw Pact forces.[94]

What distinguishes the military's interest in defensive operations from the new thinkers' ideas about non-provocative defense is the relative role of defensive operations in war. The military sees defensive operations as merely a component of a larger offensive-oriented strategy. Defensive operations hold the enemy and buy time until the appropriate forces and means can be assembled for transition to the counteroffensive. Defensive operations, then, are a worst-case option in theater war. At the tactical level there may be defensive actions as Soviet divisions off the main axis of attack attempt to contain NATO counterstrikes. At the operational level there may also be a considerable number of defensive operations along certain sectors of the front. There may even be strategic defensive operations at the beginning of the war, especially if the Warsaw Pact is caught by surprise. But this defensive phase of the war would be temporary, a transition phase, in the view of traditional thinkers.

It seems, therefore, that there is an "unstable" convergence point between the views of the new thinkers and those of the military leadership towards increased emphasis on defense in Soviet theater planning. Here political weight is unlikely to be of much use to the new thinkers. Conventional forces

---

93. See, for example, G. Ionin, "Sovremennaya oborona," *Voyennyy vestnik*, No. 4 (1981), pp. 15–18; V. Galkin, "Oboronyaetsya batal'on," *Voyennyy vestnik*, No. 3 (1982), pp. 16–19; V. Kravchenko and Yu. Upeniyek, "Vzvod PTUR v oborone," *Voyennyy vestnik*, No. 5 (1984), pp. 67–68.

94. Soviet air defenses were reorganized several times between 1978 and 1985. These changes were intended to improve the integration of strategic and tactical air defense capabilities in general, and the defensive capabilities of Soviet ground forces in particular. See International Institute of Strategic Studies (IISS), *The Military Balance 1984–1985* (London: IISS, 1984), p. 14; U.S. Department of Defense, *Soviet Military Power—1985* (Washington, D.C.: Government Printing Office [GPO], 1985), pp. 48–49. During the early 1980s the Soviet Ground Forces began experimenting with corps structures, the equivalent of two divisions but with a smaller logistical support requirement. IISS, *The Military Balance 1987–1988*, p. 27; *Soviet Military Power—1986*, pp. 65–66. If this corps structure is adopted, then it would imply a reduction in Soviet military manpower without a reduction in military capability. It may be that General Gareyev was thinking of these types of changes when he claimed that defensive concepts are affecting Soviet force structure already. See Gareyev's statement in "Voyennaya doktrina organizatsii Varshavskogo Dogovora."

are complex organisms, and are not as easily disassembled as are strategic nuclear forces. In this respect, the military still has no analytic rivals comparable to the civilian expertise on nuclear forces that grew up in the Foreign Ministry and the Academy of Sciences during twenty years of strategic arms negotiations.[95] While there are indications of efforts to develop civilian expertise in conventional warfare, the substantive and institutional hurdles suggest a long, uphill process.[96] However, no matter how strong a cadre of civilian conventional force analysts eventually emerges in the Soviet Union, the military will remain the dominant actor in planning and implementing changes in the basic structure and organization of Soviet theater forces.[97]

Moreover, conventional force planning—more than any other aspect of defense policy—cuts to the heart of Soviet military professionalism. It would seem that this is one battle that would ignite the institutional ire of the armed forces.[98] This, in turn, would be a fairly potent force for Gorbachev's political rivals on the Politburo to employ if they could organize opposition.

Over the long term, any movement in Soviet theater strategy towards the new thinkers' notions of defensive defense will most likely fit within the military's rubric for a more balanced theater strategy. The new thinkers may have to be content with declaring "victory" as the military sets about the task of improving the capabilities of the armed forces to undertake defensive actions.

Conclusions

The new political thinking on security is neither a methodology for force development nor a system of criteria for defining security requirements. It is

---

95. Interviews.
96. Within the Academy of Sciences there is some interest in establishing international security as a recognized field of scientific inquiry. See Kokoshin, "Razvitiye voyennogo dela," p. 20. This would enable the Academy to set up research and training departments under its auspices to create a generation of civilian defense intellectuals. (Interviews.) General Gareyev, however, seems to have suggested that civilian scientists do not have the proper training to be involved in such issues. See Gareyev, *Sovetskaya voyennaya nauka*, p. 32.
97. This does not preclude a political decision to cut troop strength, move to lower readiness levels, or rebase certain forces. However, such changes are not in any way comparable to the kinds of radical restructuring of theater forces proposed by the new thinkers. In fact, such activities have occurred in both NATO and Warsaw Pact forces in the past.
98. This might explain the lessening of Marshal Akhromeyev's support for the new political thinking. As it moved from the abstract to the concrete and began encroaching on the professional domain of the military, he may have found himself drawn to defend his institution.

a set of notions that, *ex post facto,* can be used by the general secretary to justify, doctrinally and ideologically, his efforts to manipulate the Soviet defense agenda. The various elements of the new thinking could be used to rationalize almost any force posture and defense policy. Thus, it would be fruitless to use this framework to attempt to predict specifically what Soviet forces might look like in ten years, since neither Soviet Minister of Defense Yazov, Chief of the General Staff Akhromeyev, nor Gorbachev himself could do this objectively. It is not surprising in this respect that Yazov found it difficult to spell out in concrete terms the thrust of "reasonable sufficiency" in his March 1988 conversations with U.S. Secretary of Defense Frank Carlucci.

Gorbachev's new thinking does, however, reflect his regime's liberation from the conceptual and ideological baggage that has so heavily influenced Soviet defense policy in the past. It also provides clues about the general directions in which Gorbachev would prefer to steer Soviet defense policy in the 1990s.

Some of the notions now hailed under the banner of Gorbachev's new political thinking on security are likely to become enduring elements of Soviet defense policy. The emphasis on avoiding nuclear war, attention to the dangers of inadvertent nuclear war, and acknowledgment of strategic and theater nuclear sufficiency all fit well within established trends in Soviet political and military thinking.

However, the extent to which the Soviet Union will pursue solutions to its security problems that represent significant departures from past policy will depend on the acceptability and durability of the more controversial ideas of the new political thinking: the mutuality of security, the centrality of political means for guaranteeing security, reasonable sufficiency in general purpose forces, and defensive defense. The thesis of this article is that this has much more to do with leadership politics than with strategic thinking.

While Gorbachev remains in power, for example, the defense policy impact of his new thinking will be sensitive to the performance of his other programs, most notably economic and social *perestroika.* Should Gorbachev's much-heralded economic and social reforms fail to produce the significant improvements that were promised, or should they spawn new problems, then more traditional elements in the leadership would have an opening to attack the full spectrum of new political thinking—including new political thinking on security. The turmoil in Azerbaijan during 1987–88 is one case in point. Equally ominous—and perhaps more directly connected with external security—would be another burst of political self-assertion, tinged with anti-Soviet behavior, in Eastern Europe. Powerful members of the Politburo seeking to contain the power and authority of the general secretary could use such events to create a consensus against the new political thinking, whether the links were real or trumped-up.

Similarly, Western behavior, and American behavior in particular, can affect the long-term impact of the new thinking. This is because the most outstanding difference between the new thinkers and the old thinkers is their divergent perceptions of the threat posed by the United States and NATO. Western actions that can be perceived as invalidating the assumptions of the new thinking would be potent tools for those opposed to Gorbachev's security framework. For example, NATO's contemplation of compensating nuclear deployments in the wake of the INF Treaty—whether appropriate or not—undermines the credibility of the new thinking: the threat to the Soviet Union has not been controlled or reduced by the treaty, merely redirected.

In the short term, then, Gorbachev does not need a political consensus supporting the new thinking on security. He only needs to prevent the formation of a political consensus against it. He must prevent the emergence of an issue that will galvanize opposition.

Looking beyond Gorbachev, there is no reason to expect that future general secretaries—or other members of the Politburo—will be "new thinkers." In the absence of truly noteworthy achievements in the near term, especially in economic-industrial performance, subsequent leaders could simply write off the new thinking as a desperate measure that, in retrospect, was ill-conceived. Indeed, if one traces the policy history of the Soviet leadership from Lenin to Stalin, Stalin to Khrushchev, Khrushchev to Brezhnev, and Brezhnev to Gorbachev, such behavior is the rule for transitions. The same political mechanisms that enabled Gorbachev to push aside many of the "Brezhnevite" members of the Politburo could be used by a wily future general secretary to oust any remnants of the Gorbachev coterie.

For the longer term, then, Gorbachev must institutionalize the new thinking within the Soviet national security decision-making structure—a lesson he must have learned from Khrushchev's failures. Indeed, Gorbachev's entire agenda-setting strategy for the new thinking seems explicitly designed to build a multi-institutional constituency.[99] But agenda-setting is only the first

---

99. In their zeal, however, some of the new thinkers are having just the opposite effect. In particular, the writings of Zhurkin, Karaganov, and Kortunov, and of Kokoshin are probably

stage of the process: The history of Soviet defense policy-making shows quite clearly how the intended course of policy can be severely altered in the transition from agenda-setting and option formulation to decision to implementation.

Barring resort to Stalin's preferred strategy of killing off and replacing everyone occupying Party and government posts, Gorbachev will have to play off institutions against one another to prevent a consensus against the new thinking from forming, while attempting to convince the institutions that they will ultimately benefit from his programs. While Gorbachev may be able to depend heavily on the Foreign Ministry, the Central Committee Staff, and the Academy of Sciences for new ideas during the agenda-setting phase of his restructuring of defense, ultimately he will have to turn to the Ministry of Defense for implementation. In particular, Gorbachev will need the military's support if he is to tackle successfully the largest and, from a resource-saving perspective, potentially most fruitful element of restructuring the Soviet military posture: general purpose forces. There is some evidence that Gorbachev recognizes this fact and that the military has been told that their willingness to support the new thinking and forthcoming limitations on defense spending will yield technologically superior weapons in the longer run.[100]

With these caveats about the durability of the new thinking in mind, let us assume that Gorbachev remains general secretary over the next five years or more, that his political clout remains about as strong as it appears today, and that his other programs proceed without major reversals. What might we expect of Soviet defense policy and behavior?

THE ROLE OF NUCLEAR WEAPONS

If one considers the major convergence points described above, then the relative de-emphasis of nuclear weaponry in Soviet military policy is one of

---

alienating the military. More ideological elements in the political leadership are being unnerved by the sudden reversal of formerly sacrosanct ideological concepts appearing in the works of Yu. Zhilin and others.

100. "27th s'ezd KPSS o dal'neyshem ukreplennii oboronosposobnosti stray i povyshenii boyevoy gotovnosti Vooruzhennykh Sil," *Voyenno-istoricheskiy zhurnal*, No. 4 (1986), pp. 3–12; B.A. Zubkov, "Zabota KPSS ob ukreplenii ekonomicheskikh osnov voyennoy moshchi sotsializsticheskogo gosudarstva," *Voyenno-istoricheskiy zhurnal*, No. 3 (1986), pp. 3–8. At least one military official seems to accept this line of argument. See V. Shabanov, "Shchit rodiny," *Ekonomicheskaya gazeta*, No. 8 (February 1988), p. 18. General of the Army Shabanov is the Deputy Minister of Defense for Armaments.

the strongest parallels between the new thinking and trends in the old thinking. I stress the word "relative" because this de-emphasis is in terms of the Soviet military's past preferences for strategy and operations, not of any putative NATO or U.S. use of nuclear weapons.[101]

STRATEGIC NUCLEAR FORCES. As noted earlier, the top Soviet military leadership (the General Staff and the Collegium of the Ministry of Defense) has come to see strategic parity as the best strategic nuclear posture that the Soviet Union can hope to attain in the foreseeable future. This is primarily because very high levels of nuclear armaments are already in the stockpiles and it is implausible that either side could prevent a retaliatory second strike by the other.[102]

Given that there is a ceiling on the total amount of resources going to Soviet defense procurement and given the relative scarcity of some precious resources (e.g., micro-electronics), the Soviet military faces a number of tradeoffs and opportunity costs as it pieces together its procurement program. What is put into one system is not available for others. The Soviet defense constituency recognizes that the United States can easily match any additional strategic nuclear buildup by the Soviet Union. At the same time, the obvious and complete vulnerability of modern industrial societies to the immense destructiveness of nuclear weapons produces a fairly sharp decline in their marginal utility. Thus, the marginal increment in usable military power from each defense ruble allocated to more strategic nuclear weapons is quite small, while the opportunity costs may be high. Strategic parity, then, becomes a reasonable goal.

In this respect, strategic parity at lower levels of forces might not necessarily appear to detract from Soviet security. Although the military establishment might not have proposed 50% reductions in strategic nuclear forces, it is not obvious why it should necessarily oppose such cuts initiated by others—if at least some of the freed high technology resources could be channeled to general purpose force modernization programs.[103] Indications are that this is one of the few concrete parts of Gorbachev's defense agenda with

101. Meyer, "Soviet Perspectives on the Paths to Nuclear War"; John G. Hines, Phillip A. Petersen, and Notra Trulock III, "Soviet Military Theory from 1945–2000: Implications for NATO," *Washington Quarterly*, Vol. 9, No. 4 (Fall 1986), pp. 117–137.
102. Ogarkov, "Zashchita sotsializma"; Yazov's statements in "K miru bez yadernogo oruzhiya," *Pravda*, February 10, 1988, p. 2; P.A. Zhilin, *Istoriya voyennogo iskusstva*, p. 407.
103. For a discussion of this problem see Stephen M. Meyer, "The Role of Economic Constraints in Soviet Defense," paper presented at the Conference on the Soviet Defense Economy, Hoover Institution, Stanford University, March 23–24, 1988.

which most of the military establishment does agree.[104] In this respect, the litmus test of Gorbachev's new thinking should be the manner in which the Soviet Union implements its strategic force cuts. Specifically, if the new thinking is in force, then the Soviet Union should be willing to make disproportionately large cuts in its most potent counterforce capabilities.

Quite naturally, then, we arrive at the issue of complete denuclearization. The idea of a nuclear-free world was put on the Soviet foreign policy agenda by Gorbachev in January 1986.[105] There is no serious enthusiasm for this notion within the Soviet national security establishment and it is highly doubtful that the majority of the Soviet political leadership shares this vision. (In fact, the degree of political opposition is likely to increase in direct proportion to the size of the cuts contemplated.)[106]

Some Western analysts have argued that the Soviet military would be in favor of a denuclearized world because it would leave the Soviets with overwhelming conventional military superiority. The image of this superiority is, however, a Western perception not readily shared by those in Moscow. Without strategic nuclear weapons, the Soviet Union would instantly lose its global military power status. It would be unable to project significant and decisive military force beyond the Eurasian landmass, and most importantly, it would not be capable of posing any significant military threat to the U.S. homeland. For the foreseeable future—well beyond 2000—Soviet superpower status requires strategic nuclear weapons.

THEATER NUCLEAR FORCES. The situation is different for theater denuclearization. The Soviet military began more than 20 years ago to move away from heavy reliance on nuclear fire support in theater warfare planning. The strong preference for fighting an all-conventional war—should war arise at all—is well documented.[107] It would not be surprising, therefore, that most of the General Staff, the commands of the Ground Forces, the Air Forces,

---

104. See Akhromeyev's comments in "Za bez'yadernyy boleye bezopasnyy mir," *Vestnik Ministerstva inostrannykh del SSSR*, No. 3 (February 15, 1986), pp. 42–49; Gareyev, *Sovetskaya voyennaya nauka*, p. 15.
105. Gorbachev's January 15, 1986 statement can be found in "Zayavleniys general'nogo sekretarya Tsk KPSS M.S. Gorbacheva," *Za novoya politicheskoye myshleniye v mezhdunarodnykh otnosheniyakh* (Moscow: Politizdat, 1987), pp. 220–233.
106. There has already been a rebuttal of the new thinkers' recommendation for 95% cuts in strategic forces: Sergei Vybornnov, Andreo Gusenkov, and Vladimir Leontiyev, "Nothing is Simple in Europe," *New Times*, March 1988, pp. 37–39.
107. Stephen M. Meyer, *Soviet Theater Nuclear Forces*, Adelphi Papers No. 187 and 188 (London: IISS, Winter 1983/84); Hines, Peterson, and Trulock, "Soviet Military Theory."

and the Air Defense Forces would perceive the *mutual* large-scale denuclearization of theater forces to be a gain.[108]

CONVENTIONAL FORCES

The major implications for general purpose forces can be readily deduced from the discussion of defensive defense. There can be little doubt that Soviet military strategy (as it pertains to theater operations) was already moving towards increased attention to defensive actions and operations. The intent was to raise the status of defensive operations, not, as the new thinkers would have it, to lower the status of offensive operations.

Soviet military studies of defensive operations point unambiguously to the forces and means required for a stable defensive posture. Mobile tank forces, mobile and deployed artillery, extensive fighter and fighter-bomber air support are the most prominent.[109] While the basic weapons types will remain the same, new generations with improved capabilities—currently in testing—will enter service. It is quite possible that we will also witness important changes in the structure and composition of ground combat units in the years ahead. Interestingly, this used to be called "force modernization"; now it seems less threatening to refer to it as "unilateral restructuring." There also appears to be renewed interest in fortifications and other forms of defensive engineering work, but only as an adjunct to help stabilize the overall theater position.[110] In particular, an increase in defensive engineering work throughout Eastern Europe is likely.

At the same time, there is increasing interest in high-technology conventional weaponry where quality dominates quantity. There is widespread recognition that conventional weapons technologies are on the verge of a major revolution in capabilities. Nothing better characterizes the Soviet perception than the often-encountered description that these new weapons will have capabilities "equivalent to battlefield nuclear weapons," not in explosive

108. At the same time, one should also not be surprised that the Soviet military continues to try to work out credible applications of nuclear weapons on the battlefield. In particular, nuclear weapons have been the subject of increased interest in *defensive* operations. See P.A. Zhilin, *Istoriya voyennogo iskusstva*, pp. 412–417; G. Reznichenko, ed., *Taktika* (Moscow: Voyenizdat, 1984), pp. 152–173, on offensive actions, and pp. 174–221 on defensive actions.
109. See sources in notes 91 and 93, as well as A.I. Yevseyev, "Opyt osushchestvleniy manyovra s tsel'yu sosredotocheniya usiliy protiv udarnoy gruppirovki protivnika v khode oboronitel'noy operatsii fronta," *Voyenno-istoricheskiy zhurnal*, No. 9 (1986), pp. 12–23; L. Zaytsev, "Ognevoye porazheniye protivnika v oborone," *Voyenno-istoricheskiy zhurnal*, No. 9 (1983), pp. 20–24.
110. See, for example, V.I. Pevykin, *Fortifikatsiya: proshloye i sovremennost'* (Moscow: Voyenizdat, 1987).

firepower, but in lethality to forces in the field. Indeed, some in the General Staff appear to believe that a new phase in the scientific-technical revolution in military affairs is on the horizon.[111] Nevertheless, the Soviet military continues to believe that more traditional systems of conventional war will dominate the battlefield in the near term—especially given the great quantities of these systems in both sides' arsenals. At best, then, the new and old technologies of theater war will exist side by side for decades to come.

Any major changes likely to occur in the next decade will most closely fit the traditional approach, not the new thinking.[112] In fact, the wholesale transition from offense-dominance to defense-dominance in the theater, preferred by the new thinkers, would still require passing through the kinds of changes currently desired by the more traditional thinkers. Given the sheer mass of Soviet theater forces, any such change would take more than a decade; the Soviet weapons procurement process would require at least that to fill orders. Retraining of commanders and troops is a very slow process, and thus a more rapid change could pose serious risks to the Soviet military posture in Europe and Asia. Therefore, it might not be possible to distinguish the two approaches for another decade.

In sum, one should expect to see noticeable changes in the Soviet theater force posture that reflect increased emphasis on defense, but not at the expense of offense. For the most part, however, Soviet military thinking on defensive operations is characterized by changes in the "software" of war, not the hardware.

ARMS CONTROL

It is fair to say that Soviet arms control behavior in the last year has been uncharacteristically flexible, even accommodating. But it would be a mistake

---

111. Marshal Ogarkov is the Soviet military man most closely identified with this view, due to his numerous pronouncements on the subject while he was chief of the general staff. In fact many in the Ministry of Defense shared his view, but Ogarkov was the only one who spoke out publicly on the subject. (Interviews.) Ogarkov did not, however, advocate scrapping current weapons systems and moving rapidly to new technologies—a position often ascribed to him and used to explain his removal as chief of the general staff. Better than anyone, Ogarkov understood that new technologies—qualitative improvements in weaponry—have a minimal initial impact on military capabilities. The accumulation of quantities of weapons based on new technologies sufficient to make a difference takes a decade or more. See Ogarkov, *Vsegda v gotovnosti k zashchite otechestva* (Moscow: Voyenizdat, 1982), pp. 37–41.

112. One can never exclude the possibility that Gorbachev will order the withdrawal of several combat divisions, or even an entire tank army, from Eastern Europe. This, however, is a token gesture that would not seriously affect the military balance.

to take such behavior for granted. First, if one steps back to view the larger picture of Gorbachev's arms control initiatives of the past two years, one gets the image of a juggler dashing madly to keep a dozen plates spinning in the air. Why Gorbachev has felt compelled to offer up so much so quickly is unclear. Some of his compulsion can be explained by the fact that while the new political thinking is supposed to validate the new approach to arms control, the "success" of arms control in moderating the military threat is in turn supposed to validate the new political thinking. Again, threat perception is at the heart of the old thinkers' critique, and Gorbachev must demonstrate an ability to reduce that threat via the tools of the new thinking. Thus, in the early stages of the new political thinking Gorbachev needs to keep arms control at the forefront of Soviet policy. It is hard to imagine, however, how he can continue to keep all his plates in the air through the whole show.

Second, there appears to be considerable sentiment among the political and military leadership that some of Soviet arms control actions and "concessions" have been ill-advised. The Soviet unilateral nuclear test moratorium was interpreted by many—including initial supporters—to have been a humiliating failure because the United States flaunted its continued testing while Soviet nuclear test sites were dormant.[113] The asymmetry of the INF cuts has been implicitly criticized in many corners of the Soviet Union, as has the agreement's failure to control British and French nuclear forces.[114]

Third, as already mentioned, professed Western interest in compensating actions to shore up NATO capabilities in the wake of the withdrawal of U.S. INF missiles from Europe has tarnished some of the new thinking's luster. Even with significant Soviet concessions, it is argued, the West is finding ways to expand the threat to the Soviet Union. In short, it may be that the period of Gorbachev's greatest freedom of action in arms control is passing.

---

113. Interviews.
114. The issue surfaces repeatedly in Soviet official and public settings. See, for example, the interview with General-Colonel Chervov, "Dogovor, kotoryy povyshayet uroven' bezopasnosti," *Krasnaya zvezda*, December 19, 1987, p. 1; and the letter to the editor of *Pravda* by H. Prozhogin, "Dogovor po RSD-RMD: za ili protiv," *Pravda*, February 20, 1988, p. 4.

Part II:
Nuclear Weapons and
Soviet Doctrine

Contrasts in American and Soviet Strategic Thought

Fritz W. Ermarth

$\mathbf{W}$e are having trouble with Soviet strategic doctrine. Soviet thinking about strategy and nuclear war differs in sigificant ways from our own. To the extent one should care about this —and that extent is a matter of debate—we do not like the way the Soviets seem to think. Before 1972, appreciation of differences between Soviet and American strategic thinking was limited to a small number of specialists. Those who held it a matter of high concern for policy were fewer still. Since that time, concern about the nature, origins, and consequences of these differences is considerably more widespread, in large measure as a result of worry about the Soviet strategic arms buildup and the continued frustrations of achieving a real breakthrough in SALT.

Heightened attention to the way the other side thinks about strategic nuclear power is timely and proper. The nature of the Soviet buildup and some of our own previous choices have locked us out of pure "hardware solutions" to our emerging strategic security problems that are independent of the other side's values and perceptions. Whatever one thinks about the wisdom or folly of the manner in which we have pursued SALT so far, it is desirable that management of the U.S.-Soviet strategic relationship have a place for an explicit dialogue. That dialogue should include more attention to strategic concepts than we have seen in past SALT negotiations. Moreover, whatever the role of SALT in the future, the existence of "rough parity" or worse almost by definition means that we cannot limit strategic policy to contending merely with the opponent's forces. In the cause of deterrence, crisis management, and, if need be, war, we must thwart his strategy. That requires understanding that opponent better.

The Need to Understand Strategic Doctrine

Let us define "strategic doctrine" as a set of operative beliefs, values, and assertions that in a significant way guide official behavior with respect to strategic research and development (R&D), weapons choice, forces, operational plans, arms control, etc. The essence of U.S. "doctrine" is to deter central nuclear war at relatively low levels of arms effort ("arms race stability") and strategic anxiety ("crisis stability") through the credible threat of catastrophic damage to the enemy

Fritz W. Ermarth has been an analyst of Soviet and American strategic policies at the Central Intelligence Agency and the Rand Corporation. Most recently he has directed Rand's Strategic Studies Program. Since submission of this article, Mr. Ermarth has become a member of the National Security Council staff to work on U.S. strategic and arms control policy.

should deterrence fail. In that event, this doctrine says it should be the aim and ability of U.S. power to inflict maximum misery on the enemy in his homeland. Making the world following the outbreak of nuclear war more tolerable for the United States is, at best, a lesser concern. Soviet strategic doctrine stipulates that Soviet strategic forces and plans should strive in all available ways to enhance the prospect that the Soviet Union could survive as a nation and, in some politically and militarily meaningful way, defeat the main enemy should deterrence fail—and by this striving help deter or prevent nuclear war, along with the attainment of other strategic and foreign policy goals.

These characterizations of U.S. and Soviet strategic doctrine and the differences between them are valid and important. Had U.S. strategic policy been more sensitive over the last ten years to the asymmetry they express, we might not find ourselves in so awkward a present situation. We would have been less sanguuine than we were about prospects that the Soviets would settle for an easily defined, non-threatening form of strategic parity. We would not have believed as uncritically as we did that the SALT process was progressing toward a common explication of already tacitly accepted norms of strategic stability.

It is, if anything, even more important that these asymmetries be fully appreciated today. They are a crucial starting point for strategic diagnosis and therapy. But they are only a starting point. The constellations of thought, value, and action that we call, respectively, U.S. and Soviet strategic doctrine or policy are much more complicated, qualified, and contradictory than the above characterizations admit by themselves. To be aware of these other ramifications without fully understanding them could lead to dangerous discounting, on one hand, or distorting, on the other, the real differences between U.S. and Soviet strategic thinking.

Comparative Strategic Doctrine

The following discussion is intended only to suggest some of the contrasts that exist between U.S. and Soviet strategic thinking. The issues raised are not treated exhaustively, and the list itself is not exhaustive. Our appreciation of these matters is not adequate to the critical times in the U.S.-Soviet strategic relationship we are facing. It would be highly desirable to develop the intellectual discipline of comparative military doctrine, especially in the strategic sphere. Systematic comparative studies of strategic doctrine could serve to clarify what we think and how we ourselves differ on these matters, as well as to organize what we know about Soviet strategic thinking.

Although many have and express views on how both the United States and the

Soviet Union deal with strategic problems, there is in fact little systematic comparison of the conceptual and behavioral foundations of our respective strategic activity. In this area, more than other comparative inquiries into communist and non-communist politics, there are the obstacles of secrecy in the path of research. Perhaps as vital, neither government nor academic institutions appear to have cultivated many people with the necessary interdisciplinary skills and experience.

The most influential factor that has inhibited lucid comparisons of U.S. and Soviet strategic thinking has been the uncritically held assumption that they had to be very similar, or at least converging with time. Many of us have been quite insensitive to the possibility that two very different political systems could deal very differently with what is, in some respects, a common problem. We understood the problem of keeping the strategic peace on equitable and economical terms —or so we thought. As reasonable men the Soviets, too, would come to understand it our way.

Explaining this particular expression of our cultural self-centeredness is itself a fascinating field for speculation. I think it goes beyond the American habit of value projection. It may result from the fact that post-war developments in U.S. strategy were an institutional and intellectual offspring of the natural sciences that spawned modern weapons. Scientific truth is transnational, not culturally determined. But, unfortunately, strategy is more like *politics* than like science.

The next five to ten years of the U.S.-Soviet strategic relationship could well be characterized by mounting U.S. anxieties about the adequacy of our deterrent forces and our strategic doctrine. There seems to be little real prospect that the SALT process, as we have been conducting it, will substantially alleviate these anxieties. Even if a more promising state of affairs emerges, however, it is hard to see us managing it with calm and confidence unless we develop a more thorough appreciation of the differences between U.S. and Soviet strategic thinking. Things have progressed beyond the point where it is useful to have the three familiar schools of thought on Soviet doctrine arguing past each other: one saying "Whatever they say, they think as we do;" the second insisting, "Whatever they say, it does not matter;" and the third contending, "They think what they say, and are therefore out for superiority over us."

Comparative strategic doctrine studies should address systematically a series of questions:

—What are the central decisions about strategy, force posture, and force employment or operations that doctrine is supposed to resolve for the sides examined?

—What are the prevailing categories, concepts, beliefs, and assertions that appear to constitute the body of strategic thought and doctrine in question?

—What are the hedges and qualifications introduced to modify the main theses of official thinking?

—What are the "non-strategic," e.g., propagandistic, purposes that might motivate doctrinal pronouncements? Does the doctrinal system recognize a distinction between what ideally ought to be, and what practically is (a serious problem in the Soviet case)?

—In what actions, e.g., force posture, does apparent doctrine have practical effect? Where does it lie dormant?

—To what extent are doctrinal pronouncements the subject of or the guise for policy dispute?

—What perceptions does one side entertain as to the doctrinal system of the other side? With what effect?

Answering these questions for both the United States and the Soviet Union is admittedly no easy matter, especially in a highly politicized environment in which many participants have already made up their minds how they want the answers to come out with respect to assumed impact on U.S. strategic policy. But we have the data to do a good deal better than we have to date.

U.S. and Soviet Doctrine Contrasted

What is U.S. strategic doctrine and policy? What is Soviet strategic doctrine and policy? The Soviets provide definitions of doctrine (doktrina) and policy (politika) that state they are official principles, guidance, and instructions from the highest governing authorities to provide for the building of the armed forces and for their employment in war.

The most useful thing about these definitions is that they remind us—or should —that we do not have direct and literal access to Soviet strategic doctrine and policy through the most commonly available sources, i.e., Soviet military literature and various pronouncements of authoritative political and military figures. Our insight into Soviet strategic policy is derived by inference from such sources along with inferences from observed R&D and force procurement behavior, what we manage to learn about peacetime force operations and exercises, and occasional direct statements in more privileged settings, such as SALT, by varyingly persuasive spokesmen.

The value of all these sources is constrained by the limitations of our perceptive apparatus, technical and intellectual, and the fact that Soviet communications on strategic subjects serve many purposes other than conveying official policy, such as foreign and domestic propaganda. For all that, we have gained over the years a substantial degree of understanding of the content of Soviet strategic thinking, of the values, standards, objectives, and calculations that underlie Soviet decisions. It is this total body of thinking and its bearing on action that are of concern here.

Where lack of access complicates understanding of Soviet strategic doctrine, an overabundance of data confuses understanding of the American side, a point that Soviets make with some justice when berated with the evils of Soviet secrecy. If, in the case of the United States, one is concerned about the body of thinking that underlies strategic action it is clearly insufficient to rely on official statements or documents at any level of classification or authority. Such sources may, for one reason or another, not tell the whole story or paper over serious differences of purpose behind some action.

One of the difficulties in determining the concepts or beliefs that underlie U.S. strategic action is that strategic policy is a composite of behavior taking place in at least three distinguishable, but overlapping arenas. The smallest, most secretive, and least significant over the long-term, assuming deterrence does not fail, is the arena of operational or war planning. The second arena is that of system and force acquisition; it is much larger and more complex than the first. The most disorganized and largest, but most important for the longer-term course of U.S. strategic behavior is the arena of largely public debate over basic strategic principles and objectives. Its participants range from the most highly placed executive authorities to influential private elites, and occasionally the public at large. Strategy-making is a relatively democratic process in the United States.

To be sure, may areas of public policymaking can be assessed in terms of these overlapping circles of players and constituents. But the realm of U.S. strategic policy may be unusual in the degree to which different rules, data, concerns, and participants dominate the different arenas. These differences make it difficult to state with authority what U.S. strategic policy is on an issue that cuts across the arenas. For example, public U.S. policy may state a clear desire to avoid counter-silo capabilities on stability grounds. The weapons acquisition community may, for a variety of reasons, simultaneously be seeking a weapons characteristic vital to counter-silo capability, improved ballistic missile accuracy. As best they can with weapons available, meanwhile, force operators may be required by the logic of their task to target enemy missile silos as a high priority.

Despite these complexities, however, it is possible to generalize a body of policy concepts and values that govern U.S. strategic behavior. There are strong tendencies that dominate U.S. strategic behavior in the areas of declaratory policy, force acquisition, and arms control policy. Again, the case of U.S. counter-silo capabilities may be cited. Today, the United States lacks high confidence capabilities against Soviet missile silos; it may continue to lack them for some time or indefinitely. This is in part the result of technological choice, the early selection of small ICBMs and the deployment of low-yield MIRV weapons. It is also the result of Soviet efforts to improve silo hardness. But the main reason for this lack is that we have abided by a conscious judgment that a serious counter-silo capability, because it threatens strategic stability, is a bad thing for the United States to possess.

The situation seems more straightforward, if secretive, on the Soviet side. Soviet strategic policymaking takes place in a far more vertical and closed system. Expertise is monopolized by the military and a subset of the top political leadership. Although elites external to this group can bid for its scarce resources to some extent, they cannot seriously challenge its values and judgments. Matters of doctrine, force acquisition, and war planning are much more intimately connected within this decision group than in the United States. Policy arguments are indeed possible. Public evidence suggests a series of major Soviet debates on nuclear strategy from the mid-1950s to the late 1960s, although identification of issues, alternatives, and parameters in these debates must be somewhat speculative.

These considerations make difficult, but not impossible, the comparative treatment of U.S. and Soviet strategic belief systems and concepts. One may describe with some confidence how the two very different decision systems deal with certain concerns central to the strategic nuclear predicament of both sides. Much about U.S. and Soviet strategic belief systems can be captured by exploring how they treat five central issues: (1) the consequences of an all-out strategic nuclear war, (2) the phenomenon of deterrence, (3) stability, (4) distinctions and relationships between intercontinental and regional strategic security concerns, and (5) strategic conflict limitation.

CONSEQUENCES OF NUCLEAR WAR

For a generation, the relevant elites of both the United States and the Soviet Union have agreed that an unlimited strategic nuclear war would be a sociopolitical disaster of immense proportions. Knowing the experiences of the peoples of the Soviet Union with warfare in this century and with nuclear inferiority since 1945, one sometimes suspects that the human dimensions of such a catastrophe are more real to Russians, high and low, than to Americans, for whom the prospect is vague and unreal, if certainly forbidding.

For many years the prevailing U.S. concept of nuclear war's consequences has been such as to preclude belief in any military or politically meaningful form of victory. Serious effort on the part of the state to enhance the prospect for national survival seemed quixotic, even dangerous. Hence stems our relative disinterest in air defenses and civil defenses over the last fifteen years, and our genuine fear that ballistic missile defenses would be severely destabilizing. Growth of Soviet nuclear power has certainly clinched this view of nuclear conflict among critical elements of the U.S. elite. But even when the United States enjoyed massive superiority, when the Soviet Union could inflict much less societal damage on the United States, and then only in a first strike (through the early 1960s), the awesome destructiveness of nuclear weapons had deprived actual war with these weapons of much of its strategic meaning for the United States.

The Soviet system has, however, in the worst of times, clung tenaciously to the belief that nuclear war cannot—indeed, must not—be deprived of strategic meaning, i.e., some rational relationship to the interests of the state. It has insisted that, however awful, nuclear war must be survivable and some kind of meaningful victory attainable. As most are aware, this issue was debated in various ways at the beginning and end of the Khrushchev era, with Khrushchev on both sides of the issue. But the system decided it *had* to believe in survival and victory of some form. Not so to believe would mean that the most basic processes of history, on which Soviet ideology and political legitimacy are founded, could be derailed by the technological works of man and the caprice of an historically doomed opponent. Moreover, as the defenders of doctrinal rectitude continued to point out, failure to believe in the "manageability" of nuclear disaster would lead to pacifism, defeatism, and lassitude in the Soviet military effort. This should not be read as the triumph of ideological will over objective science and practical reason. From the Soviet point of view, nuclear war with a powerful and hostile America was a real danger. Could the state merely give up on its traditional responsibilities to defend itself and survive in that event? Their negative answer hardly strikes one as unreasonable. Their puzzlement, alternating between contemptuous and suspicious, over U.S. insistence on a positive answer is not surprising.

In recent years the changing strategic balance has had the effect of strengthening rather than weakening the asymmetry of the two sides' convictions on this matter. Dubious when the United States enjoyed relative advantage, strategic victory and survival in nuclear conflict have become the more incredible to the United States as the strategic power of the Russians has grown. For the Soviets, however, the progress of arms and war-survival programs has transformed what was in large measure an ideological imperative into a more plausible strategic potential. For reasons to be examined below, Soviet leaders possibly believe that, under favorable operational conditions, the Soviet Union could win a central strategic war today. Notwithstanding strategic parity or essential equivalence of force, they may also believe they could lose such a conflict under some conditions.

DETERRENCE

The concept of deterrence early became a central element of both U.S. and Soviet strategic belief systems. For both sides the concept had extended or regional dimensions, and a good deal of political content. There has, in short, been some functional symmetry between the deterrence thinking of the two sides: restraint of hostile action across a spectrum of violence by the threat of punishing consequences in war. Over time and with shifts in the overall military balance, latent asymmetries of thinking have become more pronounced. For the United States, strategic deterrence has tended to become the only meaningful objective of strategic policy, and it has become progressively decoupled from regional security. For the Soviets, deterrence—or war prevention—was the first, but not the only and not the last objective of strategy. Deterrence also meant the protection of a foreign policy that had both offensive and defensive goals. And it was never counterposed against the ultimate objective of being able to manage a nuclear war successfully should deterrence fail. The Soviet concept of deterrence has evolved as the strategic balance has improved for the Soviet Union from primary emphasis on defensive themes of war prevention and protection of prior political gains to more emphasis on themes that include the protection of dynamic processes favoring Soviet international interests. Repetition of the refrain that detente is a product of Soviet strategic power, among other things, displays this evolution.

STABILITY

Strategic stability is a concept that is very difficult to treat in a comparative manner because it is so vital to U.S. strategic thinking, but hardly identifiable in Soviet strategic writings. In U.S. thinking, strategic stability has meant a condition in which incentives inherent in the arms balance to initiate the use of strategic nuclear forces and, closely related, to acquire new or additional forces are weak or absent. In an environment dominated by powerful offensive capabilities and comparatively vulnerable ultimate values, i.e., societies, stability was thought to be achievable on the basis of a contract of mutually vulnerable societies and survivable offensive forces. Emphasis on force survivability followed, as did relative uninterest in counterforce, active, and passive defenses.

Soviet failure to embrace these notions is sufficiently evident not to require much elaboration. One may argue about Soviet ability to overturn stability in U.S. terms, but not about Soviet disinclination to accept the idea as a governing principle of strategic behavior. Soviet acceptance of the ABM agreement in 1972 is still frequently cited as testimony to some acceptance of this principle. It is much more probable, however, that the agreement was attractive to Moscow because superior U.S. ABM technology plus superior U.S. ABM penetrating technology would have given the United States a major advantage during the mid- to late 1970s. In a unilateral sense, the Soviets saw the ABM agreement as stabilizing a process of strategic catch-up against a serious risk of reversal. But it did not mean acceptance of the U.S. stability principle.

The United States has always been relatively sensitive to the potential of technology to jeopardize specific formulae for achieving stability, although it has been relatively slow to perceive the pace and extent to which comparative advantage has shifted from passive survivability to counterforce technologies. The Soviets have also been sensitive to destabilizing technologies. But they have tended to accept the destabilizing dynamism of technology as an intrinsic aspect of the strategic dialectic, the underlying engine of which is a political competition not susceptible to stabilization. For the Soviets, arms control negotiations are part of this competitive process. Such negotiation can help keep risks within bounds and also, by working on the U.S. political process, restrain U.S. competitiveness.

Soviet failure to embrace U.S. strategic stability notions as strategic norms does not mean, as a practical matter, that the Soviets fail to see certain constellations of weapons technology and forces as having an intrinsic stability, in that they make the acquisition of major advantages very difficult. What they reject is the notion that, in the political and technical world as they see it, those constellations can be frozen and the strategic competition dimension thereby factored out of the East-West struggle permanently or for long periods.

INTERCONTINENTAL AND REGIONAL POWER

Defining the boundary line between strategic and non-strategic forces has been a troubling feature of SALT from the beginning. It is one of diplomacy's minor ironies that forward capabilities the United States has long regarded as part of the general purpose forces we have been hard pressed to keep out of the negotiations. But peripheral strike forces the Soviets have systematically defined and managed as strategic seem very difficult to bring into the picture.

Geography imparted an intercontinental meaning to the term strategic for the United States. The same geography dictated that, for the Soviet Union, strategic concern began at the doorstep. Soviet concern about the military capabilities in the hands of and on the territory of its neighbors is genuine, although Soviet arguments for getting the United States to legitimatize and pay for those concerns at SALT in terms of its own central force allowances have been a bit contrived. They are tantamount to penalizing the United States for having friends, while rewarding the Soviet Union for conducting itself in a manner that has left it mostly vassals and opponents on its borders.

Underlying these definitional problems are more fundamental differences between U.S. and Soviet doctrines on what is generally called "coupling." It has long been U.S. policy to assure that U.S. strategic nuclear forces are seen by the Soviets and our NATO allies as tightly coupled to European security. Along with conventional and theater nuclear forces, U.S. strategic nuclear forces constitute an element of the NATO "triad." The good health of the alliance politically and the viability of deterrence in Europe have been seen to require a very credible threat to engage U.S. strategic nuclear forces once nuclear weapons come into play above the level of quite limited use. For more than twenty years NATO's official policy has had to struggle against doubts that this coupling could be credible in the absence of clear U.S. strategic superiority. Yet the vocabularly we commonly employ itself tends to strain this linkage in that theater nuclear forces are distinguished from strategic. Ironically, the struggle to keep so-called Forward Based Systems out of SALT, because we could not find a good way to bring in comparable Soviet systems, tended to underline the distinction. In our thinking about the actual prosecution of a strategic conflict, once conflict at that level begins we tend to forget about what might be the local outcome of the regional conflict that probably precipitated the strategic exchange.

The Soviets, on the other hand, appear to take a more comprehensive view of strategy and the strategic balance. Both in peacetime political competition and in the ultimate test of a central conflict, they tend to see all force elements as contributing to a unified strategic purpose, national survival and the elimination or containment of enemies on their periphery. The U.S.S.R. tends to see intercontinental forces, and strategic forces more generally, as a means to help it win an all-out conflict in its most crucial theater, Europe. Both institutionally and operationally, Soviet intercontinental strike forces are an outgrowth and extension of forces initially developed to cover peripheral targets. Land combat forces, including conventional forces, are carefully trained and equipped to fight in nuclear conditions. In the last decade, the emergence of a hostile and potentially powerful China has more firmly riveted the "rimland" of Eurasia into the Soviet strategic perspective. Whatever the consequence of a central U.S.-Soviet nuclear conflict for their respective homelands, it could well have the effect of eliminating U.S. power and influence on the Eurasian landmass for a long time. If, by virtue of its active and passive damage-limitation measures, the Soviet Union suffered measurably less damage than did the United States, and it managed to intimidate China or destroy Chinese military power, the resultant Soviet domination of Eurasia could represent a crucial element of "strategic victory" in Soviet eyes. In any case, regional conflict outcomes seem not to lose their significance in Soviet strategy once strategic nuclear conflict begins.

CONFLICT LIMITATION

Nuclear conflict limitation is a theme on which influential American opinion is divided. After much thought and argument, the previous administration adopted a more explicit endorsement of limited strategic nuclear options as a hedge against the failings of a strategy solely reliant on all-out war plans for deterrence or response in the event of deterrent failure. The present administration has appeared more doubtful about the value of limited nuclear options because it appears generally to doubt the viability of nuclear conflict limitations. It may also share the fear of some critics that limited options could seem to make nuclear use more tolerable and therefore detract from deterrence.

Theories of nuclear conflict limitation entertained in the United States tend to rest on concepts of risk management and bargaining with the opponent. We are interested in limited options because they are more credible than unlimited ones in response to limited provocation. Whether or not they can be controlled is uncertain; hence their credible presence enhances the risk faced by the initiator of conflict. Should conflict come about, then limited options might be used to change the risk, cost, and benefit calculus of the opponent in the direction of some more or less tolerable war termination. This would not be a sure thing, but better have the limited options than not.

How the Soviets view the matter of nuclear conflict limitations is obscure. The least one can say is that they do not see it in the manner described above. From the early 1960s, after McNamara's famed Ann Arbor speech, Soviet propagandists have denounced limited nuclear war concepts as U.S. contrivances to make nuclear weapons use more "acceptable" and to rationalize the quest for counterforce advantages. They have replayed the criticism that such concepts weaken deterrence and cannot prevent nuclear war from becoming unlimited.

To some degree, Soviet propaganda on this theme is suspect for being aimed at undermining U.S. strategy innovations that detract from the political benefits of Soviet strategic force improvement. Given differences of view in the United States on this subject, moreover, the Soviets could hardly resist the temptation to fuel the U.S. argument. There are several reasons why Soviet public pronouncements should not be taken as entirely reflecting the content of operative Soviet strategic thinking and planning regarding limited nuclear use. For one thing, qualified acceptance in doctrine and posture of a non-nuclear scenario, or at least a non-nuclear phase, in theater conflict displays some Soviet willingness to embrace conflict limitation notions previously rejected. Soviet strategic nuclear force growth and modernization, in addition, have given Soviet operational planners a broader array of employment options than they had in the 1960s and may have imparted some confidence in Soviet ability to *enforce* conflict limitations. It would not be surprising, therefore, to find some Soviet contingency planning for various kinds of limited nuclear options at the theater and, perhaps, at the strategic level.

One may seriously doubt, however, whether Soviet planners would approach the problem of contingency planning for limited nuclear options with the conceptual baggage the U.S. system carries. It would seem contrary to the style of Soviet doctrinal thinking to emphasize bargaining and risk management. Rather the presence of limited options planning in the Soviet system would seem likely to rest on more traditional military concepts of economizing on force use, controlling actions and their consequences, reserving options, and leaving time to learn what is possible in the course of a campaign. The Soviet limited options planner would seem likely to approach his task with a more strictly unilateral set of concerns than his American counterpart.

Methods of Assessing the Strategic Balance

Comparative study of U.S. and Soviet strategic doctrine should give attention to a closely related matter: how we perceive and measure force balances. Allusion has already been made to asymmetries between U.S. and Soviet definitions of strategic forces, what should be counted in SALT, etc. This is by no means the heart of the matter. U.S. and Soviet methodologies for measuring military strength appear to differ significantly.

Many rather amateurish and misleading beliefs about the way the Soviets measure and value military strength prevail; for example, that the Soviets have some atavistic devotion to mass and size. Mass they do believe in because both experience and analysis show that mass counts. They can be quite choosey about size, however, as a look at their tank and fighter designs reveals. Within the limits of their technological potential, they have been quite sensitive and in no way primitive in their thinking about quality/quantity tradeoffs.

Another widespread notion is that the Soviets have an unusual propensity for worst-case planning or military overinsurance. This is hard to demonstrate convincingly in Soviet behavior. The Soviet theory of war in central Europe, for example, is daring, not conservative. Despite much rhetoric on the danger of surprise and the need for high combat readiness, Soviet strategic planning has not accorded nearly the importance to "bolt-from-the-blue" surprise attack that the United States has. This does not look like overinsurance.

The problem of measuring strength goes more deeply to differing appreciations of the processes of conflict and how they bear on force measurement. U.S. measures of the overall strategic balance tend to be of two general types. First come the so-called static measures of delivery vehicles, weapons, megatonage and equivalent megatonage, throwweight, and, perhaps, some measure of hard-target kill potential (such as weapon numbers times a scaled yield factor divided by the square of Circular Error Probability). Comparisons of this type can display some interesting things about differing forces. But they say very little about how those forces, much less the nations that employ them, will fare in war. By themselves, static measures can be dangerously misleading.

We then move on to the second, or quasi-dynamic, class of measures. Here the analyst is out to capture the essential features of a "real war" in terms general enough to allow parametric application, frequent reiteration of the analysis with varying assumptions, and easy swamping of operational and technical details which he may not be able to quantify or of which he may be ignorant. Typically, certain gross attributes of the war "scenario" will be determined, e.g., levels of alert, who goes first, and very general targeting priorities. Then specified "planning factor" performance characteristics are attributed to weapons. Because it is relatively easy (and fun), a more or less elaborate version of the ICBM duel is frequently conducted. The much more subtle and complicated, but crucial, engagement of air and sea-based forces is usually handled by gross assumption, e.g., n percent of bomber weapons get to target, all SSBNs at sea survive. Regional conflicts and forces are typically ignored. Of course, all command/control/communications systems are assumed to work as planned—otherwise the forces, and even worse, the analyst would be out of business. Finally, "residuals" of surviving forces, fatality levels, and industrial damage are totaled up. A popular variant is to run a countermilitary war in these terms and then see whether residual forces are sufficient to inflict "unacceptable damage" on cities. If so, then deterrence is intact according to some. Others point to grossly asymmetric levels of surviving forces to document an emerging strategic imbalance.

Most specialists agree and explicitly admit that this kind of analysis does not

capture the known, much less the unknown complexities, uncertainties, and for-
tuities of a real strategic nuclear conflict of any dimension. Such liturgical admissions are usually offered to gain absolution from their obvious consequences,
namely that the analysis in question could be, not illuminating, but quite wrong.
However, more heroic analytic attempts at capturing the real complexity and
operational detail of a major nuclear exchange are usually not made because they
are: a) usually beyond the expertise of single analysts or small groups, b) not
readily susceptible to varied and parametric application, and c) *still* laden by
manifold uncertainties and unknowns that are very hard to quantify. Hence they
are very hard to apply to the tasks of assessing strategic force balances or the
value of this or that force improvement. The more simplistic analysis is more
convenient. The analyst can conduct it many times, and talk over his results with
other analysts who do the same thing. The whole methodology thereby acquires
a reality and persuasiveness of its own.

The influence of this kind of analysis in our strategic decision system has many
explanations. It has sociological origins in the dominance of economists and engineers over soldiers in the conduct of our strategic affairs. It conforms with the
needs of a flat and argumentative policy process in which there are many and varied
participants, from generals to graduate students. They need a common idiom that
does not soak up too much computer time and can be unclassified. And finally,
in part because of the first explanation cited, when it comes to nuclear strategy,
we do not believe much in "real" nuclear war anyway. We are after a standard of
sufficiency that is adequate and persuasive in a peacetime setting.

Two things about this style of strategic analysis merit stating in the context of
this paper. First, on the face of it, the value of simplistic, operationally-insensitive
methodologies is assuredly less in the present strategic environment than it was
when the United States enjoyed massive superiority. Not only are weapons, force
mixes, and scenarios more complicated than these methodologies can properly
illuminate, but the relative equality of the two sides going into the conflict makes
the subleties, complexities, and uncertainties all the more important for how they
come out. Second, the Soviets do not appear to do their balance measuring in this
manner.

One can gain a fair insight into the manner of Soviet force balance analysis from
public sources, particularly Soviet military literature. Additional inferences can
be drawn from the organization and professional composition of the Soviet defense
decision system, and from some of the results of Soviet decisions. On the whole
it appears that Soviet planners and force balance assessors are much more sensitive
than we are to the subtleties and uncertainties—what we sometimes call "scenario

dependencies"—of strategic conflict seen from a very operational perspective. The timing and scale of attack initiation, tactical deception and surprise, uncertainties about weapons effects, the actual character of operational plans and targeting, timely adjustment of plans to new information, and, most important, the continued viability of command and control—these factors appear to loom large in Soviet calculations of conflict outcomes.

The important point, however, is a conceptual one: Unlike the typical U.S. planner, the Soviet planner does not appear to see the *force* balance prior to conflict as a kind of physical reification of the war outcome and therefore as a measure of strategic strength by itself. Rather he seems to see the force balance, the "correlation of military forces," as one input to a complex combat process in which other factors of great significance will play, and the chief aim of which is a new, more favorable balance of forces. The sum of these factors is strategy, and strategy is a significant variable to the Soviet planner.

As a generalization, then, the Soviet planner is very sensitive to operational details and uncertainties. Because these factors can swing widely, even wildly, in different directions, a second generalization about Soviet force analysis emerges: a given force balance in peacetime can yield widely varying outcomes to war depending on the details and uncertainties of combat. Some of those outcomes could be relatively good for the Soviet Union, others relatively bad. The planner's task is to improve the going-in force balance, to be sure. But it is also to develop and pursue ways of waging war that tend to push the outcome in favorable directions.

This kind of thinking occasions two very unpleasant features in Soviet military doctrine: a strong tendency to preempt and a determination to suppress the enemy's command and control system at all costs. The Soviets tend to see any decision to go to nuclear war as being imposed on them by a course of events that tells them "war is coming," a situation they bungled memorably in June 1941. It makes no difference whose misbehavior started events on that course. Should they find themselves on it, their operational perspective on the factors that drive war outcomes places a high premium on seizing the initiative and imposing the maximum disruptive effects on the enemy's forces *and* war plans. By going first, and especially disrupting command and control, the highest likelihood of limiting damage and coming out of the war with intact forces and a surviving nation is achieved, virtually independent of the force balance.

This leads to a final generalization. We tend rather casually to assume that, when we talk about parity and "essential equivalence" and the Soviets about "equal security," we are talking about the same thing: functional strategic stability. We are not. The Soviets are talking about a going-in force balance in which they have an equal or better chance of winning a central war, if they can orchestrate the right scenario and take advantage of lucky breaks. It is the job of the high command to see that they can. If it fails to do so, the Soviet Union could possibly lose the war. This is not stability in our terms.

Again, this is not to argue that the Soviets do not foresee appalling destruction as the result of any strategic exchange under the best of conditions. In a crisis, Soviet leaders would probably take any tolerable and even some not-very-tolerable exits from the risk of such a war. But their image of strategic crisis is one in which these exits are closing up, and the "war is coming." They see the ultimate task of strategy to be the provision of forces and options for preempting that situation. This then leads them to choose strategies that, from a U.S. point of view, seem not particularly helpful in keeping the exits open, and even likely to close them off.

It is frequently argued—more frequently as we become more anxious about the emerging force balance—that the Soviets could not have confidence in launching a strategic attack and achieving the specific objectives that theoretical analysis might suggest to be possible, such as destruction of Minuteman. Particularly because they are highly sensitive to operational uncertainties they would not, in one of the more noteworthy phrases of the latest Defense Department posture statement, gamble national survival on a "single cosmic throw of the dice." This construction of the problem obscures the high likelihood that decisions to go to strategic war will be made under great pressure and in the face of severe perceived penalty if the decision is not made and the war comes anyway. They are not likely to come about in a situation in which the choice is an uncertain war or a comfortable peace. It also obscures the fact that the heavy weight of uncertainty will also rest on the shoulders of U.S. decisionmakers in a crisis.

Dangers of Misunderstanding

In sum, there are fundamental differences between U.S. and Soviet strategic thinking, both at the level of value and at the level of method. The existence of these differences and, even more, our failure to recognize them have had dangerous consequences for the U.S.-Soviet strategic relationship.

One such might be called the "hawk's lament." Failing to appreciate the character of Soviet strategic thinking in relation to our own views, we have underestimated the competitiveness of Soviet strategic policy and the need for competitive responsiveness on our part. This is evident in both our SALT and our strategic force modernization behavior.

A second negative effect might be termed the "dove's lament." By projecting our views onto the Soviets, and failing to appreciate their real motives and perceptions, we have underestimated the difficulties of achieving genuine strategic stability through SALT and over-sold the value of what we have achieved. This has, in turn, set us up for profound, perhaps even hysterical, disillusionment in the years ahead, in which the very idea of negotiated arms control could be politically discredited. If present strategic trends continue, it is not hard to imagine a future political environment in which it would be difficult to argue for arms control negotations even of a very hard-nosed sort.

The third and most dangerous consequence of our misunderstanding of Soviet strategy involves excessive confidence in strategic stability. U.S. strategic behavior, in its broadest sense, has helped to ease the Soviet Union onto a course of more assertive international action. This has, in turn, increased the probability of a major East-West confrontation, arising not necessarily by Soviet design, in which the United States must forcefully resist a Soviet advance or face collapse of its global position, while the Soviet Union cannot easily retreat or compromise because it has newly acquired global power status to defend and the matter at issue could be vital. In such conditions, it is all too easy to imagine a "war is coming" situation in which the abstract technical factors on which we rest our confidence in stability, such as expected force survival levels and "unacceptable damage," could crumble away. The strategic case for "waiting to see what happens," for conceding the operational initiative to the other side—which is what crisis stability is all about—could look very weak. Each side could see the great operational virtues of preemption, be convinced that the other side sees them too, and be hourly more determined that the other side not have them. This, in any case, could be the Soviet way of perceiving things. Given the relative translucence of U.S. versus Soviet strategic decision processes, however, our actual ability to preempt is likely to be less than the Soviets', quite apart from the character of the force balance. Add to that the problem of a vulnerable Minuteman ICBM force and you have a potentially very nasty situation.

What we know about the nature of our own strategic thinking and that of the Soviet Union is not at all comforting at this juncture. The Soviets approach the problem of managing strategic nuclear power with highly competitive and combative instincts. Some have argued that these instincts are largely fearful and defensive, others that they are avaricious and confident. My own reading of

Russian and Soviet history is that they are both, and, for that, the more difficult to handle.

The United States and the Soviet Union share two awesome problems in common, the creation of viable industrial societies and the management of nuclear weapons. Despite much that is superficially common to our heritages, however, these two societies have fundamentally different political cultures that determine how they handle these problems. The stamp of a legal, commercial, and democratic society is clearly seen in the way the United States has approached the task of managing nuclear security. Soviet styles of managing this problem bear the stamp of an imperial, bureaucratic, and autocratic political tradition. While the United States is willing to see safety in a compact of "live and let live" under admittedly unpleasant conditions, the Soviet Union operates from a political tradition that suspects the viability of such deals, and expects them, at best, to mark the progress of historically ordained forces to ascendancy.

It is not going to be easy to stabilize the strategic competition on this foundation of political traditions. But if we understand the situation clearly, there should be no grounds for fatalism. Along with a very uncomfortable degree of competitiveness, Soviet strategic policy contains a strong element of professionalism and military rationalism with which we can do business in the interest of a common safety if we enhance those qualities in ourselves. The Soviets respect military power and they take warfare very seriously. When the propaganda and polemics are pared away, they sometimes wonder if we do. We can make a healthy contribution to our own future, and theirs, by rectifying this uncertainty.

Mutual Deterrence and Strategic Arms Limitation in Soviet Policy

Raymond L. Garthoff

One of the most controversial—and important—questions underlying debate on Soviet intentions, detente, and strategic arms limitations (SALT) in particular, has concerned the Soviet view on mutual deterrence. Do they, or don't they, believe in mutual deterrence? Do the political and military leaders in Moscow accept mutual deterrence as an underpinning to strategic arms limitation? Or do they hold a fundamentally different view of the strategic relationship between the two superpowers, and are they "taking us for a ride" in SALT? Although some decisionmakers and commentators have expressed judgment on this matter as though there were no doubt as to the answer, many others have been unsure and concerned. In particular, the continuing Soviet military buildup, and the continuing expressions in published Soviet military writings of the pursuit of a war-waging and war-winning military doctrine, have convinced some and troubled others as to Soviet views of mutual deterrence, and as to Soviet aims.

The present essay will seek to illuminate Soviet thinking on this subject, with a view to the interrelationship of Soviet ideological beliefs, political imperatives and calculation, military views and doctrine, and their intersection and reconciliation in Soviet policy.

The central conclusion of this analysis is that by the late 1960s, when SALT was launched, and since that time, the Soviet political and military leadership has recognized that under contemporary conditions there is a strategic balance between the two superpowers which provides mutual deterrence; that the nuclear strategic balance is basically stable, but requires continuing military efforts to assure its stability and continuation; and that agreed strategic arms limitations can make a contribution, possibly a significant one, to reducing these otherwise necessary reciprocal military efforts.

More broadly, the Soviet leaders believe that peaceful coexistence—with continued political and ideological competition—*is* the preferable alternative to an unrestrained arms race and to recurring high-risk politico-military confrontation; that detente and a relaxation of tensions is in the interests of the Soviet Union; and that nuclear war would not be. This does not mean that Soviet foreign policy is passive or based on satisfaction with the status quo. But the Soviet leaders

Raymond L. Garthoff is U.S. Ambassador to Bulgaria. He has been a policy analyst and practitioner in the field of dealing with the Soviet Union since 1950, and is a frequent contributor to this journal. The opinions expressed in this article are his own and do not represent official views of the Department of State.

demonstrate their recognition that the need to avoid a nuclear war can best be served by prudent actions within a framework of mutual strategic deterrence between the Soviet Union and the United States.

Questions of War and Peace in Soviet Ideology and Policy

Marxism-Leninism is based on historical determinism, a belief that socio-economic forces, through a struggle of classes, are the driving force of history. With the advent of the Soviet Union as a socialist state, the question of war between states as a possible form of class struggle arose—indeed, it was the central fact of life to the Bolshevik leaders. The Soviet leaders have seen the greatest danger to the socialist cause (identified with the Soviet Union) as coming from the capitalist military threat—and the one mortal danger faced during the first half-century of Soviet rule after the victorious conclusion of the Russian Civil War was the attack by Germany in World War II. Since World War II, the greatest threat in Soviet eyes has been the unparalleled destructive power of the American nuclear arsenal. Marxist-Leninist ideology sanctions the use of military power (and any other means) available to the socialist (Soviet) leaders whenever, *but only if,* expedient in advancing the socialist cause and not jeopardizing the security of achievements already gained, above all the security of the Soviet Union. Military power is considered necessary to *defend* the socialist cause, may be used if expedient to *advance* it, but is *not* seen as the decisive element in advancing the historical process, which will progress when conditions are ripe through indigenous action by the rising working class.

With the failure of "world revolution" after the successful conclusion of the Russian Civil War, the new Soviet state turned to recovery and then to achievement of "socialism in one country." Priority was given to economic development and to assurance of political control. Military power was secondary; the key role of military power on behalf of world socialism was seen as guaranteeing the survival of the first socialist state. Although the term was not then in vogue, *deterrence* of renewed military intervention by the capitalist powers was the underlying strategic conception. Later, when attacked, the role of the armed forces was of course defense and defeat of the attacker. The same deterrent conception has governed the period since World War II, except that there now exists a socialist camp or commonwealth, and of course it is recognized that military power in the nuclear age is enormously more dangerous and important. The principal role of Soviet military power has consistently been to dissuade imperialist powers from resort to *their* military power against the Soviet Union (and, later, also against the other countries of the socialist camp) in an effort to thwart the progressive course of history driven by social-economic revolutionary dynamics—not by military conquest.

The Soviets also see other important ideologically sanctioned *uses* of military force, but the basic Marxist-Leninist ideological framework predicates a fundamentally deterrent role for Soviet military power.[1]

The Soviets have, nonetheless, faced a doctrinal dilemma. While jettisoning Stalinist views on the inevitability of war and the necessary or desirable role of war as a catalyst of socialist advance in the world, the Communists must assume that socialism is destined to survive and to triumph, even if a world nuclear catastrophe occurs. If they openly discarded that view, it could place in question their whole world-view, and their basis for legitimacy. Hence there are reaffirmations of confidence in the ultimate triumph of socialism even if a world nuclear war should, despite Soviet efforts to prevent it, occur.

Military Views

Lenin embraced the observation of Clausewitz that "war is a continuation of politics by other means," and this indeed represents a natural Marxist-Leninist conception.[2] Remarkably, some Soviet writers (mainly but not exclusively civilians) have over the past decade and a half been so impressed by the inexpediency and enormous dangers of any nuclear world war (or indeed any war which could escalate into such a war) that they have challenged this view. They, in turn, have been criticized and refuted by other spokesmen, mainly military. Yet the question keeps arising. Why? Mainly because the two sides are not engaged in a theoretical disputation, but in political argument with considerable potential importance for military programs if not policy. In fact, both sides accept the real basic premise that war is a matter of politics or political motivation; both sides even accept the fact that nuclear war is not expedient as a matter of policy. The real underlying debate is whether war is recognized as so unpromising and dangerous that it can never occur. Such a question has profound implications for

---

1. In addition to the very summary discussion in these paragraphs, see Raymond L. Garthoff, *Soviet Military Policy: A Historical Analysis* (New York: Praeger, 1966), chapters 1, 4, 10 and 12.
2. See Raymond L. Garthoff, *Soviet Military Doctrine* (Glencoe, Ill.: Free Press, 1953), pp. 9–19 and 51–57.

military requirements. Is a deterrent force enough? And if war were to occur, is a war-fighting capability needed to seek a pyrrhic "victory"?

In the early and mid-1960s, after general acceptance of the theses on the non-inevitability, non-necessity, and non-expediency of nuclear war, Khrushchev and many lesser advocates of his views began to argue further that nuclear war would spell the end of world civilization, and was therefore not only unacceptable but unthinkable. One civilian commentator on political-military subjects carried this argument to the point of paraphrasing Clausewitz (and Lenin) to say "War can only be the continuation of madness."[3] This statement, along with a number of others, was made in the context of ideological-political Soviet polemics with the Chinese Communists. The more orthodox Soviet military line was, while agreeing that nuclear war made no sense as a continuation of politics *as a policy option for the Soviet Union*, to insist on the risks that such a war could occur and on the need for powerful Soviet military forces to deter such a war.[4]

Other military spokesmen distinguished between war as a continuation of politics, which was reaffirmed, and war as a useful instrument of politics, which it was found increasingly not to be.[5] Yet others stressed the need to be able to wage and win war if it could not be averted.

In 1965, the late Major General Nikolai Talensky, former editor of the military theoretical journal *Military Thought* (at the time of military doctrinal rejuvenation after Stalin's death in the mid-1950s) and an outspoken "revisionist," argued: "In our days there is no more dangerous illusion than the idea that thermonuclear war can still serve as an instrument of politics, that it is possible to achieve political aims by using nuclear weapons and still survive . . ."[6] Several Soviet military writers subsequently attacked General Talensky's position (and criticized him by name), arguing not that his position was theoretically wrong but that it was practically dangerous because it undercut the rationale for maintaining necessary large military forces.[7]

3. Boris Dmitriyev, "Brass Hats: Peking and Clausewitz," *Izvestiya*, 25 September 1963.
4. For example, Marshal Sergei Biryuzov (then Chief of the General Staff), "Politics and Nuclear Weapons," *Izvestiya*, 11 December 1963.
5. For example, Maj. Gen. N. Sushko and Major T. Kondratkov, "War and Politics in the 'Nuclear Age'," *Kommunist vooruzhennykh sil* [Communist of the Armed Forces], no. 2, January 1964, pp. 14–23. (Kondratkov, as a colonel, was to return to this theme in the late 1960s and 1970s.)
6. Maj. Gen. N. A. Talensky, "The Late War: Some Reflections," *Mezhdunarodnaya zhizn'* [International Affairs], no. 5, May 1965, p. 23.
7. Lt. Col. Ye. I. Rybkin, "On the Nature of Nuclear Missile War," *Kommunist vooruzhen-*

Subsequently, other civilian writers have stressed the cataclysmic nature of a nuclear world war, and clearly indicated there would be no meaningful "victor" in such a war. Some of these writers have held positions close to political leaders.[8] And there have been a number of counter-argumentations, usually by military theoretical writers, mainly challenging implications of these discussions for Soviet military strength as a deterrent, but also as a war-fighting and war-winning force if a world nuclear war should ever come.[9] (More recently, however, as shall be considered later, some of these writers have made a rather sharp turn toward accepting the view they had criticized.)

Some discussions have sought to reconcile the two opposing views. Dr. Trofimenko, for example, in a recent discussion has cited "the Leninist thesis on the fact that war is a continuation of policy . . . by forcible means," but one which is no longer "in practice a usable instrument of policy when an aggressor in the course of struggle for 'victory' can himself be annihilated."[10] He finds the chief reason for the abandonment of war as an expedient usable instrument not in the destructive nature of the weapons themselves, arguing that "imperialism would not hesitate to resort to any weapon to realize its designs," but rather in the fact that "the other side has analogous means at its disposal in a potential con-

---

nykh sil, no. 17, September 1965; Col. I. Sidel'nikov, "V. I. Lenin on the Class Approach in Determining the Nature of Wars," *Krasnaya Zvezda* [Red Star], 22 September 1965; Col. I. Grudinin, "On the Question of the Essence of War," *Krasnaya Zvezda*, 12 July 1966; and Editorial, "Theory, Politics, and Ideology: On the Essence of War," *Krasnaya Zvezda*, 24 January 1967.

8. In particular, Aleksandr Bovin, Georgy Arbatov, and Veniamin Dolgin. See A. I. Krylov, "October and the Strategy of Peace," *Voprosy filosofii* [Problems of Philosophy], no. 3, March 1968; G. A. Arbatov, "The Stalemate of the Policy of Force," *Problemy mira i sotsializma* [Problems of Peace and Socialism], no. 2, February 1974; A. Bovin, "Internationalism, and Coexistence," *Novoye vremya* [New Times], no. 30, July 1973, and "Peace and Social Progress," *Izvestiya*, 11 September 1973 (only in the first edition, substituting a *different* article, also by Bovin, in later editions!), and "Socialist, Class Politics," *Molodoi kommunist* [The Young Communist], no. 4, April 1974; and V. G. Dolgin, "Peaceful Coexistence and the Factors Contributing to its Deepening and Development," *Voprosy filosofii*, no. 1, January 1974. There have been many others, usually with references not developed so fully as these key articles.

9. For example, see Maj. Gen. K. Bochkarev, "Nuclear Arms and the Fate of Social Progress," *Sovetskaya Kirgiziya* [Soviet Kirgizia], 25 August 1970; Maj. Gen. A. Milovidov, "A Philosophical Analysis of Military Thought," *Krasnaya Zvezda*, 17 May 1973; Col. I. Sidel'nikov, "Peaceful Coexistence and the People's Security," *Krasnaya Zvezda*, 14 August 1973; Col. Ye. Rybkin, "The Leninist Conception of Nuclear War and the Present Day," *Kommunist vooruzhennykh sil*, no. 20, October 1973; Rear Adm. V. Shelyag, "Two World Outlooks—Two Views on War," *Krasnaya Zvezda*, 7 February 1974; and Col. T. Kondratkov, "War as a Continuation of Policy," *Soviet Military Review*, no. 2, February 1974.

10. G. A. Trofimenko, *SShA: Politika, voina, ideologiya* [The US: Politics, War and Ideology] (Moscow: Mysl', 1976), pp. 292–293.

flict,"[11] thus justifying the need to maintain a strong (and perhaps even war-waging) military force as a deterrent in order to buttress mutual deterrence.[12]

Military Thought, the important confidential Soviet General Staff journal, is a particularly revealing source for illuminating the "debate" on the role of war in the nuclear age. Its circulation is restricted to Soviet officers, and it can therefore be comparatively free of concerns over effects on less sophisticated mass military and lay Soviet readerships—or on non-Soviet audiences. The then Minister of Defense, Marshal Rodion Ya. Malinovsky, in an unpublished Order (No. 303 of November 6, 1965) noted that *Military Thought* is "the main military theoretical organ of the Ministry of Defense of the USSR," and that "it plays an important role in the working out of military-theoretical problems."[13]

It is clear in official directives and other discussions in *Military Thought* that since the mid-1960s the Soviet military command has seen a need to prepare for various possible wars, including both non-nuclear and nuclear. But this requirement is framed exclusively in terms of flexible response options to meet various possible Western military actions. Moreover, to cite Colonel General Povaly, then Chief of the Operations Directorate of the General Staff,

But no matter what character the war assumed, it would represent a great danger for all mankind. This is why our Party and Government are conducting a determined struggle for the exclusion of wars from the life of human society in order that no state will ever use against other states means of force for achieving its political aims, for resolving disputed international questions.[14]

There are, to be sure, many discussions of Soviet military doctrine for waging a nuclear war should one come. Usually these do not also address the *role* of war. One such discussion, however, directly addresses frankly and in some detail the debate over "the end of civilization," and provides further insights. It appeared in 1968, after the round of debate in the public press in 1965–67, and was specifically addressed to the article by A. I. Krylov in *Problems of Philosophy* which had appeared in March 1968 (cited earlier). Six months after the latter article had appeared, Major General K. Bochkarev, Deputy Commandant of the General Staff Academy, published a scathing polemical rebuttal.

---

11. Ibid., p. 293.
12. See also [Col.] T. R. Kondratkov, "Social-Philosophical Aspects of Problems of War and Peace," *Voprosy filosofii*, no. 4, April 1975.
13. "Fifty Years of Military Thought," *Voyennaya mysl'* [Military Thought], no. 6, June 1968, p. 26.
14. Col. Gen. M. I. Povaly, "Development of Soviet Military Strategy," *Voyennaya mysl'*, no. 2, February 1967, p. 74.

General Bochkarev states that a "great popularity" has been enjoyed in the West by the view that "a world nuclear war would signify 'the end of the world', and the death of all civilization, that in such a war 'there would be neither victors nor vanquished'."[15] He then says these ideas had also "made their way into our press," citing in particular the Krylov article. Bochkarev argues that imperialism has lost forever its military superiority, and has "to some degree" recognized the new military-strategic situation in the world. Written precisely at the time that the SALT talks had been scheduled to begin, he notes that "the ruling circles of the imperialist states are even making some concessions on questions of nuclear disarmament."[16] But, he stresses, the imperialists have not given up ideas of preemptive or even preventive war. "This," he notes, "unquestionably is an adventuristic gamble, but there is no serious proof that it has already been discarded by the general staffs of the Western powers, and above all by the Pentagon."[17] Krylov had not so argued, but it is clear that Bochkarev and no doubt many of his colleagues would take some convincing or are reluctant to allow that the West was in fact reliably deterred. The language suggests the latter: he does not want to give up this rationale for further Soviet military buildup.

Bochkarev asserts (not unfairly) that Krylov sees no victor in a world nuclear war—both sides would perish. He then states that "*subsequently* we will return to an evaluation of this position. *Now*, we will stress that from the point of view of the defense of the socialist homeland, this question cannot be posed and solved in this manner."[18] In this revealing formulation, Bochkarev admits that *apart* from the question of the validity of Krylov's position, even posing the question in this manner is disadvantageous to justification for Soviet defense requirements. He then goes on to admit:

Unquestionably, a world nuclear war would bring unprecedented calamities to all mankind, and our Party and Government are doing everything to prevent it. This is one of the primary tasks of the foreign policy of the Soviet Union. . . . However, *if* international imperialism unleashes a nuclear war the progress of the socialist states and their Marxist-Leninist Parties will not be paralyzed in terror and will not drop their arms as the enemies of peace and socialism would desire.[19]

15. Maj. Gen. K. Bochkarev, "The Question of the Sociological Aspect of the Struggle Against the Forces of Aggression and War," *Voyennaya mysl'*, no. 9, September 1968, pp. 3–4.
16. Ibid., p. 7.
17. Ibid., p. 7.
18. Ibid., p. 7; emphasis added.
19. Ibid., p. 7.

Bochkarev agrees with Krylov that "it is inadmissible" to ignore the conclusions of scientists on the catastrophic effects of the use of "even a part" of the vast existing nuclear stockpiles. But, he argues, there is more to war than stockpiles of nuclear weapons, including "resolution to employ the weapon" and "the socio-political base" on which they operate.[20]

In turning to his "evaluation," General Bochkarev argues "it is absolutely obvious" that "one cannot take at their face value" the admissions of Western military men "concerning the lack of prospects for a world nuclear war"; such statements are intended in part "to camouflage the preparations of the imperialist aggressors for world war," as is the doctrine of "flexible response." He then tallies the (1968) military forces of the Western blocs together at: 1560 strategic missiles, 600 heavy and 220 medium bombers, 37 aircraft carriers, 625 escort ships, 265 submarines including 70 nuclear, and regular ground forces totalling 4,735,000 men. "It is also common knowledge that the ruling circles of the United States are devoting major attention to the development of strike forces intended for war against the Soviet Union and the other socialist countries."[21] He notes the "plan" to spend $30–40 billion on deployment of an ABM system.

Bochkarev argues that "the military might of the USSR and the entire socialist camp deters imperialism but does not create an absolute guarantee against . . . war."[22] War, while deterred and unlikely, is not seen as inconceivable, and it must be prepared against with "vigilance" and with "capabilities to repel aggression."

Bochkarev then turns to the *effect* of Krylov's arguments and conclusions.

. . . The reader may get the idea of the doom of the socialist countries and all mankind in a world thermonuclear war . . . the assumption that there will be no general nuclear war and that if it does break out, struggle in it is in general excluded . . .

Well, and what if the indicated condition does not happen, if the imperialists nevertheless do unleash general nuclear war? In such a situation, will there be any kind of foreign policy goals for the socialist states and can they be attained? . . . it is assumed that with general nuclear war the "end of the world" sets in, when there can be no talk of policy in general.[23]

Bochkarov then cites Krylov on the need for realization of the enormous destruc-

20. Ibid., pp. 8–9.
21. Ibid., p. 12.
22. Ibid., p. 13.
23. Ibid., pp. 13–14.

tive consequences of a world nuclear war, in order to help prevent such a war. He is most unhappy with this formulation. Rather the General believes:

In explaining the truth of the nature of nuclear war *to the masses* it is necessary, consequently, to bring them to an understanding not only of the criminality of unleashing such a war on the part of imperialism, but also on the justice of the corresponding retribution against the aggressor. In this way, *and only in this way*, can this problem be posed and solved *from the view* of defending the socialist homeland and the interests of international communism and all progressive mankind.[24]

He is also troubled by another aspect of Krylov's stress on the improbability of world nuclear war, and his very brief reference to military strategy as applicable essentially only to possible limited wars. Again, the General:

What if the possibility of a world nuclear war nonetheless becomes a hard reality and turns into actual war? In that case—the entire content of the [Krylov] article leads us to this—a situation arises in which the concept of "military victory" is unacceptable and "military strategy, the strategy of conducting war, loses its significance." In other words, the armed forces of the socialist states at the present time, in principle, will not be able to set for themselves the goal of defeating imperialism and the global nuclear war which it unleashes and the mission of attaining victory in it, and our military science should not even work out a strategy for the conduct of war since the latter has lost its meaning and its significance ... *In this case, the very call to raise the combat readiness of our armed forces and improve their capability to defeat any aggressor is senseless.*[25]

It is clear what is troubling General Bochkarev. The entire rationale for supporting Soviet military efforts is seen as undermined.

Another aspect of Krylov's position greatly disturbs Bochkarev. Krylov contends that knowledge of the true situation strengthens the morale of the armies of socialism. The General comments:

Surprising logic: to strengthen the morale of the troops on the basis of their recognition of the hopelessness of the struggle for which they are preparing: The morale-combat qualities of Soviet soldiers are moulded on the basis of the ideology of Marxism-Leninism which ... instills in them unflagging confidence in the indestructability and final triumph of the forces of socialism.[26]

In summing up these latter points, Bochkarev concludes: "The positions of the

---

24. Ibid., p. 14; emphasis added.
25. Ibid., p. 15; emphasis added.
26. Ibid., p. 15.

author [Krylov] on the question of the capabilities and tasks of military strategy of the socialist countries in the world nuclear arena are unquestionably unacceptable."[27]

General Bochkarev ends his article with a ringing endorsement of the policy of renouncing world nuclear war, and of preventing a world war by deterrence.

Recognition of the possibility of the victory of the socialist states in a global nuclear war, as is perfectly clear, by no means signifies justification for its kindling or unleashing. The CPSU and other Marxist-Leninist parties decisively reject the irresponsible declarations on this account by the Peking adventurists, of those who talk profusely about the desirability of a world nuclear war from the point of view of the interests of the world proletariat revolution, that such a war allegedly is called upon to play the role of a "bridge" to the shining future of mankind. Communism does not need wars for its final assertion of a new social system. Its triumph is assured by the course of history . . . On the contrary, the actual possibility for the complete and decisive defeat of the military machine of the imperialist states which is assured by the economic, scientific-technical, and military might of the socialist countries plays the role of one of the primary factors determining the effectiveness of our policy of peace and the attainment of newer and newer positions in the struggle of international communism to prevent a world war.[28]

General Bochkarev's main conclusions were repeated (without attribution, but in virtual paraphrase) in a subsequent important article by Major General V. I. Zemskov, the Chief Editor of *Military Thought*. Zemskov acknowledged:

Yes, a possible nuclear war would, undoubtedly, bring unprecedented disaster to all mankind. It would be distinguished from all past wars, and would cause enormous devastation and millions of victims. . . .

Recognizing the extreme danger inherent in nuclear war, Marxist-Leninists at the same time oppose a pessimistic view toward the future of mankind.

If international imperialism unleashes a war, the peoples of the socialist states and their Marxist-Leninist parties will not cringe in terror and will not lose heart, as the monopolists would like. The peoples of the world of socialism will engage the enemy decisively, filled with confidence in the triumph of their just cause. This would be a just and victorious struggle.[29]

While some of the concerns expressed in *Military Thought* are to a lesser extent also indicated in open publications, such discussions have not laid out the

27. Ibid., p. 15.
28. Ibid, p. 16.
29. Maj. Gen. V. I. Zemskov, "Characteristic Features of Contemporary Wars and Possible Means of Conducting Them," *Voyennaya mysl'*, no. 7, July 1969, p. 23.

range of military concerns so clearly indicated by General Bochkarev, in particular those relating to "the tasks of military strategy."

Soviet military doctrine continues to be predicated on the assumption that if a general nuclear war occurs, all elements of the armed forces will contribute to waging a decisive struggle aimed at defeating world imperialism. The late Marshal Grechko presented the standard description of the role of the Soviet armed forces in these words:

Imperialism . . . is still in a position to throw the nations into the abyss of a new world war. One must be vigilant every day and every hour. That is why the Communist Party is constantly concerned with strengthening the State's defensive capability and with increasing the combat might of the Armed Forces. Their high state of combat readiness serves as an important guarantee of peace and security . . . [30]

Soviet military power, and the constant enhancement of its capability and readiness, is thus justified primarily for deterrence, as well as to wage a war if one should come despite Soviet efforts to prevent it. This view is held by the military and political leaders. It is not accurate, as some Western commentators have done, to counterpose Soviet military interest in a "war-fighting" and "war-winning" capability to a "deterrent" capability; the Soviets see the former capabilities as providing the most credible deterrent, as well as serving as a contingent resort if war should nonetheless come.

The three editions of the basic Soviet work on military doctrine, *Military Strategy*, edited by a commission headed by Marshal Sokolovsky, show both Soviet military recognition of the emergence of mutual deterrence and an equivocal and changing view on its public embrace. In the first edition, which appeared in 1962, there is a passage which attributes the concept to Western strategists and leaders, but also endorses it:

Thus, under contemporary conditions, when there is a "balance" (approximate "parity") in strategic means of destruction and a superiority of the USSR in conventional armed forces, American strategists are compelled to reconsider their previous attitude toward general nuclear war.

They began to understand that where both sides have extremely large stocks of nuclear weapons and various means of delivery to targets, mainly strategic means, general nuclear war involves enormous danger of complete mutual anni-

---

30. Marshal A. A. Grechko, *Vooruzhennye sily Sovyetskogo gosudarstva* [The Armed Forces of the Soviet State], 2nd edition (Moscow, 1975), and in translation by the USAF in its series *Soviet Military Thought*, No. 12, p. 75.

hilation. Consequently, the greater the buildup of means of mass destruction, the greater the conviction in the impossibility of their use. Hence the growth of nuclear-missile power is inversely proportional to the possibilities for its use.

There was created, as they put it in the West, a "nuclear stalemate": on the one hand a full-scale increase in the quantity of nuclear-missile weapons, and on the other the inconceivable danger in their use. In this situation, according to the evaluation of political and military circles in the United States and NATO, both sides find themselves in a position of "mutual deterrence."[31]

In the second edition, appearing in 1963, the second paragraph above was deleted; there were no changes to the text of the other two paragraphs.[32]

In the third (and latest) revised edition, issued in 1968 (shortly before Marshal Sokolovsky's death) there are three small changes to the first sentence. Instead of "contemporary conditions" the revised text refers to "conditions which have developed"; the statement that American strategists "are compelled" is changed to "have been compelled" (i.e., the situation is seen as now an accomplished fact); and the whole reference to a "balance" and "parity" is now modified by the phrase "according to Western evaluation." Otherwise there are no changes in the cited passages.[33]

In discussion of "Contemporary Means of Armed Combat and Their Effect on the Nature of War," all three editions stress the colossal and unacceptable consequences of a world nuclear war. In addition to citing American and other sources on tens of millions of casualties, the second edition added a quotation from Khrushchev (made in the interval after publication of the first edition) stating that at the beginning of 1963 the United States had more than 40,000 nuclear weapons, and "the USSR also has more than enough of these means," so that "scientists have calculated that 700–800 million people would die as a result of the initial strikes alone, and all the large cities of many countries."[34] In the third edition this (as well as all other references to or statements by Khrushchev) was deleted. But a new passage was added which, while less graphic and precise, is even more clear on the *unacceptability* of a world nuclear war to the Soviet Union:

The losses in a world nuclear war would be suffered not only by the United States

---

31. Marshal V. D. Sokolovsky, ed., *Voyennaya strategiya* [Military Strategy] (Moscow: Voen-izdat, 1962), pp. 74–75. The second and third paragraphs appear in the original text as a single long paragraph.
32. Ibid., 2nd edition, 1963, p. 80.
33. Ibid., 3rd edition, 1968, p. 72.
34. Ibid., 2nd edition, 1963, p. 244.

and its NATO Allies, but also by the socialist countries. The logic of a world nuclear war is such that in the sphere of its effect would fall an overwhelming majority of the world's states. As a result of the war many hundreds of millions of people would perish, and the majority of the survivors would in one or another degree be subject to radioactive contamination.

This is why we speak of the unacceptability of a world nuclear war, of the necessity for its prevention, of the achievement of general disarmament and the destruction of the stockpiles of nuclear weapons.

The extreme catastrophic threat of a world nuclear-missile war is hovering like a spectre over mankind. It can break out suddenly as the result of some initially local military conflict. The alternative to a devastating world nuclear war is the peaceful coexistence of states with different social orders.[35]

Thus, the most authoritative Soviet open military publication of the 1960s, with changing shadings, was quite forthright in recognizing the fact of mutual deterrence, despite some reticence to endorse the concept as formulated in the West.

Mutual deterrence in Soviet writings is usually expressed in terms of assured retaliatory capability which would devastate the aggressor, because this formulation (rather than "mutual assured destruction" capability) is more responsive to ideological sensitivity over the idea that the Soviet Union could be considered a potential aggressor and thus needs to be deterred—only adversaries (the United States, more broadly the imperialists, and also the Chinese Communists) are described as potential aggressors. In addition, this formulation avoids identification with the specific content of the American concept of "mutual assured destruction," often expressed in terms of a countervalue capability for destroying a specified percentage of the opponent's industry and population. This American interpretation is much more limited than the Soviet recognition of mutual deterrence resting on mutual capability for devastating retaliation unacceptable to a rational potential initiator of war, without calculations of arbitrary industrial and population losses which theoretically would be acceptable costs.

It is of interest that the political leaders in their programmatic statements endorse the idea that *deterrence* requires strong and ready combat capability, but do not go on to discuss meeting requirements for waging and winning a war. Brezhnev, for example, states: "Any potential aggressor is well aware that any attempt to launch a nuclear missile attack on our country would be met by devastating retaliation."[36]

---

35. Ibid., 3rd edition, 1968, p. 239.
36. L. I. Brezhnev in *Materialy XXIV s'yezda KPSS* [Materials of the Twenty-Fourth Congress of the CPSU] (Moscow: Politizdat, 1971), p. 81, and see A. N. Kosygin, ibid., p. 186.

It is also of interest that the action deterred is limited to any nuclear missile attack (or sometimes, any attack) on the Soviet Union itself (sometimes broadened to include the socialist states, meaning the countries of the Warsaw Pact, but not such countries as Vietnam or Cuba).

Mutual Deterrence and the Soviet SALT Decision

There is reason to believe that the American proposals in 1967 and 1968 to hold bilateral strategic arms limitations talks (SALT), and in particular the emphasis on avoiding an arms race in ABM systems, coincided with internal Soviet consideration of the implications for their own security, and for their future military programs, of the emerging attainment of mutual deterrence. While the transition to *mutual* deterrence had been long anticipated in the United States, it nevertheless meant a shift from prior American superiority and an unmatched American assured retaliatory capability. For the Soviets, however, it meant the achievement for the first time of a real second-strike capability, and in their view greatly enhanced security not only against a possible American first strike but also against diplomatic-military pressures supported by the superior American "position of strength" based on its monopoly of a secure second-strike capacity.

This Soviet perspective has recently been stated with unusual clarity by one of the leading Soviet commentators on the Soviet-American strategic relationship, Dr. Genrikh Trofimenko, in the following passage:

In his time, when McNamara advanced his theory of "deterrence" or "mutual deterrence" by means of a second strike dealing "unacceptable losses," he conceptually postulated parity in the capabilities of the two sides for "mutual assured destruction." The Pentagon leaders, however, calculated privately that the U.S. had greater capabilities in the sense that only the U.S. had a "full-valued capability" for a second strike, while the USSR disposed of such a capability only conditionally, "in embryo," and that this imbalance in fact and in real capabilities (with their parity theoretical) gave the U.S. an opportunity to translate it into "tangible political advantages," continuing a policy of pressure "from positions of strength" against the USSR. But no matter what illusions American strategists built on this calculation in the 1960s, and no matter what political capital they attempted to draw from it, the 1970s completely scattered such hopes: in the U.S. now no one doubts that the USSR can deal "unacceptable losses" in a second strike even under circumstances of a massive American nuclear attack on the Soviet Union.[37]

37. G. A. Trofimenko, *SShA: Politika, voina, ideologiya*, pp. 318–319.

In the exchanges in 1967–1969 leading up to the SALT talks and in their critical opening phase, the Soviet leadership showed an increasingly clear acceptance of and commitment to mutual deterrence, and awareness of the role strategic arms limitations could play in reinforcing mutual deterrence and dampening the arms race.

In the earliest Soviet responses to the American SALT proposal, the discourse was primarily in traditional disarmament terms. By the time the Soviets were prepared to meet, in 1968, both sides had expressed interest in a wider dialogue on the strategic relationship and in confidential exchanges had agreed that a main objective of the strategic arms talks would be to achieve and maintain stable strategic deterrence between the United States and the Soviet Union through agreed limitations on the deployment of strategic offensive and defensive arms, balanced so that neither side could obtain any military advantage and so that equal security should be assured for both sides.[38]

In the very first business meeting of the two SALT Delegations in Helsinki (on November 18, 1969), both sides—and not by prearrangement—stated that mutual deterrence was the underpinning of strategic arms limitation. The Soviet Delegation, in a prepared statement cleared by the highest political and military leaders in Moscow, expressed the Soviet view that:

Even in the event that one of the sides were the first to be subjected to attack, it would undoubtedly retain the ability to inflict a retaliatory strike of crushing power. Thus, evidently, we all agree that war between our two countries would be disastrous for both sides. And it would be tantamount to suicide for the ones who decided to start such a war.[39]

The Soviets prior to SALT had often described their own posture as one of deterrence, and had in their open military publications described deterrence, avoidance of war, and readiness to rebuff any aggressor as the main objectives of their defense policy and posture.[40] But the above-cited explicit formulation of mutual deterrence had never before been so clearly expressed by authoritative

---

38. See Raymond L. Garthoff, "SALT I: An Evaluation," *World Politics*, October 1978.
39. See Ambassador Gerard C. Smith, *SALT: The First Strategic Arms Negotiation* (New York: Doubleday, forthcoming) for his report on the initial Soviet presentation at SALT. By happenstance, the initial Soviet statement—though not made public—can be cited, as it was the only one not stamped "SEKRETNO"; from that time on, copies of formal statements exchanged between the delegations were marked SECRET (SEKRETNO).
40. For an example that coincided closely with the first Soviet response to the American proposal for SALT, see "Theory, Politics, and Ideology: On the Essence of War," *Krasnaya zvezda*, 24 January 1967.

Soviet spokesmen. The public military press, in particular, has avoided positive references to *mutual* deterrence and *mutual* assured destruction, for reasons discussed earlier.

It is, therefore, of considerable interest and significance that during the key formative period of Soviet policy toward negotiated strategic arms limitation there were a number of very clear and explicit endorsements in *Military Thought* by influential Soviet *military* leaders of the concepts of mutual assured retaliation and mutual deterrence.

At the very time the decision on whether to enter SALT talks was still being debated and decided in Moscow, although without reference to that fact, Marshal Nikolai I. Krylov, Commander-in-Chief of the Strategic Missile Forces, wrote in November 1967:

Under contemporary circumstances, with the existence of a system for detecting missile launches, an attempt by an aggressor to inflict a surprise preemptive strike cannot give him a decisive advantage for the achievement of victory in war, and moreover will not save him from great destruction and human losses.[41]

Later, in mid-1968, another article stated:

Everyone knows that in contemporary conditions in an armed conflict of adversaries comparatively equal in power (in number and especially in quality of weapons) an immediate retaliatory strike of enormous destructive power is inevitable.[42]

These professional discussions, soberly stated in terms clearly applying to *both* sides, are quite different from the tone of articles in the public military press with their political purposes and stress on deterring the *other* side. Similarly, in May 1969, General of the Army Semyon P. Ivanov, Commandant of the prestigious Military Academy of the General Staff, and previously Deputy Chief of the General Staff and Chief of its Operations Division, wrote:

With the existing level of development of nuclear missile weapons and their reliable cover below ground and under water it is impossible in practice to destroy them completely, and consequently it is also impossible to prevent an annihilating retaliatory strike.[43]

41. Marshal N. I. Krylov, "The Nuclear Missile Shield of the Soviet State," *Voyennaya mysl'*, no. 11, November 1967, p. 20.
42. Maj. Gen. N. Vasendin and Col. N. Kuznetsov, "Contemporary War and Surprise," *Voyennaya mysl'*, no. 6, June 1968, p. 42.
43. General of the Army S. P. Ivanov, "Soviet Military Doctrine and Strategy," *Voyennaya mysl'*, no. 5, May 1969, p. 47.

In the same May 1969 issue of *Military Thought,* its Chief Editor, Major General (now Lt. General) V. I. Zemskov, after citing American sources (including Secretary McNamara) that "the Soviet Union would be in a position to destroy all America after having withstood the first powerful strike on the part of the United States," went on to cite the buildup of American strategic forces from 1963 to 1968. He then declared:

This growth in nuclear potential, in the estimate of foreign specialists, led to the situation whereby a kind of "nuclear balance" was created between the major nuclear powers. In military-political circles of the United States, there has long been a lack of confidence in the supremacy of their nuclear-missile capabilities. Precisely for this reason they talk about a nuclear balance, the essence of which consists in the following: The capabilities for mutual destruction in a limited time by nuclear strikes on the main vitally important regions of the countries and the main groupings of armed forces are relatively equal. The presence of stockpiles of nuclear weapons and means of their delivery are such that their complete use theoretically makes it possible to destroy every living thing on our planet.
    A nuclear war, states the Declaration of the Conference of Representatives of Communists and Workers Parties of 1960, "can inflict unprecedented destruction on entire countries and turn the largest centers of world production and world culture into ruins. Such a war would result in the death and suffering of hundreds of millions of people, including those in countries not participating in the war." A nuclear war, as in general any war, cannot and must not serve as a method of resolving international disputes.
    Realistically considering this, the Communist Party of the Soviet Union and the Soviet Government are pursuing a consistent line toward preventing a world war, including a nuclear war, and toward excluding it from the life of society.[44]

The passage cited makes an interesting transition from attribution of concepts of a "nuclear balance," parity and mutual deterrence to Western sources, to the Soviet and other Communist Parties' Declaration of the devastation that would be caused by a world nuclear war, and from that to the Soviet policy aim of prevention of a world nuclear war. Later in the article, in discussing Soviet military policy, he states:

The degree of probability of a particular type of war does not, of course, remain the same for each historical period, and changes under the influence of a number of political and military-technical factors. Of special importance in this connection can be the disruption of the "nuclear balance." It is possible, for example, in case of further sharp increase of nuclear potential or *the creation by one of the*

---

44. Maj. Gen. V. I. Zemskov, "Wars of the Modern Era," *Voyennaya mysl',* no. 5, May 1969, p. 57.

sides of highly effective means of anti-ballistic missile defense while the other side lags considerably in solution of these tasks. A change of the "nuclear balance" in favor of the countries of imperialism would increase manifold the danger of a nuclear war.[45]

It is clear from these passages that General Zemskov believed in 1969 that there was a "nuclear balance" providing mutual potential destruction and therefore mutual deterrence, but that it was at least at that time a somewhat precarious balance from the *Soviet* standpoint, and particularly if the United States, which was well ahead of the Soviet Union in developing anti-ballistic missile technology, should deploy an effective ABM defense. There is a clear relationship between this discussion and the Soviet decision, taken by that time and soon to become evident in SALT, that ballistic missile defenses of the two sides should if possible be sharply limited through a strategic arms limitation agreement so as not to risk restoring the United States to a position of superiority that could imperil the still unstable state of mutual assured destruction and mutual deterrence.

A related point of considerable interest was made explicit in these same confidential General Staff discussions. The reader may have noted the reference by Marshal Krylov to "the existence of a system for detecting missile launches" as one element in his conclusion on mutual deterrence. In his discussion, he explains further that he has in mind, and the Soviet Union had under at least some unspecified contingency guidance, a policy of "launch on warning" (though he does not use that Western expression), as well as some "fallback" reliance on hardening of missile launchers.

It must be stressed that under present conditions, when the Soviet Armed Forces are in constant combat readiness, any aggressor who begins a nuclear war will not remain unpunished, a severe and inevitable retribution awaits him. With the presence in the armament of troops of launchers and missiles which are completely ready for operation, as well as systems for detecting enemy missile launches and other types of reconnaissance, *an aggressor is no longer able suddenly to destroy the missiles before their launch on the territory of the country against which the aggression is committed. They will have time during the flight of the missiles of the aggressor to leave their launchers and inflict a retaliatory strike against the enemy. Even in the most unfavorable circumstance, if a portion of missiles is unable to be launched before the strike of missiles of the aggressor, as a result of the high degree of protection of the launchers from nuclear explosions,*

---

45. Ibid., p. 59; emphasis added.

these missiles will be preserved and will carry out the combat missions assigned to them.[46]

Again, the previously cited 1968 article by General Vasendin and Colonel Kuznetsov also is explicit on the importance (and existence) of contemporary means of reconnaissance, detection, warning, and control of one's own forces in assuring retaliation (in a passage immediately preceding the one earlier quoted):

With contemporary means of reconnaissance, early detection, warning, and control should an aggressor succeed in placing into action the chief means of destruction (mass missile launches, takeoffs of aircraft, launch of space vehicles, etc.), this does not mean that he will not receive deserved retribution.[47]

General of the Army Ivanov also states:

Contemporary means of *early detection*, moreover, make it possible to discover the *initiation* of an enemy nuclear attack and to take necessary retaliatory measures in a timely manner.[48]

Although a little less precise, the "launch on warning" concept is unmistakable in these passages as well.

The Minister of Defense, Marshal Rodion Malinovsky, may have referred more obliquely to this same launch on warning concept in an openly published article in January 1967, when he wrote of "practical elaboration of methods of conducting armed conflict under conditions of contemporary warfare" in a "nuclear missile war," stating that "Soviet military thought in devoting special attention to the study of methods for increasing combat readiness of the forces in every way possible . . . for frustrating the enemy's aggressive intentions."[49]

During the SALT I negotiations, in 1970, the Soviet Delegation referred to the existence and continuous improvement of early-warning systems, owing to which ICBM silos might be empty by the time they were hit by an attacker's strike, the ICBMs having been launched by that time. The American Delegation commented later on this statement and expressed the hope that no government would launch its ICBM force solely on the possibly fallible reading of signals from its early-warning systems. It expressed the view that such a strategic doctrine seemed inconsistent with a proper concern for the problems of acciden-

---

46. Krylov, "The Nuclear Missile Shield," p. 20; emphasis added.
47. Vasendin and Kuznetsov, "Contemporary War," p. 42.
48. Ivanov, "Soviet Military Doctrine," p. 47; emphasis added.
49. Marshal R. Ya. Malinovsky, "October and the Building of the Armed Forces," *Kommunist*, no. 1, January 1967, p. 35.

tal or unauthorized launches or provocative third-party attack. The Soviet Delegation clearly was not authorized to enter a discussion of this subject, and had not intended its initial statement to do so. Accordingly, it replied with an attempt to disassociate the question from accidental, unauthorized or provocative attacks, and to refer to *American* statements (not made in SALT) about possible launch on warning. The U.S. Delegation then provided an official American disavowal of the concept by the Secretary of Defense, with further criticism of the idea as potentially dangerous for automatic escalation or even for starting a war by accident.[50] But efforts to elicit a statement on Soviet policy with respect to the concept met with silence, and an unofficial comment by a senior military representative that such matters went beyond the proper purview of SALT, and should not be discussed with civilians.

These indications in *Military Thought* and in the exchanges in SALT that the Soviet authorities, at least in 1967–70, were prepared to consider seriously a launch on warning concept helps to explain their relatively less excited concern over ICBM silo vulnerability. It raises the further question whether a concept which may have arisen at a time of relative Soviet inferiority may have continued since as a justification for keeping such a large ensiloed ICBM force (still today constituting 75 percent of Soviet strategic force capability) even after the United States has considerable counterforce capacity, and its further developing and planning to deploy highly effective counterforce capabilities which could threaten the entire Soviet ICBM force—*if* it remained in its silos and tried to "ride out" an American attack. U.S. pursuit of such a capability with the MK 12A warhead for Minuteman III, the MX missile, and Trident II may serve only to increase Soviet reliance on a launch on warning concept.

It should be noted that in the mid-1950s the Soviet military (initially through discussions in the same General Staff organ) developed a concept of preemptive Soviet action in response to a Western imminent intention to attack.[51] This concept, developed in the pre-missile age, was evidently modified, if not super-

---

50. Secretary of Defense Harold Brown, in 1977 and 1978, was much more ambiguous in Congressional testimony as to conditions under which the United States might or might not launch its ICBMs before Soviet missiles struck the United States. See George C. Wilson, "Brown Cautious on Response to Attack," *Washington Post*, 24 October 1977, and Brown's speech of June 23, 1978, stating: "The Soviets would have to consider the possibility that our minuteman missiles would no longer be in their silos when their ICBMs arrived. We have not adopted a doctrine of launch under attack but they surely would have to take such a possibility into consideration."
51. See Raymond L. Garthoff, *Soviet Strategy in the Nuclear Age* (New York: Praeger, 1958), pp. 84–87.

seded, in the 1960s by the launch on warning concept (although there are hints of the possibility under some circumstances of preemption, as in the second passage from the 1968 article cited earlier). From this standpoint, launch on warning is a step forward toward stability from preemption, but it remains a potentially destabilizing and dangerous possibility and the United States should seek ways to discourage the Soviets from any degree of reliance on it—as well as not succumbing to its temptations as a "shortcut" way to maintain a deterrent. Inherently, the *possibility* of launch on warning (or launch on first impact, or on multiple impacts, etc.) *does* contribute to the uncertainties any potential attacker must consider and that is good, but it is dangerous if in fact resorted to in defense against anything except a massive assault.

In April 1969, an article by Anatoly A. Gromyko (son of the Foreign Minister and a distinguished "American expert" in the Soviet Ministry of Foreign Affairs, then at the Academy of Sciences Institute of USA Studies) appeared in *Military Thought*. Articles in this journal by non-military contributors are rare; clearly the purpose of Gromyko's contribution was to present a rationale for SALT in terms appealing to its select military readership. The thrust of his argument was that American reaction to the buildup in Soviet strategic power (ICBMs were specifically noted) had led not only to the need for the United States to shift from "massive retaliation" to "flexible response" concepts and to accepting "mutual assured destruction," but also had compelled the United States to seek strategic arms limitations and to curb the strategic arms race. (Incidentally, he suggested that Secretary McNamara had been forced out of his position as Secretary of Defense because of hard-line opposition by "the military-industrial complex" and others to his "realism" in recognizing the emergence of mutual deterrence.) More broadly, he argued in terms of differentiation among various elements of the American policymaking and policy-influencing elite which—by implication—should be recognized by the military readers, rather than assuming all are single-mindedly hostile to any improvement of relations with the Soviet Union.[52]

Soviet military theorists and leaders, including those we have cited above, continue to discuss ways and means of waging and seeking to win a general nuclear war should one come. For reasons discussed earlier, they see no inconsistency in recognizing that such war would be an unprecedented disaster endangering all mankind, and therefore in supporting mutual deterrence based on

---

52. Anatoly A. Gromyko, "American Theoreticians Between 'Total War' and Peace," *Voyennaya mysl'*, no. 4, April 1969, pp. 86–92.

mutual retaliatory destructive capability, while also preparing to attempt to cope with the eventuality of such event if it should come and to seek to emerge from it victorious, that is, less totally destroyed than "capitalism."

Accordingly, too, the Soviet military have had an active interest and role in SALT.[53] The strong endorsement of mutual deterrence made by the Soviet side from the very outset of the SALT talks, including by senior Soviet military representatives at SALT, was noted earlier. This was backed up by further concrete signals, including above all the Soviet indications (also from the very outset of SALT in late 1969) that they were opposed to a nation-wide ABM deployment which not only could fuel the competition in strategic offensive arms, but also could upset mutual assured destruction. The explicit prohibition on such nation-wide ABM deployments contained in Article I of the ABM Treaty was, in fact, included on Soviet initiative.[54]

In sum, we see that far from having to *infer* from such things as the Soviet acceptance of the ABM Treaty that there is a Soviet interest in mutual deterrence based on assured mutual retaliatory capability, there is a clear case for it in previously unavailable confidential Soviet General Staff discussions preceding the opening of SALT, and from the SALT negotiating history as well.

Maintaining Mutual Deterrence

The Soviet leadership, as the American, continues to look in the first instance and in the final account to its own unilateral military strength as the guarantor of deterrence of the other side and of mutual deterrence. In both cases, the professional military leadership in particular remains somewhat skeptical of the role that arms control—especially bilateral (or multilateral) negotiated commitments to strategic arms limitations—can play in securing such deterrence. At the same time, there is good evidence that national leaderships, including at least some professional military men, have increasingly come to accept negotiated strategic arms limitations as a contributing element in providing more stable and less costly deterrent military forces. As one of the few established Soviet civilian commentators on strategic matters put it (in 1976): "Under contemporary circumstances a real possibility to find a common interest with a poten-

---

53. See Raymond L. Garthoff, "SALT and the Soviet Military," *Problems of Communism*, January-February 1975, pp. 21–37.
54. See Raymond L. Garthoff, "Negotiating with the Russians: Some Lessons from SALT," *International Security*, 1, no. 4, (Spring 1977): 17.

tial adversary is to be found in the area of . . . the stabilization of the military balance by means of limiting the arms race."[55]

In the Soviet view—shared by military and civilian leaders—just as in the mainstream of American thinking in the 1970s, overall "parity" has existed for about a decade. There are those—again in Moscow and in Washington—who are apprehensive as to whether this parity will be upset by some successful effort of the other side. But successive U.S. Secretaries of Defense and Chairmen of the Joint Chiefs of Staff have agreed, even when sometimes sounding such an alarm for the future (fortunately, one that seems each few years to recede to a few years hence), that "at present" there is an overall strategic parity—that while each side has certain areas of superiority they balance out to yield an overall parity.

Parity was of course for the Soviet side an improvement over the previous American unilateral superiority. Soviet political leaders had from the ebullient Khrushchev of the late 1950s on been claiming superiorities, and overall parity. But only in the early to mid-1970s did the Soviet military leaders admit that an assured retaliatory capability for the Soviet Union had come about only in the 1960s—actually, the late 1960s. And the Soviet military have acknowledged throughout the 1970s, as have the American, that while each side has certain areas of superiority, these balance out to yield an overall parity. Nevertheless, there remain uncertainties as to the future.

The Soviet military leaders, and other Soviet leaders and commentators, with varying degrees of alarm continue to display considerable suspicion of American intentions and concern over growing American capabilities *and* as to why this continued increase in capabilities is sought. To be sure, some of these expressions of concern serve other purposes, such as argument to support requested Soviet military programs. But many have the ring of sincerity about them and many cite incontrovertible evidence to support their arguments on capabilities, as well as "evidence" which to a Soviet reader (and writer) may seem convincing in allegations of nefarious American objectives and intentions.

Much of this may sound familiar to an American reader as a description of the obverse *American* suspicions of Soviet military buildup and hostile designs. A description of an adversary in terms of a "mirror image" of oneself (either as equally benign *or* belligerent) based on unverified assumptions, often unconscious ones, must be eschewed; when, however, there *is* a parallel perception of the other side it is important to recognize that fact.

---

55. Trofimenko, *SShA: Politika, voina, ideologiya*, p. 324.

In the Soviet perception, the United States has continued, notwithstanding SALT and detente, to seek military superiority. Although some highly placed American leaders and others have or are considered to have "soberly" evaluated the strategic situation and given up pursuit of supremacy, powerful forces are believed to continue to seek advantage and superiority in order to compel Soviet acquiescence in American policy preferences. Moreover, actual American military policy and programs are seen as seeking to upset or to circumvent the nuclear mutual deterrent balance.

A series of developments since the SALT I agreements were signed in 1972 are seen in this light, above all the open pursuit of counterforce capabilities through increasingly accurate and numerous MIRV systems. The existing 1046 Poseidon and Minuteman III missiles with their 6000–7000 independently targettable warheads (to say nothing of having in addition the vastly superior American strategic bomber force, the other 664 ICBMs and SLBMs, and American theater nuclear forces capable of striking the Soviet Union) *do* currently provide a superior counterforce capability against the Soviet ICBM force (and, for that matter, against the Soviet bomber and submarine missile forces, since these are not kept on the same degree of airfield alert or deployment at sea as are their American counterparts). This superiority is evident in two senses: first, greater than present Soviet capability (although the Soviets are, not surprisingly, moving to upgrade their capacity); and second, more ominous for the Soviet side because far more Soviet than American strategic eggs are in the fixed land-based ICBM force basket. Also, as noted above, other Soviet intercontinental forces are less numerous, less capable, and more vulnerable. Given the concerns in the United States over the growing—but still future—Soviet threat to American ICBMs, is it any wonder that conservative Soviet military planners and responsive political leaders would be concerned over the growing *existing* American capabilities? And the full currently planned and announced American programs for the Mark 12A warhead for Minuteman III, the MX ICBM, and the Trident I and II submarine and missile systems—to say nothing of strategic cruise missiles—would result in a still *greater* American overall (and counterforce) advantage ten years from now than we have today, *even* with all Soviet programs estimated to be deployed within that period!

It is not the purpose of the present discussion to argue for or against particular American military programs. Moreover, the Carter Administration has declared its readiness to foreclose at least some future programs in balanced strategic arms limitations in SALT II or III. But from the vantage-point of Moscow, while a general nuclear balance had come into being by the late 1960s, and parity was recognized and supported in the SALT I accords, continued major Soviet military efforts are needed to keep up the balance.

Soviet generals often cite a statement made by General Secretary Brezhnev in 1970:

We have created strategic forces which constitute a reliable means of deterring any aggressor. We shall respond to any and all attempts from any quarter to obtain military superiority over the USSR with a suitable increase in military strength to guarantee our defense. We cannot do otherwise.[56]

This of course remains a postulate of Soviet policy (as, indeed, of parallel American policy).

What effect has SALT had on the applicability of this postulate, and what is the potential role for SALT in the future?

Let us recall the important discussion by General Zemskov in the General Staff journal in 1969. He spoke of a "nuclear balance" and of the particular importance of the possible "disruption" of that balance in case of "the creation by one of the sides of highly effective means of anti-ballistic missile defense while the other side lags considerably in solution of these tasks" and that it would "increase many times the danger of a nuclear war" if the West achieved such an advantage.[57] It is clear that this reflected a view held at the highest political and military levels, and the congruence of Soviet and American views and objectives led to the ABM Treaty in SALT signed in May 1972.

Many Soviet writers have noted in general terms the effect of SALT in reflecting and supporting parity and even the nuclear balance. Trofimenko expressed with particular precision the effect of the ABM Treaty on mutual deterrence, as seen by the Soviets. He described "a situation of equality of strategic capabilities of the USSR and the U.S. stemming from the essential equality in the balance of strategic arms (in particular, since each of the sides under any circumstances retains the capability for a retaliatory strike on the vital centers of the other)." While this situation had developed by the late 1960s, and was only implicitly codified in the SALT I agreements in 1972, Trofimenko does speak of "the equalizing of the capabilities of the USSR and the U.S. for a retaliatory strike (in particular as a result of the prohibition on the creation of nation-wide ABM systems through the 1972 Treaty) . . ."[58] and most specifically, he writes:

---

56. L. I. Brezhnev, *Leninskim kursom* [The Leninist Course] vol. 3 (Moscow: Politizdat, 1970), p. 541.
57. Zemskov, *Voyennaya mysl'*, no. 5, May 1969, p. 59.
58. Trofimenko, *SShA: Politika, voina, ideologiya*, pp. 318 and 317.

The conclusion of the ABM Treaty and its subsequent Protocol [reducing the number of permitted ABM defense areas from two to one for each side] for all practical purposes cast off the key link of 'offense-defense' in the field of strategic systems. By relinquishing deployment of nation-wide ABM systems, the two sides eliminated one of the main motivating stimuli to the further buildup of efforts in the field of offensive systems.[59]

This recognition of the key significance of the ABM Treaty in "preventing the emergence of a chain reaction of competition between offensive and defensive arms" was specifically cited by Marshal Grechko, then Minister of Defense, and General of the Army (now Marshal) Kulikov, then Chief of the General Staff, in endorsing the Treaty when it was formally considered by the Supreme Soviet in the ratification process.[60]

In viewing broadly the overall current situation, Trofimenko (and others, including Brezhnev) continue today to refer to "contemporary conditions, when Soviet-American strategic parity exists."[61]

But there was another element in General Zemskov's analysis in 1969. In addition to noting the possibility of the disruption of the nuclear balance if "one side" (the United States) obtained an effective ABM capability and the other did not, he also noted such a danger "in case of a further sharp increase of nuclear [strike] potential" by one side.[62] And this is the risk some Soviet military planners have seen in the qualitative and quantitative superiority of the United States in MIRVed systems throughout the 1970s. If Soviet discussions in *Military Thought* in the mid and late 1970s were available there is no doubt this would appear as an explicit concern, notwithstanding recognition of the contribution of the SALT ABM Treaty to strategic stability.

There are many indications of this concern in Soviet discussions. Albeit without specific reference to MIRV, one worth citing is the statement by the now retired former General Staff Colonel Vasily M. Kulish, writing soon after the SALT I agreements had been reached:

The appearance of new types of weapons could seriously affect the relation of military forces between the two world systems. . . . Far-reaching international consequences could arise in the event that one side possessed qualitatively new

59. Ibid., pp. 324–325.
60. The quotation is from General of the Army Viktor G. Kulikov, cited in *Izvestiya*, 24 August 1972; a similar statement by Marshal Andrei A. Grechko appears in *Pravda*, 30 September 1972.
61. Trofimenko, *SShA: Politika, voina, ideologiya*, p. 323.
62. Zemskov, *Voyennaya mysl'*, no. 5, May 1969, p. 59.

strategic weapons which could serve to neutralize the ability of the opposing side to carry out effective retaliatory operations . . . even a relatively small and brief superiority by the United States over the Soviet Union in the development of certain "old" or "new" types and systems of weapons that significantly increase the strategic effectiveness of American military power could exert a destabilizing influence on the international political situation throughout the entire world and present extremely unfavorable consequences for the cause of peace and socialism.[63]

The main concern of the Soviet leadership is American political-military strategic *intentions*. They are concerned over growing American counterforce *capabilities* and parallel American advocacy of counterforce *concepts* both because of their impact threatening destabilization of the existing balance and because of what they suspect as to the underlying American intentions. Dr. Trofimenko, for example, concludes that the "genuine parity" reflected and bolstered by the SALT ABM Treaty "does not suit American military theoreticians." He argues that "the true nature of American strategic missile targeting is a most important state secret, and the American command can target its missiles in any way it wishes without speaking out publicly about it. Hence the public campaign of the Pentagon connected with the advertised 'retargetting' [of the Schlesinger Doctrine] is . . . a conscious effort to put psychological pressure on the other side . . ."[64]

The reversal of American stated policy on the destabilizing nature of counterforce capabilities, and the open pursuit of such capabilities since 1974 has considerably raised Soviet suspicions, especially as it accompanied the failure to reach a SALT agreement based on the Vladivostok accords.

At the outset in SALT II in late 1972, the Soviet side did probe for reciprocal restraints on MIRV (and MARV) as well as more generally on new strategic programs of both sides. These efforts were swamped by the tough overall Soviet position in SALT II, the lack of synchronization of MIRV technology (with the United States unwilling to restrain its advantages for early deployment, particularly since the Soviets could then catch up and gain from the greater MIRV potential of their larger throw-weight missiles), and the U.S. priority on efforts in SALT to move toward equalization of missile throw-weight.

In short, despite some efforts on both sides, SALT II has not yet succeeded (as of this writing) in reinforcing and moving beyond the modest restraints estab-

---

63. V. M. Kulish, in *Voyennaya sila i mezhdunarodnye otnosheniya* [Military Force and International Relations] (Moscow: IMO, 1972). p. 226.
64. Trofimenko, *SShA: Politika, voina, ideologiya*, p. 319.

lished in the SALT I Interim Agreement of 1972 on strategic offensive weapons. Accordingly, while both sides continue to seek SALT limitations on strategic offensive arms, success in this effort—in contrast to the success of the ABM Treaty —has eluded them. And accordingly, both sides continue to place reliance on their respective unilateral programs to ensure not falling behind in the strategic balance. Differences in these programs, in turn, make increasingly difficult any agreement on meaningful limitations.

Recent years have, however, seen hopeful developments in Soviet acceptance of the implications of mutual deterrence for strategic and political objectives. This may in time facilitate strategic arms limitation, or at least mute and stabilize the competition.

Soviet military and political leaders have ceased to call for strategic superiority as an objective since the 24th Party Congress in April 1971, which also marked a turning point in SALT. Instead, mutual deterrence, a balance, parity, and equal security are advocated. To be sure, this is often expressed in terms implying that it is only the West which had aggressive aims which are restrained by mutual deterrence. But it is nonetheless an important advance. Brezhnev stated the general Soviet political view in 1975 in these words:

International detente has become possible because a new relation of forces has been established in the world arena. Now the leaders of the bourgeois world can no longer entertain serious intentions of resolving the historic dispute between capitalism and socialism by force of arms. The senselessness and extreme danger of further tension are becoming increasingly obvious under conditions where both sides possess weapons of colossal destructive power.[65]

Notwithstanding the fact that each side sees only a need to deter the other, both recognize the fact of mutual strategic "sufficiency" and assured retaliatory capability and the resulting mutual deterrence.

On the eve of the Carter Administration, in a major policy address at Tula, Brezhnev authoritatively disavowed the aim of military superiority aimed at a first strike, reaffirming security as an aim, deterrence and the goal of disarmament:

Of course, comrades, we are improving our defenses. It cannot be otherwise. We have never neglected and will never neglect the security of our country and the security of our allies.

But the allegations that the Soviet Union is going beyond what is sufficient

---

65. L. I. Brezhnev, "In the Name of Peace and Happiness for Soviet People," *Pravda*, 14 June 1975.

for defense, that it is striving for superiority in arms, with the aim of delivering a "first strike," are absurd and utterly unfounded . . .
   Our efforts are aimed at preventing both first and second strikes and at preventing nuclear war altogether . . . The Soviet Union's defense potential must be sufficient to deter anyone from disturbing our peaceful life. Not a course aimed at superiority in arms but a course aimed at their reduction, at lessening military confrontation—that is our policy.[66]

The Soviet position was spelled out more fully in *Pravda* shortly after the Tula speech by the American affairs expert, Academician Arbatov. He vigorously refuted arguments that the Soviet Union was seeking superiority, and accurately described in some detail areas of the strategic balance in which the Soviet Union leads (the overall number of ICBM and SLBM missile launchers; strategic missile "throw-weight") and in which the United States leads (numbers of strategic bombers and bomber "throw-weight"; numbers of missile warheads; forward submarine bases; "and much else"). Thus, he notes, "while enjoying an approximate equality (parity) in general, the two countries have within this parity considerable differences (asymmetries) in various components of their armed forces, connected with differences in geographic situations, the nature of possible threats to their security, technical characteristics of individual weapons systems, and even in traditions of military organization." The main thing, though, is "the existence of an approximate balance, that is, a parity in the relation of forces about which the USSR and the United States came to agreement with the signing of the principle of equal rights to security."[67]

Public acceptance of parity began to be stressed in early 1977, even prior to Brezhnev's speech. For example, TASS political correspondent Kornilov noted that "there exists parity, equality of military might. It is precisely this principle, the principle of parity and the principle of equal security stemming from it which is steadily and persistently upheld by the Soviet Union . . ."[68] Viktor Berezin, another commentator, also noted:

. . . there can only be approximation and never absolute balance in military potentials of the two great powers. . . . if we look at the general relation of forces between East and West, we will not see any basic advantages [to either side] . . .

---

66. L. I. Brezhnev, "Outstanding Exploit of the Defenders of Tula," *Radio Moscow*, 18 January, and *Pravda* and *Izvestiya*, 19 January, 1977.
67. G. A. Arbatov, "The Great Lie of the Opponents of Detente," *Pravda*, 5 February 1977. Arbatov repeated this point in a broadcast interview on *Radio Moscow* on February 12, 1977.
68. Yury Kornilov, TASS Commentary, *Radio Moscow*, 12 January 1977.

with powerful strategic arms being possessed by both sides, any small advantage by either is seen as illusory.[69]

Again late in 1977, on the occasion of the Sixtieth Anniversary of the Bolshevik Revolution, Brezhnev returned to this theme, stating:

The Soviet Union is effectively looking after its own defense, but it does not and will not seek military superiority over the other side. We do not want to upset the approximate equilibrium of military strength existing at present . . . between the USSR and the United States. But in return we insist that no one else should seek to upset it in his favor.[70]

This is a more far-reaching statement than the earlier one denying an aim of superiority "with the aim of a first strike"; it denies superiority as a current or future aim for *any* purpose.

A major Soviet statement on the SALT negotiations, which appeared as an unsigned editorial in *Pravda* on February 11, 1978, noted approvingly "the objectively existing equilibrium of strategic forces between the USSR and the U.S."[71] Similarly, Marshal Kulikov wrote:

The Soviet state, effectively looking after its defense, is not seeking to achieve military superiority over the other side, but at the same time it cannot permit the approximate balance which has taken shape . . . between the USSR and the U.S. to be upset, to the disadvantage of our security.[72]

Many other authoritative commentators have echoed these themes of parity, equal security, and the non-pursuit of superiority.

Especially interesting have been a number of commentaries and discussions in the open military press. Before Brezhnev's Tula speech, in early 1977, *Red Star* carried two commentaries asserting that "parity" was a reality and had been the basis for U.S.-Soviet relations "in recent years," and that the military power of the United States and the Soviet Union was said to be regarded by "unbiased experts" as "about equal."[73]

69. Viktor Berezin, *Radio Moscow*, 31 January 1977.
70. L. I. Brezhnev, "The Great October Revolution and the Progress of Mankind," *Radio Moscow*, (live) 2 November 1977; also in *Pravda* and *Izvestiya*, 3 November 1977.
71. Editorial, "The Task of Limiting Strategic Arms: Prospects and Problems," *Pravda*, 11 February 1978.
72. Marshal Viktor G. Kulikov, "Sixty Years on Guard over the Achievements of the October Revolution," *Partiinaya zhizn'*, no. 1, January 1978.
73. TASS unsigned, "Who Sets the Tone?" *Krasnaya Zvezda*, 12 January 1977, and Yury Kornilov, "Myths and Facts," *Krasnaya Zvezda*, 14 January 1977.

Appearing about the same time as Brezhnev's Tula speech, although signed to press a month earlier (December 17, 1976) was an interesting article in the *Military-Historical Journal* by Colonel Ye. Rybkin, long regarded in the West as a "Red Hawk." Colonel Rybkin, a professor on the Lenin Military-Political Academy staff, citing Lenin that "war is a continuation of politics," but in almost direct refutation of Rybkin's earlier expressed views, cited the essential need for the possibility of peaceful coexistence and the prevention of war.[74] The point of particular interest to the present discussion is not only Rybkin's conclusion that "Rejection of a nuclear war . . . is dictated by the new realities of the era," but that "a so-called 'nuclear parity' has been established between the USSR and the United States, that is, a certain balance of power, which was officially recognized at the Soviet-American talks in 1972–74, with a mutual agreement not to disrupt the balance."[75] Moreover, in arguing that there is "an objective need to end the arms race," Rybkin cites the argument that "the quantity of nuclear weapons has reached such a level that a further increase would in practice make no change," and he cites Brezhnev's statement of July 1974 that "a sufficient quantity of arms has been amassed to destroy everything alive on earth several times over."[76] (Brezhnev, incidentally, had echoed his own 1974 remarks a few weeks earlier in a speech in Bucharest.[77])

Another prominent Soviet military writer, Major General Rair Simonyan, a professor at the Frunze Academy, has argued:

Given the priority of strategic forces, when both sides possess weapons capable of destroying many times over all life on earth, neither the addition of new armaments nor an increase in their destructive power can bring any substantial military—and still less political—advantage.[78]

He also cites and explicitly agrees with an American statement that: "In the contemporary world it is impossible to insure security by means of an arms build-up."[79]

An editorial in *Red Star* in mid-1977, in arguing the need not to be complacent

74. Col. Ye. Rybkin, "The 25th Congress of the CPSU and the Problem of Peaceful Coexistence Between Socialism and Capitalism," *Voyenno-istoricheskii Zhurnal* [The Military-Historical Journal], no. 1, January 1977, pp. 5 ff.
75. Ibid., p. 8.
76. Ibid., p. 8. (The original Brezhnev statement is in *Pravda*, 22 July 1974.)
77. L. I. Brezhnev, *Radio Moscow*, TASS, 24 November 1976.
78. Maj. Gen. R. Simonyan, "Disarmament—Demand of the Times: Concerning the Risk of Confrontation," *Pravda*, 14 June 1977.
79. Ibid.

in the quest for peace, commented: "After all, it is a case of the fate of world civilization and the future of all mankind."[80]

We thus see a new readiness even by military commentators to accept strategic parity, mutual deterrence, and the inadmissibility of nuclear war publicly.

It is of some interest and significance that there is now also a campaign to go *beyond* codification of a nuclear balance on the basis of parity at the very high levels currently existing. This criticism from "the left" so to speak is more noticeable with the quieting of reservations from the "right" so sharply dramatized by Colonel Rybkin's "conversion." A writer in *Pravda* in late 1976 argued:

Trying to justify the arms race, certain political circles in Western countries propagandize some sort of balance of terror which is supposedly necessary to maintain peace and insure the security of peoples. But such a balance is an unreliable foundation for security. The real way to achieve security is to observe the principle of the non-use of force . . .[81]

This does not *oppose* a nuclear balance based on parity; it argues a need to go beyond it. Others arguing this point usually stress the need to proceed to disarmament.

The accumulated means of mass destruction are such that an exchange of nuclear strikes contradicts even the most narrowly construed national security interests and seriously threatens the lives of peoples . . .

The "balance of terror" cannot guarantee security . . . There is a danger of their [the accumulated weapons] accidental or unsanctioned use. The numbers of these weapons are constantly growing . . .

In other words, if one wants to live in security, struggle to resolve the problems of disarmament.[82]

Even Brezhnev's major speech on the Sixtieth Anniversary of the Bolshevik Revolution, after renouncing an aim of superiority and stating that the Soviets "did not want to upset the approximate equilibrium of military strength that now exists," went on to state: "Needless to say, maintaining the existing equilibrium is not an end in itself. We are in favor of starting a downward turn in the curve of the arms race and of gradually reducing the level of the military confrontation. We want

---

80. Editorial, "Vigilance Must Be Raised Higher!" *Krasnaya Zvezda*, 22 June 1977.
81. V. Larin, "A Topical Proposal," *Pravda*, 27 October 1976.
82. Yu. Nilov, "The Time Has Come to Call a Halt," *Novoye vremya*, no. 23, June 1977, p. 6.

to reduce substantially, and then to eliminate, the threat of nuclear war—the most formidable danger for mankind."[83]

Perhaps the most sophisticated argument along this line was made several years ago by two retired military men now with the Institute of the USA and Canada, General Milshtein and Colonel Semeyko. They stressed the importance of the Soviet-American agreements of 1972 and the Prevention of Nuclear War Agreement of 1973, which they said were made possible only by "proceeding from their mutual recognition of the fact that nuclear war would have devastating consequences for mankind and from the need to reduce and in the final analysis to eliminate the danger of nuclear war . . ."[84] Milshtein and Semeyko are realistic in their criticism of mutual deterrence as not being an "ideal solution."

Of course, the concept of "mutual deterrence," which presupposes the existence of enormous nuclear forces capable of "assured destruction" is not an ideal solution to the problem of peace and the prevention of nuclear conflict.[85]

They argue that some influential elements in the United States have tried to escape mutual deterrence by pursuing "acceptable" limited nuclear options, "selective targetting" concepts and the like. This course they reject, while endorsing the effort to move from mutual deterrence on the path of detente, arms limitation, disarmament and peaceful coexistence. "Preventing nuclear war in any of its forms, large or small, and the limitation of the arms race, are the central problem of Soviet-American relations."[86]

Another analyst at the USA Institute, Dr. Trofimenko, has argued that the United States was led into SALT only by "a realization of the impossibility of the United States achieving a position of strategic military superiority over the Soviet Union" and readiness to accept parity, and by recognition of "the inevitability of a crushing counter-strike if the United States delivered a nuclear missile strike on the USSR . . ."[87] But he is led by consideration of military developments over the period 1972 through 1976 to conclude that:

---

83. L. I. Brezhnev, *Radio Moscow*, TASS English translation, 2 November 1977; *Pravda* and *Izvestiya*, 3 November 1977. This supplementary passage was omitted in the speech as delivered live on Radio Moscow, but was included in subsequent broadcasts in translation and in all printed versions of the speech.
84. [Lt. Gen.] M. A. Milshtein and [Col.] L. S. Semeyko, "The Problem of the Inadmissibility of a Nuclear Conflict (On New Approaches in the United States)," *SShA*, no. 11, November 1974, p. 4.
85. Ibid., p. 9.
86. Ibid., pp. 10–12.
87. G. A. Trofimenko, "US Foreign Policy in the Seventies: Words and Deeds," *SShA*, no. 12, December 1976, pp. 15 and 19.

Indeed, the matter of preventing nuclear war is not a policy of passive temporizing based on a presumption that a certain formal codification of the Soviet-American nuclear balance carried out in recent years is necessary and sufficient to maintain military stability, but only major new constructive steps in the sphere of military detente are able really to prevent a gradual slide toward nuclear catastrophe.[88]

A number of discussions in 1977 and 1978 have reflected disappointment and concern at the U.S. position. As Brezhnev put it in a speech in May 1977, "I am convinced that not a single statesman, or public figure, or thinking person can avoid his share of responsibility in the struggle against the threat of war, for this means responsibility for the very future of mankind itself. I shall not conceal the fact that our concern over the continuing arms race, including the strategic arms race, has grown in connection with the positions adopted in these matters by the new American Administration."[89]

A commentator commemorating the fifth anniversary of the first Nixon-Brezhnev Summit in May 1972, noted:

Both our powers possess tremendous economic and military potential, and because of this a state of conflict between them, which would be fraught with the risk of an armed clash, could lead to fatal consequences for the entire world.
. . .

For thousands of years war has been a continuation of policy, only by other, forcible, means. When diplomacy was unable to achieve one or another objective, armed force was used. A rejection of the use of armed force and the threat of its use together with a commitment to resolve differences by peaceful means would mean, at least in prospective—clearly not yet in the near run—transition to a completely new and unprecedented method of conducting international relations, where armed force and war cease to be instruments of policy . . .
. . .

Whereas in previous eras whole peoples were sometimes exterminated and great civilizations perished as a result of wars, at that time an aggressor, having well prepared for the attack could calculate that in case of victory his country had a chance of surviving, even after a very destructive war. In our age there is no such chance.[90]

Soviet thinking, increasingly expressed by military as well as political leaders and spokesmen, even in open publications, reflects the readiness to give an im-

---

88. Ibid., p. 27.
89. L. I. Brezhnev, *Radio Moscow*, 29 May 1977.
90. V. M. Berezhkov, "The Basic Principles of Soviet-American Relations," *SShA*, no. 4, April 1977, pp. 3, 5, 8 and 8–9.

portant place to agreements on strategic arms limitation and on political relations with the United States—if such agreements can be reached on a mutually acceptable basis. In the United States there is a similar readiness. But there are substantial difficulties in negotiating such agreements, even given a compatibility of aims, and success is by no means assured. Moreover, there are skeptics and recalcitrants on both sides. And there is prudence, hedged by desire for a margin of insurance, and fed by suspicions and fears—to say nothing of technical and intelligence uncertainties—all affecting respective unilateral military programs designed to safeguard deterrence, and negotiating stance and objectives. Maintaining mutual deterrence is not easy, even though mutual deterrence is a desirable situation. And negotiating agreed restraints is, while the best way to support it, also the most difficult.

Conclusion

A number of American commentators have argued that the Soviets, and in particular the Soviet military, reject or at least do not accept the concept of mutual deterrence, and they sometimes go on to question the basis for possible strategic arms limitation. These writers may not have been sufficiently aware of the record. It has sometimes been alleged that Soviet statements on such propositions as mutual deterrence and the unacceptability of general nuclear war are "for export," and they are contrasted with open Soviet military discussions. The evidence from such sources as the confidential General Staff organ *Military Thought* dispels such erroneous conclusions.

The record indicates that the Soviet political and military leadership accepts a strategic nuclear balance between the Soviet Union and the United States as a fact, and as the probable and desirable prospect for the foreseeable future. They are pursuing extensive military programs to ensure that they do not fail to maintain their side of the balance, which they see as in some jeopardy given planned American programs. They seek to stabilize and to maintain mutual deterrence.

In Marxist-Leninist eyes, military power is not and should not be the driving element in world politics. With "imperialist" military power held in check, the decisive social-economic forces of history would determine the future of the world. In their view, the United States has come to accept mutual deterrence, and some strategic arms limitations, not because it is our preference, but because we have no alternative given the general world "relation of forces," and Soviet military power in particular.

Strategic arms limitation achieved one signal concrete success in the SALT I

ABM Treaty. The absence of success to date in limiting effectively strategic offensive arms is seen as requiring continuing unilateral efforts, even strenuous ones, to prevent upsetting the strategic nuclear balance—which is generally stable, but is not assured without continuing efforts primarily though unilateral military programs but also potentially through agreed arms limitations.

Much of what has been said in the preceding paragraphs could easily be turned around to describe American views of the situation. This is not because of any careless resort to a "mirror image." There are, in fact, at this juncture a number of parallel perceptions—and misperceptions—held by both sides. Despite greatly differing ultimate objectives, the principal problems in arms control accommodations are *not* due to differing operative aims of the two sides, but to differing perceptions, to suspicions, and to the difficulties of gearing very different military forces and programs into balanced and mutually acceptable strategic arms limitations. To illuminate Soviet thinking on this matter is one step to understanding the problem and to finding its solution.

Deterrence and Coercion in Soviet Policy

Dimitri K. Simes

$\mathbf{P}$residential Directive 59 has added a new element to mutual U.S.-Soviet recriminations. Both sides accuse each other of being unwilling to live with nuclear parity, of seeking unilateral advantages, and of trying to develop capabilities to fight and win a nuclear war. On the surface, there is indeed some convergence in American and Soviet strategic concepts. And it may even appear that instead of educating the Soviet Union about the virtues of Mutual Assured Destruction, the United States has moved closer to the Soviet view that there can be no credible deterrence without the capacity to fight in the case of its failure.

But here the similarities between U.S. and Soviet strategic pronouncements end. The more impressive the Soviet nuclear arsenal becomes, the more the Kremlin tends to follow Teddy Roosevelt's advice to walk softly and carry a big stick. Moscow's claims of its military superiority and ability to win a nuclear war have become increasingly rare. This has happened at precisely the time when those American strategists who originally warned that the Soviets intended to prevail in a nuclear war now argue that it is the United States which should adopt a war-winning nuclear strategy.[1]

It is important to realize that like the actual Soviet strategic posture, Soviet strategic thinking has its own cycle of development, is influenced by different traditions and beliefs, responds to differently perceived challenges, intends to exploit a different combination of opportunities, and is formulated in a different institutional fashion through very different procedures than in the American case. Similarly, there is a need to view the Soviet concept of deterrence in the context of the aging Kremlin leaders' world outlook. These people do know first-hand how catastrophic war can be, and are not inclined to play with fire. But there is another, far less encouraging, aspect to their international philosophy, namely, a deeply felt commitment to achieve what

---

1. See for example, "Victory is Possible," by Colin S. Gray and Keith Payne, *Foreign Policy*, Summer 1980, Number 39, pp. 14–28.

The author is indebted to Abraham Brumberg, Michael Moodie, Vladimir Petrov, and Thomas Wolfe for their useful comments and suggestions on an early draft of this paper.

Dimitri Simes is a member of the Faculty at Johns Hopkins University's School of Advanced International Studies. He was formerly associated with Georgetown University's Center for Strategic and International Studies, and until 1972, with Moscow's Institute of World Economy and International Relations (IMEMO).

International Security, Winter 1980/81 (Vol. 5, No. 3) 0162-2889/81/030080-24 $02.50/0

amounts to almost absolute security. And absolute security for the USSR means very little security for everybody else. The Soviet elite constantly feels obliged to prove the legitimacy of its rule, both abroad and to the Russian empire's own citizens. As stagnation of the Soviet economy, discontent in Eastern Europe, and the international communist movement itself increasingly raise questions about the future of the Soviet model of communism, Moscow is particularly tempted to seek compensation through the use of force and coercion to obtain a greater role. And the Soviet interpretation of deterrence is inevitably influenced by the general offensive orientation of the USSR's foreign policy.[2]

It would require an extreme believer in technological determinism to expect that similar developments in weaponry would dictate identical strategic concepts, and to be surprised that in addressing nuclear warfare, the Kremlin gerontocracy thinks and acts differently from successive White House administrations. In fact, Soviet writers sometimes complain about the American tendency to impose on the USSR rules of nuclear warfare that are convenient and comprehensible to the United States. The Soviets make clear that they are not going to give the United States the luxury of—as they put it— "orchestrating its own strategic combination," so that the USSR would be reduced to following a scenario designed by American strategic planners.[3]

There is a seeming contradiction between the vocal Soviet rejection of the possibility of a limited and controlled nuclear conflict on the one hand and the ever-growing capabilities to engage in one on the other. To understand the subtleties and ambiguities of the Soviet attitude toward deterring and fighting nuclear war, it is imperative to take into account the existence of different levels in Soviet national security thinking—philosophical/strategic, and operational/technical—as well as the intricacies of the Soviet decision-making process with its notorious compartmentalization.

Misleading Dichotomies

The discussion of Soviet strategic doctrine and security planning has been seriously imperilled during the last 10 to 15 years by a number of false

2. "Actually, coercion is the ultimate form of deterrence," states the USA and Canada Institute's Foreign Policy Department chief, Henry Trofimenko. "Changing Attitudes Toward Deterrence," Center for International and Strategic Affairs, University of California, Los Angeles, *ACIS Working Paper* No. 25, p. 1.
3. G. A. Trofimenko, *SShA, Politika, Voyna, Ideologiya*, Moscow, 1976, p. 82.

dichotomies. These have often prevented analysts not only from reaching the correct conclusions but also from asking the truly relevant questions. It is not that incisive research has been unavailable. But polemical and exaggerated notions rather than scholarship have primarily shaped the American debate about Soviet national security culture and machinery.

First, there is the supposed contrast between the U.S. commitment to Mutual Assured Destruction (MAD) and the conflicting Soviet desire for a capability to fight and win a nuclear war. There is undoubtedly a great discrepancy between U.S. and Soviet thought, but deterrence and war-fighting ability *per se* are hardly incompatible in principle. If anything, the ability to fight a war has traditionally been considered one of the more reliable ways to deter aggression. The American approach developed in the 1960s—that it would be enough to deny an opponent victory even at the price of self-annihilation to achieve credible deterrence—is not the only way responsible leaders may want to protect their states. Moreover, the whole debate about the deterrence/war-fighting dichotomy tends to obscure a truly crucial question, namely, how strategic nuclear weapons complement the overall Soviet military design. Is it a principal task of the USSR's strategic nuclear forces to preserve the Soviet homeland or is it instead designed to paralyze U.S. opposition to the Kremlin's geopolitical advances?

Whether Moscow would be satisfied with parity (whatever it means) or whether it is determined to achieve superiority over the United States in strategic nuclear forces has become the subject of a second controversy among Western analysts. But surely U.S. and Soviet definitions of equality are bound to differ considerably. It is futile to try to determine legitimate defense requirements for another state. Because of different traditions and images of threat, Soviet decision-makers are bound to have a markedly different view than their U.S. counterparts of how much is enough. The fact that one power seeks superiority in strategic nuclear weapons does not necessarily tell very much about its overall foreign policy intentions. A country with superior strength on all lower levels of the military balance may seek strategic supremacy in order not just to buy over-insurance, but also possibly to acquire the status of an undisputed manager, if not arbiter, of the international process. On the other hand, a state which for a variety of reasons is incapable of matching its rival's conventional capabilities may perceive nuclear, including strategic nuclear, superiority as a last resort to avoid defeat or surrender. In addition, the United States and the Soviet Union pursue different foreign policies, enjoy different advantages in international competition (geographical, resource availability, alliance systems, etc.) and also have different vulnerabilities. Static indicators of strategic power are insufficient to establish who can inflict greater damage on whom, particularly in a confrontation short of total war.

A third dichotomy supposes the existence of and conflict between "doves" and "hawks" in Soviet ruling circles. These categories, born of U.S. Vietnam era divisiveness, have been artificially projected onto the Soviet Union. It has never been adequately explained how Soviet domestic forces or external influences were supposed to produce fundamental disagreements among apparatchiks, technocrats, and military commanders whose formative experiences went back to Stalin's era, when democratic centralism was clearly the name of the game in Soviet institutional politics. No serious effort has been made to explain how these supposed doves and hawks were able to oppose each other constantly without losing their positions and/or bringing about any sudden shifts in Soviet policy. Such effects would be expected if a constant, intensive struggle among the elite were taking place.

Even if there were doves and hawks in the Kremlin, what are the implications for U.S. policymakers? Those who believe in such a dichotomy among Soviet leaders somehow tend to assume that greater flexibility and generosity would favor the Soviet softliners.[4] Conversely, those who argue that the Soviet leadership represents a generally like-minded group disagreeing primarily over questions of hierarchy suggest that Soviet rulers only understand force; concessions would be met with contempt and perceived as naive at best and weak at worst. The policy implications of both interpretations of Soviet politics are obscure. Assuming there are indeed hawks and doves in the Kremlin, is it not possible that excessive accommodation could strengthen the hawks who may push for greater assertiveness? If, on the other hand, the Kremlin leadership is monolithic, can it be discounted that manifestations of hostility could confirm the Soviets' worst fears but not necessarily lead to any additional willingness to compromise?

A similar case can be made in connection with a fourth dichotomy between the single, rational actor (totalitarian) and pluralistic models of Soviet policy formulation. Despite many serious analyses of the Soviet decision-making process and domestic politics in general, the U.S. political debate seems to emphasize two extreme points of view. One emphasizes the pluralistic nature

---

4. For instance, this approach to relations with the USSR was eloquently advocated in Victor Zorza's column which used to appear in the *Washington Post*.

of Soviet policy formulation and expresses hopes that a greater interaction with the West would lead to further Soviet adaptation of Western political values and standards. A less benign view suggests that changes in the Soviet political *modus operandi* since Stalin's death have been essentially cosmetic and that Soviet foreign and domestic policies have developed not through complex bureaucratic bargaining but as some sort of grand strategy dictated either by the Russian historical predicament or by communist ideology, or by some combination of the two. Few responsible students of Soviet affairs would identify with either of these two exaggerated positions, but it is precisely these ideas, rather than a more sober and multi-dimensional analysis, that have had a profound impact on the creation of American public images of the Soviet Union during the last decade.

The greatest fallacy in studying Soviet policy formation is founded in the assumption that a movement toward pluralism in the USSR should by definition lead to a more restrained Soviet foreign policy. Adherents of a totalitarian model, on the other hand, seem to believe that strong centralized authoritarian controls are likely to result in more belligerently anti-Western international activities. While these assumptions, rooted in the U.S. political tradition, are commendable for their faith in pluralism and democracy, they would hardly survive the scrutiny of history. There are numerous examples of strong authoritarian rulers who conducted policies of peace and caution (and conversely of democracies which launched crusades and even revolutionary wars). Khrushchev, for example, on a number of occasions overruled the military, proceeded with an impressive demobilization of the armed forces, and initiated a dialogue with the United States. In 1968, the Soviet Union, conversely, was governed by a collective leadership with a greater margin for defense of bureaucratic and functional interests than under Khrushchev. As some thoughtful studies indicate, it was precisely this vested interest of individual Soviet power complexes which contributed to the Kremlin's decision to crush the Prague Spring.[5] There is therefore no conclusive correlation between pluralism in policy formulation and a moderate foreign policy.

A fifth dichotomy is represented by serious disagreements between those who have made a case for domination of military considerations in the Soviet political process and those who feel there is a strong tension, if not outright

---

5. Jiri Valenta, *Soviet Intervention in Czechoslovakia, 1968: Anatomy of a Decision*, (Baltimore: Johns Hopkins University Press, 1979).

conflict, between the Soviet military and the civilian leadership. Assertions are often made that the latter somehow exercises a moderating influence on overassertive marshals and admirals. Again, there is a clear element of mirror-imaging which attributes the American tradition of civil/military division to Soviet society. In terms of policy implications, what is the evidence that Soviet party apparatchiks and technocrats are necessarily a voice of caution, while the uniformed military supports foreign adventures? Could not an equally plausible argument be made that the military, precisely because of its professionalism and responsibility for war-fighting, would be particularly careful not to get involved in international situations that they did not have the military capability to handle or that could lead to a major confrontation with possibly disastrous consequences? And in light of the necessity for the civilian leadership to legitimize its regime by advancing and protecting socialism abroad, it could also be argued that the civilian authorities, to an even greater extent than the military leadership, have every incentive to favor military action that serves that end.

In sum, the collapse of American consensus on foreign policy in the late 1960s and early 1970s has led to polarized and often mistaken debate about the nature of the Soviet Union and its national security planning. Sometimes it seemed that those academics who left their ivory towers to help Washington formulate its foreign and defense policies were losing their scholarly grasp of nuance in order to score points in political battles. However noble were the partisan causes for which they fought, our understanding of the genesis and direction of Soviet national security policy has suffered immensely.

Rejecting Nuclear War

According to contemporary declaratory Soviet policy, nuclear war is inherently unwinnable, would lead to the destruction of civilization, and consequently cannot serve any rational political ends. As retired Lieutenant General Mikhail A. Milshtein, director of the Political-Military Department of the Institute of the United States and Canada Studies, states, "nuclear war will bring no advantage to anyone and may even lead to the end of civilization. And the end of civilization can hardly be called 'victory.'"[6] Such unqualified rejection of nuclear war as a continuation of policy developed only gradually

---

6. Quoted in an interview in the *New York Times*, August 25, 1980, p. 2.

in the Soviet Union and not without an intensive domestic debate. Even today, traces of the old nuclear war-winning school of thought may be found in some Soviet military writings. Nevertheless, an assessment of Soviet literature strongly suggests that during the last 15 to 20 years, the Soviet leadership has gradually but steadily, albeit with zigzags, moved toward acceptance of mutual deterrence and a rejection of prior claims that the Soviet Union possesses superior forces capable of assuring victory in a nuclear war.[7]

If Leonid Brezhnev is to be believed, the Soviet Union "is not seeking military superiority." He claims that "Soviet strategic doctrine is strictly defensive in nature."[8] The Soviet leader says that Soviet foreign policy makes every effort to avoid nuclear war and would not consider a first strike against the United States.[9] That is because, as Politburo candidate member and Central Committee Secretary in charge of the International Department, Boris N. Ponomarev explains, "Both quantitatively and qualitatively, the means of destruction of people have reached such a level that world war as a vehicle to achieve a political objective has become impossible."[10] Soviet civilian analysts go much further than that. Georgiy Arbatov, member of the Soviet Academy of Sciences and director of the Institute of the USA and Canada Studies in Moscow, paraphrases Clausewitz by saying "with the emergence of nuclear missiles, 'any correspondence between the political ends of war' and the means was lost, since no policy can have the object of destroying the enemy at the cost of self-annihilation."[11] Professor A. Feoktistov, corresponding member of the Soviet Academy of Sciences and a former astronaut, declares that, "Nuclear war in terms of its consequences would be terrible and senseless." He rejects arguments of some Western strategists that counterforce strikes would not necessarily lead to unacceptable civilian casualties. The Soviet scientist reminds us that there are about 1000 major cities in the USSR and that the majority of urban population and almost all industry and other "material valuables" are concentrated in them. Thus, there is no way to avoid "huge, incomparable casualties in case of a surprise nuclear strike."[12] It is rather remarkable, to say the least, for a senior Soviet

---

7. This view is articulated particularly strongly in the FBIS Analysis Report *President Brezhnev and the Soviet Union's Changing Security Policy*. May 25, 1979, FB 79-10009.
8. *Pravda*, September 7, 1979.
9. Leonid Brezhnev, *Leninskim Kursom*, Moscow, 1979, p. 294.
10. *Pravda*, September 25, 1980.
11. Georgiy Arbatov, "The Stalemate of the Policy of Force," *Problemy Mira i Sotsialisma*, No. 2, February 4.
12. *Literaturnaya Gazeta*, April 23, 1980.

scientist to argue in a mass circulation newspaper that his country is so vulnerable to enemy attack.

Another Soviet commentator declares that world war increasingly becomes an anachronism as a tool to reach political objectives. Referring again to Clausewitz, who is much respected by Soviet theoreticians, V. Kortunov states in the Communist Party's main journal *Kommunist* that at a certain point, "war may go outside the margins of policy and begin to act according to its own laws, and as soon as that happens, war stops being a tool of rational policy and becomes an end in itself."[13] In the same issue of *Kommunist*, Aleksandr Bovin, a serious and influential political commentator for *Izvestia*, is even more categorical. Citing Clausewitz, he speaks about "the change in the very nature of war, connected with the scientific technological revolution and the emergence of nuclear missile weaponry."[14] Bovin goes on to say that general nuclear war cannot be considered a rational policy tool because an aggressor would be subjected to a devastating second strike. Consequently, "aggression would become suicide, a self-destruction of the aggressor."[15] A young, but already noted Soviet analyst, Alexei G. Arbatov (son of the Institute director), points out in his recent book that the revolution in weaponry has transformed the very nature of security. In his view, "ways to improve the security of a state changed fundamentally under conditions wherein tremendous arsenals of the means of destruction capable of finishing our civilization are accumulated on earth."[16]

Not only civilian analysts but also Soviet military officers seem to admit that nuclear war could become an unqualified disaster, even if the latter use less dramatic language. As Major General Raer Simonyan says in *Pravda*, "Soviet people from their own experience know better than anyone else what war is and what tremendous casualties and devastation could be caused by the actions of an aggressor."[17] And Soviet Minister of Defense Dmitriy Ustinov in an authoritative article recalls the 20 million dead the Soviet Union had to pay for victory in World War II. According to Ustinov, "A clear appreciation by the Soviet leadership of what a war under contemporary conditions would mean for mankind determines the active position of the USSR" (against nuclear war).[18]

---

13. *Kommunist*, No. 10, July 1980, p. 97.
14. *Ibid.*, p. 77.
15. *Kommunist*, No. 10, July 1980, p. 78.
16. A. Arbatov, *Bezopastnost' v yaderniy vek i politika Vashingtona*, Moscow, 1980, p. 4.
17. *Pravda*, March 19, 1979.
18. *Pravda*, October 25, 1979.

These unequivocal statements are duly acknowledged by those who argue that the Soviet Union thinks it can fight and win a nuclear war. But they dismiss them as propaganda designed to delude the West into a false sense of security. It is suggested instead that the real Soviet doctrine is reflected in the missile-rattling evident in what might be called the war-winning school in Soviet nuclear theory.

The majority of Soviet writers who claim that nuclear war is winnable, however, are neither top statesmen nor leading military personalities. As a rule, they are professors of Marxist-Leninist philosophy or of communist party history and are associated with the Military-Political Academy or with political indoctrination departments of other military educational institutions. This group of "military commissars" plays an important role in what the Soviets call "moral political preparation" for a possible war. It would be rather illogical for indoctrination experts to accept easily that there is no hope whatsoever in case of a major nuclear exchange. As spokesmen for the military establishment in general, these commissars may perform a function of warning about the sinister plans of "imperialist forces" on the one hand, and on the other, improving the morale of the Soviet armed forces and population by telling them that even a nuclear war may be won by their country.

Military commissars may be earnest in their optimistic war-winning pronouncements, but their views for one reason or another are more and more overshadowed by a new orthodoxy closer to the Arbatovs and Milshteins.

Milshtein suggests in his New York Times interview that the book on military strategy edited by Marshal Vasiliy Sokolovskiy and other writings dating back to the 1960s and early 1970s which imply the possibility of victory in nuclear war are now obsolete; they cannot be viewed as reflecting current Soviet doctrine. General Milshtein, allowed by his superiors to grant an unusual interview to The New York Times, undoubtedly serves the purpose of reducing U.S. concern over Soviet nuclear theories and acquisitions. And yet, there is evidence that while he could have overstated his case, a modern nuclear war-winning orientation has indeed become less dominant in Soviet national security philosophy.

An interesting example of this shift may be the third edition (1979) of Major General Sergei K. Il'in's book, The Moral Factor in Modern Wars. General Il'in is one of the more hardline Soviet strategic official writers, claiming that nuclear war would once and forever settle the issue of imperialism's existence.[19] He declares that the outcome of a nuclear war would be first determined by the "strength of moral spirit of the people and the army" and also by "perfection of military organization" and "the level of military art." On the basis of all these factors, and especially the moral spirit of the troops, according to him, supremacy will undoubtedly be on the side of the Soviet Army and of the other socialist countries.[20] While these disturbing statements should not be taken lightly, a comparison between the second (1969) and third editions of General Il'in's book offers a less alarmist perspective. On the very first page of the second edition, he talks about "strengthening Soviet Army and Navy readiness to wage a victorious war against any aggression."[21] This sentence is deleted from the third edition. Similarly, in the second edition, Il'in says that "the Soviet Union is doing everything to ensure military technological superiority of our armed forces over the imperialist armies."[22] In the third edition, the sentence reads: "The Soviet people do everything to ensure a high level of technological equipment for the Soviet armed forces in the spirit of current requirements."[23] An obvious effort is made to de-emphasize but not eliminate a war-fighting, superiority-oriented theme in the general's monograph.

The differences between the second and third editions of Il'in's book illustrate a trend in Soviet military writings against boasting about Soviet ability to win a nuclear war. This trend is evident at the highest levels. The late Soviet Defense Minister Marshal Andrei A. Grechko described the task of the Soviet military in the following way: "In this stage, the armed forces should be able in any situation to ensure failure of an aggressor's surprise attack, relying for that on nuclear as well as conventional forces. Quick devastating strikes would destroy its main nuclear missile means and groups of forces would guarantee favorable conditions for further conduct and a victorious conclusion of the war."[24] Grechko's successor, Marshal Dmitriy Ustinov, on the other hand, says simply that "retribution for attack against the Soviet Union and other countries of the socialist commonwealth will be inevitable."[25] The difference between the language of the two defense min-

19. C. K. Il'in, *Moral'niy Faktor v Sovremennikh Voinakh*, Moscow, 1979, p. 55.
20. *Ibid.*, p. 72.
21. C. K. Il'in, *Moral'niy Faktor v Sovremennoy Voine*, Moscow, 1969, p. 3.
22. *Ibid.*, p. 122.
23. C. K. Il'in, *Moral'niy Faktor v Sovremennikh Voinakh*, Moscow, 1979, p. 169.
24. A. A. Grechko, *Na Strazhe Mira i Stroitelstva Kommunisma*, Moscow, 1971, p. 64.
25. *Pravda*, October 25, 1979.

isters is meaningful. If Grechko still promised victory, Ustinov talks only about assured punishment of the enemy. The shift from war-fighting to a Soviet style of deterrence is self-evident.

Of course, declaratory policy does not necessarily reflect the real thinking of the Soviet (or for that matter, American) leadership. Significantly, a less belligerent tone in the Soviet discussion of war gradually developed in the 1970s, during the period of détente and SALT.[26] The Soviets had sound reasons of public relations to restrain their militaristic rhetoric. As the Soviet Union increasingly enjoyed international recognition as a strategic equal to the United States, boasting about military capabilities could lead to fears of USSR superiority. The Kremlin wants its power to be respected and even feared. But once satisfied that its military capabilities are recognized, it has an interest in being careful not to provoke the West into rearmament.

Self-serving and even misleading as they are, statements about the impossibility of winning a nuclear war in any meaningful way cannot be dismissed. The Soviet media, after all, cannot entirely subordinate its pages to the requirements of domestic indoctrination and foreign policy misinformation. Soviet media comment is also an important channel of communication between the leadership and the second echelon of the elite, as well as to the Soviet people as a whole. To tell the Soviet population that contrary to the teachings of Marx and Lenin, its civilization may disappear rather than spread and flourish, has consequences for public morale. If the USSR indeed was seriously thinking about launching missiles to achieve an international "moment of truth," one would expect a greater effort to prepare its subjects psychologically for an ultimate test of the Soviet regime.

The Soviets' strong desire to avoid nuclear war, however, does not mean that they are entirely persuaded that it will not take place. During the heyday of détente in the mid-1970s, representatives of the Soviet leadership frequently suggested that the likelihood of nuclear war had been reduced.[27] But as the deterioration of the U.S.-Soviet relationship began to accelerate in the

---

26. The exchange between those who argue that nuclear war would mean an end to civilization (Arbatov; Bovin) and their commissar-type critics (Admiral Shelyag; Colonel Rybkin) who insist that despite great sacrifices for both sides, only capitalism would be destroyed, took place in late 1973–early 1974. The first unequivocal statement by Brezhnev himself that "man dies only once. However, in recent years, a quantity of weapons has already been amassed sufficient to destroy everything living on earth several times" was made in July 1974, one month after his summit meeting in Moscow with Richard Nixon, which resulted in some SALT-related agreements. (*Pravda*, July 22, 1974).

27. *XXV S'ezd Kommunisticheskoy Partii Sovetskogo Soyuza*, Moscow, 1976, volume 1, p. 43.

latter part of the decade, the expression of this sentiment became increasingly rare among Politburo members. Relative moderates from the ranks of foreign policy commentators as well as analysts like Bovin still say that the "probability of global nuclear missile conflict has been reduced."[28] But "reduced" is not excluded. As Politburo candidate member Ponomarev has declared, "We are convinced that there is no fatal inevitability of nuclear war. But this does not mean unfortunately that its occurrence is excluded."[29] And while the Soviets are not at all sure that they could fight and win a nuclear war,[30] they are making every possible effort to prepare for it.

Decisions of peace and war are the prerogative of the top political leadership. It is on this level that one finds a delineation between nuclear and conventional, primarily local, wars. How to deter nuclear war is a separate issue and is handled in a different manner. It is less philosophical and more operational. Development of the Soviet deterrence policy involves both the foreign policy establishment and the military/industrial complex. Undoubtedly, there are particularly drastic differences between the writings of the academics of the Institute of USA and Canada Studies and the Institute of World Economy and International Relations, or of commentators such as Bovin on the one hand, and the military/political commissars on the other. Nevertheless, deterrence and war-fighting are two sides of the same coin. In a paradoxically integrated way, the Soviets pursue deterrence through détente and arms control but simultaneously through a unilateral military effort; they act on the assumption that only a credible war-fighting capability can assure adequate deterrence.[31]

It would be a gross understatement to imply, however, that the Soviets developed their formidable war-fighting capabilities strictly to enhance deterrence. Once a judgment is made that there still exists a threat of nuclear war, the Soviet military is authorized to develop strategy and weapons to

---

28. *Kommunist*, No. 10, July 1980, p. 76.
29. *Pravda*, September 25, 1980.
30. An eloquent case to the contrary is made in Richard Pipes "Why the Soviet Union Thinks It Could Fight and Win a Nuclear War," *Commentary*, July 1977.
31. Fritz Ermath, "Contrasts in American and Soviet Strategic Thought," *International Security*, Fall 1978. Raymond L. Garthoff, "Mutual Deterrence and Strategic Arms Limitations in Soviet Policy," *International Security*, Summer 1978. Arnold Horelick, "The Strategic Mind-Set of the Soviet Military," *Problems of Communism*, March-April 1977. Robert Legvold, "Strategic 'Doctrine' and SALT: Soviet and American Views," *Survival*, January/February 1979. Dennis Ross, "Rethinking Soviet Strategic Policy: Inputs and Implications," ACIS Working Paper No. 5, June 1977. Jack Snyder, "The Soviet Strategic Culture: Implications for Limited Nuclear Operations," RAND, 1977.

fight it in the most efficient way possible. In the USSR, "strategic warfare is seen as less distinct from other forms of warfare."[32] Despite all their pronouncements that nuclear weapons can serve only purposes of deterrence, or failing that, of massive retaliation against an aggressor, the Soviets still have not articulated "in operationally meaningful terms a benign rationale for the military deployments they make and the new strategic arms they are acquiring."[33]

The current posture of Soviet strategic forces reflects the decisions of the late 1960s and early 1970s, when the war-winning school dominated Soviet military and even civilian writings. To impute current Soviet nuclear thinking on the basis of today's strategic posture may lead to alarming misjudgments if this time gap between decision and deployment is not considered. Among both superpowers, force posture is not always the most reliable guide to assessing attitudes of decision-makers to issues of war and peace. It is more important to make a clear distinction between the Soviet view of nuclear war avoidance and the conviction that as long as the possibility of nuclear war cannot be excluded, the Soviet Union should be well prepared for it. According to a highly authoritative Soviet military manual edited by Colonel General N. A. Lomov of the General Staff, use of nuclear weapons in a modern war would "threaten the lives of tens if not hundreds of millions of people."[34] As Lomov and his military colleagues see it, a limited nuclear war—a contingency they do not preclude—would result in disasters of unprecedented magnitude. This hardly looks like evidence of the war-winning mentality. But on the other hand, the manual provides clear suggestions regarding Soviet strategy in a nuclear war, and these are based on surprise, damage limitation, and strikes against nuclear forces and command centers of the enemy.[35] And even the usually "moderate" Trofimenko does not dispute the legitimacy of this dual approach. He points out that "the military in the United States and the Soviet Union must be ready for war-fighting," and consequently "if actual engagement of the main forces should occur, the

---

32. Andrew Marshall, "Sources of Soviet Power: The Military Potential in the 1980s," Adelphi Paper No. 152, IISS, 1978, p. 13. "Military operations (on land, in the air, and at sea) are conducted through joint efforts of all the armed services in the interests of a single goal—victory over a possible enemy," declares Chief of the General Staff Marshal Nikolai Ogarkov, Kommunist, No. 7, 1978, p. 116.
33. Arnold Horelick, op. cit., p. 80.
34. A. N. Lomov, ed., Nauchno-technicheskiy Progress i Revolyutsiya v voennom dele. Moscow, 1973, p. 260.
35. Ibid., pp. 272–273.

Soviet Union would undoubtedly act in accord with its own military doctrine, aimed at eliminating the opponent's marginal benefits and defeating the aggressor."[36] Michael MccGwire explains this disjunction by stating that an assessment of both actual Soviet deployments as well as the literature supplies "unambiguous evidence that Soviet military planners take the possibility of nuclear war very seriously and plan to fight such a war should deterrence fail." But he wisely cautions that "the evidence does not, however, support the thesis that there is an urge to war in the Kremlin.[37]

Deterrence as Offensive

It seems that one important reason Moscow stresses the irrationality of strategic nuclear war is that it has grounds to be increasingly hopeful about its ability to change the international status quo with the use of conventional forces. Not illogically, the Kremlin may be interested in convincing the United States that a nuclear response is hardly a credible option in dealing with an increasingly assertive Soviet global diplomacy of force.

The Soviet concept of strategic deterrence does not at all imply less reliance on military force as an important foreign policy instrument. If anything, recent trends suggest the opposite conclusion. Unlike analyses of Soviet nuclear planning, there is much evidence surrounding Moscow's use of military power at lower levels of confrontation. From arms shipments and military training for left-leaning nationalist movements in the 1960s, Soviet foreign policy proceeded to reliance on proxy forces in the 1970s, and the 1980s dawned with the first post-World War II direct Soviet use of ground troops outside of Moscow's traditional sphere of dominance.

New Soviet capabilities of displaying military force—whether through arms transfers, by proxy troops, or directly—are a precondition for increased Soviet assertiveness in the third world. And Moscow's perception that the balance of strategic forces has shifted considerably in its favor has probably influenced calculations of costs and benefits in areas of international turmoil. What could be viewed as an outright adventure 10 to 15 years ago now may be seen by the Kremlin leadership as an innovative and assertive, but still prudent step.

---

36. Henry Trofimenko, "Changing Attitudes Toward Deterrence," *op. cit.*, pp. 22, 25.
37. Michael MccGwire, "Commentary—Soviet Intentions," *International Security*, Summer 1979, p. 139. For a good discussion of peculiarities and ambiguities in Soviet thinking, see Robert Legvold, "Strategic 'Doctrine' and SALT: Soviet and American Views," cited above.

Steady progress in changing the military balance, coupled with successful meddling in troubled international situations, apparently contributed to greater self-confidence and boldness among the Soviet elite. While the view of the correlation of forces goes beyond a simple calculation of the military balance, the latter is perceived as an extremely important element of the equation. "America consistently lost its monopoly on nuclear weapons, then on the means of their delivery, then its 'geographic invulnerability' and finally, by the early 1970s, was forced to acknowledge a state of nuclear missile parity with the USSR," states Vitaliy V. Zhurkin, deputy director of the Institute of USA and Canada Studies.[38] According to Zhurkin and many other Soviet authors, it is superpower parity that persuaded U.S. "ruling circles" to take a more realistic approach to relations with the Soviet Union. From Leonid Brezhnev's standpoint, the very shift to détente in the superpower dialogue was caused primarily by "a general change in correlation of forces in the world arena."[39] Still other Soviet sources elaborate further on the meaning of pro-Moscow shifts in the military balance.[40]

The Soviets have been concerned that U.S. nuclear superiority could encourage Washington to be more forthcoming in opposing Soviet foreign policy exploits.[41] Soviet analysts acknowledge a possibility of superpower conflicts in the third world, and they have indicated that the United States may have a tendency to approach future superpower confrontations in the fashion of the 1962 Cuban missile crisis.[42] It would not be unreasonable for Moscow to try to assure that whenever the United States and the Soviet Union are on a collision course, Washington would not think in terms of a repetition of the Cuban crisis's decisive stand and would instead hesitate to challenge the Soviets too boldly.

The credit for the clearest explanation of the Soviet view on the military role of nuclear deterrence possibly belongs to Bovin. Writing in *Kommunist*, he states, "It is impossible to ban civil and national liberation wars. It is

---

38. Vitaliy V. Zhurkin, *SShA i Mezhdunarodno-Politicheskie Krizisi*, Moscow, 1975, p. 7.
39. *Pravda*, October 27, 1973.
40. "The Soviet Union and other socialist countries, through their growing military potential change the balance of military forces in the world arena in favor of the forces of peace and socialism. This has a sobering impact on extremist circles of imperialist states and creates favorable conditions for implementation by Soviet foreign policy of its objectives in the world arena on the basis of the principles of peaceful coexistence." *Voennaya Sila i Mezhdunarodnye Otnosheniya*, Moscow, 1972, p. 222.
41. Yu. Listvinov, *Obychnoe Oruzhie v Yadernom Veke*, Moscow, 1975, p. 27.
42. *Ibid.*, p. 5.

impossible in general to ban revolution as a way of changing the political and social order."[43] This, in turn, in Bovin's view can lead to local wars, which he finds dangerous in their potential for going out of control and leading to a superpower confrontation. But the Soviet columnist is quick to emphasize that the responsibility for avoiding local wars is entirely on the West, and primarily on the United States. The Soviet Union is by virtue of its revolutionary Marxist-Leninist tradition entitled to support national liberation movements. It is up to the United States, then, to display common sense and moderation. In this context, "nuclear missile parity is a condition contributing to the policy of peace" because it allows a more hospitable environment for success of the Soviet global offensive, short of war with the United States and particularly short of nuclear disaster.[44] In brief, it seems that one essential function of nuclear deterrence, Soviet-style, is to discourage the West, primarily the United States, from risking military opposition to Soviet advances in the third world.[45]

In the United States, the concept of Mutual Assured Destruction was developed in the charged political environment of the 1960s, when not only nuclear force but military power in general began to be viewed by a dominant segment of the national security establishment as increasingly ineffective and even distasteful. Only a doctrine that would preclude *any* use of military force short of unacceptable devastation could be politically palatable to Americans. The Soviets on the other hand did not have a period of prolonged suffering leading to a humiliating defeat that became the formative experience in their current national security thinking. Consequently, as genuinely concerned as they are with the implications of nuclear war, members of the Soviet ruling group approach nuclear deterrence not as a way to *preclude* use of military force, but on the contrary, as a means of allowing greater operational flexibility below the nuclear threshold. When Moscow talks about strategic stability, it does not mean stability on all levels of military competition; rather, it seeks stability that deters action only on the highest (holocaust) level of superpower confrontation to create more favorable conditions to exploit its conventional military advantages.

While U.S. strategic doctrine, as manifested in Presidential Directive 59, has moved in recent years from reliance on Mutual Assured Destruction to

43. *Kommunist*, No. 10, July 1980, p. 79.
44. *Kommunist*, No. 10, July 1980, p. 78.
45. V. A. Kremenyuk, *Politika SShA v Razvivayushchikhsya Stranakh*, Moscow, 1977, p. 156.

selective targeting, the Soviets insist that nuclear war, once started, will be uncontrolled. "As far as arguments about the possibility of fighting a 'limited nuclear war against the USSR,' they cannot sustain any criticism and are designed for uninformed people. The very nature of nuclear weaponry as a means of mass destruction which can be delivered in a short time over huge distances predetermines a decisive and quick response, a full-scale response," declares Yuriy Zhukov, *Pravda*'s best known political commentator.[46] The Soviet position against limited nuclear war has a logic going beyond the fear that nuclear exchanges, unlike a game of chess, are hard to manage and would not necessarily allow both players to calculate rationally their gains and losses, assess the consequences of their next step, and either accept a stalemate or admit defeat in time.

Another concern the Soviets have (or at least articulate forcefully) is that the combination of retargeting, greater precision and yield of nuclear weapons required for limited nuclear options may provide the United States with first-strike capability.[47] More important is the apparent Soviet belief that U.S. adoption of limited nuclear war options is connected with "long-term efforts to transform the nuclear force into an effective foreign policy instrument."[48] Soviet leaders worry that the United States may be tempted "to play its nuclear 'muscles'" in some regional conflicts such as possible Persian Gulf contingencies, and especially in case of a war in Europe.[49] Moscow by contrast is interested in de-coupling nuclear and conventional war. As Richard Burt observes, the threat of escalation will continue to provide both sides incentives for exercising restraint in local conflicts. But the degree of Soviet restraint will depend, in large part, on American possession of credible options for escalation."[50] And it is precisely such options, especially nuclear options, the Soviets are determined to deny the United States.

---

46. *Pravda*, August 14, 1980.
47. *Krasnaya Zvezda*, August 8, 1980.
48. *Mirovaya Ekonomika i Mezhdunarodnye Otnosheniya*, No. 4, April 1979, p. 39. Also, as Tom Wolfe reports, at a U.S.-Soviet symposium on strategic issues, a Soviet participant stated that "while it was true that Soviet doctrine has called for counterforce strikes in the event of 'all-out nuclear war,' there was no Soviet doctrine for 'limited nuclear warfare' in that part of the spectrum between general nuclear warfare and small-scale conventional conflict. What the Schlesinger approach was aimed at, he charged, was to restore 'the political leverage' of strategic forces in this part of the spectrum and, thereby, to 'intimidate' and 'dictate' to the Soviet Union." (Thomas W. Wolfe, *The SALT Experience: Its Impact on US and Soviet Strategic Policy and Decisionmaking*, RAND, 1975, p. 153.)
49. V. Zhurkin. "In Search of an Unreachable Goal: About the 'New Nuclear Strategy' of the USA," Literaturnaya Gazeta, Sept. 17, 1980.
50. Richard Burt, "Reassessing the Strategic Balance," *International Security*, Summer 1980, p. 50.

There is no conventional threat to the Soviet Union which it could not handle with its non-nuclear weapons. The same is true of Eastern Europe. Vietnam and Cuba, as well as more remote Soviet allies such as Angola, Ethiopia, and South Yemen, are a different case in point. The United States in the Caribbean or China in Southeast Asia could probably overwhelm Soviet clients, and Moscow would be unable to respond locally in a conventional mode. And in Africa, combined Western projection of power capabilities are still superior to anything the Soviets can offer. The declaratory Soviet position has long been that nuclear weapons can be used in support of the Soviet Union and her Warsaw Pact allies; that does not include any of the nations above. Precisely because the Soviets do not appear to have confidence in control of nuclear conflict escalation, even Cuba and Vietnam hardly amount to justification for risking a holocaust.

Because of this articulated lack of faith in escalation control, Moscow probably does not feel that the perception of more flexible use of nuclear weapons is on balance in the Soviet interest. Soviet strategists are concerned that a belief in the feasibility of limited counterforce strategy would make U.S. policymakers more inclined to challenge Soviet advances in the third world.[51] In short, the Soviet approach to deterrence is designed to serve Moscow's overall geopolitical objectives by becoming a nuclear umbrella over the determined Soviet drive to modify the international status quo by using, among other tools, enhanced conventional forces.

The Making of Soviet National Security Policy

The peculiarities of Soviet strategic thinking are in many ways connected with the nature of the Soviet national security formulation process. The institutional background of Soviet decision-making, as well as the bureaucratic procedures and informal arrangements which establish the rules of the game, guarantee a privileged position for military considerations and the military itself. This is not to suggest that marshals and generals control or even dominate the Soviet leadership in deliberations over national security policy. Nor does it imply that the Soviet top command is always unanimous on crucial foreign policy and defense matters. However, an impressive body of evidence indicates that as far as basic principles of national security are concerned, there exists an essential consensus among the Soviet leadership.

51. Henry A. Trofimenko, "Moscow Isn't Worried," *New York Times*, September 22, 1980.

Furthermore, compartmentalization of the Soviet decision-making process puts the uniformed military, together with some elements from the defense industries and defense research establishments, in a position of almost total monopoly over crucial information about the USSR's acquisition of weapons and actual deployments.

It is important to know how much leeway different Soviet institutions and interest groups have in arguing their cases, to what extent Soviet national security policy represents a rational collective judgment of the leadership, and to what degree it reflects compromises.

The fact is that several considerations inhibit the expression of pluralism in Soviet foreign policy formulation, irrespective of whether that would or would not result in lesser emphasis on accumulation of military power and foreign policy activism. A particularly prominent role is played by the consensus among Kremlin leaders about the fundamentals of the Soviet world outlook. This does not amount to an absolute likemindedness, but is rooted in a shared image of the basic challenge confronting the Soviet Union and of the main international objectives the USSR should pursue. A similar consensus in some respects was present in the U.S. policy of containment from the late 1940s to the mid-1960s.

In the United States, that consensus was finally destroyed by the war in Vietnam, and the emergence of new foreign policy elites both to the right and left of the traditional foreign policy establishment. Brezhnev and his associates, on the other hand, represent a remarkably homogeneous group of people with quite similar formative experiences and education. There is a shared preoccupation with security. The leadership also shares what Vladimir Petrov calls "fierce patriotism" and a view "that the Soviet Union leads the world-wide struggle against the fundamentally hostile West and that this hostility is predetermined by the conflict between two drastically different socio-economic systems."[52]

Naturally, there are constraints on the Soviet military effort. But this collective view of the Soviet elite ensures that defense requirements are perceived not as an unfortunate societal burden but rather as a crucial and in many ways beneficial (if expensive) function of the Soviet regime's leadership role in the socialist movement.[53] Moscow's national security philosophy

---

52. Vladimir Petrov, *Formation of Soviet Foreign Policy*, Institute for Sino-Soviet Studies, February 1974 (reprinted from *ORBIS*, Fall 1973, p. 846).
53. In his discussion with American officials, Leonid Brezhnev himself has frequently engaged in reminiscences of his World War II experiences. He left the impression that he was very proud

virtually ensures that the Soviet view of deterrence will include offensive overtones and would rely more on unilateral military efforts than on any abstract calculations or assumptions shared with a potential enemy about the rules of the game in international conflict.

Another important influence is that the military is well positioned in the Soviet decision-making process to block civilian contributions to operational doctrines. The military's relationship with the Party apparatus is more and more of a two-way street, with a division of labor rather than a clear-cut preponderance of the Party, as represented by the Central Commitee Secretariat.

Officially, the supreme Party organ is the Politburo, but this ultimate policymaking body—a sort of *de facto* executive-legislative committee of the whole Soviet bureaucratic structure—is in fact composed of leading representatives of all major power groups and not just the Party apparatus. On the Party side, the principal authority just below the Politburo level is in the hands of the Central Committee Secretariat. Significantly, there is no Central Committee unit which would deal with matters of military operations, deployments, and infrastructure. The Main Political Administration of the Armed Forces—simultaneously part of the Ministry of Defense and the Central Committee—and the Central Committee's Administrative Organs and Defense Industry Departments have responsibilities for political indoctrination, clearing promotions, and procurement for the military. But none of them separately and not even all of them together are qualified to give guidance on matters of a purely military nature, for which the marshals are responsible only to the Politburo itself. To a lesser degree, the same situation occurs in relations between the Central Committee and the Foreign Affairs Ministry and the KGB.

In the seventies, Brezhnev's personal Secretariat—a small group of top aides to the General Secretary—gradually emerged as substitute substantive staff for the Politburo.[54] But while some of these assistants are senior foreign policy experts, none of them is a specialist on defense issues or on internal security. There is one Major General on Brezhnev's personal staff, an aide de camp without known substantive responsibilities.

---

of his association with the military during the war and later when he served with the Main Political Administration of the Armed Forces in the early 1950s, and when he acted as Central Committee Secretariat supervisor of defense industries in the late 1950s.

54. The Central Committee's General Department handles technical and administrative arrangements. For more about the General Department, see Leonard Shapiro, "The General Department of the Central Committee of the CPSU," *Survey*, Summer 1975, pp. 53–65.

Similarly, the Council of Ministers' Presidium coordinates defense industries and is responsible for allocating resources for weapon acquisition. But
it is not involved in military-operational matters. While the Ministry of Defense is officially subordinate to the Presidium, abundant circumstantial evidence suggests that in fact it reports directly to the Politburo.[55] It appears
that "although civilian decisions are ultimately shaped by values and perceptions over which the army has no control, civilians do not have the
substantial nonmilitary sources of military information found in American
politics." And indeed "there are no Soviet equivalents for the Central Intelligence Agency, the Arms Control and Disarmament Agency, or private
consulting firms such as the Rand Corporation."[56]

The absence of an alternative assessment of Soviet defense requirements
and capabilities is an important consideration in evaluating the role of the
USSR's Defense Council, chaired by Brezhnev. On paper, members of the
Defense Council are appointed by the Supreme Soviet Presidium, where
Brezhnev also now serves as chairman.[57] In fact, the membership itself of
the Defense Council is likely to be determined by the Politburo. In the
absence of reliable evidence, it is usually assumed that in addition to Brezhnev, Prime Minister Alexei Kosygin (or rather, his successor Nikolai Tik-
hanov), Defense Minister Dmitri Ustinov, Foreign Minister Andrei Gromyko,
Central Committee Secretaries Andrei Kirilenko, and Mikhail Suslov may be
members.[58] American officials who negotiated the Strategic Arms Limitation
Talks with Brezhnev report that on several occasions the Soviet leader mentioned that he had to consult the Defense Council. There are also indications
that the Defense Council, like its war-time predecessor, the Main Defense
Council (GKO), is responsible for integrating the military effort into Soviet
economic development, together with such agencies as the Central Committee's Department of Defense Industry, the Council of Ministers' Military-
Industrial Commission, the Committee of Science and Technology, and the
State Planning Committee.

It is reasonably well established, however, that the Defense Council does

---

55. The same is true with respect to the Ministry of Foreign Affairs and the KGB, which are
also directed by full Politburo members well-placed to circumvent the Council of Ministers.
56. Timothy J. Colton, *Commissars, Commanders, and Civilian Authority: the Structure of Soviet
Military Politics* (Harvard University Press, 1979), p. 244.
57. *Konstitutsiya (Osnovnoy Zakon) Soyusa Sovetskikh Sotsialisticheskikh Respublik.* Moscow, 1977,
p. 34.
58. Harriet Fast Scott, William F. Scott, *The Armed Forces of the USSR.* (Boulder, Colorado:
Westview Press, 1979), p. 99.

Soviet Military Policy | 228

not have its own substantive staff. Accordingly, it is not a Soviet counterpart of the U.S. National Security Council, but more likely a kind of top-level interagency panel for policy planning and coordination.[59] Like everyone else, it has no alternative to relying on information supplied by the military.

The same is apparently true with respect to Brezhnev personally in his role as Commander in Chief. During World War II, the Soviet High Command, *Stavka* as it was called at the time, had to rely on the General Staff for determining Soviet force structure, developing operational plans, and monitoring their implementation.[60] It seems that under the Brezhnev-dominated leadership, with its emphasis on consensus and institutionalization of the policymaking process, the uniformed military is placed better than ever to exploit its traditional prerogatives in formulating national security decisions.

Several Soviet think tanks on foreign affairs, such as the Institute of World Economy and International Relations, the Institute of the USA and Canada Studies, the Institute of Oriental Studies, the Institute of the International Labor Movement, and several lesser establishments focusing on specific regions supply the Central Committee and to a lesser extent, the Defense and Foreign Ministries and the KGB with information and analyses. But the need-to-know principle, coupled with excessive compartmentalization and secretiveness, does not allow these Soviet academics access to information about their own country's military capabilities. Soviet foreign affairs institutes may help the leadership to understand the international environment, and such an understanding certainly influences deliberations regarding the Soviets' own military programs. Still, despite the wide publicity enjoyed by top Soviet officials from these institutes visiting the United States, their ability to seriously affect Soviet defense debates is highly questionable.

More influence is probably concentrated in the hands of Soviet scientists associated with defense-oriented research laboratories and research and development bureaus. Coordinated by the State Committee on Science and Technology and to a lesser extent, by the Academy of Sciences, the Soviet scientific community by necessity cannot be denied information about Soviet

59. Thomas Wolfe, *The SALT Experience: Its Impact on US and Soviet Strategic Policy and Decision-making*, Santa Monica, CA: Rand, Sept. 1975, R-1686-PR, pp. 58, 160. Wolfe's information is supported by this author's interviews with visiting Soviet scholars of foreign affairs, who unanimously indicated a rather restricted role for the Defense Council. They argue that it was not sufficiently institutionalized and lacked staff expertise to be an effective decision-making body outside the military procurement area.
60. G. K. Zhukov, *Vospominaniya I Razmyshleniya*, Moscow, 1969, pp. 291–292; S. M. Shtemenko, *Generalniy Shtab v Godi Voyni* Book II, Moscow, 1973, pp. 5–6; Ogarkov, *op. cit.*, *Kommunist*, No. 7, 1978, p. 114.

military technology.[61] But as is the case of foreign affairs, compartmentalization prevents natural scientists from getting involved in policy debates beyond their immediate, narrowly defined areas of responsibility. Control over information is no less an advantage in influencing policy in Moscow than in Washington. The Soviet military remains virtually unchallenged in advising the top leadership on issues of force structure and actual combat, under the conditions of Brezhnev's controlled pluralism and within the margins of the national security consensus. While evidently concluding that nuclear war is difficult to control and next to impossible to win, civilian members of the Politburo do not have much choice but to allow the military a great deal of autonomy in determining Soviet operational concepts within the limits of available resources and technology.

Unless one hopes for a fundamental restructuring of the Soviet political process, what may be required to restrict prerogatives of the Soviet military and its defense industry allies is not greater pluralism but the emergence of a strong decisive leader.[62] However, this is unlikely during the early stages of the Soviet succession. Only after a new leader managed to consolidate power could he think about challenging the military-industrial complex. The current deterioration of the U.S.-Soviet relationship and acceleration of Western defense program will create a rather inhospitable environment for any ambitious Soviet statesman to experiment with constraining military momentum or even to question the recommendations of marshals and admirals on matters over which they are accustomed to having a dominant influence.

"The Army should be cherished," Stalin commented not long before the German invasion. He explained that it was partly a lack of attention to and appreciation of the armed forces that contributed to the easy collapse of France.[63] In spite of Stalin's purges, memoirs of many retired marshals and generals reflect satisfaction with the unquestionable priority Stalin gave to defense concerns, creating a true national security state.

After the rough days the military (and many of the bureaucracies) suffered during the Khrushchev interlude, Brezhnev's regime has restored the military's sense of satisfaction. He and his Politburo associates appear to share,

61. For instance, academician Aleksandr N. Shuchukin, specialist in radio electronics, became Paul Nitze's counterpart on the Soviet SALT team. American delegates were uniformly impressed with his performance, and more specifically, his knowledge of the Soviet data. See more about him in John Newhouse, *Cold Dawn: The Story of SALT*, (Holt, Rinehart and Winston, 1973).
62. Helmut Sonnenfeldt and William G. Hyland, *Soviet Perspectives on Security*, Adelphi papers, No. 150, p. 20.
63. G. K. Zhukov, *op. cit.*, p. 236.

as Jack Snyder points out, "many of the military's values and policy preferences."[64] Détente and arms control, as practiced by the General Secretary and his colleagues, have not reduced the emphasis on unilateral military effort as the principal way to assure Soviet security and promote geopolitical ambitions. And the orderly, highly institutionalized and compartmentalized policymaking process that has prevailed during the Brezhnev years has benefited the military in bureaucratic bargaining.

Conclusion

The privileged position of the military is not set in concrete. Brezhnev's successors will inherit not only tremendous military power but also an accumulation of problems demanding urgent solutions. A combination of economic slowdown, energy shortages, and consumer pressures, coupled with fears of a growing technological gap with the West, may persuade a future leadership to constrain military appetites. Faced with the dilemma of investing in economic modernization or in further military acquisitions, the Kremlin may (depending on the international situation) opt for the former.

But for this to happen, the leadership that succeeds Brezhnev will have to resist a temptation to enhance domestic legitimacy through a global diplomacy of force. The disillusionment with détente apparently shared by the majority of the Soviet elite will make it harder for contenders for power to invest too much prestige in cooperation rather than rivalry with the West. Moreover, the tradition, mythology, and inertia of the national security state could represent another obstacle. In short, any attempt to eliminate the warfighting aspects of the Soviet strategic traditions would encounter considerable bureaucratic and cultural odds and may dearly cost those Soviet statesmen who would dare to challenge it (especially during an initial stage of succession).

The dual nature of the Soviet view of deterrence, emphasizing both offense and war-avoidance, is thus not a result of Moscow's lack of sophistication or of its bureaucratic inertia and confusion. Rather, Soviet coercive deterrence, as contradictory as it may appear to Westerners, represents a logical outcome of Soviet conceptions of national security and war on the one hand, and of domestic political organization on the other. As far as the Soviets themselves are concerned, it is entirely consistent in their terms. More importantly, it works.

---

64. Jack Snyder, *op. cit.*, p. 33.

The Soviet Union and Strategic Missile Guidance

Donald MacKenzie

Few issues have been of greater importance in Western, especially American, defense debates than Soviet missile accuracy and its implications for nuclear strategy. For thirty years the magnitude of the threat posed to the American deterrent by the Soviet missile force has been the subject of fierce if intermittent controversy.[1] How accurate Soviet missiles are, and how accurate they may become, have been central topics in this controversy.[2]

Soviet missile accuracy is of intellectual as well as policy importance. The relative roles in the arms race of technology and of politics is a persistent question. Missile accuracy has been a key case for those who argue that technology is the determining factor. An inherent logic of technical advance, so this argument goes, has pushed missile accuracies beyond the relatively modest requirements for the retaliatory destruction of cities. This technical advance has thus made possible—even required—new nuclear strategies focusing on the more demanding counterforce role: more demanding because very high accuracies are required to destroy missiles in their silos.[3]

I would like to thank the Nuffield Foundation, who supported the research drawn on here, and my colleagues at the Centre de Sociologie de l'Innovation, Ecole Nationale Supérieure des Mines de Paris, who provided me with hospitality while the paper was being written. I am indebted to David Holloway for help in the early stages of this research, to Wolfgang Rüdig for assistance with the German materials, and to Lynn Eden for perceptive comments on the original draft of the paper. Above all, I am grateful to the members of the guidance and intelligence communities without whose generous cooperation this paper could not have been written. Responsibility for the arguments in it, however, of course remains mine.

Donald MacKenzie, Lecturer in Sociology at the University of Edinburgh, researches the sociology and social history of science and technology.

1. See, for example, the conflicting analyses of George Rathjens and Albert Wohlstetter, and the resulting controversy: Operations Research Society of America, Ad Hoc Committee on Professional Standards, "Guidelines for the Practice of Operations Research," *Operations Research Letters*, Vol. 19 (September 1971), pp. 1123–1258.
2. One of the major issues raised by the so-called "B-team" of critics of the CIA was whether the latter was systematically underestimating the accuracy of Soviet missiles. See John Prados, *The Soviet Estimate: U.S. Intelligence Analysis and Soviet Strategic Forces* (Princeton: Princeton University Press, 1986), pp. 251–252.
3. The best sources on the technical issues involved in high-accuracy missile guidance and counter-silo attacks are D.G. Hoag, "Ballistic-Missile Guidance," in Bernard T. Feld, et al., eds., *Impact of New Technologies on the Arms Race* (Cambridge: MIT Press, 1971), pp. 19–108; Matthew

Proponents of this "technological determinism" are countered by those who see the armament process as ultimately shaped by strategic doctrine, or more generally by politics. There has, in particular, been a deep and abiding Western suspicion that the Soviet Union embraces a dangerous and threatening doctrine. The Soviet Union, it has been argued, is prepared to fight, and plans to win, a nuclear war.[4] If this were correct, then extreme accuracy in Soviet missiles might be less the product of an inherent logic of technology than a disturbing symptom of the dominance of a war-fighting, perhaps even a first-strike, nuclear strategy.

Soviet strategic writings have been anxiously scrutinized for omens on these matters.[5] Some attempts have also been made to correlate these writings with Soviet operations research and with the evidence of Soviet deployments and exercises.[6] Yet while voluminous estimates of the accuracy of Soviet missiles have been compiled,[7] there has been no systematic attempt

---

Bunn and Kosta Tsipis, *Ballistic Missile Guidance and Technical Uncertainties of Countersilo Attacks,* Program in Science and Technology for International Security, Report No. 9 (Cambridge: MIT Program in Science and Technology for International Security, August 1983); and Kosta Tsipis, *Arsenal: Understanding Weapons in the Nuclear Age* (New York: Simon and Schuster, 1983), ch. 5. These form useful technical background reading for much of what is discussed below. Among authors who have seen increased missile accuracy as a cause of counterforce strategy are Deborah Shapley, "Technology Creep and the Arms Race: ICBM Problem a Sleeper," *Science,* Vol. 201 (September 22, 1978), pp. 1102–1105; and Frank Barnaby, "The Military Tail wagging the Political Dog," *The Guardian,* October 23, 1980, p. 16. This is obviously simply one instance of a more general "technologically determinist" analysis of the arms race, for which see (with varying degrees of "determinism"), Dietrich Schroeer, *Science, Technology and the Nuclear Arms Race* (New York: Wiley, 1984); Marek Thee, *Military Technology, Military Strategy and the Arms Race* (London: Croom Helm, 1986); Edward Thompson, "Notes on Exterminism, the Last Stage of Civilization," *New Left Review,* No. 121 (May/June 1980), pp. 3–31; John Turner and Stockholm International Peace Research Institute (SIPRI), *Arms in the '80's: New Developments in the Global Arms Race* (London: Taylor and Francis, 1985); Lord Zuckerman, "Science Advisers and Scientific Advisers," *Proceedings of the American Philosophical Society,* Vol. 124 (1980), pp. 241–255.
4. Richard Pipes, "Why the Soviet Union thinks it could Fight and Win a Nuclear War," *Commentary,* July 1977, pp. 21–34.
5. Important contributions to this debate include ibid.; Raymond L. Garthoff, "Mutual Deterrence and Strategic Arms Limitation in Soviet Policy," *International Security,* Vol. 3, No. 1 (Summer 1978), pp. 112–147; Donald G. Brennan, "Commentary," *International Security,* Vol. 3, No. 3 (Winter 1978/79), pp. 193–198; Benjamin S. Lambeth, "The Political Potential of Soviet Equivalence," *International Security,* Vol. 4, No. 2 (Fall 1979), pp. 22–39; John Baylis and Gerald Segal, eds., *Soviet Strategy* (London: Croom Helm, 1981); John Erickson, "The Soviet View of Deterrence: A General Survey," *Survival,* Vol. 24, No. 6 (November/December 1982), pp. 242–249; David Holloway, *The Soviet Union and the Arms Race* (New Haven, Conn.: Yale University Press, 1983), ch. 3: Michael MccGwire, *Military Objectives in Soviet Foreign Policy* (Washington, D.C.: Brookings, 1987).
6. An excellent example is Stephen M. Meyer, *Soviet Theatre Nuclear Forces,* Adelphi Papers No. 187 and 188 (London: International Institute for Strategic Studies [IISS], Winter 1983/84).
7. Barton Wright, *World Weapon Database,* Vol. 1, *Soviet Missiles* (Lexington, Mass.: Lexington

to bring the historical record of Soviet missile guidance technology to bear on these issues. That is one prime function of this article.

I shall argue that the historical record of Soviet technology allows us largely to dispose of technological determinism in accounting for the development of Soviet missile accuracy. Strategic goals have shaped the technology, rather than vice versa.[8] But these goals are more complex than the "nuclear war-winning" view of Soviet strategy—or its inverted twin, the view of the Soviet Union as committed to "Mutual Assured Destruction" deterrence[9]—would allow. Missile accuracy has been given a very high priority for the counter-force capability that it provides, but not uniformly so; it has not had high priority in all systems and under all circumstances.

It would be foolish, however, to imagine that strategic goals have been the sole factor shaping Soviet guidance technology. Within the limitations of available data, I shall also address a range of other potential shaping forces. One is the role of the technological inheritance from the German work of the 1930s and 1940s. This has been influential—even 1980s Soviet guidance systems may bear its stamp—but it interacted with an important indigenous tradition of Soviet research. A further shaping force may have been the social structure of Soviet work in this area. Like most Soviet military research and development,[10] this turns out to be highly compartmentalized both vertically (among applied research, design, and production) and horizontally (among different organizations doing the same, or closely related, tasks). There is a good case to be made that this compartmentalization has affected the development of Soviet missile guidance and related navigation technologies; how-

Books and Institute for Defense and Disarmament Studies, 1986) is an extraordinarily useful source for this and other characteristics of Soviet missiles.

8. For a general discussion, with examples, of the way technological change is influenced by social, political and economic factors, see Donald MacKenzie and Judy Wajcman, eds., *The Social Shaping of Technology* (Milton Keynes, U.K.: Open University Press, 1985).

9. Garthoff, "Mutual Deterrence." Garthoff does, however, distinguish what he believes to be the Soviet position from Mutual Assured Destruction in the specific 1960s American meaning of the term (p. 124). The Soviets did not accept that *they* needed to be deterred and would have regarded as too narrow and technical its definition as the capacity to destroy, after an opponent's first strike, a certain unacceptably high proportion of that opponent's industry and population.

10. See Holloway, *The Soviet Union and the Arms Race*; David Holloway, "The Soviet Style of Military R & D," in Franklin A. Long and Judith Reppy, eds., *The Genesis of New Weapons: Decision Making for Military R & D* (New York: Pergamon Press, 1980), pp. 137–157; Arthur J. Alexander, *Weapons Acquisition in the Soviet Union, United States and France*, P-4989 (Santa Monica, Calif.: RAND, 1973); John A. McDonnell, "The Soviet Weapons Acquisition System," *Soviet Armed Forces Review Annual*, Vol. 3 (1979), pp. 175–203; and, of course, the eye-witness account of Mikhail Agursky, *The Soviet Military-Industrial Complex*, Jerusalem Papers on Peace Problems, No. 31 (Jerusalem: Hebrew University, 1980).

ever, the evidence available does not permit us fully to weigh the relative extent to which "organizational politics" and targeting requirements have shaped the Soviet arsenal.

Another shaping force is, of course, technical constraint. Some apparent constraints on Soviet guidance technology have been exaggerated in Western debate about Soviet acquisition of Western technology. Precision metal machining (e.g. of ball bearings) has not really been an overwhelming problem for the Soviets. Indeed, this Western debate tends to be based on a naive view of the nature of technology transfer. The well-documented Soviet lag in computer technology and microelectronic miniaturization has been a significant constraint. But there may also be a Soviet *preference* for "hardware" rather than "software" solutions to guidance problems. This may explain why Soviet designs for stellar-inertial guidance systems for submarine-launched ballistic missiles are quite different from American designs. In any case, computer power is a constraint of declining significance: ballistic missile on-board computers no longer represent a "state-of-the-art" problem in miniaturization.

What appears to be a combination of constraint and preference has led to what may be significant limitations in the flexibility with which the Soviet missile arsenal could be used. The mathematics of how the Soviets guide their missiles, for example, makes them harder to retarget than American missiles are. This inflexibility is not nearly as strong as it once was, but it should be borne in mind by any Western leader imagining that a nuclear war could be fought in a controlled and limited way. There would be strong pressures on the Soviets to execute a large-scale, coordinated attack on Western targets early in any nuclear exchange.

Soviet disadvantage is not the whole story, however. For socio-political rather than purely geographic reasons, the Soviets enjoy a major advantage currently denied the Americans—the ability to test strategic ballistic missiles on an overland rather than an ocean range. Because the "accuracy" of a missile is a more complex matter than is commonly understood, this Soviet advantage is more important than it may sound. It should also give Western leaders reason for pause before they attempt to "cash in" the Western lead in microelectronic miniaturization in a possible next technological stage of accuracy enhancement—the deployment of maneuvering strategic missile reentry vehicles. Instead, there is good reason to take seriously the possibility that for the first time in thirty years the growth of strategic ballistic missile accuracy could realistically be brought within the scope of arms control agreements.

Sources of Information

The internal workings of Soviet guidance systems are hidden from even the most high-resolution photo-reconnaissance satellite, and to my knowledge no demonstrably reliable high-level human intelligence has been received from an agent or emigré privy to the technical secrets of Soviet guidance.[11] How, then, can anyone in the West speak of a history of Soviet guidance technology?

The key source of information, of course, is telemetry—a by-product of the Soviet missile development and testing process. For a missile test to be of maximum use to the missile's designers and users, as much information as possible on the in-flight performance of key components such as the guidance system must be gathered. A continuous record of the performance of these components is, therefore, transmitted from the missile to the ground. From relatively early on in the Soviet missile program, this telemetry has been more-or-less comprehensively intercepted by Western intelligence. Telemetry can be coded before transmission, but the Soviet Union has started to do this only relatively recently, and even now this encryption does not completely prevent the making of inferences.[12]

---

11. In Peter Wright's celebrated *Spycatcher: The Candid Autobiography of a Senior Intelligence Officer* (New York: Viking/Penguin, 1987), he discusses the intelligence received from the British agent Oleg Penkovsky and two later defectors called "Top Hat" and "Fedora." Fedora in particular gave Western intelligence detailed information about guidance, but this information, says Wright (p. 211), later came to be regarded as deliberately misleading. Wright also suggests that the Soviets "doctored" test telemetry, and may have "introduced a fake third gyro on their missiles to make them appear less accurate than they in fact were" (p. 211). But no direct evidence for these latter claims is cited, and the passage leaves one in doubt as to Wright's grasp of the technical issues involved.

12. As early as 1948 a team from British intelligence, posing as archaeologists in Iran, reportedly intercepted telemetry from Soviet testing of V-2s. See Prados, *The Soviet Estimate*, p. 57. In recent years, however, the United States has charged that Soviet encryption of telemetry has increased to the point where it impedes verification of Soviet compliance with the unratified SALT II treaty. For a discussion of this issue, see James A. Schear, "Arms Control Treaty Compliance: Buildup to a Breakdown?" *International Security*, Vol. 10, No. 2 (Fall 1985), pp. 162–164. Schear concludes that "the loss of such data will degrade—perhaps irretrievably—U.S. estimates of Soviet strategic missile capabilities" (p. 164).

Particularly important is telemetry of on-board computation, which reveals the nature of the guidance formulation—the "mathematics" of the guidance system—which, in turn, allows inferences about the nature of the technology. If stellar-inertial guidance is being employed, for example, an on-board calculation has to be made to turn the information from the star fixes into the requisite guidance correction. In modern guidance systems the on-board computer is programmed to correct for predictable instrument errors (e.g. "drift" in the gyroscopes or "bias" in the accelerometers), and if telemetry representing this can be intercepted, then something of the nature of Soviet beliefs about the errors of their guidance systems can be determined.

Identifying and interpreting telemetry channels is not a simple matter. Although the analysts' experience and intuition are indispensable, their inferences can be checked, both against the radar record of actual missile trajectories (and sometimes satellite photographs of impact craters), and in the internal debates of the intelligence community. The question of encryption aside, experienced analysts reckon that 95 to 98% of the telemetry channels from Soviet missile testing can be identified with confidence.

Of course, this does not answer all questions. For example, it does not suffice for production of an unequivocal accuracy figure for a Soviet missile of a given type (see Appendix), though it is at least as important an input to that process as identifying final impact points. Nor does telemetry permit clear identification of the type of gyroscope being employed, although something of a consensus answer to that question has emerged after detailed study.

The Western records of intercepted telemetry, radar tracking and impact point analysis naturally remain classified. So there is a double indirectness in our knowledge of Soviet missile guidance. Nevertheless, over the years some of the conclusions reached by the intelligence community about Soviet missile guidance—chiefly estimates of Soviet missiles' Circular Error Probable (CEP, or radius of the circle around the target within which 50% of warheads would be expected to fall, see Appendix), but also very occasional comments about the nature of Soviet guidance technology[13]—have appeared in the

13. See, especially, "Soviets' Nuclear Arsenal Continues to Proliferate," *Aviation Week and Space Technology*, June 16, 1980, pp. 67–76, a remarkable compendium of Soviet missile accuracies and yields. The correspondence of the figures in this article to more recently declassified official estimates strongly suggests an authoritative leak, possibly from someone with access to Defense Intelligence Agency (DIA) estimates, given the closeness of the article's estimate of the CEP of the SS-19 (see Appendix hereto) to the DIA estimate.

specialist press and literature, most frequently *Aviation Week and Space Technology*. In addition, some early estimates of CEP have now been declassified.[14] Soviet technical writings should not be wholly dismissed as a source of information, even though inference from them to design details of deployed systems is normally (and, obviously, deliberately) impossible. Ballistic missile guidance, at least the dominant inertial variety (see below), is part of a wider field of inertial guidance and navigation that has applications for space, submarine, military and civil aircraft, and land as well as missile guidance. The history of this overall field in the Soviet Union, in at least its theoretical aspects, can to some extent be traced from the technical literature.[15]

Aside from these published sources, in researching Soviet missile guidance I was able to make use of interviews with people who had had direct contact with missile guidance and inertial navigation in the Soviet Union.[16] Even more helpful were discussions with members of the U.S. intelligence community, especially guidance system analysts, which, though of course unclassified, considerably supplemented what I was able to glean from the published record.[17]

All of this evidence must be viewed with caution. Western intelligence does not know as much as it would like to about Soviet guidance.[18] The intelligence community is also notoriously divided in the conclusions it draws from the available evidence,[19] so in interviewing or use of published "leaks" one must take into account the source's likely position in these controversies. What follows is thus based upon "soft" data, and in all probability stands in

---

14. Wright, *Soviet Missiles*.
15. There is an extremely useful historical survey of this literature in V.D. Andreev, I.D. Blyumin, E.A. Devyanin and M. Klimov, "Obzor Razvitiya Teorii Giroskopicheskikh i Inertsial'nykh Navigatsionnykh Sistem," (Survey of the development of the theory of gyroscopic and inertial navigation systems)," in *Razvitie Mekhaniki Giroskopicheskikh i Inertsial'nykh Sistem* (The development of the mechanics of gyroscopic and inertial systems) (Moscow: Nauka, 1973), pp. 33–72.
16. This included interviews with a Soviet emigré computer engineer, a German gyroscope specialist who worked in the Soviet Union after 1945 (conducted by my colleague, Dr. Wolfgang Rüdig), and several American specialists who were in contact with their Soviet counterparts.
17. "Factual" claims about Soviet guidance in what follows for which no source is given in the footnotes are from these interviews; I have preferred to avoid repetitive citation of anonymous interviews.
18. One intelligence analyst told me of a repeated dream he had, in which he was shown around the Soviet missile test center at Tyuratam, and allowed to look at whatever he wanted. Alas, in the morning he could never quite remember what he had seen!
19. Prados, *The Soviet Estimate*, and Lawrence Freedman, *U.S. Intelligence and the Soviet Strategic Threat* (London: Macmillan, 1977).

need of correction; I hope, indeed, that it may spark debate that will deepen our understanding of these important issues.

The German Inheritance

Like the Americans, the Soviets were "second wave" entrants to the field of ballistic missile guidance. The first ballistic missile genuinely to be guided—not simply stabilized as it flew along its unguided trajectory—was the Second World War German V-2.

Two radically different approaches, developed for the guidance of the V-2, continued to compete in the United States until the end of the 1950s, and even later in the Soviet Union. Both radio and inertial guidance of V-2s performed essentially the same two tasks, but by quite different means. The first task was to keep the missile flying in the direction of its target. The second was to detect its velocity and shut off its rocket motor when it had reached a speed such that it would neither fall short of its target nor overshoot it.

In radio guidance, two transmitting antennas were placed some distance behind the launch site, symmetrically on either side of the missile's plane of flight. The signals received from them enabled detection and correction of deviation from the plane of flight. The Doppler effect—the shift in frequency when source and receiver are in motion relative to one another—was used to detect missile velocity.[20]

In inertial guidance, these two functions were performed in a wholly self-contained way, with no contact, after firing, between the missile and the ground station. The basic inertial system, the "LEV-3,"[21] contained two gyroscopes that detected deviations from the desired direction of flight, and also controlled the process of tilting the missile after its vertical launch down to the required angle. Velocity was determined by measuring the acceleration of the missile, using accelerometers further discussed below.

In the LEV-3 these sensors were physically fixed to the body of the missile. But the Germans also experimented with, though they did not use opera-

---

20. Walter Haeussermann, "Developments in the Field of Automatic Guidance and Control of Rockets," *Journal of Guidance and Control*, Vol. 4, No. 3 (May–June 1981), pp. 225–239, especially pp. 226–228.
21. F.K. Mueller, *A History of Inertial Guidance* (Redstone Arsenal, Ala.: Army Ballistic Missile Agency, n.d. but c. 1960). This has now been reprinted in the *Journal of the British Interplanetary Society*, Vol. 38 (1985), pp. 180–192.

tionally, a more sophisticated kind of inertial guidance that more closely prefigures its modern form.[22] In this, gyroscopes and accelerometers are mounted on a "stable platform" (see Figure One for the basic principle). The gyroscopes detect any rotation of the platform, and a feedback system corrects it. So the platform remains fixed in its orientation in space, regardless of the movement of the missile carrying it.

By modern standards, the V-2 was a short-range missile, with a maximum range less than 200 nautical miles, or around 350 kilometers. Its developers seem to have hoped for an accuracy under ideal circumstances of a tenth of

Figure 1. Stable Platform Inertial Guidance System (schematic).

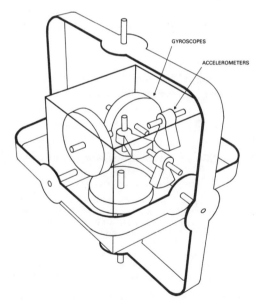

22. Ibid., also Otto Müller, "The Control System of the V-2," in Th. Benecke and A.W. Quick, *History of German Guided Missile Development* (Brunswick: Appelhans, 1957), pp. 80–101.

one per cent of its range[23]—0.2 nautical miles or 350 meters at maximum range. But operational accuracies were many times worse than this. The CEP was on the order of 3.5 nautical miles (6.5 kilometers).[24]

Given that CEP was roughly proportional to range, this meant that neither Americans nor Soviets could hope to guide even medium-range missiles, much less possible ICBMs, by simply using the V-2 technology they were both able to capture in 1945. The V-2 was important as an exemplar. It showed that the ballistic missile was feasible as a weapon, and its existence was certainly a crucial factor in the post-1945 Soviet decision to place great priority on ballistic missile development.[25] But V-2 technology had to be improved considerably for this development to be of long-term strategic significance.

Germany in 1945 contained, however, not just hardware that could be captured, examined and copied, but also people with skills, knowledge and ideas for improvement of guidance accuracies. These included those who had worked directly at the V-2 development base at Peenemünde and a wider set of specialists in navigation and the application of gyroscopes. The German navy, in particular, had in the 1920s and 1930s sought to compensate for the small size of its vessels, limited by the Treaty of Versailles, by placing high priority on ultra-accurate navigation and gunnery. Among these specialists were two groups, one working for the naval navigation and fire control suppliers Kreiselgeräte GmbH, the other for Luftwaffe suppliers Siemens, both of which had taken a serious interest in developing self-contained, inertial navigation for submarines, ships and aircraft.[26]

23. Ernst A. Steinhoff, "Development of the German A-4 Guidance and Control System, 1939–1945: A Memoir," in R. Carghill Hall, ed., Essays on the History of Rocketry and Astronautics: Proceedings of the Third through Sixth History Symposia of the International Academy of Aeronautics, Vol. 2 (Washington, D.C.: National Aeronautics and Space Administration, 1977), pp. 203–215, on p. 206.
24. Herbert K. Weiss, "Influence of the Guidance Designer on Warfare," in Sidney Lees, ed., Air, Space and Instruments: Draper Anniversary Volume (New York: McGraw Hill, 1963), pp. 32–74, on p. 64: Lawrence Freedman, The Evolution of Nuclear Strategy (London: Macmillan, 1981), p. 25.
25. For the history of the Soviet ICBM program, see David Holloway, "Military Technology," in Ronald Amann, Julian Cooper and R.W. Davies, eds., The Technological Level of Soviet Industry (New Haven, Conn.: Yale University Press, 1977), pp. 407–489; David Holloway, "Innovation in the Defense Sector: Battle Tanks and ICBMs," in Ronald Amann and Julian Cooper, eds., Industrial Innovation in the Soviet Union (New Haven, Conn.: Yale University Press, 1982), pp. 368–414; and Holloway, The Soviet Union and the Arms Race, pp. 150–154.
26. For various perspectives on the German work of this period, see H. Hellman, "The Development of Inertial Navigation," Navigation: Journal of the Institute of Navigation, Vol. 9, No. 2 (Summer 1962), pp. 83–94; Johannes G. Gievers, "Erinnerungen an Kreiselgeräte" (Recollections of Kreiselgeräte), Jahrbuch der Deutschen Gesellschaft für Luft- und Raumfahrt (Bonn: Deutsche

As is well-known, while the Americans obtained most of the technical experts from Peenemünde, a certain number, led by Helmut Gröttrup, assistant to the Director of the Guidance, Control and Telemetry Laboratory, chose—it appears for personal and career reasons rather than out of ideological preference[27]—to work for the Soviets. They reopened the V-2 production line, and by autumn 1946, when they were forcibly transferred to the Soviet Union, had produced some 30 V-2s.[28]

Though this group contained, aside from Gröttrup himself, several guidance specialists and the gyroscope expert Kurt Magnus, it would probably have been insufficient—even had it been more trusted by the Soviets than it was—to sustain a major guidance development effort. But this group was not the only source of Soviet access to German navigation and gyroscope technology.

Of possibly greater long-term significance were the links between the Soviet Union and naval suppliers Kreiselgeräte. As well as supplying the Reichsmarine with gyroscopic navigational and fire-control equipment, Kreiselgeräte had lent its expertise to the V-2 program. Its visionary but idiosyncratic first technical director, Johannes Maria Boykow, who died in 1935, had been an early enthusiast for the idea of fully self-contained inertial navigation.[29] His successor Johannes Gievers developed Boykow's ideas for an inertial "Übergrundkompass" (over-ground compass).[30]

Both practical inertial navigation, and more accurate missile inertial guidance, shared a common problem in the inaccuracy of the basic gyroscopes and accelerometers. This inaccuracy was believed to be in large part due to friction in the mechanical bearings they employed. Gievers, along with other Kreiselgeräte specialists F. Müller and H. Rothe (who ended up in American hands), came to the conclusion that the way to solve this problem was to replace mechanical bearings by a film of gas supplied by an external gas-

Gesellschaft für Luft- und Raumfahrt 1971), pp. 263–291; G. Klein and B. Stieler, "Contributions of the late Dr. Ing. Johannes Gievers to Inertial Technology," paper presented at Symposium Gyro Technology 1979, Stuttgart, FRG; M. Pütz, "Contributions of the Late Professor Dr. Eduard Fischel to Gyro Technology," paper presented to Symposium Gyro Technology 1984, Stuttgart, FRG.

27. Frederick I. Ordway III and Mitchell R. Sharpe, *The Rocket Team* (Cambridge: MIT Press, 1982), pp. 318–319.
28. Ibid., p. 321.
29. J.M. Boykow, "Instrument for Indicating Navigational Factors," U.S. Patent No. 2,109,283, February 22, 1938.
30. Klein and Stieler, "Contribution of Gievers," p. 1.4.

bottle or pump.[31] By the end of the war Kreiselgeräte was working on gas-supported gyroscopes to improve V-2 accuracy, and had built a miniature submarine gyrocompass, designed by Gievers, incorporating an air-supported accelerometer.[32]

Soviet access to this gas bearing technology is of some importance. As we shall see, this became the dominant Soviet approach to inertial instrument design, while remaining a minority approach in the U.S., where its use ceased by the end of the 1960s. It could conceivably have been developed independently in the Soviet Union, but it seems much more likely that the inspiration for Soviet work in this field was German.

Links between Kreiselgeräte and the Soviet Union predated the war. During the time of the Hitler-Stalin pact, Kreiselgeräte contracted to provide gyroscopic instruments and fire-control systems for German warships to be supplied to the Soviet Union. From 1939 to 1941, therefore, Soviet "acceptance officials," well versed in gyro technology and fluent in German, were present in the Kreiselgeräte plant in Berlin. These officials returned with the occupying forces in 1945 to obtain navigational devices, gain the cooperation of Kreiselgeräte employees and find out more about German developments. Among those who worked temporarily for the Soviets was Gievers, who provided them with a detailed description of the miniature gyrocompass. The Soviets also obtained a working prototype of it, including the air bearing accelerometer.[33]

It would, however, be quite mistaken to see the Soviets as simply "acquiring" advanced German technology. A high level of indigenous technical expertise must have existed to assimilate and make use of it. Gievers testifies that the Soviet "acceptance officials" were "more knowledgeable of certain aspects of gyroscope technology than we were: they could tell us a lot about gyro development in American firms that we had no knowledge of."[34] Certainly, the Soviet Union was careful not to become reliant on captured Ger-

---

31. Gievers, "Erinnerungen an Kreiselgeräte"; Cdr. W.E. May, W.G. Heatly and H.C. Wassell, "Draft Report of Visit to B.N.G.M., Minden, June 12th, 13th, 1946," in the file on Gievers at the Admiralty Compass Observatory, Slough, U.K.; Haeussermann, "Developments in Guidance and Control of Rockets," pp. 232–233.
32. Klein and Stieler, "Contribution of Gievers," pp. 1.5–1.6.
33. Gievers, "Erinnerungen an Kreiselgeräte," p. 28. I am quoting from the Defense Intelligence Agency translation of this article (DIA Translation No. LN 040–82, oddly titled "History of the Gyroscope").
34. Ibid., p. 27.

man personnel. The Gröttrup group became aware that their efforts were being paralleled by Soviet teams: the technical questions they were asked, as their work proceeded in the late 1940s, could only have emanated from people directly involved.[35]

The visible evidence of this indigenous Soviet expertise in the guidance field is a powerful tradition, flourishing after 1945 but with roots stretching back well before the war, of work in the theoretical analysis of gyroscopic systems. From the publications of this school it is hard to detect the status of Soviet practical work in the pre-war period; the concrete analyses that were published concerned foreign devices such as the German Anschütz gyrocompass or the American Sperry aircraft gyrohorizon. But this school was confident enough to correct German analyses of the Germans' own devices.[36]

It seems likely, however, that practical Soviet technology, like that of almost all the rest of the world, lagged behind German, although there is some tentative evidence of advanced Soviet work even under the extremely adverse conditions of the war. There was theoretical research on inertial navigation prior to 1945, and some practical work in the Automation Department of the Moscow Power Engineering Institute appears to have begun in 1943.[37] If that is correct, Soviet practical work was temporarily in advance of American, which began only after the end of the war.

So the Soviet Union had both the capacity and the desire to learn from German work, not merely to copy it. German work thus contributed to post-1945 indigenous Soviet development rather than being a straightforward determinant of it. Its importance, however, can be seen by the fact that as late as 1953, when the bulk of the Gröttrup group was allowed to return to Germany, twelve guidance specialists were retained for a further five years "with good salaries and excellent accommodation."[38] By then, though, the Soviets' own research and development effort in missile guidance must have been well on the way to maturity.

---

35. Interview with member of Gröttrup group. See also Irmgard Gröttrup, *Rocket Wife* (London: Deutsch, 1959).
36. Andreev, et al., "Obzor Razvitiya."
37. L.I. Tkachev, *Sistemy Inertsial'noi Orientirovki* (Inertial Navigation Systems) (Moscow: Moskovskiy Energeticheskiy Institut, 1973), trans., Joint Publications Research Service No. 67629, July 20, 1976, p. 102.
38. Ordway and Sharpe, *The Rocket Team*, p. 342.

Social Organization of Guidance System Research, Development, and Production

The indigenous Soviet effort that emerged in missile guidance has three layers: one public (the research institutes) and two hidden from view (design bureaus and production facilities). The public face of Soviet guidance and navigation technology is the active and sophisticated theoretical effort, openly published, referred to above. The best-known source of this effort is the Institute for Problems in Mechanics of the Academy of Sciences, the head of which is the leading Soviet theoretician, Academician A.Yu. Ishlinsky. Born in Moscow in 1913, Ishlinsky worked on the theory of elasticity before he moved to work on the applied mathematics of gyroscopes and inertial systems.[39] Ishlinsky has, since the 1950s, been in close touch with developments in the United States, and he maintained frequent contact with the leading Western inertial proponent, Charles Stark Draper.[40] Overseas specialists can visit Ishlinsky's institute, and freely discuss with Ishlinsky and his staff the work done there.

This institute is, however, not responsible for missile guidance systems. Development and design work for these is the business, in missile guidance as in other fields in the Soviet Union, of design bureaus; in the case of guidance these are "closed" (i.e., secret) bureaus.

There are three guidance design bureaus. One specializes in work for Soviet navy missiles; the other two in different kinds of work for the Soviet Strategic Rocket Forces. The guidance bureaus are separate from the missile bureaus headed by Korolev (until 1966), Yangel (until 1971), Nadiraze and Chelomei.[41] One Soviet source notes a problem that flows from this separation:

---

39. See, for example, A. Yu. Ishlinsky, *Mechanics of Gyroscopic Systems* (Jerusalem: Israel Program for Scientific Translations, 1965), which is a translation of Ishlinsky's *Mekhanika Giroskopicheskikh Sistem* (Moscow: Izdatel'stvo Akademii Nauk SSSR, 1965); Ishlinsky, *Inertial'noe Upravlenie ballisticheskimi Raketami* (Inertial guidance of ballistic missiles) (Moscow: Nauka, 1968).
40. A congratulatory telegram from Ishlinsky is, for example, to be found in the volume published in 1963 to celebrate Draper's 60th birthday. Lees, *Air, Space and Instruments*, p. vi.
41. For these bureaus, see Holloway, *The Soviet Union and the Arms Race*, p. 151; Holloway, "Innovation in the Defense Sector," p. 399; and Robert P. Berman and John C. Baker, *Soviet Strategic Forces: Requirements and Responses* (Washington, D.C.: Brookings, 1982), pp. 53–55 and 102–107. According to the latter, Korolev's bureau, which seems to have stopped strategic missile work on his death, designed the SS-6 and SS-8. Yangel's bureau designed the SS-7, SS-9, SS-17, and SS-18, as well as the early medium range missiles, SS-4 and SS-5, and submarine-launched missiles SS-N-4 and SS-N-5. The Nadiraze bureau designed the SS-13, the unsuccessful solid-fueled SS-16, and the SS-20. The Chelomei bureau designed the SS-11 and SS-19, and seems to have taken over responsibility for the later SLBM program.

During the course of experimental development the problem of individual determination of the probability of reliable missile operation P^*_m and dispersion of impact points $(\sigma^*)^2$ is often encountered. Sometimes this is caused by the fact that the guidance system, which determines $(\sigma^*)^2$, and the missile design are produced by different organizations.[42]

The guidance bureaus are not tied to particular missile bureaus—a guidance bureau can work with more than one missile bureau, although as the latter have also tended to specialize (into "heavy" ICBMs, "light" ICBMs, solid-fuel systems, etc.), the pattern of interconnections cannot be wholly random.

The third level of the Soviet guidance effort is separate yet again: the plants that produce guidance components and systems are distinct from both the design bureaus and the research institutes. So the social organization of guidance system technology in the Soviet Union appears highly compartmentalized vertically.

It is also compartmentalized horizontally. Each of the guidance bureaus has developed its own style, and there appears to be little communication or crossover of technology between them. Further, there appear to be barriers between design of missile guidance systems and work in the related technologies of submarine and aircraft inertial navigation. Only at the level of theory and applied research does "inertial guidance and navigation" seem to exist as a unified entity in the Soviet Union.

This vertical and horizontal compartmentalization contrasts with the situation prevalent in the West,[43] though perhaps not quite as strongly as it first appears. "Inertial guidance and navigation" is viewed in the West as a largely unified field, dominated by commercial firms rather than government plants or laboratories. These firms typically perform research and development, design, and production: all major firms straddle at least two or three of the full range of inertial activities (strategic and tactical missile guidance, space, submarine navigation, military and civil aircraft navigation and land navigation), although perhaps only one, the major French firm SAGEM (Société

42. V.I. Varfolomeyev and M.I. Kopytov, *Proyektirovaniye i Ispytaniye Ballisticheskikh Raket* (Design and Testing of Ballistic Missiles) (Moscow: Military Publishing House of the Ministry of Defense, 1970). I am quoting from the Joint Publications Research Service translation, No. 51810, November 19, 1970, p. 305.
43. Unreferenced information on Western developments is drawn from a wider study of the history of missile guidance, which I am preparing for publication under the title *Technology of Power: An Historical Sociology of Nuclear Missile Guidance*.

d'Applications Générales d'Electricité et de Méchanique), is involved in the whole gamut.

The major exception to this pattern is the dominant Western institution in ballistic missile guidance system design, the Charles Stark Draper Laboratory, Inc., of Cambridge, Massachusetts (until 1973 it was the MIT [Massachusetts Institute of Technology] Instrumentation Laboratory). This is a not-for-profit organization, not a commercial firm, and it does only research and design work, not volume production. Although involved in the late 1940s and 1950s in aircraft and submarine navigation, and in the 1960s in the Apollo space program, the Draper Laboratory has come to specialize in ballistic missile guidance, being responsible for the design of the guidance systems for all the generations of American submarine-launched ballistic missiles (SLBMs), and for the Air Force's Thor, Titan II, MX and Small ICBM (the latter better known as "Midgetman").[44] It had important competitors in the German guidance specialists who designed the guidance for the U.S. Army's Redstone, Jupiter and Pershing I missiles, NASA's Saturn booster, and also in the designers of the Minuteman guidance system at the Autonetics Division of North American Aviation, now Rockwell International. But the 1960s Saturn was the Germans' last major program, as well as the last American system to use externally-pressurized gas bearing gyroscopes of the kind used in the Soviet Union; Autonetics is now involved in MX inertial measurement unit production only as second-source producer for what is essentially a Draper-designed system.

The American technology that most directly compares with Soviet missile guidance is thus predominantly the product of an institution largely insulated from the commercial marketplace, vertically separated from production, and specialized in missile guidance rather than other applications of inertial technology. This we will need to bear in mind when we consider the effects on Soviet guidance technology of the social organization of its research, design, and production.

Soviet Land-Based Missile Guidance Technology

After 1945, the Soviet Union moved much more decisively than the United States to give a high priority to ballistic missiles. In the United States, cruise

---

44. Despite considerable expenditure on the development of alternatives for the Small ICBM, its guidance system will essentially be the same as that of MX. "News Briefs," *Aviation Week and Space Technology*, February 29, 1988, p. 34.

missiles, analogues of the German V-1 rather than V-2, received higher priority initially, and a powerful lobby defended the strategic bomber as a primary weapon system.[45] Land-based missiles—first medium-range, later of intercontinental range—were and still are of primary importance in that Soviet effort, so it is appropriate to begin our more detailed review of Soviet ballistic missile guidance with land-based systems.

RADIO VERSUS INERTIAL GUIDANCE

As we have seen, two guidance technologies could be inherited from the V-2: radio and inertial. Radio appeared to be more accurate than inertial, but suffered from an obvious military disadvantage—an enemy could perhaps jam or interfere with it.

Nevertheless, given the very great difficulties involved in developing inertial components accurate enough to guide missiles of substantially longer range than the V-2, radio guidance appeared to many to be the more immediately feasible proposition. So while American medium-range missiles of the 1950s were inertially guided (Redstone and Jupiter by a system designed by the German team, Thor by a Draper system), the first American ICBMs—Atlas D and Titan I—were radio-guided. Only in the early 1960s, with Atlas E and F, Minuteman and Titan II, did inertial guidance supplant radio. Even as this was happening, radio guidance was seen by many as the more accurate. But as the missiles themselves began to be emplaced in underground silos, guiding them from vulnerable above-ground radio antennas or radars could easily be argued to be foolish.

From the earliest times, both radio and inertial guidance were pursued in the Soviet Union. Irmgard Gröttrup, who accompanied the German technologists who went to the Soviet Union, has described their use of radio guidance in 1948.[46] There, too, radio guidance seemed to have had the initial edge, even for missiles well short of ICBM range.

The first seriously operational[47] Soviet nuclear missile was the medium-range SS-3 "Shyster." It first entered service around 1955, and although Sovet-designed it incorporated much V-2 technology, some of it improved.

---

45. Robert L. Perry, *The Ballistic Missile Decisions*, P-3686 (Santa Monica, Calif.: RAND, 1967).
46. Gröttrup, *Rocket Wife*, pp. 87–88.
47. Earlier, two versions of the V-2 had been built: one by the Gröttrup group, the other, known as the R-1, by a Soviet group under designer Sergei Korolev. Then a longer-range, improved version of the R-1, the R-2, was built, followed by the SS-3. See Holloway, "Military Technology," pp. 455–458.

It appears to have been radio-guided.[48] Its successor, the SS-4, deployed from 1959 onwards, was also radio-guided. But its radio guidance was replaced, possibly as early as by 1962, by inertial guidance.[49] The 1961 SS-5 may well have been inertially-guided from deployment onwards.[50] All subsequent Soviet medium- and intermediate-range ballistic missiles have been inertially-guided.

A similar pattern is to be found in ICBM development. Khrushchev's memoirs indicate use of radio guidance for the first experimental Soviet ICBM, the SS-6, deployed in very small numbers around 1961.[51] The widely deployed second generation ICBM, the SS-7, operational from 1962–63 onward, may, like the SS-4, have had its early radio guidance replaced by inertial;[52] radio guidance may also have been used on the less successful SS-8.[53] Only with the third generation Soviet ICBMs, the SS-9, SS-11 and SS-13, first deployed in the latter half of the 1960s, is there evidence of an irreversible shift to inertial.[54] With the fourth (SS-17, SS-18 and SS-19) and fifth generation ICBMs, pure inertial guidance has certainly been universal.

The pattern, found first in medium-range missiles and repeated slightly later for ICBMs, is thus of initial use of radio guidance and its gradual replacement (possibly including retrofitting) by inertial guidance. It suggests that inertial guidance in the Soviet Union was, as in the U.S., considered the less mature technology, but because of its self-contained nature, the militarily superior one. Though the USSR, like the United States, would very likely have viewed radio guidance as having advantages in accuracy, these were apparently not taken as sufficient to outweigh its greater vulnerability. The lag in the switch from radio to pure inertial—it took place a good five years later in the Soviet Union—suggests either that the trade-off was seen as closer there or, perhaps more likely, that Soviet inertial technology matured more slowly than American.

48. Wright, *Soviet Missiles*, p. 309.
49. Ibid., p. 314.
50. Ibid., p. 323.
51. Nikita Khrushchev, *Khrushchev Remembers: The Last Testament*, trans. and ed., Strobe Talbott (London: Deutsch, 1974), p. 109.
52. Wright, *Soviet Missiles*, p. 114.
53. Berman and Baker, *Soviet Strategic Forces*, p. 104.
54. However, one of the sources quoted by Wright, *Soviet Missiles*, p. 152, suggests radio guidance of (presumably early versions of) the SS-11, which entered service in 1966, and Prados, *Soviet Estimate*, p. 206, suggests radio guidance of the SS-9.

SOVIET INERTIAL INSTRUMENT TECHNOLOGY

In both America and the Soviet Union, great efforts were made, after 1945, to overcome the major barrier to accurate inertial guidance and navigation: inadequacy of gyroscopes and accelerometers. The form taken by this effort was painstaking gradual improvement of a single basic type of device. But the basic type chosen differed. The Soviets chose the externally-pressurized gas bearing inertial instrument inherited, most likely, from Kreiselgeräte. While, as indicated above, this was also pursued until the 1960s in the United States, there it was a Draper device that became hegemonic. In this, the single-degree-of-freedom floated rate-integrating gyroscope, the gyro rotor is enclosed in a hermetically sealed can which is then floated in fluid heated to achieve near-neutral buoyancy and so minimize friction in the bearings supporting the can (see Figure Two). This device has more or less successfully fought off a series of competitors for missile guidance (although it is largely being supplanted in other inertial applications). These competitors included not just the German design, but an Autonetics design involving "self-activating" rather than externally-pressurized gas bearings (the Autonetics gyroscope was adopted for Minuteman but not for MX), "dry" gyroscopes and

Figure 2.   A floated single-degree-of-freedom integrating gyroscope (highly schematic).

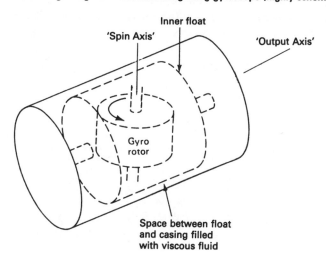

most recently the laser gyroscope.[55] So the accelerometers for Trident and MX, and also the MX gyroscopes, are Draper fluid-floated instruments—linear descendants of a design first adopted in the 1940s.

The reason for the dominance of the fluid-floated instrument in the U.S. is that its proponents have won the argument that it is more accurate than its competitors. For example, the only exception to its dominance in the current generation of U.S. strategic missiles is the Trident gyroscopes, where accuracy is argued to be less crucial because an in-flight starsight is used in part to correct gyro "drift" (see below). Thus it is of some interest that the Soviets have not adopted the fluid-floated gyroscope.

This cannot be a decision taken in ignorance. The fluid-floated gyroscope has been described in detail in open Western literature from the mid-1950s onward, and through Ishlinsky the Soviets have had close contact with its most enthusiastic proponent, Stark Draper. The Soviet Union would have had little difficulty in obtaining actual examples of at least medium-accuracy fluid-floated gyros fifteen years ago—they are to be found in the standard navigational equipment of the widely-sold Boeing 747. Nor is the Soviet Union ignorant of more modern types of gyroscope. Soviet theoretical work exists on dry gyroscopes, laser gyroscopes and even the "wine glass" hemispherical resonator gyro[56] that is currently exciting some Western interest. There is evidence from a visitor to the Soviet Union of quantity production of the dry gyroscope, but not for missile guidance (presumably it is for aircraft navigation); there is also apparently at least development, if not production, of laser and fiber-optic gyroscopes.[57] So it appears that a single basic instrument design (the externally-pressurized gas bearing gyroscope) probably inherited from German work of the 1940s, has been selected and subjected to evolutionary improvement. All three Soviet guidance bureaus seem to

55. In a "self-activating" gas bearing gyroscope the necessary pressure is derived from the spin of the gyroscope rotor—see below, notes 81 and 82, for how this differs from the German design. A "dry" gyroscope uses neither fluid nor gas bearings. In modern "dry" gyroscopes, known as tuned-rotor gyroscopes, a sophisticated mechanical design is used to "decouple" the spinning rotor from the gyroscope casing. In the laser gyroscope, the task of the mechanical gyroscope—the detection of rotation—is performed using not a spinning rotor, but beams of coherent light passing around an enclosed path in opposite directions. Rotation of the device causes a shift in the optical interference patterns when the two beams are combined.
56. This is a mechanical gyro, but more of a "solid-state" one, in that it vibrates rather than rotates. It is being developed by Delco, the division of General Motors that produced the first successful civil air inertial navigation system, the "Carousel" used in the Boeing 747.
57. The fiber-optic gyroscope is based on the same optical principle as the laser gyroscope, but uses optical fiber rather than gas-filled cavities in a solid block.

have followed this course. The Western situation with different organizations promoting different basic designs (albeit with success in the long run tending to flow to Draper and the fluid-floated instrument) seems not to have prevailed in the Soviet Union.

Are Soviet inertial instruments, then, inherently inferior to Western, given the dominance of an instrument type abandoned in the West twenty years ago? Apart from one important area, discussed below, the answer appears to be no. In the sensing of acceleration and in-flight rotation, the best Soviet instruments appear to those I interviewed to be in the same league as the best Western ones.

Despite this overall allegiance to gas bearing instruments, Soviet inertial instrument design is not completely uniform. One important difference among the guidance bureaus is in accelerometer design. This is of considerable interest, because in ballistic missile use (where high accelerations must be measured accurately, but the stable platform must be kept in known orientation for only a short period of time) it is accelerometer accuracy that is commonly understood to be more crucial to overall CEP than is gyroscope accuracy.

In strategic missile accelerometers there is a choice between two fundamental designs, both of which were used, in early form, in the V-2 program.[58] In the pendulous integrating gyro accelerometer (PIGA), a gyroscope is constructed in an unsymmetrical way so as to make it sensitive to acceleration, not just rotation. Its precession[59] under the effects of acceleration can directly yield the missile's velocity; i.e., it has a mathematically integrating action. The first PIGA, as used in the V-2, is shown in Figure Three. The other simpler type of design is the "restrained pendulum." This contains no gy-

---

58. Thomas M. Moore, "German Missile Accelerometers," *Electrical Engineering*, November 1949, pp. 996–999. Other forms of accelerometer have been proposed, but have not yet found strategic missile use.

59. "Precession" is the distinctive movement of the spin axis of a gyroscope wheel (or a spinning top) under the influence of an applied torque. The mechanical gyroscope shown in Figure Two, for example, will precess around its "output axis" when movement of the stable platform on which it is based causes a torque around its "input axis." This precession is turned into an electrical signal by a signal generator internal to the gyroscope. This electrical signal is then fed back to rotate the platform, canceling out its initial movement.

The deliberate mass unbalance in the PIGA means that a torque arises when the device is subject to acceleration. The angle through which the gyro wheel precesses is proportional to the time integral of the applied acceleration. This precession can be turned into an electric input to an on-board computer (in modern guidance systems) or can directly initiate rocket motor cut-off (as in the much simpler V-2 system).

Figure 3. Pendulous Integrating Gyro Accelerometer, as Designed for V-2.

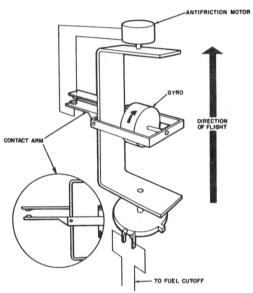

Source: F. K. Mueller, *A History of Inertial Guidance* (Redstone Arsenal, Ala.: Army Ballistic Missile Agency), p. 19. This history, undated but c. 1960, has been reprinted in the *Journal of the British Interplanetary Society*, Vol. 38 (1985), pp. 180–192.

roscope, simply a mass. When the mass is subjected to acceleration, a re-straining force has to be applied to prevent it moving from its equilibrium position. The size of this force is then the measure of acceleration.

Although in the V-2 program the restrained pendulum design appears to have been the more accurate,[60] since then consensus appears to have emerged that the PIGA is inherently the more accurate device. On the other hand it is also inherently more complex, and so tends to be much more difficult to make and much more expensive. In U.S. programs the PIGA has dominated, except in Navy missiles of the 1960s and 1970s,[61] a period during

---

60. Ibid., pp. 966–997.
61. See Donald MacKenzie and Graham Spinardi, "Weapons Technology in Social and Historical Perspective: U.S. Navy Fleet Ballistic Missile Guidance from Polaris to Trident," *Social Studies of Science*, Vol. 18, No. 3 (August 1988).

which Navy missile designers did not give accuracy highest priority. With Trident II D5, where counterforce accuracy is for the first time a clear priority, the PIGA has, however, been chosen.

Soviet ICBM programs use both PIGAs and restrained pendula; the two types of device are characteristic of different bureaus. This divergence is an important contributor to a vital aspect of Soviet ICBMs to which I now turn: within the same generation of ICBM, "high-accuracy" missiles, using PIGAs, can be differentiated from "medium-accuracy" missiles using restrained pendula.

ACCURACY, INSTITUTIONAL INTERESTS AND STRATEGIC ROLES

This differentiation in accuracy can be seen in Soviet ICBMs of the first all-inertial generation, the SS-9, SS-11 mod 1, and SS-13 mod 1 of the late 1960s. The SS-9, although the earliest missile of the generation, seems to have been the most accurate (see Appendix). The estimates in the classified versions of the Secretary of Defense's Reports to Congress, for example, gave an SS-9 CEP of 0.5 to 1.0 nautical miles, but an SS-11 CEP of only 1 to 1.5 nautical miles.[62]

A similar differentiation, albeit less clearly seen amongst a welter of leaked and guessed CEPs, may be found in the next (fourth) generation of Soviet ICBMs—the SS-17, SS-18 and SS-19—although by then what both "high" and "medium" accuracy meant had changed. One source suggested to me that, in round terms, the SS-18 was a "tenth of a nautical mile system," while the SS-17 and SS-19 were "quarter of a nautical mile systems." Taken wholly literally this would probably overestimate the accuracy of the SS-18 and underestimate that of the others (see Appendix), and would certainly not be a consensus judgment among guidance system analysts. But there is, I believe, good reason to think that the fourth generation of ICBMs, like the third generation, includes both high- and medium-accuracy missiles.[63]

One possible explanation for this lies in institutional interests and competences. Perhaps the two guidance bureaus specializing in ICBM guidance have simply evolved different technical styles, one prioritizing accuracy, the other "producibility." Or perhaps one is simply better at its job than the other, but the inferior one is too well-entrenched politically to be done

---

62. Wright, *Soviet Missiles*, pp. 60 and 61.
63. See Appendix, though it will be noted that this conclusion is dependent on the judgment there that the SS-19 is a medium- rather than high-accuracy missile.

without. Institutional processes can shape military technology in this way, confounding analysis of the technology in terms of "rational" policy goals.[64] Without the detailed interview evidence that could be gathered on equivalent U.S. technical decisions, we cannot further investigate Soviet decisions directly. But it is interesting to correlate the nature of guidance design with overall missile design in third-generation ICBMs. The SS-9 was much larger physically than the other ICBMs of its generation, and it carried a warhead with a yield estimated officially in the U.S. at around 18 megatons,[65] while the yield of the SS-11 mod 1 was around one megaton and that of the SS-13 mod 1 probably less than that.

So the "high-accuracy" missile was also "high-yield," while the "medium-accuracy" missiles were "medium-yield." This suggests a deliberate design policy: to optimize the SS-9, even at considerable expense, for hard-target-kill capability, while designing the SS-11 and SS-13 more cheaply for attacks on softer targets.[66] In other words, the medium accuracy of the latter systems might be the result in part of a deliberate policy decision.

The pattern in the fourth generation is, however, not so clear. The high-accuracy missile is again the "heavy ICBM," the SS-18. But the distinction in yields is not clear-cut.[67] More recent developments are interesting in this respect. During 1987 the Soviet Union reportedly began testing a follow-on

---

64. See, for example, the famous M-16 rifle fiasco, graphically described by James Fallows, *National Defense* (New York: Random House, 1981), pp. 76–95.
65. Wright, *Soviet Missiles*, p. 60.
66. That appears to have been the judgment at the time of the U.S. intelligence community: "Savage [SS-11] is intended as a city buster while Scarp [SS-9] is directed towards neutralization of specific hardened targets such as Minuteman silos." Donald C. Winston, "SS-9 seen spurring Nixon ABM Effort," *Aviation Week and Space Technology*, March 31, 1969, p. 18.
67. The single-warhead versions of the SS-18 (mod 1 and mod 3) still had enormous yields—they may indeed simply have used the SS-9's thermonuclear device. But the single-warhead versions of the SS-17 and SS-19 are also large, if not *as* large: perhaps 2 and 3.5 megatons respectively. There is some evidence that in the first MIRVed subgeneration (SS-17 mod 1, SS-18 mod 2, and SS-19 mod 1), the SS-18 carried both more *and* heavier warheads. But in the second, current subgeneration (SS-17 mod 3, the SS-18 mod 4, and SS-19 mod 3), the evidence suggests very similar yields, possibly even the same approximately 500-kiloton warhead, with the SS-18 simply carrying more of them. As that later generation was being developed, a new factor may have been important: the haste resulting from the need to test any warhead of more than 150 kilotons, if it was to be test-fired at full yield, before the Threshold Test Ban Treaty came into effect on March 31, 1976. See Lynn R. Sykes and Dan M. Davis, "The Yields of Soviet Strategic Weapons," *Scientific American*, Vol. 256, No. 1 (January 1987), pp. 29–37, on this point; and ibid., together with Wright, *Soviet Missiles*, pp. 62–68, on the above yield estimates. So we have to be much more tentative in suggesting a differentiation of intended strategic roles for fourth generation Soviet ICBMs than for third generation. While the SS-18 was clearly intended for a counterforce role, it is harder to infer an unambiguous role for the SS-17 and, especially, SS-19.

to the SS-18 mod 4; whether Western intelligence will designate it "SS-18 mod 5," or argue it to be a wholly new missile, is not yet clear. This was said to have greater accuracy than the SS-18 mod 4.[68] On the other hand, much current effort is devoted to making a portion of the Soviet ICBM force mobile for the first time. There is little indication that either the multiple-warhead, rail-mobile SS-24 or the single-warhead, road-mobile SS-25 is more accurate than the best existing fourth generation ICBMs: it is hard to avoid a degradation in accuracy with a mobile, compared to a silo-based, missile. So there is some continuing, albeit highly tentative, evidence of differentiation of strategic roles, with some of the ICBM force being given the greater protection of mobility, at a cost in accuracy, while the best silo-based counterforce missile is improved even further in its accuracy.

THE MATHEMATICS OF GUIDANCE

The guidance "mathematics" used by the Soviets also differs from the American, both overall and in the lesser extent to which the Soviets seek to compensate mathematically for instrument errors. Pre-launch alignment of ICBM guidance systems is achieved differently, and Soviet and American systems differ also in certain significant physical respects.

The most basic question in the mathematics of guidance is how the missile is to be guided so that the warhead will end on or near target. Two opposite extremes can be envisaged. In the first, the requisite trajectory is calculated in advance, on the ground, and the guidance and control system is then required simply to return the missile to the pre-planned trajectory when it apears to deviate: "fly-the-wire" guidance, it is sometimes called. In the second, known as "explicit" guidance, the missile guidance system is given only the coordinates of the launch point and target, continuously calculates its instantaneous position and velocity, and constantly recalculates the changes in velocity required to bring the missile to the target.

The questions of mathematics are closely connected to other aspects of system design. Fly-the-wire guidance minimizes, and explicit guidance maximizes, the demands on on-board computer capacity. Guidance formulations are also constrained by the type of propulsion used. Liquid-fueled missiles are more flexible in this respect than solid, since by adjusting the flow of

---

68. Brendan M. Greeley, Jr., "Soviets Increase Deployment of Mobile Ballistic, Cruise Missiles," *Aviation Week and Space Technology*, March 30, 1987, pp. 24–25, and "Washington Roundup," *Aviation Week and Space Technology*, October 5, 1987, p. 17.

fuel the rocket engines can be throttled. Solid fuel rocket engines, on the other hand, are not throttled: so only the direction, and not the magnitude, of velocity increments is within the control of the guidance system. A common metaphor is that it is like having to drive with the gas pedal stuck to the floor: fly-the-wire is thus seen as much more difficult for solid rockets. Furthermore, weather conditions, notably temperature, affect solid rocket thrust, so a pre-planned trajectory is seen as harder with solids for this reason too.

It is therefore not surprising that the Soviets have remained much closer to the fly-the-wire end of the continuum than have the Americans. On-board digital computers were introduced to the Soviet ICBM program only with the fourth generation ICBMs (SS-16, SS-17, SS-18, SS-19) of the 1970s; [69] while the greater flexibility of the liquid-fueled motors that dominated (and still dominate) the Soviet ICBM program made a fly-the-wire system straightforward to implement. This was particularly evident in the testing of early Soviet ICBMs. The SS-6s and SS-9s would shut off their rocket motors at the same place and same time in one test after another.

Even early American systems moved some distance away from fly-the-wire guidance. Thor (which had an on-board analog computer) and Polaris (which began with an on-board digital differential analyzer rather than a full digital computer) used an ingenious scheme called Q-guidance, which permitted most of the calculations to be done on the ground while avoiding the worst of the inflexibility of fly-the-wire guidance. [70] Titan, some versions of Atlas, and Minuteman I and II used "delta guidance," involving what mathematicians call a Taylor series expansion around a nominal rocket-motor cut-off point. [71] With Minuteman III and MX, the Americans have moved much closer to explicit guidance, although the impossibility of storing on board an accurate model of the earth's gravitational field, comprehensive enough to cover all possible trajectories, means that fully explicit guidance still cannot be pursued without compromising accuracy.

Soviet guidance formulations have remained similar to delta guidance, and the flexibility of liquid propulsion makes it possible for them to use mostly the simple linear terms of the Taylor series. But the price of this in-mission

---

69. Berman and Baker, *Soviet Strategic Forces*, p. 104.
70. See R.H. Battin, "Space Guidance Evolution—A Personal Narrative," *Journal of Guidance and Control*, Vol. 5, No. 2 (March/April 1982), pp. 97–109.
71. Delta guidance is briefly described, ibid., pp. 98–99; and in more detail in G.R. Pitman, ed., *Inertial Guidance* (New York: Wiley, 1962), pp. 253–260.

simplicity is a great deal of on-ground computation, especially with multiple independently-targetable re-entry vehicles (MIRVs). A Soviet guidance system will need to be pre-programmed with as many as 50 to 100 constants for a complex mission including many re-entry vehicles. The capacity for rapid, fully flexible retargeting of the Soviet ICBM force, especially in wartime conditions, must therefore be quite limited. This is a point of some importance, because it must be expected to generate some pressure to execute a war plan before the conditions for its use disappear.[72]

CALIBRATION AND ERROR-COMPENSATION SOFTWARE

In modern American ICBMs, the on-board digital computer does not simply carry out in-flight guidance calculations. It is also used to reduce the effect of errors in the gyroscopes and accelerometers. These instruments are calibrated *in situ*, and a mathematical model is used to compensate in flight for predictable errors in their output. Thus accuracy comes to depend, not on the size of the "absolute" errors in gyroscopes and accelerometers, but on the predictability of those errors together with the sophistication of the calibration and compensation algorithms used.

Mathematical error modeling is used considerably less in Soviet than in American systems. Even in fourth generation ICBMs it compares, in level of sophistication, to that employed in Minuteman I and II (systems of the 1960s),

---

72. In another aspect of the need to pre-program a guidance system, the Soviets are in a worse situation than the Americans for geographical rather than computational reasons. An inertial guidance system, despite its apparent autonomy, has to be pre-programmed with data on the relevant portions of the earth's gravitational field. Global gravity models, in relatively easily computer-stored mathematical format, are available, but these begin to be insufficient when high accuracies (better than around 0.15 nautical miles or 300 meters) are demanded, as for the current Minuteman force, MX and the best Soviet missiles. Detailed gravity survey data are therefore needed for a region several hundred miles down-range of the launch point, and also behind it. For the U.S. this is an expensive but not intractable problem; it is also easily solved on the Soviet missile test ranges, which run east-west across the Soviet Union. But for operational trajectories from some Soviet ICBM fields, the necessary regions include parts of India, the Himalayas and relatively inaccessible regions of Northern Siberia; see the map of ICBM fields in Berman and Baker, *Soviet Strategic Forces*, pp. 16–17. A trade-off may, however, be involved. The southernmost Soviet ICBM fields, where the problems of "backwards" gravity data will be greatest, have for the last decade been the least vulnerable, since they are out of range of the section of the Minuteman III force equipped with the large Mark 12A warhead rather than the original lighter Mark 12. (It is, incidentally, indicative of the difficulties faced by Western intelligence's guidance system analysts that they have to take into account, in their estimates of Soviet ICBM accuracies, the likely quality of the gravitational data possessed by the Soviet Union for operational trajectories.)

rather than to that of Minuteman III or, certainly, MX, the accuracy of which is heavily dependent upon error modeling.

In large part, of course, this may be due to a restriction in the capacity of Soviet on-board computers. There is, apparently, little spare computation capacity in some systems. Nevertheless, it appears that the Soviets could do more in this direction, but have chosen not to.

Given that missile accuracy could be significantly increased by greater use of modeling, according to the currently dominant viewpoint in the United States, its "under-use" by the Soviets is a matter of some interest. Three possibilities, not necessarily mutually exclusive, suggest themselves: One, the relevant Soviet authorities may be satisfied with the accuracies their systems currently possess. Second, there may be a difference in technical philosophy involved—a reluctance to make operational performance too dependent on complex software and mathematical modeling. Third, it may be a result of the compartmentalization of Soviet research and development: instrument designers have continued myopically to seek to minimize absolute errors, while there has not been a strong enough overall system perspective to pursue, instead, mitigation of the consequences of these errors.

The available evidence does not enable us to offer these explanations other than tentatively. It does, however, render implausible the implied account in the official "American Intelligence Community Report on Soviet Acquisition of Western Technology," that the Soviet Union cannot write sufficiently good calibration and compensation algorithms.[73] In fact, the theoretical analysis of guidance systems is, perhaps, the area of greatest indigenous Soviet strength, as noted above.

PRE-LAUNCH ALIGNMENT

An even more striking difference between American and Soviet approaches, one much debated within the U.S. intelligence community, is pre-launch alignment of ICBM guidance systems. Prior to launch, a missile guidance system needs to "know where it is pointing" in the horizontal plane: a tiny error in alignment—say 3 arc seconds—is incompatible with hard-target-killer accuracy.

In all early missile systems, alignment was performed externally. The early American Minuteman force, for example, was serviced periodically by "op-

73. "Intelligence Community Report on Soviet Acquisition of Western Technology," *U.S. Export Weekly*, April 13, 1982, pp. 58–70, on p. 69.

tical alignment crews" who ensured the alignment of the guidance system using pre-surveyed external landmarks. Gradually, however, this function was moved "inside" the missile, by means of "gyrocompassing," analogous to the way the gyro is used to find north in a ship's gyrocompass.[74] In Minuteman III this is accomplished by a separate gyroscope, unnecessary for in-flight guidance. In the "elegant" MX guidance system, this added complexity is done away with, and the guidance system's own gyroscopes are used for gyrocompassing.

There is, however, a considerable penalty to pay: gyroscopes good enough to permit high-accuracy gyrocompassing have to be two orders of magnitude more accurate (drift rates on the order of 10^{-5} degrees per hour) than required for high accuracy in-flight guidance (about 10^{-3} degrees per hour). This, for example, is the rationale for the use of the ultra-low-drift Draper-designed Third Generation Gyroscopes on MX. It was also a major barrier, perhaps the most significant, faced by the laser gyroscope in its unsuccessful struggle for acceptance for the Small ICBM.[75]

The Soviet Union has not taken this path, and has adopted an approach that failed when experimented with in the U.S.: a gyrocompass, external to the missile but within the silo, is used to determine orientation in the horizontal plane, and the information is transferred optically to the guidance system.

The Soviets use a gyrocompass of Hungarian manufacture, known as MOM after the maker, Magyar Optikai Müvek (Hungarian Optical Works). It is commercially available, so it is known to the West. It is the best commercial gyrocompass in the world; its performance level indicates that requirements other than the normal demands of survey work have shaped it. An MOM gyrocompass was purchased in Canada and subjected to detailed analysis by American specialists. It employs a wire-suspended gyro, powered by a different kind of electric motor[76] than that used on the failed Western attempt to use the same technology.

---

74. There is a useful history in J.M. Wuerth, "The Evolution of Minuteman Guidance and Control," *Navigation: Journal of the Institute of Navigation*, Vol. 23, No. 1 (Spring 1976), pp. 64–75.
75. Thus an Air Force Scientific Advisory Board study, headed by ICBM pioneer General Bernard Schriever, concluded that: "Current [laser gyroscope] instruments do not . . . have the capability of gyrocompassing to the accuracy required to establish the initial conditions for an unaided ICBM flight." Quoted in C.A. Robinson, "Parallel Programs Advance Small ICBM," *Aviation Week and Space Technology*, March 5, 1984, pp. 14–17, on p. 17.
76. It is of the type known as an "induction motor" rather than the "hysteresis synchronous" motor more conventionally used in Western gyros.

The external gyrocompass approach offers advantages to the Soviets. It avoids the need to complicate guidance system platform design with an additional instrument for gyrocompassing, without placing on Soviet external gas bearing gyros the same drift rate demands as are placed on the MX floated Third Generation Gyroscopes. Some of the disadvantages this approach would carry in the United States may not be so pressing in the Soviet Union: it requires highly skilled operators, and, given the tedium of the task and the recruitment difficulties of the U.S. armed services, this might prove a major problem. It would add significantly to the running costs of the ICBM fields, a non-negligible feature in the strange world of strategic system economics.

Nevertheless, the external gyrocompass approach must add to the vulnerability of the Soviet ICBM force: the integrity of the system, in the immediate aftermath and vicinity of a nuclear blast, would presumably be less than the wholly internal Minuteman III and MX systems. This could form a pressure for preemptive launch, or especially for launch-on-warning, that has not been recognized in the Western open literature.

The implications of external gyrocompassing for the accuracy of Soviet ICBMs are controversial among guidance systems analysts. No one doubts that the MOM gyrocompass can, in principle, provide the requisite alignment accuracies. It is reckoned by Western intelligence to be an excellent instrument. The device bought in Canada gave evidence, for example, of extremely high quality machining; the ball-bearing raceway grinding was reckoned to be superior to that available in the West at the time. The question is, how much accuracy is lost in the process of optical transfer? My view is that those analysts who believe this is significant are probably correct. If they are, then Soviet retention of external gyrocompassing becomes of particular interest. While instrument performance limitations may block the MX path of using the guidance system's gyros to gyrocompass, a Minuteman-style solution—a single additional high-quality gyro—would seem feasible. That it has not been adopted may indicate that the accuracies achieved have been seen as "good enough," and any increase is not worth the price of a move away from a well-established solution toward greater guidance system complexity.

REDUNDANCY AND "SCRUNCHING"

A further aspect of Soviet guidance system design that has attracted comment, some of it wry,[77] is redundancy in Soviet systems—the use of more

---

77. A German guidance specialist in the U.S. recalls joking with a Soviet colleague that the

than one device to perform a task. While American ICBMs have only one on-board computer, redundancy in on-board computers is universal in Soviet ICBMs, even those of the fifth generation. While American missiles and space boosters have never employed more than one accelerometer for each of the three axes in space, it has been common in Soviet systems to employ more than one, with some kind of "voting" system to average their results.[78]

The guidance bureau that specializes in high-accuracy systems, however, seems much less inclined to use redundancy: in particular, the fourth generation hard-target-killer ICBM, the SS-18, is in Soviet terms a low-redundancy system. The other bureau, by comparison, employs greater redundancy. The correlations of a "high-accuracy, low-redundancy" approach and a "medium-accuracy, greater-redundancy" approach may well not be accidental. Given the expense and production difficulties of the PIGAs used in the high-accuracy approach—difficulties all too familiar to those responsible for Minuteman, MX and Trident D5 guidance—one can understand a reluctance not to multiply the number of them that a given system requires.

Soviet guidance system design also differs from American, at least in some systems, in the optimization of instrument orientation—the Soviets place the three accelerometers, not mutually at right angles, but "scrunched" around the dominant direction of rocket thrust. The principle is known in the West;[79] its rationale is to increase accuracy, not by adding extra accelerometers, but by having all three accelerometers measure at least a component of the acceleration in the most crucial thrust direction. Its value is not universally accepted in the West—Draper was not an enthusiast—and any advantage it possesses would be reduced to the extent that one moves away from a predictable fly-the-wire trajectory. Its adoption in the Soviet Union, however, indicates that at least some specialists there believe that it increases accuracy.[80]

GUIDANCE, BALL BEARINGS AND THE ALERT STATUS OF SOVIET ICBMS
The Soviet use of externally-pressurized gas bearing gyroscopes and accelerometers is interesting not only because it is a significant difference from

---

American way was political democracy and dictatorship within guidance systems, while the Soviet way was political dictatorship but democracy within guidance systems!
78. A simple "voting" system, for example, would initiate warhead separation when the second of three thrust-axis accelerometers indicated that the required velocity had been reached.
79. See G.A. Harter, "Error Analysis and Performance Optimization of Rocket Vehicle Guidance Systems," in Pitman, *Inertial Guidance*, pp. 326–328.
80. See Ishlinsky, *Inertial'noe Upravlenie*, for indication of detailed consideration in the Soviet Union of the effect of accelerometer orientation on accuracy.

current Western designs. It also has an important effect in reducing what might otherwise be a serious operational constraint on Soviet ICBMs: the speed with which the force can be brought to operational alert, and the length of time it can be maintained there. Fluid-floated gyros would have to be brought to the correct temperature if they have cooled down, and they are extremely sensitive to temperature fluctuations, while this is much less of a problem with the Soviet style of gyro. The latter is also believed to have a better "turn-on repeatability" (predictability of performance from one period of use to the next) than the fluid-floated gyro.

The Western solution to this has been, since the beginning of the 1960s, to maintain ICBM guidance systems in the field in continuous operation. Many Western design decisions can be related to this, most obviously those to do with the spin-axis bearings in gyroscopes and PIGAs.[81] Although ball bearings have had their proponents for this task, notably Draper himself, the Western consensus has been for a shift to "self-activating gas bearings." In these there is no physical contact between the moving parts; they are kept separate by gas pressure generated by the spin of the rotor.[82] This kind of design permits continuous running—as there is no mechanical contact—and avoids the obvious problem that when the rotor stops spinning the bearing ceases to work.[83]

Continuous operation does bring its problems, however. The most serious of these affected the Minuteman II force, when the early integrated circuits began to fail at a high rate, rendering large portions of the force temporarily inoperable and necessitating an urgent and expensive replacement program. The externally pressurized gas bearing permits the Soviet Union to avoid the potential problems of continuously running guidance systems, since it means that the force, while kept "dormant" most of the time, can be brought quickly to alert status.

In the early years of the Soviet force, spin-axis ball-bearing life appears to have been a major concern, limiting sharply the length of the time the force could be kept on alert, and potentially making it highly vulnerable—in its

---

81. Note that this is a different question from flotation versus external gas bearings, which concerns support of what is conventionally called the output axis, not the spin axis. See Figure 2.
82. Again note that we are here dealing with quite a different principle than the output axis bearings, where there is no spin to use, and where if gas is to be used, as it is in the Soviet design, the pressure must come from an external source.
83. Gyros with self-activated gas spin axis bearings can, nonetheless, be stopped and restarted, apparently without damage even if this is done fairly frequently.

above-ground, "soft" configuration of the early 1960s—to an American preemptive attack in a situation such as the Cuban missile crisis. It is not clear whether the Soviets have responded by moving from ball bearings to spin-axis gas bearings: that sort of shift would not show up in telemetry. Certainly, though, the problems of maintaining the force on alert seem to have diminished since then.

Equally certainly, however, the import of American ball-bearing grinding machines has had little to do with this, or with increased Soviet missile accuracy, despite the oft-repeated story that it has.[84] The very size of the controversial Soviet purchase suggests a quite different purpose: just one grinding machine would have supplied the inertial guidance needs of the entire Soviet Union. The Soviet Union had in any case other sources of supply, notably a long-standing history of purchases from Swiss precision machine-tool manufacturers; further, the quality of the MOM gyrocompass suggests that high-accuracy machining was also available within the Warsaw Pact. Nor has it been properly noted in the public debate on this purchase that improving ball-bearing grinding is, according to dominant American beliefs, the wrong way to try to achieve high accuracy. The proponents of gas spin-axis bearings would claim that adopting these, and discarding ball bearings altogether, brought a ten-fold improvement in the accuracy of U.S. missile gyroscopes and accelerometers.[85]

RE-ENTRY VEHICLE DESIGN

The design of re-entry vehicles is as important to missile accuracy as that of guidance systems. Unlike many of the features of guidance system design, however, this has been relatively widely noted in the West,[86] and so needs only brief mention here. In all currently deployed ICBMs, and also submarine-launched ballistic missile systems, Soviet and American, the re-entry vehicles are unguided. If re-entry is not as predicted—if, for example, uneven

---

84. See, e.g., Charles Levinson, *Vodka-Cola* (Horsham, U.K.: Biblios, 1980), p. 223. A version of the story—admittedly with significant qualifications—is even to be found in the official "Intelligence Community Report." For a discussion of the ball bearing episode, see Julian Cooper, "Western Technology and the Soviet Defense Industry," in Bruce Parrott, ed., *Trade, Technology, and Soviet-American Relations* (Bloomington: Indiana University Press, 1985), pp. 169–202.
85. So the most relevant area of potential technology transfer might not have been ball bearings but, for example, ceramics that could be used in self-activating gas bearings and technology for high accuracy machining of ceramics.
86. See, for example, R.J. Smith, "An Upheaval in U.S. Strategic Thought," *Science*, Vol. 216 (April 2, 1982), pp. 30–34.

ablation of the re-entry vehicle's shielding causes unforeseen aerodynamic forces, or if an unpredicted upper atmosphere jet stream is encountered—then errors will be introduced.

Historically, this was a second-order concern to the designers of re-entry vehicles. The original goal was simply to protect the contents of the re-entry vehicle from destruction or damage by the heat generated during re-entry. For this, a blunt re-entry body (one with a low "beta," or ballistic coefficient) is better than a streamlined one, since the heat generated is dissipated better in slow re-entry. So a move to high beta can be taken as indicative of a desire for increased accuracy, even at the cost of tougher requirements for heat protection. (Fast re-entry also brings benefits in terms of evading endo-atmospheric anti-ballistic missiles, but beyond a certain beta, accuracy rather than penetration seems the more plausible rationale, especially in the post-1972 context of the Anti-Ballistic Missile Treaty.)

It would appear that the Soviet Union attempted to move to high beta re-entry vehicles before that technology was mature. For some time they had to go back to low beta, before a successful return to high beta. This pursuit of high beta can hardly be seen as anything other than an attempt to increase accuracy.

OVERLAND TESTING AND MANEUVERING RE-ENTRY VEHICLES

Missile accuracy is not simply a product of the guidance and re-entry vehicle hardware used. A well-verified mathematical model of system errors is needed to achieve high accuracy, and also to be able reliably to extrapolate test-range CEP to an operational CEP. The quality of test-range instrumentation is thus a vital contributor to accuracy.

Here is an area where the Soviets may have profited from acquired Western technology.[87] But of at least equal significance is the Soviet possession of an ICBM test range that is wholly or partially overland (partially, in the case of longer-range firing into the Pacific rather than to the Kamchatka Peninsula). For legal and political rather than geographical reasons, overland ballistic missile testing in the U.S. is restricted to military reservations, such as the White Sands Missile Range, New Mexico.[88] When tests are performed outside

87. The "Intelligence Community Report," p. 64, asserts that the Soviets have acquired from the West "missile test range instrumentation systems and documentation and precision cine-theodolites for collecting data critical to post flight ballistic missile analysis."
88. Cruise missile testing, where the missile can be "shadowed" by an aircraft, is a little more widespread, but still controversial.

these reservations, as they occasionally are from Green River, Utah, towards White Sands, the residents along this remote flight path are apparently sent a check in advance to permit them to move into a motel for the day! But even with this extension, the available overland ranges are far too small for ICBM testing. So U.S. ICBM testing is done on ranges over the ocean, primarily from Vandenberg Air Force Base on the California coast to Kwajalein Atoll in the Marshall Islands (where the local inhabitants lack the political clout of mainland U.S. citizens).

An ocean range is harder to instrument than a land-based one, and the development of satellite-based instrumentation systems has so far only partially reduced this problem. The Soviet Union's ability to test over land is thus a considerable advantage, one it has built upon by heavy investment in test-range instrumentation. Such investment makes sense only in terms of enhancing and verifying missile accuracies: similar technology is used for space tracking, but its level of accuracy need not be so great.

This Soviet advantage will grow considerably in significance if, as is possible, further advances in missile accuracy are sought, not by incremental improvements to existing guidance systems (these seem, at least to U.S. decision-makers, already to have reached a point of rapidly diminishing returns[89]), but by introducing terminally-guided maneuvering re-entry vehicles. Although miniaturization (of inertial components and especially microelectronics) counts in such a technology, so does the capacity to test over a variety of terrains at ICBM ranges. That would pose the Soviet Union no problem, while the United States might well be restricted to simulating ICBM re-entry over military reservations. A ban on such a technology—currently perhaps unattractive because of the Western lead in it[90]—might therefore nevertheless be in the West's longer-term interests.

Submarine Navigation and Submarine-Launched Ballistic Missile Guidance

As in the United States, the development of a Soviet land-based missile force was followed by the development of a submarine-launched force. The term "submarine-launched," though, contains an ambiguity when applied to the

---

89. See Donald MacKenzie, "Missile Accuracy—An Arms Control Opportunity," *Bulletin of the Atomic Scientists,* Vol. 42, No. 6 (June–July 1986), pp. 11–16.
90. Though the Soviet Union is interested in the more tractable technology of shorter-range ballistic missile terminal guidance, there is no evidence of Soviet testing of ICBM-range accuracy-enhancing terminally-guided re-entry vehicles.

earliest Soviet missile of this type, the SS-N-4, first deployed in 1958 or 1959, because the submarine carrying it had to come to the surface to fire it. Only with the SS-N-5, first deployed in 1963, did submerged launch become possible, and only with the 1968 SS-N-6 did the Soviet Union possess a system comparable in range to America's Polaris, first deployed in 1959.[91]

All three of these missiles, the SS-N-4, -5 and -6, were inertially guided; radio guidance from a submarine is a much less attractive proposition than from a land-based site. In this, they paralleled the American submarine-launched missiles of the period, although they lagged behind these in both range and accuracy. Even the mod 3 of the SS-N-6, introduced in 1974, was no more capable a missile than the previous decade's A3 version of Polaris.[92]

Aside from the generally more demanding character of designing a missile to be launched underwater, both Americans and Soviets faced a particular problem in making submarine-launched missiles accurate—knowing the orientation, position and velocity of the submarine at time of launch. In the United States, this problem was partially solved by the development of highly accurate submarine inertial navigators (Ships Inertial Navigation Systems, or SINS), which are periodically updated using the land-based radio navigation system Loran-C, the satellite-based Transit system and sonar images of seabed features.[93]

The Soviets appear to have had great difficulty with SINS technology. One source suggests Soviet ballistic-missile submarines may not have had SINS as late as 1966 or even 1976.[94] This is implausible.[95] But even in the 1980s the Soviets seem to have lagged significantly behind the United States in SINS technology. This lag parallels a lag in the other main non-missile, non-space application of inertial technology: aircraft navigation.[96]

91. Wright, *Soviet Missiles*, especially p. 33.
92. See the estimates for range and accuracy, ibid., p. 50.
93. See Owen Wilkes and Nils Petter Gleditsch, *Loran-C and Omega: A Study of the Military Importance of Radio Navigation Aids* (Oslo: Norwegian University Press, 1987).
94. K. J. Moore, Mark Flanigan and Robert D. Helsel, "Developments in Submarine Systems, 1955–1976," in Michael MccGwire and John McDonnell, eds., *Soviet Naval Influence: Domestic and Foreign Dimensions* (New York: Praeger, 1977), pp. 157 and 170.
95. Without SINS, ballistic missile submarines would suffer severe limitations on operational flexibility. Either they would have to come to or near the surface for some minutes before firing in order to take a stellar or radio navigation fix, or they would be restricted to areas where seabed features had been mapped accurately. It seems unlikely that these limitations would not have been noted in the literature, were they true, but they have not been.
96. "Intelligence Community Report," p. 69. The Soviets also have lagged in systems to update SINS. The Soviet Union operates an update system equivalent to Loran-C in only one of the patrol areas of its ballistic missile submarines, the Sea of Okhotsk, and a Soviet satellite-based

Why should the Soviets do well in one version (missile guidance) but badly in other versions (submarine and aircraft navigation) of what in Western eyes is essentially the same technology? One possible explanation is that the Soviets have awarded these latter areas lower priority. But another explanation is compartmentalization. American SINS technology has benefited enormously from direct inputs from other areas of inertial technology. The first U.S. operational SINS was essentially a converted missile guidance system, the directly developed SINS having proved unsatisfactory. The major subsequent revolution in SINS technology—the move to gyroscopes in which the spinning rotor is supported by an electrostatic field—involved the adaptation of a system that had been designed as an aircraft navigator, with the variant directly developed as a SINS again proving a partial failure.[97] So if compartmentalization of the Soviet research, development and production system inhibits such "horizontal" transfers of technology, this may be the cause of the Soviet lag in SINS technology.

STELLAR-INERTIAL GUIDANCE

In the early 1960s the Americans began to experiment with a technology that promised greatly to reduce the accuracy problems suffered by submarine-launched missiles. In stellar-inertial guidance, the attempt is made to correct uncertainties in initial launchpoint and orientation by taking a fix, in flight, on a star or stars.

This technology did not win immediate acceptance in the United States. Some SLBM guidance engineers did not like the added complexity that a star-tracker involved. This objection was largely overcome by the development of the "unistar" system. This greatly reduces the added complexity by involving only a single sighting of a single star, it being argued that there is no loss of accuracy if the star is in an "optimal" location.[98] But other design-

system equivalent to the U.S. Transit system has been in continuous operation only since 1971. See Wilkes and Gleditsch, *Loran-C and Omega*, pp. 304–305, who reckon the accuracy of this system, known as Tsikada, less than that of Transit. The new Soviet global navigation satellite system, Glonass, analogous to the U.S. Global Positioning System, will certainly improve on Tsikada's accuracy, but is not yet operational. Note that deficiencies in Soviet SINS increase the vulnerability of Soviet missile submarines to Western anti-submarine warfare, because these submarines will need more frequently to surface an antenna (ibid., p. 307), or make frequent use of sonar to identify seabed features.
97. MacKenzie and Spinardi, "Weapons Technology."
98. See Donald MacKenzie, "Stellar-Inertial Guidance: A Study in the Sociology of Military Technology," in Everett Mendelsohn, M. Roe Smith and Peter Weingart, eds., *Sociology of the Sciences Yearbook 1988* (Dordrecht, Netherlands: Reidel, forthcoming).

ers, especially at the Draper Laboratory, remained committed to pure inertial rather than aided inertial systems. There were also those, in both the Navy and Congress, who did not want to see submarine-launched ballistic missiles rival ICBMs in accuracy—some because they feared the consequences of overt inter-service rivalry in accuracy, others because they did not wish the fleet ballistic missile system to become a counterforce rather than a Mutual Assured Destruction weapon.[99] The result was the cancellation of a stellar-inertial guidance option for Poseidon, and operational introduction of the technology only with Trident I C4 in 1979.

The Soviets introduced stellar-inertial guidance six years earlier, with the SS-N-8 which became operational in 1973.[100] The main novel characteristic of the SS-N-8 was a quantum leap in range. With nearly three times the range of its predecessor (7,800 km, or 4,200 nautical miles, as against the 2,500–3,000 km range of the SS-N-6),[101] the SS-N-8 made it possible for Soviet ballistic missile submarines to strike the U.S. from the relatively safe waters of the Barents Sea and the Sea of Okhotsk, rather than open ocean areas closer to the U.S., where they would be more vulnerable to Western anti-submarine warfare.

Stellar-inertial guidance was used by the Soviets to achieve this increase in range rather than to reduce the SS-N-8's CEP, which may be little better than that of the SS-N-6.[102] To achieve the same CEP at tripled range would, in the absence of stellar-inertial guidance, have meant a roughly three-fold increase in the performance of both the missile guidance system and the submarine's SINS. The SS-N-8's stellar-inertial system seems to have been a simple one, directed merely at correcting the dominant azimuth errors (errors of orientation on the horizontal plane), but nevertheless in terms of that result must be counted a successful technology.

The successor to the still-operational SS-N-8 was the SS-N-18. This first Soviet MIRVed submarine-launched missile entered service in 1978. It too was equipped with stellar-inertial guidance, but of a much more sophisticated

---

99. Ibid.
100. The first published reference to Soviet stellar-inertial guidance that I have found is William Beecher, "SIG: What the Arms Agreement Doesn't Cover," *Sea Power*, December 1972, pp. 8–11, although it is unclear whether the article is referring to the SS-N-8.
101. Wright, *Soviet Missiles*, pp. 50–51 and 272.
102. *Aviation Week and Space Technology*, February 25, 1974, quotes unnamed "U.S. officials" who believed that "stellar-inertial guidance . . . has done little to improve the accuracy of the missile." See also Wright, *Soviet Missiles*, p. 50.

type than that of the SS-N-8. The SS-N-18's system has the capacity for multiple star-sightings.[103]

There is a very interesting difference in approach here between the Soviets and Americans. The latter have designed both the Trident C4 and the new D5 stellar-inertial guidance around the unistar principle, taking only one fix on one star. The Soviets, on the other hand, appear to design for both sightings of two stars and multiple sightings of the same star. This means increased mechanical complexity, and if the American theory is correct, cannot bring with it enhanced accuracy; indeed a proponent of unistar would argue that the Soviet design could reduce accuracy, because the greater mechanical complexity increases the risk of instability in the line-of-sight.

Again, ignorance cannot be the cause of the Soviet choice here: the unistar principle has been available in open literature since 1971,[104] while the SS-N-18's tests did not begin until 1975,[105] and there has been no sign of a subsequent Soviet shift to the American design.

At least two possible rationales for the divergence suggest themselves. One is that the relevant Soviet design bureau does not accept the American theory, and is pursuing maximum possible accuracy by avoiding the "trap" into which the Americans have fallen. It is, for example, acknowledged by the proponents of unistar that an optimally located star will generally not be available, and use of a non-optimum star will lead to a reduction (albeit a small one, they would argue) in accuracy. Another possible explanation is distrust of complex software and sophisticated mathematical algorithms. The American system requires the maintenance, within the submarine, of a large computerized star map, since it is important to have a near-optimum star always available. It also relies on *a priori* knowledge of system error statistics. For example, a deviation in the horizontal plane between the actual and predicted images of the chosen star could be caused by error in the knowledge of initial orientation obtained from the submarine's inertial navigator, or by in-flight drift of the relevant gyro in the missile guidance system. To achieve the optimum correction, the system must "know" the likely magnitudes of errors of the two types.

103. Richard T. Ackley, "The Wartime Role of Soviet SSBNs," U.S. Naval Institute *Proceedings*, Vol. 104, No. 6 (June 1978), pp. 34–42, on p. 41, describes the guidance system of the SS-N-18 (an unfortunate but obvious misprint has this as "SS-N-8") as having the "capability for two celestial observations."
104. See Hoag, "Ballistic-Missile Guidance," pp. 91–94.
105. Wright, *Soviet Missiles*, p. 289.

The Soviet system, on the other hand, demands less in terms of star map "bookkeeping" (since any two bright enough stars sufficiently separated will suffice), and attempts a deterministic, rather than a statistical correction. By taking two sightings at different points in time, errors in initial information can be separated from in-flight gyro drift (since the effects of the former are constant, while the latter vary with time).

Despite the early success of the SS-N-8 star tracker system, the subsequent attempt at a quantum leap in sophistication led to problems, but these appear now to have been solved. Nevertheless, the Soviet Union's SLBM force does not (at least yet) appear to have evolved in the same direction as the American. The U.S. force has shifted from Poseidon (designed as a soft-target, "ABM-saturating," Mutual Assured Destruction weapon), through Trident I C4 (a complex intermediate case, but one in which stellar-inertial guidance was initially justified by the need to maintain Poseidon accuracies at longer ranges and longer periods between updates of the SINS from external sources), to Trident II D5, where hard-target kill capability, and thus high yield and extreme accuracy, have become unequivocal priorities. Despite their use of stellar-inertial guidance, the Soviets do not seem likely to deploy a "hard-target-killer" submarine-launched missile, at least for some time to come.[106] This may be due to technical difficulties. Perhaps, however, that has not been seen as the appropriate role for this portion of the Soviet strategic force.

Discussion: Accuracy, Strategy, Technology and Social Organization

What overall picture emerges of the development of Soviet missile accuracy and of its relationships to Soviet nuclear strategy, to the technological situation of the Soviet Union and to its distinctive social organization of military technology?

First and foremost, there can be no doubt that increasing missile accuracy has been a very high priority goal of the Soviet Union. The general development of inertial instruments; the quality of the MOM gyrocompass; the investment in range instrumentation; the introduction of high beta re-entry

106. See ibid., especially pp. 76–77, on developments more recent than the SS-N-18. The 1988 version of *Soviet Military Power* (pp. 48–50), hedging its bets by the use of the conditional, states that: "Improved accuracy of the Soviets' latest SLBM systems, as well as possible efforts to increase SLBM reentry vehicle size and warhead yield, would confirm Moscow's plans to develop a hard-target-kill capability for its SLBM force."

vehicles; the increased sophistication of Soviet stellar-inertial guidance—all these point in the same direction.

Second, there is little plausibility in the "technologically determinist" suggestion that this is simply some natural trajectory of technical change. Rather, it has been achieved with considerable difficulty and very likely at great expense. Unlike the situation in the West, there is no dynamic wider inertial industry for missile guidance to draw upon.[107] Nor, even more evidently, is there a burgeoning indigenous computer industry creating sweet technologies that present themselves effortlessly to guidance system designers.[108]

There is nothing in the evidence we have examined to disprove decisively the idea that this effort is the result of the "capturing" by ambitious guidance engineers of national policy. There have, indeed, been frequent suspicions that many aspects of the Western contribution to the arms race can be explained in this way.[109] But this explanation is implausible. It would require a group of technologists to have the capacity to seize a significant proportion of Soviet national resources for purposes essentially their own; and to continue to be able to do so despite the damage their activities did to East-West relations, for the threatening nature of the SS-9 and SS-18 has unquestionably fueled "hawkish" Western policies and analyses.

It seems difficult to avoid the conclusion that the search for accuracy has been possible, rather, because the Soviet military and perhaps political elite have desired the counterforce capability that accuracy brings. And there is direct evidence for this. As long ago as the early 1960s, when the effort to increase accuracy was only in its infancy, Marshal Sokolovskii's authoritative *Military Strategy* made it quite clear that the military elite saw counterforce targeting as perfectly proper.[110] Certainly there is little evidence of Soviet adherence to Mutual Assured Destruction if, by that, we mean acceptance of the idea that counterforce targeting, and particularly the possession of weapons accurate enough effectively to be so targeted, is destabilizing and

---

107. In actuality, though, the development of missile accuracy in the U.S. is not an accidental byproduct of this either. As explained above, Western missile guidance technology has come to be quite sharply differentiated from the other applications of inertial sensors.
108. Again, this should not be read as the cause of increased missile accuracy in the West either. See MacKenzie, *Technology of Power.*
109. See, for example, Zuckerman, "Science Advisers and Scientific Advisers."
110. V.D. Sokolovskii, ed., *Military Strategy: Soviet Doctrine and Concepts* (New York: Praeger, 1963), for example, p. 280: "The targets in a modern war will be the enemy's nuclear weapons, his economy, his system of government and military control, and also his army groups and his navy in the theaters of military operation."

is injurious even to the security of the side deploying them. This study does not, however, lend any support to a simplistic "first strike" interpretation of Soviet policy. In at least two crucial episodes, the Soviets have had to choose between accuracy and the security of their forces—in the choice between radio and inertial guidance, and in the current deployment of mobile ICBMs. In each case they have chosen security, at the cost of a reduction—or at any rate less than maximum growth—in the accuracy, and hence first-strike capability, of their arsenal. Similarly, the existence of both high-accuracy and medium-accuracy ICBMs suggests a more differentiated approach to nuclear targeting than any simple reliance on a first strike would imply. For the simplest interpretation of this pattern is the allocation of different types of weapons systems to different types of target: high-accuracy ICBMs for hard counterforce and countercommand targets, and medium-accuracy ICBMs for softer military, economic, and population targets.

Third, if strategic requirements are shaping the Soviet arsenal, these requirements are patently diverse. The arsenal includes the high-accuracy missiles needed for a preemptive strike against Western forces. But the presence—in greater numbers—of medium-accuracy systems would indicate that the Soviet authorities do not believe that a war would terminate after counterforce strikes alone. And the measures taken to protect Soviet forces would indicate no confidence that the Soviet Union would be able to preempt. This picture, interestingly enough, is very similar to what an outsider, deprived of detailed information on the processes that have created it, would deduce from inspection of the current U.S. arsenal: that it departs from the requirements of Mutual Assured Destruction, but not in a way wholly consistent with full priority to first-strike capability.

At the level of the assessment of Soviet intentions—even before the current wave of disarmament proposals—the analogy is perhaps reassuring. But it ought also to stand as a methodological warning. For what we learn from investigation of the processes that have led to the current U.S. arsenal is that, in some cases, *no* consistent strategic philosophy underlay its shaping.[111] So we must be cautious in concluding that the Soviets' differentiated arsenal is simply the result of "rational" shaping of different portions of that arsenal

---

111. Trident I C4 is the best example, being essentially a compromise between the proponents of Mutual Assured Destruction and those of counterforce, together, perhaps, with the weariness of Navy targeting staffs at Air Force jibes about Poseidon's "firecrackers" (40 kiloton warheads!). See MacKenzie and Spinardi, "Weapons Technology."

to have the optimum characteristics for attacks on different portions on the spectrum of Western targets. It could be, for example, that the Strategic Rocket Forces contain factions embracing different strategic philosophies, and that a differentiated arsenal is an outcome of their conflict, rather than the result of logical deduction from a single set of targeting requirements. We simply lack the evidence necessary to be sure.

Fourth, the Soviet structure of research, development and production has influenced guidance system design. From organizational sociology,[112] we can infer that a highly compartmentalized structure should be best at an "incremental" form of technical change, involving continuous refinement of essentially the same technical system. Though this form of change is not universal in Soviet military technology,[113] it certainly seems prevalent in the guidance sphere, with, most noticeably, a history of some forty years' refinement of the same basic type of inertial sensor.

This pattern, however, is almost as strongly to be found in the United States. The Draper fluid-floated instrument has a history of continuous evolution from the 1940s onward similar to the German-Soviet gas-supported instrument. The recent adoption of Draper gyroscopes and accelerometers for the Small ICBM is testimony to their hegemony, whatever the fate of the missile itself. Despite the many differences in detail reviewed above, in their overall form of technical change within missile guidance, the similarities of the Soviet and American cases strike one more forcibly than the differences.[114] In both, accuracy has been steadily increased by evolutionary refinement of the same basic technology.

Significant differences in the form of technical change are thus to be found primarily in the applications of inertial technology other than missile guidance, such as submarine and aircraft navigation. Here there appears to be a much greater Soviet disadvantage, and it could well be that compartmentalization is part of the problem. For these applications in the West have been characterized by major changes in basic technology, and by technology transfer from one application to the other.

---

112. See, for example, the classic by Tom Burns and G.M. Stalker, *The Management of Innovation* (London: Tavistock, 1962).
113. Holloway, "The Soviet Style," pp. 139, 150–153.
114. As suggested above, this may be related to the fact that U.S. and Soviet differences in social structure of research and development are less in missile guidance than elsewhere. In its structural position, the Draper Laboratory resembles a Soviet design bureau more closely than it does a capitalist firm.

Fifth, what we have found forces us to be highly skeptical about the significance of technology acquired from the West in enhancing Soviet missile accuracy, and thus about the role of even the tightest control on such acquisition as a restraint on it. Almost certainly, access in the 1940s to German technology and technologists was important, but even then, it was a powerful Soviet indigenous tradition of research that made possible assimilation of the knowledge gained. Thereafter, acquisition of Western technology in missile guidance has not been crucial. The key apparent instance of it—the famous ball bearing case—is spurious.

Much Western debate on this topic is not rooted in the realities of technology transfer, especially in an area such as inertial guidance and navigation. The U.S. "Intelligence Community Report on Soviet Acquisition of Western Technology" asserts that "The Soviets will . . . give top priority to acquiring information on the latest generation of U.S. inertial components upon which the MX ICBM and the Trident SLBM guidance systems are based."[115] This may well be so; but even were the Soviets to acquire actual MX or Trident instruments, the effect on Soviet programs would not necessarily be large. There is no reason to expect such an acquisition to disturb the well-established Soviet preference for sensor technology of a different type. Nor, in any case, is the transfer of inertial component technology simply a matter of acquiring blueprints or samples. The production processes of such technology remain difficult and "art-like," requiring highly specific know-how that is difficult to transfer without transfer of actual personnel.

The same report also asserts that "the Soviets have yet to demonstrate a capability to deploy reliable, accurate airborne inertial navigation systems for long-range navigation and weapons delivery. Thus, while long used in the West, these systems are still prime candidates for acquisition."[116] But such Western systems, especially the Delco "Carousel" used in the Boeing 747, have been widely disseminated since the early 1970s, and it is hard to believe Soviet acquisition of one to have been impossible. Were technology transfer in the inertial area the straightforward matter the report seems to imply, then the Soviet difficulty referred to would surely have vanished by now.

This is not to say that the Soviets have not encountered technical constraints in seeking to increase missile accuracy. Most obviously, they have

115. "Intelligence Community Report," p. 69.
116. Ibid.

been limited by the state of their digital computer technology and microelectronic miniaturization. Yet even an apparently fundamental constraint can be "designed around"—this is, for example, one interpretation of the way Soviet stellar-inertial design differs from American. It may also be that different technical styles, such as the apparent Soviet distrust of complex software solutions to guidance problems, will make what one set of designers would see as a great constraint seem much less onerous to another. Nor should we forget that the level of miniaturization to be found in ballistic missile on-board computers no longer represents a state-of-the-art problem. The Trident II on-board computer, for example, represents the lower end of large-scale integration (up to 1,500 devices per chip) rather than the very large scale integration currently available.

A more fundamental issue than technology transfer, finally, is the overall situation of high-accuracy inertial and stellar-inertial missile guidance. In the United States, development of this technology is widely perceived as having become asymptotic. Significant advances in accuracy using this technology, beyond the CEPs achieved with MX and Trident II, are seen by many as impossible, at least without expenditures that would overstrain even the generous finances of strategic systems.

It would be of great interest to know whether Soviet technologists feel themselves to be facing the same asymptote. If so—if only a radical shift in guidance technology could realistically be hoped to increase accuracy greatly—then an apparently constant feature of the last thirty years of the arms race may be about to disappear. That feature is the steady, incremental growth of missile accuracy on both sides, and the impossibility of finding a verifiable way of constraining it. In this situation there are opportunities for arms control[117] as well as risks, chiefly of a new qualitative arms race towards "zero CEP" using terminal guidance or revived radio-guidance (using the new U.S. Global Positioning System and Soviet Glonass satellite systems); such a race could be made more, not less, dangerous by an agreement to cut the numbers of strategic weapons. It is not too late for decision-makers, East and West, to consider which path they wish to follow.

---

117. See MacKenzie, "Missile Accuracy"; my argument, in brief, is that it would be possible to verify a ban on testing of either terminal guidance or radio-aided systems, thus potentially "freezing" missile accuracies at around current U.S. levels. See also Matthew Bunn, "The Next Nuclear Offensive," *Technology Review*, January 1988, pp. 28–36.

Appendix: *A Possible History of American and Soviet Ballistic Missile CEPs*

A missile does not "have" a CEP in the absolute sense in which we might say it has a diameter. Rather, results from test-firings on specific ranges have to be combined with laboratory tests of components and assumptions about errors in models of gravity and geodesy to form an "error budget" for the missile—a far-from-straightforward process, even for the U.S.'s own missiles. This "error budget" is then used to predict CEP for operational trajectories— indeed, strictly, multiple CEPs, since accuracy varies with distance to the target and angle of atmospheric re-entry.

Two points about this process require special emphasis. First, it is inherently statistical. Estimation of test-range CEP, for example, is based upon a finite (and in recent years actually quite small) number of test-firings. So, even for U.S. missiles there is a statistical "confidence interval" around any CEP figure; the interval is obviously much larger when it comes to U.S. knowledge of Soviet missile accuracy. During the 1960s, U.S. intelligence estimates, some of which I have quoted in the text, seem to have been explicitly of this form.

Although the practice now seems to be for different agencies to offer single point estimates of CEP, persistent differences among these estimates indicate that uncertainty remains. Although the range of uncertainty has been reduced through time by improved intelligence techniques, its fall has of course been paralleled by that of CEP itself. One intelligence analyst told me that the band of "honest disagreement"[1] had remained constant in relative size at around plus-or-minus ¼ to ½ of CEP.

The second point is that because a CEP is not a physical characteristic of a missile, but the product of a theoretical model, it can change through time even if there are no modifications to the guidance hardware. Typically CEPs fall as error processes become better understood and compensated for, and error budgets are accordingly revised. The history of Minuteman guidance and control accuracy is a case in point (see Figure Four).

Even leaving aside the practical difficulties caused by the classified nature of CEP estimates, and the diversity of figures for the same CEP that appear

---

1. By "honest disagreement" I mean the range of estimates that guidance system analysts take as possessing *some* warrant, even though they obviously have preferences within that range.

Figure 4. Minuteman Guidance Accuracy Evolution.

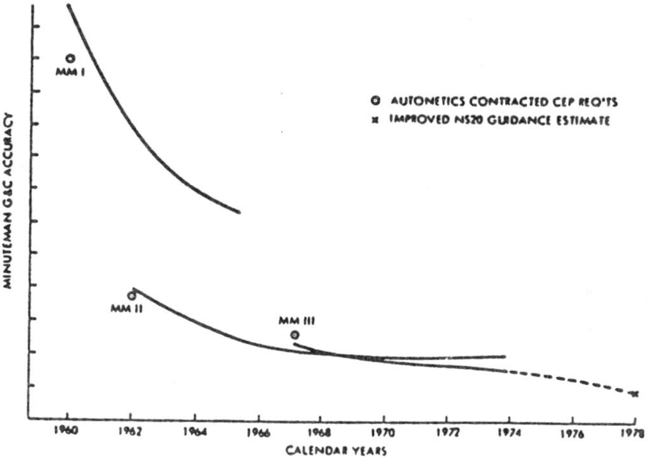

Source: J.M. Wuerth, "The Evolution of Minuteman Guidance and Control," *Navigation: Journal of the Institute of Navigation*, Vol. 23, No. 1 (Spring 1976), pp. 64–75.

in the open literature, any history of U.S. and Soviet CEPs can for these two reasons be put forward only tentatively, which is what I have done in Tables One and Two.

I have derived the U.S. figures primarily by "chaining"—starting from declassified CEPs of early missiles, and using "relative" data (such as Figure Four) to work forward to the accuracies of currently deployed missiles. The details of this are discussed elsewhere.[2] The method leads sometimes to accuracy bands, rather than single accuracy figures; in the tables I have used the medians of such bands.

For the Soviet figures I have almost never found good reason to depart from the "best estimates" of Barton Wright. The exception is the accuracy of the SS-19, which Wright seems to overestimate considerably, perhaps being too influenced by a 1981 Defense Intelligence Agency (DIA) figure for the mod 3 of 245 meters (0.13 nautical miles) that was released through a mistake

---

2. MacKenzie, *Technology of Power*, Appendix.

Table 1. Hypothetical CEPs of ICBMs

Year of First Deployment	U.S. ICBMs	CEP[a]	Soviet ICBMs	CEP[a]
1958				
1959	Atlas D	1.8		
1960				
1961	Atlas E	?	SS-6	2.0
	Atlas F	?		
1962	Minuteman 1	1.1	SS-7	1.5
	Titan 1	0.65		
1963	Titan 2	0.65		
1964			SS-8	1.0
1965				
1966	Minuteman 2	0.26	SS-9	0.5
			SS-11 mod 1	0.75
1967				
1968				
1969			SS-13 mod 1	1.0
1970	Minuteman 3	0.21		
1971				
1972				
1973			SS-11 mod 3	0.6
			SS-13 mod 2	0.81
1974			SS-11 mod 2	0.6
			SS-18 mod 1	0.23
1975			SS-17 mod 1	0.24
			SS-19 mod 1	0.25
1976				
1977			SS-18 mod 2	0.23
			SS-18 mod 3	0.19
1978			SS-17 mod 2	0.23
			SS-19 mod 2	0.23
1979	Minuteman 3[b]	0.12	SS-18 mod 4	0.14
1980				
1981			SS-17 mod 3	0.20
			SS-19 mod 3	0.21
1982				
1983				
1984				
1985				
1986	MX	0.06	SS-25	?
1987			SS-24	?
1988				
1989			"SS-18 mod 5"[c]	?

Notes:
a. Unit = nautical miles (nmi).
b. Guidance improvements.
c. Follow-on to SS-18 mod 4, tested in 1987. See text, pp. 28–29.

Table 2. Hypothetical CEPs of SLBMs

Year of First Deployment	U.S. SLBMs	CEP and Range[a]	Soviet SLBMs	CEP and Range[a]
1958			SS-N-4 (surface launched)	2.0 at 350
1959				
1960	Polaris A1	2.0 at 1,000		
1961				
1962	Polaris A2	2.0 at 1,500		
1963			SS-N-5	1.5 at 700
1964	Polaris A3	0.5 at 2,500		
1965				
1966				
1967				
1968			SS-N-6 mod 1	1.0 at 1,300
1969				
1970				
1971	Poseidon C3	0.25 at 2,500		
1972				
1973			SS-N-6 mod 2	1.0 at 1,600
			SS-N-8 mod 1	0.84 at 4,200
1974			SS-N-6 mod 3	1.0 at 1,600
1975				
1976				
1977			SS-N-8 mod 2	0.84 at 4,900
1978			SS-N-18 mods 1&3	0.76 at 3,500
1979	Trident C4	0.25 at 4,000[b]		
1980				
1981				
1982				
1983	Trident C4	0.12 at 4,000[c]	SS-N-20	0.5 at 4,500
1984				
1985				
1986				
1987			SS-N-23	? at 5,000
1988				
1989	Trident D5	0.06 at 4,000[d]		

Notes:
a. Unit = nautical miles (nmi).
b. Accuracy goal.
c. 1983 flight tests.
d. Accuracy requirement at 4,000 nmi range. As with C3 and C4, longer ranges are physically possible, but accuracy will degrade.

in declassification.[3] A March 1985 National Intelligence Estimate (NIE), how-ever, put the SS-19's CEP at 435 yards (0.215 nautical miles). Although the DIA dissented from this Central Intelligence Agency–influenced figure, it appears to have defended not its 1981 figure but only a more moderate 325 yards (0.16 nautical miles).[4] In Table One I use the 1985 NIE figure, and have made corresponding upwards adjustments to the CEPs of the earlier mods of the SS-19.

A minor annoyance in CEP discussions is the use of a multiplicity of units, which can on occasion seriously mislead.[5] Because of its dominance in early American discussions where we have access to actual estimates, now declas-sified, I have used the traditional nautical miles.

One nautical mile = 1,852 meters, = 2,025 yards = 6,076 feet = 1.151 statute miles.

---

3. Wright, *Soviet Missiles*, p. 68.
4. Bill Keller, "Imperfect Science, Important Conclusions," *New York Times*, July 28, 1985, p. 4E; and Jeffrey T. Richelson, "Old Surveillance, New Interpretations," *Bulletin of the Atomic Scientists*, Vol. 42, No. 2 (February 1986), pp. 18–23.
5. In Richelson, "Old Surveillance," CEPs which ought to be in yards are quoted as feet.

Part III:
Soviet Conventional
Forces and Strategy

Stalin's Postwar Army Reappraised

Matthew A. Evangelista

$\mathbf{A}$t the end of World War II, the Soviet army was considered a major threat to the security of Western Europe, one that could be deterred only by U.S. possession of the atomic bomb. In the words of Winston Churchill, "it is indeed a melancholy thought that nothing preserves Europe from an overwhelming military attack except the devastating resources of the United States in this awful weapon."[1]

The perception of Soviet conventional armies as overly large, offensively oriented, and invincibly strong was the driving force behind the formation of a Western military alliance and a major determinant in the evolution of U.S. nuclear strategy.[2] In the United States, the popular press supported the notion that a Soviet conventional invasion of Western Europe could be countered only by U.S. strategic air power and nuclear weapons. As one *Newsweek* article from 1948 described the situation:

In the great Washington debate on American defense requirements, the chief emphasis is put on knocking out Russia in any future war. The temporary overrunning of Europe by the Red Army is taken for granted.[3]

The balance of East–West conventional forces presented—175 Soviet divisions and 75 East European divisions to less than a score of Western divisions—did indeed make the prospects for a nonnuclear defense of Western Europe appear bleak.[4]

I would like to thank Randall Forsberg for encouragement and support during the preliminary stages of my research on this topic, conducted at her Institute for Defense and Disarmament Studies in Brookline, Mass. from 1980–1981. I am also grateful to David Holloway of the University of Edinburgh, Jane Sharp, Ben Miller, and Walter LaFeber of Cornell University for their helpful comments and suggestions.

Matthew A. Evangelista is a Graduate Student and an Andrew D. White Fellow in the Department of Government at Cornell University.

1. Winston Churchill, "The Peril in Europe," a political party broadcast, August 26, 1950, in *The Collected Works of Sir Winston Churchill* (London: Cassell, 1975), Vol. 29, p. 29.
2. For a discussion of other factors bearing on early U.S. nuclear weapons decisions, see Gregg Herken, *The Winning Weapon: The Atomic Bomb in the Cold War 1945–1950* (New York: Knopf, 1980).
3. *Newsweek*, May 10, 1948, p. 32.
4. A typical presentation is an article entitled "Russia's Edge in Men and Arms," *U.S. News and*

International Security, Winter 1982/1983 (Vol. 7, No. 3) 0162-2889/83/030110-29 $02.50/0
© 1983 by the President and Fellows of Harvard College and of the Massachusetts Institute of Technology.

This study attempts to refute the common perception of an overwhelming Soviet conventional threat to Western Europe during the early postwar period by assessing the military capabilities of Stalin's army for launching a successful invasion. The analysis focuses on the period 1947–1948, which coincides with the completion of Soviet demobilization and the beginning of discussions in the West leading to the formation of the North Atlantic Treaty Organization in 1949. It seems now that the Soviet military threat was considerably exaggerated during this period. Indeed, the notion of an overwhelmingly large Soviet army facing only token Western forces was inaccurate. Moreover, it appears that Soviet troops were not capable of executing the kind of invasion feared in the West during the late 1940s, due in part to strictly military considerations, and also to the fact that many of them were engaged in nonmilitary tasks instead of in training for an offensive.

Early Estimates of Soviet Conventional Forces

As a starting point for assessing Soviet ground forces' capabilities and comparing them to those of the West during the early postwar years, one should consider the overall size of forces. This is the aspect of Soviet military power that dominated public discussion at the time, and does to a large extent today as well. Public perceptions of Soviet preponderance of ground forces divisions corresponded in general to U.S. intelligence reports of the time. For example, in 1948 the Joint Chiefs of Staff (JCS) estimated Soviet divisions at about 175, the same number that most frequently appeared in the press.[5]

Unfortunately, U.S. intelligence reports of Soviet manpower in the early postwar period did not specify whether the 175 estimated Soviet divisions were full-strength, combat-ready divisions, or whether they were only partial-strength or cadre (paper) divisions. All 175 divisions were referred to as

---

World Report, April 2, 1948, pp. 23–25, the first paragraph of which reads: "Russia, at this stage, is the world's No. 1 military power. Russia's armies and air forces are in a position to pour across Europe and into Asia almost at will."

5. For JCS estimates, see Joint Intelligence Committee, "Soviet Intentions and Capabilities 1949, 1956/7," December 2, 1948; Joint War Plans Committee, " 'BROILER': Joint Outline War Plan for Fiscal Year 1949," December 18, 1947; "Planning Guidance for Medium-Range Emergency Plan," April 6, 1948. Nearly all of the intelligence documents cited in this essay are available either through a microfilm collection, *Records of the Joint Chiefs of Staff, Part II: 1946–1953, The Soviet Union*, ed. Paul Kesaris (Frederick, Md.: University Publications of America, 1979), or a microfiche collection, *Declassified Document Reference Service* (Arlington, Va.: Carrollton Press, U.S. Historical Documents Institute, various years).

"line divisions," with no definition of the term.[6] During the mid-1950s, the Central Intelligence Agency (CIA) in its classified reports began to describe line divisions as having about 70 percent of their average wartime strength. In 1957, a CIA estimate revealed what is now generally accepted about contemporary Soviet divisional strength—that actual manpower levels vary according to location of divisions. The report evidently went on to give more specific details, but these have been "sanitized" from the declassified version.[7]

Not until the Kennedy Administration did the public finally learn that not all Soviet divisions were full-strength and combat-ready, but even this information pertained solely to Soviet strength at that time.[8] Only recently have some observers questioned the notion that the Soviet army during the early postwar years fielded 175 full-strength divisions. Paul Nitze not long ago suggested that the breakdown at the time was on the order of one-third full strength, one-third partial strength, and one-third cadre.[9]

Despite this revelation, it is still commonly believed that the Soviet Union did not demobilize its ground forces at the end of World War II. This is not the case. The first two stages of demobilization took place during 1945, following a decree of the Supreme Soviet issued on June 23 of that year. Thirty-three classes of conscripts and 28,700 officers were demobilized. The

6. See for example JIC Report, December 2, 1948, p. 22.
7. For estimates of line division strength, see CIA National Intelligence Estimate 11-3-55, "Soviet Capabilities and Probable Soviet Courses of Action through 1960," May 17, 1955, p. 49, and NIE 11-4-57, "Main Trends in Soviet Capabilities and Policies 1957–1962," November 12, 1957, p. 29. The latter is the report with information on Soviet deployments removed. In addition, most information on Soviet nuclear weapons development has been "sanitized," along with all CIA evidence for the "bomber gap," later disproved. Regarding Soviet divisional strength, one JCS report from 1946 suggested that 68 out of an estimated 156 rifle divisions were at only 75-percent strength, but this information never made it into subsequent reports or public discussion. See JWPC 432/7, "Tentative Over-All Strategic Concept and Estimate of Initial Operations—Short Title: 'PINCHER,'" June 18, 1946, p. 22.
8. See speech of Assistant Secretary of Defense Paul Nitze to Council on World Affairs, March 2, 1963, cited in Richard J. Barnet and Marcus G. Raskin, *After 20 Years* (New York: Vintage Books, 1966), p. 4. Also see Chapter 4 in Alain C. Enthoven and K. Wayne Smith, *How Much Is Enough? Shaping the Defense Program, 1961–1969* (New York: Harper and Row, 1971), pp. 117–164.
9. See Samuel F. Wells, "Sounding the Tocsin: NSC 68 and the Soviet Threat," *International Security*, Vol. 4, No. 2 (Fall 1979), pp. 116–158, and Paul Nitze's reply, "NSC 68 and the Soviet Threat Reconsidered," *International Security*, Vol. 4, No. 4 (Spring 1980), pp. 170–176, esp. p. 173. Enthoven and Smith wrote that, in the early 1960s, a "detailed review of the 175 [Soviet] divisions indicated that at least half of them were cadre divisions (that is, essentially paper units) with perhaps 10 percent of their manpower on board and far from 100 percent of their equipment." Enthoven and Smith, *How Much Is Enough?*, p. 136.

Table 1. Soviet Manpower Strength 1948			
	Early U.S. Intelligence Predictions*	Later U.S. Intelligence Estimates**	Soviet Figures***
Total	4,500,000–4,750,000	4,000,000	n/a
Navy	700,000–950,000	1,100,000	
Air Force			2,874,000
Ground Forces	3,200,000	2,500,000	
Security Troops	600,000	400,000	n/a

n/a = not available
* Joint War Plans Committee Reports, June 18, 1946; May 15, 1947.
** Joint Intelligence Committee Report, December 2, 1948.
*** Speech by Nikita Khrushchev in *Pravda*, January 15, 1960.

third stage of demobilization was carried out from May to September 1946, and the final stages completed by the beginning of 1949.[10] The Western press at the time followed these developments while playing down their significance. Contemporary Western analysts now believe that Soviet reports of the pace of postwar demobilization are by and large accurate.[11] The main problem in public perceptions of Soviet demobilization is the fact that emphasis was always placed on the still large numbers of Soviet divisions instead of on the declining numbers of troops, an issue that will receive more attention below.

There is some evidence to suggest that the extent of Soviet demobilization took the American intelligence services by surprise. Following each stage of Soviet demobilization, U.S. intelligence reports announced downward revisions in both current estimates and predictions of Soviet strength. For example, JCS reports of June 1946 predicted that the Soviet Union would retain an armed force of 4,500,000 men, including 3,200,000 in the ground forces exclusive of security troops (see Table 1): "This figure is nearly commensurate

10. *Sovetskaia Voennaia Entsiklopediia* [Soviet Military Encyclopedia] (Moscow: Voenizdat, 1976), Vol. 2, p. 351. Also see *Sovetskie vooruzhenye sily* [The Soviet armed forces] (Moscow: Voenizdat, 1978), p. 374.
11. See Thomas W. Wolfe, *Soviet Power and Europe, 1945–1970* (Baltimore, Md.: Johns Hopkins University Press, 1970), pp. 10–11. For contemporary coverage of Soviet demobilization, see Jerry S. Addington, "The Postwar Russian Army," *Field Artillery Journal*, March–April 1949, p. 81. For an example of downplaying Soviet demobilization, see *Newsweek*, March 29, 1948, p. 28. For a current example of the same, see *Time*, November 30, 1981, p. 40, in which a figure of 210 Soviet divisions is claimed for 1949.

Table 2. Soviet Division Strength 1948

	Early U.S. Intelligence Predictions*	Later U.S. Intelligence Estimates**	Contemporary Western Estimates***
Full-Strength	208	175	60
Partial-Strength	—	—	58
Cadre	—	—	57
Total	208	175	175
Occupation divisions in Europe	66	31	30
Occupation divisions available for an invasion of Europe	55	25–31	n/a
Additional divisions immediately available ("strategic reserve")	12	[12?]	n/a
Total divisions available for a surprise invasion of Europe	67	24–43	n/a

n/a = not available
* Joint War Plans Committee Report, June 18, 1946.
** Joint Intelligence Committee Report, December 2, 1948, except the figure of 25 which is from CIA Report, November 15, 1950.
*** Paul Nitze, in *International Security*, Vol. 4, No. 4 (Spring 1980), except the figure of 30 which is from Thomas W. Wolfe, *Soviet Power and Europe*, p. 39.

with immediate occupation and security requirements, and it is doubtful if further large-scale reductions in total armed forces are contemplated during the first occupation years." The report estimated that 66 divisions out of a total 208 would be employed in Europe "on occupation duties" for several years (see Table 2).[12]

By 1948 it became clear that the Soviets had demobilized considerably more troops than U.S. intelligence reports had predicted. JCS estimates of that year (see Tables 1 and 2) began to place Soviet ground forces strength at 2,500,000 (out of a total armed forces strength of 4,000,000), and the number of Soviet divisions occupying Eastern Europe and Germany at 31 out of a total of 175. In other words, the Soviets were now deploying less than half as many divisions in Europe and altogether 700,000 fewer ground troops than the JCS had earlier deemed appropriate for security needs during the

12. JWPC Report, June 18, 1946, pp. 22–23.

first years of occupation. At this time, however, the JCS no longer described Soviet troops in terms of their occupation function, but rather as offensively oriented combat forces: "They are so disposed as to provide a highly mobile and armored spearhead for an offensive in Western Europe in the event of a war."[13]

Although most observers agreed on a figure of about 30 for Soviet divisions deployed in Eastern Europe in the late 1940s,[14] the final total for postdemobilization forces remained in dispute. Nikita Khrushchev claimed in a speech before the Supreme Soviet in January 1960 that the size of the Soviet armed forces (including, presumably, the ground forces, navy, and air forces) had decreased from 11,365,000 in 1945 to 2,874,000 in 1948.[15] This latter figure is considerably less than most Western estimates of the time, which fell around 4,000,000 for total Soviet armed forces (see Table 1).[16]

Most contemporary Western observers now agree that Khrushchev's numbers were generally accurate and that overall manpower strength of the Soviet armed forces was considerably exaggerated in the West during the early postwar years.[17] The more striking point, however, is that the U.S. Joint Chiefs of Staff at first predicted that the Soviets would need these large numbers of troops simply for occupation needs. Later, when the JCS was planning Soviet invasion scenarios, they used their overinflated estimates to predict invasions that the Soviets were incapable of executing, due to the decreased manpower levels resulting from earlier demobilization. The general conclusions resulting from these early studies—that the Soviets could easily sweep across Western Europe—were never revised to account for lower estimates of Soviet divisional and manpower strength.

THE INVASION SCENARIO AND THE CENTRAL BALANCE OF FORCES
In order to consider in more detail the prospects for a successful Soviet invasion, one must understand the type of attack envisaged and the forces that would be involved on both sides. Western military officials expected that the Soviets would launch a surprise attack primarily with standing forces

13. JIC Report, December 2, 1948, p. 22.
14. Wolfe writes that this number remained fairly constant through the early 1950s, *Soviet Power and Europe*, p. 39. European military analysts, writing in the mid-1950s, expressed the same view. See, for example, *Allgemeine Schweizerische Militärzeitschrift*, December 1956, p. 928.
15. Khrushchev's speech is printed in *Pravda*, January 15, 1960.
16. See Wolfe's discussion, *Soviet Power and Europe*, pp. 10–11, esp. footnotes 3–6, where he reviews the sources of information on Soviet armed forces strength during the period.
17. Wolfe, *Soviet Power and Europe*, pp. 38–39.

in Europe (fearing that a major mobilization would spoil the surprise) and that they would employ a *blitzkrieg* strategy.

In 1947, the Joint War Plans Committee (JWPC) of the JCS described the probable attack as "developing in three thrusts, i.e., (1) across the north German plain, (2) from Thuringa [*sic*] southwest through the Lorraine Gap and thence, down the Rhone Valley, and (3) into the Danish Peninsula."[18] Soviet troops deployed in such an attack would presumably be those stationed in Germany, Austria, Poland, and the western USSR, and perhaps some transferred from occupation duty in the Balkans. The Soviets had no troops deployed in Czechoslovakia during these years (until 1968), although such deployments would have made sense for an invasion through southern Germany into France.[19]

The JCS considered the native troops of Poland and Czechoslovakia too unreliable to participate in a Soviet invasion, and expected that Soviet troops would most likely have to contend with uprisings in those countries in the event of war. With respect to Poland, for example: "The estimated 100,000 armed members of the underground would be joined by the majority of the Polish population in the event of an armed conflict between Russia and the Western Powers."[20] Another source considered the reliability of the Czechoslovak army "highly questionable."[21] The JCS made similar assessments of the armies of Bulgaria, Romania, and Hungary. It should be noted that these views were in marked contrast to the popular perceptions of the time (and of the present), which envisaged 75 fully armed satellite divisions fighting loyally alongside the Russians.[22]

The JWPC estimated that about 67 Soviet divisions would be employed in an invasion of Western Europe. This figure was derived from the assumption that Soviet postdemobilization strength would be 208 divisions, 66 of which would be deployed on occupation duty in Europe (see Table 2). The report suggested that 55 of these divisions, plus 12 divisions "in strategic reserve"

18. Joint War Plans Committee, "Strategic Study of Western and Northern Europe," May 15, 1947, p. 36.
19. JWPC, December 18, 1947, p. 71.
20. JWPC, May 15, 1947, p. 62.
21. *Brassey's Annual: The Armed Forces Yearbook* (London: William Clowes and Sons, 1951), p. 265. The JWPC Report, May 15, 1947, p. 36, expresses the same opinion in much the same words.
22. JCS 2073/7, "Intelligence Guidance for the US Representatives on the Regional Planning Groups of the North Atlantic Treaty Organization," n.d. [1949?], p. 92. For popular descriptions of the satellite divisions, see *Newsweek*, March 29, 1948, p. 28, or May 17, 1948, p. 30.

in the western USSR, would be "available for offensive operations outside the USSR within a relatively short time."[23]

Thus, 67 divisions would be available, but only on two conditions: (1) "provided some satellite divisions could be used to relieve Soviet divisions," and (2) "provided no serious disturbances occurred in occupied countries." The remaining Soviet divisions (estimated at 120), the report suggested, would "be utilized to run the complicated training and military administration within the USSR, and to perform the necessary garrison supply and security functions."[24]

Although U.S. military planners used estimates of Soviet divisions in their war scenarios and in public presentations of the Soviet military threat, these are not the relevant measure of Soviet conventional strength. The reason is that Soviet divisions are not equivalent to Western divisions. They are much smaller in manpower and lack the extensive logistical and support services of Western divisions.

Soviet division strength during the early postwar period ranged from 9,000–12,000 men, depending on type of division. A "division slice," including supporting troops, was estimated at 13,000–15,000.[25] Western division strength ranged from 16,000–18,000, while the strength of a Western division slice averaged about 40,000.[26]

Systems analysts of the Defense Department during the Kennedy Administration claimed that the support "tail" of Western divisions contributed significantly to the effectiveness of the combat "teeth," such that a Western division slice, if nearly three times larger than its Soviet counterpart, should be that much more effective as well.[27] The argument also holds for the earlier period. Thus, a relevant comparison of Soviet and Western forces should be based on manpower strength instead of division strength.

To test the plausibility of JCS war scenarios, it makes sense to translate their divisional estimates into manpower figures and compare these to the forces deployed in the West.

23. JWPC Report, June 18, 1946, p. 23. Another JWPC Report, from May 15, 1947, suggested that 58 Soviet divisions would be employed in an invasion of Western Europe.
24. JWPC Report, June 18, 1946, p. 23.
25. Joint Intelligence Staff, "Logistics Requirements of Soviet Divisions," November 4, 1946, pp. 1–6. See also Louis B. Ely, *The Red Army Today* (Harrisburg, Pa.: Military Service Publishing Co., 1949), esp. Appendix 1, "Comparison of Soviet and Western Divisions," pp. 211–219.
26. Joint Intelligence Committee, "A Comparison of Fighting Values of Russian and Allied Forces," September 21, 1948. See also Enthoven and Smith, *How Much Is Enough?*, p. 140.
27. Enthoven and Smith, *How Much Is Enough?*, p. 140.

How many men, then, would have been available for a Soviet invasion of Western Europe? If most Soviet forces in Eastern Europe were not required for occupation functions, the maximum number of divisions available throughout occupied Europe and the Balkans would be 31. In the original scenarios, the JCS estimated that 55 out of a total 66 occupation divisions would take part in an invasion, but by 1948 had revised the estimate for total divisions down to 31 without specifying how many of these would now be used in an invasion (see Table 2). CIA estimates of the time suggested an attacking force of about 25 divisions.[28]

If 25 or 30 divisions were at full complement with supporting troops, they would represent a force of about 500,000, the figure usually given for total Soviet manpower in occupied Europe.[29] If the 12 divisions in "strategic reserve" were added to this figure, assuming full strength and support, this would mean a total of 700,000–800,000 troops. It is doubtful, however, that such a strategic reserve force, if it existed, would have been at full combat strength. Even in 1955, when according to Khrushchev the Soviet armed forces were at a postwar peak in manpower, the CIA estimated "line divisions" at only 70 percent of wartime manpower complement.[30] In any case, if the Soviets did have 700,000–800,000 troops immediately available for an invasion of Western Europe, what troops were deployed in the West to oppose them?

The Western forces available to face a Soviet attack of the type described by the JCS would be those on occupation duty in Germany and Austria, plus those in the countries being invaded: Belgium, the Netherlands, Denmark, and France.[31]

The Western occupation forces on duty in Germany and Austria in 1947–1948 consisted of those of the following countries: United Kingdom (140,000),

28. CIA National Intelligence Estimate, NIE-3, "Soviet Capabilities and Intentions," November 15, 1950, p. 5. None of these documents gave more detailed information on Soviet deployments in Europe other than an overall number of divisions, without even a breakdown by country. This is even true for the document cited above, JCS 2073/7, that was supposedly intended to assist NATO regional planning.
29. See Wolfe, *Soviet Power and Europe*, p. 39.
30. See Khrushchev's speech in *Pravda*, January 15, 1960. For the CIA estimate, see NIE 11-3-55, May 17, 1955, p. 49.
31. In one 1947 JCS Report, some doubt was expressed as to the reliability of the French forces, due to the presence of Communists in the French government and Communist strength in the trade union movement. By 1948, however, with Communists no longer represented in the government, JCS reports included French forces in the Western totals without reservation. See JIC Report, December 2, 1948, p. 30, or a later JIC Report, "Most Likely Period for Initiation of Hostilities between USSR and the Western Powers," August 22, 1950, p. 25.

United States (126,000), France (80,000), Belgium (24,000), Norway (4,400), and Denmark (4,000). To these nearly 400,000 troops should be added the home armies of France (270,000), the Netherlands (108,000), Belgium (50,000), and Denmark (22,000), for a grand total of somewhat more than 800,000.[32]

In short, the tally of East–West forces appears quite different from the one commonly accepted. Part of the difference consists simply in counting soldiers instead of divisions. It has been and still is common practice, especially in the popular press, to compare only numbers of divisions in assessing the East–West balance. For the early postwar period, such a method suggested a Soviet numerical superiority of a magnitude of ten. When one considers, however, that Soviet divisional manpower has historically numbered 50 to 60 percent of Western divisional manpower, and that Soviet divisions have far fewer support troops, the picture looks different. Considering the 700,000–800,000 Soviet troops estimated by the JCS as likely to take part in an invasion of Europe, and the 800,000 Western troops available to oppose them, an image of rough parity emerges.

One may argue, however, that as the JCS overestimated the number of Soviet divisions that would be used to occupy Europe, so they may have overestimated the number that would need to remain in the interior of the Soviet Union in the event of an invasion. It is also possible to disagree with the JCS evaluation of Eastern European armies, and to suggest that they could have been employed successfully in a Soviet invasion.

Even with the addition of such a sizable contingent of forces, however, the Soviets would not have had the three-to-one numerical superiority generally considered necessary for military commanders to feel confident of the success of an invasion. They would be far from the superiority in manpower,

---

32. These figures are taken primarily from JIC Report, December 2, 1948, supplemented by a major *New York Times* study published in that paper on May 12, 1947, pp. 1, 14. The estimates given here are the lowest of those found in any of the studies—higher figures are possible. For example, the *New York Times* estimated British forces stationed in Germany as high as 250,000. Not included in the figures presented here are about 100,000 French forces fighting in Indochina, another 100,000 French forces stationed in North Africa, 60,000 Dutch troops stationed in Indonesia, and 17,000 Belgian troops stationed in the Congo. See *New York Times*, p. 14. The indigenous armies of Norway and Italy are not counted in this comparison, since they would not immediately be involved in a Soviet invasion of Central Europe. Nor are the British and American forces stationed in Italy included, although in the event of an invasion, they would most likely be transferred quickly, as would indigenous forces from Britain and the United States. Even with these forces excluded, the image is not the commonly accepted one, as described in one popular article: "Military strength [in Western Europe] is almost negligible. Except for England, there is no military establishment worth the name in all Western Europe. France is without an Army." *U.S. News and World Report*, March 19, 1948, p. 12.

weapons, and airpower that Soviet military writers credit with allowing the Soviet Army to drive back the Germans during World War II.[33]

Soviet Military Capabilities

Although, based on their capabilities or functions, the Western forces in early postwar Europe were not particularly suited to wage another war, the Soviet forces were even less so.[34] Soviet troops were not capable of executing the type of invasion that many Western observers expected during the early postwar period. Soviet forces were severely lacking in many important components of military capability, including transportation, equipment, and troop morale. They were not the "highly mobile and armored spearhead" of many Western popular and military writings.

Perhaps the most obvious major indication of an army's ability to execute a rapid invasion is military transport. Thus, if the Soviet army were oriented toward or capable of a *blitzkrieg* invasion of Europe during the early postwar period, this should be reflected in the transport capabilities of its forces.

One analyst of military affairs describes the Soviet transport situation during the war as follows:

33. For example, in the drive from Warsaw to Berlin in the spring of 1945, Soviet sources claim an initial superiority of 5.5:1 in manpower, 7.8:1 in guns, 5.7:1 in tanks, and 17.6:1 in planes. See *Istoriia Velikoi Otechestvennoi Voiny Sovetskogo Soiuza* [History of the great patriotic war of the Soviet Union] (Moscow: Voenizdat, 1960–1963), Vol. 5, p. 57, cited in Alexander Werth, *Russia at War 1941–1945* (New York: E.P. Dutton, 1964), p. 953. German estimates are even higher—11:1 in infantry, 7:1 in tanks, and 20:1 in guns. See Albert Seaton, *The Russo–German War 1941–1945* (New York: Praeger, 1970), p. 527.
34. The notion of complete lack of coordination among the Western forces before the formation of NATO is not completely accurate. Already toward the end of 1946, the British and American military leaders in charge of the occupation of Germany were in such close collaboration that they began planning to merge their zones into "Bizonia," coordinating their political and economic policies. France added its zone in 1948. See Daniel Yergin, *Shattered Peace: The Origins of the Cold War and the National Security State* (Boston, Mass.: Houghton Mifflin, 1977), pp. 230, 333–334, 366, 370. Military coordination was proceeding as well. A National Security Council document of early 1949 instructed the American commander in Europe "to take offensive action against the USSR if the USSR attacks the forces or installations of other Western European occupying powers, even without actual attack on United States forces or installations," to "notify the Commander of the occupation forces of the United Kingdom and France of your intentions," and to "effect with them all practicable coordination measures." See NSC 39, "A Report to the National Security Council by the Secretary of Defense on Proposed Directive to the Commander in Chief, European Command, on Implementation of Emergency Plans," January 24, 1949, pp. 1–2. An NSC memorandum of the following day stressed that these coordination measures were in no way related to the Brussels Treaty or to discussions on the formation of NATO. See "Analysis of the Implications Involved in the Issuance of the Directive to CINCEUR Proposed in NSC 39," January 25, 1949, p. 3.

The quick support of tanks by infantry elements, and mobile combination between the two, was hindered by the lack of any armored carriers or other cross-country vehicles. That meant waiting until infantry brigades or divisions could be brought up in trucks—and these might be stuck far behind when the sandy roads turned into mud. . . . The mass of the army was much worse equipped. Even the volume of American supplies did not go far in making up the shortage of trucks, and most of them were needed to carry the infantry parts of the armored corps or for the rear services. The ordinary infantry divisions had to scrape along with a make-shift collection of horse transport—and little of that.[35]

In the immediate postwar years, the transport situation was no better. As late as 1950, half of the transport of the standing army was horse-drawn.[36] Horse transport was phased out by 1954–1955, but continued to be utilized in the reserves.[37] During the first five years of the postwar period, although the Soviet forces were extensively reorganized, they were still equipped with World War II materiel.[38] Such a state of affairs may have allowed the Soviets to drive back the Germans in a long war of attrition, but it indicates no serious capability for a *blitzkrieg*.

In addition to the poor state of Soviet transport equipment, the conditions of the roads and railways in the Soviet Union and Eastern Europe would certainly have hindered an invasion of Western Europe. One report of the U.S. Joint Chiefs of Staff described the state of road transportation in Eastern Europe in 1947 as follows:

Highways are in a very low state of repair. Practically all bridges of any consequence on east–west routes were destroyed during the war and are being replaced very slowly. There is little maintenance work in evidence in

35. B.H. Liddell Hart, "The Red Army: A Searching Analysis of Russian Men and Tactics," in *Ordnance*, July–August 1949, p. 27.
36. Edgar O'Ballance, *The Red Army* (London: Faber & Faber, 1964), p. 192.
37. A. Dunin, "Razvitie sukhoputnykh voisk v poslevoennyi period" [The development of the ground forces in the postwar period], in *Voenno–Istoricheskii Zhurnal* [Military–historical journal], Number 5 (May 1978), p. 33. Also, *Sovetskie vooruzhenye sily*, p. 393.
38. Wolfe, *Soviet Power and Europe*, p. 38, fn. 15. See also M. Povalii, "Development of Soviet Military Strategy," in *Voennaia Mysl'* [Military thought], Number 2 (February 1967), p. 68 (translation of the Foreign Broadcast Information Service). It should also be noted in regard to equipment that, as World War II demonstrated, Soviet weapons systems did not achieve nearly the high level of technical sophistication as their American and British counterparts. The most notable examples are in radar and radar beam technology, night fighter aircraft, and jet engine technology. See R.V. Jones, *The Wizard War: British Scientific Intelligence 1939–1945* (New York: Coward, McCann, and Georghegan, 1978).

Poland. Speeds on some of the principal roads are limited to from 10 to 15 m.p.h. because of rough surfaces and temporary bridge construction.[39]

Conditions in the Western regions of the USSR were equally bad:

At the conclusion of hostilities, the road system constituted a serious weakness in motor transport capabilities. Wartime demolition and excessively heavy use by the Germans without adequate maintenance damaged a total of 91,000 km. of main Soviet roads and destroyed 90,000 road bridges measuring 930 km. Although this damage in many places had been temporarily repaired or by-passed, a substantial volume of more permanent construction of roads and bridges is still needed to attain even the low prewar level.[40]

In the event of a Soviet invasion of Western Europe, troops in the western USSR would rely on the railway system, "the basic framework for military transportation,"[41] in order to travel to the front. During the early postwar years, they would have faced the same kind of problems as with the road transport system, due to extensive wartime destruction. From 35,000 to 65,000 km of railway track was destroyed during the war, and 80 percent of the railway bridges seriously damaged.[42]

Another major impediment to a rapid advance to the front would have been simply that Soviet and Eastern European track gauges are not the same. The Eastern European tracks are of standard European gauge (4 ft. 8 1/2 in.), whereas Soviet track is wider (5 ft.).[43] Thus, troops traveling from the western Soviet Union into Poland, for example, would have to stop at the border and transfer all of their equipment from Soviet to Polish cars before continuing the journey. As one JCS report stated, "The additional problems involved in transshipment between the Soviet Union and satellite areas resulting from gauge differences cannot be overemphasized."[44]

---

39. Joint Intelligence Staff, "Soviet Logistics Capabilities for Support of Iberian Campaign and Air Assault on Great Britain," March 5, 1947, p. 22.
40. Joint Intelligence Staff, "Capabilities and Intentions of the USSR in the Post-War Period," July 9, 1946, p. 34.
41. Raymond L. Garthoff, *Soviet Military Doctrine* (Santa Monica, Calif.: The Rand Corporation, 1953), p. 292. According to the JCS as well: "Movement of Soviet troops and military reserves from widely dispersed points in Western USSR and satellite countries depends primarily upon rail transportation." See JCS, "Estimate of the Over-all Effect of Air Bombing on the Industrial Capacity of the USSR on the Soviet Capability to Prosecute a Campaign in Western Europe," May 28, 1952, p. 309.
42. JIS Report, July 9, 1946, for the figure of 35,000 km and the bridge damage assessment, pp. 29–30. For the figure of 65,000 km, *Tyl Sovetskoi Armii* [The rear services of the Soviet army] (Moscow: Voenizdat, 1968), p. 274.
43. JCS Report, May 28, 1952, pp. 328–329.
44. JIC Report, December 2, 1948, p. 18.

Those problems would be further compounded by the fact that the Soviet reparations effort had entailed removal of a good deal of Eastern Germany's rails.[45] Such factors do not indicate the ability to execute a rapid invasion. In addition to their transport problems, the very structure and equipment of postwar Soviet divisions would not have allowed for the flexibility and mobility necessary to carry out a successful *blitzkrieg*. This is due to the fact that, in achieving a high "tooth-to-tail ratio" (combat troops to support troops), Soviet divisions sacrificed important communications, reconnaissance, and logistics capabilities that Western units maintained. For example, each American artillery battalion of the late 1940s used two light airplanes for observation purposes and a radar system for locating enemy mortar. The Soviets, on the other hand, relied on the captain of a battery serving at an observation post, "seeing all he can, but seldom seeing enough."[46]

Western divisions, by utilizing more men to support their communications systems (nearly 1,500 per division compared to about 500 for the Soviets) were better able to maneuver their forces and achieve a quick massing of fire at the appropriate time and place—capabilities required by a *blitzkrieg* strategy.[47] Soviet maneuverability was hampered by the small number of personnel, relative to Western divisions, intended to handle ammunition, and the fact that Soviet divisions provided no replacements for the killed and wounded. As one contemporary observer described the consequences:

A Red Army unit commander is likely not to have sufficient ammunition at the right place at the right time in a rapidly moving, fluid situation. . . . When [personnel] losses occur, weapons move more slowly, fire control bogs down, ammunition fails to arrive. The Russian commander seeks to overcome this through demands for superhuman exertion, but his men are not superhuman. . . . Ultimately, a division engaged for long in serious fighting must be withdrawn from the line, refilled, perhaps retrained, and restored to combat.[48]

---

45. In regard to the rail situation in eastern Germany, J.P. Nettl writes that, "by the end of 1946 some 5,500 km. of track had been dismantled, consisting of 1,800 km. of single or double track totally removed, and 3,700 km. of double or single track reduction. This is 29 per cent of the total system, and includes some 9,000 switches, or 35 per cent of the total. As far as track installations are concerned, dismantling was not confined to removed track, but extended to most of the central German main lines, Berlin–Leipzig, Magdeburg–Berlin, Berlin–Frankfurt/ Oder and Berlin–Stettin, etc. Signalling installations, safety devices, and telephone facilities were mainly affected." See Nettl, *The Eastern Zone and Soviet Policy in Germany, 1945–50* (London: Oxford University Press, 1951), p. 185.
46. Ely, *Red Army Today*, p. 215.
47. Ibid.
48. Ibid., pp. 215–216. Another contemporary observer, British Major General J.F.C. Fuller

Another important consideration in assessing the effectiveness of Soviet troops for executing an invasion is morale. Stalin recognized the significance of morale in listing it as one of his five "permanently operating factors" necessary for victory in war.

If Stalin truly judged his army on the basis of morale, he had much cause for dissatisfaction with his troops on occupation duty in Europe. CIA reports of the late 1940s noted a "high rate of disaffection and desertion prevalent among present Soviet occupation forces."[49] Low morale was the product of the extremely harsh conditions under which Soviet troops were forced to live, in countries quite hostile to Soviet occupation.[50] Desertions numbered in the tens of thousands.[51] Within the USSR too there were evidently serious

---

made the following comment: "Although Russia may have from 200 to 300 divisions, it is highly improbable, should it come to war, that the Soviets could maintain more than 20 to 25 divisions on a fighting footing in Western Germany because of the inefficiency of their communications." Quoted in *Newsweek*, February 28, 1948, p. 28.

49. CIA, "The Strategic Value to the USSR of the Conquest of Western Europe and the Near East (to Cairo) prior to 1950," ORE 58-48 (Appendices), October 27, 1948, p. 44.

50. One observer describes the Soviet soldiers' lot, even in the later postwar period of 1949–1952, as follows: "These years were the harshest for the ordinary conscripts and officers . . . especially those who were stationed abroad. . . . Rations normally consisted of a meat or fish soup and bread, with small quantities of coarse tobacco for cigarette and pipe smokers; canteens for enlisted men were poorly stocked, and items like tea or sugar were at this time almost impossible to obtain. During his first two years of service an enlisted man received about 95 kopecks a day, 25 cents at the official exchange rate in 1951, and no marriage allowance was payable unless he had five or more children; on top of this he was required to 'volunteer' part of his meager pay to state loans. . . . Enlisted men stationed in Europe were subjected to an exceptionally harsh code of discipline. They were permanently confined to barracks, except when marching out on duty in groups, and punishments for fraternizing with the local population ranged from demotion with short terms of imprisonment to twenty years of hard labor in Siberia." J.M. Mackintosh, *Juggernaut: A History of the Soviet Armed Forces* (London: Secker and Warburg, 1967), pp. 280–281.

51. "The wave of desertions which affected the Soviet forces in Germany and Austria in particular was unique in history for it concerned a victorious army, which did not include professional troops, in peacetime. A significant detail was that among the deserters there were many officers and a high percentage of Great Russians. It is obviously difficult to evaluate the number of desertions: the figure of 75,000 which is not impossible, has been suggested." Michel Garder, *A History of the Soviet Army* (London: Paul Mall Press, 1966), p. 129. Another historian mentions "the desertion of thousands of Red Army men in Rumania in the summer of 1944," and suggests that most Soviet soldiers deserted out of fear of returning to the USSR: "The main body of soldiers was submitted to a purge, which reached its height in 1947. Soviet troops who had been prisoners of war were treated very severely. Special attention was paid to military forces abroad, and large numbers of men were recalled for interrogation. One Soviet defector estimates that at least 20 percent of the Soviet administration in East Germany was arrested over a period of three years." R.W. Pethybridge, *A History of Postwar Russia* (New York: New American Library, 1966), pp. 28, 66. The numbers of desertions are impossible to determine accurately because so many deserters did not report to Western authorities, fearing the forced repatriation policies of Russia's allies. The scale of desertions may have some mitigating influence on the force estimates discussed in the first part of this paper, but probably not on more than

problems with morale and discipline.[52] This information suggests that, in terms of morale and reliability, the Soviet occupation forces were not likely to be the effective instruments of an all-out blitz against Europe, about which so many contemporary observers warned.

Functions and Activities of the Soviet Army

Soviet forces were employed for so many diverse functions during the early postwar period that training and preparation for an invasion of Western Europe clearly could not have been their primary activity.

Soviet military forces played a central occupation role in Eastern Europe and Germany, were agents of Soviet reparations policy, and carried out Stalin's campaign of political repression in Eastern Europe and among the national minorities in the Soviet Union. Finally, the Soviet army was a major source of labor, upon which Stalin relied for restoring the extensive damage left in the wake of the German armies. Soviet troops were engaged in activities ranging from de-activating German land mines, to working on collective farms, to rebuilding destroyed industrial facilities and apartment complexes. These largely civilian tasks are rarely taken into consideration when assessing Soviet military capability or the size of the Soviet armed forces.

Many Soviet troops in Germany were extensively engaged in occupation duties, to a much greater extent than their Western counterparts.[53] In addi-

---

a short-term basis. Rather, it may serve as a partial rationale for the large body of trained reserves conscripted annually in the Soviet Union during this period—a point often emphasized by those who feared a Soviet ground forces invasion. In light of the notion that the Soviet military was forced to replace as many as several thousand deserters each month during the period 1945–1948, it was quite sensible to want to replace them with fresh, young, well-indoctrinated conscripts. These would not have suffered the rigors of battle and would be less inclined to flee the continued oppression of occupation duty in hostile countries.

52. This impression is obtained by reading between the lines in the official histories of the Soviet military districts. For example, from the Kiev district history: "It was necessary to subdue demobilization moods among a certain part of the soldiers, eliminate elements of self-satisfaction and presumptuousness, convince the personnel that even in peacetime high degrees of organization, discipline, and improvement of military mastery are needed." *Istoriia krasnoznamennogo Kievskogo voennogo okruga* [History of the Red Banner Kiev Military District] (Moscow: Voenizdat, 1974), hereafter cited as *Kiev MD*, p. 303. Similar reports are found in the histories of the other military districts, for example in *Istoriia ordena Lenina Leningradskogo voennogo okruga* [History of the Order of Lenin Leningrad Military District] (Moscow: Voenizdat, 1974), hereafter cited as *Leningrad MD*, p. 454.

53. One observer, who served as Chief of the British Mission in the Soviet-occupied zone of Germany, describes their role in the following manner: "In contrast to the methods of the Western Allies, all Russian occupation control at this period rested in military hands, and no civil officials were to be seen, except for a limited number of political officers at higher head-

tion, they played a role which had no parallel in the Western zones, by carrying out the Soviet reparations policy.

The issue of reparations was an extremely important one for the Soviets, one "on which the Soviet claims were strongest and most justified," according to Adam Ulam.[54] J.P. Nettl considered reparations "the most important reason for [Soviet] presence in Germany," and described the extent to which the Soviet Military Administration and the Red Army were obliged to assist Soviet reparations teams. At times, work was handled exclusively by untrained army personnel, resulting in considerable damage to the facilities being dismantled.[55]

Soviet soldiers carried out a "reparations policy" of sorts in Eastern Europe as well, and economic exploitation of this region served as a means of rebuilding the devastated Soviet economy.[56] The main role of Soviet military

---

quarters, easily recognizable by their distinctive uniform. The occupational military government and administration was, in fact, carried out by entirely separate military headquarters and troops, the military governorships corresponding to the former provincial and lander [sic] divisions of the zone." Many of the staff officers serving occupation duty were either elderly or medically unfit due to having been wounded. The troops themselves were "of poor quality, indifferently clothed, and, as regards transport, at any rate, ill found in equipment." L.C. Manners-Smith, "The Soviet Army in Occupation: The Second Phase," in B.H. Liddell Hart, ed., *The Soviet Army* (London: Weidenfeld and Nicolson, 1956), pp. 190–191. The potential of these troops for combat duty was apparently not great.

54. Adam B. Ulam, *Expansion and Coexistence: Soviet Foreign Policy, 1917–1973* (New York: Praeger, 1974), p. 392.

55. According to Nettl, over a thousand factories were dismantled and more than 500,000 wagonloads of reparations goods were shipped from Germany to the Soviet Union by mid-1947. See *Eastern Zone and Soviet Policy*, Chapter 7, esp. pp. 200–201, 232–234, 299–305. See also Frank A. Keating, "The Soviet Army's Behaviour in Victory and Occupation: The First Phase," in Liddell Hart, *Soviet Army*, p. 185.

56. Soviet sources discuss the nonmilitary functions of Soviet troops in Eastern Europe, particularly in regard to the Rear Services or *Tyl*. Needless to say, it is their role in economic reconstruction, not exploitation, of Eastern Europe that is emphasized: "To restore the economy of European countries, liberated by our army from the German fascist occupation, which had been ravaged and plundered by Hitler's armies, the Soviet Union delivered machines, machine tools, motor vehicles, fuel and industrial raw materials. Poland received a large amount of aid, especially in the restoration of the Upper Silesian coal basin, and so did the petroleum-extracting and petroleum-processing industry of Rumania." While there may be some doubt as to the nature of the Rear Services' work in Eastern Europe, the system was certainly quite extensive. During the early postwar period, 400 *Tyl* officers were stationed in Berlin alone. They supervised "the operation of transport, telegraph stations, bath houses, laundry establishments, bakeries, water supply systems, and other public services." In addition, the *Tyl* was responsible for handling the massive shipments of grain from the Soviet Union to Czechoslovakia in 1947, following U.S. refusal of food aid, and for salvaging works of art from the Dresden and Berlin museums. See I. Bagramian, "Development of Rear Services of Soviet Armed Forces," in *Voennaia Mysl'*, Number 4 (April 1967), p. 31 (FBIS translation). On the grain shipment issue, see Yergin, *Shattered Peace*, p. 345.

force in Eastern Europe, however, seems to have been political repression. Stalin stationed his troops in those countries in which the potential for or reality of anti-Soviet activity was most evident, and did not do so in countries, such as Czechoslovakia and Finland, which he considered more reliable.[57]

Some Soviet sources acknowledge the explicitly political role of Soviet troops stationed in Europe. One such source describes in typical Soviet formulation the function of the Southern Group of forces in suppressing anti-Soviet activity in Bulgaria and Romania. Soviet troops were "entrusted with one of the most important political tasks—protecting the workers of Bulgaria and Romania from internal counter-revolution and external intervention, rendering them fraternal help in the construction of socialism." Their role in economic reconstruction, "carried out together with the population," is also stressed.[58]

Troops stationed in the western military districts of the Soviet Union during the early postwar years functioned much like Soviet occupation forces in Europe—to control hostile, anti-Soviet populations. Most estimates have set the number of Soviet troops deployed in the western USSR at 50–60 divisions, but there is no evidence that these were full-strength, combat-ready divisions.[59] The military districts in which they were most likely stationed correspond to the contemporary Baltic, Belorussian, Carpathian, Kiev, and North Caucasus districts. These five western districts represent areas populated by non-Russian nationalities: Lithuanians, Latvians, and Estonians in the Baltic district; Belorussians and Poles in the Belorussian district; Poles and Ukrainians in the Carpathian and Kiev districts; and Ukrainians, Moldavians, and others in the North Caucasus district.

Many of these national groups had strong traditions of anti-Russian sentiment and harbored irredentist claims to territories annexed by the Soviets before and during World War II.[60] Some groups had formed anti-Soviet

57. For a discussion, see Matthew A. Evangelista, "Soviet Military Capabilities and Objectives in the Early Postwar Period, 1945–1953," Occasional Paper Number 2 of the Institute for Defense and Disarmament Studies, Brookline, Mass., pp. 18–20.
58. V. Tolubko, *Nedelin* (Moscow: Molodaia Gvardiia, 1979), p. 145. This is a biography of Marshal Nedelin, the Soviet rocket specialist who served for a time as Commander of Artillery for the Southern Group of Soviet forces.
59. Wolfe, *Soviet Power and Europe*, p. 39.
60. The Baltic states had been independent from 1918 until the Soviets forcibly annexed the three countries in June and July of 1940, on the basis of the Molotov–von Ribbentrop agreements. From the late eighteenth century, Belorussia had been part of the Russian empire, and it became one of the first Soviet republics. However, some Belorussians had inhabited eastern Poland from the fourteenth century, when all of Belorussia was incorporated into the Polish–Lithuanian

partisan bands during the war, and others had sided with the Germans.[61] The Soviets could only expect a similar situation in the event of another war with the West. Indeed, CIA reports from 1948 predicted mass desertions from the Soviet army and "anti-Soviet guerrilla action by Ukrainians and other Soviet peoples" in the event of war.[62]

Resistance to Soviet rule continued throughout the early postwar period. Soviet and Western sources alike mention the existence of armed, anti-Soviet groups active in the western regions of the USSR from the mid-1940s well into the 1950s. Such groups were particularly strong in the Baltics[63] and in the western regions of Belorussia and the Ukraine.[64] The Soviets relied on border guards, regular army units, and the political troops of the Ministry of Internal Affairs (MVD) to put down anti-Soviet activity.

---

kingdom. The descendants of these Belorussians came under Soviet rule for the first time in 1939, when Stalin and Hitler divided Poland between themselves, and then again after the defeat of Germany.

The same is true for the Carpathian district. L'vov itself was ethnically Polish, whereas the surrounding countryside was overwhelmingly Ukrainian. In winning this region, Stalin won a potentially troublesome irredenta as well as several thousand more Ukrainian subjects.

The bulk of the Ukrainians were located in the Kiev military district. To the Russians these people presented a serious security problem. From the time of the Cossacks, Ukrainians had opposed Russian rule. During both world wars, many Ukrainians favored the Germans and formed anti-Soviet partisan groups to fight the Russian armies. See N. Galay's chapter, "The Partisan Forces," in Liddell Hart, *Soviet Army,* for a historical review of the major uprisings in western Russia from the fifteenth century through the Second World War, esp. pp. 165–168.

61. During World War II, many of these groups were active deep in the rear of the Soviet armies, in territory never occupied by the Germans. In addition to the unknown numbers of these partisans, over one million Soviet citizens served in auxiliary troops directly under German command. See Galay, "Partisan Forces," pp. 167–168.

62. CIA Report, October 27, 1948, p. 39. See also the discussion of anti-Soviet guerrilla activity during World War II, p. 41.

63. Pethybridge writes: "The critical situation in western Russia after 1945 was due partly to the havoc left by the German occupation and partly to discontent among the national minorities. Disciplinary measures that were applied throughout the USSR had to be applied with particular severity in this region. After the end of hostilities the state of war was declared to be still applicable in the Baltic republics and in those western provinces of the Ukraine and the Belorussian Soviet Socialist Republics that had been under Polish sovereignty. Military courts of the Ministry of the Interior (the secret police) continued to apply criminal law in these areas. . . . Wartime dislocation and apathy or outright hatred on the part of the local population hampered the work of the party and government." *History of Postwar Russia,* p. 67. This somewhat understates anti-Soviet sentiment. Another source, citing anti-Soviet partisans, claims that in Lithuania from 1945–1952 over 100,000 Soviet MVD, NKVD, and regular army troops were killed by guerrillas. See Albertas Gerutis, ed., *Lithuania 700 Years* (New York: Manyland Books, 1969), p. 392.

64. In regard to the latter republic, Pethybridge writes that, "Armed resistance to the Soviet regime went on long after the Red Army had occupied the western Ukraine, and there were official references to fighting by underground groups as late as 1954 in the Ukraine, and well into 1956 in Lithuania." *History of Postwar Russia,* p. 67. Soviet sources claim that two predom-

A more extreme case of Stalin's political repression of non-Russian nationalities is found in the forced relocation program, by which large segments of the populations of Latvia, Lithuania, and Estonia were removed from their homes and resettled in Siberia. The program was largely carried out by military forces, particularly those of the MVD, and met with considerable resistance from the local populations. Hundreds of thousands of people were deported in a series of campaigns which lasted through the early fifties.[65]

While many of the deportees were resettled in distant Siberian towns, as many as 25 percent were sent to prison labor camps. The army participated extensively in the system of prison camps, guarding German prisoners of war, deportees, and Soviet citizens as well. In conscript labor camps, soldiers were posted in every factory. Repatriation camps for Russians returning from Germany were also heavily guarded. Thus, from the time of arrest and deportation through the internment of hundreds of thousands of prisoners, Soviet army soldiers played a central role.[66]

In order to consider the potential of Soviet troops for participating in an invasion of Europe, one must first make the improbable assumption that they would no longer be necessary to fulfill their roles of political repression and control. In fact there were many other such activities, unrelated to

inant Ukrainian guerrilla organizations operated until 1954: the Organization of Ukrainian Nationalists (*Organizatsiia ukrainskikh natsionalistov*, or OUN), which had been in existence since 1929; and the Ukrainian Insurrectionary Army (*Ukrainskaia povstancheskaia armiia*, or UPA), formed during the war. One Soviet source claims that "leaders of the OUN and UPA tried to set up ambushes of border guards, mine roads, blow up bridges, set Soviet office buildings afire, and commit sabotage at factories. . . . Fearing the inevitable punishment for their numerous crimes, they rarely laid down their arms voluntarily. For this reason, the struggle with them was complicated, demanded great vigilance, firmness, and courage, and took a long time." See *Pogranichnye voiska SSSR, 1945–1950: Sbornik dokumentov i materialov* [Border troops of the USSR, 1945–1950: collection of documents and materials] (Moscow: Nauka, 1975), hereafter cited as *Border Troops*, pp. 7, 19, 31, 33, 37.

65. David J. Dallin and Boris I. Nicolaevsky, *Forced Labor in Soviet Russia* (New Haven, Conn.: Yale University Press, 1947), pp. 270–272, 288. Also, Aleksandr I. Solzhenitsyn, *The Gulag Archipelago*, trans. Thomas P. Whitney (New York: Harper and Row, 1974), esp. pp. 90–92, and *Border Troops*, pp. 6–7. In Lithuania, mass deportations continued through 1951 and included about 350,000 persons—12 percent of the population. See Gerutis, *Lithuania*, p. 387. The peak year for Latvia was 1949, when wholesale deportations of urban populations as well as kulaks were carried out. See J. Rutkis, ed., *Latvia: Country and People* (Stockholm: Latvian National Foundation, 1967), pp. 260–261. JCS Reports include references to "removal of ethnic minorities" from Poland and Czechoslovakia as well. See JIS Report, July 9, 1946, p. 158. Nettl writes of mass transfers of German laborers in 1947–1948, conducted by the Soviet military administration, involving as many as 100,000 Germans during a single two-month period. See *Eastern Zone and Soviet Policy*, p. 141.

66. See Chapter 14 in Dallin and Nicolaevsky, *Forced Labor in Soviet Russia*, esp. pp. 269–274.

offensive military preparations, in which Soviet forces were engaged in the early postwar period.

One branch of the Soviet armed forces, the *Tyl* or Rear Services, has traditionally served nonmilitary purposes in peacetime, carrying out much work in the civilian sector. While no estimates for the size of the Rear Services are available for the early postwar period, contemporary estimates range from 100,000 to 400,000 troops.[67] According to Soviet sources, many of the tasks that technically fell within the purview of the *Tyl* during the early postwar years were handled by regular army troops, due to the vast quantities of work required. The most notable examples are those concerning restoration of war damage. One major task, for which the Soviet army was responsible, was the de-activation and removal of mines dispersed throughout the western regions of the USSR by the retreating German armies. All of the official Soviet histories of the western military districts discuss in some detail the extent of this work, which involved tens of thousands of soldiers and lasted until the mid-1950s. The engineer troops of the *Tyl* were nominally responsible for this work, but the volume was far too great for them to handle alone.[68]

As with the engineer troops, the construction and billeting troops of the *Tyl* were forced to rely on regular army units for assistance. Even for the rebuilding and maintenance of military facilities, their participation was required. One Soviet source reports that "the soldiers themselves often repaired barracks, built dining halls, set up military posts, camps, and sports fields."[69]

---

67. See Chapter 7 in Harriet Fast Scott and William F. Scott, *The Armed Forces of the USSR* (Boulder, Colo.: Westview Press, 1979), pp. 227–253.

68. One source reports that from 1944–1953 soldiers in Estonia and in the Leningrad, Pskov, and Novgorod regions (*oblasti*) de-mined 27,000 square kilometers of land, removing 30 million explosive devices. The Leningrad district command was obliged to call in regular army units to assist the engineer troops of the *Tyl*. During the first several years, 50,000 soldiers were assigned to de-mining work. See *Leningrad MD*, pp. 455–456. In Belorussia, military units cleared 36,000 square km of territory and 4,826 km of road. See *Krasnoznamennyi Belorusskii voennyi okrug* [The Red Banner Belorussian Military District] (Minsk, 1973), p. 480. In the Kiev district, over 300,000 square km were cleared of nearly 14 million "mines, aviation bombs, shells, and fougasses." See *Kiev MD*, p. 306. Other districts report comparable figures. See *Ordena Lenina Moskovskii voennyi okrug* [The Order of Lenin Moscow Military District] (Moscow: Voenizdat, 1971), hereafter cited as *Moscow MD*, pp. 318–319. See also *Krasnoznamennyi severo-kavkazskii: Ocherk istorii krasnoznamennogo severo-kavkazskogo voennogo okruga* [The Red Banner Northern Caucasus: An outline of the history of the Red Banner Northern Caucasus Military District] (Rostov: Rostovskoe knizhnoe izdatel'stvo, 1971), hereafter cited as *No. Caucasus MD*, p. 305.

69. Another source reveals that, although housing construction for the troops of the Baku air defense district was put under the command of a Lieutenant Colonel of the Military Construction Administration in 1947, military personnel were obliged to do much of the work themselves.

Many Soviet soldiers were engaged in activities completely unrelated to the military, let alone to preparation for offensive combat. Such is the case with the practice of *shefstvo* (literally "patronage"), which refers to the use of soldiers in civilian industry and agriculture. Although *shefstvo* had been common since the time of the revolution, some Western analysts felt that it was rendered unnecessary by Stalin's use of prison labor in the early 1950s, and was not revived until the mid-1950s when much of the prison camp system was dismantled under Khrushchev. In fact, Soviet military histories of the postwar period abound in references to the role of *shefstvo* during the years immediately following World War II. The accounts refer to the use of soldiers in construction work, as skilled labor in factories, as agricultural workers, and in disaster relief operations.[70]

The rebuilding of cities and towns destroyed by the Germans was a major task of the early postwar period: "Builders alone could not carry out the huge volume of this work. It demanded a broad call for troops as well."[71] By Soviet count, over 70,000 villages and 1,710 towns were destroyed during the war. In the Moscow district alone, troops were used in rebuilding, among others, the towns of Smolensk, Voronezh, Kalinin, Kursk, and Briansk, in addition to Moscow itself.[72]

This included construction of apartment buildings, cooking and dining facilities, and bath houses, and was not completed until 1954; the experience was considered valuable for training soldiers in civilian skills. See *Bakinskii okrug protivovozdushnoi oborony: Istoricheskii ocherk 1920–1974 gg.* [Baku Anti-air Defense District: An historical outline, 1920–1974] (Baku: Azerbaidzhanskoe gosudarstvennoe izdatel'stvo, 1974), hereafter cited as *Baku PVO*, pp. 205–206.

70. Agricultural *shefstvo* took many forms. Soldiers worked in the fields during sowing and harvesting times, local bases lent military equipment, especially trucks, to nearby collective and state farms, and military mechanics worked on farm machinery and even in tractor factories. See *No. Caucasus MD*, pp. 305–308, and *Leningrad MD*, pp. 457–459. The results suggest the extent of the work: during a 40-day period in 1948, soldiers stationed in the Ukraine threshed 8,000 tons of grain and transported another 155,000 tons. Soviet army troops were instrumental in harvesting and transporting grain during the 1947 and 1948 harvests in the Stalingrad *oblast'*. Border guards made such a substantial contribution that in several regions collective farms were named *Pogranichnik* ("Border Guard") in their honor. See *Kiev MD*, p. 307; *No. Caucasus MD*, p. 307; *Border Troops*, p. 43. For an example of Western underestimation of *shefstvo* in the Stalin period, see Roman Kolkowicz, *The Use of Soviet Military Labor in the Civilian Economy: A Study of Military "Shefstvo"* (Santa Monica, Calif.: The Rand Corporation, 1962).

71. *Leningrad MD*, p. 454.

72. *Moscow MD*, p. 319. See also *Inzhinernye voiska v boiakh za Sovetskuiu rodinu* [Engineer troops in the battles for the Soviet homeland] (Moscow: Voenizdat, 1970); and A.I. Romashko, *Voennye stroiteli na stroikakh Moskvy* [Military builders in the building of Moscow] (Moscow: Voenizdat, 1972). In the Kiev district, "troops cleared streets, restored dwelling places and cultural-community establishments, laid streetcar lines, secured the supply of electricity and water," participated in restoration of the 25 largest coal mines of the Donbass region, and installed industrial machinery in factories. "It is possible to name tens or hundreds more plants, factories, mines

The purpose here is not to claim that these troops would be unable to fight in the event of war. Rather, it is to suggest that preparation for an offensive war against Western Europe was not the major activity for the bulk of Soviet troops. Rebuilding of the war-torn economy and control of political dissent within the USSR and bordering countries took precedence.

One branch of the Soviet military that clearly was preparing for war in the early postwar period was the PVO Strany, or Air Defense, forces. Their task was to defend the Soviet Union from atomic air attack. Discussion of the PVO troops is relevant to this analysis in that their numbers have traditionally been included by Western observers in assessing ground force strength and potential for a Soviet invasion.

Estimates of the size of the PVO forces during the postwar period have always fallen within the 500,000–600,000 range.[73] According to Western sources, half this amount consists of ground elements (and the other half of fighter–interceptor forces). They are usually counted with army manpower estimates despite the fact that the PVO has been a separate branch of the Soviet armed forces since 1948, with a status equal to that of the ground forces, air force, or navy.[74] Including the PVO ground elements in an assessment of the offensive capabilities of the Soviet ground forces is extremely misleading, since their major function consisted of operating anti-aircraft artillery in defense of important industrial and economic centers.[75] In the

and pits, the restoration of which is connected with the self-sacrificing, truly heroic work of the district troops. Soldiers, non-commissioned officers [*serzhanty*], and officers denied themselves rest, and worked as much as circumstances demanded." *Kiev MD*, p. 307.

73. See, for example, Garthoff, *Soviet Military Doctrine*, p. 357; Asher Lee, "Strategic Air Defense," in Asher Lee, ed., *The Soviet Air and Rocket Forces* (New York: Praeger, 1959), p. 125; *The Military Balance* (London: International Institute for Strategic Studies, various years); David R. Jones, "National Air Defense Forces," in David R. Jones, ed., *Soviet Armed Forces Review Annual* (Gulf Breeze, Fla.: Academic International Press, various years).

74. In fact, the PVO was long considered an elite branch, and its personnel were given special benefits and treatment. See Garthoff, *Soviet Military Doctrine*, p. 357, and Matthew A. Evangelista, "The Evolution of Soviet Tactical Air Forces," in David R. Jones, ed., *Soviet Armed Forces Review Annual* (Gulf Breeze, Fla.: Academic International Press, forthcoming).

75. During the Second World War, 60 to 90 percent of medium calibre and one-third to two-thirds of small calibre anti-aircraft artillery fulfilled this function exclusively (the rest being used primarily in defense of railroad junctions and troop formations). More than 40 percent of the AA batteries were assigned to the defense of three major centers: Moscow, Leningrad, and Baku. G. Zimin, "PVO Strany troops in the Great Patriotic War" (FBIS translation), in *Voennaia Mysl'*, Number 5 (May 1965), pp. 102, 105. It is possible to use anti-aircraft artillery in roles other than air defense of strategic objectives. I am grateful to Ben Miller for pointing out that the Germans used anti-aircraft artillery for direct-fire roles in support of their ground forces during World War II. During the first months after the invasion of the Soviet Union in June 1941, Soviet front commanders also used PVO forces for nonstrategic roles, such as air defense

event of a Soviet invasion of Western Europe, it is hardly likely that these forces would have been diverted from their roles of strategic air defense, especially considering the Western preponderance of air power.[76]

Evaluations of the Soviet Conventional Threat

This essay has attempted to demonstrate that Stalin's postwar army was not capable of a successful *blitzkrieg* invasion of Western Europe during the period preceding the formation of NATO. The argument has been based on a numerical comparison of available Soviet and Western forces and a consideration of the type of invasion expected by U.S. military planners, as well as on an analysis of Soviet military capabilities and nonmilitary functions.

Although the conclusions of this paper are in contrast to the prevailing wisdom concerning the postwar Soviet army, they are consistent with many early postwar intelligence reports regarding Soviet military capabilities and intentions. One such report, from November 1945, enumerated the Soviet Union's "important weaknesses which seriously limit her military capabilities," and estimated "the time required to remedy them to a degree sufficient to make the USSR willing to risk a major armed conflict":

a. War losses in manpower and industry and the set-back in a far from fully developed industry. (15 years)
b. Lack of technicians. (5–10 years)
c. Lack of a Strategic Air Force. (5–10 years)
d. Lack of a modern navy. (15–20 years for a war involving major naval operations)
e. Poor condition of railway and military transportation systems and equipment. (10 years)

---

of their troops and sometimes anti-tank defense, leaving defense of strategic centers as a secondary concern. Stalin responded in November 1941 by putting all ground elements of the PVO under the command of a central PVO administration in order to preserve their role in strategic defense. Even during the last year of the war, when some ground and air elements of the PVO were used in offensive operations, the main task of the PVO remained air defense of the large centers. See Zimin, "PVO Strany troops," p. 110, and *Voiska PVO strany v Velikoi Otechestvennoi voine, 1941–1945* [Troops of the PVO Strany in the Great Patriotic War] (Moscow: Voenizdat, 1981), p. 264.

76. For U.S. plans for strategic air retaliation against the USSR, see Part II of Herken, *Winning Weapon*. Some observers felt that Western air power provided considerable defense capability against a possible Soviet invasion as well. This was the opinion of several Chiefs of the British Air Staff, one of whom declared, "I cannot believe that 500,000, 1,000,000, or even 2,000,000 men could advance without being stopped by the power of the Royal Air Force, backed by the power of the American Air Force." Quoted by Liddell Hart, "The Red Army," p. 28.

f. Vulnerability of Soviet oil, rail and vital industrial centers to long-range bombers.

g. Lack of atomic bomb. (5–10 years, possibly less)

h. Resistance in occupied countries. (5 years or less)

i. Quantitative military weakness in the Far East—especially naval. (15–20 years)

The report concluded that the Soviets would be unlikely to risk a major war for at least fifteen years.[77]

Similar assessments of the likelihood of a Soviet-initiated war were made by the CIA well into 1949 and were supported by reports from foreign observers.[78] Subsequently, estimates by the CIA and other U.S. intelligence agencies exaggerated Soviet capabilities and intentions to such a great extent that it is surprising that anyone took them seriously.[79]

---

77. Joint Intelligence Staff, "Soviet Capabilities," November 9, 1945, Appendix C.

78. In an untitled report from August 1946, the CIA mentioned a personal communication between Marshal Zhukov and Viacheslav Molotov, somehow obtained, in which the former insisted that his armies were unprepared to fight a war. A CIA report of 1948 suggested several reasons why the Soviets would not initiate a war, including, "The resulting global conflict would place the entire Soviet system at stake in a war to the finish at a time when the USSR is inferior to the West in potential military power." The report also mentioned the risk of engendering popular discontent at home and creating internal security problems. See ORE 58-48, October 27, 1948, p. 39. In a report from 1949, the CIA stated, "There is no conclusive evidence of Soviet preparation for direct military aggression during 1949," and "A deliberate Soviet resort to direct military action against the West during 1949 is improbable." See ORE 46-49, "The Possibility of Direct Soviet Military Action during 1949," May 3, 1949, p. 1. Following a trip to the USSR in 1947, British Field Marshal Montgomery made these remarks in a letter to General Eisenhower: "The Soviet Union is very, very tired. Devastation in Russia is appalling and the country is in no fit state to go to war. . . . It will be 15 to 20 years before Russia will be able to remedy her various defects and be in a position to fight a major world war with a good chance of success." Letter dated February 1, 1947, p. 3. According to Milovan Djilas, Stalin also expected that the Soviet Union would not be involved in another war for 15 to 20 years. See his *Conversations with Stalin*, trans. Michael B. Petrovich (New York: Harcourt, Brace & World, 1962), pp. 114–115.

79. While the CIA claimed in 1948 that the West was militarily superior to the USSR, and in 1948 and 1949 that the Soviets would not deliberately provoke a war and were "likely to exercise some care to avoid an unintended outbreak of hostilities with the United States" (CIA Report, May 3, 1949, p. 1), in 1950 the agency made the following assessment: "In the belief that their object cannot be fully attained without a general war with the Western Powers, the Soviet rulers may deliberately provoke such a war at the time when in their opinions the relative strength of the USSR is at its maximum. It is estimated that such a period will exist from now through 1954. . . . From the point of view of military forces and economic potential, the Soviet Union is in a position to conduct a general war now . . . if the Soviet rulers should consider it desirable or expedient to do so." A *partial* list of the operations the Soviets would undertake "simultaneously" followed later in the report: "(1) A campaign against Western Europe including Italy, (2) An aerial bombardment against the British Isles, (3) Campaigns against the Near and Middle East including Greece and Turkey, (4) Campaigns in the Far East, (5) Attacks against Canada and the United States, including Alaska and the Aleutians, (6) A sea and air offensive against Anglo–American sea communications. . . ." CIA National Intelligence Estimate, NIE-3, "Soviet Capabilities and Intentions," November 15, 1950, pp. 1–2, 66.

One may well ask how Soviet conventional forces could have been so exaggerated during the early postwar period. Why were divisional figures used instead of manpower figures, when the latter would have made for more relevant comparisons?[80] Why were the striking weaknesses in Soviet military capabilities—in transport, communications, and logistics—never discussed, and the extensive role of the military in postwar reconstruction and in political control of Eastern Europe ignored? It is difficult to avoid the impression that many in the West intentionally exaggerated the Soviet conventional threat to Europe, for a number of reasons.

In order to gain U.S. congressional and popular support for the NATO alliance, the State Department and the military emphasized NATO's role as a counter to a potential Soviet military offensive, although according to U.S. intelligence documents, such an event was unlikely in the near future.[81] In addition, Soviet-supported political actions, such as the communist coup in Czechoslovakia, were described as if they were no different from outright military aggression and indicative of Soviet military intentions.[82] It seems

---

80. Part of the reason the CIA relied primarily on divisional estimates instead of overall manpower estimates is that the former were more dependable. Although it is never easy to obtain information concerning CIA research methodologies, recently declassified reports offer some hints regarding the agency's estimates of Soviet manpower. It seems that the number of 175 Soviet divisions was derived from Soviet tables of organization and equipment (TO&E) and was considered reliable. Estimates of number of men per division were evidently less so, considering that they were constantly revised downward from the mid-1950s until the present interpretation of three classes of divisional readiness was agreed upon. Unfortunately, there was no attempt made by intelligence analysts to reveal the tentative nature of some of these estimates, and all were consequently accepted as equally reliable. See CIA Special Intelligence Estimate Number 11-6-60, "Strength of the Armed Forces of the USSR," May 3, 1960, pp. 1–2.

81. See Ambassador George F. Kennan's discussion in a telegram sent from Moscow in 1952 and reprinted in his *Memoirs, 1950–1963* (Boston, Mass.: Little, Brown, 1972), pp. 327–351. Kennan gives this reason for the formation of NATO: "Large numbers of people, both in Western Europe and in the United States, were incapable of understanding the Russian technique of penetration and 'partial war' or of thinking in terms of this technique. They were capable of thinking about international developments only in the old-fashioned terms of full-fledged war or full-fledged peace. It was inconceivable to them that there could be real and serious threats to the independence of their countries that did not come to them in the form of foreign armies marching across frontiers; and it was natural that in undertaking to combat what they conceived to be a foreign threat they should have turned to the old-fashioned and familiar expedient of military alliance." See pp. 333–334.

82. Not only Americans were prone to confuse, deliberately or not, Soviet political threats for military ones. Winston Churchill best expressed this confusion over the Communist coup in Czechoslovakia in a speech at the Massachusetts Institute of Technology in March of 1949: "I must not conceal from you tonight the truth as I see it. It is certain that Europe would have been Communized like Czechoslovakia, and London under bombardment some time ago but for the deterrent of the atomic bomb in the hands of the United States." If Churchill feared that Europe would be "Communized" by Soviet-backed coups, as in Czechoslovakia, then the deterrent effect of the U.S. atomic bomb would be negligible, since it had failed to prevent the

clear that most American proponents of NATO actually valued it primarily
as a way of solidifying America's political commitment to Western Europe,
but felt that NATO could be better sold by emphasizing its military necessity,
with constant reference to the Soviet conventional threat.[83]

Elements of the U.S. military, particularly the proponents of strategic air
power and a 70-group Air Force, found it desirable to exaggerate the Soviet
conventional threat, because this left American atomic weapons as the only
alternative to Soviet ground forces. In 1949, Air Force Chief of Staff Hoyt S.
Vandenburg expressed this early version of nuclear deterrence of conventional threats in the following manner:

A prime objective of this country must be to find a counterbalance to the
potential enemy's masses of ground troops other than equal masses of American and Allied ground troops. No such balancing factor exists other than
strategic bombing, including atomic bombs.[84]

In the late 1940s and early 1950s, most Americans were unwilling to support a conventional defense of Western Europe because their military leaders
presented the prospects as hopeless. As Enthoven and Smith wrote much
later,

In a perverse sense it is rather comforting to be outnumbered 5 to 1 [in
conventional forces] by your enemy, because then there is no point in making
the effort to deploy your forces in the right place, or to ensure that your
forces are ready, or to insist on proper training standards. If, however, the
opposing force numbers are approximately equal, these factors become more
important. We have more incentive for making sure that our forces are ready,
well trained, and well equipped.[85]

The U.S. military gave the American people no incentive to favor improving
conventional forces for Europe's defense during the 1940s and 1950s. Stra-

---

coup in Prague. If, on the other hand, the Soviet threat was of a military nature, one that would
include "London under bombardment," then there is no sense in using the case of Czechoslovakia as an analogy. Churchill's speed is reprinted in *His Complete Speeches, 1897–1963* (London:
Chelsea House, 1974), Vol. 7, p. 50. It is certainly true in any case that the Czechoslovak coup
gave special impetus to the move to form an anti-Soviet alliance. See Claude Delmas, *L'O.T.A.N.*
(Paris: Presses Universitaires de France, 1969), pp. 18–21. For further discussion, see Evangelista,
"Soviet Military Capabilities and Objectives," pp. 3–8.
83. See Walter LaFeber, *America, Russia, and the Cold War 1945–1975* (New York: John Wiley and
Sons, 1976), pp. 83–87. See also Barnet and Raskin, *After 20 Years*, esp. Chapter 1.
84. U.S., Congress, House, Committee on Armed Services, *Hearings on National Defense Program*
(Washington, D.C.: U.S. Government Printing Office, n.d.), Vol. 1, pp. 454–456. See also
Herken, *Winning Weapon*, pp. 291–293.
85. Enthoven and Smith, *How Much Is Enough?*, p. 141.

tegic air power with atomic weapons was proposed as the solution to American security problems, and the popular press and the public generally supported the policy and the assumptions about Soviet conventional superiority that led to it.[86]

The evidence provided here, however, indicates that these assumptions were unfounded and consequently that American security policy, in the late 1940s at least, was based on an illusory conception of the Soviet threat. It is interesting to note in this context that recurrently over the last two decades analysts attempting to appraise the NATO–Warsaw Pact conventional balance have argued that NATO is in much better shape than is commonly believed. During the early 1960s, for example, the Defense Department reexamined the European balance and concluded that NATO was *not* hopelessly outmanned and outgunned in Central Europe; this analysis contributed to the adoption of NATO's new policy of "flexible response."[87]

During the 1970s, some analysts again presented evidence to support the notion of NATO–Warsaw Pact parity in conventional forces, based primarily on the introduction into Western forces of sophisticated precision-guided munitions, particularly anti-tank weapons.[88] More recently, several analyses have found the prospects quite good for conventional deterrence in Europe and favor less reliance on nuclear weapons in NATO military policy.[89]

Such analyses hint at the possibility that the exaggeration of Soviet military power has continued down to the present day. Could it be possible that the

86. See John Lewis Gaddis, *Strategies of Containment* (New York: Oxford University Press, 1982), pp. 121–122, 147–150. See also David Alan Rosenberg, "'A Smoking Radiating Ruin at the End of Two Hours': Documents on American Plans for Nuclear War with the Soviet Union, 1954–55," *International Security*, Vol. 6, No. 3 (Winter 1981–1982), pp. 3–38.
87. At the same time, however, the number of U.S. tactical nuclear weapons in Europe increased by 60 percent. See Gaddis, *Strategies of Containment*, pp. 220–221. Also Chapter 4 in Enthoven and Smith, *How Much Is Enough?*
88. For example, John J. Mearsheimer, "Precision-guided Munitions and Conventional Deterrence," *Survival*, March–April 1979, pp. 68–76; Phillip A. Karber, "The Soviet Anti-Tank Debate," *Survival*, May–June 1976; and Karber, *The Impact of New Conventional Technologies on Military Doctrine and Organization in the Warsaw Pact*, Adelphi Paper, Number 144 (London: International Institute for Strategic Studies, 1978).
89. John J. Mearsheimer, "Maneuver, Mobile Defense, and the NATO Central Front," *International Security*, Vol. 6, No. 3 (Winter 1981/1982), pp. 104–122; and Mearsheimer, "Why the Soviets Can't Win Quickly in Central Europe," *International Security*, Vol. 7, No. 1 (Summer 1982), pp. 3–39. Mearsheimer's work was discussed in a series of articles by Tom Wicker in *The New York Times* in April 1982. See also Jane Sharp, "Nuclear Weapons and Alliance Cohesion," *The Bulletin of the Atomic Scientists*, June 1982; McGeorge Bundy, George F. Kennan, Robert S. McNamara, and Gerard Smith, "Nuclear Weapons and the Atlantic Alliance," *Foreign Affairs*, Vol. 60, No. 4 (Spring 1982) pp. 753–768.

current conventional wisdom about Soviet superiority in Europe is the legacy of the original overestimation of the Red Army in the late 1940s? Given the extent to which powerfully formed impressions can persist, it seems plausible that the origins of our views of Soviet military power in Europe today can be traced to the misconceptions of the early postwar period. And whatever the truth about the balance today, the evidence now available shows that in the late 1940s the "Red Juggernaut" was anything but.

The Soviet Offensive in Europe

The Schlieffen Plan Revisited?

Richard Ned Lebow

Over the years a substantial literature has developed about the conventional military balance in Europe and the respective strategies of NATO and the Warsaw Pact. A certain asymmetry exists in this literature. NATO strategy has always been controversial; students of the subject concur in its content but disagree as to its wisdom. Many critics contend that a Soviet conventional offensive would probably succeed in its objective, generally assumed to be the destruction of NATO forces behind the Rhine River line.[1] Studies abound that propose a

The author wishes to acknowledge the support he received from the German Marshall Fund and the Rockefeller Foundation, which permitted him to work out the ideas for this article at the Villa Serbelloni in Bellagio and to discuss them there with Robert Jervis and Gert Krell. Useful assistance was subsequently provided by Matthew Evangelista, Michael MccGwire, Craig Nation, Edward Rhodes, Myron Rush, and Jack Snyder. This article is part of a book-length study, *Away from the Abyss: Managing Superpower Strategic Relations*, to be published in January 1986 by Cornell University Press.

Richard Ned Lebow is Professor of Government and Director of the Peace Studies Program at Cornell University.

1. The 1950s conventional wisdom was that NATO could be overwhelmed in a matter of days. Matthew A. Evangelista, "Stalin's Postwar Army Reappraised," *International Security*, Vol. 7, No. 3 (Winter 1982-83), pp. 110–138, has demonstrated that this judgement was based on a distorted assessment of Soviet military power. Western views of the balance did not begin to change until the late 1960s, when a more realistic view of Pact capabilities began to emerge. Thomas W. Wolfe's *Soviet Power and Europe, 1945–1970* (Baltimore: Johns Hopkins University Press, 1970), was particularly influential in this regard. Some authorities, among them, Alain C. Enthoven and K. Wayne Smith, *How Much is Enough?* (New York: Harper & Row, 1971), contended that a successful conventional defense of Europe was now possible and that NATO's most glaring deficiencies could be corrected at relatively little cost. This assessment was challenged not only by the traditionalists but by younger defense analysts. Steven L. Canby, *NATO Military Policy*, Rand Report R-1088-ARPA (Santa Monica, Calif.: Rand Corporation, 1973), and *The Alliance and Europe: Part IV, Military Doctrine and Technology*, Adelphi Paper No. 109 (London: International Institute for Strategic Studies, Winter 1974-75), and Richard D. Lawrence and Jeffrey Record, *U.S. Force Structure in NATO* (Washington, D.C.: Brookings Institution, 1974), argued that NATO would be unable to halt a Pact offensive because of its static defensive strategy, slow reinforcement rate, and relative lack of logistical and equipment standardization. A good review of this early literature is provided by Robert Lucas Fischer, *Defending the Central Front: The Balance of Forces*, Adelphi Paper No. 127 (London: International Institute for Strategic Studies, Autumn 1976). The 1970s witnessed across-the-board improvements in Pact firepower, mobility, and command and control. This led some critics of NATO strategy to assert that Soviet-led forces could overwhelm NATO without proper reinforcement. The threat of a "standing start" attack was publicized by Senators Sam Nunn and Dewey F. Bartlett, *NATO and the New*

International Security, Spring 1985 (Vol. 9, No. 4) 0162-2889/85/040044-35 $02.50/0

variety of military "fixes" or even alternative strategies for European security. In recent years the subject has become something of a cottage industry.[2]

Soviet Threat, U.S. Senate, Armed Services Committee, 95th Congress, First Session (Washington, D.C.: U.S. Government Printing Office, 1977). It was also the principle theme of Phillip A. Karber, *The Impact of New Conventional Technologies on Military Doctrine and Organization in the Warsaw Pact*, Adelphi Paper No. 144 (London: International Institute for Strategic Studies, Spring 1978). Within the government, a recent CIA report has rekindled the current administration's interest in the problem. See the *Washington Times*, July 26, 1984, p. 1. The most cogent critique of this scenario remains Les Aspin, "A Surprise Attack on NATO: Refocusing the Debate," *Congressional Record*, February 7, 1977, pp. H911–914. Less pessimistic views of the conventional balance have also been advanced by: Gert Krell, *Der Rüstungswettlauf in Europa: Mittelstreckensystem, Konventionelle Waffen, Rüstungskontrolle* (The Arms Race in Europe: Medium Range Systems, Conventional Weapons and Arms Control) (Frankfurt/Main: Campus-Verlag, 1982); John J. Mearsheimer, "Why the Soviets Can't Win Quickly in Central Europe," *International Security*, Vol. 7, No. 1 (Summer 1982), pp. 3–39 (revised and expanded version: *Conventional Deterrence* [Ithaca: Cornell University Press, 1983], pp. 165–189); Anthony H. Cordesman, "The NATO Central Region and the Balance of Uncertainty," *Armed Forces Journal International*, July 1983, pp. 18–58; and William P. Mako, *U.S. Ground Forces and the Defense of Central Europe* (Washington, D.C.: Brookings, 1983). The European Security Study Group, *Strengthening Conventional Deterrence in Europe: Proposals for the 1980s* (New York: St. Martin's Press, 1983), paints a far gloomier but also more superficial picture of the balance. A somber but more carefully reasoned portrayal of the balance is to be found in Phillip A. Karber, "The Growing Armor/Anti-Armor Imbalance in Central Europe," *Armed Forces Journal International*, July 1981, pp. 37–48, and "In Defense of Forward Defense," *Armed Forces Journal International*, May 1984, pp. 27–50.

Assessments are political documents offered in support or opposition to demands for more spending for conventional forces, or they are designed to show the viability, or lack of it, of specific military strategies. Robert Shishko, *The European Conventional Balance: A Primer*, Rand Paper P-6707 (Santa Monica, Calif.: Rand Corporation, 1981), p. 7, rightly observes that they may tell the reader more about the political-military orientation of their author than they do about the balance itself. Henry Stanhope, "New Threat or Old Fears?," in Derek Leebaert, ed., *European Security: Prospects for the 1980s* (Lexington, Mass.: D.C. Heath, 1979), p. 46, observes that the more realistic the assessment, the less unfavorable to NATO it becomes. This is a result of the fact that NATO's advantages lie in qualitative characteristics that are not taken into account by facile quantitative comparisons.

2. Among these are proposals for a German territorial militia to function as an anti-tank force. Basil Liddell Hart, *Deterrent or Defense: A Fresh Look at the West's Military Position* (New York: Praeger, 1960); Kenneth Hunt, *The Alliance and Europe: Part IV: Military Doctrine and Technology*, Adelphi Paper No. 109 (London: International Institute for Strategic Studies, 1975); and F.W. von Mellenthin and R.H.S. Stolfi with E. Sobik, *NATO Under Attack* (Durham: Duke University Press, 1984). In recent years one set of proposals, put forward mostly by Germans, urges an even more defensive orientation than NATO has traditionally followed. See, for example, Horst Afheldt, *Verteidigung und Frieden* [Defense and Freedom] (Munich: C. Hanser Verlag, 1976), and *Defensive Verteidigung* [Defensive Defense] (Reinbeck bei Hamburg: Rororo Aktuell, 1983); Komitee für Grundrechte und Demokratie, *Frieden mit anderen Waffen: Fünf Vorschläge zu einer alternativen Sicherheitspolitik* [Peace Through Other Weapons: Five Proposals for a New Security Policy] (Reinbeck bei Hamburg: Rororo Aktuell, 1981); J. Löser, *Weder rot noch tot. Überleben ohne Atomkrieg—eine Sicherheitspolitische Alternative* [Neither Red nor Dead. Surviving Without Nuclear War—an Alternative Security Policy] (Munich: G. Olzog Verlag, 1981); Egon Bahr, *Gemeinsame Sicherheit. Gendanken zu Entscharfung der nuklearen Konfrontation in Europa* [Mutual Security: Thoughts about the Intensification of the Nuclear Confrontation in Europe], *Europa Archiv*, July 25, 1982, pp. 421–430. At the other end of the spectrum, proposals, authored mostly by Americans, advocate a much more offensive strategy, including all the variants of the "Deep Strike"

By contrast, almost all studies of Soviet strategy are descriptive. Controversy surrounds the content of that strategy rather than its wisdom. Recent articles have debated the Soviet preference for a purely conventional offensive as opposed to a mixed one that employs nuclear and conventional weapons.[3] There is also a lively dispute about the meaning and importance of operational maneuver groups.[4] Most students of the subject seem to take for granted that Soviet conventional strategy, whatever its content and objectives, is a reasonable reflection of Soviet interests.[5]

A careful analysis of Soviet strategy, nuclear or conventional, would suggest that it is based on a number of unrealistic military and political assumptions and is therefore inconsistent with or even counterproductive to Soviet interests. Soviet notions of theater nuclear war have always been preposter-

strategy, and the recent proposal for a retaliatory offensive strategy by Samuel P. Huntington in his "Conventional Deterrence and Conventional Retaliation in Europe," *International Security*, Vol. 8, No. 3 (Winter 1983-84), pp. 32–56.

3. Karber, *The Impact of New Conventional Technologies*, argued that after 1973 the Soviets came to believe that conventional warfare could be carried out with increasing impunity below the nuclear threshold. In a more recent review, David M. Glantz, "Soviet Offensive Ground Doctrine Since 1945," *Air University Review*, March-April 1983, pp. 25–35, finds that Soviet doctrine now stresses the possibility and perhaps a preference for a non-nuclear phase of conventional operations. Stephen M. Meyer, *Soviet Theatre Nuclear Forces, Part I: Development of Doctrine and Objectives*, Adelphi Papers No. 187 (London: International Institute for Strategic Studies, 1984), pp. 21–34, argues that the principal wartime mission of Soviet conventional forces in Europe would be to destroy NATO's theater nuclear forces. Soviet nuclear forces would be husbanded in rear areas, safe from enemy conventional strikes, but would be used preemptively if the West appeared on the verge of launching a nuclear attack. Phillip A. Petersen and John G. Hines, "The Conventional Offensive in Soviet Theater Strategy," *Orbis*, Vol. 27, No. 3 (Fall 1983), pp. 695–739, advance the same portrayal of Soviet strategy and argue that Moscow has always preferred to achieve victory by conventional means alone. Michael MccGwire, *Soviet Military Objectives in a World War* (Washington, D.C.: Brookings, forthcoming), chapter 1 concurs with this analysis. Contrasting interpretations are offered by Joseph D. Douglass, Jr. and Amoretta M. Hoeber, *Conventional War and Escalation: The Soviet View* (New York: Crane, Russak, 1981), and Ilana Kass and Michael J. Deane, "The Role of Nuclear Weapons in the Modern Theater Battlefield: The Current Soviet View," *Comparative Strategy*, Vol. 4, No. 3 (1984), pp. 193–213.

4. See, for example: Christopher N. Donnelly, "The Soviet Operational Maneuver Group—A New Challenge for NATO," *International Defense Review*, Vol. 15, No. 9 (September 1982), pp. 1177–1186; Petersen and Hines, "The Conventional Offensive in Soviet Theater Strategy"; Earl F. Ziemke, "The Soviet Theory of Deep Operations," *Parameters*, Vol. 13 (June 1983), pp. 23–33; C.J. Dick, "Soviet Operational Manoeuvre Groups: A Closer Look," *International Defense Review*, Vol. 16, No. 6 (June 1983), pp. 769–776; and Peter H. Vigor, *Soviet Blitzkrieg Theory* (New York: St. Martin's Press, 1983).

5. Notable exceptions are German scholars affiliated with the Frankfurt Peace Research Institute: Stephan Tiedtke, *Rüstungskontrolle aus sowjetischer Sicht. Die Rahmenbedingungen der sowjetischen MBFR-Politik* [Arms Control from the Soviet Perspective: The Background to Soviet MBFR Policy] (Frankfurt: Campus-Verlag, 1980), and "Alternative Military Defense Strategies as a Component of Détente and Ostpolitik," *Bulletin of Peace Proposals*, Vol. 15, No. 1 (1984), pp. 3–12; Krell and Schmidt, *Der Rüstungswettlauf in Europa*; Peter Schlotter, "Reflections on European Security," *Bulletin of Peace Proposals*, Vol. 15, No. 1 (1984), pp. 3–12.

ous from a purely technical standpoint. They also stand in stark contradiction to any presumed Soviet interest in winning largely intact the prize of Western Europe or in limiting damage to the Soviet homeland by controlling escalation. As I will try to show, Soviet plans for a conventional offensive are no more realistic. In striking ways, they mirror the faults of the infamous Schlieffen Plan, which, most historians agree, was both an important cause of the First World War and a principal reason for Germany's ultimate defeat.

Soviet Conceptions of Military Power

The Soviets give every indication of believing in the necessity of maintaining military superiority over their neighbors. Attempts to do so have often created friction with neighboring states even if they were designed to do the opposite. When this approach to international relations is wedded to a propensity for the offensive, it can convey an even greater impression of threat.

The preferred Soviet response to external threat has been whenever possible to flex superior military muscle in the hope of moderating an adversary's behavior. Occasionally this strategy has worked admirably. The trouncing the Red Army administered to the Japanese in Mongolia in 1939–40 convinced Tokyo to abandon its plans for further conquests in Central Asia and turn instead against the French, British, and Dutch in Southeast Asia and the United States in the Central Pacific. But efforts to cow an adversary by intimidation can also backfire. Sino–Soviet relations are a case in point.

In response to the steady deterioration of relations with China in the late 1960s and early 1970s, Moscow carried out a major military buildup along the Soviet Union's long frontier with China. By the time of Mao's death in 1976, there were forty-three Soviet divisions in place supported by numerous modern combat aircraft, pre-positioned munitions, and an expanding communications and transportation network. Moscow had also redeployed one-quarter of its SS-4 and SS-5 missiles from the Western military districts to the Far Eastern theater.[6] The Soviet buildup failed to moderate Chinese foreign policy. Instead, it encouraged Peking to accelerate its own military

6. Harry Gelman, *The Soviet Far East Buildup and Soviet Risk-Taking in China*, Rand Report R-2943-AF (Santa Monica, Calif.: Rand, 1982); Lawrence Freedman, "The Dilemma of Theatre Nuclear Arms Control," *Survival*, Vol. 23, No. 1 (January-February 1981), pp. 2–10; Douglas T. Stuart, "Prospects for Sino–European Security Cooperation," *Orbis*, Vol. 26, No. 3 (Fall 1982), pp. 721–747; Vernon Aspaturian, "The Domestic Sources of Soviet Policy Toward China," in Douglas T. Stuart and William T. Tow, eds., *China, the Soviet Union and the West* (Boulder, Colo.: Westview Press, 1982), pp. 39–57. On the Chinese response, see Kenneth G. Lieberthal, *Sino–*

modernization, conventional and nuclear, and to seek political rapproche-
ment with the United States. The Chinese also shifted the bulk of their army
from the South, where it had faced American forces in Indochina, to the
North, opposite the Soviet force deployment. These moves only heightened
Soviet concern for their security in the Far East.

Moscow's fascination with awesome military power reflects in part its long-
standing adherence to a rather crude approach to conflict management.
Almost since its inception, the Soviet regime has correlated its ability to
pursue a wide range of foreign policy objectives with its military strength.
M.V. Frunze, a leader in efforts to modernize the Red Army in the 1920s,
declared quite bluntly: "The stronger and more powerful [the army] is, and
the more it is a threat to our enemies, then the more our interests will be
served."[7] For Frunze and his successors, military power was therefore envisaged as having a dual function. It served *defensive* ends by discouraging
military challenges of the Soviet Union. At the same time it was seen to
confer *political* advantages as intimidated neighbors were expected to be more
pliable.

In a deeper sense, Soviet interest in military superiority is also a response
to Russia's history of humiliating defeats, many of which threatened the very
existence of the country. In a speech delivered in 1931, Stalin himself revealed
the extent to which memories of those traumas influenced Soviet conceptions
of security. "Those who fall behind," he warned, "get beaten."

But we do not want to be beaten. No, we refuse to be beaten! One feature
of the history of old Russia was the continual beatings she suffered for falling
behind, for her backwardness. She was beaten by the Mongol Khans. She
was beaten by the Turkish beys. She was beaten by the Polish and Lithuanian
gentry. She was beaten by the British and French capitalists. She was beaten
by the Japanese barons. All beat her—for her backwardness; for military
backwardness, for political backwardness, for industrial backwardness. . . .
Such is the jungle law of capitalism. You are backward, you are weak—
therefore you are wrong; hence you can be beaten and enslaved. You are
mighty—therefore you are right; hence we must be wary of you. That is why
we must no longer lag behind.[8]

Soviet Conflict in the 1970s: Its Evolution and Implications for the Strategic Triangle, Rand Report R-2342-NA (Santa Monica, Calif.: Rand, 1978); and Melvin Gurtov and Byong-Moo Hwang, *China Under Threat: The Politics of Strategy and Diplomacy* (Baltimore: Johns Hopkins University Press, 1980).
7. M.V. Frunze, *Sobranie sochinenii*, 3 vols. (Moscow and Leningrad: Gosizdat, 1925-26), Vol. 1, p. 365.
8. Quoted in Nathan Leites, *The Operational Code of the Politburo* (New York: McGraw-Hill, 1951), p. 79.

Despite Stalin's commitment to avoid future defeats by overcoming Soviet backwardness, World War II once again revealed serious military deficiencies. However, the costly initial setbacks suffered by the Red Army cannot be attributed to technological backwardness. In June 1941, the Russians possessed more planes and tanks than the Germans. And the newer models of Soviet tanks and infantry weapons, albeit few in number at that time, were by no means inferior to their German counterparts. The Red Army was overwhelmed because Soviet political authorities and military leaders made the worst possible use of their men and weapons. The Soviet Union emerged victorious in the end only because of its nearly inexhaustible reservoir of manpower and its ultimate ability to outproduce the German enemy.

The experience of World War II reinforced the Soviets' tradition of relying upon numbers to offset their expected technological and organizational backwardness. A.N. Tupolev, one of the foremost Soviet postwar aircraft designers, articulated this philosophy in his call for "long production runs" of simple, "black bread" aircraft. "If these aircraft fall somewhat behind Western ones in terms of technology," he explained, "to hell with them; we'll get by on quantity."[9] Other Soviet services appear to be motivated by the same outlook; it is probably one important reason why they continue to field impressive numbers of all kinds of weapons. This proclivity may also be encouraged by the existence of powerful vested bureaucratic interests, which make it difficult to shut down an assembly line once production has begun.[10]

The continuing Soviet penchant for large numbers of everything to compensate for their expected battlefield inferiority may now be atavistic; most Western military analysts are impressed by both the training of the Red Army and the equipment with which it would fight. Deficiencies certainly exist in Soviet organization, doctrine, and equipment—as they do in the West—but Soviet forces compare quite favorably in most respects with their Western counterparts. If their weapons do not exactly incorporate state-of-the-art technology, they are nevertheless often capable, durable systems. Where a significant technological gap still exists, for example, with regard to aircraft or electronic countermeasures (ECM), Soviet superiority in numbers occasionally compensates for it.

---

9. Quoted in G. Ozerov, *Tupolevskaya sharaga* [The Tupolev Design Bureau], 2nd ed. (Frankfurt: Posev, 1973), p. 57.
10. Arthur J. Alexander, *Decision-Making in Soviet Weapons Procurement*, Adelphi Paper No. 148 (London: International Institute for Strategic Studies, Winter 1978-79); Karl F. Spielmann, Jr., *Analyzing Soviet Strategic Arms Decisions* (Boulder, Colo.: Westview Press, 1978); David Holloway, *The Soviet Union and the Arms Race* (New Haven: Yale University Press, 1983).

Improvements in Soviet military organization, training, and weapons together with the traditional penchant for large numbers have created a novel
situation. In the past, Soviet numerical superiority made up for Soviet operational and technological backwardness. Today, Soviet numerical superiority complements Soviet operational and technical competence. The Soviet
Union's military power has accordingly become much more threatening in
the eyes of its neighbors.

The perception of Soviet military prowess is evident in most Western
assessments of the military balance in Europe. What is important in this
connection is not the comparison of NATO and Warsaw Pact forces or specific
components of them: this is inevitably a subject of considerable controversy.
It is rather the base line for those comparisons. In the 1930s, this was the
Red Army's ability to defend the Soviet Union. For the last several decades
it has been the Soviet Union's putative ability to conduct offensive operations
in Western Europe, to break through NATO defenses and reach the Rhine
River line or even the Channel ports. Opinions differ widely as to whether
the Red Army could accomplish this, but nobody in the West doubts its
ability to defend Eastern Europe from NATO.

If the strength of the Pact armies appears to many Western analysts as
greater than that required by any legitimate defensive needs, these forces
probably do not appear strong enough in the eyes of Moscow. For a start,
Soviet military planners are known to estimate their needs on the basis of
very conservative criteria. Like their Western counterparts, they are most
sensitive to the capabilities of their adversary and the deficiencies of their
own forces. They must also base their comparisons on uncertain and incomplete data about the performance characteristics and operational reliability of
weapons on both sides, but especially those of the adversary. The less that
is known about the qualities of the other side's weapons, the greater the
tendency to assign high values to them in order to be on the "safe side." In
dynamic analyses, this bias can be further compounded by the choice of a
war scenario that is particularly favorable to the enemy. In a conventional
European war, this would be a situation in which the other side had gained
a significant head start with its mobilization. Rigging the scenario in this way
results in an extremely threatening picture of the strategic balance.

When worst case analysis is used by both sides, it means that they will
interpret a situation of strategic parity as one of imbalance favoring their
adversary. This will encourage both of them to augment or modernize their
arsenals in order to redress the balance. This in turn will aggravate the

tensions between them as each side will interpret any arms buildup as proof of the other's hostile intentions, given its belief that its adversary already possesses an advantage. The current Soviet and American inability to agree about either the conventional or nuclear balance in Europe offers a telling example of just how this dynamic operates.[11] It illustrates how asymmetrical perceptions of military balance are an important structural cause of arms races.

Exaggeration of the military threat posed by the West encourages exaggerated notions of the force requirements necessary to meet it. This tendency is further abetted by the pervasive feelings of military inadequacy already described. Both these factors contribute to the adoption of very conservative yardsticks for military planning. Soviet authorities stress the need for a "decisive superiority" before taking the offensive. This they estimate to be a theater-wide advantage of 3–5:1 in infantry, 6–8:1 for artillery, 3–4:1 for tanks and self-propelled artillery, and 5–10:1 in aircraft.[12] By contrast, NATO planners work on the assumption of a 1.5–2:1 theater force ratio and at least a 3:1 superiority at the point of attack. Israeli forces, which rely upon significant qualitative superiority over any adversary, have carried out successful large-scale offensives with force ratios of 1:1 or even less.

The numerical advantage required by Soviet planners rather accurately reflects the Soviet experience in World War II, when a staggering numerical preponderance in men and weapons was almost always an essential condition of success in any offensive waged against the German army. In their drive from Warsaw to Berlin in the spring of 1945, the Soviets acknowledge an initial superiority of 5.5:1 in infantry, 7.8:1 in artillery, 5.7:1 in tanks, and 17.6:1 in aircraft.[13] Although the quality of Soviet forces has improved sub-

---

11. For analyses of this phenomenon, see Raymond L. Garthoff, "The Soviet SS-20 Decision," *Survival*, Vol. 25, No. 3 (May–June 1983), pp. 110–119, and "The NATO Decision on Theater Nuclear Forces," *Political Science Quarterly*, Vol. 98, No. 2 (Summer 1983), pp. 197–214; Gert Krell, *Deterrence in the 1980's: Part X, The Limitations of Nuclear Deterrence: Criteria for Restraint*, Adelphi Paper (London: International Institute for Strategic Studies, forthcoming). On the conventional balance, see John C. Keliher, *The Negotiations on Mutual and Balanced Force Reductions: The Search for Arms Control in Central Europe* (New York: Pergamon, 1980).
12. See V.Ye. Savkin, *The Basic Principles of Operational Art and Tactics* (Washington, D.C.: U.S. Government Printing Office, 1974) [originally published in Moscow in 1972], pp. 119–152, 201–229, for a discussion of the importance of achieving superiority along the axes of advance; A.A. Sidorenko, *The Offensive* (Washington, D.C.: U.S. Government Printing Office, 1976) [originally published in Moscow in 1970], pp. 5–39, for force ratios.
13. *Istoriia velikoi otechestvennoi voiny sovetskogo soiuza* [History of the Great Patriotic War of the Soviet Union], 6 vols. (Moscow: Institute of Marxism–Leninism, 1960–63), Vol. 5, p. 57. German officers of the period claim that the Soviet advantage was even greater—11:1 in infantry, 7:1 in

stantially in comparison with those of their likely adversaries, Soviet staff officers continue to employ World War II force ratios for their planning purposes. Because the Soviet Union's defense of Eastern Europe is predicated upon the ability of the Red Army and the armies of its allies to conduct an offensive in Western Europe, Soviet planners cannot be content with the existing balance of forces in Europe. From their perspective, their forces are insufficient for the political-military task assigned to them, especially if NATO is able to mobilize its forces in advance of any war. From the Western perspective, of course, Warsaw Pact forces are threatening, as they appear larger than would be required for any legitimate defensive needs.

The Appeal of the Offensive

It is readily apparent that the asymmetrical notions of military sufficiency that exist between East and West are made much more acute by the Soviet commitment to an offensive strategy. This can be explained with reference to both Soviet military tradition and the particular strategic requirements Soviet leaders believe that a war in Europe would impose upon them. The overall concept of the postwar Red Army has been defensive; its objective has been to deter Western aggression. Soviet forces have been postured to repel any Western attack and then to take the offensive or to initiate an offensive from the outset. This approach reflects the Soviet view that victory can only be achieved through offensive operations, a belief that was reinforced by the experience of World War II.[14] It is fair to inquire whether or not this offensive orientation is really in the Soviet interest.

Offensives are usually appealing because they promise to carry the war into the enemy's territory and away from one's own. If even partly successful, they put the initiator in a better bargaining position at the end of hostilities because of the territory he controls. An offensive orientation also appeals to soldiers; it is seen as more "manly" than the defensive and generally requires

---

tanks, and 20:1 in guns. Albert Seaton, *The Russo–German War 1941–45* (New York: Praeger, 1970), p. 527. Soviet military authorities also stress the continuing relevance of the lessons of this campaign as well as those of the Vistula–Oder operation of January 1945 and Manchurian invasion of August 1945 to contemporary conventional strategy. On this, see Glantz, "Soviet Offensive Ground Doctrine Since 1945"; and Peter W. Vigor and Christopher Donnelly, "The Manchurian Campaign and Its Relevance to Modern Strategy," *Comparative Strategy*, Vol. 2, No. 2 (1980), pp. 159–178.
14. MccGwire, *Soviet Military Objectives*, chapter 1, traces the evolution of postwar Soviet strategic concepts with regard to Europe.

a larger and better-equipped military organization. In practice, however, offensives are usually more difficult to execute. They may also entail greater political risks. The trade-offs between the two military strategies are important and interesting to consider in the case of the Soviets in Europe.[15]

The notion of defense through offensive has been central to Soviet military doctrine since the 1930s. Ever since, the Red Army's training and equipment have been geared to that end.[16] Beyond doctrinal and organizational incentives, all of which point towards the offensive, Soviet leaders probably also perceive a number of important political and military rewards associated with an offensive strategy. Offensives can be planned in detail in advance and thereby maximize central control over military operations. In a war with NATO, a successful offensive, by demonstrating Soviet military prowess, would quell any thoughts of opposition or resistance in Eastern Europe.[17] If the Red Army actually succeeded in reaching the Rhine, the Soviet Union would also gain the prize of West Germany and could be in a position to dictate peace terms.

The peacetime payoffs of an offensive strategy are also great. To the extent that it is seen to reflect a conventional military balance in favor of the Soviets, it acts as something of a check on both internal dissent in Warsaw Pact countries and the desires of at least several of the communist regimes in those countries to pursue more independent domestic and foreign policies. The Red Army, moreover, has become an increasingly important mechanism for the Soviet domination of Eastern Europe as ideological and economic means of leverage have either eroded or become more uncertain.[18] The same

15. On the appeal of the offensive, see Jack Snyder, *The Ideology of the Offensive: Military Decision Making and the Disasters of 1914* (Ithaca: Cornell University Press, 1984); and Stephen Van Evera, "Causes of War," Ph.D. dissertation, University of California, Berkeley, 1984.
16. M.V. Frunze, *Izberannyye proizvedeniye* [Selected works] (Moscow: Military Publishing House, 1950), p. 206, who constantly stressed the offensive, declared that: "The victor will be the one who finds within himself the resolution to attack: the side with only defense is inevitably doomed to defeat." Both Sidorenko, *The Offensive*, pp. 5–39, and Savkin, *Operational Art and Tactics*, pp. 39–45, emphasize the historical Soviet commitment to offensive operations. For Western authorities on the Soviet offensive orientation, see John Erickson, *The Soviet High Command: A Military–Political History, 1918–1941* (New York: St. Martin's Press, 1962), *passim*; Edward L. Warner, III, *The Military in Contemporary Soviet Politics* (New York: Frederick Praeger, 1977), Chapter 4; and Holloway, *The Soviet Union and the Arms Race*, pp. 29–39.
17. Klaus-Peter Stratmann, *NATO–Strategie in der Krise?* (Baden-Baden: Nomos, 1981), pp. 28, 29, 29 note 5, documents the concern of the leaders of the German Democratic Republic in the 1950s regarding the political consequences of a NATO attack.
18. See the following: Robin Alison Remington, "The Changing Soviet Perception of the Warsaw Pact" (Cambridge: MIT Center for International Studies, November 1967); Roman Kolkowicz, "The Warsaw Pact: Entangling Alliance," *Survey*, No. 70/71 (1969), pp. 86–101; A. Ross Johnson,

holds true for Western Europe, where Soviet political influence has declined precipitously since the early postwar years.

Communist parties throughout Western Europe have experienced repeated electoral setbacks and are on the whole on the decline. Most of them have also established their independence from Moscow; in some cases they have actually been expelled from the Soviet-dominated Communist International Movement. The relatively powerful Italian Communist Party is the most recent example of the latter. In the absence of influential parties responsive to Soviet directives, Moscow has fallen back upon the military threat it poses to Western Europe as its principal if unsatisfactory means of political leverage. Soviet force modernization in the 1960s and 1970s triggered fears among some Americans and Europeans that the military balance has become so one-sided as to threaten "Finlandization"—defined as an accommodation with the Soviet Union by its neighbors verging on political subservience. These fears seem greatly exaggerated, but their expression could conceivably convince the Soviets of the political efficacy of maintaining impressive force levels in Eastern Europe and, with it, a putative ability to conduct a successful offensive in the West. Such an outcome would be ironic, given the intentions of those who voice fears of Finlandization.

The drawbacks to an offensive strategy are also great if perhaps less obvious to Moscow. Offensives are difficult to conduct because of the greater demands they place on communications, control, and logistics and because of the tactical advantages that usually accrue to the defender fighting from covered, prepared positions. These disadvantages can sometimes be offset by surprise. In the context of Europe, the Soviets might achieve surprise but certainly cannot count upon it. Warsaw Pact forces are kept at a relatively low state of readiness, and efforts to bring them up to full operational status in terms of men and equipment are almost certain to be detected by NATO's sophisticated electronic and photographic surveillance capabilities. According

"Soviet–East European Military Relations: An Overview," in Dale R. Herspring and Ivan Volgyes, eds., *Civil–Military Relations in Communist Systems* (Boulder, Colo.: Westview, 1978), pp. 243–266; Dale R. Herspring, "The Warsaw Pact at 25," *Problems of Communism*, Vol. 29, No. 5 (September-October 1980), pp. 1–15; Kent N. Brown, "Coalition Politics and Soviet Influence in Eastern Europe," in Jan F. Triska and Paul M. Cocks, eds., *Political Development in Eastern Europe* (New York: Praeger, 1977), pp. 241–255; Christopher D. Jones, *Soviet Influence in Eastern Europe* (New York: Praeger, 1981); Malcolm Mackintosh, "Military Considerations in Soviet–East European Relations in the 1980s," in Karen Dawisha and Philip Hanson, eds., *Soviet–East European Dilemmas: Coercion, Competition, and Consent* (New York: Holmes & Meier, 1981), pp. 134–147; and David Holloway, "The Warsaw Pact in Transition," in David Holloway and Jane M.O. Sharp, eds., *The Warsaw Pact: Alliance in Transition?* (Ithaca: Cornell University Press, 1984), pp. 19–38.

to General Alexander Haig, former supreme allied commander in Europe, NATO could count on at least eight days' warning of attack.[19] Surprise rests rather with the possibility that, for a combination of psychological and political reasons, NATO countries will be unwilling to believe or act upon the information their sensors provide.[20]

The Soviets must also face the reality that recent and ongoing technological developments will significantly enhance the prospects for NATO's defense of the central front in Europe. Precision guided munitions (PGMs) of the "fire and forget" variety, sub-munitions, bomblets that autonomously home in on separate targets, and more sophisticated means of electronic surveillance, target acquisition, and command and control will make the battlefield a much more dangerous place for the kinds of tank concentrations upon which the Soviets base their offensives.[21] Demographic change in West Germany, which has transformed the once relatively open North German plain into a densely populated region of urban and suburban sprawl, also works to the disadvantage of the Soviets. It severely limits the mobility of armor while increasing its vulnerability by offering the defender countless positions for siting anti-tank weapons for long-range attack or short-range ambush.[22]

19. Drew Middleton in *The New York Times*, September 15, 1977. Nunn and Bartlett, *NATO and the New Soviet Threat*, pp. 4–6, contend that the Warsaw Pact would only need two days to organize a two-front attack. Mako, *U.S. Ground Forces*, pp. 45–48, compares and evaluates estimates for various attack scenarios and concludes that "a prudently conservative" estimate would be four days preparation for a two-front attack and eleven days for a three-front attack.
20. Richard K. Betts, *Surprise Attack: Lessons for Defense Planning* (Washington, D.C.: Brookings Institution, 1982), offers the best analysis of this problem in the context of Europe.
21. The most thorough treatment of the technical, military, and political implications of new technologies remains the series of articles published in *New Conventional Weapons and East–West Security*, Adelphi Papers Nos. 144 and 145 (London: International Institute for Strategic Studies, 1978). Other useful literature includes Richard Burt, *New Weapons Technologies: Debate and Directions*, Adelphi Paper No. 126 (London: International Institute for Strategic Studies, 1976); Paul F. Walker, "Precision-guided Weapons," *Scientific American*, August 1981, pp. 37–45; Neville Brown, "The Changing Face of Non-nuclear War," *Survival*, Vol. 24, No. 5 (September-October 1982), pp. 211–219; Edgar Ulsamer, "Smart and Standing Off," *Air Force Magazine*, November 1983, pp. 56–62; Phil Williams and William Wallace, "Emerging Technologies and European Security," *Survival*, Vol. 26, No. 2 (March-April 1984), pp. 70–78. There is also some evidence that Soviet military leaders have reached the conclusion that armored warfare has become much more difficult as the direct result of new weapons technologies. In the second edition of his book, *The Armed Forces of the Soviet State*, trans. U.S. Air Force (Washington, D.C.: U.S. Government Printing Office, 1975), former Soviet Defense Minister Marshal A.A. Grechko reported that this was the conclusion of two conferences held by the defense ministry to evaluate the lessons of the 1973 Arab–Israeli War.
22. Paul Bracken, "Urban Sprawl and NATO Defence," *Survival*, Vol. 18, No. 6 (November-December 1976), pp. 254–260; Steven L. Canby, *Short [And Long] War Responses: Restructuring, Border Defense, and Reserve Mobilization for Armored Warfare* (Santa Monica, Calif.: Technology Service Corporation, 1978), pp. 51–53; Peter H. Vigor, "Doubts and Difficulties Confronting a

Both these developments, if properly exploited by NATO, would diminish the prospects for a successful Soviet blitzkrieg across the North German plain or through the Fulda Gap, especially one that aims to reach and secure the Rhine River line within a matter of days or a week at most.

Another Schlieffen Plan?

The scope and nature of the Soviet Union's offensive strategy is reminiscent of the Schlieffen Plan, that daring and ill-fated offensive upon which Germany pinned its hopes at the outbreak of World War I. Like the Schlieffen Plan, the Soviet offensive strategy is a high-risk venture that seems to gamble everything on one throw of the "iron dice." The Schlieffen Plan failed, largely because of command and control breakdowns that prevented advancing German armies from exploiting numerous military opportunities. Many experts allege that if a Soviet offensive fails, it will probably be for the same reason.[23]

The Schlieffen Plan is most often described as the outcome of the German general staff's belief that the Reich was almost certain to find France and Russia arrayed against it in any continental war. The generals doubted Germany's ability to wage war successfully on two fronts and therefore concluded that their adversaries would have to be dealt with sequentially. According to the war plan devised initially by General Alfred von Schlieffen, France, the stronger of the two adversaries, was to be attacked first, while a delaying action was fought in the east against the more slowly mobilizing Russians. When France was defeated, German might would be turned against Russia. Schlieffen's war plan staked everything on Germany's ability to knock France out of the war quickly in order to free German armies for redeployment in the East in time to stop the Russians before they advanced too far into Prussia. To do this, Schlieffen devised a daring strategy: almost

Would-be Soviet Attacker," *RUSI*, Vol. 125 (June 1980), pp. 32–38; James H. Polk, "The North German Plain Attack Scenario: Threat or Illusion?," *Strategic Review*, Vol. 8 (Summer 1980), pp. 60–66; Mearsheimer, *Conventional Deterrence*, pp. 178–179; Gary L. Guertner, "Nuclear War In Suburbia," *Orbis*, Vol. 26, No. 1 (Spring 1982), pp. 49–69.

23. See, for example, Joshua M. Epstein, "On Conventional Deterrence in Europe: Questions of Soviet Confidence," *Orbis*, Vol. 26, No. 1 (Spring 1982), pp. 71–86; Vigor, *Soviet Blitzkrieg Theory*; and Cordesman, "The NATO Central Region and the Balance of Uncertainty." Andrew Cockburn, *The Threat: Inside the Soviet Military Machine* (New York: Random House, 1983), pp. 169–176, describes other similar assessments. Richard Simpkin, *Red Armour: An Examination of the Soviet Mobile Force Concept* (Oxford: Pergamon Press, 1984), emphasizes the rigidity of the Soviet command structure.

all ready and mobilized forces were to be thrown into the battle against France, leaving only a thin screen of covering forces in the east. As the Franco–German frontier was largely unsuited to the rapid advance of large armies, Schlieffen made the equally fateful decision to direct the main axis of the offensive through Belgium. The German army was to overrun that country and then wheel south in order to outflank and encircle the French army behind Paris.[24]

Despite impressive early advances, the German offensive ran into serious difficulty in northern France and ultimately ground to a halt after a costly but inconclusive battle along the Marne, no more than two days' march from Paris. The Schlieffen Plan failed for many reasons. Historians have pointed to the physical exhaustion of the troops, stiff Anglo–French opposition, and most importantly, a series of poor command decisions that failed to exploit the several opportunities offered to the Germans to outflank their adversaries.[25] The poor control and coordination of the German armies has often been attributed to irresolute leadership; Helmuth von Moltke, commander of the German armies, remained in his headquarters far beyond the fast receding front line, from where he fretted about his own ability to direct the offensive. This allowed his front line commanders, who were deeply jealous of each other and often uninformed and even uninterested in each other's movements, to conduct an increasingly uncoordinated campaign. But perhaps an even more fundamental cause of the German failure was the structural gap between mobility and control.

The kinds of technological and administrative developments that permitted the rapid advance of large armies—e.g., a large professional civil service, an expanding network of railways and paved roads, the standardization of weapons and their ordnance—were not matched by innovations that facilitated their command and control.[26] Field telephone systems were very rarely

24. See Gerhard Ritter, The Schlieffen Plan, trans. Andrew and Eva Wilson (New York: Praeger, 1958); L.L. Farrar, Jr., The Short War: German Policy, Strategy, and Domestic Affairs, August–December 1914 (Santa Barbara, Calif.: ABC-CLIO, 1973), pp. 1–33; and Snyder, The Ideology of the Offensive, pp. 107–156.
25. Ritter, The Schlieffen Plan, passim; Correlli Barnett, The Swordbearers: Supreme Command in the First World War (Bloomington, Ind.: Indiana University Press, 1964), pp. 300–302; B.H. Liddell Hart, A History of The World War (Boston: Little, Brown, 1935), pp. 84–88; and Snyder, The Ideology of the Offensive, pp. 111–116.
26. Martin Van Creveld, Supplying War: Logistics from Wallenstein to Patton (Cambridge: Cambridge University Press, 1977), pp. 109–141, convincingly documents the staggering logistical problems created by the rapid advance of large modern armies and the inability of the Germans to keep them supplied. Van Creveld argues that, for this reason, the German advance would not have been able to progress much beyond the Marne even if they had won the battle.

used; they were in short supply, and most often deactivated by accidental damage or sabotage, and ill-suited to rapid maneuver as they took some hours to set up. Radio communication provided a better link between headquarters and the field, but Moltke's headquarters in Coblenz had only one receiving set, and the First Army, on the crucial right wing of the advance, had but two transmitters, only one of which was useful for communicating with Coblenz. That transmitter had such a restricted range that a series of relay stations were required at intervals only a little further apart than would have been the case for a mechanical semaphore. The radio link was so uncertain and overloaded that only the briefest and most urgent messages could be sent. Even then, the process of coding, transmission, and decoding could take up to 24 hours, and the messages that emerged were often so garbled as to be useless.[27]

Because of the difficulties of radio transmission in 1914, both sides relied heavily on horse cavalry for reconnaissance and communication. This was haphazard and slow. To make matters even worse, all of the armies were hampered by antiquated command structures that could not make good or rapid use of what intelligence they did receive. Commanders made important strategic decisions on the basis of incomplete, often inaccurate, information that was almost always so delayed in transmission as to be overtaken by events. In the German case, this meant that their two armies advancing on Paris were largely ignorant of each other's position as well as of the whereabouts of the enemy's main forces, thought to be somewhere in front of them. The allies also suffered from this blindness, but its effect was mitigated by internal lines of communication and the significantly shorter distance between the front line and their headquarters in Paris. The allied victory on the Marne more than anything else reflected their ability to respond more rapidly to changing battlefield conditions.

Like the Schlieffen Plan, the Soviet war plan is, by most accounts, based on the hope of achieving a rapid victory by means of a conventional offensive that destroys or envelops the bulk of NATO's combat forces to the East of the Rhine River line.[28] The incentive to do this also appears to derive from a

27. Barnett, The Swordbearers, p. 67.
28. For Soviet sources on the commitment to take the offensive, see Savkin, The Basic Principles of Operational Art and Tactics; Sidorenko, The Offensive; and V.D. Sokolovskiy, Soviet Military Strategy, ed. Harriet Fast Scott, 3rd ed. (New York: Crane, Russak, 1968). Further evidence in support of the contention that the Soviets hope to win any war in Europe quickly is provided by the configuration of their army: its organization, training, equipment, and logistics are all

similar concern for the political and military difficulties that a longer war of attrition would entail.

The parallels are really quite striking in this regard. For the Germans, a war of attrition meant a two-front war against a combination of powers which, if we include Britain, possessed superior economic resources and free access to the sea. For the Soviet Union, the economic imbalance would be even more pronounced as the gross national product (GNP) of the Warsaw Pact is a mere 31 percent of NATO's. Since the Sino–Soviet split, Soviet leaders have also become keen to forestall the prospect of a two-front war and are said to worry that China would be tempted to intervene against them in the east if a war in the west became stalemated. Like the Schlieffen Plan, the Soviets' strategy also seems designed to take advantage of their faster mobilization rate, a function in this case of the fact that the bulk of NATO's reinforcements must come from overseas.[29] Finally, the German offensive orientation was influenced by concern for the reliability of their Austro–Hungarian ally.[30] So, too, must the Russians fear for the loyalty of their Eastern European allies.

As did the Schlieffen Plan, the Soviet Union's war plan puts a premium on the capability of its forces to carry out a coordinated offensive that successfully exploits every major opportunity presented by allied weakness or confusion. The Germans learned, to their bitter disappointment, that such an expectation was unrealistic in the extreme.[31] So too does the Soviet concept

geared to fight a short conflict, not a war of attrition. On this point, see John Hemsley, "The Soviet Ground Forces," in John Erickson and E.J. Feuchtwanger, eds., *Soviet Military Power and Performance* (Hamden, Conn.: Archon Books, 1979), pp. 47–73. The most up-to-date and comprehensive description of what a Soviet offensive in Europe would look like is Petersen and Hines, "The Conventional Offensive in Soviet Theater Strategy." Both authors are analysts for the Defense Intelligence Agency.

29. On reinforcement rates and force ratios at various stages of mobilization, see Fischer, "Defending the Central Front," pp. 15–24; and Mako, *U.S. Ground Forces*, pp. 52–58. Fen Osler Hampson, "Groping for Technical Panaceas: The European Conventional Balance and Nuclear Stability," *International Security*, Vol. 8, No. 3 (Winter 1983-84), pp. 64–69, compares and evaluates the estimates of five different studies of mobilization under varying attack scenarios.

30. The Germans feared that a defensive, and the longer war that this would of necessity entail, would exacerbate political tensions within the already deeply divided Austro–Hungarian Empire. Austrian leaders also favored a German offensive but not one directed against France, as this would leave Austria to face the Russians by itself. The Germans tried to assuage Vienna's concern by considerably exaggerating the number of troops they planned to commit to the East at the onset of war.

31. Van Creveld, *Supplying War*, pp. 109–141. In World War II, by contrast, German successes in blitzkrieg warfare were attributable, according to most authorities, to improved doctrine, command and control, and the striking degree of initiative exercised by NCOs. This latter factor, discussed elsewhere in the text, is quite contrary to Soviet traditions.

appear to make insufficient allowance, numerical advantage aside, for what Clausewitz called "friction": everything in real war, as opposed to exercises or simulations, that will degrade an army's performance. For Clausewitz, friction was such a serious impediment to campaigning that he defined greatness in generals not in terms of strategic brilliance but rather as the ability to overcome friction.[32] The Iran rescue operation, the Falklands campaign, and the Iran–Iraq War each give vivid testimony to the fact that friction remains the most serious obstacle to success in modern warfare as well.

Most Western assessments of Warsaw Pact conventional strength, based as they are on numbers of tanks, men, planes, and the like, take insufficient account of the problems the Soviets would confront in actual offensive operations in Europe. The most serious causes of friction in this context would almost certainly be command and control breakdowns, logistical failures, and the physical exhaustion of troops and commanders alike. The unopposed Soviet invasion of Czechoslovakia gave ample evidence of all of these problems. Soviet armored units quickly outran their rail-based logistical system and could not be resupplied by trucks as there were too few of them. According to one authority,

during the first week of the occupation . . . a breakdown of transportation and supply services threatened to paralyze the Soviet armies in Czechoslovakia [and] the situation was saved by . . . [an] airlift which delivered fuel, food, and essential equipment. . . . Under actual combat conditions . . . [Soviet divisions] would have lacked many essential items after the first 24 hours.[33]

Friction would impede battlefield responsiveness, so essential to the kind of offensive the Soviets contemplate. The problem the Soviets confront in this regard is already pronounced because of the rigid and hierarchical command structure that remains a distinctive feature of all branches of the Soviet military. A military tradition and chain of command that discourage or actually deny battlefield initiative by subordinate commanders is hardly suited to the needs of mobile warfare; if anything, it is likely to hinder its conduct. John Mearsheimer writes:

A blitzkrieg is not a steamroller: success is ultimately a consequence of commanders' ability to make rapid-fire decisions in the fog of battle that

---

32. Carl von Clausewitz, *Vom Kriege* (Frankfurt: Verlag Ullstein, 1981), pp. 77–79.
33. Leo Heiman, "Soviet Invasion Weakness," *Military Review*, August 1969, pp. 38–45. This point is also made by Jeffrey Record, *Sizing Up the Soviet Army* (Washington, D.C.: Brookings, 1975), p. 46.

enable the attacking forces to make the crucial deep strategic penetrations. Should the Soviets attack NATO, there is a chance that the Soviets will open one or more holes in the NATO front. Naturally, NATO will try to close those holes and to seal off any penetrations as quickly as possible. The key question is: Can the Soviets exploit such opportunities before NATO, which is well prepared for such an eventuality, shuts the door?[34]

The answer, Mearsheimer argues, will not be determined by the amount of firepower the Soviets have at their disposal but rather by the ability of NCOs and officers to make the kinds of decisions that will permit their armored spearheads to penetrate NATO's rear and envelop its front-line forces. Success in a blitzkrieg depends upon split-second timing as battlefield opportunities are so fleeting.

Rigidity also constitutes a serious potential vulnerability as enemy interference with or actual destruction of important links in the chain of command could transform a breakthrough by even the most potent striking force from an asset holding out the prospect of victory into a liability threatening disaster. The fate of the Egyptian Third Army in the October 1973 War, cut off from resupply on the far side of the Suez Canal by an Israeli counteroffensive that capitalized on the sluggishness of the Soviet-trained Egyptian army's response to changing battlefield conditions, gives striking testimony to this danger. Former Secretary of Defense Harold Brown has indicated his belief that such a disaster could overtake the Soviets as well.[35]

Fully aware of Soviet vulnerabilities in this regard, NATO has tried increasingly to gear its defensive effort to exploit them to its advantage. In doing so, it is placing more emphasis on the importance of its own more flexible command structure and access to state-of-the-art communications technology—a field in which the West retains a distinct advantage—as a means of improving its own battlefield responsiveness and of degrading that of the Warsaw Pact through attrition and electronic countermeasures.

There is also growing support, especially in the United States, for adopting a more offensive strategy in order to exploit the possibilities of these technologies to the fullest extent. The Follow-On Forces Attack concept of NATO

---

34. Mearsheimer, *Conventional Deterrence*, p. 185.
35. Department of Defense, *Annual Report*, Fiscal Year 1982 (Washington, D.C.: U.S. Government Printing Office, 1981), pp. 74–75. Epstein, "On Conventional Deterrence," pp. 76–80; Mearsheimer, *Conventional Deterrence*, pp. 184–187; Mako, *U.S. Ground Forces*, p. 62; John Hemsley, *Soviet Troop Control* (Oxford: Brassey, 1982), pp. 197–201; Cockburn, *The Threat*, pp. 169–176; and von Mellenthin and Stolfi, *NATO Under Attack*, pp. 83–96, also comment at length about the impediment that command rigidity constitutes for Soviet offensive operations.

(FOFA) envisages the use of "emerging technologies" and special ground units to strike at Soviet forces and their command and transportation networks before they enter the battle zone. Air and ground forces would be expected to make extensive use of recent technological developments such as the NAVSTAR Global Positioning System, high speed, jamming-proof digital communications systems, electronic jammers, laser-guided missiles, and the overall increased mobility of all ground forces.[36]

To this point in the analysis, I have emphasized the military and organizational impediments to a successful Soviet blitzkrieg in Western Europe. If we assume for the moment that these can be overcome and that the Red Army can succeed in breaking through Western defenses, it is by no means clear that such a military victory would be conducive to the political objectives sought by Soviet leaders. Here again, an analogy to the Schlieffen Plan is enlightening.

Win, lose, or draw, the Schlieffen Plan threatened disaster for Germany. As it failed in practice to envelop and destroy the French army, it ushered in a long and costly war of attrition, which Germany lost because of the greater material resources of the Allies. If the Plan had succeeded, German armies would have encircled their French adversaries and occupied Paris. Schlieffen assumed that such a victory would prompt a French surrender or at least cessation of French military resistance. This was a highly questionable surmise. As in 1870, new French armies could have been raised and those in reserve brought into action. While these forces would have had little initial likelihood of scoring any major successes against the Germans, they would have tied down large numbers of German troops as Moltke's armies would, of necessity, have been drawn deeper and deeper into France. An active

---

36. In addition to NATO's FOFA strategy, the U.S. Army has adopted a new, more offensive doctrine, best known as "AirLand Battle" and later called "Army 21" and "Force 21." It is described in U.S. Army, *Operations: Field Manual 100-5* (Washington, D.C.: Department of the Army, 1982). Both concepts are discussed in detail in Boyd D. Sutton et al., "Deep Attack Concepts and the Defense of Central Europe," *Survival*, Vol. 26, No. 2 (March–April 1984), pp. 50–70. More information is available in a special edition of *Current News*, January 18, 1983, which brings together many of the technical expositions and commentary publicly available at that time. A favorable analysis of deep strike strategies is presented in ESECS, *Strengthening Conventional Deterrence in Europe.* Compelling critiques of the ESECS study and of deep strike strategies are made by Matthew A. Evangelista, "Offense or Defense: A Tale of Two Commissions," *World Policy Journal*, Vol. 1, No. 1 (Fall 1983), pp. 46–69; Hampson, "Groping for Technical Panaceas"; Williams and Wallace, "Emerging Technologies and European Security"; Joel S. Wit, "Deep Strike: NATO's New Defense Concept and Its Implications for Arms Control," *Arms Control Today*, Vol. 13, No. 10 (November 1983), pp. 1, 4–7, 9; and Jeffrey Record, "NATO's Forward Defense and Striking Deep," *Armed Forces Journal International*, November 1983, pp. 42–48.

resistance in the German rear would also have limited the effectiveness of future German offensives by interfering with a long and vulnerable line of supply. Protection of their exposed rear would have required growing numbers of occupation troops.

In 1870, post-Sedan French resistance was ineffective because of poor leadership and a myriad of political divisions within Paris and between Paris and the countryside. Even so, continued resistance threatened to deny Prussia the fruits of military victory because it led to the overthrow of the monarchy and the creation of a tenuous Republic. None of the leaders of the new Republic felt politically secure enough at first to surrender, let alone to grant the kinds of territorial and other concessions that a peace treaty would have entailed. Continued warfare also raised the enticing prospect of the intervention of other important European powers. The French will to resist collapsed before this materialized. Even so, the real lesson of 1870 was not the potency of modern armies but rather the difficulty in an age of nationalism of using armies in Europe to achieve far-reaching political goals.[37]

In contrast to 1870, the French in 1914 were politically united—to the extent that unity is ever possible in France. This sense of common national purpose could have provided the foundation for continuing resistance and the obvious sacrifices that this would have entailed. French resistance to Germany could have assumed a character and scale similar to that of Spanish resistance to France a century earlier. Unlike 1870, the French would not have been fighting alone. Britain and Russia among the great powers were their allies. Their involvement in the war would have provided the French with a strong incentive to continue fighting, as it had the Spanish in their struggle against revolutionary France.

Anglo–French forces might not have defeated Germany in the end, as victory would have been made that much more difficult by the assumed German occupation of much of France. Continuing French willingness to fight would, nevertheless, have denied Germany the expected political rewards of its initial military triumph. It would also have forced Germany to wage a two-front war, the very prospect the Schlieffen Plan was designed to forestall. As both sides would have continued to raise new armies, the situation might have come to resemble the war of attrition that actually

---

37. For sources, see Lonsdale Augustus Hale, The "People's War" in France (London: H. Rees, 1904); Michael Howard, The Franco–Prussian War (New York: Methuen, 1961), pp. 224–256, 371–456; Otto Pflanze, Bismarck and the Development of Germany: The Period of Unification (Princeton: Princeton University Press, 1963), pp. 458–479.

occurred—with the major difference that Germany would have been in a stronger position because of its control of more French territory including, presumably, Paris and the Channel ports. Victory, assuming the Germans finally triumphed over their adversaries, might have proved just as pyrrhic as it did for the Allies in 1918.

Soviet offensive plans, whether successful or not, also seem to court disaster, albeit for somewhat different reasons. If the Red Army broke through NATO defenses and threatened to trap the bulk of NATO's forces forward of the Rhine, the Alliance would be hard pressed to use tactical nuclear weapons. Any nuclearization of the conflict, regardless of who initiated it, would almost certainly provoke reprisals and could easily and rapidly escalate to the strategic level. Even a limited nuclear war in Europe, assuming for the moment that such a conflict is politically possible, would be incredibly costly to both sides regardless of who, if anyone, emerged the victor. It would also be certain to destroy much of the population and economic assets of Central and Western Europe, certainly an important prize of any war.

Conventional military success therefore carries with it an acute risk of nuclear destruction. The only way the Soviets could secure a meaningful victory would be for NATO to accept defeat and not to resort to nuclear weapons. This outcome is not inconceivable; as we have observed, much of the recent literature stresses the Soviet intention to wage a conventional offensive with this end in mind. Numerous Western authorities also question whether NATO would initiate the use of nuclear weapons to stave off defeat.[38] A purely conventional war is nevertheless certainly not a circumstance

38. On Soviet strategy, see references 3 and 4. Doubts that NATO would initiate first use of nuclear weapons have been expressed by such diverse American political figures as Henry A. Kissinger, "The Future of NATO," in Kenneth A. Myers, ed., *NATO: The Next Thirty Years* (Boulder, Colo.: Westview, 1980), p. 7; McGeorge Bundy, George F. Kennan, Robert S. McNamara, and Gerard Smith, "Nuclear Weapons and the Atlantic Alliance," *Foreign Affairs*, Vol. 60, No. 4 (Spring 1982), pp. 753–768; George W. Ball, "The Cosmic Bluff," *The New York Review of Books*, July 21, 1983, pp. 37–40; and Paul C. Warnke, "The Illusion of NATO's Nuclear Defense," in Andrew J. Pierre, ed., *Nuclear Weapons in Europe* (New York: Council on Foreign Relations, 1984), pp. 75–97. The current first use strategy also lacks support among Western European publics. For data and discussion, see: Leo P. Crespi, "West European Perceptions of the U.S.," Paper presented at the annual meeting of the International Society of Political Psychology, June 4, 1982; Bruce Russett and Donald R. DeLuca, "Theater Nuclear Forces: Public Opinion in Western Europe," *Political Science Quarterly*, Vol. 98, No. 2 (Summer 1983), pp. 179–196; David Capitanchik, "Public Opinion and Nuclear Weapons in Europe," *Arms Control*, Vol. 4, No. 2 (September 1983), pp. 111–133; Gert Krell, Thomas Risse-Kappen, and Hans-Joachim Schmidt, "The No-First-Use Question in West Germany," in John D. Steinbruner and Leon V. Sigal, eds., *Alliance Security: NATO and the No-First-Use Question* (Washington, D.C.: Brookings Institution, 1983), pp. 147–172. Petersen and Hines, "The Conventional Offensive in Soviet Theater Strategy," pp. 701–702, cite Soviet sources that predict a declining probability of NATO initiating the use of nuclear weapons in combat.

that the Soviets can count upon. NATO might resort to nuclear weapons in the aftermath of a Soviet breakthrough despite prewar expectations to the contrary. Even if it did not, a Soviet effort to keep the war conventional would require Moscow to forgo all the expected advantages of preemption in a situation in which NATO would certainly seriously consider going nuclear. Soviet doctrine and military logic make it very unlikely that Soviet forces would exercise restraint in such circumstances. NATO's dispersal of the Pershing II missiles in Germany in order to protect them from attack could easily be misinterpreted by the Soviets as a prelude to preemption and trigger their own nuclear attack.[39]

The other possible outcome of a Warsaw Pact offensive is failure, defined as an offensive that falls short of its objective of defeating NATO's armies or breaking the alliance's will to fight. This would also be a highly unpalatable outcome from Moscow's perspective. Soviet land, sea, and air forces are geared for the short offensive. Their doctrine, training, equipment, and logistics are not in any way suitable for a war of long duration nor for one in which they would have to go over to the defensive. Soviet industry would also find it difficult to compete with the West in a war of attrition.[40] A stalled offensive, moreover, would create serious political problems for the Soviet Union in Eastern Europe.

Even in the best of times, Warsaw Pact reliability must be considered questionable. It is unclear which, if any, of the Pact countries could be persuaded to participate in an invasion of Western Europe. The available evidence indicates that this task would be entrusted almost entirely to the Red Army, while the ground forces of the Pact allies were relegated to air defense, logistical support, and other behind-the-lines responsibilities. Large numbers of Soviet troops would also have to be left in these countries to protect their lines of communication and to ensure the continued loyalty of indigenous armies and peoples. Poland, the most likely place for such op-

---

39. Meyer, *Soviet Theatre Nuclear Forces*, Part I, pp. 27–28, writes "that most Soviet military writers explicitly link the decision to employ TNF to an assessment of the likelihood of imminent use of nuclear weapons by the enemy." Barry R. Posen, "Inadvertent Nuclear War? Escalation and NATO's Northern Flank," *International Security*, Vol. 7, No. 2 (Fall 1982), pp. 28–54, argues that even in the absence of a NATO decision to go nuclear, the battle in Europe would threaten Soviet command and control centers and degrade strategic air defenses. The belief that NATO might use the resulting confusion to launch an attack against Soviet strategic assets could provoke almost irresistible pressures for preemption by Moscow. Petersen and Hines, "The Conventional Offensive in Soviet Theater Strategy," pp. 730–731, argue that the Soviets are not at all sanguine about their ability to prevent NATO use.

40. It is interesting to observe that many in the West also fear a long war. A case in point is William W. Kaufmann, "Nonnuclear Deterrence," in Steinbruner and Sigal, eds., *Alliance Security*, pp. 43–90, who worries about the relative ability of NATO to sustain a long war.

position to arise, is also astride the most essential rail and communication links from the Soviet Union to East Germany and beyond that to the battle-front. Any Soviet setback, and worse still, a stalemated conventional war, could be expected to encourage behind-the-lines resistance in Poland, supported perhaps by some elements of the Polish army. Resistance could spread to neighboring countries and constitute an intolerable strain upon already overburdened Soviet forces.[41]

In retrospect, it is quite apparent that Germany in 1914 would have been better served by a defensive strategy.[42] Had the German army of Schlieffen and Moltke's day adopted such a strategy, it would have been in a enviable position. The First World War might never even have occurred as a Russian mobilization would not necessarily have triggered a German invasion of France as it did. Nor would German leaders have been as concerned as they were at the time about exploiting their closing "window of opportunity."[43] This concept only had meaning for an offensive strategy.

Had war nevertheless broken out in 1914, Germany would have been unassailable. In the West, Britain would surely have remained neutral in the absence of a German invasion of France via neutral Belgium.[44] The French

---

41. Warsaw Pact reliability is evaluated by Dale R. Herspring and Ivan Volgyes, "Political Reliability in the Eastern European Warsaw Pact Armies," *Armed Forces and Society*, Vol. 6, No. 2 (Winter 1980), pp. 286–291; A. Ross Johnson, Robert W. Dean, and Alexander Alexiev, "The Armies of the Warsaw Pact Northern Tier," *Survival*, Vol. 23, No. 4 (July-August 1981), pp. 174–182; Mackintosh, "Military Considerations in Soviet–East European Relations"; Richard Ned Lebow, "The Soviet Response to Poland and the Future of the Warsaw Pact," in Arlene Idol Broadhurst, ed., *The Future of European Alliance Systems: NATO and the Warsaw Pact* (Boulder, Colo.: Westview, 1982), pp. 185–236; David Holloway, "The Warsaw Pact in Transition"; and Daniel N. Nelson, *Soviet Allies: The Warsaw Pact and the Issue of Reliability* (Boulder, Colo.: Westview, 1984). All of these assessments are admittedly speculative but they all voice doubts about the reliability of the Eastern European armies in any war with NATO.
42. The elder Moltke in the 1880s had planned to fight a two-front war in just this manner. For details of his war plan see Ritter, *The Schlieffen Plan*, pp. 17–27; and Helmuth Karl Bernhard von Moltke, *Die deutschen Aufmarschpläne, 1871–1890*, ed. Ferdinand von Schmerfeld (Berlin: Mittler, 1929). This approach lost favor in the 1890s because Russian deployments in Poland became larger and less exposed. A 1912 war game also indicated that on M+45 the French could turn the flank of the Metz fortress without the Germans having won a decisive victory in the East. One German general, Sigismund von Schlichtung, did insist on the feasibility of Moltke's plan for a limited offensive in the East while holding the Metz–Strasbourg line in the West. On this subject, see Snyder, *The Ideology of the Offensive*, pp. 116–117; and Egon von Gayl, *General von Schlichtung und sein Lebenswerk* (Berlin: Stilke, 1913), p. 367.
43. For a discussion of this question, see Richard Ned Lebow, "Windows of Opportunity: Do States Jump Through Them?," *International Security*, Vol. 9, No. 1 (Summer 1984), pp. 147–186.
44. Both Paul M. Kennedy, *The Rise of the Anglo–German Antagonism, 1860–1914* (London: Allen & Unwin, 1980), pp. 425–465, and Zara Steiner, *Britain and the Origins of the First World War* (New York: St. Martin's, 1977), pp. 211, 228–237, make the case for British neutrality in absence of an invasion of Belgium.

army would have exhausted itself, as it began to do in 1914, in a series of unsuccessful and costly assaults against the strong, natural German defensive position in Alsace. In the East, where Germany initially took the defensive, the Russian offensive into Prussia was repulsed in disorder with grave losses. If, after a series of defensive victories of this kind, German leaders had declared their commitment to a peace on the basis of the *status quo ante bellum*, they probably would have prevailed. It seems unlikely that there would have been much support in France or Russia for continuing the war after a series of disheartening and crushing defeats. Nor could these two powers have resisted British and perhaps even American pressures to lay down their arms and accept an equitable peace. The Austro–Hungarian Empire would thus have been preserved, although the Russian Empire might have succumbed to revolution. German preeminence on the continent would not only have been maintained but immeasurably strengthened.

It is often argued that Germany pursued an offensive strategy in the First World War because it had far-reaching territorial aims.[45] Such aims would

---

45. This thesis is most forcefully argued by Fritz Fischer in two books: *Griff nach der Weltmacht* (Düsseldorf: Droste Verlag, 1961), antiseptic English translation: *Germany's Aims in the First World War* (New York: W.W. Norton, 1967); and *Krieg der Illusionen* (Düsseldorf: Droste Verlag, 1969), English translation: *War of Illusions* (New York: W.W. Norton, 1975). Fischer argues that German leaders pursued an aggressive policy in order to overcome the stresses generated by the unstable political, economic, and social structure of the Reich. This interpretation has been developed further by Arno Mayer, "Domestic Causes of the First World War," in Leonard Krieger and Fritz Stern, eds., *The Responsibility of Power* (Garden City, N.Y.: Doubleday, 1967), pp. 308–324; and Hans-Ulrich Wehler, *Der Deutsche Kaiserreich, 1871–1918* (Göttingen: Vandenhoeck and Ruprecht, 1977). Fischer's student, Imanuel Geiss, *German Foreign Policy, 1871–1914* (London: Routledge and Kegan Paul, 1976), argues that Sarajevo was "hardly more than the cue for the Reich to rush into action"; Volker R. Berghahn, *Germany and the Approach of War in 1914* (New York: St. Martin's Press, 1973), offers a more balanced approach. The Fischer thesis has been contested by other German historians, among them: Gerhard Ritter, *Staatskunst und Kriegshandwerk: Das Problem des Militarismus in Deutschland*, 2nd ed. rev. (Munich: R. Oldenbourg Verlag, 1965), Vol. 2; Wolfgang Mommsen, "Domestic Factors in German Foreign Policy Before 1914," *Journal of Central European History*, Vol. 6 (March 1973), pp. 11–43; Geoff Eley, *Reshaping the German Right: Radical Nationalism and Political Change After Bismarck* (New Haven: Yale University Press, 1980); and Richard Ned Lebow, *Between Peace and War: The Nature of International Crisis* (Baltimore: Johns Hopkins University Press, 1981), pp. 101–147. David E. Kaiser, "Germany and the Origins of the First World War," *Journal of Modern History*, Vol. 55, No. 3 (September 1983), pp. 442–474, makes a strong case that the literature from Fischer on has grossly exaggerated the extent to which German foreign policy before 1914 was designed to achieve domestic goals. Mommsen, "Domestic Factors in German Foreign Policy Before 1914"; Michael R. Gordon, "Domestic Conflict and the Origins of the First World War: The British and German Cases," *Journal of Modern History*, Vol. 46, No. 2 (June 1974), pp. 191–226; Eley, *Reshaping the German Right*; and Isabel V. Hull, *The Entourage of Kaiser Wilhelm II, 1888–1918* (New York: Cambridge University Press, 1982), all rightly criticize the tendency among German historians to explain events in terms of abstract social forces without explaining how these forces actually influenced policy in practice.

obviously have required the conquest of the coveted provinces during the course of the war. The literature on the controversy that surrounds the question of German aims in World War I is vast and entirely beyond the scope of this article to treat. Two observations are nevertheless in order. The first of these concerns the danger of inferring cause from effect.

The "September Program," a quasi-official list of war aims prepared by the German government in cooperation with German industry in the autumn of 1914, called for the annexation of Belgium along with control of northern France and much of Eastern Europe. Fritz Fischer and others cite it as compelling evidence of Germany's aggressive intentions. However, the September Program was prepared *after* German armies had occupied Belgium and struck deep into France. It was an expression of the euphoria that briefly reigned in Germany when it appeared that Moltke's army was on the threshold of victory. The extravagant war aims it gave expression to were at least as much a response to Germany's military strategy as they were a cause of it. Sensitive to this criticism, Fischer and his followers have in subsequent works documented prewar expressions of expansionist war aims and have interpreted them as responses to the many structural problems of the Reich.[46] But they still have failed to unearth convincing evidence to the effect that German policymakers actually pursued an aggressive foreign policy for these reasons. Recent research indicates that German political leaders in 1914 were probably much more influenced by strategic considerations, in particular by their fear that Russian military reforms and railway construction would soon make the Schlieffen Plan unworkable.[47]

It is worth considering that Germany's strategy in August 1914 may have been primarily an expression of a strong organizational bias on the part of the military in favor of the offensive. This bias derived in the first instance from the fact of Germany's successful invasion of France in 1870, which established a pattern of expectations within the military and society at large that the next war, also assumed to be against France, would end once again with the German army marching into Paris. Beyond this, the German army (together with every other major army in Europe) valued the offensive as an end in itself; it was seen to be an expression of all those values, among them courage, sacrifice, and honor, from which the officer corps of the day derived

46. This literature is discussed above.
47. Lebow, *Between Peace and War*, pp. 229–265; Kaiser, "Germany and the Origins of the First World War"; and Snyder, *The Ideology of the Offensive, passim.*

its very *raisons d'être*. Defense, by contrast, was scorned as unmanly.[48] For these reasons even a state like Belgium, whom nobody has accused of harboring any aggressive war aims, was drawn to the offensive.[49] We also know that German war planning as a whole took place in a political vacuum; it reflected a narrow military outlook upon the world and was demonstrably insensitive, if not blind, to the political implications of strategic decisions. All of this points to the conclusion that Germany's offensive strategy in 1914 was conceived of as a military solution to a military problem. Historians must accordingly be careful in drawing political inferences from it.

A Defensive Strategy for the Warsaw Pact

The Soviet offensive strategy in Europe may also have little to do with any Soviet plans for conquest.[50] It too may be largely an expression of organizational biases, some of which have already been discussed. To the extent that this is true, it is at least theoretically feasible to consider the alternative of a defensive strategy.

A defensive strategy would appear to offer many important advantages to the Soviet Union. By all accounts, the Red Army could defend Eastern Europe against any possible combination of opposing forces. It also seems inconceivable that NATO would ever be in a position to mount an offensive against the Warsaw Pact. Even assuming that the Alliance possessed the military capability to do so, the political opposition to such a venture would be enormous in Holland, Belgium, Norway, Denmark, and Italy not to mention among the British and German left. Political constraints seem more than sufficient to preclude a NATO offensive under almost any conceivable circumstances.

Let us nevertheless assume that NATO, or at least German and American elements of NATO, did attempt some kind of penetration of Pact territory, say in response to a revolution in East Germany. This is probably the scenario

---

48. Lebow, *Between Peace and War*, pp. 247–254; Snyder, *The Ideology of the Offensive*, pp. 107–154; and Van Evera, "Causes of War," review the evidence to this effect.
49. Stephen Van Evera, "The Cult of the Offensive and the Origins of the First World War," *International Security*, Vol. 9, No. 1 (Summer 1984), p. 61.
50. MccGwire, *Soviet Military Objectives in Wartime*, argues that, while Soviet leaders do not want war, they nevertheless see their occupation of Western Europe as an essential prerequisite to victory in any war with international capitalism. According to MccGwire, control and exploitation of European industrial resources would be necessary before the Soviets could successfully challenge the United States.

that Moscow fears the most. However, even this situation would favor the Soviets militarily and politically. For a start, the Western side would be fighting at a disadvantage because it had taken the offensive. Western forces would be in more exposed positions, further removed from their supplies and air defense network. A military setback would threaten NATO's survival, given the political controversy that any offensive would have sparked within and among its member countries. Within Eastern Europe, the Soviets would reap important political benefits. Nothing is quite so likely to generate support for the Russians in these countries as the fear, however remote in reality, of another German *drang nach osten*. Even the Poles, and almost certainly the Czechs, could be expected to put aside their differences with Moscow and rally round to the extent that they felt threatened in this way. A West German offensive capability would therefore act as a potent source of Warsaw Pact cohesion, the very last thing NATO wishes to encourage.[51]

A defensive strategy for the Soviet Union would place greater emphasis on infantry and artillery than on armor and attack aircraft and would allow the withdrawal of a number of tank armies from Central Europe. This could be accomplished through the Mutual and Balanced Force Reduction (MBFR) negotiations in Vienna, where NATO could probably be made to pay a high military price to secure the withdrawal of these forces. At the very least, Moscow could demand that NATO disband a significant number of its armored formations in return. The German army alone has over 6,000 tanks (including those on order)—more, Soviet military authorities are fond of pointing out, than they had when they attacked the Soviet Union in June 1941.[52] Such a mutual reduction in force levels would still leave the Soviets with more than enough forces to maintain their hegemony in Eastern Europe. It would also bring great political rewards.

The perception of a serious Soviet military threat to Western Europe provided the initial incentive for many countries of that region to band together with the United States in a military alliance. More recently, a decade-long

51. This point is made by Johnson, "Soviet–East European Military Relations"; Herspring and Volgyes, "Political Reliability in the Eastern European Warsaw Pact Armies"; and Holloway, "The Warsaw Pact in Transition," pp. 29–31.

52. West German Minister of Defense, *White Paper 1979: The Security of the Federal Republic of Germany and the Development of the Federal Armed Forces* (Bonn: Minister of Defence, 1979); and *The Military Balance, 1983–1984* (London: International Institute for Strategic Studies, 1983), p. 34. In June 1941, the *Wehrmacht* committed 2,434 tanks against 24,000 Red Army tanks. After three months of fighting, the Red Army had lost 17,500. Raymond L. Garthoff, *Perspectives on the Strategic Balance* (Washington, D.C.: Brookings Institution, 1983), pp. 27–28.

Warsaw Pact conventional force buildup and modernization acted as the catalyst for NATO to improve its own conventional military capability. The transformation of the Warsaw Pact into a much more tightly integrated and better-armed fighting force also contributed to the general deterioration in East–West relations. More to the point, it has helped advocates of greater defense spending sell their case to the American public. A defensive strategy by contrast, especially if coupled with an MBFR agreement, would take much of the wind out of the sails of the American, British, and German defense lobbies. It is also possible that the relaxation in tension that would follow upon even a partial mutual drawdown of forces would do even more to encourage centrifugal forces within the NATO alliance than any perception of Soviet threat. The resulting decline of NATO, in both a military and a political sense, would more than offset any loss of Soviet military muscle mandated by such an agreement.

A variety of objections might be raised to the argument that Soviet interests would be served better by a defensive strategy. A defensive strategy is likely to result in a longer war, something that is generally described as inimical to Soviet interests. David Holloway writes: "If the Soviet General Staff's evaluation of its allies coincides with Western assessments, Soviet military planners will be reinforced in their belief that a long war would be unpredictable and might lead to disaster and that consequently, if there is a war, the Soviet Union must try to achieve its goals as quickly and decisively as possible."[53]

Two reasons, one political, the other military, are usually given for why a long war is not in the Soviet interest. The political explanation revolves around the well-documented Soviet sensitivity to their political position in Eastern Europe. A defensive strategy is undeniably more likely to result in East Germany, or at least parts of it, becoming a battlefield in a European war. It is sometimes alleged that the very presence of Western troops on Warsaw Pact territory could act as a powerful catalyst for rebellion or resistance, as many Eastern Europeans might interpret it as the harbinger of their liberation. In this connection, it is important to distinguish among possible scenarios of Western intervention. A NATO attack in which Germany could be made to appear the aggressor would, as noted earlier, facilitate Pact cohesion. The reverse would be true in a situation where the Soviet bloc

---

53. Holloway, "The Warsaw Pact in Transition," pp. 30–31.

appeared to be crumbling and NATO intervened in support of an uprising in one of the Warsaw Pact countries. A rebellion might also be even more likely to occur in a long war because of the greater damage Eastern European countries would suffer in the course of the fighting. This could be expected to generate more intense hostility towards the Soviet Union and would also allow more time for resistance movements to organize.

Despite these indisputable drawbacks to a defensive orientation, it is by no means clear that an offensive strategy offers any better guarantee of the Soviet position in Eastern Europe. It certainly offers no immunity from attack as the northern tier countries, and the Soviet forces within them, would be subject to aerial bombardment and perhaps even nuclear assault. Most students of the Warsaw Pact argue that the event most likely to trigger active opposition to the Soviet Union in Eastern Europe is a Red Army setback or defeat. For reasons already discussed, the danger of this happening seems much greater in an offensive as opposed to a defensive campaign against NATO. Moreover, an uprising under such circumstances would pose a greater threat to Soviet forces because they would almost certainly be in a more precarious military situation if this happened and also more dependent upon a longer and more vulnerable line of supply.

All of these scenarios for both defensive and offensive strategies are admittedly speculative. However, they do highlight the extent to which the two strategies represent contrasting approaches to the problem of maintaining control over Eastern Europe. The offensive strategy constitutes a high payoff-high risk option. If the attack against NATO succeeds, Eastern Europe can be expected to remain quiescent; but there is also a significant probability that the attack would fail and that the Soviets would confront major uprisings behind their lines in its aftermath. The defensive strategy by contrast represents a kind of "minimax" solution to the problem. It seems more likely to invite behind-the-lines resistance but resistance on a less threatening scale because the prospect of a major military defeat is more remote. The trade-offs between these two approaches cannot be assessed with any degree of confidence beforehand. It may be that the offensive strategy is more appealing to Soviet policymakers because it does hold out the prospect of forestalling altogether any political or military problems in Eastern Europe, an outcome whose probability the Soviets may for this reason be prone to exaggerate. A defensive strategy may nevertheless be a more realistic choice, if less palatable psychologically.

The military reason for a short war pertains to the Soviet need to defeat NATO before reinforcements from the United States deprive the Warsaw Pact of its initial numerical advantage. Giving the Warsaw Pact a head start of seven days, the figure used by the U.S. Defense Department for planning purposes, it achieves its most favorable force ratios on or about the tenth day of mobilization, relatively early in the war, and later, between forty and sixty days, when forces brought forward from the western military districts of the Soviet Union enter the battle. There is disagreement in the West—and quite possibly in the Soviet Union as well—about the ratios that would actually obtain at these times and whether or not they are sufficient for Soviet purposes.[54] Some analysts have also questioned the relevance of force ratios to the outcome of any campaign.[55]

For our purposes here, these controversies about force ratios can be set aside. They are most pertinent to a scenario in which the Red Army is poised for a do-or-die offensive against the West. For defensive or limited offensive operations, the need for an overall numerical advantage is less critical. What counts are local tactical advantages, and these depend more on such factors as planning, intelligence, and surprise than they do upon theater-wide force ratios. Soviet forces would in any case retain some kind of numerical edge even after full NATO mobilization. William Mako estimates that this would be in the range of 1.2:1 to 1.8:1 after full mobilization, depending upon NATO's force posture at the time. NATO may actually have denied itself some of the forces, weapons, and logistics it would need to fight a longer war in order to develop greater capability to meet the perceived short-warning, short-war threat.[56]

Strategies are not only means of fighting wars; they can also serve important peacetime purposes. Soviet conventional strategy and force structure unquestionably advance Soviet political goals in Europe under peacetime

54. See footnote 25 for references.
55. Jack N. Merritt and Pierre M. Sprey, "Negative Marginal Returns in Weapons Acquisition," in Richard G. Head and Ervin J. Rokke, eds., American Defense Policy, 3rd ed. (Baltimore: Johns Hopkins University Press, 1973), pp. 486–497, among others, argue that doctrine, training, tactics, and morale are more important components of combat capability. Donn A. Starry, "A Tactical Evolution—FM 100-5," Military Review, Vol. 58, No. 8 (August 1978), pp. 2–11, reports that the U.S. Army found that force ratios had only the most marginal correlation with the outcomes of 1,000 tank battles.
56. Mako, U.S. Ground Forces, pp. 38–55, provides the most thoughtful comparison of force ratios over time under different mobilization scenarios. See also Kaufmann, "Nonnuclear Deterrence," pp. 43–90.

conditions. The Red Army's capability and visible presence in most Warsaw Pact countries contribute to the pacification of Eastern Europe and are also an important source of Soviet political influence in Western Europe.

Christopher Jones argues that an offensive strategy is an essential component of Soviet efforts to maintain their influence in Eastern Europe. According to Jones, Moscow wants to prevent other Warsaw Pact members from following the example of Yugoslavia, Albania, and Romania, all of which have adopted a territorial defense strategy in order to better resist Soviet intervention. The varying degrees of political independence these three countries possess rest to a large extent upon this capability. Integration of Warsaw Pact armies into an offensively oriented strategy is therefore necessary, he claims, if the Soviets are to retain the capability to intervene rapidly and successfully in any of these Eastern European countries.[57] As Jones portrays it, Soviet doctrine is an imperial political weapon, a fact which, if true, would hardly speak well for its quality as a military instrument.

If, as Jones asserts, the main objective of Pact strategy has been to prevent the emergence of national armies capable of defending national territory, it would not really have been necessary for the Soviet Union actually to develop and field all the forces and equipment required to invade Western Europe. Some half-way effort toward this end would have been quite sufficient. Even an avowedly defensive strategy would not be inconsistent with a Soviet capability for military intervention in Eastern Europe. Nor would a defensive strategy ineluctably result in more independent national armies; every military justification would remain to keep these forces tightly integrated with Soviet forces and under Soviet command. This integration, which is independent of an offensive or defensive strategic orientation, is the key to Soviet control.

A defensive strategy would, in any case, require some offensive preparations as limited offensive operations are an important component of any good defense. Defensive fortifications, assuming they were constructed, would face West not East and would almost certainly be restricted to the inter-German and Czech–German frontier provinces. Eastern European countries would remain just as vulnerable to Soviet intervention. If a defensive strategy led to a mutual reduction in armor negotiated through the MBFR forum, it could even facilitate Soviet intervention by reducing disproportion-

---

57. Jones, *Soviet Influence in Eastern Europe*; and Jones, "National Armies and National Sovereignty," in Holloway and Sharp, eds., *The Warsaw Pact: Alliance in Transition?*, pp. 87–110.

ately the armored forces of the Pact allies in comparison to those of the U.S.S.R.

The final objection to a defensive strategy concerns the political payoffs in Western Europe that the Soviet Union currently derives from an offensive strategy. Some American and European commentators contend that this offensive orientation encourages intra-NATO conflicts and prompts greater European accommodation to Soviet political wishes. Other analysts, rightly so in my opinion, have doubted the prospects of Finlandization. They have argued, moreover, that the minor indications of accommodation with the East that have taken place as a result of détente are a function of economic and political as opposed to security motives.[58] As we observed earlier, there are also important political advantages to be gained in Western Europe from a defensive strategy. These trade-offs would by no means be unfavorable to the Soviets, as they might intensify the centrifugal forces within NATO even more effectively than an offensive strategy.

Conclusions

The offensive military strategy of the Soviet Union and the military force requirements it engenders constitute a fundamental cause of the dangerous spiral of insecurity and arms competition in Europe.[59] Because an offensive strategy requires a Soviet military advantage, Soviet security requires Western insecurity. This precludes any kind of arrangement under which both sides could feel secure. Offensive strategies are not only dangerous but are often unnecessary. I have tried to demonstrate that this was true for Germany in 1914 and is for the Soviet Union today. The kind of offensive the Soviets plan for may also be increasingly unrealizable militarily.

Unfortunately, logic, no matter how compelling, is unlikely in and of itself to act as a catalyst for change. When policies achieve institutional expression, they assume new importance as justifications for the continued existence of

---

58. For a good discussion of "Finlandization, its several meanings in the context of broader European foreign policy, and an independent analysis of Finnish foreign policy, see Erling Bjøl, *Nordic Security*, Adelphi Paper No. 181 (London: International Institute for Strategic Studies, 1983), pp. 7–16.
59. For a theoretical discussion of the security dilemmas produced by offensive strategies, see Robert Jervis, "Cooperation Under the Security Dilemma," *World Politics*, Vol. 30 (January 1978), pp. 167–214; and Jack L. Snyder, "Perceptions of the Security Dilemma in 1914," in Robert Jervis, Richard Ned Lebow, and Janice Gross Stein, eds., *Psychology and Deterrence* (Baltimore: Johns Hopkins University Press, forthcoming).

the routines or even organizations they have spawned. Soviet offensive doctrine has given rise to a mighty military establishment, equipped with large numbers of tanks, artillery, mobile infantry, and a command and logistical setup that reflects this offensive orientation. Re-orientation to the defensive would require a reallocation of military resources, something which would bring about a shift in relative status within the armed services. This would be resisted fiercely by those who stood to lose out. As status, resources, and influence are disproportionately allocated at the moment to those responsible for offensive operations, the tank armies in particular, the Soviet military constitutes a powerful impediment to doctrinal change.

Military opposition does not of necessity preclude new doctrine and associated organizational reforms. Nikita Khrushchev implemented a major reorganization of the Soviet military establishment in the early 1960s. After rising to power with the support of the military, he turned on them, embraced the doctrine of "Peaceful Coexistence," and sought to reduce the overall level of military spending by relying more heavily on nuclear deterrence. He also created the Strategic Rocket Forces as a full-fledged military service and gave it responsibility for missiles carrying nuclear weapons despite the strenuous opposition of the air force and elements of the army. Khrushchev antagonized the traditional military power structure, and they were instrumental in bringing about his fall from power. However, Khrushchev's forced retirement is generally believed to have been brought about primarily as a result of other policy failures; as long as he retained power, he dominated the military and succeeded more or less in imposing his will on it.[60]

The key to Khrushchev's military reforms lay in his undisputed primacy in the Kremlin. In the absence of the authority that such ascendancy brings, major military reforms seem unthinkable in the face of military opposition. Even the theoretical possibility of a reorientation of military strategy towards the defensive must therefore probably await resolution of the current succession crisis and the emergence of a leader strong enough and secure enough to impose his will on the military.

What incentive would a Soviet leader have for forcing the military to adopt a more defensive orientation? In addition to the political and military arguments we have explored—and the military ones at least ought to become

---

60. Nikita S. Khrushchev, *Khrushchev Remembers*, trans. and ed. Strobe Talbott (Boston: Beacon Press, 1970), p. 540.

increasingly apparent to the Soviets themselves—there is the question of money. This was apparently a principal motivation for Khrushchev.[61] It might be an even greater incentive in the future when, according to most predictions, the Soviet economy will become hard pressed to satisfy both military and civilian needs. Adopting a defensive strategy as a means of justifying large cuts in the conventional military budget could conceivably become an attractive option for the civilian leadership.

Major institutional reform is sometimes possible only in the aftermath of a policy disaster. When disaster exposes the stupidity of entrenched policies or the incompetence of the policymakers responsible for implementing them, it provides an opening for opponents to exploit. But given the likely repercussions of a war in Europe, neither side may be granted the opportunity for *ex post facto* reform. It is therefore imperative for both superpowers to rethink their respective strategies *prior* to a fatal confrontation. The Soviets in particular would be well advised to reconsider their offensive strategy, which constitutes a serious threat to their own security.

In this connection, it is important to recognize the extent to which Western statements and policies influence Soviet perceptions of the threat they face and the forces that are necessary to confront it. AirLand Battle, FOFA, and other offensive strategies can only intensify Soviet perceptions of this threat for exactly the same reasons that the Soviet commitment to the offensive has done this in the West for forty years. Samuel Huntington's recent call for a retaliatory offensive, a NATO advance deep into East Germany, is a particularly egregious example of this kind of provocation.[62] It is also foolish, as there is no possibility, for both political and military reasons, that such an operation could be mounted.

There is little likelihood that any of the deep strike strategies will be implemented in the near future as they are dependent upon expensive and as yet underdeveloped technologies. A doctrinal commitment to these strategies will nevertheless be perceived by the Soviets as evidence of the West's

---

61. See Timothy J. Colton, *Commissars, Commanders, and Civilian Authority: The Structure of Soviet Military Politics* (Cambridge: Harvard University Press, 1979), pp. 200, 221–249; David Holloway, "The Role of the Military in Soviet Politics," in *The Soviet Union in Europe and the Near East: Her Capabilities and Intentions* (London: RUSI, 1970), pp. 7–15; and Matthew A. Evangelista, "Military Influence in Soviet Politics: Red Militarism or National Security Consensus," Paper presented at conference on political–military relations, Bellagio, Italy, July 1984.
62. Huntington, "Conventional Deterrence and Conventional Retaliation in Europe." For a critique of Huntington, see Keith A. Dunn and William O. Staudenmaier, eds., *Alternative Military Strategies for the Future* (Boulder, Colo.: Westview, forthcoming).

hostile intentions. An American or NATO commitment to a more offensive doctrine can therefore only have the effect of confirming Soviet opinion as to the rectitude of their own offensive strategy. This is just the reverse of what the West ought to be striving to do.

Perhaps the greatest irony is that many American military officers and defense intellectuals are attracted to offensive strategies at a time when an effort should be made to dissuade the Soviets from *their* commitment to the offensive. Surely, if there is anything more dangerous than one side committed to an offensive strategy, it would be both sides committed to it. Such a situation would dramatically intensify East–West tensions and make the contemporary security dilemma in Europe even more reminiscent of the situation that prevailed in the years before 1914. It would also constitute folly to the extreme, for, as we have seen, offensive strategies are not only destabilizing but quite contrary to the real interests of both superpowers.

Uncertainties for the Soviet War Planner

Benjamin S. Lambeth

$\mathbf{D}$uring the years when American strategic superiority overshadowed Soviet power, most Western observers tended to dismiss Soviet military doctrine as an anachronism. Its stress on such themes as preemption and victory, given the incapacity of Soviet forces to lend them credibility, was generally interpreted as little more than routine military incantation. The true measure of Soviet strength was felt to lie in such observables as the Soviet backdown during the Cuban Missile Crisis and Moscow's indisposition to challenge the United States to a race for strategic preeminence immediately thereafter. Under these circumstances, the bombast of Soviet pronouncements tended to resonate with hollow tones. Aside from occasional voices urging a more concerned view of Soviet ambitions, the consensus held that the Soviets had finally come to recognize their place in the nuclear relationship and could be counted on to conduct themselves with circumspection.

Since that time, the pendulum of U.S. assessments has swung from complacency to near-alarm as a result of the steady gains in Soviet force modernization over the past 15 years. Although Soviet doctrine itself has remained largely unchanged since the 1960s, the force posture has moved toward such close congruence with that doctrine that many commentators are now convinced that the Soviet leaders actually believe they are within reach of being able to fight and win a nuclear war. This image of Soviet robustness has fostered growing concern that the Soviet leaders may see a lucrative connection between their achievement of parity and their potential for assertive behavior at the expense of the West. A prominent journalist not normally given to brooding over the Soviet threat, for example, voiced concern well over a year before the invasion of Afghanistan that the Soviets might eventually "talk themselves into the most dangerous of all positions: the self-intoxicating position of believing that they can get away with anything."[1]

Benjamin S. Lambeth is a Senior Staff Member of the Rand Corporation, specializing in Soviet political and military affairs. He served previously in the Office of National Estimates and Office of Political Research, Central Intelligence Agency.

1. Joseph Kraft, "Russia's Winning Streak," The Washington Post, May 4, 1978.

International Security, Winter 1982/1983 (Vol. 7, No. 3) 0162-2889/83/030139-28 $02.50/1

In principle, such concern over Soviet military programs and conduct is both proper and long overdue. At the same time, we must take care not to overdramatize Soviet prowess. Not only would an exaggerated image of Soviet strength engender needless Western paralysis in the face of Soviet misbehavior, it would also undermine acceptance by the American public of the argument that feasible improvements in the U.S. defense posture will make a difference; without public support, essential improvements will be impossible. Furthermore, such an image would be contradicted by long-standing evidence of Soviet leadership conservatism and risk-aversion.

In isolation from political context, Soviet doctrinal rhetoric projects a stark image of singularity of purpose. On closer examination, however, the message transmitted by this rhetoric is not quite as threatening as it first sounds. For one thing, Soviet leaders view the world just as darkly as Americans do. Having never fought a nuclear war and thus lacking any experience at it, they appreciate that strategic planning operates in a realm of vast obscurity. Moreover, although Soviet forces and concepts reflect an undeniable combat orientation, their principal purpose remains deterrence rather than war. The fact that, through tradition and preference, the Soviets have sought security in hedges against failures of deterrence rather than in stability through "mutual assured destruction" in no way bespeaks any underlying disposition to put those hedges to the test.

Most assessments of Soviet capability emphasize elements that contribute to Soviet strength. By contrast, vulnerability analysis remains undeveloped in strategic research.[2] This essay aims to provide an exploratory venture in the latter direction. It seeks to illuminate some of the unknowns, uncertainties, and doubts that would be likely to temper Soviet incentives to use force in any confrontation laden with risks of nuclear war. Some of these concerns find occasional expression in Soviet military writings. Others are observable in characteristic modes of Soviet crisis behavior. Their net effect is to portray an adversary less assured of its combat virtuosity than a superficial review of its doctrine and forces might suggest. These sources of anxiety and doubt in Soviet planning are the focus of the following discussion. Its objective is to explore a variety of factors conducive to Soviet strategic nervousness that place the more strident refrains of Soviet doctrine in a less distressing light.

---

2. See, however, Major General Jasper A. Welch, Jr., USAF, "The Role of Vulnerability Analysis in Military Planning for Deterrence and Defense of Invasion Threats to NATO" (unpublished paper, June 1976).

The result should help reduce the image of Soviet strength projected by the raw evidence of Soviet force development down to the more manageable proportions it deserves.

Ambivalence in Soviet Doctrine and Style

The most obvious indication of uncertainty in Soviet force planning can be found in the important qualifications contained in Soviet military doctrine itself. In Soviet parlance, doctrine is commonly defined as a set of organized views on "the nature of contemporary wars that might be unleashed . . . against the Soviet Union and on the resultant demands, which flow from such views, for the preparation of the country and its armed forces for war."[3] Not surprisingly, Soviet writings display more confidence on the second score than the first. Where such matters as the basic nature of the security dilemma and the required concepts and hardware for dealing with it are concerned, the Soviets show little confusion. In their view, although the destructiveness of nuclear weaponry has made major war highly unlikely, it nonetheless remains possible because the opposing social systems have irreconcilable incompatibilities. This possibility must be duly accommodated in Soviet defense planning. A force capable of merely inflicting punitive retaliation following an enemy attack is considered insufficient because it is unreliable and could fail to compel enemy restraint in a crisis precisely when it was most needed. From the Soviet perspective, the only sensible foundation of national security is a force capable of decisively seizing the initiative at the brink of war and actually fighting toward specific political and military objectives. Such a posture is not only likely to offer the strongest guarantee of continued deterrence; it will also provide the military wherewithal that would be needed for coping responsibly should deterrence fail.

In contrast to these certitudes about the imperatives of weapons procurement, Soviet commentary on what a nuclear war might actually look like is highly imprecise. Soviet authorities manifest unresolved feelings about such crucial but imponderable questions as how such a war might be triggered in the first place, how long it might last, whether it would be containable at the conventional level, how rapidly it would escalate to theater nuclear operations, what dynamics the transition to intercontinental warfare would entail,

---

3. Lieutenant General I. Zavialov, "On Soviet Military Doctrine," *Krasnaia zvezda*, March 30, 1967.

and, most of all, what the endgame would look like in terms of American behavior and ultimate Soviet prospects for victory. Soviet military spokesmen have been consistently frustrated in their efforts to grapple with these issues since their discourse on strategic nuclear matters began in the 1950s.

In practical terms, all doctrine does for Soviet planners, aside from pre-scribing broad guidelines for force procurement, is to indicate the most sensible modes of combat in the best of all worlds. Because of its irresolution about the precise contours a war might assume and its appreciation that things could go badly despite the best efforts of the leadership to control events, doctrine scarcely offers a hard prediction of how the Soviets would actually respond, or much comfort in the way of "instant courage" for Soviet strategic decision-makers.

To suggest this, of course, is not to deny the importance of doctrine as a reflection of Soviet strategic logic or as a factor significantly affecting the way the Soviets go about force development and modernization. Nor, most em-phatically, is it to deprecate the threat to U.S. interests posed by recent Soviet force improvements or to "excuse" them on the ground that they somehow constitute a legitimate outgrowth of Soviet paranoia.[4] Nonetheless, we must be careful not to misread Soviet doctrine as a categorical predictor of Soviet behavior. The Soviet armed services can readily accept injunctions about the need for large weapon inventories with not only equanimity but enthusiasm, so long as they do not impose an intolerable drain on resources or provoke the United States into determined offsetting measures. Doctrinal insistence on preemption as the only key to Soviet survival, however, would probably

---

4. This point warrants elaboration. Some analysts have downplayed the significance of the Soviet buildup on the ground that it has been driven more by legitimate security concerns than by aggressive hegemonial ambitions. In the words of one such proponent, "the firmly rooted Russian–Soviet sense of insecurity . . . has very likely bred a natural inclination to overcompen-sate and overinsure on security matters." Because of this underlying motivation, he argues, the resultant Soviet quest for strategic advantage "should not be interpreted in a totally offensive threatening light" and "need not be destabilizing if [properly] understood." Dennis Ross, "Rethinking Soviet Strategic Policy: Inputs and Implications," *The Journal of Strategic Studies*, Vol. 1, No. 1 (May 1978), pp. 4–5. Pushed to the extreme, such formulas amount to apologetic pleas to "pity the poor Russians" because of their unfortunate historical experiences. This viewpoint may have logical attractions, but it ignores the severe consequences the fruits of perceived Soviet "insufficiency" can have for vital Western interests. Whether or not recent Soviet policy has had "aggressive" underpinnings, Moscow's insistence on forces capable of assuring absolute security for the Soviet Union necessarily implies an unacceptable condition of absolute insecurity for everybody else. It is one thing to *explain* Soviet behavior as a manifestation of security. It is something quite different to *condone* such behavior solely on the strength of the explanation. Whatever the motivations for continued Soviet force improvement, the capabilities for coercive diplomacy they permit can scarcely escape the concern of responsible Western planners.

find less ready acceptance in the crisis deliberations of political leaders ultimately responsible for decisions about war and peace. Those leaders would be disciplined by an appreciation of the severe opportunity costs of miscalculation and of the proclivities of best-laid plans to go astray.

The ambiguity of formal doctrine as a guide to Soviet action is matched by strong tendencies toward restraint and caution in Soviet political–military style. In his account of the Soviet political character written in the early 1950s, Nathan Leites advanced the proposition that, when all the returns are examined, "the Politburo's question for any major operation is whether it is required or impermissible . . . rather than whether it is tough or easy."[5] This proposition suggests a Soviet standard of behavior fundamentally unlike that familiar to most Westerners and touches the heart of the reason why the Soviets have failed to develop sophisticated "theories" of coercive diplomacy comparable to those prevalent in U.S. strategic discourse. Although the Soviets are masters of opportunism, they have avoided indiscriminate muscle-flexing. Instead, their tendency has been to talk tough as a matter of practice, yet to reserve actual intervention for cases where they have supreme interests at stake, a high probability of U.S. noninvolvement, and a comfortable prospect of success with moderate investment of military capital.[6]

Given this Soviet instinct to avoid meddling in areas where intervention could threaten to boomerang and to engage militarily only after weighing the costs of inaction against the possibility for success with an economy of force, it is hardly surprising that the Soviet leaders were so perplexed by the piecemeal and ultimately disastrous American involvement in Vietnam. Everything we know about the Soviet philosophy of intervention suggests that they saw the initial U.S. decision to escalate as a headlong leap into a quagmire and the ultimate U.S. acceptance of defeat as a testament to Americans' lack of "seriousness" about war, neither of which they would likely countenance in their own military conduct. In contrast to U.S. experience, the Soviets have generally regarded military power primarily as a static

5. Nathan Leites, *A Study of Bolshevism* (Glencoe, Ill.: The Free Press, 1953), p. 34.
6. A considerable body of literature on Soviet crisis comportment generally supports the notion that despite their frequent rhetorical excesses, Soviet political leaders have pursued risk-minimizing strategies more or less regardless of variations in the East–West military balance. See, in particular, Hannes Adomeit, *Soviet Risk-Taking and Crisis Behavior: From Confrontation to Coexistence*, Adelphi Paper, Number 101 (London: International Institute for Strategic Studies, 1973); and Jan F. Triska and David D. Finley, *Soviet Foreign Policy* (New York: Macmillan, 1968), pp. 310–349. See also Jack L. Snyder, *The Soviet Strategic Culture: Implications for Limited Nuclear Options*, R-2154-AF (Santa Monica, Calif.: The Rand Corporation, September 1977), pp. 13–15.

guarantor of deterrence on terms congenial to Soviet diplomatic interests, and only marginally as an instrument for underwriting adventures not deemed essential to the preservation of Soviet security.

What, then, of the Soviet decision to emplace ballistic missiles in Cuba in 1962? A critic of the thesis outlined above might argue that Khrushchev's gambit was a gesture totally out of keeping with the idea that Soviet conduct has been characteristically risk-averse. A reasonable reply would be that Khrushchev's initial calculations were probably based on an honest belief that he could get away with his move, given previous U.S. irresolution in Vienna and at the Bay of Pigs, and that the real demonstration of Soviet crisis behavior came only after the U.S. imposition of a naval blockade made it clear that he had grossly underestimated the intensity of the American response.

The Soviet concept of security has always featured a prominent element of expansionism. Yet Soviet leaders from Lenin onward have repeatedly shown sublime faith that time is on their side. As a consequence, they have been reluctant to "push" history with attempts to reap political gains on the cheap before the natural convergence of the right conditions. In the case of the Cuban crisis, Khrushchev, in all likelihood, genuinely felt he had tested the waters and found them safe. Once he realized that the American commitment to getting the missiles out was greater than his own interest in keeping them in, he immediately reverted to a strategy of prudent loss-cutting by withdrawing the offending weaponry in return for a face-saving U.S. guarantee not to invade the island.

In each phase, the initial deployment and the ultimate backdown alike, he acted with characteristic Soviet rationality, "pushing to the limit" (in Leites's formulation) where he perceived an opportunity to do so at low cost, yet yielding to U.S. resistance when he discovered, doubtless to his astonishment, that the game was not worth the gamble. In the bill of particulars brought against him by his successors, his cardinal sin was probably not so much his failure to stand firm in the face of American opposition (which would have been gravely foolhardy under the circumstances) as his colossal misjudgment of the American temper that caused the Soviet Union to suffer such humiliation. In the Soviet system, no less than in the criminal underworld and other communities based on unmoderated power, mistakes of that magnitude are rarely forgiven, not so much for reasons of callous insensitivity but precisely because of the threat they pose to the institutions they represent.

Sources of Soviet Strategic Anxiety and Doubt

Probably to its credit, the Soviet Union has never developed refined theories about the use of strategic power in coercive diplomacy comparable to such Western notions as "compellence," graduated escalation, and selective nuclear options. The Soviets regard such concepts as dangerous usurpations of the proper role of military power—namely, the prompt securing of objectives deemed essential to the national interest but unattainable through less extreme measures. As Soviet reluctance to commit forces beyond the immediate periphery of Soviet hegemony attests, these sorts of objectives have, at least until now, remained extremely limited. These narrow circumstances (the Hungarian and Czechoslovak invasions of 1956 and 1968, the Sino–Soviet border clashes of 1969, and the ongoing Afghanistan operation) have entailed what the Soviet leadership considers intolerable pressures on its own doorstep. They have also been distinguished by a very low probability of U.S. military opposition.

The caution that has tended to deter Soviet leaders from indulging in adventures of dubious necessity or prospect for success would probably assert itself forcefully in a future confrontation where direct superpower combat loomed as a serious possibility. It would also be reinforced by several important operational concerns regarding the many ways Soviet plans could become upset due to weaknesses in such areas as combat readiness, command and control, alliance solidarity, and military morale. Such sources of hesitancy would be especially likely to counsel Soviet restraint in crises where Soviet leaders were convinced that continued inaction or carefully measured exploratory probing, whatever their long-term political costs, would promise less risk than would proceeding with dramatic initiatives that could backfire in unexpected ways. Although it would be imprudent to overstate this point, it seems reasonable to suggest that these elements of anxiety and uncertainty could exert a powerful self-deterrence in future crises short of one where Soviet decision-makers were so convinced that major war was coming that *some* decisive preemptive move was required.

The Soviets are uniquely prone to approach–avoidance conflicts in crisis decision-making because of divergent strains in their political culture. On the one hand, their offensive military orientation, their belief in the commanding importance of initiatives, and their compulsion to check undesirable trains of events before they become unmanageable incline them toward rejecting passivity and treating forceful preemption as the supreme measure of leadership rectitude. On the other hand, their faith in the inevitability of socialism, their abhorrence of momentary acts that might threaten to undo their existing gains, their tendency to draw sharp distinctions between the desirable and the necessary, and their associated confidence that time is on their side impose a powerful braking influence on their willingness to seek radical solutions when events might be safely left to continue for another day.

These conflicting pressures have saddled the Soviet leadership with dilemmas probably far more deeply felt than comparable influences on the crisis decision-making of Western political leaders. Even in Hungary and Czechoslovakia, where perceived necessity and the local balance of forces strongly supported positive action and offered confident prospects for Soviet success, the decision to intervene was preceded by excruciating rumination over potential risks and costs, in which arguments for delaying were strong and the final choice was anything but foreordained.[7] In light of that experience, similar indecision could be expected to weigh on Soviet policymakers with vastly greater effect in any challenge where the Soviet Union stood at the brink of full-scale combat involvement with U.S. forces. In such a case, the preeminent Soviet concern would probably not be over the threat of a "credible first strike," or any of the other niceties of American strategic parlance, so much as over the more undifferentiated specter of "just plain war," to use Thomas Schelling's apt formulation.[8] Given this prospect, Soviet planning, at least initially, would probably emphasize identifying and evaluating those uncertainties about Soviet military performance and the possible interplay of uncontrollable variables that would threaten the success of *any* Soviet option, rather than detailed force capabilities and exchange ratios in specific scenarios. At this level of policy deliberation, with the basic question of war or peace yet undecided, the weight of evidence from past Soviet behavior suggests that consideration of prospective gains would be overshadowed by contemplation of the various things that could go awry.

---

7. In the case of Hungary, Khrushchev recounted that, until the final decision to invade was consolidated within the Party Presidium, "I don't know how many times we changed our minds back and forth." *Khrushchev Remembers*, ed. and trans. Strobe Talbott (Boston: Little, Brown, 1971), p. 148. As for Czechoslovakia, Brezhnev related after the event that one major concern among diverse Politburo members was that "this step would threaten the authority of the Soviet Union in the eyes of the people of the world." Jiri Valenta, *Soviet Intervention in Czechoslovakia, 1968: Anatomy of a Decision* (Baltimore: Johns Hopkins University Press, 1979), p. 142.
8. Thomas C. Schelling, *Arms and Influence* (New Haven: Yale University Press, 1966), pp. 98–99.

This is not to say that in all crises involving the possibility of war with the United States, the Soviets would invariably find themselves mired in immobility. Much would depend on the situation, its proximity to Soviet lines of communication, its relevance to Soviet security interests, and the balance between political stakes and military risks. Much would also hinge on authoritative Soviet assessments of U.S. seriousness and capacity for concerted action. The Chinese expression for "crisis"—a compound of the words "danger" and "opportunity" (*wei-chi*)—neatly captures the conundrum that would beset Soviet leaders in contemplating any direct use of military force against the United States. Obviously they would feel conflicting pressures toward boldness and caution. Their choice would probably hinge as much on what they thought they could get away with as on any detailed assessment of comparative strategic strengths.

Nonetheless, in any Soviet–American confrontation where major escalation appeared possible, Soviet deliberations would be strongly influenced by numerous concerns generally muted in peacetime. The following remarks will survey some of the uncertainties that could generate worry in the minds of Soviet decision-makers if they embarked on a potentially dangerous course, yet still commanded some initiative and could make the outcome go either way. These should be read neither as confident forecasts of Soviet caution in all circumstances nor as an exhaustive account of every conceivable source of concern that might counsel Soviet restraint. Rather, they should be regarded as an abbreviated checklist of fears that could arise in any circumstance where Soviet military forces might actually be required to fight. Although these anxieties scarcely vitiate the importance of doctrinal verities or diminish the seriousness with which those articles should be viewed by Western planners, they suggest that Soviet elites are far less confident than an isolated reading of their doctrinal professions might indicate.

OPERATIONAL CAPABILITIES OF SOVIET FORCES

Apart from uncertainty about such poorly understood aspects of weapons phenomenology as electromagnetic pulse and fratricide and other technical imponderables of force performance that afflict all nuclear states, the Soviet leadership probably senses a whole range of deficiencies in its arsenal that are unobservable to the West yet figure significantly in Soviet planning. Just to cite one example, we assume that Soviet authorities command fairly accurate knowledge of their ICBM force's reliability as a result of their extensive experience with operational training launches.[9] We are necessarily less certain about the extent of confidence that knowledge inspires, but it may be less than comforting to decision-makers who are obliged to worry about worst cases and would have to shoulder the responsibility for their mistakes. Various sources indicate that ostensibly "no-notice" Soviet operational readiness inspections are carefully stage-managed so that all participants earn high marks.[10] If this practice is widespread throughout the Soviet military, it provides Soviet planners with not only a good feel for what their forces can do under controlled peacetime conditions, but also with grounds for legitimate concern about the degradations they might encounter in a combat situation marked by confusion and a requirement for improvising under duress. If global war appeared a foregone conclusion, such uneasiness might urge prompt preemption while adequate time remained to bring Soviet forces to full readiness under the cover of secrecy. In most situations, however, it would more likely engender profound distress reminiscent of Khrushchev's legendary "smell of burning in the air" at the height of the Cuban crisis.[11] Professional soldiers, if not their civilian superiors, are the least confident of their preparedness the closer they edge toward war. Such foreboding would probably afflict Soviet commanders as intensely as it would comparable military elites the world over.

Similar sorts of brooding, easily sublimated in peacetime yet difficult to suppress in crises, might also surface in connection with Soviet nonnuclear forces. Despite their extensive investments in air defense, we know from the testimony of Lieutenant Victor Belenko that the Soviets have little confidence in the ability of their front-line interceptors to deal with the U.S. low-altitude bomber threat.[12] For many force categories, Soviet planners may not have developed certain theoretically feasible employment options occasionally attributed to them in worst-case Western threat assessments, such as the use

---

9. Unlike the United States, the Soviet Union routinely conducts ICBM tests and training firings from operational silos. As of early 1974, it had carried out approximately one hundred such launches. See Secretary of Defense James Schlesinger, *Annual Defense Department Report, FY 1975* (Washington, D.C.: U.S. Government Printing Office, March 4, 1976), p. 56.
10. See Herbert Goldhamer, *The Soviet Soldier: Soviet Military Management at the Troop Level* (New York: Crane, Russak, 1975), pp. 116–124.
11. "Khrushchev's Report on the International Situation," *Current Digest of the Soviet Press,* Vol. 14, No. 51 (January 16, 1963), p. 7.
12. John Barron, *MiG Pilot* (New York: McGraw–Hill, 1980), p. 72.

of bombers on one-way missions against the United States. In his memoirs, Khrushchev graphically recounted the derision that met proposals to have the BISON recover in Mexico from bombing missions against U.S. targets. This casts at least some suspicion on more recent Western intimations that the BACKFIRE might be slated for similar one-way missions terminating in Cuba.[13]

These and other indicators are, of course, merely straws in the wind and scarcely constitute conclusive evidence of Soviet shortcomings. All the same, they remind us that Soviet decision-makers know themselves far better than the Americans know them and are likely to be far more sensitive to their operational inadequacies than they are frequently given credit for. How these perceived inadequacies would affect Soviet crisis behavior would depend on Soviet judgments about the nature of the strategic imperatives. They could never be completely ignored and might constitute major factors advising restraint if the necessity for decisive military action had not been clearly established in the minds of the Soviet leaders.

OPERATIONAL CAPABILITIES OF U.S. FORCES
Just as U.S. policymakers tend to exaggerate Soviet strengths, so may the Soviets exaggerate the Americans'. Henry Kissinger has likened both super-powers to "heavily armed blind men feeling their way around a room, each believing himself in mortal peril from the other whom he assumes to have perfect vision."[14] This characterization not only reflects the Americans' occasional urge to overstate unpleasant turns of Soviet behavior as components of a coherent "master plan"; it also reflects both countries' tendency to view their opponent's strategic developments in the gloomiest light while depreciating their own considerable advantages in the process. The Soviets have deep admiration for American technological prowess. This contributes to a Soviet perspective on U.S. weaponry at substantial odds with their general contempt for U.S. strategic doctrine and concepts. As a consequence, Soviet

---

13. On the matter of the BISON, Khrushchev noted: "This plane failed to satisfy our requirements. It could reach the United States, but it couldn't come back. Myasischev [the designer] said the Mya-4 could bomb the United States and then land in Mexico. We replied to that idea with a joke: 'What do you think Mexico is—our mother in law? You think we can simply go calling anytime we want? The Mexicans would never let us have the plane back.'" *Khrushchev Remembers: The Last Testament* (Boston: Little, Brown, 1974), p. 39.
14. Henry A. Kissinger, *White House Years* (Boston: Little, Brown, 1979), p. 552.

threat assessments could well be colored by an unconscious propensity to attribute larger-than-life performance capabilities to American military forces.

At first glance, such a suggestion runs counter to the popular notion that, because of the vast dissimilarities between American and Soviet societies, the Soviets enjoy the twin advantages of secrecy to cloak their own operational deficiencies from Western intelligence purview and freedom to scrutinize every detail of U.S. strategic capabilities like an open book. Yet Moscow's image of American power resulting from this so-called "information asymmetry" may not be nearly so confidence-inspiring as this stark depiction would have us believe. Much has been made about the amount of damaging military data Americans freely provide the Soviets through such open sources as annual Posture Statements, Congressional testimony, technical journals, and press reports. As a result of this hemorrhage of information, so the argument goes, it would take an obtuse Soviet observer indeed not to be able to piece together a mosaic of U.S. programs, capabilities, and plans with a degree of exactitude that Western analysts are only rarely capable of replicating for the Soviet Union, even with the most rigorous and sophisticated intelligence collection techniques.

Although the difficulty of protecting military information in a democratic society is a proper concern of U.S. defense planners and undoubtedly exacts some toll in the effectiveness of the American military posture, there are plausible grounds for wondering whether it uniformly provides advantages to those Soviet officials responsible for keeping track of American force developments. The Soviet military bureaucracy is highly stratified and compartmentalized, and unimpeded data flow is anything but routine. Given the pervasiveness of an acute "left hand knoweth not" syndrome through the Soviet defense community, one can fairly ask how capable its evaluation network is to filter information about U.S. capabilities and draw appropriate connections. The Soviet intelligence subculture has long been known to harbor profound distrust of open-source material on the grounds that it could constitute purposely distorted "disinformation." Instead, it has tended to rely on hard-copy data secured through classic espionage channels as the only authoritative sources of insight into enemy capabilities and plans. Coupled with Moscow's traditional stress on uprooting enemy "secrets" as the ultimate proof of intelligence virtuosity and the KGB's reputed disdain for analysis (which a former Soviet officer once dismissed as "a job for lieutenants and women"), this trait suggests that the Soviet Union may be less effective in assimilating evidence about U.S. strengths and weaknesses than the darker fears of some Americans might suggest.[15]

If there is any truth to this notion, high-level Soviet defense officials may regard U.S. capabilities as being far less imperfect than Americans are frequently inclined to view them. To note only one possibility, the Soviets are probably less impressed by the much-heralded "Minuteman vulnerability problem" than most U.S. defense analysts, since they apparently retain considerable faith in hardened silos to protect their own ICBMs and show little concern—at least yet—about the need for new basing modes to accommodate the impending hard-target capabilities of MX and Trident. If Soviet decision-makers derive any comfort at all from this impending U.S. liability, it probably stems more from U.S. expressions of anxiety over it than from any independent technical evaluations of their own counterforce capabilities. Soviets, like Americans, tend to be fixated by worst-case projection in their contingency planning. It is thus probable that their own uncertainties about how successful a Soviet disarming attack might be, rather than vicarious reassurance from U.S. nervousness about Minuteman survivability, would play the commanding role in any Soviet consideration of the first-strike option in a crisis.

The effect of this Soviet approach to threat assessment is far from congenial to U.S. interests as far as peacetime force planning is concerned, because it probably accelerates rather than moderates Soviet force improvement activities. Yet during a grave crisis in which the Soviet Union's livelihood lay at risk, it could induce caution rather than boldness in military initiatives that could backfire catastrophically in the event of miscalculation. The broad chasm that separates perceptions of Soviet capability on the part of professional intelligence specialists from the more basic images held by senior officials is a characteristic feature of American defense politics.[16] In the Soviet Union, such disparity is probably even more pronounced because of the rigid

---

15. According to one authoritative account, although "the KGB strives to verify the authenticity of stolen documents and the accuracy of agent reports," it completely lacks "any independent body of professional analysts who attempt to distill the underlying meaning and import from intelligence." John Barron, *KGB: The Secret Work of Soviet Secret Agents* (New York: Reader's Digest Press, 1974), pp. 76–77.

16. As Henry Kissinger has observed, "One of the key problems of contemporary national security policy is the ever-widening gap that has opened up between the sophistication of technical studies and the capacity of an already overworked leadership group to absorb their intricacy." Quoted in E.S. Quade and W.I. Boucher, eds., *Systems Analysis and Policymaking: Applications in Defense* (New York: American Elsevier Publishing Company, 1968), p. v.

compartmentalization and hierarchical structure of the Soviet policy apparatus. Accordingly, those party authorities who would be held responsible for gross errors of judgment in a crisis would probably be more disposed to give U.S. capabilities the benefit of the doubt than would intelligence experts commanding a more finely grained appreciation of deficiencies in the U.S. military posture.

AMERICAN RATIONALITY UNDER PRESSURE

One of the more ironic sources of Soviet hesitation in past times of East–West tension has been Moscow's bewilderment at the often cryptic character of American conduct. As a result of their ideological convictions and the abiding constancy of purpose they have inspired, Soviet leaders have come to follow a definite logic in their own political behavior over the years and to acquire a clear set of derivative expectations about the forms of comportment their "capitalist" adversaries ought to observe. Just as conservative Western analysts have been tempted to interpret the most unconnected Soviet moves as parts of a coherent "grand design," so the Soviets have had their own compulsions to perceive all facets of U.S. foreign behavior as being unswervingly inimical to Soviet security interests.

It has long been a familiar cliché that the Soviets would prefer to deal with hardcore Wall Street bankers than romantic liberals in their relations with the United States, because the former are at least conditioned to act in the predictable fashion Soviet *apparatchiks* are schooled to expect. Liberals, by contrast, have frequently adopted policies out of phase with Soviet expectations and thus highly perplexing in their underlying motivations. The numerous instances of inconsistency and vacillation in U.S. behavior during the Carter years directly occasioned the undoubtedly genuine Soviet expressions of frustration over the so-called "zigs and zags" of U.S. policy and probably fostered great uncertainty about how the United States might respond to future Soviet policy initiatives. Despite the embarrassment of riches nominally available to Soviet intelligence analysts, the Soviet estimator responsible for forecasting future U.S. behavior probably has no easier lot than his American counterpart.

Although Soviet doctrinal writings have long underscored the tactical virtues of preemption at the edge of war, their associated image of "victory" (both theater and intercontinental) has hinged on the tacit assumption that the United States would be unable or unwilling to muster an effective retaliation. If the Soviets have been reassured in their defense planning by the notion that nothing succeeds like success, they cannot have escaped the collateral axiom that nothing fails like failure. Their doctrinal refrain that nuclear weapons now permit the achievement of fundamental strategic aims at the very outset of an unrestricted war ultimately entails making a virtue of necessity, for it almost *requires* those objectives to be attained as a precondition of victory. The rational response for the United States in the wake of a massive Soviet counterforce attack would almost have to be a rejection of counter-city retaliation in favor of using surviving forces to try to bargain for a reasonably acceptable postwar settlement from a position of severe military disadvantage. Yet it is far from clear that a U.S. leadership driven by confusion, desperation, and inflamed passion for revenge would choose (or be able) to exercise such supremely disciplined self-control.

In the unlikely case that U.S. unpredictability caused the Soviets to be concerned that the United States might initiate the large-scale use of nuclear weapons, the Soviet urge to preempt would probably overwhelm any arguments for hesitancy. In most circumstances, however, the Soviets would have little cause to fear such a U.S. move (at least at the intercontinental-war level). Any Soviet decision to preempt would accordingly have to account for the possibility that the United States might respond by executing the countervalue portion of the Single Integrated Operational Plan (SIOP)—or worse yet, launch the entire component of its nonreserve forces under assessment of incoming attack—with all the consequences such a possibility would imply for Soviet prospects for success. Even though such a U.S. response under conditions of adversity might leave the Soviet Union with a favorable outcome in purely military terms, Soviet decision-makers would have to inquire searchingly whether such an outcome would constitute any practical "victory" worth having, given the far greater rewards that would accrue from not triggering such devastation in the first place.

At the height of the Vietnam War, President Nixon remarked that the United States had a vested interest in cultivating an image of unpredictability.[17] Carried to extremes, such an attitude could risk provoking just the sort of Soviet impulsiveness it was intended to prevent. Within limits, however,

17. After his departure from office, the former president expanded this point into a general principle of strategic diplomacy: "International relations are a lot like poker—stud poker with a hole card. . . . Our only covered card is the will, nerve, and unpredictability of the President—his ability to make the enemy think twice about raising the ante. . . . If the adversary feels that you are unpredictable, even rash, he will be deterred from pressing you too far. . . . We should not make statements that we will never launch a preemptive strike. Whether or not we would ever exercise that option, we should always leave open the possibility that in extreme circumstances we might." Richard M. Nixon, *The Real War* (New York: Warner Books, 1980), pp. 253–256.

U.S. efforts to exploit the "rationality of irrationality" principle by stressing the inevitability of retaliation and alluding periodically to launch-on-warning as a last-ditch nuclear option could reinforce deterrence, so long as they were not substituted for continued investments in U.S. strategic capability. Even though the most ardent American enthusiasts of "assured destruction" might doubt whether such a threat would actually be consummated, there is enough evidence that things could go the other way to make Soviet first-strike proponents unsure about testing their luck. Soviet doctrine may emphasize such principles as surprise, momentum, and victory, but it does not commit Soviet leaders to modes of action that would go against common sense. Insofar as the Soviets can not *count* on U.S. passivity in situations where logic would suggest it as the only sensible alternative, their doctrinal rhetoric must provide them cold comfort at best.

THE DANGER OF DISORIENTATION AND DERAILMENT

Nathan Leites has observed that "Bolsheviks intensely fear their own disposition toward fear."[18] Although this assessment was ventured during the 1950s when inferiority and enemy encirclement were the entirety of Soviet historical experience, it remains valid and continues to explain much of the Soviet Union's distinctive style of military behavior. Much of the bravado in Soviet doctrine can be read as reaction against Moscow's feelings of insecurity and doubt, as can the "gigantism" of Soviet weapons programs stressing size and brute force (exemplified by the SS-18) and the pursuit of numerical abundance in armored vehicles and fighter aircraft, which would sustain high attrition in modern combat. Indeed, almost every feature of Soviet doctrine, arms acquisition, and manpower recruitment lends itself to partial explanation as evidence of Soviet overinsurance against the possibility of wartime events unfolding in unexpected ways.

To a certain extent, such concerns are generic to all military commanders regardless of their ideology or political culture. They are particularly influential in Soviet planning, however, because of the Soviet Union's adherence to an operational doctrine that relies so heavily on initiative and surprise. It is not uncommon to encounter expressions of mild resentment in Western circles over the Soviet Union's apparent luxury to choose the time and complexion of any war it might fight. Yet along with that luxury goes a burden of responsibility unique to holders of offensively oriented doctrines

18. Leites, *Study of Bolshevism*, p. 38.

to weigh the prewar situation with extraordinary prescience, since the chances of success are heavily bound up with the correctness of planning assumptions and opportunities for regrouping are likely to be few and far between. Countries on the receiving end that are politically bound to defensive and reactive strategies have options for flexibility generally denied to those who would start a war. In many cases, the defender might need only be capable of disrupting the attacker's designs to forestall defeat.

None of this has been lost on the Soviets, and evidence of the unease it inspires can be found across a broad range of Soviet military writing and planning activity. Soviet articles on military training and troop management brood over the danger of *rasteriannost'* ("losing one's bearings") in the heat of the battle.[19] Concern over getting caught up in a train of events that cannot be controlled has long preoccupied Soviet commanders and political officers. This respect for the corrosive influence that uncontrolled events could exert on leadership voluntarism was neatly captured in a high-level Soviet political injunction over a decade ago that "the time has long passed when a general could direct his troops while standing on a hill."[20] It goes far toward explaining the unusual stress on redundancy in Soviet command and control arrangements. It also accounts for the preoccupation shown by Soviet commanders and training officers over the difficulty of maintaining motivation and discipline among rank-and-file troops to endure the dislocations that would attend any battlefield use of nuclear weapons. There is little indication of concern over the political loyalty of the armed forces (even though that loyalty may attach more to national than to party symbols), but there is ample evidence of Soviet uncertainty over the extent to which those forces could sustain adequate performance under conditions of unprecedented duress. As a consequence, routine training patterns show signs of an acutely felt need to assure such performance in the event of war through peacetime psychological conditioning and example-setting.[21]

---

19. A representative example of this fixation may be seen in the remark by Army General Pavlovskii that a major objective in the training of officers must be to ensure that "they do not lose their bearings when events develop unfavorably." *Krasnaia zvezda,* February 13, 1974. Also pertinent is the following editorial comment that "of active deeds in battle, capable above all is the man who knows how to subdue not only the feeling of fear—that assertion is hardly distinctive—but also the feeling of *rasteriannost'*." *Krasnaia zvezda,* January 24, 1974.
20. Major General V. Zemskov, "An Important Factor for Victory in War," *Krasnaia zvezda,* January 5, 1967.
21. A detailed and sophisticated marshalling of evidence from Soviet source materials bearing on this concern may be found in Nathan Leites, *What Soviet Commanders Fear from Their Own Forces,* P-5958 (Santa Monica, Calif.: The Rand Corporation, May 1978).

This preoccupation has origins running back to the earliest days of the Bolshevik Revolution and has persisted as a dominant theme in Soviet military education ever since. The "quality of commanders," one may recall, figured prominently among Stalin's five "permanently operating factors" affecting the outcome of war,[22] and inspirational leadership remains a critical precondition of victory in the current Soviet litany of operational desiderata. As early as the 1930s, Soviet training doctrine depicted "political steadfastness and moral attitudes" as indispensable ingredients of operational effectiveness and affirmed the vital importance of assuring that "whatever the difficulties, the army knows what it is fighting for."[23] As a consequence, much of the party's political work in the armed forces has been directed less toward fulfilling watchdog roles (as is often assumed in the West) than toward what Timothy Colton has called the "internalization of civic virtue" among troops that would bear the brunt of losses in combat.[24]

Unfortunately for Soviet planners, merely recognizing the importance of discipline and pursuing measures to instill it can provide little assurance that the results will weather the test of war, particularly one where nuclear weapons might be involved. The Soviets harp about morale, yet fear losing it just when it would be most urgently needed. Their reported policy of whole-unit replacement in the event of major battlefield losses to nuclear effects testifies to their determination to avoid contaminating fresh troops with the resignation that would afflict the survivors of any such catastrophe.[25] Nonetheless, despite their efforts to inculcate strong moral fiber among their troops and their associated measures to contain the more corrosive effects of nuclear shock on unit performance, the specter of confusion, defeatism, and even mass desertion must be an enduring source of uncertainty to any Soviet commander or decision-maker who would have to count on Soviet ground forces to secure victory.

A related malaise that periodically crops up in Soviet military writing

---

22. The other four included the stability of the rear, the morale of the army, the quantity and quality of divisions, and the armament of the army. For discussion, see Herbert S. Dinerstein, *War and the Soviet Union* (New York: Praeger, 1962), pp. 6–8; and Raymond L. Garthoff, *Soviet Military Doctrine* (Glencoe, Ill.: The Free Press, 1953), pp. 34–35.
23. V.K. Triandafillov, *Kharakter operatsii sovremennykh armii* [The operational character of modern armies] (Moscow: Voenizdat, 1932), pp. 50–63.
24. Timothy J. Colton, *Commissars, Commanders, and Civilian Authority: The Structure of Soviet Military Politics* (Cambridge: Harvard University Press, 1979), p. 71.
25. See Colonel A.A. Sidorenko, *The Offensive* (Moscow: Voenizdat, 1970), translated and published by the U.S. Air Force, p. 143.

concerns the perils of overconfidence and the danger that inadequate flexibility at the threshold of war could draw the Soviet Union into a cul-de-sac from which graceful extrication would be impossible. Western analysts often miss this factor and look solely to the surface manifestations of doctrine for insight into Soviet assumptions and expectations. Although it is hardly routine in Soviet discourse on operational matters, one can find sufficient warnings about the dangers of *shapkozakidatel'stvo* ("misplaced belief in the prospect of an easy victory") in Soviet writings to demonstrate that the Soviets do not necessarily believe in the self-fulfilling quality of their doctrinal prescriptions. This applies with particular force to the controversial question of whether the Soviet leadership confidently "thinks it could fight and win a nuclear war."[26] It is a far cry from traditional Soviet military thought to say that Soviet officials are so self-assured that they are prepared to contemplate threats against bedrock U.S. interests in cases other than those where Soviet survival lay equally at risk. Even in dire emergencies where "striking first in the last resort" was the Soviet leadership's least miserable option for attempting to control rapidly unravelling events, Soviet deliberation over such a decision would still be dominated by the most awesome doubt about the future of the socialist vision.

At almost every level of conventional force employment, Soviet commentary emphasizes the importance of such critical intangibles as leadership, awareness, and flexibility, none of which can be counted on in adequate measure at the proper time. It is common to find criticisms of commanders who allow their crews to train repetitively in stereotyped scenarios where targets, terrain features, and the disposition of the "enemy" are all well known in advance, yet who persuade themselves that their impressive results would be repeated in a combat environment.[27] Whether comparable concerns attach to higher-level exercises involving nuclear forces is not ascertainable

---

26. Richard Pipes, "Why the Soviet Union Thinks It Could Fight and Win a Nuclear War," *Commentary*, Vol. 64, No. 1 (July 1977).

27. A candid illustration may be seen in the following comment by the Soviet air commander for the North Caucasus Military District: "Once we investigated a case where a team of experienced pilots carried out a bombing mission which was rated very low. . . . In this case, the pilots had been flying the same routes for a long time and had only worked out the combat problems for their own range under normal target conditions. They did not work out the tactical background. In training, the pilots imitating the target fly only on a straight line, without changing altitude or speed. . . . These people are assuming that the simulated enemy air defense system has been destroyed, but they have simply not thought out the situation. How can someone go into real combat without the necessary skills?" Lieutenant General of Aviation G. Pavlov, "The Inexhaustible Reserve," *Krasnaia zvezda*, August 4, 1976.

from Soviet writings, but it would scarcely be surprising given the Soviet penchant for training across the board in highly routine and unimaginative ways.

A final source of uncertainty involves the appreciation by many Soviet commanders of the potential cost of overcentralization that pervades the Soviet armed forces from the General Staff down to field units. This uncertainty is closely linked with the broader problems associated with the Soviet Union's offensively oriented doctrine discussed above. The Soviet command structure is stratified almost to ossification, with each echelon highly dependent on authority from above and little allowance provided for initiative at lower levels. This hierarchical quality of Soviet military life affects planning and operations in equal measure and heavily influences Soviet military performance. It has the virtue of providing an environment in which roles and missions are carefully allocated in advance and plans can be put into operation with maximum orderliness and singularity of purpose.

Unfortunately, this strength can also constitute a paralyzing weakness when command and control links have been broken, original plans have been derailed, and improvisation becomes required to salvage some measure of control from a rapidly eroding situation. As long as events unfold as anticipated, centralization and command integration can compensate for insufficiencies in the more tangible ingredients of military power. Yet, highly orchestrated war plans requiring careful coordination for mission effectiveness have had a rich record of becoming snarled beyond repair.[28] In the face of such a possibility, one of the least likely sources of versatility and strength would be to have principals on the front line who had been programmed never to think for themselves.

A glimpse of the penalties that can ensue from such overcentralization and inflexibility was displayed in the July 1970 air battle between Soviet and Israeli pilots over the Suez Canal, in which five MiG-21s were destroyed with no Israeli losses in an intense engagement lasting less than five minutes. The day before, Soviet-flown MiGs had attacked and damaged an Israeli A-4 on a deep interdiction sortie near the Egyptian airfield at Inchas. The Israelis sought retribution by launching a diversionary feint. As expected, the MiGs rose to the bait and were promptly engaged by eight Israeli F-4s and Mirages.

---

28. Particularly notable in this regard are the well-known failures of the German Schlieffen Plan and the British amphibious assault on Gallipoli during World War I, both of which involved elaborate schemes that were impressive in concept yet foundered in execution because of various deficiencies in leadership. See B.H. Liddell Hart, *The Real War, 1914–1918* (Boston: Little, Brown, 1930), pp. 46–49, 159–174.

As described in various published accounts, the Soviet formation rapidly broke up in confusion and chaos once the first MiG was shot down. Throughout the engagement, the Soviets showed little evidence of air combat proficiency or air discipline. Having presumably been trained solely for radar intercepts against passive targets, they simply found themselves out of their element once they became unexpectedly caught in a hard-maneuvering visual fight in which the initiative was no longer theirs.[29]

Naturally, one must guard against overgeneralization from such an isolated example. Yet the inflexibilities that caused those Soviet aircrews to experience such a rude lesson in tactical surprise were precisely of the sort that regularly elicit criticism throughout Soviet military articles on operational training to this day. Such criticism is particularly visible in Soviet commentary on matters pertaining to pilot training, but it addresses a cultural trait that probably exists to some degree at all levels of Soviet military activity and constitutes one of the most deep-seated weaknesses of the Soviet armed forces.

Other Uncertainties

The sources of uncertainty in Soviet operational planning examined above apply mainly to questions affecting the performance of Soviet forces and command structures under the strains that would accompany any superpower showdown involving risk of major war. They encompass those concerns that would most immediately bedevil high-level Soviet planners tasked with recommending whether, when, and how to commit Soviet forces to major actions involving danger of nuclear escalation.

Beyond these operational–tactical sources of hesitancy is a broader array of nightmares that might give equal or greater pause to Soviet civilian leaders. Each higher-order concern could be extensively explored in a separate inquiry. This discussion merely identifies them and briefly indicates how they might constrain Soviet assertiveness at the brink of war.

APPRECIATION OF SOVIET COMBAT INEXPERIENCE

Prior to Afghanistan, the Soviet armed forces had never fought on any respectable scale in their entire postwar history. Their only significant involvement had been against neighboring "allies" in policing actions featuring

---

29. For a rare first-hand account of this engagement, see Zeev Schiff, *A History of the Israeli Army* (San Francisco: Straight Arrow Books, 1974), pp. 199–202. Additional details may be found in "Israel: Preparing for the Next Round," *Air Enthusiast*, Vol. 1, No. 7 (December 1971), p. 344.

little risk of military opposition. Soviet spokesmen have gone to remarkable lengths in recent years to express grudging admiration for the operational seasoning U.S. armed forces acquired in Vietnam and that which the Israelis have gained in their various combat trials in the Middle East.[30] The Soviet Union, for better or worse, has enjoyed no comparable opportunity to test its mettle against a determined adversary since its triumph over Nazi Germany in the Great Fatherland War. Although the Afghanistan episode may yet remind the Soviets what it means to live with casualty lists on a daily basis, it is scarcely likely to provide much of an opportunity for gauging how Soviet forces would perform in high-intensity combat against a technologically sophisticated adversary like the United States. Undoubtedly, the Soviets have gained some instructive baseline data about operational resource management through their various power-projection activities in recent years, but there is a limit beyond which these fringe experiences (and such routine peacetime practices as summer training exercises) cannot replicate the demands and uncertainties of sustained military conflict. This inexperience must inspire nagging unease in the minds of Soviet decision-makers, especially those who do not routinely concern themselves with military matters. It may assume heightened significance if the Soviet Union eventually proves to be as inept at counterinsurgency warfare in Afghanistan as the United States seems to have been in Southeast Asia.[31]

CONCERN OVER PREMATURE NUCLEAR WEAPONS RELEASE

The Soviets are at least as obsessive about nuclear weapons control as their American counterparts are. The alert rate of Soviet nuclear forces is generally believed to be far lower than that of the United States.[32] In the Warsaw Pact forward area, nuclear weapons may not even be collocated with, let alone mated to, their delivery systems in peacetime.[33] And, even for periods of tension, it is far from explicit what measures might threaten to remove

---

30. See Drew Middleton, "Soviet Officers Said to Admire American Army," *The New York Times*, December 19, 1977.
31. See Kenneth H. Bacon, "Russian Army Has Been Good But Not Perfect in Combating the Insurgents in Afghanistan," *The Wall Street Journal*, April 24, 1980.
32. John Newhouse, *Cold Dawn: The Story of SALT* (New York: Holt, Rinehart and Winston, 1973), p. 23. See also Robert Berman and John Baker, *Soviet Strategic Forces: Requirements and Responses* (Washington, D.C.: The Brookings Institution, forthcoming).
33. Thomas W. Wolfe, *Soviet Power and Europe: 1945–1970* (Baltimore: Johns Hopkins University Press, 1970), p. 487; and Jeffrey Record, *U.S. Nuclear Weapons in Europe: Issues and Alternatives* (Washington, D.C.: The Brookings Institution, 1974), p. 37.

nuclear weapons from the direct supervision of the Soviet national command authorities. During the Cuban crisis, for example, it was never clear whether nuclear warheads were actually emplaced on the island alongside the missiles.[34] In peacetime, responsibility for nuclear weapons security is reportedly not assigned to operational commands but instead is vested in the KGB, an independent civilian institution.[35]

These and related indicators suggest that Soviet nuclear arms are scarcely poised on a hair trigger. On the contrary, the Soviet nuclear arsenal appears to be so securely disciplined by party authority as to raise a legitimate question whether the Soviet decision-making apparatus is actually capable of supporting the requirement for timely preemption reflected in formal Soviet strategic doctrine. During the terminal phase of the party–military debate over institutional roles following Khrushchev's ouster, an authoritative party spokesman reminded the armed forces that nuclear weapons were so laden with political importance that the party could never allow them "to escape its direct control."[36] Given the unique instabilities of the Soviet political system, many reasons beyond command and control could account for this insistence on civilian monopoly over nuclear armaments at all times. One may be a justifiable leadership concern that premature release of such armaments in a crisis might jeopardize not only Soviet national security but continued party preeminence as well.

TRUSTWORTHINESS OF SOVIET "FRATERNAL ALLIES"

Western analysts generally assume that Soviet forces alone would bear the *initial* burden of air and ground operations in a European conflict. At the same time, a major role in the ensuing phases of combat would probably be

---

34. At the time the crisis broke, the missile launch sites were nearing completion, but only 42 MRBMs had been delivered and none of the IRBMs had been introduced. Moreover, although nuclear weapons storage bunkers were in various stages of construction, the missiles were far from operationally ready when the dismantling of the sites began. In *Essence of Decision: Explaining the Cuban Missile Crisis* (Boston: Little, Brown, 1971), Graham Allison reports that MRBMs had not been observed with warhead sections during their shipboard transportation (p. 103). All of this involves compound speculation, and none of it should be taken to suggest that the Soviets were not prepared to introduce nuclear weapons once their overall deployment effort succeeded. Nonetheless, the notion that they were in no hurry to move nuclear warheads prematurely to Cuba is consistent with general evidence of Soviet concern over the maintenance of close nuclear command and control.
35. Oleg Penkovskiy, *The Penkovskiy Papers* (New York: Doubleday and Company, 1965), p. 331. See also Barron, *KGB*, p. 15, and Allison, *Essence of Decision,* p. 110.
36. Major General V. Zemskov, "An Important Factor for Victory in War," *Krasnaia zvezda*, January 5, 1967.

assigned to various indigenous Warsaw Pact forces. Since the prospect and character of their support would depend heavily on the circumstances that occasioned the war in the first place, they have been topics of intense speculation in Western defense circles ever since the Warsaw Pact was first constituted. The Soviet leadership could never be completely confident of effective Pact support in any circumstances that directly threatened independent East European security interests.[37] Any plan to commit Soviet forces against NATO that required organized Pact involvement as a precondition of success would entail a particularly thorny Soviet decision as a consequence of this uncertainty. Most East European elites are beholden to Soviet power and support for their continued tenure, but they are scarcely obliged to squander their political fortunes or otherwise sacrifice the interests of their domestic constituencies in blind obeisance to Soviet ambitions.[38]

THE THREAT OF MILITARY BONAPARTISM

Since the dismissal of Marshal Zhukov in 1957, the Soviet military has never even remotely challenged the preeminence of party rule. Nonetheless, its interests are frequently at odds with those of the civilian party apparatus and it does command a monopoly on arms. During the 1960s, Western analysts of Soviet party–military relations tended to characterize the two organizations as natural rivals because of their divergent interests and images of how best to deal with Soviet security.[39] More recently, it has become apparent that this tension principally reflected transitory incompatibilities between Khrushchev and his marshals and that party and military interests in fact now overlap a great deal. Persisting differences typically remain limited to matters of resource allocation and show little evidence of deeper contention over institutional roles and power distribution within Soviet society.[40]

---

37. For one of the few serious attempts to examine this commonly expressed but rarely documented proposition in detail, see Dale R. Herspring and Ivan Volgyes, "Political Reliability in the East European Warsaw Pact Armies," *Armed Forces and Society*, Winter 1980, pp. 279–296. See also A. Ross Johnson, Robert W. Dean, and Alexander Alexiev, *East European Military Establishments: The Warsaw Pact Northern Tier*, R-2417/1-AF/FF (Santa Monica, Calif.: The Rand Corporation, December 1980).
38. See, for example, Eric Bourne, "Kremlin Allies Grumble over Afghan War," *The Christian Science Monitor*, June 4, 1980.
39. This thesis was most prominently expounded by Roman Kolkowicz, *The Soviet Military and the Communist Party* (Princeton: Princeton University Press, 1967).
40. See, for example, William E. Odom, "The Party Connection," *Problems of Communism*, September–October 1973, pp. 12–26; and Odom, "Who Controls Whom in Moscow," *Foreign Policy*, Number 19 (Summer 1975), pp. 109–123.

All the same, the Soviet Union remains a nonpluralistic social organism with no formal mechanism for the orderly transfer of political power. Accordingly, in times of leadership transition or external stress, the military could play a major role in domestic politics either by throwing its weight behind its favored contender or directly insinuating itself into the processes of decision-making in cases that threatened its image of Soviet security interests. Because the party enjoys no natural tradition of civilian rule and lacks the constitutional legitimacy of elected governments in Western democratic societies, it might face the added problem of having to worry about its *internal* sources of support alongside the choices and dilemmas imposed by external events.

Would the armed forces be disposed to supplant party authority in the event of a nuclear crisis in which the domestic instruments of social control had fallen apart and the survival of the regime lay in the breach? Perhaps not, given almost everything we know about their past patterns of political conduct. Yet, such a situation would be unprecedented in Soviet experience, and the party leadership could never know for sure.

INTERNAL NATIONALIST INSURRECTIONS

An associated question that could beset Soviet leaders in an incipient wartime situation concerns ethnic forces that might threaten to fragment the Soviet Union. The USSR is not a naturally cohesive nation–state but a quasi-imperial conglomeration of diverse cultures held together far more by Soviet power than by any feelings of national identity. The Slavic component of the Soviet armed forces might indeed fight to the finish for "Mother Russia" in most conditions of national crisis, but similar devotion could hardly be counted on from those non-Russians who increasingly constitute the majority of Soviet military manpower.[41] Soviet leaders have long been sensitive to the threat of insurgent nationalist movements within Soviet borders as a consequence of external encouragement. Indeed, a major component of their rationale for moving into Afghanistan was a felt need to head off any prospect, however remote, of radical Muslim fundamentalism infecting Soviet Central Asia. In recent years, Western defense writings have suggested that the United States might have much to gain by capitalizing on Soviet ethnic rivalries and thus fragmenting the Soviet Union politically in the event of

---

41. See S. Enders Wimbush and Alex Alexiev, *The Ethnic Factor in the Soviet Armed Forces*, R-2787 (Santa Monica, Calif.: The Rand Corporation, March 1982).

war.[42] Although there are severe difficulties concerning how one might actually carry out such a plan to significantly influence war outcomes, even the slightest hint of such reasoning in U.S. planning would cause acute discomfort in the minds of the Soviet leaders. After all, one of their predominant goals in any crisis would be the preservation of the Soviet state. This interest would scarcely be served by actions that threatened to unleash internal forces beyond the ability of Soviet domestic power to contain.

THE YELLOW PERIL

Perhaps the most deeply rooted fear of Soviet leaders and ordinary Russians alike is the specter of a billion Chinese on the southern flank of the Soviet Union, armed with nuclear weapons and animated by consuming anti-Soviet hatred, major territorial claims against the USSR, and global ambitions aimed at undercutting Soviet influence and presence. The Soviet leadership is acutely concerned about the prospect of a two-front war and could never be assured that the Chinese would not try to capitalize on a Soviet–American confrontation, either as an ally of the United States or independently, with a view toward exploiting the Soviet Union's predicament. The urgency of Soviet concern over China's propensity for irrationality that was felt at the height of the Cultural Revolution has almost surely abated dramatically now that Mao has departed and a more secular and moderate leadership has assumed the reins of power. At the same time, China remains a natural enemy of the Soviet Union in a way the United States never has been. The thought least likely to inspire composure in the minds of the Soviet leaders is the prospect of being reduced to China's stature and thus prey to Chinese revanchism as the necessary price for strategic "victory" in a war with the United States.

Concluding Warnings

After all is said and done, a great deal of uncertainty remains about Soviet strategic uncertainty. There is much we do not know (and cannot know)

42. Colin Gray, for example, has noted the potential deterrent value of a U.S. targeting plan aimed expressly at critical Soviet social control mechanisms whose widespread disruption during the course of a war might allow "the centrifugal forces within the Soviet empire to begin to bring that system down from within." "Soviet Strategic Vulnerabilities," *Air Force Magazine*, March 1979, p. 64. See also the reference to possible use of nuclear weapons "to achieve regionalization of the Soviet Union" in Walter Pincus, "Thinking the Unthinkable: Studying New Approaches to a Nuclear War," *The Washington Post*, February 11, 1979.

about how Soviet leaders would act in the face of a major test. Uncertainty can cut two ways, depending on how the Soviet leadership perceives the risks and stakes of a situation. It can counsel circumspection and hesitancy— but it can also provide strong incentives toward forceful action aimed at seizing the initiative, defining the rules of engagement according to Soviet preference, and dominating events before they have a chance to slip irretrievably out of grasp.

An example of the latter phenomenon might be sought in the hypothetical case of a major European war in which nuclear weapons had not yet been used, yet where things were plainly going badly for NATO. A sweeping Soviet conventional victory could contain the seeds of disaster in that it would threaten to trigger NATO nuclear escalation as a last-ditch move to forestall utter military defeat. Such a prospect would be almost certain to give Soviet decision-makers compelling grounds for theater nuclear preemption, a major move entailing manifold implications the Soviets might genuinely prefer to avoid.

Conversely, in a conventional war in which NATO had succeeded in disrupting Moscow's offensive momentum, the Soviets themselves could feel powerful urges to raise the ante with nuclear escalation to head off the possiblity of not only losing the military campaign but also watching their East European empire crumble away in the process. If nuclear employment appeared unavoidable sooner or later, the Soviets might well see good reasons for *starting* with nuclear operations and forgoing the conventional phase altogether.

This uncertainty is why, in reasoning far more conclusive than indications drawn from Soviet force posture or doctrine, it is so hard for Western analysts to generate persuasive scenarios for a NATO contingency involving solely conventional arms. However gratifying it may be intellectually, U.S. planners and researchers who indulge in elaborate exercises of manipulating fighter sortie rates, tank exchange ratios, and comparable battlefield minutiae as though the analytical problem simply entailed a grand replay of World War II with modern technology are living in a world of sublime unreality. Soviet incentives for nuclear weapons use, to the extent they would be felt at all, would stem less from doctrinal preference than from operational necessity. If the Soviet leaders felt any mental conflict whatever in such a predicament, it would, in all likelihood, turn on the question of whether to go to war in the first place, not on whether they had a choice between conventional or nuclear options.

Whatever way Soviet decision-makers choose to resolve such uncertainties will depend heavily on the particular crisis they face. In the remote event the Soviets decided the time was right for a full-fledged invasion of Europe and had carefully planned for such an attack in advance, they would also have reconciled themselves to the possibility of a broader superpower war and accepted the risks of such a war as a fair price for the fruits of theater victory. In such a case, there would be little the United States and NATO could usefully do in the way of threat manipulation and "intrawar bargaining." The operational challenge for the West would reduce simply to fighting the war as well as possible and hoping the Soviets had misjudged their chances for success. In the more likely event that both superpowers found themselves inadvertently caught in a conventional skirmish that neither side was eager to pursue, however, there might be considerable room for the sorts of uncertainties discussed here to help lead the Soviets toward some face-saving settlement before the point of no return had been reached.